Rails
Across Dixie

RAILS
ACROSS DIXIE

*A History of Passenger
Trains in the American South*

Jim Cox

McFarland & Company, Inc., Publishers
Jefferson, North Carolina

385.22

The present work is a reprint of the illustrated case bound edition of Rails Across Dixie: A History of Passenger Trains in the American South, *first published in 2011 by McFarland.*

LIBRARY OF CONGRESS CATALOGUING-IN-PUBLICATION DATA

Cox, Jim, 1939–
Rails across dixie : a history of passenger trains
in the American South / Jim Cox.
p. cm.
Includes bibliographical references and index.
softcover : acid free paper ∞
1. Passenger trains— Southern States— History. 2. Passenger
trains— Technological innovations— Southern States— History.
3. Passenger trains— Southern States— Pictorial works. I. Title.
TF570.C69 2011   385'.220975 — dc22   2010036662

BRITISH LIBRARY CATALOGUING DATA ARE AVAILABLE

ISBN (print) 978-1-4766-6601-3
ISBN (ebook)978-0-7864-6175-2

Front cover: FEC 6, now a dieselized and streamlined South
Wind with EMD 1005 on the point (A-A-A configuration),
running north of Eau Gallie, Florida, April 1960 (photograph
by David W. Salter, courtesy of Chuck Blardone)

Manufactured in the United States of America

*McFarland & Company, Inc., Publishers
Box 611, Jefferson, North Carolina 28640
www.mcfarlandpub.com*

For Pi
my soul mate and seatmate
for a whole lot of miles

CONTENTS

I. The Manufacture of Transportation

II. Dixie Legends

III. The Human Dimension

IV. Present and Future

Appendices

ACKNOWLEDGMENTS

The risk of attempting to cite all the people and organizations that are partially responsible for executing a project like this is inevitably to overlook somebody whose contribution is equally worthy. If I'm at fault here it is purely unintentional and I apologize up front. So many gifted people have made inestimable additions to this work for which I am profoundly grateful. The time and effort they put into supplying my requests have been of sizeable and valued significance in the outcome. I'm better positioned to realize it than anyone. I've never worked on a similar project with a more genuinely selfless group of volunteers; their help has made the unequivocal difference.

I'm sincerely grateful to the following individuals for their input into this finished product: Charles Anderson, Ken M. Ardinger, E.G. Baker, Richard C. Beall, Chuck Blardone, Fred Carnes, Charles B. Castner, Jr., Hugh M. Comer, Kim Andersen Cumber, Susan L. Gordon, Frank Gregg, Irene Heinstein, John Jensen, R. Lyle Key, Jr., Erik Landrum, John Landrum, Robert Malinoski, Karina McDaniel, Peter C. McLachlan, Jay Miller, David H. Noble, Al Perez, Joe Postove, Michael B. Robbins, Ben Roberts, Rob Rousseau, David W. Salter, William Sheild, Jeff Smith, Jay T. Thomson, Robert W. Thomson, Allen Tuten, Michael C. R. Wall, Cal Winter, and Clyde Woodruff.

A handful of fraternal and professional groups also have been particularly helpful in these pursuits. I credit the Central of Georgia Railway Historical Society, Florida East Coast Railway Society, Louisville & Nashville Railroad Historical Society, National Railroad Historical Society, Norfolk Southern Historical Society (the original carrier by that name dating to 1883), North Carolina State Archives, Pennsylvania Railroad Technical and Historical Society, and Tennessee State Library and Archives.

Beyond these who shared materially I wish to recognize my late father and mother who planted this trains-mania initially. It was they who inspired me with the joy of railroading and gave me frequent opportunities to pursue it. They encouraged my fascination with "all things trains" and supported my insatiable quests to explore what was down the tracks and around the bend on some of Dixie's most intriguing routes and carriers.

Finally, to my supportive spouse, I issue my deepest appreciation. She, too—without much chance to be a railfan before entering my life—has been utterly enthralled by the trappings of passenger rail. The fact that we share this passion for trains together has made the journey so much sweeter. On one of our earliest treks, as we settled into our compartment, she grabbed my hand and exclaimed, "Thank you for doing this for me!" I don't think she realized I was so buoyant because I was doing this *for us*! That was many trips back. Today we both expectantly look toward our adventures over the tracks with just as much gusto. I'm grateful for the encouragement she extends in this as well as in my writing endeavors.

A word about illustrations is probably in order. The modern historical associations of every major and several minor passenger carriers traversing the American South during the heyday of that traffic were solicited for pictorial inclusion. So were the archives of all the states within the territory. Some either didn't respond or were unable to participate for sundry reasons. As a result a few carriers are underrepresented. Be assured it was my intent to encompass them all and regrets are extended for any excluded or underplayed. In a perfect world, all would be equally embodied. Hopefully the illustrations that are here will help you properly interpret what has transpired in passenger rail across the South.

INTRODUCTION
A Sentimental Journey

Train travel in the United States has had a great deal going for it. Particularly was that true during the first half of the 20th century. Aside from the freedom from driving — whatever one's intended distance might be — aside from being relatively inexpensive, reliable, comfortable, safe, secure, and speedy, passenger rail has invariably proffered myriad additional intrinsic benefits.

Where else, for example, could you gain the extraordinary perspective on the American scene that is supplied by so many incredibly riveting panoramas afforded by generously endowed picture windows? And where could a traveler reap so many prospects for as much human interaction and camaraderie as on a journey by train? Where, for instance, could a rider be exposed to the language, customs and backgrounds of so many locals (and far-flung travelers) as happens when they are linked together by rails? (Perhaps by steamship, possibly — what percentage actually did that in the past? And how many flew back then? Few. Even if they did, would their travels have led to the verbal exchanges on a par with those that patrons experience aboard trains?) Trains were (and are) often the setting of fleeting interface. Sometimes they have been the spot where long-term friendships, productive business contacts, and romantic interludes incubated. Trains had few rivals and maybe no equals in the wonders they performed while transporting collective masses of the population to their destinations.

And still more fundamental gains occurred in natural ways.

What about the mesmerizing effects of a train whistle blowing in the night? What about the clickety-clack of iron wheels racing along tracks separated by crossties? When a train intersects a road or enters a metropolitan district (even a rural township), all the other traffic comes to a standstill — in some kind of pattern that doesn't seem in the least implausibly in salute. What other form of public transportation earns that kind of respect? There is something profoundly captivating about a trip by train that other modes of transit could never lay claim to. The potential for so many good times awaits the traveler who takes a journey by rail. And so much of it segues into unbelievably warm fuzzy feelings that for many linger throughout a lifetime.

If I had not been fittingly inspired earlier, my zeal for trains was to acquire added momentum by the time I completed my foundational training. My high school in Tampa, Florida, is named after a 19th century railroader who spearheaded a quest to almost unilaterally cultivate and advance Florida's Gulf coast and central districts. More than any other individual, entrepreneurial financier H. B. Plant (1819–1899) is credited with the awesome expansion that blanketed the western half of the Sunshine State in the 20th century. "The business success of Henry Bradley Plant and the loyalty of his men were largely the result of the personal interest that he took in the affairs of all of his companies," insisted one historian. "Never was there labor strife on the Plant System, which was for the most part run by this one man."[1]

Plant's unrelenting efforts to develop the region while significantly increasing accessibility to it coupled with clever marketing ability resulted in a foundation many enterprising successors were to capitalize on. As a result he caused this largely untamed tract of future paradise to be adapted to a highly desirable playground, beckoning in particular affluent people ensconced in the cold climes to the north. At the same time, the region was transformed into a conspicuously bustling trade zone with flourishing commerce. Through its portals people, foodstuffs, raw materials and manufactured goods passed to and from stateside and global destinations.

Plant left his native Connecticut in 1854, moving south to manage a soon-to-be booming express concern at Augusta, Georgia. From little acorns, big trees grow. Demonstrating incisive business acumen, he was to ultimately preside over an enterprise whose branches extended into diversified disciplines: railroads, steamship lines, hotels, express trade, investments, real estate, promotion, and a plethora of auxiliary interests gathered under the Plant System umbrella. By the time of his death, Plant owned more than 2,200 miles of rail right-of-way that extended northeast from Tampa to Charleston, South Carolina, and northwest to Montgomery, Alabama. His steamship lines, connecting with Plant rails at Tampa, ran south to Key West and Havana, Cuba, and north to Mobile, Alabama. From Winter Park to Fort Myers, eight hotels and resorts owned by the Plant System were prime wintertime destinations of prosperous Yankees every year. One of those palaces, the magnificently ornate Tampa Bay Hotel, a five-story edifice of Spanish and Moorish architecture, is today the centerpiece of the downtown University of Tampa campus. The exposure to academia extends H. B. Plant's link with education well beyond the local high school named after him.

"Although Mr. Plant specified in his will that the Plant System should remain an independent enterprise, these wishes were ignored by his family, who promptly disposed of the various properties when so allowed by the court. However, one development, Plant City, Florida, named in honor of this great railroad man, lives on today and keeps the name of Henry Bradley Plant alive for future generations as the man who did the most to promote the west coast and central sections of Florida."[2]

In 1902, Atlantic Coast Line Railroad (ACL) bought the Plant System rails. Absorbing his routes, ACL was able to move passengers and goods on its own network all the way from Richmond, Virginia, to Tampa, a distance of 929 miles. North of Richmond, passengers and freight continued their journeys unimpeded to Washington, New York and Boston on the routes of cooperating rail carriers. While Plant's desires weren't honored as he requested, his accomplishments—combined with those of other entrepreneurs—were applied to greatly extend the transportation systems in which he invested so much of his life.

Henry B. Plant was one of the most successful of the lot yet was but one of legions of wealthy rail tycoons living in 19th and 20th century America. Several of them will be encountered in this book. Their stories are told from the perspectives of authenticity and objectivity with occasional splashes of anecdotal footnotes. While this text is purportedly a historical account that concentrates heavily on the railway passenger service of the Southeastern quadrant of America, it is also an attempt to make this journey fascinating and gratifying at the same time.

Speaking for me, it was always easy to love trains. That goes back to a very early age. Two houses we lived in during some of my formative years backed up to the east-west tracks of the Seaboard Air Line Railroad (SAL) in Charlotte, North Carolina. At a parallel freight siding, I became familiar with the names of distant railroads emblazoned on the boxcars and tank and grain cars that were frequently set aside there until summoned for more important service: Soo Line, Santa Fe, Great Northern, Frisco, New York Central, Baltimore & Ohio, Southern Pacific, Milwaukee Road, Rock Island, and many others. Once, as an adolescent, I convinced my parents it was safe for me to hike those tracks as far as I could toward Monroe (the next town, 25 miles distant), at least until I got tired enough to turn around and retrace my steps. I recall it now as one of the more memorable adventures of my youth.

Best of all, as I was drifting off to sleep most nights, I awaited the familiar clickety-clack announcing the arrival of the untitled passenger train number 13 from Wilmington to Charlotte. How I wished I was aboard, returning from some remote destination! That train, and number 14, which departed for the coast at dawn every morning, met other trains intersecting at Hamlet, a busy but suitably christened rail burg in eastern North Carolina. At Hamlet one could catch a northbound local for Raleigh, Richmond, Washington and New York. Or transfer to the southbound *Palmland* streamliner for Columbia, Savannah and Florida points on two coasts. I was never lucky enough to ride numbers 13 or 14. On occasion, nonetheless, I went outside to catch a glimpse of the blur of those travelers lucky enough to be aboard the consist whizzing by that included a locomotive, mail car and coaches. Was that any way to put aside foolish notions of destinations uncharted? Hardly.

Those unshakable images began to take root when some friends from Birmingham, Alabama, paid us a visit by rail. Their family had four kids. The dad was a dispatcher for Southern Railway and one of his job perks allowed his family free rail travel, one they frequently applied. As they recited an enviable travelogue, my absorption with trains instantly escalated. My parents subsequently agreed I could make a trip to Birmingham alone. In the late 1940s and early 1950s, it was quite safe to stick a lad of nine or 10 on a through streamliner (no change of trains en route), dispatching him on a 421-mile 10-hour journey. That prompted more trips between Charlotte and Birmingham for both their kids and me via Southern Railway, my dad always paying my fare.

In the same epoch, on occasions I also traveled on Southern Railway alone between Charlotte and Atlanta to visit our Georgia relatives. At 10, I accompanied my dad on a business trip to Richmond, Virginia. Traveling overnight by train, we slept in a sectional Pullman car each way, the kind with curtains that buttoned up — my singular experience in putting my tootsies in an upper berth! Without doubt, those trips were some of my favored recollections of pubescent years. Such journeys did little to dissuade the passion I had harbored for railroads since my preschool days.

After our family left Charlotte for Tampa during my teen years, I made several jaunts on Atlantic Coast Line and Seaboard Air Line routes out of and into Tampa. Those carriers seamlessly connected with other railways for intriguing venues. Rail transit was cheap and certainly was my preference whenever possible in traveling between home and college and worksites, especially if time wasn't a pressing factor.

Settling in later at Nashville, Tennessee, I was employed by an outfit situated directly across the street from Union Station. That terminal was a charming structure that possessed magnetic qualities sporadically drawing me through its portals to do little more than observe the flow of traffic on foot and on rail. My firm purchased the "air rights" in the railroad gulch. The "air rights" were above numerous parallel tracks that were set below the city streets running to and from Union Station. Adjacent to and north of the terminal my employer erected a nearly three-block-long office-warehouse situated on pillars high above the rails. It was a novel idea that added to the local train lore and to the allure for me. From then on I was a sporadic patron of the Louisville & Nashville Railroad (L&N). One of my joys was to introduce my young bride to her first rail journey over the Nashville, Chattanooga & St. Louis route to Atlanta (NC&StL was by then already absorbed into L&N). A bonus occurred in later years when I took our three offspring on train adventures of their own.

But the icing on the cake has been that my wife — who hadn't been on any rail journey but that single one in the 1960s— never completely dismissed it from her mind. Three decades later the two of us climbed aboard Amtrak for a cross-country escapade. That was almost a decade-and-a-half ago. We have repeated our initial long-distance rail experience together annually and sometimes twice a year. Our trips include deluxe sleeping car accommodations with private bath and shower and meals in the dining car included in the fare, plus— on western trains— access to an observation car enclosed by glass on three sides.

For us, the destinations haven't ever been what the travel was about: getting there is inevitably more than half the fun! We are pure and simple railway fanatics. We have been almost everywhere Amtrak runs and to some of the same places multiple times. Yet we believe there's nothing to compare with the breathtaking vistas rolling by our picture windows.

I have authored other books prior to this one (my 19th). This is my first venture in capturing in print what railways have to offer. As a native southerner, I've longed for an opportunity to pen a volume that honors my beloved South. This is the vehicle (no witticism intended) to do it. Parenthetically, the South in this treatise refers to 12 states. (I fully realize there may be some differences of opinion on this topic. I've tried to be inclusive without eliminating any that clearly don't fit the mold.) For these purposes, the following dozen are included: Alabama, Arkansas, Florida, Georgia, Kentucky, Louisiana, Mississippi, North Carolina, South Carolina, Tennessee, Virginia, and West Virginia.

Trains— and our captivation with them —continue to make significant inroads in the world's economy as they transport goods to market to improve our lives and contribute to commerce, education and government. At the same time, trains move us literally and figuratively. While conveying commodities is the bulk of what railroads do, passenger rail is exhibiting a manifest resurgence. This portends optimistic promise for the future, particularly as overtaxed airways and highways and safety hazards and environmental concerns come into play.

When I launched the investigation that has netted this book, I had little idea that the wealth of information I was to encounter existed. Yet as I quickly discovered researchers were at work almost at railroading's inception, amassing prodigious details of rail history and documenting them for posterity. In addition to trains still running and depots still operating and locomotives and rolling stock still being exhibited in many mediums, I also learned the modern railfan is supported through diverse opportunities for scratching a sometimes insatiable itch: there are rail museums, excursion trains, other rail-themed attractions, traveling train shows, libraries, Web sites, publications, and a whole lot else.

There are numerous organized clusters, too, mainly contingents of volunteers that are dedicated to the expansion and preservation of railroadiana memorabilia. It's like a subculture within society's fabric and focused passionately on an area that draws possibly tens of thousands of zealous Americans. It's also impressive to observe the dedication some give to their cause.

It occurs to me that the judicious railfan or modern researcher will discover an unintentional factual error or inconsistency within these pages and say to himself: "Ah-ha!" I will, therefore, admit my guilt even before my lapses are found out. While I was completing this volume, a sharp railfan I am good friends with said to me: "I've never read a book without errors." He assured me one or more clever practitioners of the craft will turn up a handful of grievous shortcomings. For those I beg your indulgence in advance. They are commissions of the head and not of the heart, and no one laments their inclusion to the extent this author does, I assure you.

As already noted, this volume turns the spotlight on passenger trains in Dixie during the 19th, 20th and 21st centuries. While a dozen major carriers of the past headline separate chapters, there are many more that traversed Southern roadbeds which are also highlighted. There is still much more. Ten appendices supply additional material to augment what is encountered in the chapters. A few numbers are reflective: There is a glossary with 244 railroad definitions, 13 railroads receive intensive scrutiny beyond the 12 introduced in chapters, 47 railroad attractions are highlighted, there are histories of railway terminals in 53 cities, a chronology contains 69 historical entries, biographies of 22 individuals who heavily influenced Southern railroading are presented, citations of 358 important and not-so-important rail carriers in the South are introduced, 19 present and future local and regional passenger transit systems that embrace a variety of models are detailed, and 6 monorail systems now in operation are identified. The volume isn't limited to intercity rail, therefore; there's multiple forms of intracity rail from a past, present and future perspective, along with an examination of high speed rail possibly just over the horizon.

Now, come along to the land of cotton, old times there are not forgotten. For some reading this, I suspect it will be a sentimental journey we're taking, too.

I

The Manufacture of Transportation

1

MAKING TRACKS
Cumbersome Methodology Gets the Shaft

In its most primitive form, the blueprint of contemporary railroading may be traced all the way back to medieval feudalism. Antecedents of the common rail systems now in use in some of the world's leading industrialized nations are credited by some authorities to practices initially applied during the days of the Roman Empire. Did people living then determine the gauge on which the tracks of both English and American rail lines were to lie? Some theorists argue so while there is disagreement in other camps.[1]

The measurement between the wheels to the left and right sides of carts, wagons and carriages, for instance, was originally set by the ancient Greeks and Romans, at least one faction insists. Those cultures operated pushcarts over carefully defined tracks hewn from roadways. The notion of providing an even, unrestricted path to steer the wheels along parallel ruts was to thwart their vehicles from running off roads or callously rumbling on uneven stones. In manifold examples of this model the ruts measured 4 feet, 8.5 inches (56.5 inches) apart. More than 2,000 years later, that precise expanse was adopted as the common spread between the rails on train tracks in most of the world's developed nations.

The advocates of this opinion acknowledge, meanwhile, that — after the fall of the Roman Empire — the paradigm of the guided track that controlled the wheels evidently vanished for hundreds of years. It did not resurface, in fact, until the 15th century. Some modern railroad historiographers have recently alluded to rituals indicating that those basic designs— still lying dormant after a very long interval — were at last exposed. Labor-intensive forces living in the 1400s believed the idea had merit.[2] Contingents of industrious Western European miners extrapolated that nascent concept in a contrivance that made gaining their livelihoods infinitely easier.

To that point those unremitting tradesmen pushed their weighty wagons encumbered with their metal tonnage through twisting, narrowly defined sub-ground passageways. Relying on sheer physical stamina and exertion, they mustered enough collective endurance to ram those carts up steep shafts to reach the surface with their precious cargos. This was often over rough, lopsided and sometimes muddy terrain that added markedly to their struggles.

But here's an inescapable fact: until John Watt's steam engine — the first apparatus capable of turning wheels— was channeled into widespread use following its appearance in 1782, the load, speed and endurance factors in surface transportation were clearly limited to human or animal propulsion.[3] They had no other methods of accomplishing their burdensome tasks.

Those who champion the carts-and-ruts hypothesis insist that by the late 15th century — weary of repetitive, cumbersome duty — a few practical, imaginative thinkers applied the Greeks' and Romans' innovative skills to radically improve their wearying lot. In a two-part facsimile, they (a) carved grooves in the middle of broad wooden wagon wheels, and (b) made parallel guides for rolling those conveyances— using slim, horizontally level tree trunks to create a railing system. A 1513 artists' rendering depicts the unique design of their pursuit. And as word of their triumph spread, others under similar duress adapted their good fortune to their own circumstances.

Around 1550, horse-drawn wagonways appeared in Germany, maybe adding credence to the carts-and-ruts theory.[4] By the 1590s, miners throughout Western Europe adopted comparable labor-saving tactics.[5]

But what of the aforementioned opposing supposition? "We can't connect our railway age back to bits of surviving stone road," a modern historian maintains. "During the intervening thousand or so years most knowledge of the ancient world disappeared. Modern track gauge relates to the dimensions of a horse's hind end only to the extent that draft animals pulling wagons on the early tramways of Great Britain and Europe needed a path. That meant placing rails between 4 and 5 feet apart."[6]

The *real* instigator of the widely accepted 56.5-inch gauge, according to persuasive contemporary pundits, is an early English locomotive fabricator, George Stephenson (1781–1848). John P. Hankley writes, "Stephenson was a brilliant, self-taught engineer who, with his son Robert, built railways throughout the world. George was headstrong, opinionated, and arrogant. When he regarded a design as established, he tolerated no dissent. Stephenson used a ... "Northumbrian" gauge for the 1830 Liverpool & Manchester Railway, making 56-$^1/_2$ inches a formal specification. Stephenson decided the issue was settled."[7]

His insistence upon a 56.5-inch track gauge eventually gained momentum on both sides of the Atlantic. To the consternation of a few challengers using wider scales, Stephenson's choice was ultimately adopted by Parliament as the standard track gauge for Great Britain (1846). After visiting England to observe early rail operations, in 1830, founders of the Baltimore & Ohio Railroad returned to America with confidence that Stephenson's 56.5-inch scale was also good enough for them. When Congress authorized completion of a transcontinental route across the United States in 1863, the same scale was authorized for that road. Its decision had the effect of unification: other roads with varying widths (both narrower and wider) found the will, the money and the opportunity to fall into line or eventually went out of business. The necessity for consistency was compelling for innumerable reasons.

It would seem then that two schools of thought on the origins of the railway gauge are still in session. One offers a colorful reverie steeped in fabled lore, conceived in enchanting ritual. The other is perhaps more practical and tinged with realism as the basis for the system adopted by the industry so long ago.

> The belief in progress has been one of the dominant forces in Western Civilization from the Scientific Revolution of the seventeenth century to the present. Embodied in the idea of progress is the conviction that each generation will be better off than the one that preceded it. Eventually, all peoples will benefit from and share in this better world. R. R. Palmer, in his *History of the Modern World*, calls this belief in progress "a kind of nonreligious faith that the conditions of human life" will continually improve as time goes on.[8]

For more than a millennium, until the 17th century, science nevertheless advanced only modestly. Inquiry was discouraged while experimentation was practically nonexistent. If anything, science retreated while breakthroughs were pronounced irrelevant. "There had arisen a conception of science as a cycle of liberal studies for a privileged minority," historian Benjamin Farrington conjectured. Humanity's future appeared to offer little promise beyond replicating its past.

But ... surprise!

The 17th and 18th centuries ushered in sweeping changes that fashioned a climate of openness and acceptance of radical ideas. Many structures were steeped by social mobility, democracy and popular sovereignty. With that came a rebirth of scientific pursuit as centuries of stagnation eroded, overcome by a spirit of inquiry that spawned unimaginable technological advances. The resulting discoveries and inventions fundamentally increased humankind's ability to control nature and at last to actually direct a portion of it.

The Industrial Revolution arrived on the heels of this epoch of intensely visionary scientific breakthroughs, commonly designated by scholars as the decades between the years 1760 and 1840.[9] The tidal wave of changes it introduced brought incredible technological improvements that netted capabilities and efficiencies never before seen. Most of these advancements were launched in England, although they rapidly swept across Western Europe, North America and — in the first half of the 19th century — Russia, Japan and some Third World lands.

Technological, socioeconomic and cultural shifts occurred. Until then economies were almost exclusively dependent on manual labor for serious advance. In many quarters that reliance was replaced by power-driven machinery that appreciably strengthened commerce. The development was initiated by mechanizing textile production and deriving iron-making skills that wholly multiplied the ability to manufacture machinery. Trade expansion followed with the introduction of improved waterways, roads and railroads. Steam power and sophisticated equipment were responsible for dramatic growth in productive competence. "The development and application of the steam engine was probably the most important single element that characterized and contributed to the success of the Industrial Revolution," affirmed a student of the pioneering applications.[10]

The railroads were, as just observed, among those transformations. And with their emergence came — as an early informant branded the phenomenon — *the manufacture of transportation*.[11] Initially in many minds this was envisioned as a commercial means of hauling freight across (at times, vast) geographical distances with greater ease, efficiency and speed than anyone to that date believed possible. To that notion was added the capability of moving ordinary people from place to place — further, faster and often more cheaply than the usual methods relied upon in the past: foot, animals, pushcarts, wagons, carriages and waterway vessels. One observer added yet another requisite for the development of rail transit: "The War of 1812, which saw the U.S. coastline dotted with British ships, increased the necessity for a system of overland transportation."[12]

While the manufacture of transportation began with the invention of the railroad, it is more properly depicted as an outcome of the proliferation of rail networks connecting far-flung points.[13] As with so much evolving technology of the period, the English — among the world's leading powers, proffering long-established and advanced properties of culture, education, economy, order, stability and military prowess — were at the forefront of railway innovation.

A timeline of rail history signifies several key dates that were watershed moments in the development of the manufacture of transportation.[14]

1761 — Initial iron rails are laid at Bath, England.

1782 — Scottish mechanical engineer and inventor James Watt (1736–1819) crafts the first steam engine that is capable of turning wheels.

1797 — The steam locomotive is devised in England.

1802 — The Surrey Iron Railway, with horse-drawn carts, commences in south London, the world's first public freight railway.

1804 — Relying upon horse-drawn wagons, a public passenger railway is introduced for the first time anywhere in Wales.

1804 — Inventor and mining engineer Richard Trevithick (1771–1833) of Cornwall, England, constructs the world's first steam locomotive; it's financed by his cousin, mechanical engineer, inventor and mine captain Andrew Vivian (1759–1842) for the narrow gauge Penydarren Tramway in Wales.

1825—The Stockton and Darlington Railway, the first *public* railway, is launched on September 27 in England powered by a steam-driven locomotive running on rails, dubbed *Locomotion* and built by inventor and colliery enginewright George Stephenson (1781–1848) of Newcastle-upon-Tyne; the 33-car train travels 21 miles and totes more than 600 riders, most of them standing up, some crowded by freight.

1830—In the U.S., the Baltimore & Ohio Railroad, chartered by Baltimore entrepreneurs in 1827, begins passenger service May 22, initially running on literal horse power with animals pulling carriages reminiscent of mule-drawn buckboards; seeking better, the B&O discards wind-driven sails as alternate motive power in favor of a steam loco, the *Tom Thumb*, designed by industrialist-inventor Peter Cooper (1791–1883) of New York City, pulling a carload of 36 B&O executives its first time out on August 28 at 18 miles per hour.

1830—On December 25, the South Carolina Canal & Railroad Company demonstrates its *Best Friend of Charleston* steam-powered locomotive; in less than three weeks, on January 15, 1831, SCC&R initiates America's first regular rail passenger service by steam over a six-mile track, launching a new dimension in scheduled transportation. (This epic leap forward is detailed in Chapter 2.)

1868—Confederate Major Eli H. Janney (1831–1912), a dry goods store clerk following the Civil War, crafts the knuckle-coupler that today connects most passenger and freight cars, eliminating a link-and-pin system that maimed and killed railroad workers for years, a major step in safety for railway occupations.

1869—The first transcontinental railroad is completed in the United States when rail-laying crews from the western Central Pacific Railroad and eastern Union Pacific Railroad converge May 10 at Promontory in Utah territory.

1872—Machinist, engineer, inventor George Westinghouse (1846–1914) of New York patents the first automatic air brake, essentially the same system in use today; he had invented the straight air brake in 1869, perfecting it later—until then, brakemen walked the rooftops of moving trains to manually apply brakes to each car, a highly dangerous maneuver.

1881—Germany launches the world's first public electric railway.

1883—Railroad Standard Time, heralded by rail tycoons, begins at noon on November 18, dividing the United States into four time zones; after the nation follows it for 35 years, the prototype is officially sanctioned as Congress adopts the Standard Time Act on March 18, 1918, with a quartet of time zones across the continental U.S.

1887—Congress establishes the Interstate Commerce Commission (ICC) to regulate the railroad industry; ICC remains opaque and harmless for two decades until the Hepburn Act bestows it with radically larger authority in 1906, the agency thereafter issuing stringent directives to carriers with severe penalties for infractions which profoundly figure in the railroads' undoing after the mid 20th century; Congress abolishes the ICC in 1995, replacing it with the Surface Transportation Board to resolve railroad rate and service disputes and review proposed mergers.

1912—Germany's industrialist, engineer, inventor Rudolf Diesel (1858–1913) fabricates the internal-combustion locomotive engine to which his name is ultimately given.

1913—Diesel-powered railcars enter service in Sweden.

1926—Diesel-powered locomotives enter service in Canada.

1934—On October 12, the Association of American Railroads, a trade bloc with antecedents extending to 1867, formally pools a handful of diverse units into a single alliance focused on railway industry issues.

1964—Bullet train service is inaugurated in Japan with the debut in October of the Tōkaidō Shinkansen rail route running between Osaka and Tokyo.

1965—High speed rail arrives in Europe with the exhibition of 125 mile-per-hour trains sprinting between Munich and Augsburg.

1971— Amtrak officially begins on May 1, authorized by Congress in the wake of drastically diminished passenger loads and the railroads' harsh economic turbulence attributed to multiple factors; all but a handful of freight carriers trade their passenger business to Amtrak as the new entity moves travelers over some of those same freight rights-of-way.

1981— France premiers the world's first high-speed TGV line.

2000— Acela Express trains introduce North America to high speed rail at a velocity of 150 miles an hour in limited spots.

2009— President Barack Obama outlines a plan to share high speed rail with pockets of Americans into large metroplexes. Appropriating $8 billion as seed money for the system with a pledge for more, Obama vows: "We must start developing clean, energy-efficient transportation that will define our regions for centuries to come."

As the first big business to emerge in America, the railroads helped create a modern economy based on commerce and trade instead of farming. At the same time, the railways offered an efficient method of running big business that set a pattern for many other forms of industry. U.S. railroads established new professions for many citizens and provided jobs for nearly two million people. From the mid 19th century to the early 20th century, the railroads provided a livelihood "to more people than any other industry, agriculture excepted."[15] By 1916, railroads employed one out of every 25 working people in America.[16] But the contributions of railways weren't limited to mere transportation and employment.

Before the rails' existence, news of something as important as the death of an English king could take up to three months to reach all of Great Britain. The commencement of radio, you recall, was yet another century into the future while newspapers weren't yet that widespread. Following the advent of rail, however, virtually every citizen learned of such commanding news bulletins within days. In the United States, meanwhile, railroads "served as the dominant spur to technology and innovation.... Their need for high technology (of that time) advanced technology development and accelerated its diffusion into the general society."[17]

Once again, prior to the arrival of the rail lines, urban residents— generally unable to obtain a continuous stream of fresh provisions from the crops grown on farmlands in remote regions— languished as victims of frequently poor health. Freight trains changed some of that, delivering just-picked produce and fruits and farm-fresh milk to the cities and villages where people often pursued industrialized occupations. Those same trains carried the raw materials needed by the factories and then took manufactured commodities to distant places where end consumers bought and used them in their own homes and businesses.

The rails provided all of this and more. By transporting military personnel quickly and efficiently, they aided countries in their national defense. Rails helped in other ways, too, like tying solitary and sometimes inaccessible geographical territories together. The railroad gave a poorly located settlement — one not on a navigable river that could offer communication with the interior — a chance it improve its circumstances.

Andrew Jackson (1767–1845) was among the nation's earliest leaders to recognize the potential offered to the homeland by the railroads. He regularly advocated that an insufficiency of internal improvements in the country could endanger its cohesiveness and future existence as a formidable confederation. Jackson, the nation's seventh president (1829–1837), was the first of the chief executives— in an address to Congress— to officially call attention to the railroads. On December 6, 1831, he affirmed: "In the construction of railroads and the application of steam power we have a reasonable prospect that the extreme parts of our country will be so much approximated and those most isolated by the obstacles of nature rendered so accessible as to remove an apprehension that the great extent of the Union would endanger its permanent existence."

Ultimately, the rails played a critical role in forming nations, providing logical spots for hamlets, towns and cities to be established along their routes. Along those rail lines came farms, homes, schools, churches, businesses and industries. There can be no mistaking it: the coming of the railroads was a colossal factor in determining the allocations of land in new countries such as ours. The location of the rails was a crucial deciding factor in settling how and where many people lived in America in the 19th and early 20th centuries and, thereby, indisputably influencing the geography of the 21st century.

In spite of all the laudable aforementioned outcomes that can be attributed to making tracks, historiographer Stewart Holbrook, who chronicled the first century of rail operations in this country, was right on target when he allowed: "The main achievement of the railroads was to help enormously to build the United States into a world power and do it well within the span of one man's lifetime."[18] Is there any skepticism that the effects of laying those rails during that epoch were absolutely unparalleled in their achievements?

Most of the early railroads, established in the 1830s, 1840s and 1850s, were succinct and didn't link to one another. Independently owned and managed, there was little inducement for them to merge the ends of their lines together. Nevertheless, some of those early railways selected names that hinted at long-range aspirations. By the turn of the century, consolidation was the name of the game. A handful of enterprising rail barons, sensing impending rewards by developing cohesive systems reaching across long distances, began connecting the loose ends of many of the short lines. By forming circuits that traversed much of the length and breadth of the nation, they provided the capability of moving raw materials, manufactured goods, mail and people across vast stretches of land that had not been previously allied.

The growth of the railroads was frequently measured in the number of track miles in operation at a given time.[19] In 1830, the first year of rail service in the United States, a total of 23 miles was completed. That paled quickly as the industry took off. By 1840, some 409 U.S. railroad companies maintained 2,800 miles of trackage.[20] The mileage increased to nearly 9,000 within a decade. The railway revolution began in earnest in 1850 with new construction averaging 2,300 miles annually over the next score years minus the period of the War Between the States (1861–1865). Yet the railroads progressed even then.

Besides moving men and material, they acutely influenced life on the frontier. From an accustomed northerly-southerly route along the Mississippi River, the railroads swung the focus of a great deal of these denizens to a westerly-easterly course. The shift persisted following the war as the first transcontinental line was completed in 1969. President Abraham Lincoln had signed a bill in 1862, the Pacific Railway Act, authorizing the cross-country rail connection in an effort to finally unify the nation coast-to-coast. The extension of the railroad played a significant role in the settlement of more and more people across the western plains and deserts and in the mountainous areas of the West.

The average annual addition of new track laid in America in the 1880s was 7,030 miles. In the exceptional year of 1887, nearly 13,000 miles of new tracks were completed. More and more track was recorded as the years elapsed. By 1900, 193,346 miles had been laid; 16 years afterward, at what some historians consider the summit of the railroads' existence, 254,000 miles were in use.

As we have witnessed, the manufacture of transportation introduced an imposing new trade wherever it surfaced. Arriving in the United States only a half-century after it embarked on a national enterprise, the railways fostered a manner of life that symbolized a spirit of optimism, determination and pride among the new inhabitants. The locomotives and the cars pulled behind them became a hallmark affecting not merely our transit of material and people but influencing how we occupied our new home.

Can there be any doubt? In so many ways, what we are today was effectively shaped by the coming of the trains.

2

BELLE ÉPOQUE
The Golden Age of Train Travel

As previous references have shown, the application of railroading as a form of moving people from place to place wasn't among the chief considerations of those who initially envisioned an easier, faster or even cheaper method of transport. The Greeks, Romans and Western Europeans sought better hauling methods for their raw materials and — eventually — their manufactured goods. Nothing more. They had no time to consider transferring segments of the population over short and long distances.

Despite their primitive capabilities, nonetheless, their laudable intents would ultimately supply the impetus for an entire new industry. The bulk of revenues that would be realized from the ensuing trade were to be derived by moving freight rather than human beings. Still, the addition of mass transit provisions for people would be, in many instances, icing on the cake. Passenger service — for all of the many headaches that would be tied to it — would produce even more profits in some cases that could be applied to carriers' bottom lines, and substantially boost proceeds under the most favorable conditions. In transit's halcyon days, both travelers and carriers would benefit from the relationship. And it only took a few centuries to get there!

The modern philosophers of railroad history have been unable to agree on what constitutes the heyday of railroading in America. Dubbing it the *belle époque*, or golden age of train travel, one scholar attests that the epoch is bracketed by 1890 on the front end and the outbreak of the Second World War on the back end, or about 1941, extending it a full half-century. In that period, "Dozens of railroads vied for passenger business with crack trains that featured every manner of luxury and service."[1] Another source maintains that railroading's golden age in this country began about 1900 and persisted at least to 1950: "It certainly was the period in our nation's history that nearly everyone was exposed to railroads in one shape or form particularly because it was the fastest and preferred method of travel."[2] While other informants submit that the halcyon days probably lasted five decades, in their opinion, the projected timeframe shifts to an earlier era.

One advocates that "the passenger train probably reached its peak share around the mid–1890s when it is thought to have provided some 95% of intercity trips."[3] Another insists that trains carried "95% of all intercity transportation through 1910."[4] Yet another notes that public railroads were "the king of transportation" for 120 years, from their institution in 1925 in England to the end of the Second World War in 1945 with their crest arriving in 1916.[5] Track mileage in this country reached an all time high of 254,037 miles in 1916.[6] But did so long a period equate with rail's heyday? That uncertainty may have to be left to one's personal evaluation after multiple factors are considered.

One wag spilled the beans: "The fact is that during all those so-called glory years of rail travel, most Americans rode on trains that were quite ordinary — slow and probably neither

FEC Southbound #5 *City of Miami* arrives at a new Fort Lauderdale terminal powered by E9 1032 in 1962, a few decades following rails' 1920s pinnacle. In a dieselized epoch, however, "All Aboard" with trains' modern accouterments was as enticing to many travelers as the rails had been to those who experienced the preceding steam age (***photograph by Fred Carnes, courtesy Richard C. Beall***).

very clean nor very comfortable. Then as now, luxury was for the fortunate few."[7] Actually, some would be quick to depict Amtrak today in comparable fashion.

Across the years railroads have practiced open seating in their dining cars, a tradition from the bygone epoch not lost on Amtrak. On a journey from Chicago to Washington, D.C., aboard the *Capitol Limited* in late 2008, my wife and I were seated at a table opposite a couple from Mississippi. "Are you all regulars on the trains?" I respectfully probed. "No, we aren't," the husband replied. "This is our first and last trip by rail." His pronouncement, and the brief moment of silence accompanying it, spoke volumes.

There can be no denying the fact that trains aren't for everyone. And Amtrak, just like its passenger-hauling predecessors, doesn't get everything right. While trains may be for the foolhardy, they're a traveling lifestyle that one either easily embraces or doesn't. For the latter deputation, it can turn into an utter nightmare. Anybody who is put off by physical jostling or incessant rattles while en route, or who comes unglued when a menu item isn't available, or who gets upset when the published timetable isn't followed to the letter (or, at times, even close), probably isn't going to be a happy camper aboard Amtrak. It takes a special individual in no particular hurry, willing to let most grievances slide, in order to find train travel satisfying and rewarding. There is more said about this in Chapter 18 on Amtrak.

As time went on, meanwhile, the railroads became weighted down with increasing federal oversight and legislation. While offered under the argument of partially protecting the industry, it frequently netted the opposite effect. The regulatory agency created by the U.S. Congress in 1887, the Interstate Commerce Commission, was a sleeping giant during its initial couple of decades. But it waked up when the Hepburn Act took effect on June 19, 1906. Railroads "lost the greatest battle in their history," the National Association of Railroad Passengers reported, "and, with it, the right to control their own industry."[8] In the first full year of the act's application, 1907, "Formal complaints filed by shippers increased six-fold. So virulent was the anti railroad fever in the heartland that constituents of Senator William Peters Hepburn, the bill's sponsor, turned him out of office in his next election for not restricting the railroads even more."[9,10]

Had America's love affair with the rails dissipated so much that it had arrived at an abrupt conclusion? Well, certainly not if one considers it solely as a mode of passenger transportation. While rail would continue to dominate the means for moving large numbers of people from place to place for a long while, it would still be a viable form of personal transportation for many people beyond the midpoint of the 20th century.

According to figures released by Amtrak, in 1920, railroads carried 1.27 billion travelers some 47.4 billion miles, despite a 20 percent rise in rail fares that year.[11] That same year a typical American traveled by automobile 50 miles in intercity trips while journeying 450 miles by train. The pattern was reversed before the decade's end: in 1930, over-the-road vehicles took Americans 1,691 miles in intercity travel as trains carried them 219 miles. For the very first time, "Passenger service began to produce a net deficit for the railroads," Amtrak affirmed, although "for four consecutive years, 1942 through 1945, the railroads had positive earnings from their passenger service."[12]

By 1949, the combined passenger revenue from all U.S. railroads totaled $650 million, 48.6 percent of net earnings from freight. Hassles over decreasing passenger proceeds over the next two decades finally resulted in the creation of Amtrak. Despite the complications, most of the battles over declining intercity public transit service were fought largely between the industry and regulators and out of the public eye. Travelers came and went almost oblivious to the warring factions. That's a part of the story that you would expect to witness in an account of passenger service in the South only as it expressly affected it. For the most part, it's left to other texts that deal with issues pertaining to governmental control. A single example is included as an exhibition of this phenomenon occurring in the background.

The feds injected themselves into rail passenger service when President Woodrow Wilson issued an executive order creating the United States Railway Administration on December 26, 1917. Its purpose was to run America's transportation system during the First World War to benefit unified interests of the nation. Upon his appointment as the agency's director general of railroads, Secretary of the Treasury William Gibbs McAdoo (1863–1941)—who had wed Wilson's eldest daughter at the White House on May 7, 1914—ordered that each U.S. railroad abolish nonessential passenger service. Not only that, he barred competitive passenger service between rail lines. To whatever extent possible, he further ordered the railroads to reduce their aggregate passenger terminals and city ticket offices, combining operations into fewer facilities.[13]

In this same period, attempting to dissuade skilled railway employees from vacating their jobs in the rail shops and trains for more lucrative posts in the manufacturing sector, McAdoo increased wages 30 percent. The laborers saw their compensation rise 62.5 percent over what they were paid in 1916, in fact. To partially neutralize this, McAdoo raised freight and passenger rates by 40 percent, letting commerce and the public underwrite the increases. Protests from travelers netted deletion of a small sleeper surcharge but nothing more.[14]

In the meantime, McAdoo held the oversight post until the armistice was signed ending the war in November 1918. Despite his recommendation that the feds continue to control the railroads for another five years, in March 1920, Congress returned them to private ownership with greater watchdog oversight. More allowances were made to the labor force. The concessions, and disregarded equipment maintenance that languished during the war years, pushed the industry into a $1.2 billion deficit. McAdoo's successor, Santa Fe Railroad board chairman

Walker D. Hines, refused to act on owners' appeals for increases in passenger and freight rates, fearing angry reprisals from both domains.

As spelled out here, regulation — which had virtually lain dormant until shortly after the turn of the century — was suddenly alive and well. Sometimes to the consternation and utter amazement of the railroad tycoons, it made an overwhelming impact on private enterprise.

Now let us turn the spotlight on the South and the passenger service that crisscrossed it. For the uninitiated, and for our purposes in this tome, we are focusing on the region extending from the Mason-Dixon Line separating Virginia and West Virginia from Maryland, and Kentucky from Ohio and Indiana to the Gulf Coast; and from the Atlantic Ocean to the borders distinguishing Arkansas from Oklahoma, and Louisiana from Texas.

The dozen states that encompass our concentration here include Alabama, Arkansas, Florida, Georgia, Kentucky, Louisiana, Mississippi, North Carolina, South Carolina, Tennessee, Virginia, and West Virginia. Unambiguously, this is Dixie Land. And the railroads that traverse it today are modern versions of generations of predecessor systems that left enduring marks upon the region — geographically, occupationally, politically, socially, commercially — as powerful evidence of their impressive legacies.

In addition to the bureaucracy of federal oversight that was to emerge to handicap all of the railroads in the 20th century, the Southern railways experienced their own set of complex circumstances in the latter decades of the 19th century.

> From its earliest beginnings, railroading in the Deep South reflected the character of the region it served in that it was archaic, feudal, individualistic and at times eccentric.... The institutions of landholding and the merging of public and private law in a feudal system of interlocking obligations between landholder and landlord had close parallels in the ante-bellum South and after the War Between the States many parts of the South clung to this unreconstructed economy in an effort to resist Northern dominance and the industrial age it represented. As the most effective vehicle of industrialization, the railroads were feared and hated by the planter aristocracy, and in many instances these influential men were able to prevent the building of carriers into their ancestral domains so that the tracks were forced to bypass communities which in a few years found continued economic existence impossible without them. The result was the construction of a vast and intricate pattern of short independent lines to connect the once-haughty but now-humbled dissident communities with the main-line carriers.[15]

Even before all of these issues surfaced, however, the South was originating the passenger train as we know it in contemporary America and that's where this story logically starts. In the previous chapter we observed that the South Carolina Canal & Railroad Company (SCC&R) was the first in the nation to offer regularly scheduled service hauling travelers on cars pulled by a steam-driven locomotive. As with other engines of its day, this one had a name: *The Best Friend of Charleston.*

Why Charleston? One source credits Boston, Baltimore and Charleston as having "led the way in establishing major railroads in their regions to tap into the inland markets that had begun to bypass them due to the lack of connecting rivers into these same areas. The relative speed and ability to travel regardless of the weather made rail travel attractive to travelers and businesses."[16]

In 1830, SCC&R awarded a $4,000 contract to Edward L. Miller to manufacture a locomotive capable of pulling three times its own weight while covering a distance of at least 10 miles an hour.[17,18] While this is dawdling by today's standards, remember that until that time Americans were dependent on their own feet or those of animals and on boats for travel. Ten miles an hour would seem like a brisk gait to them. Miller engaged Charles E. Detmold, a New Yorker, to design the machine. Detmold's plans were then fabricated by the West Point Foundry Association, a firm situated on the banks of the North River (Hudson River) in New York City. Curiously, the manufacturer was unable to assess the execution of the locomotive prior to shipping. *The New York Journal of Commerce* reported that there was "no railroad in this vicinity upon which it could be tried." Hence, the machine departed the factory with its speed in doubt.

In actual practice, however, *The Best Friend of Charleston*, which arrived by barge at the Atlantic port city for which it was named, could perform at 15 to 20 miles per hour while hauling up to 50 passengers.[19] The 0-4-0 engine (the numbers refer to its wheel arrangement) weighed between 9,000 and 10,000 pounds. Operating at 50 pounds of boiler pressure per square inch, it could produce a traction force of over 400 pounds. The *Best Friend*'s fuel, light timber, which was specified in the original quotation, was pine firewood naturally rich in pitch. It sizzled as it was consumed swiftly and generated profuse spurts of thick black smoke.

This first true railroad in the United States with regularly scheduled passenger service went for a trial run on Christmas day 1830. Six miles of track had been completed by that time. "The six miles of railroad may properly be said to have fathered all lines since in this country," one rail historian insisted while assessing *Best Friend*'s dramatic feat more than a century afterward.[20] Behind the engine ran a flag-draped cannon-toting flatcar with three men aboard, incessantly firing the cannon. Behind them were two attached wagons bearing more than 140 Charleston socialites.[21] The train was pressed into continuously scheduled service less than three weeks later on January 15, 1831.

Best Friend provided recurring passenger service for six months, purportedly reaching speeds up to 25 miles an hour.[22] But the original newsmaking engine met an untimely end on June 7, 1831. It appears that one of the firemen launching a new profession in America — responsible for habitually feeding the engine with fuel and water — got tired of listening to the repetitively piercing hissing of the safety valve. As recorded by one source, "The first Negro ashcat on record sat on the safety valve of the South's first successful locomotive, *The Best Friend of Charleston*, until the first boiler explosion eliminated both of them."[23] A contemporary Web site established the obvious: "Our country's first railroads ... used mostly trial and error to learn what worked and what did not which, unfortunately, sometimes resulted in injuries or deaths."[24]

Not to be outdone by this unanticipated turn of events, the resolute owners of the South Carolina Canal & Railroad Company immediately set about salvaging what they could of their now defunct engine. In the locomotive's brief span of continuous service, the Southern rail barons had realized a new impetus in travel never before witnessed in America, and definitely not to the extent they had been able to provide it. They would make good on their capital investment by recouping what they could of *The Best Friend of Charleston*. Within a short while they set Charleston machinist Thomas Dotterer to work creating plans for a rebuilt *Best Friend*. Charleston manufacturer Julius Petsch then went to work implementing Dotterer's schematic.[25] The finished product, appearing under the new name of *Phoenix*, pulled passenger cars along the SCC&R rails in 1831, only a few months after the horrifying accident.

Also in 1831, SCC&R added another engine to its growing motive-power inventory. The newest named *South Carolina* with a (2 - 2) + (2 - 2) wheel arrangement — the nation's first eight-wheeled engine — was designed by Horatio Allen.[26] It, too, was constructed at the West Point Foundry in New York City. That was the plant, you recall, that had fabricated SCC&R's original engine, *The Best Friend of Charleston*, in 1930.

Flush with booming success, in 1833-1834, SCC&R officials once again hired Thomas Dotterer to draw plans for yet another engine for its use. The new locomotive, branded *Native*, was the first in the South to be constructed from the ground up.[27] Dotterer's fame spread and he soon began designing and building steam engines for other railroads. So great was the demand for his services and so prosperous was his business that the Dotterer and Company plant was relocated to Reading, Pennsylvania, to take advantage of the local iron mills.

In the meantime, when SCC&R's projected total 136-mile rail trackage was finally laid in October 1833, linking the port city of Charleston with the inland settlement of Hamburg, South Carolina, the line offered the longest continuous railroad right-of-way on the planet.[28] In common use that route was identified as the Charleston & Hamburg, extending from the Atlantic to the head of navigation on the Savannah River.[29]

SCC&R's sterling achievements in passenger transit as well as in freight hauling, and that experienced by other early railroads, netted a kind of rail mania in the U.S. After Andrew Jackson made the first presidential train trip in 1833, whatever opposition there had been to the railway systems anywhere began to dissipate promptly.[30] There was, instead, a significant increase in the number of railroads. Half of those on the planet, in fact, were operating in the United States by 1835.[31]

Five years after *Best Friend* made its impressive inaugural journey, some 1,098 miles of steam railroad were operating in America.[32] Four years hence the total increased just short of 5,000 miles (1839). The need was rapidly supplied in Dixie as new lines formed and were chartered, constructed and placed into service. While Pennsylvania led all the states in completed trackage with 947 miles in 1839, and New York was next with 573 miles, five Southeastern states successively followed with a combined 1,177 miles: Virginia, 363; Alabama, 308; North Carolina, 246; Tennessee, 164; and Louisiana, 96.

Anecdotally, author Anthony Bianculli contributes some insightful asides on building, maintaining and operating the early railroad engines which you may find beguiling.[33] They apply to *The Best Friend of Charleston* as well as ensuing locomotives in that pioneering era running throughout the United States.

> Before 1850, there were no American suppliers of railroad equipment, the engineering and manufacturing talents to build steam engines were to be found in established foundries and machine shops. Because the early locomotives were rudimentary, mechanics in these organizations were able to comprehend their operation and construction and undertake to build them....
>
> In the early years, once delivered, the various railroads were faced with the need to operate and service their locomotives. Enginemen and qualified mechanics were scarce, and it was common practice to supervise them only loosely. In the case of engineers, particularly, "they started when they were ready, ran at whatever speed they wanted to, and managed the train as they desired. They were masters of the situation and were a law unto themselves." On some roads this situation became intolerable and "unsatisfactory to the patrons." Fortunately, as railroads (and railroad machinery) became more common, crews learned to conduct operations in a more responsible and restrained manner. Yet, the perception of the engineer as an individualistic, idiosyncratic figure continued in fact for many years.

As the years rolled by there were numerous innovations in passenger service that were designed to make traveling by rail safer, more convenient and more comfortable for those aboard. Of course, they affected not only trains of the South but elsewhere. Some will be delineated in greater detail in ensuing chapters. For now, mention of a handful of the most prominent service upgrades is included in the order in which they occurred.[34]

1865—George Pullman of Chicago fabricates the prototype of what for generations will be the standard Pullman sleeper, converting seats for daytime travel into beds for nighttime use; on the Chicago and Alton Railroad, Pullman turns a trio of coaches into cars with berths in 1858-1859.

1867—Canada's Great Western Railway inaugurates the first dining car.

1880—Walking between moving railway cars is enhanced when an elastic diaphragm is added at each end of passenger cars; coupling them together nets an enclosed passageway that makes travel between lurching coaches easy and safe.

1881—The addition of steam heat to rail passenger cars improves the comfort level of travelers.

1887—Solid vestibules and electric lights placate those aboard still more.

1904—The introduction of all-steel coaches adds to passengers' safety and comfort while reducing noise levels.

1934—The first streamlined diesel passenger train begins service in the United States.

1945–1970—U.S. railroads enter the postwar era with renewed optimism, investing billions in passenger cars, freight gear and new locomotives, trading final steam engines for diesels (late 1950s); upgrades fail to arrest a decline in market share experienced prior to the war which resumes following it.

1970—Congress enacts the Rail Passenger Service Act creating Amtrak effective May 1, 1971, taking over the passenger service of most intercity railroads coast-to-coast; in modern times Amtrak's 23,000 workers serve more than 20 million riders annually with the numbers categorically indicating an upward trend.

Creature comforts were an important part of the overall rail transit experience. And some of the railroads that were genuinely committed to them operated on routes below the Mason-Dixon Line. The systems that rendered superior service to their Dixie riders made definitive statements in interpreting what Southern hospitality was all about.

We may not think of livestock when creature comforts come to mind but some railways made special provisions for animals. In baggage cars at the head ends of certain passenger trains, Florida East Coast transported celebrated horses for the south Florida winter sport of thoroughbred racing. Crews took these cars to wooden platforms at Hialeah Race Track or Tropical Park Race Track for unloading and subsequent reloading. On a West Miami siding, Tropical Park activity is seen in January 1962 (*photograph by Ken M. Ardinger, courtesy Richard C. Beall*).

For the first 100 years passenger trains were merely a means of traveling from Point A to Point B, fast and efficiently (and, for the most part, safely). During that time few luxuries or conveniences were added to trains as most merely included coaches with straight-back seats which were hardly, if at all, comfortable (something similar to school buses today). And, likewise, few of the trains had names and most were not famous.

However, that all began to change in the early 1930s when a new concept emerged, streamliners. Their existence came about for a few reasons; first was the fact that railroads were beginning to lose market share to other modes of transportation (such as automobiles) and were looking for an innovative way to bring passengers back to the rails; and second was the fact that railroads were also looking for a way to bring those passengers back so that they not only wanted to ride the rails but also wanted to do so in style, comfort, and relaxation.[35]

What precisely characterized a streamliner? Many interpretations could be applied. For our purposes, here's the comprehensive answer: In the 1930s, lightweight materials, mostly aluminum and compound metals, began to appear in rail car construction. The result netted lighter cars with corresponding advantages. For one, the sleek, wind-resistant shape of the cars—tube-like with more rounded corners and edges and less rectangular boxcar-like design—plus the lightweight materials that shrouded them, permitted the cars to travel faster than ever before. The newer fabrications naturally reduced resistance to the locomotives towing them as the steel wheels turned on the rails. It was a sharp contrast to the traditional cars that had been cast in heavyweight iron or steel or other metal alloys. Moreover, the streamliners' lighter construction diminished the damage absorbed by the rails and rail beds from the punishment of trains incessantly racing over the tracks. This factor curtailed the frequency and severity of repairs along the rail lines, thereby saving the railroads money.

To these advantages for the rail owners, of course, could be added the excitement of the passengers for something fresh and original in appearance and offering luxurious appoint-

Streamliners were in vogue from the late 1930s through the halcyon days of passenger railroading. Amtrak's northbound *Champion* has just departed the 38th Avenue North station in St. Petersburg, Florida, in 1974. Beyond Lakeland it will combine with the *Silver Meteor* from Miami to form one train for the continuation of the trip north. Led by ex–RF&P EMD E8 1011 with three more E-units behind, only the first three are powering the train; the fourth is being towed for repairs. The station canopy over the walkway between platforms is in the distance above and to the train's right. Presently on the old ACL mainline, the *Champion* will turn onto ex–SAL tracks at Clearwater for the run to Tampa before picking up ACL rails again. The whole route is owned by SCL at this time, nevertheless (*courtesy Michael B. Robbins*).

ments and greater satisfaction while in transit. The diesel-powered streamliners were "with it"—featuring modern conveniences that appealed not just to the eye but to the savvy traveler wishing to be whisked between destinations in style. The allure that the streamliners proffered was commensurate with the acclaim they achieved. Here was an innovation that in one sense wasn't going anywhere—it would be around for a very long time—while at the same time, figuratively and literally speaking, really was going someplace!

The Union Pacific Railroad was at the forefront of these changes when it launched the streamliner in February 1934: "For its time the train was an entirely new and novel concept, looking somewhat like a sleek and shiny tube with no boxy features whatsoever (contrary to the standard coaches of the day)."[36] By April of the same year the Burlington Railroad joined what would be a trend very soon, converting to its own streamliners. Countless spinoff versions followed as other railroads joined the bandwagon. Before the U.S. involvement in the Second World War occurred in 1941, almost every major line operated at least one streamlined train. The railroads running across the South took to the streamliner like a duck to water.

With that foundation, we move to the Dixie Legends—the railroads that traversed the South and brought us the fabulous trains that made travel not only incomparably memorable, but bathed in unreserved anticipation.

All aboard! The journey is about to start.

II

Dixie Legends

3

ATLANTIC COAST LINE RAILROAD
Riders of the Purple Stage

Midway in the 20th century, when a preponderance of rail carriers in the passenger sector in the United States stopped making profits from that business, at least two competitive railroads in the South were enthusiastically maintaining their public transit trade without complaint. The Atlantic Coast Line (ACL) and Seaboard Air Line (SAL) companies seemed almost oblivious to the mounting losses that some of their competitors were experiencing. Insulated by favorable routes, well-maintained and modern equipment, attentive service personnel, lots of double trackage speeding trains along while boosting safety, upgraded station facilities and perceptive and responsive management, the ACL and SAL were earning revenues every year by transporting travelers. To be sure both lines experienced declines from earlier highs, yet they were kept at ease by the public's favorable impression of the product they delivered — enough so to remain firmly entrenched with it as an underpinning of their raison d'être. At a time when most other railways were beginning to realize mammoth losses in their passenger trade, the ACL and SAL exhibited a paradigm that was to persist virtually until Amtrak acquired that province of the commerce in 1971.

So how did this pair pull off their convincing coup d'état when most of the rival systems that had perfected their passenger craft over a half-century began to wither in carloads? Multiple reasons for the others' failure and the ACL's and SAL's good fortune abound. The answers may be distilled into a handful of logical clarifications.

For one, both systems— operating in the same geographical territory in the same half-dozen states (Virginia, North and South Carolina, Georgia, Florida and Alabama) with mainlines paralleling one another between Richmond, Virginia, and most major Florida points— were widely recognized for their concern with creature comforts. Both carriers, staunch opponents until they merged in 1967, doggedly fought to attain and retain loyal patrons. Each competitor offered shiny trainsets that had eye appeal both inside and out. Modern conveniences abounded which added to the comfort and contentment of the traveling public.

The onboard staffs of both lines, meanwhile, were comprised of well-trained service-oriented individuals who routinely demonstrated professionalism above and beyond the call of duty. To most of those personnel it was obviously more than a mere job, as it showed in the way they went about performing their tasks. They liked the patrons whom they served and they wanted to keep them coming back. It was a hallmark of distinction that couldn't be accorded every member of the industry in the 1950s and 1960s. Indeed, some other systems made little attempt to hide the fact they would like to see passenger business go away forever.

Although some carriers allowed their service and equipment to deteriorate progressively, the ACL and SAL maintained theirs with utmost attention to detail. At least until the mid 1960s, ACL also added new depots and renovated existing stations along its routes; some other lines failed to properly preserve theirs or simply abandoned them altogether.

Thundering beside Southern pines, leaving a trail of smoke in its path, is #1716, a 4-6-2 leading ACL 5, the illustrious *South Wind*, southbound at Callahan, Florida, in March 1948. The famous passenger train between Chicago and Florida's two coasts hasn't yet been dieselized or streamlined with light-weight cars — that will happen in the early 1950s. So it's still huffing and puffing at its first stop in the Sunshine State, 19 miles northwest of Jacksonville. The *South Wind* isn't exclusive to ACL, of course; partners FEC, L&N and PRR propel it along their rights-of-way, too (***photograph by Hugh M. Comer, courtesy Chuck Blardone***).

Beyond the upgraded equipment, stations and service, both of these contending companies had an advantage that most other U.S. rail systems did not. "The ACL and SAL were perhaps the only two railroads in the country to serve markets so highly demanded by passengers," noted a source surveying trends affecting key U.S. rail systems.[1] Beginning in the late 1800s with the inception of through train service to Florida, the Sunshine State became readily accessible to those living outside its boundaries. "Vacationers and travelers, particularly from the northern states, were enamored with its tropical weather, warm breezes, and beautiful beaches. This tropical climate gave both railroads an unprecedented marketing advantage not found on most other systems."[2] This approbation is easily verified in the growing proliferation of trains both railroads offered from the North to points south.

In SAL's case, in its heyday there were no fewer than nine daily trains from the North (New York City, Washington, D.C., Cincinnati) to the South (Miami, Tampa, St. Petersburg, Atlanta, Birmingham) plus another daily trainset operating east-west between Jacksonville and New Orleans. ACL, meanwhile, responded with eight daily north-south streamliners originating on the upper end of the route in New York City and bound for diverse destinations that included Miami, Tampa, St. Petersburg, Sarasota, Key West, Augusta, Savannah, Wilmington and Jacksonville. Between the dual carriers, they had the Sunshine State sewed up.

Yet another crucial asset in ACL's portfolio that it relied upon heavily was a staunch com-

FEC 6, now a dieselized and streamlined *South Wind* with EMD 1005 on the point (A-A-A configuration), is running north of Eau Gallie, Florida, in April 1960, en route to Chicago. Departing Miami a few hours earlier, on reaching Jacksonville it will unite with two more sections of the *South Wind* that originated in Sarasota and St. Petersburg and persist as one train out of Florida. Eau Gallie, a tiny burg in coastal Brevard County and that jurisdiction's seat of government in the 1870s, is now a minuscule district in Melbourne into which it merged in 1969 (*photograph by David W. Salter, courtesy Chuck Blardone*).

mitment to creative marketing and advertising. Throughout its lifetime the company constantly poured huge sums into innovatively selling its passenger wares. Those efforts can't be minimized when interpreting why ACL was so successful in regularly drawing legions of travelers to its coach seats and sleeping car bedrooms. Understanding well that spending money to make money is an absolute essential, not being afraid to do so separated ACL from some of its more lackluster contemporaries.

In the glory days of 20th century passenger rail service, southbound trains were handed over to the Atlantic Coast Line Railroad at the firm's northern terminus at Richmond. The trains had reached that point via two other lines. Out of New York City they traveled the Pennsylvania Railroad's (PRR) mainline into Washington, D.C. Between the nation's capital and Richmond they journeyed over the Richmond, Fredericksburg & Potomac Railroad (RF&P).

It was commonplace, as you will observe, for adjacent railroads to unify their operations in moving freight, mail and passengers over long distances. Travelers might ultimately ride on lines owned by three or four different carriers before their trips concluded. Yet the car in which they had begun their journey often was the one in which they arrived at their final destination, barring any change of train necessitated en route. It was all done seamlessly without riders being automatically aware that they were switching to other companies or directions at some point along their route. Cars were routinely uncoupled and shifted, then attached behind different locomotives so they could continue uninterrupted to their destinations. Meanwhile, the originating locomotive pulled other cars in that consist to a separate terminus altogether.

The Atlantic Coast Line owned a very extensive set of tracks that traversed most of Florida's west coast and interior, yet it had no similar direct line of its own on the Sunshine State's east coast. To accomplish that feat ACL relied heavily upon the tracks of the Florida East Coast Railway (FEC). Geographically, the FEC hugged the Atlantic beachfront from Jacksonville to Miami and — in some early decades of the 20th century — persisted from Miami through the island keys to Key West.[3] That made it possible for Havana-bound travelers to reach the southernmost tip of the continental U.S. by rail before continuing aboard a steamship plying the Caribbean Ocean for 90 miles to reach Cuba.

In addition to the prolific human traffic it generated daily between the East Coast and Florida, the Atlantic Coast Line Railroad was in an enviable spot to channel riders between the Midwest and Florida's tropical paradise. Many of those denizens were also seeking their own places in the sun. The ACL dubbed the trainsets originating over other lines in far-flung cities like Chicago, Detroit, Cincinnati and St. Louis as its "western" system. Those trains generated less revenue than ACL's "eastern" fleet. For one reason, ACL controlled less trackage on Midwest-to-Florida runs. Yet the passengers transported back and forth between those northwestern metropolises and the sunny seacoasts could anticipate similar service to that enjoyed by riders of the purple stage up and down the eastern seaboard.[4]

As in the East, a series of Midwestern partner outfits originated the long-distance trips or carried their passenger cars along diverse routes to somewhere. They principally included the Baltimore & Ohio, Central of Georgia, Chicago & Eastern Illinois, Illinois Central, Louisville & Nashville, and Pennsylvania lines. The "western" passengers were delivered to an ACL gateway at Atlanta or Albany, Georgia, or Montgomery, Alabama, where their cars were flawlessly hooked to ACL locomotives for continuation of their trips south. Reverse exchanges at the same points transpired on northbound treks.

The remarkable passenger tradition of the Atlantic Coast Line Railroad — a flag that was diminished by the 1967 amalgamation with the SAL Railroad (as the newly-named Seaboard Coast Line) and which went out of existence altogether with the inception of the CSX Corporation on November 1, 1980 — may still be witnessed in the current Amtrak enterprise.[5]

Despite Amtrak's variable fortunes as a commercial entity, its present New York–Southeast route persists as the only long-distance corridor with multiple daily service, e.g. New York–Jacksonville, 977 miles; New York–Tampa, 1,223 miles; New York–Miami, 1,389 miles.[6] As this is written, two daily trains serve the Sunshine State from the Northeast while a third runs every day to Savannah, Georgia, a briefer 829 miles. Noteworthy is the point that, south of Richmond, much of the route the coastal trains pursue is over rails that comprised the Atlantic Coast Line system. Starting in the 1990s and at least to 2010, Amtrak's timetables brand all of these trains — plus two more exclusively serving North Carolina destinations — as *Atlantic Coast Service*. The label produces a familiar (and to ACL railfans, satisfying) ring.

The *Atlantic Coast Line* appellation has been traced as far back as 1871. That year a Baltimore, Maryland, capitalist-investor, William T. Walters, and a few of his cohorts applied that nomenclature to their most recent purchase. (We'll learn more about Walters and his heirs presently.) The troupe bought a plethora of small self-reliant railroads connecting Richmond — only six years before, the capital of the Confederacy — with the major port city of Wilmington, North Carolina. Over the next three decades the structure of the separate railways was simplified. These investors christened their compound organization "Atlantic Coast Line of Railroads" and "Atlantic Coast Line System" and, by 1893, "Atlantic Coast Line Company." In 1900, they repositioned it as a uniform entity with a name that was to stick for two-thirds of a century: Atlantic Coast Line Railroad.

But the story of this rising juggernaut has ties extending much earlier than 1871. Railroad historians cite the Petersburg (Virginia) Railroad Company as the oldest of the component lines that culminated in the ACL. The commonwealth of Virginia granted a charter to the firm in 1830, the same year the South Carolina Canal and Railroad Company invested in steam engines.[7] Residents of Petersburg, south of Richmond in Virginia's midsection, were seeking to increase their trade with North Carolina suppliers that were then heavily focused on the Tidewater area grazing Virginia's coastline. They were convinced the railroad could appreciably stimulate their local economy. Subsequently, the Richmond & Petersburg Railroad, chartered in 1836 and opened in 1838, provided the necessary extension that was to feed rail cars into the commonwealth's capital at Richmond.

At about the same time all of this was transpiring in the Old Dominion State, the Tar Heel State — just below it — was witnessing some absorbing railroad activity of its own. The Wilmington & Raleigh Railroad, chartered in 1833 (some sources claim 1835), was completed in 1840. It tied the crucial port city of Wilmington to Weldon in the eastern upstate a few miles below the Virginia border. There was a connection at Weldon with the Petersburg Railroad, allowing traffic to proceed unimpeded to Petersburg, Virginia. In 1855, this important link was renamed the Wilmington & Weldon Railroad. In less than a half-century it, too, was folded into the Atlantic Coast Line Railroad.

Of the final member of that early trio of railways, the Wilmington & Weldon, an informant wrote: "This was one of the most important roads in the South, being the mainline for carrying supplies from the deep south to Richmond and the main route for sending blockade runner supplies from Wilmington to Richmond."[8] The completion of the Wilmington & Weldon, Petersburg, and Richmond & Petersburg railroads a couple of decades prior to the start of the War Between the States (1861–1865) was to prove a godsend to the Confederacy. Along its compound route, soldiers, equipment and provisions arriving in the port of Wilmington by freighter were transported to the Southern cause's headquarters at Richmond.

On March 1, 1898, the commonwealth of Virginia approved a merger of the Petersburg and Richmond & Petersburg railroads, renamed the Atlantic Coast Line Railroad Company of Virginia. A few months later, on July 18, 1898, a pool of short lines in the Palmetto State organized into the Atlantic Coast Line Railroad Company of South Carolina.[9] Consolidated into the fold were the Wilmington, Columbia & Augusta Railroad, the Northeastern Railroad and several more: Fayetteville & Florence Railroad, Cheraw & Darlington Railroad, Manchester & Augusta Railroad and the Charleston, Sumter & Northern Railroad. In August 1899, the ACL Railroad Company of South Carolina acquired half interest in the Georgia Railroad and Banking Company from the Louisville & Nashville Railroad, giving it access to Atlanta and Macon, Georgia. That same year ACL also purchased the Charleston and Western Carolina Railway, extending from Port Royal, South Carolina, northwesterly to Augusta, Georgia, and continuing to Anderson, Greenville and Spartanburg, South Carolina. In 1899, meanwhile, the legislature in the Tar Heel State approved an application by several local concerns to form the Atlantic Coast Line Railroad Company of North Carolina. It isn't difficult to see a pattern developing here.

By 1900, all of these interests joined their operations, emerging on April 21 as the rebranded Atlantic Coast Line Railroad. Possessing the most favorable regulatory climate among the states named, Virginia was initially selected by the ACL ownership as headquarters for the new company. The ACL Railroad Company of Virginia deleted any reference to the locality in its appellation and absorbed the other companies. The Atlantic Coast Line Railroad was officially on the books.

Very early the directors of the fledgling outfit decided to consolidate their operations in headquarters facilities at Wilmington, North Carolina, nonetheless. At the start they acquired rental space. Eventually they occupied several downtown city blocks of prime real estate adjacent to both sides of the ACL tracks. The concentration in Wilmington began as early as the

1880s, expanding in the 1890s.[10] It persisted in that location through 1960. The ACL office complex included edifices labeled A, B, C, D, and a records facility. Accounting was housed in A and B, the two structures nearest the waterfront; general offices and the passenger depot waiting room occupied building C; and the rest of the ACL enterprise filled D, now the city police station.

From those structures came orders running a line that extended from Richmond to Naples, Florida, and from Wilmington to Montgomery. ACL maintained a major presence in Richmond, the northern terminus of its east coast service, and Jacksonville, a city where seven ACL routes converged — the virtual gateway to and from Florida with the notable exception of the Perry cutoff beginning in 1928. That alternate gateway allowed some Florida west coast traffic to bypass Jacksonville on its north-south journey.

There was yet another tactical burg through which almost all ACL north-south mainline traffic passed. A hefty portion of the east-west traffic went there, too. That insuperable cross-point was Florence, South Carolina, which was centralized in both importance to the ACL and in its strategic geography. In addition to a foremost freight yard and shop operation, Florence was a principal crew-change venue on the ACL. The city hardly could have been better chosen. It was situated 383 miles north of Jacksonville and 298 miles south of Richmond on the mainline. It was 110 miles west of Wilmington and 167 miles east of Augusta. And it was the southern terminus of a 63-mile freight line that ran northwest to Wadesboro, North Carolina, with connections there to Winston-Salem and major industrial centers of the North.

Florence was active into the 1960s as a servicing and refueling stop for the ACL east coast fleet. In the mid 1950s, streamliners were permitted 10 minutes for servicing, a wait reduced to five minutes a little later. Conventional trains tarried up to 35 minutes at Florence as mail and express was dispatched. Passengers often left Florence in new directions (south to west, north to east, for example). This crossroads seemingly in the middle of little else was crucial

Concentration of assets in Wilmington, North Carolina, predated ACL's formation in 1900 maybe by 20 years, an early harbinger of the role that city played in the road's life. With structures on manifold downtown blocks, ACL's passenger station, platforms and engine roundhouse (background). at mid 20th century hint at the depth of influence Wilmington had on ACL's extensive route system — and vice versa (*courtesy The North Carolina State Archives*).

At mid 20th century passenger train 55 eases out of ACL's headquarters city of Wilmington in the late afternoon and within moments approaches the Cape Fear River. It's on a 110-mile journey to Florence, South Carolina, where it will meet other trains schlepping travelers to Columbia or to Charleston, Savannah and Florida points. The originating consist will proceed another 338 miles from Florence to Atlanta. It's hauling a through sleeper and coach to the Peach State capital and a café-lounge car to Florence, where it will pick up a like diner bound for Augusta (*courtesy The North Carolina State Archives*).

to ACL's mid-route operations. Coincidentally, just a few miles north, the SAL maintained a similar junction at Hamlet, North Carolina. SAL's north-south mainline crossed there with east-west local and express traffic and passenger service to Atlanta and Birmingham.

For a few moments let's pause to examine some of the chief personalities that were involved in the formation of the ACL and in running it during its early years. We'll begin with W. T. Walters, previously mentioned.

Born at Liverpool, Pennsylvania, on May 23, 1819, William Thompson Walters moved to Baltimore about 1840.[11] He opened a wholesale liquor business there in 1847. This led him into other prospering mercantile interests. He later became president of the first steamship line operating between Baltimore and Savannah and was a director of the Northern Central Railway. Walters was absolutely convinced that the South would rise again following the War Between the States and was persuaded that the territory would not be unduly impeded by the setback. Upon his death in Baltimore on November 22, 1894, a newspaper acknowledged that he "was prominent in every great Southern company organized for transportation of freight and travel."[12]

Having developed an interest in art, Walters spent most of the Civil War era in Europe (1861–1865) acquiring costly paintings and sculptures for a personal collection. After his death, his treasures were placed in a Baltimore museum that bears his family name today. In the meantime, returning to Baltimore following the war, Walters was elected vice president of a bank and took an active role in refinancing several railroads in the South. Operating a produce commercial enterprise, W. T. Walters & Company, in 1871, he was intensely interested in raising and transporting fresh vegetables for eastern markets. With his earlier involvement in transportation, he purchased a number of short rail lines in multiple southern states. Yet it would take W. T. Walters' son, Henry Walters, to realize his father's ultimate dream: connecting a railroad that would extend from the agricultural fields of the Deep South to the markets of the North.

Born in Baltimore on September 26, 1848, Henry (nicknamed "Harry") grew up to inherit a large portion of the material possessions his father had amassed. It was he, for example, who established the art museum that included the family collection. He also possessed a similar vision to that of his dad, plus the resolve and opportunity to make it happen. Following the patriarch's death, the younger Walters formed a permanent friendship with a New York City financier of international acclaim, J. Pierpont Morgan.

Not long before, Morgan had gained control of the Richmond & Danville Railroad. Effective July 1, 1894, he and other investors initially reorganized it as the Southern Railway Company. It was renamed the Southern Railway System around the turn of the century. What began as a 140-mile local rail connection — chartered in 1847, completed in 1856, linking two Virginia cities and interim points — was to encompass 8,883 miles throughout the Southeast in the Southern empire.[13] Thus, while Henry Walters and J. P. Morgan were contemporaries, both became rail tycoons in Dixie land. A harmonious relationship between the pair improved their respective railroads by warding off some of the competition.

A contemporary rail historian provided insights into some of Walters' and Morgan's business dealings.[14]

> The Coast Line and the Southern had one common enemy, the Seaboard Air Line, which expanded to Florida in 1900. With the wealthy Southern on one side and the rich Coast Line on the other, the Seaboard Air Line Ry. was driven into Bankruptcy in 1908 (and again in December of 1930) while trying to compete with those two superior railroad systems.
>
> The friendly Morgan-Walters relationship proved very profitable for both the Coast Line and the Southern.... The Coast Line shared in the joint ownership of the Chesapeake Steamship Company of Baltimore, and received the support of J. Pierpont Morgan when acquiring the Plant System in 1902. Back in 1899 the two gentlemen had generously divided the old bankrupt Cape Fear & Yadkin Valley Ry. between themselves in a splendid spirit of co-operation.
>
> However, the choice plum granted "Harry" Walters later in 1902 by the House of Morgan was the control of the entire Louisville & Nashville RR along with its subsidiary, the NC&StL Ry., and the L&N's share in the lease of the Georgia RR (ACL of SC had become half lessee about three years previously). Included in the prize was a half interest in the Monon Route (Chicago, Indianapolis & Louisville Ry.) as a freight entrance into Chicago. The other half ownership in the Monon was held by the Southern Ry.... The close relationship between Mr. Morgan and Mr. Walters caused the Atlantic Coast Line to be dubbed for many years as a "Morgan" road.

The assignment of the Louisville & Nashville Railroad to the Atlantic Coast Line bears brief detail. It didn't produce comparable revenues or exhibit the strategic influence produced by another acquisition that year (which will be detailed momentarily), yet its importance cannot be minimized. The majority-stock gain (51 percent) of the L&N gave the ACL a steady, dependable income stream while it presented hospitable linkage to the Midwest. For all of its existence following that procurement, the L&N was operated under its own flag, clearly identified as the L&N. The L&N also controlled the Nashville, Chattanooga & St. Louis Railroad (NC&StL). In 1899, the ACL and L&N jointly leased the Georgia Railroad which controlled the Atlanta & West Point Rail Road and the Western Railway of Alabama. By linking them together, ACL maintained a through route between Augusta, Atlanta and Montgomery.

A further comment is apropos in regard to the business transactions between Henry Walters and J. P. Morgan. The presidential administration of Theodore Roosevelt (1901–1909) worked tenaciously to dissolve rail monopolies that existed in the United States, during a time in which these rail barons were quite active. "Both Mr. Morgan and Mr. Walters were far too intelligent than to be placed in any position that might engage the wrath of President Roosevelt, for operating a Coast Line–Southern monopoly," noted an astute observer.[15] Henry Walters died in New York City on November 30, 1931. In the meantime, in 1910, yet another member of the Walters tribe entered the Atlantic Coast Line family.

Lyman Delano, William T. Walters' grandson, joined the firm. He was the child of Jennie Walters Delano (1853–1922), the patriarch's only daughter, making him a nephew of Henry Walters. Born January 16, 1883, at Newburgh, New York, the Harvard grad served the ACL as general manager, vice president and chairman of the board, succeeding Henry Walters in the latter post until the early 1940s. During the First World War, Delano had been federal manager of the ACL. His death in a bizarre accident on July 23, 1944, occurred at Barrytown, New York.

In the 67 years that the Atlantic Coast Line Railroad operated under that flag, it was governed by seven presidents. Their names, some of whom will be highlighted in much greater detail presently, and their years of service were: Warren G. Elliott, 1900–1902; R. G. Erwin, 1902–1906; T. M. Emerson, 1906–1913; J. R. Kenly, 1913–1928; George B. Elliott, 1928–1942; Champion McDowell Davis, 1942–1957; and W. Thomas Rice, 1957–1967.

One of the trademarks of railroads, as with so many commercial ventures of almost any discipline, is to brand their product, idea or service with distinctive labels. Railroads have tended to maintain more than one signifying slogan giving them instant identification with the public. These messages—subtly or blatantly—convey whatever theme their owners wish to espouse. The Atlantic Coast Line was no different. From time to time advertising, promotional literature, public timetables, ticket envelopes, freight car signage, etc., was emblazoned with its mottoes then in effect. One appearing over a durable period in the latter years patently exclaimed: *Thanks for Using Coast Line.*

Railroads sought to capitalize on their advantages, of course, by highlighting them. In the 20th century the ACL often touted itself as maintaining *The Only Double Track Route between the East and Florida,* a fact that its principal rival could not refute.[16] This meant, hypothetically at least, that ACL's trains ran faster than those of its competitor whose locomotives might be forced to dawdle behind freight traffic and slower passenger trains on lengthy solo-track sections, or wait on sidings for other choo-choos to pass.

The catchphrase that ACL tended to repeat more faithfully throughout its decades of service, nevertheless, was *The Standard Railroad of the South.* It was a nebulous statement, one difficult to challenge, suggesting pretty strongly that ACL had achieved quality in the geographical territory it covered—while subliminally hinting that other contenders for the honor still had homework to do.

As discovered already Atlantic Coast Line and other railroads of its stature achieved some of their grandeur by buying up smaller lines. These independent railways were often disjointed, failing to link with one another or with any place of import outside their own regions. By connecting them directly with other lines or by laying added miles of rail line in doing so, ACL and its counterparts turned them into something far more important than they had been. In some cases those previously unimportant rails contributed to what was becoming a vast territorial stretch of mainlines that extended for hundreds of miles. Upon completion, travelers, raw materials, finished commodities and the U.S. mail could be transported without interruption over considerable distances.

Traffic to and from the populous industrialized Northeast was a keystone in developing ACL's commerce. North of Richmond, construction on the Richmond, Fredericksburg & Potomac (RF&P) Railroad began in 1834, closing the space that had separated the southern mainline from Washington, D.C., in 1842. The Pennsylvania Railroad, already in operation, would then receive and forward trains between the nation's capital and the nation's largest metropolis. A half-dozen railroads shared in controlling the RF&P by 1901, including the Atlantic Coast Line and five more carriers whose trainsets kept the route an escalating thoroughfare.

The ACL was to complete its core route map in 1902, absorbing into its assets the Plant System. This consortium of railways gathered by Henry Bradley Plant was indisputably the seminal acquisition of the Atlantic Coast Line Railroad across its 67 years as an independent domain.[17] Not only did the Plant System add 2,200 miles of tracks to the ACL's existing pool, it extended the line's reach from South Carolina southward and westward to increase its mounting geographical empire by tacking on the states of Georgia, Alabama and — strategically — Florida to its empire.

In the process the ACL secured its position in some cities while picking up some new ones, among them Savannah, Waycross, and Albany, Georgia; Montgomery, Alabama; and Jacksonville, Orlando, Tampa, and St. Petersburg, Florida, all of which were to play tactical roles in its future development. Of course, the Plant acquisition firmed up the ACL's seamless rail service on Florida's east coast via another carrier that included Daytona Beach, West Palm Beach, Fort Lauderdale, Miami and Key West. It also provided ACL routes into Atlanta and Birmingham.

There really can be no mistaking it: the Plant purchase, while not the last for ACL, was the crown jewel that made it possible to remain on one train all the way from New York or

As time elapsed, to compete effectively with archrival SAL, ACL realized it must trim time from its schedule between Richmond and Florida. A sure way was to bypass coastal Wilmington, breezing across the Carolinas to the west. While a disenchanted Wilmington wasn't on the mainline any longer, it was still ACL's base of operations. South of the city, passenger trains like this one continued to Augusta, Georgia. It's about to pass an ACL freight while crossing South Carolina (ca. 1950). ACL owned the Georgia Railroad headquartered at Augusta with L&N, which ACL also controlled. With more feeder routes in its inventory, from Augusta ACL had trackage rights to Atlanta and Montgomery (*courtesy The North Carolina State Archives*).

Chicago to south Florida. It put the balmy tropics within easy access of millions of frozen Yankees seeking their day in the sun in wintertime, many of whom made that trek annually.

At the same time, the purchase gave the ACL an opportunity to advance a Plant policy of incredible promotion of Florida. The railroad did so by organizing the Atlantic Land & Improvement Company. This subsidiary engaged in the sale and development of real estate and facilities over the entire system. It was another byproduct of this strategic acquisition that benefited the state, local and national commerce and ACL as well.

The accumulation of the short lines into ACL's system prompts many engrossing accounts. Space doesn't permit lots of details. In a nutshell, a brief mention of some of the more notable gains by the ACL not enumerated previously is included. These were acquired through purchases, trades, leases or management contracts. All contributed mightily to the freight and passenger behemoth that the Atlantic Coast Line was rapidly becoming. Such a large accumulation of leased and affiliated lines was soon to be known as the ACL "family" of railroads, the forerunner of the Family Lines System which was to embrace the L&N in its promotional references. In 1974, that marketing label was subsequently applied to the successor Seaboard Coast Line Railroad.

1904—The ACL purchases the Jacksonville & Southwestern Railroad, an improvement to transit between Jacksonville and St. Petersburg; addition of a trio of nearby short lines between 1904 and 1916 contributes to this endeavor.

1925—The ACL and L&N jointly lease the Carolina, Clinchfield & Ohio, thereafter known as the Clinchfield Railroad; it meets the ACL–controlled Charleston & Western Carolina Railway at Spartanburg, South Carolina, opening a doorway to the Appalachian coal fields in Tennessee, Virginia and Kentucky on Clinchfield's northerly route beyond its terminus at Elkhorn, Kentucky, with Chesapeake & Ohio Railway connections there to Ashland, Kentucky, and Cincinnati, Ohio.

1926—ACL buys the stock and assumes all debts of the bankrupt Atlanta, Birmingham & Atlantic Railway, altering the road's nomenclature to Atlanta, Birmingham & Coast though operating it independently; AB&C's mainline extends from the prime ACL junction at Waycross northwesterly to Manchester, Georgia, with one route there branching north to Atlanta and a second west to Birmingham, giving ACL new access from the Midwest, Atlanta and Birmingham to Florida, appreciably upgrading passenger service; the 641-mile AB&C is merged into ACL as its Western Division in 1946.

In 1928, the Perry cutoff opened, providing a more direct route between the Midwest and Tampa for the first time. Instead of traveling from west Georgia eastward to Waycross, Georgia, and Jacksonville, Florida, then retreating southwesterly to Tampa, the crisscrossing of two states could be eliminated. The new itinerary took southbound passengers from Thomasville, Georgia, east of Tallahassee, Florida, to Dunnellon, Florida, and on to Tampa. There were branches off the mainline leading to more distant south Florida resorts like Sarasota, Punta Gorda, Fort Myers, Naples and Everglades. The ACL's contributions in building up these vacation venues in the first half of the 20th century—and those of its counterpart, the Seaboard Air Line Railroad—cannot be adequately calculated but were doubtlessly gargantuan. As more and more people came to visit, more and more came to stay.

One of the most palpable disparities separating the SAL and the ACL was in how the two systems reached farthest south Florida from the state's dominant entry terminal at Jacksonville. With the common exception of St. Petersburg–bound trains, SAL shipped most of its passengers over a main that ran into Florida's midsection before breaking into dual directions. At Wildwood, which may have earned its most superlative distinction as "the place where they

A 1972 view of the ex–ACL Uceta railroad shop in Tampa, which was operated by SCL at that time. Diesel electric locomotives and freight cars were repaired and rebuilt here. A GE locomotive is in the center. Uceta yard is to the left (north side). of the repair shop building, then the main classification yard for ACL in central Florida. After the 1967 SCL merger, the yard was gradually downgraded to an SCL storage yard and intermodal facility, later CSX. On the right (south side) of the building is the SAL Yeoman Yard (courtesy *Michael B. Robbins*).

separate the trains," passengers arriving from the north were dispatched in opposite directions. One locomotive hauled west coast travelers southwesterly to Tampa, Sarasota, Venice and Port Boca Grande. Another carried east coast tourists in a southeasterly direction to West Palm Beach, Fort Lauderdale and Miami.

But the ACL — which had gained access to the Sunshine State's central and west coast cities and resorts with the purchase of the Plant System — had no tracks of its own to Miami, even though a freight route terminating at Okeelanta wasn't that far away. Arriving there would have deposited riders slightly south of Lake Okeechobee and not too far north of the marshy swamps of the Everglades— alligator country — and really not a good plan. The lights of the metropolitan centers may have beckoned but they were still too distant to see. Fortunately, in 1896, Henry M. Flagler's Florida East Coast Railway was completed. Fortunate again, investors in what was to become the Atlantic Coast Line Railroad struck a deal with Flagler to continue the ACL passenger trains southward over FEC tracks.[18]

While those Atlantic Coast Line officials yearned for a route to Miami that they could control altogether (freight trains ran up and down the FEC line creating a drawback that couldn't be ignored), that never happened. When the FEC fell into receivership during and following the Great Depression, in 1944, the ACL tried unsuccessfully to acquire the FEC. The pursuit persisted for 14 years; in fact, obstructions included a stubborn Interstate Commerce Commission, state claimants alarmed by potential loss of jobs and rivalry, fierce resistance by Seaboard and Southern owners, and an unenthusiastic ACL president, Tom Rice, who— shortly after coming aboard — was buddying up to Seaboard with merger on his mind. Things could be worse, and they got worse in a hurry in 1963.

Two years after the Florida East Coast Railway emerged from bankruptcy, 11 non-operating unions struck the outfit on January 23, 1963. At issue was the FEC's refusal to participate in nationwide compensation pacts. The line suffered a complete and immediate work stoppage. The ACL, its partner for 67 years, was suddenly without means of getting its trains to and from Miami. But the ice had been broken in 1958 on the possibility of merging with the Seaboard Air Line Railroad.

With lightning speed ACL officials struck another deal with longtime rival SAL to allow it to bring ACL trains down its own (ACL) trackage as far south as Auburndale, 59 miles south of Wildwood, where SAL's Wildwood-Miami main crossed at grade. There the ACL trains turned southeastward onto Seaboard tracks, joining SAL's route to the coast. The FEC strike that had prompted the changes languished for years, parts of it unsettled until the mid 1970s. Thus the detour became permanent, and ACL's trains to Miami operated over SAL trackage the final 220 miles of the trip south from Auburndale. The arrangement persisted until Amtrak took over the then combined passenger operations of the Seaboard Coast Line Railroad on May 1, 1971.

At the time no fewer than four passenger trains were operating over those tracks every day throughout the year, and sometimes no fewer than eight per day in each direction (16 trains). They included SAL's *Silver Meteor* and *Silver Star* and — in the winter months— the *Palmland* and *Sunland*. To that contingent was added ACL's daily *East Coast Champion*, *City of Miami* and *South Wind* on alternate days, and the daily seasonal *Florida Special*. All of those southbound trains originated in New York City with the exception of the pair running on alternating days, which traveled from Chicago by dissimilar routes to Jacksonville.

As noted already, the Northeast-to-Florida route was fundamental to the Atlantic Coast Line's focus, volume and profits. That priority was demonstrated as early as 1888 when precursor rail operators emphasized rapid, sumptuous transportation between prime destinations with the *New York & Florida Special*. By the 1920s, beyond the wintertime *Florida Special*— as that enduring train was designated following the First World War — and the *Gulf Coast Limited* and *Miamian*, both seasonal trains, the ACL offered the *Havana Special* every day all year long. There were years, nevertheless, that the cold weather months witnessed an assortment of nine ACL passenger trains traversing the main route. Even with that, more sections were still added to existing trains during the heavy winter months when demand was the greatest.

The duration of the seasonal operations shifted over time. It extended from mid December through May by the late 1930s, but was reduced to a late April finish following the Second World War. Departure schedules, meanwhile, at the end-of-the-line terminals in New York, Miami, Tampa, St. Petersburg and a few lesser Florida venues were scattered throughout the day. This provided accommodating service no matter what time travelers wished to leave. The multiplicity of choices lingered into the 1960s. While the ACL sent fewer trains over the route then, it persisted in providing convenient departure and arrival times at the furthermost ends of the route.

ACL's western service generated daily runs between Chicago and both Florida coasts that included the *Seminole* and *Southland* plus the seasonal *Dixie Flyer*. The *City of Miami* and *South Wind* left Chicago every other day on divergent routes while the *Dixie Flagler* traveled yet another course on opposite days— those three trains serving both Florida coasts (with Miami, St. Petersburg and Sarasota terminations). Finally, among the major western daily passenger runs, the *Flamingo* operated between Cincinnati and both Sunshine State coasts. Of course the ACL was busily engaged as an active participant in myriad other daily passenger runs, including service between New York–Atlanta, New York–Wilmington, and Wilmington–Atlanta–Memphis, Tennessee.

It's late afternoon, about 1950, as northbound ACL passenger consist 48 led by a new E8 slows for the eastern North Carolina burg of Warsaw after originating at Wilmington 55 miles back. In 68 more miles, this evening at Rocky Mount, it will meet up with ACL 76, the named *Havana Special.* The 48's cars will be attached for the rest of the journey to Richmond, Washington, D.C., and a New York terminus about 7 A.M. the next day (*courtesy The North Carolina State Archives*).

Its most provocative participation, however, was in the *Havana Special* during the years it operated over the Key West extension of the Florida East Coast Railway. Construction of that 153-mile single-track line began in 1904 and was completed in 1912. Running much of the way over open ocean trestles from the FEC's southern terminus at Homestead below Miami, it continued to Key West. It was one of the most ambitious engineering feats in the world. The complexity in its day would have rivaled the Chunnel linking England with France in modern times. The project was financed by Henry M. Flagler, who had built an empire of luxury resorts dotting the seaside landscapes along the Flagler-owned FEC rails between Jacksonville and Miami. His most stupefying challenge yet, the Overseas Railroad was to survive until it was dismantled by a hurricane that struck the keys on September 2, 1935.

Up until then the *Havana Special* ferried generally affluent travelers to Key West, where most of them were shuttled to Flagler-built piers to continue their journeys aboard steamships. There they crossed the Caribbean Sea 90 miles to the port of Havana, Cuba, where some of society's uppercrust vacationed in sumptuous tropical splendor. You'll find more about this in the Florida East Coast Railway chapter (6). After the storm-tossed carnage, however, the *Havana Special* sobriquet was retained but the trains ended their runs at Miami, St. Petersburg and Fort Myers or Naples.

The spirited nature exhibited by the ACL across the decades, especially as it vied for passengers with its closest rival, Seaboard Air Line Railroad, presents some fascinatingly gripping case studies in the application of practical business acumen. The intense penetration of both carriers into the same market caused the dual lines to labor incessantly and arduously to achieve similar calculated ends. Among their emphases was providing sleek, modern, fast, attractive, clean, comfortable trainsets. Particularly was this trend evidenced after the introduction of streamliners in the 1930s and the arrival of diesel motive power. Dieselizing and the newer lightweight cars began arriving at ACL in 1939.

By concentrating on those factors, ACL and SAL attempted to create favorable visual impressions among the uncommitted as well as their unswerving travelers; they hoped to convince both groups that their lines possessed a corner on the most elegant means of getting to their destinations consistently. One of the ways these competitors accomplished that was in rebuilding, refurbishing and replacing worn-out passenger cars while pioneering the use of new equipment as it became available wherever it was affordable and realistic.

The ACL was to gain still further competitive advantage as the 1930s drew to a close. It premiered a unique color scheme that immediately separated it from other major rail carriers. The new graphic display affected not only the company's advertising, signage and referential materials but effectively identified its trainsets. By dressing its locomotives as well as coach, baggage-dormitory, dining and observation-lounge cars in the royal purple hue that had long been emblazoned on its printed timetables, ACL created a stir within the industry. Furthermore the company accented its plum-tinted locomotives with yellow stripes and aluminum-gray bands. Stainless steel cars were adorned with matching royal purple letterboards displaying aluminum-gray lettering. As a result the ACL's trainsets were eye-catching, readily distinguished everywhere, their costumed bodies standing proudly within a sea of traditional hues (often black or silver) maintained by virtually every other line.

The celebrated scheme, which debuted in 1939, was to persist as an ACL hallmark through 1957. One of W. Thomas Rice's first acts after ascending to the railroad's presidency was to order abolishment of the royal purple livery. (We will learn more about Rice's contributions in due time.) He did so for mercenary reasons. Applications of the mauve paint were labor intensive with pigments fading frequently under unremitting southern sun. This necessitated a repainting job virtually every other year. Rice picked solid black as an alternate for ACL's locomotives and accented them with aluminum and yellow. Heavyweight cars, meanwhile, were returned to their traditional Pullman green. Lightweight stainless steel cars remained unpainted but bore black lettering. Dropping the royal purple which had long been an identifying symbol of the railroad was estimated to save it $100,000 annually. It was a cost-cutting move in an era in which travel by train was diminishing.

Returning to the rivalry that characterized the ongoing relationship between the ACL and SAL, on February 2, 1939, Seaboard was the first of the pair to move into the developing streamline epoch by inaugurating the *Silver Meteor* lightweight coach between New York and Miami. (A separate trainset peeled off at Wildwood for Tampa and St. Petersburg and at Tampa for Venice.) Sell-out crowds for nearly every trip were lured by the train's shiny smooth façade. Added to this were persuasive chair cars permitting at least minimal nocturnal rest (more so than travelers had been accustomed to), an inexpensive dining car and an observation-lounge car. The novelty of something this fresh and innovative was captivating to many.

According to rail historians ACL officials were initially dubious about the lightweight phenomenon that was gradually but inexorably invading the passenger cargo turf. Given the reaction they were now witnessing to the *Silver Meteor*, they could hardly afford to sit on the fence any longer, however. The company quickly placed an order with the Budd Corporation of Philadelphia for lightweight trainsets of its own. ACL would go SAL one better, nevertheless: not only would it compete with the original SAL innovation, it would put on *two* new trains concurrently!

The fact that Champion McDowell Davis was a longtime ACL loyalist, at the time serving as a vice president (and later president, 1942–1957) had no bearing whatsoever on the moniker finally selected in a widely touted train-naming competition, so some observers say. Before continuing, Davis is worthy of a little more elaborate introduction. Born July 1, 1879, near Hickory, North Carolina, Davis began working at 14 as a messenger in the freight office of

The southbound *East Coast Champion* is thundering to a stop as it passes people awaiting their relatives and friends at the Miami passenger station in 1958. The terminal is directly behind them to the east (*photograph by Fred Carnes, courtesy Richard C. Beall*).

In an opposite view of the accompanying photograph, FEC Pullman car *Cuba* brings up the rear of train 2, the *East Coast Champion*, as it's prepared to leave Miami for the trek north. While it begins the journey on FEC rails, #2 will roll onto ACL tracks at Jacksonville for most of the trip through Dixie. Note the white-coated porters beside the vestibules ready for departure (*photograph by Fred Carnes, courtesy Richard C. Beall*).

the Wilmington & Weldon Railroad, a forerunner of the ACL, in Wilmington. He was later a veteran of the Spanish-American War. After 64 years as a railroad man, the never-married Davis retired in 1957. He turned some of his attention to philanthropy and willed the family peanut plantation at Wilmington to charity. He died at 96 in Wilmington on January 28, 1975.

Back to naming those trains! The $300 prize awarded a Philadelphia lass for her entry of the name *Champion* superseded more than 100,000 others ACL received. The hoopla from that alone provoked incredible curiosity about ACL's plans for two new trains, a well-crafted PR strategy that netted a windfall of propitious reaction even before anybody had seen the trains. Some insiders still believed that the choice of *Champion* finally applied to those introductory streamliners' nomenclature, nonetheless, was selected by ACL's board of directors in appreciation of Champ Davis's contributions to the company.[19] According to ACL publicists, the *Champion* twins were among the fastest trains making the daily dash between New York and Florida. ACL's reputation for superior passenger service onboard was a symbol of their habitual splendor.

One of the new duo was named the *East Coast Champion* and sped down the Florida East Coast tracks from Jacksonville to Miami. The other, the *West Coast Champion*, sprinted along some of the former Plant System routes from Jacksonville to Tampa, St. Petersburg and Sarasota. ACL created a lot of hullabaloo in railroad competitiveness when it introduced the cloned *Champs* in December 1939. It capitalized on its expansion big time, seeking to accrue all of the mileage it could (literally) out of its newest innovation. The institution of a pair of streamliners bearing similar monikers was worthy of a major advertising blitz and ACL rose to the occasion.

Comparing the two competing lines' groundbreaking streamliners within a year of each other during the early 1950s, timetables reveal the following: the SAL *Silver Meteor* made the 1,389-mile trek from New York to Miami in 25 hours and 30 minutes while the ACL's *East Coast Champion* covered its 1,388-mile route in 24 hours 55 minutes, or 35 minutes less. The *Silver Meteor* to Florida's other coast, meanwhile, arrived at Tampa, 1,193 miles from New York, in 23 hours 45 minutes. The *West Coast Champion*, on the other hand, traveled 1,270 miles between New York and Tampa, arriving in 26 hours 15 minutes. At least some of the two-and-a-half hours on the ACL run presumably could be charged to a route that was 77 miles farther than the SAL's.

The dual *Champions* would persist into the merger epoch when, in late 1967, the *East Coast Champion* was discontinued. While the *West Coast Champion* remained with extensions from Tampa into St. Petersburg and Venice, St. Petersburg lost its direct service from Jacksonville. The Seaboard's *Silver Meteor* and *Silver Star* (the latter reaching both coasts) prevailed in serving Miami following the merger of the two systems into the Seaboard Coast Line.

There were many more trains beyond the *Champions* that were included in ACL's inventory proving equally popular with patrons fleeing their Northeastern and Midwestern habitats or who traveled for business purposes. At the middle of the 20th century, for instance, they included the New York–Miami *Everglades* plus the seasonal *Florida Special* and *Miamian*. Serving both Florida coasts from New York (with separate sections southbound out of Jacksonville, terminating at Miami, St. Petersburg and Sarasota) was the daily *Havana Special* plus the seasonal *Vacationer*. Meanwhile the *Palmetto* traveled ACL's mainline every day between New York and Savannah.

In the postwar epoch the ACL — like many other railroads — ordered scads of new lightweight passenger cars from fabricators. It took awhile, however, for production to return to prewar quotas and meet added demands. In 1949, the ACL, PRR, RF&P and FEC lines began

Amtrak's 11-car ***Champion*** is about to reach the downtown passenger station at Clearwater, Florida, on this 1973 day. It left its last stop, Tampa, on ex–SAL tracks but will head to its terminus at St. Petersburg over ex–ACL rails. SCL owns and maintains all the rails by now. The ***Champion's*** motive power is supplied by EMD E-units pulling a consist of conventional lightweight passenger cars that depend on steam from the locomotives (***courtesy Michael B. Robbins***).

receiving shipments of cars they had requisitioned three years earlier.[20] As of July 10, all of the coaches allocated to the dual *Champions* plus the *Miamian* were converted to lightweight. In addition, lightweight sleeping cars—then owned by ACL in the wake of some unresolved antitrust action against the Pullman Company — were dispersed to that trio of trains. By September 25, all of the trilogy's trainsets were lightweight. Prior to 1949, ACL owned just 51 lightweight cars. Two years later it had 148.[21]

While the purchase of new cars was costly, there were many rewards tied to them. Still, ACL sometimes found a way around that malaise by once again applying inventive imagination to improve its lot.

> The overwhelming popularity of Coast Line's lightweight trains made clear that railroads had to continue upgrading their rosters if they were to hold the patronage of an increasingly mobile, impatient, and affluent traveling public. The appeal of the new cars was good news, but the great contrast in the public eye between them and the conventional roster was not. ACL understood it had to upgrade its heavyweight cars but did not want to invest any additional funds into new equipment—for one reason, much of the public's demand for the lightweight trains came during peak travel periods only. ACL instead chose the better members of its considerable heavyweight fleet (which still comprised 283 passenger-carrying cars in 1950) and modernized them into close equivalents of the newer cars....
>
> The cars were stripped to their frames and completely rebuilt, using respaced side posts to allow for wide picture windows and new welded side panels that provided a smooth, streamlined exterior appearance. The refurbished interior was the equivalent of new lightweight equipment with electro-mechanical air conditioning, reclining seats, new lighting, and enlarged lounges. Seating capacity was a spacious 54 versus 88 in the cars' original configuration. Roller bearing trucks allowed the cars to move at streamliner speeds....
>
> The most striking change in appearance, however, was the cars' dramatic new Royal Purple color scheme ... the same as on lightweight cars.[22]

Yet another area in which Atlantic Coast Line radically advanced was in the facilities it offered its departing and arriving passengers. In a flurry of activity that was accelerated from the late 1940s into the early 1960s, many ACL depots were either replaced or refurbished, modernized to standards in keeping with the line's ongoing attempts to improve its image. Some stations were relocated on the fringes of urban areas, quite some distance from their established downtown digs. Bypass routing hastened train operations while diminishing cross-street tieups. Among cities receiving the makeovers were Savannah, Georgia, and the Florida municipalities of Gainesville, Lakeland, St. Petersburg and Sanford. Stations were replaced with modern facilities at Charleston, South Carolina, and Wilmington, North Carolina, while city ticket offices in a number of major metropolitan areas were upgraded.

Even though ACL's premier trains (the two *Champions*, *Florida Special* and *Miamian*) earned money in the 1950s, an Interstate Commerce Commission expense formula indicated that income from that source was lagging. Despite the figures, president Champ Davis wouldn't entertain any notion of scrapping the service: "Coast Line would lose more in passenger train revenues than it would save in operating expenses." He could cite statistics; in running passenger trains across Dixie in 1953, for instance, only the Illinois Central earned more than the ACL. And in that geographical territory ACL operated more passenger train miles than anybody with the exception of Southern.[23]

The fact that railroads were losing passengers in that epoch could be blamed on a number of factors. Most were beyond their control. The major culprit was prosperity. For the first time since 1929, before the stock market crash that provoked the Great Depression, in postwar America the economy was on the upswing. Years of economic disparity and gradual recovery followed by the outbreak of the Second World War put the nation into a tailspin. Suddenly, after it was all over, good-paying jobs returned and many people were able to make purchases they had been denied for a long while, through lack of spending power or because commodities simply weren't available. Housing was one of those. But also proliferating was the automobile.

Many found the family car within reach for the first time. That fact — and the promise of an upgraded super highway system in the 1950s — led many to explore the open road.[24] In doing so, they began to shun their accustomed means of long-distance travel, by train. There was also an appreciable increase in affordable airline service linking more and more places. For the first time for millions of travelers, aviation came within their grasp. The introduction of jet propulsion in the commercial sector added a compelling factor to that mix in the late 1950s.

The Atlantic Coast Line's passenger revenues that had reached $28.5 million in 1946 fell to $14.1 million in 1959. They recovered to $14.8 million the following year and held steady as the 1960s advanced, edging toward dissolution of the railroad as a separate concern in 1967. While earnings remained fairly stable, the number of passengers consistently declined, falling from almost 1.7 million in 1956 to slightly more than 1.1 million a decade later.[25] Despite the losses, ACL's management remained resolute and upbeat about the future.

As the years wore on, the ACL maintained several arrows in its quiver to attract passengers to its fold. Many years before, it had earned a justifiable reputation for providing quality equipment. With fewer trains operating in the 1950s and 1960s, ACL could supply virtually every run with lightweight or satisfactorily rebuilt passenger cars. The physical plant was equal to the task of maintaining hardware in matchless form, too. While portions of the Richmond-Jacksonville main were single-tracked in the early 1960s, new centralized traffic control systems and more signal upgrades contributed to safety on the line plus an increased ability to keep the traffic moving. Meanwhile, ACL persisted in giving attention to details that made its riders feel appreciated while onboard, looking out for their comfort. Dining cars, for example, remained full service with attractive menus. The company advertised three meals for $5 daily, a persuasive factor with many travelers in the 1960s.

This seems like a good time to mention the treatment of minorities on the Atlantic Coast Line in the years leading up to rulings by the U.S. Supreme Court ushering in racial equality. Most of the ACL local trains hauled at least two coaches, one designated for whites and one for blacks. This was in keeping with contemporary Southern custom and law (in some places) permitting strict segregation of the races. ACL owned some walled-off coaches and a handful of "Jim Crow" split baggage-coaches. Yet as a matter of practice, 1950s consists usually carried discrete cars. At the same time, ACL attempted to uphold the "separate but equal" mandate that the Interstate Commerce Commission and court edicts meted out in regard to public passenger transit.

In one expression in 1949, which may have been indicative of the ACL's perception and position on the matter, president Champ Davis reprimanded L. S. Jeffords, vice-president and general manager, in a letter. The scolding pertained to an "unfortunate and unnecessary incident" wherein a "colored" coach wasn't sufficiently air conditioned. An observant Davis affirmed that — in addition to their entitlement to equal accommodations — Negroes' patronage aboard ACL trains was "much more consistent" than whites'. It behooved the company to deplore such conditions and take steps to avoid replications. About that time ACL posted sizeable notices within its "colored" coaches thanking Negroes for their business. Not only did it seem the right thing to do in the climate of the times, it could possibly substantially increase that segment of travelers if they felt genuinely appreciated. It was another indication that ACL officials were attentive to details that mattered.

A follow-up is in order in regard to an earlier quote concerning the Seaboard as the "common enemy" of both the ACL and Southern Railway and the affluence of those pivotal lines when compared to the Seaboard. We have further observed that, in 1944, the Southern joined Seaboard to block the ACL's tries to purchase the Florida East Coast Railroad. Coupled with other issues, ACL's hopes were again dashed for control of trackage to Florida's southeast coast.

This all hints at an old theory suggesting that while two can play together fine, add a third party and there could be trouble. Wouldn't any two members of this commanding railroads' trio serving the same states find some stuff in common with one rival but not the other, leaving a "common enemy" as an outsider for a while? Seen in that light, there were times when competitive advantage might accrue to a line by ganging up with a partner on the third party. Whether those motives are noble and altruistic, it still sometimes works that way in business as well as in interpersonal relationships.

While the Seaboard Air Line Railroad may have fallen on hard times in the early decades of the 20th century, the Seaboard Coast Line Railroad—an amalgamation of the SAL and ACL in 1967—was a fusion of "two financially healthy, parallel systems that served the same six southeastern states.... ACL and Seaboard, together with the Interstate Commerce Commission, recognized that trucks and airlines—not other railroads—were fast becoming the railroads' major threat. Although the two roads had battled on many fronts, they realized they could best prosper together rather than apart."[26]

In 1958, the duo put aside the major sticking points that separated them to start examining whether unification might be a practical response to the challenges they encountered. Nine years hence, on July 1, 1967, having defeated legal roadblocks raised by neighboring railway systems and waded through a lengthy sanctioning process with the Interstate Commerce Commission, the ACL and SAL combined their rival ventures into the solitary Seaboard Coast Line Railroad.

The dual roads shared many mutual features. Chief among them was an analogous geographical territory with both carriers schlepping northerners over parallel routes to and from the popular resorts of Florida. In the 20th century, ACL and SAL—accompanied by heavy doses of advertising and promotion; sleek, modern, comfortable passenger equipment; convenient schedules; and inexpensive fares—turned travel experiences into pleasant journeys while contributing heavily to the development of the Sunshine State as a tourist Mecca. But the ACL and SAL had strengths that were unique to just one of those carriers, too.

The ACL established a weighty presence in transporting passengers from the Midwest to the Southeast—particularly to Florida. Without interruption in travelers' itineraries, it transferred their cars to and from ACL trains at Birmingham, Montgomery, Atlanta and Albany. The SAL had no similar comprehensive ability. While the ACL dominated markets in eastern North Carolina and south central Florida and offered leading service from almost anywhere on its line to Montgomery, the SAL was easily the predominant carrier between New York, Atlanta and Birmingham. On that route it operated an ample fleet of passenger trains over its own tracks. ACL's greatest physical weakness was its inability to control trackage from Jacksonville to Miami. It was a depressant that the line never saw reversed.

William Thomas Rice, who followed Champion McDowell Davis as ACL president in 1957, showed early signs of embracing the line's principal adversary, the Seaboard Air Line Railroad. It was a stance that wouldn't have been tolerated much earlier when the rival railways fought steadfastly, considering an opponent not only a threat but, to some degree, an enemy. Both ACL and SAL had been guided by an overarching theme of enlisting, converting and retaining every passenger possible, turning them into zealots who repeatedly picked their line for travel. If it meant taking spoils from the other side while engaged in battle, that was a part of doing business. Rice, on the other hand, also a lifelong railroad man, appeared more accommodating. While he was undoubtedly influenced by the rise of the automobile, developing interstate highway system and availability and economy of jet travel, he was quickly perceived as a different breed of leader than ACL had been accustomed to.

Born at Hague, Virginia, in the commonwealth's Tidewater region on June 13, 1912, he accepted a $155-a-month job at the Pennsylvania Railroad in 1934. He had just graduated from Virginia Polytechnic Institute with highest academic civil engineering honors. Rice was elevated by the PRR to track supervisor before moving to the presidency of the Richmond, Fredericksburg & Potomac Railroad on January 1, 1955. Two years hence, on August 1, 1957, he was elected to a similar capacity at the Atlantic Coast Line Railroad. This soon set into motion plans for a potential merger with the Seaboard Air Line Railway.

Acting with Seaboard president John W. Smith, Rice labored steadily to achieve the shared goal, working cautiously to be assured they got it right before taking any irreversible missteps. "While the two companies were fierce competitors," noted one observer, "similar to the Pennsylvania Railroad and the New York Central who would also merge during the same period, the difference between the two was that the ACL and SAL spent many years planning their new system in an effort to ensure the marriage would go smoothly."[27] It was a testament to the intents and creative abilities demonstrated by the principals of both companies.

One theorist suggested that one of the more attractive possibilities to Rice was in finding a way for ACL trains to reach Miami over their own tracks at last. While there were a variety of issues under consideration in the ongoing discussions, had the ownership of a Miami route become a near obsession with the ACL crowd? So it appears, if an endless procession of analysts who commented on the matter is to be believed.

During the Rice administration the Atlantic Coast Line Railroad divested itself of interests in several sideline enterprises. Principal among them were its holdings in the Peninsular & Occidental Steamship Company, dispatched in 1960, and the Baltimore Steam Packet Company (Old Bay Line) the following year. The signs were all there, if anyone possibly had missed them, that the ACL was preparing itself for a wedding in the not-too-distant future.

The unification of the two systems was ultimately accomplished July 1, 1967. The newly formed Seaboard Coast Line Railroad was administered from Jacksonville, Florida, the city to which the ACL had transferred its operational base from Wilmington at the end of 1960. W. Thomas Rice was elected president. Not inconsequentially, he filled the post of chairman of the Louisville & Nashville Railroad simultaneously. Rice's counterpart, meanwhile, John W. Smith, who had presided over the SAL since 1952, became chairman of the board and chief executive officer of the combined outfit. Whether by preplanned design or simply for undisclosed reasons, six months into the merged operation Smith was relieved of his CEO status, which was then added to Rice's presidential duties. Smith stayed on as chairman.

In 1970, upon Smith's retirement, Rice was elected chairman and CEO of the Seaboard Coast Line Railroad and of its parent firm, Seaboard Coast Line Industries, Inc. He retired in 1977. But Rice wasn't done yet. With one pivotal merger under his belt already, he was ready, willing and able to implement yet another. Working alongside Hays T. Watkins, Jr., chairman and CEO of Chessie System, Inc., on November 1, 1980, Rice had a large hand in establishing the CSX Corporation.[28] Incorporated in 1973, Chessie System, Inc., was a holding company owning the Chesapeake & Ohio Railway, Baltimore & Ohio Railroad, Western Maryland Railway and a few minor lines. On August 31, 1987, the Chesapeake & Ohio Railway, having absorbed the Baltimore & Ohio Railroad on April 30 of that year, completed the merger with CSX begun in 1980.[29]

CSX Corporation's base of operations was situated in Jacksonville, Florida, which had been the digs for predecessors Atlantic Coast Line and Seaboard Coast Line railroads extending back as early as 1960. The new enterprise combined the Chessie and Seaboard systems, including the Louisville & Nashville Railroad, under a single umbrella, instantly becoming the largest Class 1 railroad in the eastern United States. Rice was named CSX chairman emeritus. He died at 93 at Richmond on March 5, 2006.

The predecessor railroads' commitment to quality passenger service was reflected in the nearly four-year span in which the integrated enterprise operated. "We are running trains [for the traveling public], and folks still like them," Rice declared in 1969. "I believe we have an obligation to the passengers ... and there is a place for this service."[30] The SCL, therefore, was not among those lines frantically urging the federal government to remove its obligation to provide passenger service when the National Railroad Passenger Corporation (Amtrak) came into being in late 1970. On the contrary, because of SCL's inherently strong passenger showing, when Amtrak began deleting long distance trains, it found those on the Northeast-to-Florida route to be among the most celebrated with travelers. Outside the Northeast, there were more surviving trains there, in fact, than on most of the lines on which Amtrak took over passenger service.

Under a debuting Amtrak, the streamliners *Champion* running from New York to St. Petersburg, *Silver Meteor* from New York to Miami, and *Silver Star* between New York and both Miami and St. Petersburg operated daily as before on the "eastern route." The *Florida Special* was also retained for one more winter season (1971-1972). By 1976, the daily *Palmetto* was restored between New York and Savannah. It persisted for many years, and then disappeared only to resurface in Amtrak timetables in the present century.

On the "western route," meanwhile, from its start Amtrak preserved the *South Wind*, soon renamed the *Floridian*, turning it into a daily streamliner between Chicago and both St. Petersburg and Miami. A severe budget reduction imposed by Congress on Amtrak in 1979 brought the runs of the *Champion* and *Floridian* to a permanent end. Gone was the nomenclature of one of the most celebrated trains on its route which had traveled daily almost continually for 40 years. At the same time the only through passenger service between Chicago and Florida was eliminated. At that juncture a west coast section of the *Silver Meteor* was added. Tampa, like Miami, received both the *Silver Star* and *Silver*

After four decades of running up and down the Eastern seaboard, ACL's premier trains — those memorable purple-liveried *Champions* (both East and West Coast species) — headed for mothballs in 1979. How many tens of thousands of travelers did they tote over their timely tenure? Diesel 501, an E3 built in 1939, was one of two originals plying those tracks to 1970, schlepping passengers back and forth between cold climes and sunny times. It exceeded six million miles, reportedly earning status as "the most traveled E-unit in U.S. history." North Carolina's Department of Transportation bought it in 1998; as of June 13, 2009, it occupied an exalted stall at the Spencer museum's roundhouse (*courtesy Jay Miller*).

In 1976, at Sanford, Florida, dual Amtrak *Champions* pass one another. A boat-tail stainless steel observation car brings up the rear of the southbound *Champion* (to Tampa). while EMD SDP40F 600 leads the northbound version (to New York). Two locomotives furnish the motive power on each train. The SCL right-of-way is ex–ACL property (courtesy *Michael B. Robbins*).

Meteor daily, but service beyond Tampa to St. Petersburg was continued by bus rather than train.

In addition to all of this, the Auto-Train Corporation premiered a privately-owned passenger train hauling riders' cars in automobile carriers between Lorton, Virginia, and Sanford, Florida, on December 6, 1971. A second auto-train was instituted between Louisville, Kentucky, and Sanford from 1974 to 1977. It folded when it didn't generate sufficient income. The route between Lorton and Sanford was abandoned by its original operator on May 1, 1981. Seeing an opportunity there, Amtrak revived the Lorton-Sanford auto-train service in 1984. As this is written in 2009, the 855-mile overnight auto-train is one of that system's perpetually prime moneymakers.

By 2010, Amtrak's "Atlantic Coast Service" was dispatching no fewer than a half-dozen daily trains on portions of its eastern routes, including the auto-train with late afternoon departure and mid morning arrival, plus: *Piedmont*, a subsidized North Carolina service between Raleigh and Charlotte, southbound morning, northbound evening; *Carolinian*, subsidized North Carolina service between New York and Charlotte, leaving early morning, arriving mid evening; *Palmetto* between New York and Savannah, leaving morning, arriving night; *Silver Star* between New York and Miami via Tampa with bus connections at DeLand to Daytona Beach and from Tampa to St. Petersburg and Fort Myers, leaving New York late morning, arriving Miami early evening the following day, and leaving Miami midday, arriving New York the following night; *Silver Meteor* between New York and Miami with bus connections at DeLand to Daytona Beach and at Orlando to Tampa, St. Petersburg and Fort Myers, leaving New York mid afternoon, arriving Miami early evening the following day, leaving Miami early morning, arriving New York midday the following day. Schedules are always subject to change.

In the late 1990s, a seasoned Atlantic Coast Line historiographer observed[31]:

> As this is written Amtrak is considering a fascinating return to the past — restoration of service over the Florida East Coast.... The railroad and Amtrak are actively discussing rerouting the *Silver Meteor* as early as spring 2000. The new service would bring through passenger service back to the FEC for the first time since January 1963.
>
> The Atlantic Coast Line was officially formed in 1900, not quite a century ago. Even with that non–ACL name, a *Silver Meteor* running over the FEC would make a fitting salute to one hundred years of ACL service over the original New York–Miami route.

An optimist, no less! Things looked promising then. For one reason or another, that dream hasn't become reality. Despite that, from time to time there are still rumblings that cause even the most skeptical railfan to manifest hope that the visualization may turn into more than fantasy. In 2010, it appears as promising as ever. It *would* be a fitting tribute to the glory days. Perhaps yet!

4

CENTRAL OF GEORGIA RAILWAY
Horses of a Different Color

A couple of venerated thoroughbred steeds for which the Central of Georgia's (CofG) most fêted passenger trains were named are but two of the justifications for the railroad's celebrated status among Dixie carriers. Although CofG may not have ferried passengers over exceedingly vast stretches of track that a handful of railroads surrounding it did, nevertheless it supplied an utterly indispensable service to thousands of riders daily. By transporting travelers between their originating Midwest and mid–South carriers and their Florida-bound haulers, CofG fostered a crucial benefit as a bridge carrier. Every day for decades it filled the gap as legions of satisfied travelers seamlessly sped along its routes toward their ultimate destinations.

Beyond that redoubtable achievement — and particularly for those denizens privileged to live along its mainline — CofG was genuinely, enthusiastically, almost universally endorsed by the people who delivered its most loyal patronage. There were pockets of rural communities in Georgia where its name was practically spoken of in reverential tones as the locals who depended on it for frequent passage verbalized unequivocal pride in "their" train.

Its tradition is reflective of a handful of railroads principally rolling through one or two states that fulfilled their essential mission: they ferried produce, raw materials, manufactured goods and extraneous freight of sundry origin to and from the major cities in the territory while transporting the people who lived nearby. Those folk often came from pastoral surroundings and journeyed to the populous centers and returned to their native habitats, some doing so intermittently. In an era in which few transportation options were available to many folks in the more rustic districts, carriers like Central of Georgia signified an illustrious tradition as one of life's requisites.

CofG's two best remembered passenger consists were the *Nancy Hanks*, which ran a round trip daily between Savannah and Atlanta, and the *Man O' War*, which followed a similar pattern between Columbus and Atlanta. (The latter initially navigated its briefer route twice daily.) Both trains were branded after race horses that secured the attachment of millions of Americans who were suitably mesmerized by their rapid and durable rise to fame. And both trains became colorful legends in their own rights. Before delving into their magnitude further, let's review the history of the carrier whose routes they traveled.

The bearing of this company on its region cannot be overplayed: "The Central of Georgia Railway was one of the most significant railroads in the American South and a vital part of Georgia's transportation infrastructure for more than one hundred years. From its start the Central was a classic expression of the developmental American railroad, serving as a leader in the region's economic growth. With tracks that passed through some of the most productive cotton lands in the state, the Central was a vital element in the antebellum Georgia economy."[1] Not only does this have implications for the CofG's freight traffic, we shall see that it included the firm's people-moving endeavors, too.

An extensive and innovative roundhouse compound constructed in Savannah in the 1850s survives today as "the most complete antebellum railroad complex in the nation."[2] Accorded National Historic Landmark status, the CofG Roundhouse Railroad Museum is administered by the Coastal Heritage Society. The line's first diesel locomotive, SW1, purchased in 1939, and reacquired in August 2008, is exhibited there in an array of memorabilia that would cause an avowed railfan's heart to skip some beats.[3]

The Central of Georgia began in the minds of some Savannah entrepreneurs not long after railroading in the neighboring Palmetto State debuted in 1830. You may recall the narrative of the nation's first regularly scheduled passenger train service driven by steam engine that year, operated by the South Carolina Canal and Railroad Company.[4] By 1833, the SCC&R was extended from the Atlantic coastal city of Charleston 136 miles inland to the thriving commercial center of Hamburg, a warring trade rival with nearby Augusta, Georgia. Both of those waterway towns were situated on the Savannah River. From Hamburg and Augusta significant quantities of baled cotton were regularly dispatched to the textile mills of New England and Europe. That same year (1833), a rail connection into Augusta was completed, offering a continuous line between the important upriver market of Augusta and the port city of Charleston.

Returning now to those Savannah businessmen, they were of the resolute opinion that the new rail connection between Charleston and Augusta spelled doom for their own city, also on the Atlantic Ocean.[5] They had convinced themselves (perhaps with good reason) that their opportunities for business growth would be stymied without alternatives to barges and the like — and the geographical limitations those vessels presented — to get their state's raw goods to the world's markets. At the same time, they guessed (probably quite correctly) that the port of Savannah was about to suffer a devastating commercial loss to the one at Charleston, some 100 miles to the north. At Charleston, ships could pick up tons of materiel arriving by rail and carry them to the ends of the earth.

Before 1833 ended, nonetheless, those Peach State capitalists organized the Central Rail Road and Canal Company, chartered December 20 of that year. Their agreement permitted building rail and waterway connections from Savannah to the state's interior. Yet it would not be until the postbellum era following the War Between the States that the venture would establish a steamboat line linking Georgia to the major port cities of the Atlantic seaboard.[6] Down the road apiece the outfit's name was to be altered with some commonness. But it was predominantly identified by most natives of its home state as the Central of Georgia Railway, or simply "the Central."

Savannah was always its headquarters, with the caveat that in some years it was owned by some out-of-state carriers. Construction wasn't launched until 1835. Soon convinced that attracting capital investment would be a good thing for their rail system — and that that objective might be facilitated if they linked it with the banking trade — in 1835, those earliest investors rebranded their enterprise as the Central Rail Road and Banking Company of Georgia.

Eight years after construction began, in 1843, the railroad reached the periphery of Macon in central Georgia, one of the state's most populous centers. It did so through a combination of factors: state charters, an unending rise in local investments, and cheap labor supplied by Irish immigrants and Negro slaves. While it wouldn't hold the distinction for long, for a period of time in the early 1840s, the Central was purported to be "the longest railroad under one management in the world."[7]

It would be another eight years (1851) until a bridge over the Ocmulgee River was completed carrying the railroad from Savannah 131 miles into Macon proper. There the line tied into the Macon & Western Railroad, completed in 1846. That opened coastal traffic to and

Its location near Georgia's midpoint established Macon as a keystone in a Central of Georgia route system accessing manifold stretches of Peach State terrain. The carrier's Macon Shops were to be critical to its operations. This 1886 0-6-0 steam locomotive, for example, crafted by Baldwin Locomotive Works, was converted to a tank engine there in 1909. Number 8 persisted as a Macon switch engine to 1953, fondly dubbed "Maude" after a comic-strip character, *Maude the Mule*. A 2004 photograph shows "Maude," C&G's oldest extant locomotive, on exhibit at Savannah's Roundhouse Museum (*courtesy Clyde Woodruff*).

from Savannah into Atlanta (then called Marthasville, and earlier Terminus), less than 90 miles to the northwest. All of this would effectively become the mainline of the Central's operations.

Meanwhile, at Millen, Georgia, the Central was paired with the Augusta & Waynesboro Railroad (A&W), providing ready access to Augusta, 53 miles from Millen. The A&W, charted in 1838 and completed in 1854, was renamed Augusta & Savannah Railroad in 1856. The noteworthy aspect, of course, is that those Savannah entrepreneurs—who had, in 1833, sought a means of reaching Augusta by rail, among other objectives—finally had one, albeit more than two decades after planning to achieve it. It would be yet another half-dozen years (1862) before the Central would lease the Augusta & Savannah Railroad, nevertheless.

In December 1845, the Central was instrumental in chartering the South Western Railroad.[8] This line gave access into the notable Georgia burgs of Albany, Americus, Columbus and Fort Gaines. Under its various appellations across the latter half of the 19th century the Central acquired many more railroads through purchase or lease arrangements. Some of its expansion occurred outside its home state in bordering Alabama, Florida and Tennessee. Noted by year, trackage rights or ownership of those lines attained by the Central were[9]:

1855—Eatonton Branch Railroad
1855—Milledgeville and Eatonton Railroad
1855—Milledgeville and Gordon Railroad
1857—Augusta and Waynesboro Railroad

1857— Girard Railroad
1860— Barnesville and Thomaston Railroad
1862— Augusta and Savannah Railroad
1868— Muscogee Railroad
1869— Southwestern of Georgia Railroad
1877— North and South Railroad of Georgia
1879— Columbus and Atlanta Air Line Railroad
1879— Montgomery and Eufaula Railroad
1879— Vicksburg and Brunswick Railroad
1880— East Alabama and Cincinnati Railroad
1880— Savannah and Memphis Railroad
1886— Mobile and Girard Railroad
1887— Rome and Carrollton Railroad
1888— Columbus and Rome Railroad
1888— Columbus and Western Railway
1888— East Alabama Railroad
1890— Savannah and Tybee Railroad
1890— Savannah and Western Railroad
1890— Savannah, Griffin and North Alabama Railroad
1891— Upson County Railroad

The Montgomery and Eufaula Railroad was purchased in 1879, providing Alabama access. The road was initially placed in the hands of a trustee, then reorganized and conveyed to the Central of Georgia on December 14, 1895. The acquisition provided a mainline extending from Macon to Montgomery. Reaching Birmingham was another of the CofG's prime objectives. The Columbus and Western Railway obtained a line built by the Atlanta and West Point Railroad from Columbus to Opelika, Alabama, in 1883. It was extended from Opelika to Birmingham and reached that destination in 1888. Seven years later the Central acquired the whole line. By then it had mainlines for moving freight and passengers running west from the port of Savannah to Albany, Atlanta, Augusta, Birmingham, Columbus, and Macon among its paramount locations.

The Central set its sights on Chattanooga, Tennessee, next. On May 16, 1901, it took possession of the Chattanooga, Rome and Southern Railroad. That line was completed in 1888 linking Chattanooga with Carrollton, Georgia, 138 miles south. The Central added trackage farther south from Carrollton, intersecting with its Macon–Atlanta main at Griffin. In so doing the line finally connected Macon with Chattanooga while bypassing Atlanta in that process. It was another exalted feather in CofG's cap.

The CofG was able to maintain its operations fairly soundly during the first three years of the Civil War. To that point the line was deeply committed to the Confederate cause, fulfilling military, manufacturing and economic functions for the Rebel forces. Meanwhile, Union soldiers launched a strong offensive against the carrier in the summer of 1864, destroying bridges, tracks and rolling stock. "Sherman's bowties," a depiction applied to sections of rail that had been heated and twisted around Georgia trees, was part of Union General William T. Sherman's legacy. On his destructive rampage through the state from Chattanooga to the sea, Sherman ordered his army to destroy virtually every physical asset it encountered. To the surprise of many, following that immense devastation and the eventual cessation of the conflict, the railroad was able to meet its obligations with equal resolve. By June 1866, it was back in business.

In 1886, the CofG altered the gauge of its tracks from five feet to the prevailing width

On July 8, 1965, E8A units 812 and 811 lead CofG's *Seminole* at Opelika, Alabama, 27 miles west of Columbus, Georgia, and about 100 miles east of Birmingham. The pair constitutes the only CofG–owned E8A locomotives, painted in IC hues about 1959, retaining CofG lettering and reserved almost entirely for the *Seminole*. CofG made inroads into neighboring Alabama in 1879, although 16 years elapsed till the carrier gained title to trackage bearing trains from Savannah to Montgomery and Birmingham, CofG's dual westernmost termini (*courtesy Allen Tuten and Central of Georgia Railway Historical Society*).

adopted by most other carriers as their norm: four feet, eight and a half inches.[10] This, of course, allowed trains to run on lines of competitors where it might have been impossible to do so previously. Worth mentioning is the fact that, as the years passed by, CofG's agricultural traffic dropped sharply. In 1915, farm products, equipment and supplies accounted for 26.4 percent of haulage; that weakened to 6.9 percent in 1955.[11] The line's trackage, on the other hand, reached 1,944 miles in 1929, very nearly its peak.[12] In its last full year of passenger service, 1970, the CofG's mileage extended to only 1,729 miles.

While all of the give-and-take was transpiring in the antebellum and postbellum epochs, the Central was also positioning itself as a fundamental player in a frenzied period of takeovers, mergers and fraud that the railroad industry experienced. Things changed radically in 1888 when the Richmond (Virginia) Terminal Company, a holding firm with substantial interests in the railroads of the South, gained control of the Central. In time the Terminal Company would be acquired by Southern Railway.

> The Terminal extended all of its operating units a large degree of operating autonomy, and no efforts at physical or managerial integration occurred between the various railroads in its port-folio....
>
> The CofG had another layer of protection from the Terminal: a political and judicial environment in its home state that was protective of the railroad's interests. The Central of Georgia, therefore, was not folded into Southern Railway along with the Terminal's other railroads. Southern did have a financial stake in the company through 1907.... Not until 1963 would the Central of Georgia become part of Southern Railway.[13]

By 1890, owning or controlling some 2,300 miles of railroad trackage, the Central was considered "one of the most efficient and prosperous systems in the South."[14] Its dominion by the Richmond concern nevertheless—no matter how desultory it may have seemed—regrettably led to financial ruin.[15] Quandaries experienced by the parent firm forced the Central into liquidation. In 1892, the Georgia-based line was sold at foreclosure, the result of a bond default and a shareholder's lawsuit.[16]

The Central (which had been rebranded the Central Rail Road and Banking Company of Georgia in 1835, the reader may recall) was reorganized on November 1, 1895. Its new handle, the Central of Georgia Railway, became its most commonly recognized sobriquet. Sixty-two years transpired between the carrier's formation in 1833, and the time it was finally dubbed with its renowned appellation.

Acquisitions and divestitures continued to heavily influence the direction of the CofG. On April 1, 1896, for instance, the Seaboard Air Line Railroad, a major long-distance provider with a heavy commitment to passenger service between Richmond, Virginia, and the Carolinas, Georgia, Florida and Alabama, took a perpetual lease on the CofG's 58-mile Lyons Branch to Meldrim, Georgia. The CofG picked up the Middle Georgia and Atlantic Railway in 1897, and the Louisville (Georgia) and Wadley Railroad in 1898. A half-interest lease in the Georgia Railroad was discharged by the CofG to the Louisville (Kentucky) & Nashville Railroad in 1898.

Not only was the CofG busily engaged in acquisitions and divestitures throughout much of its history—beyond the transfer of railroad ownership—it was into many added commercial ventures that accrued still more capital for its operations. In the early 20th century, for instance, the CofG cultivated the coal, iron and steel industries of Birmingham, marketing them to potential investors seeking new venues for added expansion. Birmingham's massive concentration in the production of natural resources had given it the trademark branding "Pittsburgh of the South." At the same time the CofG was actively attempting to attract chemical and textile trades to Georgia for their peculiar operations.

All along its routes across the quartet of states it served, the CofG—well aware that cotton had diminished as a cash crop—sought to replace it. The railroad's economic investment team pushed new agricultural growth while highlighting commercial enterprises in diverse realms like clay and forestry production. In so doing the carrier capitalized on the products existing in plentiful quantities along its routes. The economic development of the territory served was usually a consequential function of the railroads of America. Filling not only freight cars but passenger coaches was a major goal as they attempted to increase growth and production along the way. The CofG was well positioned by recognizing the opportunities that existed within its region and by aggressively going after the kinds of trade concerns that could thrive on them.

In 1907, the CofG was purchased by a new owner, an individual whose whole life had been almost altogether vested in the industry, rail baron Edward Henry Harriman.[17] Born at Hempstead, New York, on February 25, 1848, young Harriman worked as an office boy and stockbroker on New York City's famed Wall Street before turning to management for the Illinois Central Railroad (IC).[18] Time would prove that he possessed an astonishing ability to transform rusting, decrepit rail systems into modern cash cows. Organizing a syndicate to obtain a bankrupt Union Pacific Railway in 1898, Harriman reversed the line's fortunes, helping it finally flourish.

He took control of the Southern Pacific Railroad and several more carriers. The Central of Georgia was but one of many small cogs in the wheel of this railroad tycoon's fortunes. Appraised among better known names with routes crossing vast expanses of space, the CofG could be considered minuscule in the Harriman empire. It nonetheless measurably contrasted in that portfolio against the geographical region where it was a prominent player. "Together, with the Illinois Central, the UP and SP formed the core of the Harriman system—three technically separate corporate entities that had similar organizational structures and philoso-phies and whose standardization and uniformity produced substantial economies in purchas-ing, operations, and maintenance."[19]

Some of Harriman's business practices were sternly criticized, leading to—in one assess-ment—a "blighted public image." One of Wall Street's grimmest financial setbacks resulted from an imbroglio involving the Great Northern Railroad's James J. Hill and Harriman. The two rail magnates established the Northern Securities Company in 1901, a holding company knitting the Great Northern, Northern Pacific and Burlington railroads together. Yet that became a lightning rod for increasing public opposition to trusts. Not only did the U.S. Supreme Court disperse Northern Securities in 1904, President Theodore Roosevelt, an ex-Harriman ally, sharply attacked his personal integrity. "This presidential condemnation did more than anything else to tar Harriman as a monopolistic robber baron and enemy of the people," a biographer allowed.[20]

In the meantime, not long after purchasing the Central of Georgia Railway in 1907, Har-riman's failing health and subsequent death in Orange County, New York, caused by stomach cancer on September 9, 1909, led to the line's sale that same year to the Illinois Central Rail-road.[21] The CofG was to remain under the IC flag for a long while. It entered receivership again in 1932, enduring a shaky financial status for the remainder of the Great Depression and post–Depression era and through the Second World War. In 1942, the Illinois Central wrote off its substantial investments—and those of Edward H. Harriman before it—and cut its ties to the Central of Georgia Railway.[22] Operating capital of the C&G improved dramat-ically following the war, and the 16-year receivership albatross was removed from its neck in 1948. Three years later the company purchased the Savannah and Atlanta Railway.

In this same era the CofG converted its locomotive power from steam to diesel engines just as other major carriers were doing. In the middle of the 20th century, that—plus con-solidation of its routes and the line's calculated physical placement—made it a prime target for takeover by a larger carrier. The railroad was a "desirable property" as a ready-made con-duit between the sizeable Midwest and Florida markets. And after several years of purchasing C&G stock, in 1956, the St. Louis–San Francisco Railway (widely identified as the "Frisco" line) finally gained control of the Savannah-based carrier.[23]

Linked with a trio of predecessor roads, the Frisco's heritage reached back to 1849. Fol-lowing its launch under its own moniker in 1876, Frisco was reorganized twice before 1916, when it reemerged in a third incarnation. That time it was to possess a handful of short lines in Arkansas, Florida, Kansas, Mississippi, Missouri, Oklahoma, Tennessee and Texas. In con-junction with the Missouri-Kansas-Texas Railroad (MKT or "Katy"), from 1917 to 1959, the Frisco jointly operated a luxury passenger train, *Texas Special*, running between St. Louis, Missouri, and San Antonio, Texas. In the meantime Frisco operated a couple of mainlines: St. Louis–Tulsa–Oklahoma City and Kansas City–Memphis–Birmingham.

It was the latter route, in 1956, that attracted it to the Central of Georgia Railway. Ter-minating its eastbound trains at Birmingham and Pensacola, Frisco sought a way to extend its access beyond those points. Obviously it had looked on the CofG with covetousness in its heart. Frisco viewed the Southeast regional as a meal ticket to reach the Atlantic seaboard with its lucrative shipping lanes and interstate rail connections running in every direction. But the Interstate Commerce Commission (ICC), the federal regulatory agency that oversaw the railroads as the government watchdog, was unconvinced by Frisco's purchase, to which it had given pending approval. The ICC was ultimately persuaded that the buy significantly weakened competition in the district. In 1961, it ordered the departure of the C&G from the Frisco portfolio. Frisco had no choice but to dispose of the stock it held in the Central.

Southern Railway, which had long been a dominant long-distance player in Dixie and an overpowering contemporary of the C&G, subsequently bought its outstanding stock.[24] But sadly, that didn't come about without some unpleasant features. In the early 1960s, Southern was on a buying spree, gobbling up regional, most often shortline railways that could be advantageous in increasing its already extensive freight-hauling trade. The pattern of those purchases had persisted throughout the 1950s, so this wasn't a new trend. Southern worked through multiple deals, buying the Interstate Railroad (Virginia) in 1961, the Georgia & Florida Railroad in 1963, and three succinct Georgia spans in 1966: Albany & Northern; Ashburn, Sylvester & Camilla; and Georgia Northern. Overshadowing those transactions in scope, significance and confrontation, nonetheless, was Southern's August 1960 bid to procure the Central of Georgia, which then encompassed 1,956 miles, its utmost trackage plateau.

The overarching debate in the looming projected fusion dealt with questions in regard to labor. The Interstate Commerce Commission had long sought to pacify workers when any two lines united their forces. Distinctly recognizing their rights and guaranteeing seniority privileges was crucial to the CofG unions. When the ICC gave its approval to the pairing in 1963, a number of provisos for that particular situation were stipulated. There was still enough abstraction in the language protocol that Southern president D. W. (Bill) Brosnan (1962–1967 in that office) construed a few matters to satisfy himself. "What the commission could not measure was Brosnan's hate for the unions on the Central of Georgia Railway," reported one wag. "They had dared to cross him, to question a merger he thought was for their own good."[25]

One assessment of Brosnan proclaimed that he was "one of the most polarizing figures in U.S. railroad history."[26] While his perseverance in improving efficiency paid off handsomely for his line, he was never loved by the labor unions or the workforce they represented. Meanwhile, on June 17, 1963, Southern fulfilled its requirements set forth by the ICC and took over the Central of Georgia. "The day the Southern got permission to take the Central," said author Richard Saunders, whose chronicle *Main Lines: North American Railroads 1900–1970* embraced the struggle, "it summarily dismissed 1,500 Central employees without prior notice, without implementing agreements, and without attempting to merge seniority rosters.... Among those run off, along with track workers and clerks, was Allison Ledbetter, the chairman of the Central board. He had once criticized Brosnan's purchase of specialized freight cars. No one criticized Brosnan without paying for it."

Did we say "polarizing"? Did we say "workforce"? It appears that boards of directors could be on that anti-labor enemy list, too. It was surely a portentous beginning of formal relations between the CofG and its new parent. After four-plus years of litigation, the ICC ruled that Southern must retroactively provide protective benefits to those affected workers. The order came down at about the same time age caught up with Brosnan. At 64, he left the Southern presidency that year (1967) to finish his time as chairman and chief executive officer. So who paid the price for Brosnan's dismissals, and who had the last laugh?

Southern turned the CofG into an auxiliary and allowed it to persist under its own eminent moniker, nevertheless. As such the CofG was permitted to join Amtrak when it took over most of the nation's rail passenger service on May 1, 1971.[27] (Amtrak has never called upon the Central to provide *any* service.) The corporate body of the Southern, however, took a stance that appeared defiant: "We didn't have to sign up with Amtrak," said Southern president W. Graham Claytor, Jr., Brosnan's hand-picked successor. "We could afford to keep our primary train and make it the finest in the country."[28] That was a price Claytor — who ironically became president of Amtrak in 1981— was unwilling to pay. Southern maintained a trio of daily passenger trains for a while —*Asheville Special*, *Piedmont Limited*, and *Southern Crescent*. The latter was the most prestigious and durable of the three. Southern kept it running between Washington and Atlanta every day with an extension to New Orleans three days a week through January 31, 1979. After that Southern bailed out of the passenger business, relinquishing its beloved *Crescent* to Amtrak.

When Southern determined in 1971 to merge four railroads into a single subsidiary, Central of Georgia Railway's nomenclature was once again affected, though only slightly. Southern labeled it the Central of Georgia *Railroad* (italics intended). The ancillary unit was comprised of the CofG and a trio of lines it had purchased years before: Georgia & Florida, Savannah & Atlanta, and Wrightsville & Tennille. The new arrangement survived the Southern's 1982 amalgamation with the Norfolk & Western Railway which formed the Norfolk Southern Railroad, a Class 1 freight carrier. The Central of Georgia Railroad remains an operating unit of the NS Corporation today, though few, if any, locomotives or rail cars still display Central markings. One observer, meanwhile, downgrades the line today as merely "a paper railroad within the Norfolk Southern Railway group."[29]

> The Central of Georgia still exists today, but only as an operating entity of the Norfolk Southern Corporation. For accounting purposes it is assigned ownership of some rolling stock and locomotives, but they are mostly indistinguishable from any other NS equipment. Some bear small "CG" sub-lettering....
>
> NS still operates sections of the former CG, but over the years significant trackage has been abandoned, handed over to short line operators or sold outright. The original CG line from Macon to Savannah is NS, but many of the branches down in southeastern Georgia have been abandoned. NS operates the Macon–Atlanta, Macon–Columbus and Columbus–Birmingham lines. The Griffin–Chattanooga main is chopped at the CSX crossing near Senoia, but NS operates it from south of Rome to Senoia. From Summerville to Chattanooga the Chattooga [*sic*] & Chickamauga Railway operates the former Central of Georgia....
>
> Except for the Columbus–Birmingham line, what is left in Alabama is also in the hands of short lines.[30]

The Central of Georgia's passenger service was dispersed in a variety of proportions.

After purchasing the Savannah and Tybee Railroad in 1890, the company lured tourists to Tybee Island — a coastal isthmus situated about 20 miles east of downtown Savannah — for romps in the sand, surf and sun.

The CofG was simultaneously providing fairly economical traveling connections linking a quintet of Georgia's largest metropolitan centers: Atlanta, Augusta, Macon, Columbus and Savannah. While the road served these communities with passenger trains into the late 1950s and some beyond, by 1950, the CofG was fielding 17 passenger round-trip runs daily. A handful of those were "name" trains. Seven of the 17 began or ended their CofG trips at Atlanta, six at Albany, five at Columbus, four at Macon and three at Savannah. Outside the state, C&G passenger service began or ended at Chattanooga, Birmingham and Montgomery plus a few more Alabama hamlets.

The most extensive passenger traffic lumbered over the mainline between Savannah and Macon and Macon and Atlanta with a trio of round-trips on the full route daily. Among the famous monikers hauled over CofG rails were the *Seminole* (1890–1969), *Dixie Flyer* (1908–1952), *Southland* (1915–1959), *Flamingo* (1925–1968), *City of Miami* (1940–1971), *Sunchaser* (1941–1949) and more than a dozen others. Often the better known labels were operated in conjunction with other railroads.

The number of passenger cars owned by the Central of Georgia fluctuated. As early as 1888, there were 173 in its stable. Before tapering off, the figure increased to a peak of 303 in 1919. Even though CofG still maintained 179 of the cars in 1948, the total fell to 107 by 1961.

The line's color scheme also varied over the years. A medium shade of Tuscan red enveloped CofG passenger cars in 1901. Before 1917, that was changed to Pullman green, a shade that persisted nearly three decades. In 1945, some heavyweight equipment was overhauled and repainted in blue and gray to match newly ordered streamliner cars that were to arrive in 1947. Theorists hint that may have been a throwback to the Confederacy nearly a century earlier. Whether it was so or not, Pullman green returned a dozen years afterward in 1959. Interestingly, the Central of Georgia Historical Society currently offers HO scale passenger cars manufactured by Rapido Trains and painted in "Central of Georgia's blue and gray scheme." Even though the blue-gray colors dominated the scene for only about a dozen years, notably missing in current Rapido promotions are references to Pullman green and Tuscan red hues.

Somewhere along the way the Central — like most of its competitors — adopted an identifying motto. It graced passenger car letterboards and signified the company on freight equipment and other rolling stock as well as on stationery, signage, timetables and advertising. The slogan was brief but was soon linked in the minds of travelers and haulers for the message it conveyed: *The Right Way*. The catchphrase remained visible even after other carriers took over CofG's operations.

Toward the end of the 1920s, CofG received delivery of 10 luxurious Pullman observation cars. The line added them to multiple consists, including those running overnight between Savannah and Augusta. Each car was equipped with 14 seats and occasional tables for the comfort and convenience of travelers. Appointments like those suggest that the Central was concerned that its patrons be content on their journeys, as it tried to supply them with the latest amenities. Those actions helped maintain a corps of travelers who were unswervingly loyal throughout the carrier's life.

For much of the first seven decades of the 20th century, the Atlantic Coast Line Railroad (ACL), one of a handful of foremost long-distance carriers in the Southeast, relied heavily on the Central of Georgia. The Central routinely moved no fewer than five of ACL's leading trains between the Midwest and Florida. Four of the five were daily runs. The *Seminole* and *City of Miami*, both with southbound originations in Chicago — the latter operating on an erratic schedule (sometimes two, sometimes three days weekly) — traveled Illinois Central (IC) tracks to Birmingham. The dual trains were handed over to the CofG there, proceeding to Albany for transfer to the ACL on the next leg of their treks. Arriving in Jacksonville, they were split into multiple sections: one continued southwest over ACL trackage to Clearwater and St. Petersburg, another followed a separate ACL route to Tampa and Sarasota, a third went on yet a different course to Fort Myers, while a fourth continued over Florida East Coast (FEC) tracks to West Palm Beach, Fort Lauderdale and Miami.

There was a trio of additional trains that depended upon the Central of Georgia as a bridge linking their far-flung destinations, too. All three were met by the CofG at Atlanta every day and ferried along its route to Albany for the continuation of Florida-bound runs over ACL trackage (with Miami connections via FEC at Jacksonville). One train's northern terminus was Cincinnati while the other two began trips south via different carriers leaving Chicago or Detroit, converging in Cincinnati before proceeding farther south. The *Flamingo* traveled between Cincinnati and Atlanta over a Louisville & Nashville (L&N) route. The *Dixie Flyer* left the Windy City over Chicago & Eastern Illinois rails to Nashville, where it met the Nashville, Chattanooga & St. Louis for its next leg to Atlanta. The *Southland* arrived in Cincinnati from Chicago via the Pennsylvania Railroad while its Detroit section traveled over the Baltimore & Ohio. The combined train sprinted from Cincinnati to Atlanta over the L&N route.

A distinctive of the *Southland* was that passengers traveling to Clearwater, St. Petersburg, Tampa, Sarasota and Fort Myers — prime west coast resorts — didn't crisscross Georgia first and retreat across Florida to reach their destinations. Using a cutoff bypassing Jacksonville and opened by the ACL in 1928, those patrons proceeded southbound from Albany via the ACL to Thomasville, Georgia, before entering Florida for the trek down its west coast.

The *Flamingo* powered by CofG steam engine 481 rolls along tracks at Macon, Georgia, in 1942.
Between 1925 and 1968, CofG supplied seamless connections for the passenger train between L&N
at the upper end (Atlanta) and ACL at the lower end (Albany, Georgia) on a route linking Cincinnati,
Louisville and upper Midwest origins with Florida points (*photograph by Hugh M. Comer, courtesy
Chuck Blardone*).

Central of Georgia — in addition to supplying favorable routes to the Atlantic Coast Line
and Southern Railways Systems for those carriers' crack streamliners between the 1940s and
the 1970s — operated a first-rate fleet of diesel-powered people-movers of its own. Not only
did the CofG gain notoriety among Georgia's citizens, it became a symbol of regional pride.

In its January 1936 issue, *The Central of Georgia Magazine*, an in-house monthly circulated
to employees of the railroad and its joint agencies, revealed that — for the 1935–1936 winter
season — still more North–South trains were to be handled by CofG for other lines. And some
were operating at a faster clip. Here's a sample of some of the news, still occurring in the
steam-driven era.

The deluxe *Floridian*, through Albany, Columbus and Birmingham en route to and from
Chicago and the West on its way to Florida, makes its first trip over our line January 3. Anticipating heavy travel to and from Florida this year it will be operated daily, instead of tri-weekly
as in recent winter tourist seasons.

Notably faster schedules, particularly northbound, will be in effect this year. Schedule of the

A lengthy *Flamingo* consist spreads its wings at Byron, a tiny burg in Georgia's central Peach County south of Macon. An octennial may have passed since the *Flamingo's* journey by steam, for it's now about 1950. Led by dual EMD E7A locomotives, including 802 built in 1946, the train persists under CofG tutelage between Atlanta and Albany (***courtesy Allen Tuten and Central of Georgia Railway Historical Society***).

Floridian ... is one hour shorter between Miami and Birmingham.... It leaves Miami at 10 P.M., one-half hour later than last year, and reaches Birmingham 5:35 P.M., or one half hour earlier than last year....

The *Seminole*, northbound over the same route, is 2 hours and 45 minutes faster from Jacksonville to Birmingham. Leaving Jacksonville at 11:55 P.M., it reaches Birmingham at 11:50 A.M., whereas formerly it left Jacksonville at 8:40 P.M., to reach Birmingham at 11:20 A.M.

The *New Southland* ... now takes one hour less than formerly from St. Petersburg to Atlanta. Leaving St. Petersburg at 3 P.M., it reaches Atlanta at 6:40 A.M. Southbound the *New Southland* is one hour and 25 minutes faster, leaving Atlanta at 5:40 P.M., arriving St. Petersburg 8:30 P.M.

With faster schedules, improved equipment and a severe winter with us already, indications are there will be a good bit of travel to Florida via the railroads, and all of us can recommend not only the trains mentioned, but our other Florida trains— the *Dixie Flyer, Flamingo* and new Atlanta–Jacksonville *Southland Express.*

Two decades later in a 1950 issue the same periodical urged its readers to take the Central of Georgia–Bay Line Railway combo for a summer vacation that would be incomparable. "If you go to Panama City this summer," gushed an enthused scribe, "you will view the whitest sand you've ever seen, and the beach — well, it stretches as far as the eye can reach, and then some."

A CofG train left Atlanta nightly at 10:30 P.M. for Panama City via Macon, Albany, and Dothan, Alabama, arriving Panama City at 10:55 A.M. It returned at 5:20 P.M. (6 P.M. Sundays in summer), arriving Atlanta at 6 A.M. The plug observed that arriving Pullman passengers could remain undisturbed until 8 A.M.

Of the passenger services proffered by CofG, nevertheless, two trains rose like cream to

Between Atlanta and Albany, Georgia, CofG's bridge-route status is reaffirmed by connecting L&N–borne *Southland* to ACL's shortcut to Florida's west coast opened in 1928. The route lets passengers leaving Midwest domiciles gain quicker access to their Sunshine State targets by avoiding a Jacksonville entrance: many miles and hours to Tampa, St. Pete, Sarasota and more sunny goals are thereby deleted. A southbound *Southland*, led by EMD E7A locomotives 808 and 805, plies the link to the cutoff below Macon at Hiley, Georgia, about 1950 (*courtesy Allen Tuten and Central of Georgia Railway Historical Society*).

the surface. Both were named after famous race horses. One was the *Nancy Hanks*, running between Savannah and Atlanta; the other, the *Man O' War*, operating between Columbus and Atlanta. Each made one round trip daily between their distant-most outposts and the state's capital, although *Man O' War* was launched with two round trips daily. Their schedules were specifically designed to accommodate the crowd wishing to shop, to visit friends and relatives, to keep medical appointments and to transact business in Atlanta before returning to their more bucolic origins in the evening.

Savvy marketers working for the Central of Georgia cooked up special promotions to increase the patronage. "Rich's Shoppers Specials," for instance, on both the *Nancy Hanks* and *Man O' War*, brought travelers virtually to the doorsteps of the resplendent "Department Store of the South" in downtown Atlanta — quite an adventure for many Georgians in the epoch prior to shopping malls in every burg. Through such methods and purposes, the dual trains became even more than a convenience, a true lifeline to the people of Georgia. It served to increase their users' dependency on the habit, as well as their respect for the conveyances themselves.

Neither of the new trains was shabby by any stretch of the imagination. On the contrary, both were luxurious in their appointments and approach to railway passage. American Car & Foundry (ACF) of St. Charles, Missouri, began delivering freshly-minted passenger, baggage-express and mail-baggage cars to Savannah in late 1945 — shipments ordered by CofG a few months earlier. Unable to let that opportunity pass unnoticed, the editors of the *Central of Georgia Magazine* mused pensively over those handsome gray and flashy blue-striped coaches: "Their modern design and coloring make them suitable for use in streamlined trains that we may later operate." Were those scribes dreaming dreams and seeing visions? Had they been privy to inside knowledge that would soon be widespread?

As it turned out, in 1947, the initial CofG streamliners materialized just as those scribes pontificated. And it was instantly apparent that little extra touches to pamper the riders not only had been considered but implemented, right down to an innovative lighting system. These were horses of a different color from anything their riders had previously witnessed. Although a half-dozen of the upgraded cars went into service on other trains, the bulk was tapped for those premiering (and premier) streamliners. They would be best remembered for marching across Georgia on the routes of the *Man O' War* and *Nancy Hanks*.

ACF had created the "Sunliner," a "revolutionary" coach for the Central of Georgia. An ACF ad revealed the secrets of the Sunliner's "wonderful new window," with a "Venetian blind" built right into the glass, that worked miracles. The secret was the clever new way that ACF handled deflected light.

ACF said that in daylight outside light struck deflector vanes placed within the window glass itself, and was thrown upward. Striking the baggage rack and ceiling, light was again deflected and diffused through the car. As a result, there was no sun glare and riders got "even, balanced light at all hours of the day," no matter which side of the coach they rode on.

At night the head-high fluorescent lights, also with Dayflector diffusers built into them, gave the same balance of light as in daytime. Late night travelers could "doze without pin-point lights to disturb them," as even the night lighting of the Sunliner was "indirect and restful."

The blinds also eliminated "eye shock" from rapidly varying light and shadow that could result from the train's motion. "Draw your drape, and you still get full, shadowless light."

Man O' War was the less flamboyant of the CofG's premier trains, perhaps as much due to its shorter 117-mile route than that traversed by its opposite number. Nevertheless it per-formed well while supplying a vital link between Columbus, on the state's western border with Alabama, and Atlanta in north central Georgia. This train zipped along to Pine Mountain, Newnan and Fairburn on its generally northeasterly trek to the state capital. It was hailed for a legendary stallion that racing fans had unofficially nick-named "Big Red."[31]

Man O' War was foaled in the heart of blue-grass race country at Lexington, Kentucky, on March 29, 1917. Until retirement following the Kenilworth Gold Cup on October 12, 1920, a contest some of that day dubbed "the race of the century," he was an irrefutable champion. Con-

From the inside looking out, here's what passengers saw in coaches on revered *Nancy Hanks* and *Man O' War* streamliners. Constructed by American Car & Foundry, the fleet offered sumptuous appoint-ments. Customized lighting, shading and other novel features resulted in comfortable travel experiences. With a maid aboard and a grill-lounge car on this *Hanks* consist, it's clear CofG spared little expense in trying to win and maintain patrons (**photograph by American Car & Foundry, courtesy Allen Tuten and Central of Georgia Railway Historical Society**).

Plying tracks between Atlanta and Columbus, *Man O' War* was among CofG's most revered passenger trains. In late 1949, a boat-tailed tavern-observation car, *Fort Benning*, is at the rear of the sleek silver aluminum consist departing Atlanta's Terminal Station. In addition to *Benning*, in 1947, dual coaches and a joint baggage-passenger car were fabricated for *Man O' War*. Named after a winning Kentucky thoroughbred race horse (1917–1947), many of the train's most loyal clientele believed they were aboard a champ, too (*courtesy Allen Tuten and Central of Georgia Railway Historical Society*).

sistently winning the impressive competitions in which he was entered (he won 20 of 21 starts), Man O' War outpaced a Triple Crown winner while establishing copious track records. Some of those are unsurpassed in the annals of world thoroughbred racing. Upon Man O' War's death on November 1, 1947, more than 2,000 people paid respects. The great steed was the first horse to be embalmed and rests today at the Kentucky Horse Park under a life-size statue in his native Bluegrass State. A major thoroughfare in Lexington is named Man O' War Boulevard, attesting to his legendary status.

    The thoroughbred is still held in awe by modern racing fans, and not merely through the heirs of his lineage. The fabled Man O' War's name and record is kept alive by hero-worshippers through vast merchandising efforts (shirts, mugs, plates, lunchboxes and many more items bearing his likeness), posters, pictures, decals, books, screensavers, online exhibits and an almost endless assortment of collectibles pursued by the faithful. Despite the marketing mania bordering on hokiness, "He is the yardstick that greatness is still measured against in horse racing," a modern observer of the industry conjectures.[32]

    With that kind of affirmation, is it any wonder — given the euphoria of the moment — that the Central of Georgia's namesake train honoring the great racing champion quickly garnered a loyal following? Implemented in the very year in which the venerated steed died, CofG's *Man O' War* was a natural winner itself, an instant hit with those traveling its route between Columbus and Atlanta. Launched in mid June 1947, *Man O' War* was the first all–Georgia streamliner.

At its inception it traversed the distance between its termini twice daily — morning for midday arrivals and late afternoon for evening arrivals — later reduced to a single round trip as demand fell off. Bearing stainless steel cars, *Man O' War*'s exterior sported an aluminum façade with shadow line striping. In 1952, a red hat band was added to its distinctive looks. From the start the train was made up of two dual 54-seat "chair cars" or open coaches (*Fort McPherson* and *Fort Oglethorpe*), a baggage-passenger car (*Fort Mitchell*) seating 44 and a tavern-observation car (*Fort Benning*) with a rounded tail, common in that era.

In many cases a railroad boasted just one flagship passenger train. Even if that consist could not be classified as the premier train of a line all by itself, there was often a foremost representative of the fleet that stood at the head of the line. That selection (perception) might be based on many factors: heritage, reputation, acclaim, speed, livery, equipment, service, exclusivity, endurance, or possibly some combination of them or all of those.

Whatever the factors that were working at the Central of Georgia in the mid 20th century, there was little doubt that the *Nancy Hanks* (affectionately labeled "The Nancy" by residents in the southeastern quadrant of the Peach State) stood a little ahead of other trains within that road's aggregate. Though its debut followed the inauguration of the *Man O' War* by nearly a month, in the minds of most Georgians, *Nancy Hanks* eventually pulled ahead of whatever was in second place. They spoke about it in near-reverent terms and the glories of the consist that rambled along the tracks separating Georgia's only coastal metropolis from the state capital.

> *Some folks say that the Nancy can't run;*
> *But stop, let me tell you what the Nancy done:*
> *She left Atlanta at half past one*
> *And got to Savannah at the settin' of the sun.*
> *The Nancy run so fast*
> *She burnt the wind and scorcht the grass.*[33]

The tale behind naming of the *Nancy Hanks* bears repeating. There were two of those trains, in fact, separated by 54 years, and their heritage stemmed from a famous president's mother.[34] The early train was steam-driven while the latter was diesel-powered. (To be precisely correct it was dubbed the *Nancy Hanks II*.) Each bore the image on the side of the famed trotter for which it was signified. On September 28, 1892, as the *Nancy Hanks* passenger train legacy began, bay mare Nancy Hanks was crowned the world's fastest trotter at 2:04 for the mile during an exhibition at Terre Haute, Indiana.

Like Man O' War, Nancy Hanks had been foaled in Fayette County, Kentucky, in pure bluegrass country, in 1886. "It's nigh on impossible to write something about this outstanding mare that will ever do her justice," allowed an equestrian historian.[35] While she lost her first heat at Harrodsburg, Kentucky, in 1889, it was the only time in Nancy Hanks' career of five seasons that any other horse beat her. She made six more races in 1889 and won them all. She won all six races in which she was entered the following year, nine the following year and three more before her record-smashing win at Terre Haute. Nancy Hanks was the first trotter to complete the mile in 2:05 or better. The celebrated mare that produced 11 foals following her retirement died on August 16, 1915. She was buried at Hamburg Place in Lexington, Kentucky.

In 1892 the Central of Georgia bought compound #1592 from Baldwin Locomotive Works and named the locomotive "Nancy Hanks" after the mare that held the world mile trotting record at the time; the mare herself was said to have been named after Abraham Lincoln's mother. The following year the locomotive was assigned to a special Savannah–Atlanta passenger train, and soon the moniker migrated from the locomotive to the entire train, which sported blue and gold coaches, with each bearing a likeness to the renowned mare. Service was cancelled, however, on

The original *Nancy Hanks,* a Baldwin-fabricated 4-4-0 steam-powered consist, was also named after a famous Kentucky horse (1886–1915). The train that took her moniker lasted from 1892 to 1893. It returned to the tracks, however, in 1947, as *Nancy Hanks II.* On that occasion it gained far more mileage, fame and appeal than its forebears, both the four-legged and eight-wheeled varieties. *Nancy* became a legend across the Peach State, at last running its final race in 1971 (***courtesy Allen Tuten and Central of Georgia Railway Historical Society***).

> August 13, 1893, after several "Nancys" trotted off the tracks, which at the time was unprepared for the speeds that Compound could make when she stretched out her long legs.
>
> Fifty four years later on July 17, 1947, Central's quick footed coast-to-capitol service returned, this time to much more capable trackage, in the form of a beautiful blue and gray four-car diesel powered streamliner, the *Nancy Hanks II.* The cars were from American Car and Foundry, the power from General Motors, and the service was an immediate success. Central applied the same sound philosophy to the *Nancy Hanks II* that it applied to the *Man O' War*—cheap fares and a ninety-notches-and-no-smoke schedule in combination to draw Georgians out of their ever more beloved automobiles.[36]

There were 12 schedule stops and a trio of flag stops between Savannah Passenger Depot and Atlanta Terminal Station along the 294-mile journey. The route carried westbound travelers to Millen, Wadley, Tennille, Macon, Forsyth, Griffin and Jonesboro.

At Millen, in the late 1940s and early 1950s, the train met up with *Little Nancy,* a separate consist which carried connecting passengers to and from Augusta. "The Nancy" was an all-coach, reserved-seat train with food service provided by a grill-lounge car, and it even had a maid aboard. Inveterate patrons found the menu's "Nancy Burgers," corned beef and eggs and Middle Georgia vegetables tasty treats. The train departed from Savannah each morning at seven o'clock, pausing just five minutes in Macon before sprinting to Atlanta, arriving at 12:40 P.M. At 6 P.M. it left the capital city for the return journey to the coast, arriving just before midnight.

Ridership soared from the start. Demand for seats was so great, in fact, that on weekdays a fifth car was added while on weekends a sixth car was required to supply the needs. Throughout the late 1940s and the 1950s, *Nancy Hanks* was a fundamental link between the points it served and the hordes of Georgians who were devoted to her. But by the 1960s, some of her luster began to wear off: "Airlines were no longer just exotic luxuries for the wealthy and every year a bridge replaced one more ferry and a few more red clay hills were cut down and smoothed over by a ribbon of asphalt. Georgians could drive their own automobiles to Rich's."[37]

You have read already of the sorrowing experience in disintegrating labor relations when the Southern Railway System acquired the Central of Georgia in 1963. Though that put a

Departing Atlanta's Terminal Station, ca. late 1949, *Nancy Hanks II* led by CofG E7A 804 begins a nightly trip to the coast by Jonesboro, Griffin, Forsyth, Macon, Tennille, Wadley, Millen and other burgs. It's expected to arrive Savannah in under six hours. The trainset will be serviced and maintained there before returning to the state capital tomorrow. For two dozen years (1947–71), *Nancy Hanks* was the chief method of travel many Georgians relied on for accessing two of their most populous cities (***courtesy Allen Tuten and Central of Georgia Railway Historical Society***).

damper on the workforce's feelings for its new corporate owners from the beginning, the Southern did what it could to help its appendage prosper anyway. Leaving the CofG to operate under its own nomenclature was a positive step. In 1968, Southern leased 85-foot steel-construction dome cars from the Wabash Railroad, renovated them and added them to the *Nancy Hanks* consist. Built by Pullman-Standard Company, the cars' dark blue exterior and blue and gray interior upholstery fit nicely into the premier passenger train's color scheme. While recurring patrons who still depended upon "The Nancy" for their travels across the state appreciated the dome cars, their addition unfortunately wasn't enough to inspire huge numbers of new riders to become repeat passengers. Having despaired by 1970, Southern officials prevailed on the Georgia Public Service Commission (GPSC) to allow it to cease operating the legendary train. But the GPSC turned a deaf ear to Southern's protestations.

"Invention is the mother of necessity," exclaimed philosopher-economist Thorstein Veblin (1857–1929). Out of its "necessity," Southern found a way to kill a train by inventing a sure-fire alternative. When Amtrak was created by Congress in late 1970, the laws surrounding it permitted that carrier to discontinue the passenger services of railroads joining its new operation. Southern Railway declined to join Amtrak at that time, preferring to continue running its passenger service itself. (Southern was to remain in the passenger business into 1979, you may recall.) In a highly unusual move, however, Southern claimed that subsidiary CofG was in principle an autonomous operation. The CofG could, therefore, join Amtrak while the parent firm remained aloof.

At Millen, Georgia, in Jenkins County, *Nancy Hanks II* is met by *Little Nancy.* The latter CofG consist connects to Augusta, about 50 miles north of Millen, hard by the Savannah River border that Georgia shares with South Carolina. This 1971 image of the *Nancy* arriving at Millen led by Southern Railway FP7A 6149 is possibly the legendary train's final call there (***photograph by Ben Roberts courtesy Allen Tuten and Central of Georgia Railway Historical Society***).

Amtrak bought into Southern's understanding of the law. The Central of Georgia was admitted to Amtrak's fold. Acting on the wishes of the parent firm, Amtrak exercised its option by discontinuing the *Nancy Hanks.* The National Association of Rail Passengers (NARP) sued Amtrak and Southern, hoping to have the pronouncement overruled. The Central was merely an operating division of the Southern, the NARP declared. But Southern prevailed in the courtroom and "The Nancy's" fate was sealed. The demise of that train was not welcome news across Georgia.

Middle Georgians by the thousands said goodbye to Miss Nancy Hanks Friday as the 24-year-old lady made her last trip through Middle Georgia.

With 500 festive passengers aboard, including several top railway officials, the Nancy left Atlanta at 6 P.M., arrived in Macon more than one hour late, and was destined to reach her final home in Savannah in the wee hours Saturday.

Crowds lined each stop and byway, many with signs bidding the Nancy a final goodbye. At least 200 Maconites were at Wesleyan Station....

Though the atmosphere on the train was festive, it was a sad crowd which waved at the Nancy along the stops between Atlanta and Macon.

In Griffin, hundreds lined the rails and displayed a sign reading "Hi and Goodby, we love you, Nancy." ...

Friday was the last run for Nancy Hanks II as well as several other famous passenger trains, due to the takeover by Amtrak of passenger service on most lines. The Nancy was one felt not to be needed after studies by Amtrak officials.

There were few tears aboard the Nancy, but many people along the tracks held hankies to their faces as the old favorite passed by.[38]

After the cutback of the *Nancy Hanks*, Southern Railway put that equipment to use rather than release it to Amtrak.[39] Coaches were reupholstered and its livery was bathed in Southern green. It became part of the *Crescent* consists, Southern's flagship streamliner still prevailing between Washington, D.C., and New Orleans via Charlotte and Atlanta. Once the *Crescent* was dispatched to Amtrak in 1979, the CofG coaches were no longer valuable as rolling stock. Southern donated them to multiple rail historical societies scattered alongside its trackage.

An era had come to an end. The old blue and gray mare, she ain't what she used to be any more.[40]

5

CHESAPEAKE & OHIO RAILWAY
The Cat's Meow

At first glance a railroad with a trio of "name" passenger trains in its portfolio may not appear to be entirely representative in an account focused on travel-by-rail.[1] "The C&O's passenger fleet can be best described as modest," claimed one historical rail source.[2] "This reserved approach can best be seen when the railroad would place a huge order of streamlined equipment in the mid–1940s to compete with the best trains across the industry for exemplary passenger service. However, it soon backed out on the plan."

The restrained slant toward travelers seems even more problematic here when one considers that the line was widely and principally recognized as a bituminous coal-hauler. In spite of the disclaimer, nevertheless, the Chesapeake & Ohio Railway (C&O) routinely pushed its restricted passenger provisions to the forefront. Maintaining a modern fleet at all times and emphasizing classy creature comforts, the C&O capitalized on its service as a 20th century long-distance conveyance through heavy investments in advertising and marketing. Those efforts paid off, resonating over the decades with tens of thousands of satisfied riders, even though its limited number of trains paled in comparison to the volume exhibited by some of its contemporaries.

Over a mainline extending from the Atlantic seaboard to the Ohio River, with multiple branches connecting major Eastern and Midwestern metropolises, the C&O nevertheless earned a solid reputation as a people-mover. That business would never begin to rival its freight-hauling commerce, of course, much of it between crucial waterways. That traffic, the line's inarguable bread-and-butter, was conducted in eight states, in the U.S. capital, and internationally when the carrier went north of the border to Ontario, Canada, following one of its impressive business acquisitions.

The Chessie System, as it would be labeled later in life, embraced much of what was good about railroading. While some of its competitors faltered or fell during the Great Depression, the C&O persevered and prospered. Although the C&O changed hands frequently over its lifetime, for much of its existence fortune smiled upon it and it was better positioned to deal with negative circumstances than were some of its peers. Over the years it was able to gain on some of its major opposites through purchases, leases, trades and other deals that gave it some strategic advantages. And in its waning days as an independent hauler, its name survived when most others didn't. By providing the "C" in CSX Corporation, it figured prominently in the nomenclature of the Class 1 rail system that succeeded a handful of major players in Eastern and Southeastern U.S. roads.

Two transportation outfits in the Old Dominion State are C&O's earliest precursors.[3] The James River & Kanawha Canal Company, established in 1785, significantly influenced transportation decisions made by some Virginia planters living a half-century later. Those 18th century Louisa County farmers banded together to organize the Louisa Railroad, incor-

In February 1981, ex–C&O Greenbrier 4-8-4 J-3-A 614 runs in central Florida to Tampa pulling an excursion train. Fabricated for C&O in 1948 by Lima Locomotive Works, the modern, powerful coal-burning steam engine is equipped with an oversize tender for extra coal and an auxiliary water tender, the result of fewer fueling facilities in contemporary times (*courtesy Michael B. Robbins*).

porated on February 18, 1836, in an effort to get their crops to market. The first train moved over tracks that had been completed between Hanover Junction (now Doswell) and Fredericks Hall on December 20, 1837. The Louisa's owners signed an agreement with the Richmond, Fredericksburg & Potomac Railroad (RF&P) to tie their short line into it at Doswell. But a decade afterward they petitioned the courts and won the right to compete with the RF&P by building their own rails to the state capital at Richmond. The Louisa Railroad also constructed a western leg to Charlottesville.

To maintain pace with its enlarging vision, at about that time the Louisa was rebranded the Virginia Central Railroad (VC). Despite an aggressive stance, the VC's backers were temporarily thwarted — mechanically and financially — when they attempted to expand the line through the Blue Ridge Mountains at Swift Run Gap. Although they may have been briefly sidetracked in reaching the other side of the hill, their unbridled ambition wasn't to be permanently denied. Building west from the west foot of those peaks, they crossed the Shenandoah Valley and Great North Mountain, reaching the foot of Alleghany [*sic*] Mountain in 1856 at Jackson's River Station (now Clifton Forge).

In the meantime the Commonwealth of Virginia had come to the rescue — and as many as three times. Reportedly "always keen to help with 'internal improvements,'" the state purchased 40 percent of VC stock while incorporating and partially financing two more railroads that could turn a longtime dream into reality. "When railroad builders employed by the Commonwealth of Virginia made their trail toward the western mountains in the 1840s, they followed the stone markings etched in the 1740s by George Washington, surveyor."[4] Yes, *that* George Washington. His name would provide a phenomenal coup d'état for that line a couple of centuries later.

The first of those chartered railroads, the Blue Ridge, was given the mission of successfully completing the trek across the Blue Ridge Mountains. It was a tricky and costly undertaking. With civil engineer Claudius Crozet as project overseer, that feat was accomplished. In the process a quartet of tunnels was bored. One of those, 4,263 feet in length, opened in 1858, was situated between Mechum's River and Waynesboro. At the time it was among the longest tunnels on the planet. It was also one of the costliest, burdening Virginia just before the Civil War with a debt that — in today's dollars — approached half a billion.[5] Tracks through the tunnel allowed western Virginia militiamen to stream into Richmond if they were needed during the war. During a ceremony at the Blue Ridge Tunnel's completion, an ecstatic Governor Henry A. Wise declared that project engineer Crozet had "acupunctured" the mountain, finally tying the capital to the Shenandoah Valley and the west.

The Blue Ridge Railroad reached Clifton Forge in 1857, and that same year it was leased to the Virginia Central. The state-chartered Covington & Ohio Railroad, meanwhile, drew the task of completing the Alleghany grading, tunneling west and providing a route into Charleston (then still in Virginia).[6] That work came to a close for a while when the War Between the States intervened (1861–1865).

> During the 1850's the railroad's biggest competitor was the canal being constructed by the James River Company started in 1785 with George Washington its president. By 1851 the canal had reached its farthest navigable point on the James River and a railroad was proposed to span the distance to the Ohio River. Construction on the Virginia Central was postponed until the fate of the Covington & Ohio was determined. The answer came in the form of the Civil War, halting construction on both lines.[7]

Because of its optimal location, the Virginia Central became a strong ally of the Confederacy during the conflict. One of the road's operations was invested in toting foodstuffs from the Shenandoah Valley to Richmond, capital of the Confederacy. The VC additionally ferried troops, military supplies and equipment where they were most needed. The campaigns penetrated VC tracks relentlessly, unavoidably pinning a target on its back. It consistently left the line as an object of Union mercenaries who tenaciously tore the living daylights out of it, destroying all but about five miles of its track.

When the battles ended company president Williams Carter Wickham tried to attract some British investors to help him rebuild the road. But it was to no avail. Realizing financially bankrupt and destitute Southerners couldn't contribute to underwriting the colossal costs of reconstruction, Wickham turned to wealthy Yankee rail entrepreneur Collis P. Huntington of New York City. From a man who was heavily invested in the Central Pacific Railway that was about to link up with the Union Pacific Railway, Wickham found the help he sought. Huntington envisioned a true transcontinental railroad traversing the nation coast-to-coast under a single operating management. His interest was piqued as he considered the possibility of the Virginia Central becoming the eastern link to this proposed nationwide rail system.

> Virginia and West Virginia, sundered by war but hoping for a miracle, had turned over all their stock and right-of-way to railway baron Collis Potter Huntington, provided that freight trains could run from the eastern Tidewater to the Ohio River by 1872. Huntington, the tall and barrel-chested Republican who created the C&O, had agents in Prussia selling ten million dollars in mortgage bonds, all beginning to pay off creditors in 1872. Huntington was accustomed to buying legislators, inspectors, even U.S. congressmen to get what he wanted. Only Virginia's western mountains stood in the way.[8]

Huntington furnished the cash to renovate the damaged line and extend it to the Ohio River across the new state of West Virginia. With a new objective of linking the Old Dominion State's Tidewater coast with the "Western Waters" — an ancient aspiration of "the Great Connection" that had never been dismissed in the Commonwealth since Colonial days — the property of the Virginia-backed Covington & Ohio Railroad was transferred to and absorbed by the VC. Actually, the majority of the Covington & Ohio was then within West Virginia, which had been admitted to the union in 1863, and was—as a result—no longer controlled by the commonwealth of Virginia.

By 1869, the road crossed Alleghany Mountain via a great deal of the tunneling and roadbed construction that the Covington & Ohio had completed prior to the war. Tracks were already laid to a mammoth mineral water resort in Greenbrier County, West Virginia, named White Sulphur Springs. More will be said about this imposing destination and its implications for railway travelers shortly. Stagecoach connections transferred passengers arriving there to Charleston and the Kanawha River, opening navigable passageways to virtually everywhere that the Ohio and Mississippi flowed.

At about this same time the Covington & Ohio and the Virginia Central combined their separate operations into a newly-named Chesapeake & Ohio Railroad.[9] The line was chartered in both Virginia and West Virginia. The year was 1868, although most historians announce the formal start of their blending as 1869. Collis Huntington assumed the presidency of the C&O on July 15, 1869.

> Construction west continued with more tunnels and massive fills. At the same time construction east was begun from the new city of Huntington on the Ohio River. The two lines were connected at Hawks Nest, West Virginia on January 28th 1873. But the promise of revenue was halted by the depression of 1873 and a steel industry that never came to Virginia. The railroad went into receivership in 1875 and came out as the Chesapeake & Ohio Railway in 1878. In 1881 the C&O connected its line to the Elizabethtown, Lexington & Big Sandy Railroad, which gave it access to Cincinnati by way of Lexington, Kentucky, over the Kentucky Central. Both lines were controlled by Huntington as were the profitable packet boats that ran from Huntington to Cincinnati. A direct line to Cincinnati was not completed until 1888.[10]

While all of this was happening the C&O was building east to the Virginia port city of Newport News, a route finished in 1882. Going eastbound from Clifton Forge, on the Jackson River, the C&O eventually controlled dual mains across the Old Dominion State. The James River Line, beginning as a canal, proffered a zigzag water-level route to the Tidewater territory where the railroad's namesake city, Chesapeake, sat only a few miles west of the Atlantic beachside. The Mountain Subdivision, on the other hand, led northeast from Clifton Forge to Washington, D.C. (and ultimately over Pennsylvania Railroad tracks into New York City).

In the meantime, if it hadn't been clear before, it certainly was to anybody persistently watching the C&O's operations that coal radically figured into a predominance of business transactions the line experienced during the bulk of its lifetime. That hadn't precisely been its intent from the start, despite the reality of its good fortune once several rival railroads began panning for black gold.

> The Chesapeake and Ohio was built out of Virginia and across the Appalachians with development of coal mining far down in its priorities. It was lucky, though, for C&O that its engineers followed the route sanctioned by George Washington out of his native Virginia to the Ohio; that is, the James River and Kanawha Turnpike and Overland Trail, for that meant the main line would go through the center of the then untapped and practically unknown New River and Kanawha fields, which in time would make the Sewell seam in the New River field the fourth most important seam in the history of West Virginia mining.
>
> But Collis P. Huntington never thought of that.... As much as Huntington worked at economic development on the new road—e.g. hiring a city planner to lay out the new city of Huntington, founding a shipbuilding company at the road's terminus on Chesapeake Bay, backing his brother-in-law in founding a car building company in Huntington—he seemed indifferent to building spurs or branches to coal mines. Part of this reticence might have been the ineptness of the geological engineer he hired to report on the natural resources of the new road upon its completion, and part might have been that Huntington was kept busy working out problems of land acquisition and construction beyond the C&O in order to achieve his transcontinental.[11]

Situated astride some of the foremost bituminous seams in the nation, the C&O would later capitalize on transitioning those precious assets between their natural habitats and waiting on cargo ships at Hampton Roads ports. There shipments could be ferried to numerous Northeastern markets for heating and other purposes. "Even during the Great Depression," affirmed one informant, "coal was something that had to be used everywhere."

Coal remained the C&O's principal transported commodity throughout most of its life as an independent carrier. In the decade between 1878 and 1888, for instance, coal resources were seriously developed and shipped eastward for the first time by the C&O. Yet in spite of the commodity's commanding dominance of C&O freight traffic over the long haul (no pun intended), in the years immediately following the Second World War, up to half of the line's cargo was derived from a growing, prospering vehicle trade.[12] A little detail will make that clearer.

In 1929, the Chesapeake & Ohio acquired controlling interest in the Pere Marquette Railroad (PM) which geographically crisscrossed Michigan while extending tracks into northern Illinois and Indiana, plus internationally eastward to Ontario, Canada.[13] Nearly two decades after becoming the PM's parent firm, that line was fully integrated into the C&O on June 6, 1947. Over the years since 1929, it had become a highly lucrative possession. It ferried raw materials to the vast number of vehicle production plants scattered throughout its territory and bore finished vehicles to sundry waterways and distant rail lines for delivery to the showrooms of America. Dependable merchandise like that fortified the C&O against the inevitable fluctuations in the coal industry, providing, at times, as much as 50 percent of the C&O's haulage.

For more than one reason, it was critical to the C&O's owners to establish a major presence along America's eastern seaboard. During the Second World War men and material in increasing numbers were transported to and from the Hampton Roads Port of Embarkation as a major gateway for troops and equipment in the European Theater. This was the loading site for the invasion of North Africa. Meanwhile, the C&O's old staple coal was required by the war-related activity to meet ever-increasing demands. A source allowed: "C&O was ready with a powerful, well organized, well maintained railway powered by the largest and most modern locomotives."

From the late 19th century through most of the decades of the 20th century the independent C&O's ownership passed through the hands of several industrialists, financiers and rail magnates. Some of those simultaneously maintained control of more than a single line. Among them was J. P. Morgan and William K. Vanderbilt (1849–1920) and siblings O. P. and M. J. Van Sweringen (1923–1942). The C&O was also guided by some powerful and occasionally flamboyant chairmen from the 1940s through the 1970s that put their "brand" of doing business not only on that company but on the railroad industry itself. Included were Robert R. Young, Walter J. Tuohy, Cyrus S. Eaton and Hays T. Watkins, Jr. The latter saw the C&O, Baltimore & Ohio Railroad (B&O) and Western Maryland Railway (WM) merge under a combined Chessie System umbrella in 1972. (A decade earlier C&O acquired operating control of the B&O.) That appellation (Chessie System), incidentally, was colloquially applied for an enduring stretch of time; its origins dated to 1933, from the introduction of one of the most memorable advertising campaigns in railroad history.

Do you recall the advent of the Cheshire cat in Lewis Carroll's *Alice's Adventures in Wonderland*? While the Cheshire wasn't an actual breed of cat, Carroll saw a representative British Shorthair illustrated on a label of Cheshire cheese; it emanated from an English county of noble cheese-making, Cheshire. That's the derivation of the application in his mythical tale. All of which seems to fit nicely into a model for "Chessie the Cat," amulet of the C&O, which appeared widely in advertising touting the line's passenger service beginning in 1933.

Brought to life by illustrator Guido Grenewald, Chessie was the inspiration of an aide to the C&O president of the Great Depression era, Lionel Probert. It was Probert who penned the most memorable slogan linked to the infamous feline, *Sleep Like a Kitten*. That aphorism soon began appearing everywhere C&O passenger trains were plugged — periodical ads, bill-boards, timetables and other company literature, and mementos of eclectic descriptions. As one of the most widely pitched and best recalled railroad ad campaigns ever in use, the C&O's success with it — and with that of its mascot — is unassailable. In fact it lives on today, as the C&O Railway Historical Society dispenses calendars and other trinkets bearing the infamous Chessie emblem. Back in the day, recalled a source, "when the kitten debuted demand was so high that the C&O could not keep enough merchandise in stock."[14]

Chessie's notoriety didn't cease with the sales commodities and promotional campaigns. The kitten became indistinguishable from the C&O itself. And never say die. In the early 1970s, it became renowned all over again when the Chessie System — holding company for the C&O, B&O and WM — superimposed the kitty's profile within the Chessie System "C" that festooned the road's new — at that time — vermillion, yellow and blue livery.

The Chessie print ads appeared in travel magazines, newsweeklies and women's period-icals from the 1930s to the 1950s, seguing into posters, prints and merchandise galore, prompted by a number of additional clever slogans. Combined with appropriate line drawings and copy, these offered persuasive arguments. For many within the traveling public, those plugs reinforced a notion that C&O held an impressive edge among providers of over-the-tracks creature comforts, particularly in surroundings accentuated by unsurpassed luxury, as those found aboard C&O's crack trains. Included were such maxims as *Chessie — Sleep Warden of the American Traveler, Let Me Call You Sleepheart, Sleep Like a Kitten and Arrive Fresh as a Daisy*, and more. Here are a few sample texts from those full page print promotions for one or all three of C&O's premier long-distance "name" trains.

Chessie Invites You

Whenever business or pleasure takes you into her territory, Chessie invites you to travel the most interesting and enjoyable way — through *The Chessie Corridor*.

Relaxed in the comfort of air-conditioned, fast trains — The George Washington, The Sports-man, The F.F.V.— you'll be enthralled by a grand scenic panorama — no two miles alike ... or refreshed at night in a clean and quiet sleeping car that lulls you to *Sleep Like a Kitten*.

Chessie especially invites World's Fair visitors to make the trip on her railroad. It will greatly add to their journey's pleasures.

—

Heartstrings of Steel

The Railroad with a heart — Chesapeake and Ohio — is truly in tune with the travel world! Upon its heartstrings of steel resounds the most responsive chord that has ever been struck in transportation...

Sleep Like a Kitten and
Arrive Fresh as a Daisy!

Discover for yourself this harmonious way of traveling. Learn on The George Washington, the most wonderful train in the world.

The George Washington • The Sportsman • The F.F.V.

The Finest Fleet of Genuinely
Air-Conditioned Trains in the World

—

America's Sleepheart
INVITES
America's Sweethearts

... to start a honeymoon aboard The George Washington! What a memorable wedding trip that will be ... a ride on the most wonderful train in the world ... a stay at one of the world's most romantic resorts — White Sulphur Springs or Virginia Hot Springs, chosen by brides and grooms for generations. Chesapeake and Ohio Lines can be trusted with your secret so why not confide in us? We'll be glad to help you make your plans — handle your reservations. *Sleep Like a Kitten* in genuine air-conditioned comfort! *Arrive Fresh as a Daisy!*

By the time those campaigns were going the C&O had long reached some pretty awesome spots along its route. Included, and sometimes mentioned in its advertising, were the cities of Baltimore, Charleston, Chicago, Cincinnati, Cleveland, Columbus, Detroit, Indianapolis, Louisville, Newport News, New York, Norfolk, Philadelphia, Richmond, St. Louis and Washington. The references to those elegant hotels weren't afterthoughts either. Shrewd moves by C&O owners in 1910 transferred the upscale White Sulphur Springs resort at Greenbrier, West Virginia, into their hands. That venue has welcomed presidents and other heads of state for a lot of pampering. Also governors, senators, congressmen and public figures of many stripes, including many from the entertainment and sports worlds, have been refreshed within its portals.

While the resort has been popular with the wealthy for decades, some of the glitter has worn off in modern times. Losing $35 million there in 2008, current owner CSX Transportation — which inherited the Greenbrier property in a deal it made in 1980 — hired a well-known investment banking firm in January 2009 to evaluate what to do with it in light of the nation's spiraling economic decline. C&O officials had used it as a corporate retreat for many years while "many of the rail mergers and acquisitions that shaped the current network of the East were forged within its walls."[15] By the time this book is published, of course, that valuable property may be out of railroad hands for the first time in a century. The C&O capitalized on it, turning it into not merely a hotel alongside the tracks but a destination for a targeted segment of chic clientele.

The C&O gained some unsolicited fame when popular impresario-vocalist Tex Benecke and his Orchestra recorded and performed a big band number in the 1940s titled *Chesapeake and Ohio*. Penned by Carl Sigman and Herb Magidson, the vocal's lyrics expressed regret for an oversight: failing to ask for a lady's address as she and the singer traveled on the C&O Railway. It created a stir, establishing the line's moniker with publics with whom it had never made much of an impression until then.

In 1963, under the oversight of chairman Cyrus S. Eaton, the Chesapeake & Ohio Railway was led to "affiliate" with an ancient modern line, the hoary Baltimore & Ohio Railroad, which — until that time, at least — might have been perceived by the industry more as a competitor and less as a colleague. "Avoiding a mistake that would become endemic to later mergers among other lines, a gradual amalgamation of the two lines' services, personnel, motive power and rolling stock, and facilities built a new and stronger system, which was ready for a new name in 1972."[16,17]

Under auspices of an imaginative Hays T. Watkins, Jr., the C&O, B&O and Western Maryland Railway were branded the Chessie System, its headquarters in Cleveland, Ohio. Again under Watkins' watchful eye, eight years hence the Chessie combined with Seaboard Coast Line Industries, Inc. to form CSX Transportation. Seaboard Industries included the Seaboard Coast Line Railroad (formerly ACL and SAL), Louisville & Nashville Railroad (including the NC&StL, portions of the Chicago & Eastern Illinois, and Monon), Clinchfield Railroad and others. Acquiring 42 percent of Conrail in 1999, CSX was assured status as one of a quartet of key Class 1 freight railroad systems in the United States.

A minuscule handful of "name" passenger trains fostered by the C&O that somehow missed most of the company's sterling promotional opportunities existed.

In the modern age a cooperative arrangement between Amtrak and the Michigan State Department of Transportation maintains a longstanding tradition by retaining the name *Pere Marquette*. With the DOT largely responsible for financing, that all-coach train currently runs daily over a 176-mile route. Leaving Grand Rapids every morning, it arrives in Chicago four hours later. Every evening it returns over the same tracks. In the "old" days the train served Wolverine cities like Lansing and Plymouth. Inaugurated as the nation's first all-new postwar streamliner on August 10, 1946, the original *Pere Marquette* plied the rails between Grand Rapids and Detroit every day.

One train actually never made it out of the gate but was on the C&O drawing boards in the late 1940s, to be christened the *Chessie*. Daylight sections from Louisville and Cincinnati were intended to hook up at Ashland, Kentucky, for a run across the mountains where they were to split again — one section proceeding to Washington, the other to Newport News. The *Chessie*, meanwhile, was to have an unusual function in just being. "The *Chessie*'s real purpose was not to supplement C&O's existing through passenger service but to ferry well heeled patrons to the famed Greenbrier in White Sulphur Springs, serving much like a five-star hotel's limousine," professed one wag.[18]

That confirmed the train's sumptuously planned appointments, including an on-board movie theater showing current Hollywood releases; a nurse specialist in the family coach to change diapers, prepare formula and babysit patrons' precious little darlings; and a juvenile playroom stocked with coloring books, crayons and furnished with a diminutive Disney cartoon theater. "The Chessie's amenities were just normal services for the 'resort crowd,'" gushed the reporter. "The train's on-board library, original oil paintings, and the industrial exhibits throughout the train weren't there for the common passenger boarding at Mineral or Mt. Carbon.... The dome cars, ceiling-height acquarium [*sic*], and soda fountains were not available for residents of Goshen or Gauley."

Even after three of its projected five steam-turbo-electric engines were delivered in 1947, the C&O backed out of this ambitious project. A less than 100 percent conviction that it would be a viable moneymaker, plus competing diesel-powered streamliners just then debuting on other lines (B&O's *Cincinnatian*, Norfolk & Western's *Powhatan Arrow*) dispelled (derailed?) the sensibility of the idea.

"Diesels came to the C&O and N&W at about the time they sought permission to abandon money losing locals and mixed trains (peddler freights that handled both freight cars and paying passengers)," noted an Appalachian scholar. "So most of these trains never underwent the transition from steam power to diesel. However, C&O and N&W had through passenger trains that kept running until the inauguration of Amtrak at the end of April 1971."[19] Passenger trains on the C&O were finally dieselized throughout the system in 1952, when the company bought 30 model E8s (originally introduced in 1949) for its mainline passenger trains.

And what about those "name" trains we've referenced that were prominently touted in C&O advertising, at times to the exclusion of other passenger services?

The *FFV*, standing for *Fast Flying Virginian*, was one. It was also the C&O's inaugural luxury passenger train. Premiering on May 11, 1889, it began just after traffic commenced across a rail bridge spanning the Ohio River linking Covington, Kentucky, with Cincinnati, Ohio. The opulent consist "flew" daily between New York and Cincinnati by way of Philadelphia, Baltimore, Washington, Charleston and Ashland.

An introspective on dining aboard the *FFV* suggests how the C&O approached passengers in general and, in particular, how *FFV* patrons were indulged. It offers insights on how dining car service may have been conducted on upscale trains of many lines.[20] "Electrically lit," the *FFV* was at times dubbed "The Vestibule Limited." It was also the first C&O trainset extending dining service to its patrons.

> The C&O laid over two diner cars every night at Hinton, WV. The railroad company served meals on a schedule both on this train and later on its other luxury trains The George Washington and The Sportsman.

The F.F.V.'s two diner cars were only on the trains during meal times, which for westbound trains would have been just after the 7:30 AM departure from Hinton....

Laying the diners over at Hinton permitted the C&O to service eight trains (4 east and 4 west) with seven diners, and permitted the diner crews to sleep at night off the railroad....

[A] ... menu from May 1900 offers up meals for a dollar that include such choices as: Baked Apples and Cream, Broiled Sea Fish, Sirloin Steak, Spring Lamb Chops, Shirred Eggs, and Saratoga [potato] Chips....

By 1948 travelers on a "coach budget" could order more humble fare in the F.F.V. diner car. They'd find Stewed Prunes with Cream (.30), Breakfast Figs in Syrup (.35), a Jelly Omelet (.65), or two Poached Eggs on Toast (.50). The Griddle Cakes with Syrup were .45 (a dime more with honey); as were French Toast with Marmalade. Milk Toast (.25), RyCrisp (.10), and Doughnuts (.10) were also on the menu. Coffee and tea came by the pot (.20), and milk by the bottle.

In September 1900, Wilbur Wright, of Dayton, Ohio, may very well have dined from the menu referenced above from that year. He rode the *FFV* between Cincinnati and Old Point Comfort, Virginia, on his way to Kitty Hawk, North Carolina. With him was much of the apparatus he and his brother Orville would use in constructing the Wright Flyer which would finally successfully take to the air on December 17, 1903.

Strangely enough the eastbound *FFV* was discontinued six years prior to the westbound *FFV*, the latter's demise occurring on May 12, 1968.[21] What happened to the westbound train every day between 1962 and 1968, upon reaching its terminus? Or better yet, from whence were the consists derived that launched those westbound journeys from the Big Apple, if we assume that no eastbound train appeared beforehand to be turned around? Such unanswered questions appear to remain in limbo.[22]

The next luxury train inaugurated by the Chesapeake & Ohio Railway was *The Sportsman* in 1930. That crack train ran daily between Virginia's coastal Tidewater region both to Detroit and Cincinnati. It persisted into the 1960s, as did all of C&O's major passenger conveyances.

The *George Washington* may have been the line's flagship operation.[23] Lionel Probert, mentioned previously, C&O marketing genius responsible for the "Chessie the Cat" advertising campaign, believed that launching it on the date of the first U.S. president's birth, precisely 200 years later, would give it the kick-start it needed.[24] So a ceremony was conducted in Washington, D.C., on that day, February 22, 1932, and the *George Washington* was off and running. The route followed the C&O's super-scenic main through the Blue Ridge Mountains of Virginia and westward across the Appalachians. To the east it connected with Newport News and Norfolk. To the west it traveled to Cincinnati and Louisville. At Cincinnati, it proceeded over the tracks of the New York Central Railroad into Chicago.

The *George Washington* was decorated in the Colonial period, from the era of George Washington himself, and featured all of the latest creature comforts for passengers, such as carpeting and even air-conditioning. The stateliness of the train, along with its spectacular scenery through western Virginia and the Blue Ridge, West Virginia and the New River Gorge, and portions of Kentucky through Appalachia country quickly propelled it as the C&O's flagship train surpassing even the railroad's *Fast Flying Virginian*, or *FFV*, its posh operation at the time. Couple this with the fact that the *George* served a number of elegant and charming hotels, such as its own world-famous Greenbrier Resort, and it's no wonder the train became so popular.

In the early 1950s the train was updated with lightweight, streamlined equipment including matching EWD E-series diesel locomotives, all of which were adorned in a beautiful livery of blue, yellow, and gray (somewhat similar to the B&O's own passenger livery). Later, after the C&O took control of the B&O in 1962 it combined the B&O's *National Limited*, which ran to Chicago, and the *George* at Cincinnati. The two trains then ran in tandem from there to Chicago and vice-versa as far south as Cincinnati, where they split and continued on their different routings as separate trains....

Today, you can still ride virtually the same route as the original George Washington under Amtrak's *Cardinal*.[25]

In addition to the *Cardinal*, another Amtrak passenger route that dips briefly into the Mountaineer State beckons the *Capitol Limited*. On its run between Washington, D.C., and Chicago, the *Limited* calls at Martinsburg, West Virginia. On April 19, 1975, it was led by Amtrak E9A 401, ex–B&O 1455 built as B&O 36. Martinsburg is 74 miles northwest of the nation's capital (*courtesy Jay T. Thomson*).

As this is written the *Cardinal* operates three trips weekly in each direction. Westbound it leaves New York's Pennsylvania Station early Sunday, Wednesday and Friday mornings, proceeds to Philadelphia, Baltimore, Washington, Charlottesville, Charleston, Ashland, Cincinnati, Indianapolis and finally to Chicago's Union Station at mid morning the following day. Eastbound it leaves Chicago in late afternoon on Tuesday, Thursday and Saturday and is in New York in late evening the following night.

In the matter of winning over, and retaining, satisfied customers in the glory days of train travel during the 20th century, C&O management assigned that top priority to the *George Washington*. In 1947, a newspaperman working in Staunton, Virginia, shared a personal recollection from a trip aboard the *George Washington*. He may have captured the train's— and the C&O's— essence of spirited passenger service about as well as any illustration might could have.[26]

What I remember most vividly of all about [1940s C&O chairman Robert R.] Young's valiant effort to make the C&O's passenger service more attractive to the riding public was something that took place on a cold early Sunday morning in late winter.... I decided to ... go over to the station, and take the *George Washington* home to Richmond. The night air was penetratingly cold, and there was snow everywhere. Tired, shivering, I waited for the train to arrive from the west. At length [it] came into the station ... and I went aboard a coach. I placed my suitcase on a seat and waited for the dining car's scheduled opening. Others were already in line. I was still chilled from my vigil on the train platform. Not long after the *George Washington* left Staunton the doors to the double-coach dining car opened. Before the waiters began taking orders they walked along the tables and poured out steaming demitasse cups of thick black railroad coffee for all present. Sipping it, watching through the fogged windows as the train moved across the snowy Blue Ridge, I was very grateful. It was a small thing, a creature comfort I have never forgotten.

There are likely millions of people whose recollections of grand passenger trains could be distilled into tales of demitasse cups and other amenities that made rail travel one of great anticipation, gratifying experience and memorable reminiscence. The C&O did this well; it might have been branded the *cat's meow*.

6

FLORIDA EAST COAST RAILWAY
The Eighth Wonder of the World

Few projects in American railroading can be considered any more ambitious than the one undertaken by the Florida East Coast Railway (FEC) from 1905 to 1912. Make that, embarked on by the road's founder and benefactor, Henry M. Flagler. It was his pure grit, buoyancy and unwavering tenacity that netted a feat which had been broadly deemed impossible: to harness nature's forces well enough to create a rail line running 128 miles into the ocean from the peninsula with only occasional sparse earth rising above the sea to support its trestles.

Compounded by the fact it was launched in an era of relatively limited technology as well as undeveloped (e.g., primitive) operational gear, it was a death-defying exercise. Flagler determined to secure a rail line that would run altogether where no man had gone before, over water between Miami and Key West. That it was achieved and completed in his lifetime is an enduring monument to the vision and consuming focus of one man. That it persisted for 23 years—until the crushing forces of the elements took their practically inevitable revenge on the intrusion into that heretofore impenetrable sanctuary—was stunning. You may be sure that the line that died at sea was an accomplishment rivaling the greatest physical triumphs in any field in its day. More will be said about that formidable feat and the colossal collapse of the impossible dream presently.

The story of the Florida East Coast Railway began a number of years before thought of reaching its oceanic conquest was precipitated. That any of it—seemingly including the FEC itself—existed at all would appear to have been pure happenstance, a sort of unimagined, unplanned phenomenon. It started with Flagler, the man at the center of the activity, the optimistic driving force behind it and the resourceful giant whose wealth made it feasible. To fully appreciate the FEC, one must attempt to know and, if possible, understand this iconic figure.

Born January 2, 1830, at Hopewell, New York, Henry Morrison Flagler was a minister's son. On completing the eighth grade at 14 in 1844, he struck out for Bellevue, Ohio, taking a $5-a-month job coupled with room and board in a kinsman's grain shop. Five years hence he was making $400 monthly as a salesman for the firm. He partnered with a half-brother in the grain business in 1852, and wed a relative, Mary Harkness, in 1853. Between 1858 and 1870, she bore him three children, two preceding him in death.

In 1862, Flagler and a brother-in-law started a salt mine refinery at Saginaw, Michigan. When that failed he returned to Bellevue in 1865—then $100,000 in the hole—rejoining the grain industry as a commission merchant the following year. It took him into friendship with John D. Rockefeller, who was in similar pursuits before launching an oil refinery in 1867. Cleveland, Ohio, was perceived as the zenith of oil refining in the United States at that time. Rockefeller selected it as the headquarters site of his new business venture.

Needing more capital to initiate it, however, he enlisted the aid of Flagler. The latter was able to sponge $100,000 off some kin on the condition that he (Flagler) would "be made a partner" in the new enterprise. With a third cohort (Andrews), Rockefeller and Flagler commenced operations in 1867. It would be the start of something grand! The firm's moniker was altered to a more memorable Standard Oil on January 10, 1870. Within two years their fledgling endeavor led the American oil refining trade, producing 10,000 barrels daily. In 1877, the firm's command center — and the Flaglers with it — moved their permanent base of operations to New York City.

While all of this was transpiring, Mary Flagler, Henry's wife, was suffering relentless health crises. This was nothing new; she had been sickly for a great deal of her life although it was becoming more pronounced as time transpired. After a physician recommended that she try a winter in Jacksonville, Florida, for physical and possibly mental rejuvenation, the Flaglers departed the Big Apple for Big Orange country in 1878. Nevertheless Mary's condition continued to deteriorate and at 47 she died on May 18, 1881. Her debilitating experience — and a few trips in subsequent winters to the Sunshine State — opened her widower's eyes to new opportunities that were to also invigorate him for the next three decades.

Two years after losing Mary, Flagler married Ida Alice Shourds. That winter the newlyweds traveled to St. Augustine, about 40 miles south of Jacksonville on the Atlantic coast.

> Arriving in the "Ancient City," Flagler found a sleepy, almost dilapidated town of about 2,500 inhabitants. While he was charmed with the climate and beauty of the old place, he found the hotel facilities quite inferior to the accommodations he and his circle of friends were accustomed to in northern cities....
> Why did St. Augustine, with such lovely weather, have such poor lodging? Why wasn't a hotel built or planned to entice weather-weary Northerners?...
> He began to have visions of what St. Augustine might be if only a little money were lavished on her....
> Flagler was well aware of Florida's poor railroads, but it was brought to his attention very distinctly when he began construction of the Ponce de Leon Hotel. The Jacksonville, St. Augustine and Halifax River Railroad [JStA&HR], which had reached St. Augustine in June, 1883, was a rickety, little narrow gauge road ... of minimal value ... in the ongoing hotel construction.
> There was, in 1884, little thought in Flagler's mind of operating a railroad. Unfortunately ... the ownership of the JStA&HR showed little inclination to upgrade their railroad.... Flagler ... knew that better transportation facilities were an absolute must, both for the immense quantities of building materials the hotels (he had begun a second hotel, the Alcazar, and purchased a third, the Casa Monica, before the Ponce de Leon was completed) would require, and later for the elegant class of people he hoped to attract to St. Augustine when the hotels were completed.[1]

A light went on in his mind. With his clever business acumen working overtime, Flagler saw enormous possibilities for attracting out-of-state visitors — and especially those with the resources and time to escape the traditionally harsh winters of the North. He knew that his gargantuan personal wealth generated from Standard Oil could not only convert, provide and upgrade lagging lodging facilities in Florida but allow him to also develop a modern rail system to ferry the upscale crowd to his pleasure palaces. Rail transit below Jacksonville was spotty, mostly a hit or miss proposition in the few places it went. Flagler would — more than anyone else — be ultimately credited with creating a winter fever among the legions of Yankees that could be satisfied by spending winters along Florida's sunny shores. With his imagination, resolve and bankroll, the fix was within reach.

Flagler relinquished his day-to-day tasks with Standard Oil yet retained his seat on its board to 1911. He had been John D. Rockefeller's closest associate in the firm's earliest development and continued as vice president to 1908. Meanwhile, in 1885, Flagler and his new bride moved to Kirkside, a mansion he had constructed for them at St. Augustine. There he oversaw a diversifying portfolio of commercial projects that included hotel properties, railroads, steamship lines and real estate management for starters. "The Oldest City in America," as St. Augustine dubs itself, was to become the hub of operations for the future Florida East Coast Railway.

Flagler's life as a rail baron began with the purchase of the narrow-gauge Jacksonville, St. Augustine & Halifax River Railway, which he soon converted to standard measure. In 1895, it was the original underpinning of the newly organized Florida East Coast Railway.

After the Ponce de Leon Hotel opened to rave reviews and a pecuniary bonanza on January 10, 1888, Flagler built a rail bridge across the St. Johns River, opening the lower half of Florida to traffic. In 1890, he purchased the Ormond Hotel at Ormond Beach. With visions of grandeur now assured, he continued extending the rail line along the coast, on several occasions buying existing short line railroads that were useful in his southern quest. Upon reaching Palm Beach in 1894, at last Flagler contented himself that his line had finally arrived at a logical terminus.

At the same time he was continuing to pepper the coastline with superlative playgrounds for the wealthy. Alongside Lake Worth in Palm Beach, for instance, he opened the 1150-room Royal Poinciana Hotel, then the largest wooden edifice on the planet. The Palm Beach Inn overlooking the Atlantic Ocean was next. Renamed The Breakers in 1901, it is the only one of his stately resorts to survive in its original business sector in contemporary times.[2]

While the railroad was supposed to end at Palm Beach, a siege of unanticipated freezing weather in the winter of 1894-1895 prompted Flagler to revisit the matter. Sixty miles south of Palm Beach lay the settlement of Fort Dallas; it was reportedly unfazed by the cold snap. Some private property owners there prevailed on Flagler's time, offering him free land in exchange for continuing his rail line another 60 miles. Not only did he do so, in 1896, with the tracks reaching Biscayne Bay, he dredged a channel, formed streets, instituted water and power systems and underwrote the area's first newspaper, *The Metropolis*. (Eventually Flagler would gain controlling interest in *The Florida Times-Union* in Jacksonville, *The Miami Herald* and *The St. Augustine Record*.)

In 1897, he opened the exclusive Royal Palm Hotel in that little burg. When the residents wanted to rebrand their town *Flagler* to honor their generous benefactor, he wisely vetoed it. A Native American sobriquet was substituted instead. Henceforth the hamlet was to be known as *Miami*. Completion of the rail line increased the population appreciably, by the way: it soared rapidly from 300 denizens to 1,500.

While all this was transpiring Flagler was experiencing trouble at home. For some time Ida Alice Flagler, his second spouse, whom he married in 1883, had suffered mental lapses. By 1895, he institutionalized her. There are sources hinting that — six years later — he urged (influenced?) the state legislature in Tallahassee to adopt a law that would make incurable insanity sufficient grounds for divorce. No matter how it came about, he and Ida Alice were legally separated in 1901, and he immediately wed a third woman, Mary Lily Kenan, 34, some 37 years his junior. She was a second wife for him whose first name was Mary.

Characterized by some as "an ideal mate for him," she was considered his equal, culturally, intellectually and socially. Whatever her heart desired, she had only to request it and he gave it to her. They soon moved into a just-completed 55-room 60,000-square-foot estate (branded Whitehall) at Palm Beach. It was Flagler's last earthly residence and cost $2.5 million to erect in 1902. That was a princely sum then and now: Inflation Calculator's Web site purports that — in 2008's dollars — Whitehall could be built for about $61.5 million. Sharing the marble mansion's premises today are the Henry Morrison Flagler Museum, open to the public, and the Palm Beach County Historical Society.

In the winter of 1898, Flagler — who was well acquainted with several U.S. presidents[3] — invited the then-current occupant of the White House, William McKinley, to visit him. Well aware of his own clout and prestige, perhaps surprisingly so, Flagler informed the nation's chief executive: "My domain begins at Jacksonville." To a minister he was acquainted with, the industrialist wrote of his posture as if Floridians were his subjects: "I feel that these people are wards of mine and have a special claim upon me." Stemming from those exclamations, a historian's estimate of Flagler's exploits to that juncture suggests he might have had no equals in the sphere of marketing as in just about everything else.[4]

> It was almost as if a Biblical scene was being recounted. What he (Flagler) saw was good. Flagler said, "Let there be hotels," and, lo, there were hotels. Then Flagler said, "Let there be railroads—and land companies—and cities—and paved roads—and water works—and visitors"—and lo, there were all of these things.
>
> But most importantly, there was Flagler. And today's promotions, by cities, by airlines, by hotels, and by development companies, as well as by Amtrak, the bus lines and the cruise companies, is derived, in both concept and appeal, from the groundwork laid by Flagler's promotions of the East coast of Florida as the "American Riviera." ...
>
> The campaigns to encourage the Northern populace to seek sunshine and good health ... was engendered by the Flagler people. There was not, nor has there been, anything to compare with the artistry and eloquence of the early FEC publicists.

By 1905, having reached a new plateau with no more uncompleted challenges before him, Flagler came under conviction that he should add a 156-mile stretch of new track to the existing line that ended in Dade County (Miami). According to one source there is actual evidence that he had pretty well committed himself to the concept as early as midsummer 1898, following the end of the Spanish-American War.[5] Flagler and his top-level assistants commissioned multiple preliminary engineering and feasibility studies. A historiographer recalled: "The 'railroad across the ocean' had at long last shed its pie-in-the-sky status, and was now being taken seriously by one of the most successful entrepreneurs in America."[6]

Flagler envisioned a course that would extend the present route 28 miles south of Miami to the end of the peninsula, then turn right and proceed 128 more miles over deep sea to Key West, sitting at the far end of an archipelago in the Gulf of Mexico with no surface transportation to take one there. There was no highway to Key West until 1938, which was at last built on the abandoned railway right-of-way. Until the rails arrived the city could be navigated only by watercraft in the pre-flight era. With more than 20,000 inhabitants calling it home already despite the transportation barriers, for more than five decades Key West had been the state's most populous Mecca.[7]

It was also the nearest American municipality to a proposed canal excavation zone fostered by the U.S. government across Panama. When that came to fruition, new trade routes linking the Atlantic and Pacific oceans would be available, eliminating the necessity of a far longer voyage around the tip of South America. And Key West was just 90 miles north of Havana, Cuba, which Flagler envisioned as a tropical vacationland beckoning the affluent tourists he was already ferrying to Florida. There might have been at least one other reason Flagler was anxious to embark on that doubtable pursuit, one he might not have widely discussed. Its origins date to some of Flagler's earliest years in Florida.

> A competitor of sorts had cropped up. On the west coast of Florida, perhaps inspired by Flagler's notoriety, a man named Henry Plant had been buying up a series of existing narrow-gauge railroads with the stated intention of extending a line all the way from Tampa to Miami. Plant had also built a deep-water pier that transformed Tampa into an important port on the Gulf of Mexico, and by 1891 he had completed his own extravagant hotel, the Tampa Bay, which, at $3 million, considerably exceeded the cost of the Ponce de Leon, a paltry $2.5 million. [Like Flagler, Plant became a rail baron, too, buying scads of railroads and earning a reputation for building a string of princely hotel palaces of his own across central and west coast Florida. See Chapter 3.]
>
> Goaded by the outspoken Plant's vow to "outdo" him, Flagler considered what he might play as a trump card.... During the grand opening of the Tampa Bay Hotel ... Flagler first [secretly]

proposed ... the notion of extending his one railroad another four hundred miles to the south, all the way to Key West.

Key West, Flagler correctly interpreted, could replace Tampa as the closest deep-water port to the new canal by more than 300 miles. What he didn't factor in was that, in 1908, the U.S. Navy refused to grant him permission to dredge the waters of Key West harbor so he could shape the massive dock he needed to turn this important segment of his long-held dream into reality. Flagler's idea for a colossal deep-water port with 12 mammoth covered piers 800 feet long and 200 feet wide simply never transpired. Minus those docking and freight transfer facilities, steamers before and after the Panama Canal opened continued to ply the waters farther north to Tampa, New Orleans, Mobile, Jacksonville and other already established deep-water ports. It was one of many blows that plagued Flagler's blueprint, a flaw he could never overcome.

For all of the aforementioned reasons, he nevertheless determined to build a railroad to sea, even when myriad skeptics labeled him crazy, classifying his notion as "Flagler's Folly." All of that was put to rest once it was a done deal of course. Newspapers touted it with blaring headlines, championing "The Eighth Wonder of the World." The fascinatingly gripping account of the extension of the rails and the practically insurmountable odds encountered — odds that would have dissuaded a lesser man — is retold by a handful of Flagler and FEC biographers. Frail of health and vision by then, Flagler lived to see his dream completed, riding

Henry Flagler's dream of rails to the sea culminated in a massive yard and dock at Key West, where he envisioned a huge enterprise. There passengers would be exchanged between the trains they arrived on and great steamers for Caribbean and Central and South American destinations. He invested in both forms of transportation plus opulent resorts to serve them in Florida and Cuba, catering to visitors' every whim. Flagler's grandiose schemes were dramatically curtailed when the Navy refused to let him dredge and develop Key West harbor next to Trumbo Point Yard, however. This setback was a foretaste of a greater disaster, the arrival of a hurricane that destroyed Flagler's Overseas Railroad (*courtesy Cal Winter*).

A southbound *Havana Special* powered by a FEC Pacific locomotive nears Bahia Honda Bridge, a 5,055-foot viaduct with approaches ranging from 23 to 35 feet deep. This channel, dubbed by Spaniards "Deep Bay," is more than two-thirds of the trip down the keys. Construction was formidable due to its depth. Track was laid above the crest of the highest recorded hurricane wave to avert washing away in storms. A rule of thumb said "the deeper the water, the higher the wave." The trestle, formed of German cement that hardened under water, netted 26 spans from 128 to 186 feet in length (*courtesy Cal Winter*).

the rails to the end of the line on January 22, 1912. He died 16 months later at 83 on May 20, 1913, following a fall down the marble stairs at his beloved Whitehall four months earlier from which he never fully recovered.

While those landmark dates are important in the history of the Florida East Coast Railway, they are likely superseded by September 2, 1935. On that Labor Day a monstrous unnamed Category 5 hurricane packing winds in excess of 200 miles an hour rose up from the Caribbean and surged over the keys. In its fury it shook the very foundations of the Overseas Railway, dismantled large chunks and carried much of it along with many lives to watery graves. Although all of the bodies were never recovered, more than 600 were. Among the known dead, at least half were permanent residents that included 63 members of a single clan (the Russell family) while another 288 were highway laborers who lived elsewhere.[8]

The rail line was never rebuilt, although some observers believed that — had Henry Flagler been alive — he would have paid to restore it. The roadbed and remaining bridges ultimately provided the impetus and the route for an Overseas Highway.[9] The paved dual-lane U.S. 1 between Miami and Key West opened in 1938. It became the inhabitants' and the tourists' lifeline to the mainland. That road has been called upon many times since in fleeing successive hurricanes packing powerful winds that struck the otherwise tropical rapture.

Assessments of Flagler's contributions are plentiful and run to extremes. A few suffice.

> Flagler's railroad across the ocean never earned a dime of profit, and it is difficult to imagine how a businessman as bright as he was ever thought it would.... While tourists made use of the line, freight shippers—the bread and butter of the railroad business—never did.[10]
>
> Had he been content to reinvest his Standard Oil dividends instead of spending them to invent Florida, Henry Morrison Flagler might be as synonymous with wealth and power as his

former partner and sales associate John D. Rockefeller. But Rockefeller did the safe and sane thing, and Flagler built his Speedway to Sunshine.[11]

•

[Flagler] made so much money from Standard Oil that he could not possibly spend it in his lifetime....

Although Flagler retired from Standard Oil before he was fifty-three, his stock in it gushed dividends like an uncapped well until the end of his life....

Perhaps only Flagler knew his true reasons for building the Key West Extension. If he had stopped at Miami, his FEC railroads would have been money-makers.[12]

•

Flagler did not consider himself a railroad man, nor did he come to Florida to build railroads or hotels. But because of the circumstances with which he was confronted, magnified by his need to create, Henry M. Flagler, the Standard Oil magnate, became Flagler the railroad builder ... hotel builder ... the land magnate. Most importantly, through design or otherwise, the man became Flagler the Empire Builder, with most of the East Coast of Florida south of St. Augustine owing its existence to him.

In addition to having a county named after him ... almost every town and city on the East Coast has a street, school, park, playground, church or library named after him.[13]

Flagler was, as biographer Edward N. Akin put it, "not so much a businessman as a visionary in businessman's clothing."

And what, coincidentally, became of Mary Lily Flagler, the financier's third spouse? Though her late husband left her $100 million in his will, she hardly lived a charmed existence following his death. She died after a brief second marriage under puzzling conditions, in fact.[14]

At the literal end of the line (as well as the country), the *Havana Special* waits alongside a steamer that has arrived from Havana at Key West. The train will haul passengers up the keys to Miami, some continuing aboard as far as New York over ACL, RF&P and Pennsy routes. From 1912 until an unnamed hurricane ended those jaunts in 1935, FEC maintained a burgeoning — albeit unprofitable — commerce ferrying a well-heeled clientele between their cold-weather Northern domiciles and sunny tropical respites south of the border. An FEC Pacific steam engine powers the *Havana Special* (*photograph by Al Perez, courtesy Cal Winter*).

And what became of the Florida East Coast Railway? It experienced both prosperous and lean years, often directly tied to the nation's economy. A branch line largely for farm products was opened from 1915 to 1947. It ran between Maytown, near New Smyrna Beach, through the interior of the state southward to Lake Okeechobee and the Everglades. It became the most important secondary route off the main, albeit exclusively for freight traffic.

In the meantime, the mainline witnessed spurts in passenger transport as well as heavy freight haulage. By 1923, for instance, five daily trains in each direction plied the tracks between Jacksonville and Miami. Two of them — still in the day of the Key West Extension — offered through service to the Island City. Timetables for the *Havana Special* and *Key West Express* called for trips from Miami to Key West in under six hours. Flagler-owned steamers waiting alongside the tracks at the end of the line simplified the transition for travelers continuing to Havana.

By 1924, tourists and new residents were pouring into Florida at such a dizzy pace that the FEC was running eight trains every day in each direction between Jacksonville and Miami as it tried to keep up with demand. Many visitors came from far-flung destinations under auspices of other roads that took them to Jacksonville, where they bonded with the FEC. New York City and points in that direction ushered in travelers via Atlantic Coast Line (ACL), Seaboard Air Line (SAL) and Southern (SOU) routes. Chicago residents and many from a plethora of Midwestern municipalities began their trips over the Chicago & Eastern Illinois, Illinois Central, Louisville & Nashville (L&N), Pennsylvania, SOU and other carriers, often supported by the Central of Georgia (CofG) connecting major trunk lines. From the West — Kansas City, Memphis, New Orleans, St. Louis and beyond — they traveled by way of the ACL, St. Louis–San Francisco, Gulf, Mobile & Ohio, L&N and SAL, often including one or more connecting carriers before their arrival in Jacksonville.

That city, more than any other in the South, was inexorably busy with rail traffic — every day of every year no matter what the hour. With the exception of the ACL's north-south Perry cutoff to Tampa opened in western Florida in 1928, and the route to Alabama and beyond from Pensacola to Mobile or Montgomery, it was almost a foregone conclusion train travelers going to or from the Sunshine State in the 20th century could count on passing through Jacksonville. As many as nine out of every 10 did so. FEC's connecting trains waited patiently there, gathering and transporting them to resorts all along the Atlantic shoreline between that north Florida feeder terminus and Miami. And from Jacksonville to Stuart, a stop just north of West Palm Beach, the FEC had no competition in running FEC passenger trains—plus those of the ACL, with whom it maintained an exclusive contract from 1896 to 1963.[15] It was a lucrative operation.

Typical of the ACL trains on those tracks in 1957, the streamlined *Miamian* was a coach and Pullman consist with limited stops— none scheduled, for instance, between Florence, South Carolina, and Jacksonville, a 383-mile trek. The *Miamian* departed New York's Pennsylvania Station at 10:30 A.M. daily and was due in Jacksonville at 3:45 the following morning. Leaving Jax on FEC tracks within a quarter-hour, it called at only a half-dozen stations before reaching Miami at 11:15 A.M. In less than 25 hours it completed a 1,047-mile journey—averaging better than 42 miles an hour including all scheduled and flag stops.

On the return trip north the *Miamian* departed its namesake city at 5 P.M., made it to Jacksonville by 12:20 A.M., left it at 12:35 and was in New York that same afternoon at 5:45 P.M. Its 1957 consist between Washington and Miami included six coaches, seven sleepers offering a mix of accommodations (sections, double bedrooms, compartments, drawing rooms), diner, and tavern-lounge car.

The *Miamian* was but one of a half-dozen interline passenger trains rolling over FEC tracks in 1957; only a few years before there had been still more. Some originated in Chicago

The year is roughly 1958 and this is a typical day as a well corralled aggregate of FEC motive power awaits its individual summons from Miami's Buena Vista Yard Roundhouse. The facility and yard are no longer there but the historic turntable now spans a canal and serves a single-lane road in Homestead, Florida (*photograph by Fred Carnes, courtesy Richard C. Beall*).

and followed a multiplicity of routes to Jacksonville. The *City of Miami* and the *South Wind*, operating on alternate days, left Chicago in this epoch around 9 A.M. Central Time before pulling into Jacksonville about 24 hours later at 9:15 A.M. Both *City* and *Wind* (on different days) departed on FEC tracks at 9:45, made 15 intermediate stops and were in Miami at 5:15 P.M.

In the reverse direction the pair left Miami on opposite days at 12:15 P.M., arrived at Jacksonville at 7:45 P.M. for a 20-minute layover, and were scheduled to be in the Windy City about 6:45 P.M. Central Time the following evening. For most of the route the *City of Miami* had two coaches, seven sleepers that exhibited a plethora of accommodations, diner, and a tavern-lounge-observation car. The *South Wind* operated likewise with six sleepers. More coaches and sleepers were aboard the consist north of Jacksonville. These continued south as a separate train over the ACL main to Tampa, St. Petersburg, Sarasota, Fort Myers and Naples.

The exclusivity to and from Miami enjoyed by the FEC and its partner roads persisted until Seaboard took notice and became a more aggressive rival than it customarily had been. A separate route to south Florida was highly desirable. ACL sought one for decades but was never able to muster it for sundry reasons.[16] It did attempt —from 1944 to 1958 — to purchase the FEC outright and thereby gain control of the route. That never came to fruition, however. But in a Florida land boom in the 1920s the SAL saw a whopping opportunity that it wasn't about to let slip through its fingers.

Seaboard president Davies Warfield was convinced that the only way the SAL could gain competitive advantage over its principal rivals (ACL, FEC, SOU) was expansion in Florida. He pushed for cross-state trackage to tie the east and west coasts together. In 1924, the SAL commenced to create a long stem off its mainline between Jacksonville and Tampa at the little

A hue and cry must have reached the ears of FEC brass after recurring clientele saw what FEC had done to the motive power. Eliminating factory-applied triple-striping that adorned its early generation diesels, including E7A 1012, the carrier cut labor costs by repainting in bland solid blue. That didn't work out well; in addition to its unfamiliarity, the new scheme didn't adapt to dirt and grime, causing FEC to halt repainting at 39 of its 110 diesels. In 1962, train 6, the *City of Miami*, sometimes known among the faithful as the *Chicago Streamliner*, sports the new livery as it's about to depart its namesake for the Windy City (*photograph by Fred Carnes, courtesy Richard C. Beall*).

central Florida hamlet of Coleman. That branch netted a 204-mile addition running southeast to West Palm Beach. Florida's cross-state railroad from Tampa to West Palm Beach became reality with the opening of that line on January 21, 1925. But that feat was just the tip of the iceberg (or top of the palm trees maybe?).

A year hence an ambitious SAL began creating roadbeds for still further development on both coasts. The western end of the mainline was continued to Clearwater, St. Petersburg, Fort Myers and Naples in southwest Florida. In southeast Florida rails were added below West Palm Beach to Fort Lauderdale, Miami and Homestead, in direct competition with FEC. The extensions on both coasts opened to traffic in January 1927. While a devastating hurricane halted Florida's land boom that year, devaluing areas into which SAL had just expanded, the company was well positioned to seize the next wave of newcomers—visitors and residents— that were certain to follow. SAL and FEC would go head-to-head fighting to serve their customers better than their opposite number on routes that led to real estate which was fast becoming some of the Sunshine State's most desirable land.

But a funny thing happened on the way to Miami. While FEC rightly professed it maintained the shortest route between Jacksonville and the end of its line (366 miles to SAL's 406 miles)—FEC never had to flaunt that before SAL showed up, of course—for some reason that 40-mile savings did not translate into *time saved*. It's a curious conundrum to anybody comparing the timetables both then and now.

Pick an era—the early 1950s, for instance—for relative purposes. ACL's top two diesel-powered streamliners plying FEC tracks alongside the Atlantic—the *East Coast Champion*

Onlookers wave as the *City of Miami* crosses Miami Shores Canal. Its head-end power is supplied by FEC E3A 1001. This is a heavily retouched photograph: one-half of each of the two visible cars were totally disfigured and have been reconstructed to present a more acceptable image (*courtesy Chuck Blardone*).

and the *Florida Special*— made the 366-mile trek with just five intermediate station stops in an even seven hours in both directions. In that same interlude SAL's top two diesel-powered streamliners— the *Orange Blossom Special* and the *Silver Meteor*— running SAL's 406-mile course, much of it through the interior of Florida with 11 (*Special*) or 15 (*Meteor*) scheduled stops en route, arrived at their destinations, north or south, between 6 hours 52 minutes and 6 hours 57 minutes. Was this purely advertising genius and little more?

How did SAL undercut the competition? Were they the instigators of a practice used by modern airlines, widespread at least until recently, in which published arrival times weren't worth the paper they were printed on? Who knows? If SAL could maintain its announced schedules, however, it may have gotten help in a couple of ways: (1) SAL passenger trains encountered fewer freights on their tracks due to more haulage up and down the shorter coastal route; and (2) by traveling mostly through rural, less populated terrain instead of beachfront resorts loaded with tourists SAL could "make time" at incredibly faster speeds. The new rivalry provided something for everybody. ACL and FEC could promote their "shortest route" while SAL touted the "fastest route" to Miami, if only by minutes. The bragging rights of both translated into money in the bank.

There's another chapter in the Florida route tale that must not be missed. On January 23, 1963, a total of 11 non-operating unions struck the FEC over the road's snubbing of compensation accords embracing railways across the country. As a result an instant, comprehensive work stoppage occurred throughout the FEC system. Not only did that affect FEC, it thwarted

In a 1958 photograph, switch engines hold their positions as the southbound *East Coast Champion* train 1 crosses N.E. 36th Street in Buena Vista Yard at Miami behind three E7s on its way to the Miami passenger station two miles south (*photograph by Fred Carnes, courtesy Richard C. Beall*).

ACL, its partner of 67 years, preventing it from sending its long distance trains between Jacksonville and Miami. Because merger talks with SAL had been progressing for five years at that juncture, the doorway to a solution to ACL's dilemma was palpable on the horizon. ACL officials prevailed on SAL to help it reach Miami when its accustomed pathway was suddenly road-blocked.

Until those lines fused in 1968, ACL took its trains down the ACL mainline serving central and west coast Florida as far south as Auburndale. The SAL main from Jacksonville to Miami crossed the ACL tracks there. It was a simple matter to turn the ACL trains onto the SAL route for the continuation of the trip to Miami. In doing so the ACL missed stops formerly served on the FEC line at St. Augustine, Ormond Beach, Daytona Beach, New Smyrna Beach, Titusville, Cocoa, Melbourne, Fort Pierce and a handful of lesser burgs. But it still called at several commanding cities: West Palm Beach, Lake Worth, Boynton Beach, Delray Beach, Deerfield Beach, Fort Lauderdale, Hollywood, Miami and more. The FEC strike that prompted that change languished for years, parts of it remaining unsettled until the mid 1970s. (More detail will follow in this chapter.) The detour became permanent, lasting to the integration of the ACL-SAL in 1968 and Amtrak's assumption of passenger travel in 1971.

In an effort to be profitable and remain solvent the Florida East Coast Railway gave considerable care to the coddling of passengers, as much as many of the larger trunk line roads were doing that were covering much greater distances through several states. FEC's emphasis on safety, comfort, impeccable service and gratifying traveler amenities resonated with patrons. Even though riders who boarded or detrained at St. Augustine, Ormond Beach, Daytona Beach, New Smyrna, Titusville, Cocoa, Vero Beach and Fort Pierce had no nearby rail alternative — they were "in between" Jacksonville and Miami, many miles from the SAL main — the FEC worked hard to keep them contented and thereby retain them. They tried to build loyalty among the locals just as they sought to do for long-distance travelers whose destinations took them well beyond the gateway at Jacksonville. In working at the pleasing and retention task, the FEC applied some unique measures.

When the *Florida Special* added a diminutive portable swimming pool to its southbound consist in 1933, it turned heads throughout the industry. "One railroad operating between New York and Florida has installed a recreation car on its southern run so passengers will not need to wait until they reach Miami to begin their sports," revealed the March 1933 issue of *Popular Mechanics.* "The club car is equipped with a small bathing pool, mechanical horses, a punching bag and other equipment for the entertainment of passengers who want to exercise." Shades of workouts in pre-fitness center, pre-spa days? In addition to the pool, there was a gymnasium, dance floor, orchestra, bridge room, barber shop and hostess-instructor who oversaw it all. Harold K. North, a FEC ticket agent in 1933 at the Miami depot, recalled that pool, though not fondly: "It was a real nuisance, as the constant motion of the train caused the pool to constantly need refilling. I ... remember the curiosity the pool generated. I don't think it ran after that one year."

The lounge car on the *Havana Special* advertised that in the center of the train one could find "a drawing room lounge, a ladies' lounge and bath, gentlemen's lounge and bath, well-equipped soda fountain with a trained Filipino attendant." Tongue-in-cheek, was that politically correct? Those baths, incidentally, surely weren't bathtub or shower-equipped, as patrons of sleepers in the Amtrak era have experienced. (There aren't any tubs but the showers, while minuscule, can be invigorating as one lunges forward and backward while attempting to remain upright at 79 M.P.H. or more!)

Mindful that some travelers sought solace beyond Florida's sunny climes in their quests for tropical splendor, FEC and partner ACL exploited the chances they had. By firmly tying the FEC to connections with steamship and airline companies, they promoted convenient, trouble-free transfers between trains, water and air routes to hip island oases. As early as 1929, FEC advertised through service to "the romantic Caribbean" that embraced Havana, the West Indies, and Central and South America. With transfers included, a trip from New York to Miami by rail continuing to Havana via Pan American Airways (PAA) was a breeze: two-and-a-quarter hours from Miami on a tri-motor propeller-driven 12-passenger airliner with crew of four. (Just 90 minutes elapsed between one's arrival at the Miami depot and departure from the airport and those venues weren't near one another! Imagine how long that would take in today's security-laden environment.) FEC sold patrons on the trip's length — 36 hours from New York to Havana, leaving New York at 10:15 P.M. and arriving Havana at 10:15 A.M. the second morning — then captured many of those riders as loyal customers by making their trips not only stress-free but memorable.

If a vacationer preferred he could remain on the train to Key West where, until 1935, he switched to Peninsular & Occidental Steamship Company (P&O) dinghies, a journey no less interesting or exciting. That put him in Havana in little more than 12 hours from Miami. For the pampered guest seeking an exclusive retreat in the tropics, it was a solution that the FEC gave constant care to in an effort to please the most discriminating traveler.

There was much more available to those with the time and money to spend, of course. By West Indies Air Limited one could depart Miami either Monday, Wednesday or Friday for a four-day package adventure by air to more than a dozen Caribbean and South American destinations with nightly accommodations included. The trip included stops at Port au Prince, Santo Domingo, San Juan, St. Thomas, Port of Spain and the three Guyanas, and ended at Belem, Paraguay. Or one might fly four days weekly on PAA from Miami to Jamaica and then to the Panama Canal Zone. PAA and P&O both hauled vacationers daily from Miami to Nassau, Bahamas, where a couple of palatial Flagler resorts, The Colonial and The Royal Victoria, awaited as part of their unforgettable experience.

When the nation's economy went bust in the Great Depression of the 1930s, to salvage as much of a sharply faltering passenger business as it could, much of the rail industry induced deep fare cuts. FEC and its partners cooperated fully to rejuvenate trade. In 1933, for example, for $24 one could journey one-way between Miami and Havana. The daily round-trip tariff between Miami and Key West was only $4.75 and that was slashed to $2.50 on Sunday. If a local family of four could scrape together 10 bucks—a tall order for many in that day—it could escape its financial woes for a few hours with a spirited jaunt over the Overseas Railway. But those leisure-seekers mustn't delay in doing so: while nobody realized it then, a fateful end to those enchanting escapades was rapidly approaching the keys. By September 1935, carnage in the wake of the unnamed hurricane would bring absolute cessation to a diversion that had charmed and entranced so many.

The Seaboard Air Line Railroad was the first carrier to introduce dieselized streamliners to Floridians when the *Silver Meteor* rolled out of Georgia on its maiden voyage southbound from New York City on February 2, 1939. More is said about that train and the reactions of the competition in chapters on the SAL (13) and Atlantic Coast Line Railroad (3). Suffice it to state here that ACL, which could generally be branded as more conservative in comparison to SAL, stood on the sidelines waiting for the next shoe to drop. The changeover from heavy metal (weighty, heavy metal, and slower steam engines and cars) would be a huge investment when it occurred, and ACL hadn't yet coughed up the cash. But the shoe dropped quickly as passengers (and even admiring potential passengers) swooned over the sleekness of the modernization that those shiny stainless steel tubes with their curved aerodynamic sides and ends displayed.

ACL and its longtime associate FEC didn't need any convincing then that they'd better get on board or be left in the dust after witnessing swift pronounced public fawning that the fancy new equipment generated. FEC and ACL placed orders at once for brand new dieselized locomotive power and streamlined coaches, sleepers, diners and tavern-observation cars. While it would be December 1939 before those components could be in operation, the roads used the time to upgrade what they had: 10 existing coaches were air-conditioned, outfitted with reclining seats, given improved toilet facilities and lighting (many cars had been previously converted), while eight 4-8-2 Mountain type engines were reconditioned to pull passenger consists at a faster clip and thereby abolish most double-heading on lengthy trains.

One of the new streamliners was to be reserved exclusively for FEC use between Jacksonville and Miami. While ACL conducted a nationwide contest to name its innovative New York–Florida train—to trump SAL there were actually *two* of them departing Jacksonville by separate routes, the *East Coast Champion* and the *West Coast Champion*—FEC solicited proposed monikers from within its company for its own Jacksonville–Miami streamliner. After exhaustive deliberations *Henry M. Flagler* was adopted and the sobriquet was etched on the engine sides by the motive power-building Budd Company of Philadelphia. The *Flagler* made its first run south on December 3, 1939. It persisted under that appellation only briefly, nevertheless.

For a number of reasons it lost its profitability. Foremost among them may have been that it was needed for too many daily trips between its terminal cities to run independently. Not only was there the ACL to consider but a trio of roads bringing trains from Chicago. Therefore with its *Henry M. Flagler* label removed, on December 18, 1940, that engine became part of a pool ferrying trains originating in Chicago between Jacksonville and Miami under the *Dixie Flagler* handle.

Two more roads were involved in schlepping passengers over the ACL route between New York and Jacksonville—Pennsylvania and the Richmond, Fredericksburg & Potomac. They joined the FEC and ACL in the equipment-furnishing alliance on the route. In subsequent years with 16 to 21 cars in tow it wasn't out of the ordinary to find a trio of diesels pulling consists with cars representing that quartet of carriers hauling riders to Miami. Even the New Haven Railroad, which provided connecting trains between New York to Boston, on limited occasions furnished some of the cars.

The *Champion* was permanently doubled on December 21, 1940, becoming a 14-car all-coach streamliner with dual diners and taverns (one in the middle, another with a rounded-end supplying an observation-lounge as the last car). At the same time the *Florida Special* and *Vacationer* were dieselized.[17] That also marked the first time all passenger trains on the FEC main were air conditioned. It was something to celebrate, for not every railroad could claim it.

After the FEC lost its Cuba connection in March 1945, the rail carrier signed a pact with the West India Fruit and Steamship Company to pick up that service between Miami, Key West and Havana. Late the following year an agreement was reached with the Florida–Havana Railroad Car Ferry to provide similar service from Palm Beach to Havana.

In conjunction with the New York Central Railroad and Southern Railway, on December 15, 1949, FEC launched a new winter season streamliner, the *New Royal Palm*. Sections originating in Buffalo, Chicago, Cleveland, Detroit and New York combined for the trip south

For a fleeting moment, it was Camelot. An artist's rendering of FEC's *Henry M. Flagler* diesel engine was a magnetic attraction wherever it appeared as a stand-alone poster and in company literature. The nomenclature resulted from a spirited internal debate and was emblazoned on one of the daily trains ferrying passengers between Miami and Jacksonville at the inception of FEC's streamliner era in late 1939. Within a year, alas, a decision was made to remove the hallowed moniker and include the locomotive in a head-end consortium furnished by varied lines powering the consists under the *Dixie Flagler* sobriquet from Miami to Chicago (**courtesy Chuck Blardone**).

In early 1958, the southbound *Florida Special* #87 has just arrived at the Miami passenger station situated in the distance behind the middle unit. The train has stopped blocking N.W. 1st Street long enough for hostlers to separate the engines from the train and take them to the Buena Vista roundhouse for servicing, leaving the cars behind for travelers to exit (*photograph by Ken M. Ardinger, courtesy Richard C. Beall*).

A labor strike on January 23, 1963, changed passenger service forever on FEC. Once trains began running with scab and management labor, they hauled only freight. Sabotage ensued including dynamiting trains to cause derailments. As a deterrent FEC equipped vehicles with rail wheels and operated "hi-rail" cars ahead of trains to try to detect vandalism. When court-ordered passenger service was restored, FEC ran one train a day each way. Few cars were supplied and officials warned travelers of potential harm or death by striker sabotage, an effort to dissuade riders. Train 2 is set to depart North Miami depot behind a "hi-rail" vehicle on August 2, 1965 (*photograph by Ken M. Ardinger, courtesy Richard C. Beall*).

with sleepers added in Cincinnati and Atlanta. In addition to the sleepers the consist included a rounded-end tavern-lounge-observation car and diner.

When the unions struck the FEC on January 23, 1963, shutting down the whole route, it prompted ACL to rapidly respond by realigning with SAL, ending a coalition that had existed with FEC nearly seven decades. The work stoppage, thought to be temporary at first, dragged on and on. While more than 200 acts of vandalism, theft, sabotage, derailment and attempted murder were conducted against the FEC by what may have been striking laborers (at least four were tried, convicted and imprisoned), a war of words raged in courtrooms, state and federal legislative halls as the FEC and unions bickered. Among the victims affected were passengers: service, on which many depended, abruptly ceased. Before 1963 ended, Miami politicians, acting in misguided haste, dismantled the FEC depot. Several other places along FEC tracks reacted similarly, city fathers believing the road's passenger days were forever over.

That wasn't the case, however. When Miami mayor (1957–1967) Robert King High, with aspirations for the governorship, discovered that the FEC's original charter, never amended, required the company to provide daily except Sunday passenger service between Jacksonville and Miami, he shouted it far and wide.[18] After airing it out before the Florida Railroad and Public Utilities Commission and the state Supreme Court, FEC announced in July 1965 that it would resume limited passenger service between those points. While FEC would live up to its legal obligations, it would offer nothing extra. Only riders paying full fare would be transported. No passes for any rail line would be honored. No checked baggage would be allowed, no remains, U.S. mail, company mail or express.

The FEC resumed the service on August 2, 1965, with one train daily Monday through Saturday in each direction. Southbound it left Jacksonville at 9:40 A.M. and arrived Miami at 5:15 P.M. The return portion left Miami at 9 A.M. and was into Jacksonville at 4:20 P.M. A one-

FEC ran one small train daily in each direction after the courts so ordered. The Miami passenger station had been torn down in the early days of the strike. The lone passenger train departed the newly acquired Hialeah, Florida, yard and ran "light" to the North Miami passenger depot for its initial departure with riders. Northbound train 2, seen here, travels through Hialeah on the way to the North Miami station behind E9 1035 (*photograph by Fred Carnes, courtesy Richard C. Beall*).

way coach ticket for the full trip cost $10.86 while first class travelers seated in the tavern-lounge-observation car paid $15.23.

The train was launched with two coaches that were quickly reduced to one. Although there were no sleepers and no diner, passengers could order box lunches en route that were picked up at a station stop along the line. Soft drinks and coffee could be purchased onboard but no alcoholic beverages were available. Six-member crews included an engineer, head end brakeman, flagman, conductor, passenger service agent and porter. It was minimal and a far cry from the "glory days" that many patrons recalled from just three years before. While one passionate historian dubbed it "America's shortest, full service streamliner," that now seems speculative and open to interpretation considering the dining experience was nontraditional in the usual sense.

Because Miami had shot itself in the foot by removing its passenger facility in 1963, an alternative had to be substituted. Making the best of a bad situation, FEC terminated its passenger service at the North Miami stop at N.E. 16th Avenue and 129th Street, a small station erected in 1955. The ambitious mayor of Miami, High, whose intervention resulted in the resumption of human cargo in the first place, fumed over the turn of events, yet was powerless to alter it.

Less than three years hence the service to that stop ceased: FEC pleaded successfully before the Florida Public Service Commission, gaining permission to delete its limited travel transportation. The final day of operation was July 31, 1968. A more prosperous future would occur for the FEC as it concentrated its efforts altogether on freight traffic. Getting people to their destinations was the impetus when Henry Flagler bought his first railroad in 1884, becoming the cornerstone of the Florida East Coast system. Times had changed dramatically in America and people had gained many more travel options 84 years later. It had been a good run, and in the halcyon days when it mattered most, FEC had proven a worthy, viable, dependable carrier as millions sought a place in the sun.

7

GULF, MOBILE & OHIO RAILROAD
Great Things Made of Little Things

Of the multiple carriers profiled in this book that plied their craft along Southern tracks, in some dimensions the Gulf, Mobile & Ohio Railroad (GM&O) earns a rung at the lower end of the ladder. If limited solely to the number of travelers it carried (as compared to neighboring systems), or its pithy interval of passenger service (about three decades; just 18 years in Dixie), the GM&O earns inferior marks as a people-hauler and may be judged as one of the region's weaker links. Perceptibly, it was a little fish swimming in a big pond.

Yet the numbers belie another aspect of the GM&O that account for some momentous inroads. This little line operating in the mid–South and also in later years the Midwest— along with a couple of its ancestors—quietly went about its efforts with an unrestrained approach in innovation. The road and its forebears, in fact, pioneered in a few areas that were to benefit rail riders far beyond its own territory. Concurrently, that threesome received their justified plaudits for such sterling contributions. Few living beyond those denizens they served had ever heard of those carriers while fewer still realized that the concepts they fostered in upgraded service and equipment were initially implemented on the routes of minuscule providers. The GM&O defied many odds, yet its largely unheralded story and legacy is compelling, worthy of deeper introspection.

Hardly thought of in connection with any mention of longevity, the GM&O wasn't even formed until a few years after diesel engines arrived on the scene. Its eventual, problematic merger with a "bitter rival"—an ascription assigned by some industry analysts—led to a posthaste retreat: that amalgamation witnessed the dismantling of most of GM&O's parallel trunk lines and branches in deference to its larger and more powerful partner. Yet during its brief span as a stand-alone railway, GM&O earned an auspicious standing as a solid freight and passenger transporter. At its peak it crossed seven states in its quest to oblige disparate, far-flung constituencies across the nation's midsection, often divided from one another by hundreds of miles. Shippers and riders from the Gulf Coast to the Great Lakes relied on GM&O. In the ephemeral timeframe in which it prospered in the middle decades of the 20th century, the line earned a reputation as a respected and responsive outfit.

The full extent of the components that ultimately encompassed the Gulf, Mobile & Ohio Railroad were legionary. The heavyweights among them may be distilled, nevertheless, into a trio of roads: (1) the Gulf, Mobile & Northern Railroad—with its mainline running between Mobile, Alabama, and Jackson, Tennessee, with a branch intersecting it running west to Jackson, Mississippi, where it turned south to New Orleans; (2) the Mobile & Ohio Railroad— with mainline running north from Mobile to East St. Louis, Illinois, and with three stems linking as many cities to the mainline—Birmingham, Memphis and Montgomery; and (3) the Alton Railroad—with mainlines extending from Chicago to St. Louis and Springfield, Illinois (off that main), west to Kansas City, Missouri, with dual offshoots to Peoria, Illinois.

Just a year beyond the creation of the Alton & Sangamon Railroad in 1847, earliest forerunner of the Alton, the Mobile & Ohio Railroad (M&O) was launched at Mobile, Alabama. Some Mobile businessmen hoped to profit from north-south trade like their river-blessed neighbor to the west, New Orleans, by organizing the M&O in 1848. With an avowed target of constructing a rail line to the Ohio River at Cairo, Illinois, the M&O investors' cash supply was depleted long before the rails got to the end of the line. Some entrepreneurs at Jackson, Tennessee, on the other hand—led by Judge Milton Brown, a future U.S. congressman—bought the weakened line. The M&O reached Jackson in 1851, and a few years later it was extended northward as far as Columbus, Kentucky. Regular passenger service between Jackson and Columbus began in 1858.

But another 16 years passed before the Mobile & Ohio finally witnessed passenger service to and from the banks of the Ohio (1874), its intended destination a quarter-century earlier. One of the chief reasons for the prolonged lapse was the War Between the States (1861–1865), which intervened with disastrous effects. The M&O's tracks were decimated during the conflict. In the strategic Battle for Pittsburg Landing—in which Union and Confederate troops clashed at a site about 65 miles southeast of Jackson near Corinth, Mississippi—the South lost some key east-west and north-south supply lines as the M&O was put out of commission. Subsequently, in the postwar years, with the South struggling to get back on its feet, replacement of those ravaged routes lagged. Nor did an 1873 economic depression help the effort to return to normalcy.

It was actually 1883, a historian maintains, when the M&O crossed the Ohio River over an Illinois Central bridge to North Cairo.[1] Three years hence Mobile & Ohio purchased a narrow gauge system, St. Louis & Cairo. Once it had been widened to standard gauge, M&O celebrated a 650-mile system that linked St. Louis with Mobile. All this transpired nearly a century after the earliest antecedents of the Gulf, Mobile & Ohio organized. There was more, much more, that happened before those outfits joined together to establish GM&O.

Another early member of those imposing lines, Gulf, Mobile & Northern Railroad, dates to the mid 1910s with the reorganization of the New Orleans, Mobile & Chicago Railroad. That system connected Mobile, Alabama, with Middleton, Tennessee. Middleton was the tiniest of hamlets (it boasted just 607 residents in 2007), a west Tennessee backwater brushing beside the Mississippi border, 40 miles south of Jackson and 74 miles east of Memphis. So what compelled a railroad to construct its terminals between the Gulf coast and Middleton?

Colonel William Clark Falkner (1826–1889), variously championed as "a Southern Gentleman, lawyer and statesman," chartered the Ripley Railroad Company in 1872.[2] His purpose was to connect his plantation interests at Ripley, Mississippi, with the Memphis and Charleston Railroad (later Southern) at Middleton. Falkner soon altered the moniker to the Ripley, Ship Island and Kentucky Railroad. When an extension was added through New Albany, Mississippi, to Pontotoc, he rebranded it again—this time to the Gulf & Chicago Railroad. That line wasn't successful as a stand-alone enterprise, by the way; eventually it segued into the Gulf, Mobile & Northern Railroad.

A historian claims that Falkner's association with the early predecessor of the GM&O "could be construed to be the basis for the GM&N's title as 'The Rebel Route.'"[3] In the 1930s, the Daughters of the Confederacy (DAC), nonetheless, vehemently protested the labeling for reasons of their own. "Peace was restored when [GM&N] President I. B. Tigrett explained that the name did not refer to the War Between the States but was intended to mark a revolutionary step in transportation."[4] That seemed to pacify the DAC.

And lest anybody mistakenly think it was the affluent plantation owner who underwrote the bills for the early rail line, that idea was only partially true. He likely subscribed some portion of the costs. But it took Jacksonians to make the impending tracks lead to a recognizable railroad town. Voting affirmatively in 1917, the Tennesseans issued bonds valued at $100,000 to extend the Gulf, Mobile & Northern Railroad from Middleton to Jackson. The finished tracks opened in September 1919, some 47 years after Falkner decided to run them from Ripley to Middleton. Sometimes things took a while in a languid culture.

A couple of decades earlier the rival Mobile & Ohio Railroad (M&O) had reached Alabama's state capital at Montgomery in 1898. From a stem off the M&O's north-south trunk line at Artesia, Mississippi, laid to Columbus, Mississippi, in 1860, work proceeded on to Montgomery in 1896. Montgomery was 181 miles southeast of Artesia. Tuscaloosa was picked as the operational hub of the Montgomery District with M&O staffers dubbing the stem the "Pea Vine."

M&O's resolve to access Montgomery was nurtured by a serious yen to increase revenue traffic between the capital, south Georgia and all of Florida. Multiple competitors maintained formidable passenger service to and from Montgomery, among them Atlantic Coast Line, Central of Georgia, Louisville & Nashville, Seaboard Air Line, West Point Route and Southern (the latter over Western Railway of Alabama and L&N tracks). By tying into established traffic patterns at Montgomery, the M&O believed it could bump up in its people-moving commerce.

It anticipated a rise in freight-hauling, too, expecting to cash in on developing coal, iron ore and steel industries that were rapidly expanding in the vicinity of Birmingham, less than 100 miles to the north of Montgomery. After the M&O negotiated with the Birmingham Southern Railroad (BS) in 1899, hoping to open a roadway connecting the pair in order to gain entrance to Birmingham proper, the Louisville & Nashville and Southern intervened. Controlling BS stock, those lines stopped the measure in its tracks, deeming it unhealthy for the owners' profitable enterprises. Parenthetically, in a sense — almost as if having awakened a sleeping giant — three years hence Southern Railway bought almost all of M&O's common stock, thereby also acquiring control of that line (1901).

Nevertheless a persistent M&O — unwilling to give up — eventually found another way to get to Birmingham. In 1908, the road gained trackage rights over the Illinois Central's route from Corinth, Mississippi, to Haleyville, Alabama, and from there to Birmingham on rails owned by M&O's parent firm, Southern Railway. M&O and its successor, Gulf, Mobile & Ohio, had access to Birmingham via that route for 44 years (to 1952). That year the Interstate Commerce Commission — over the howling protests of Illinois Central — allowed GM&O to gain access to Birmingham via L&N rails from Tuscaloosa. Recall that Southern and L&N had originally denied M&O and successor GM&O use of tracks they jointly owned in order to reach Birmingham. In the intervening years, surely with objectives and management both having altered, the pair of lines had revised their thinking. They decided to share their tracks with an old adversary. Now it was IC, an M&O/GM&O collaborator, turning into a foe. At times it seemed like the only thing certain about railroading was that in any particular situation, given enough time, things would change — for the better, or worse.

In the interim Mobile & Ohio erected an imposing depot at Mobile in 1905-1906, which also served the superseding GM&O rail system as its key southeastern terminus. Built at a cost of $575,000, the facility was large and ornate, of Spanish Colonial Revival architecture. It was abandoned by the railroad eight decades afterward in 1986. Purchased by the city of Mobile and revitalized for use as offices of the Metro Transit Authority, that city's local bus concern, it was adapted to serve several private businesses, too.

Into the life of nearly every railroad of any substance in America one or more individuals ostensibly existed who could be deemed a catalyst (or savior) for whatever greatness a particular line achieved. Exhibiting physical, mental, persuasive, emotional, political or financial muscle, and often some combination of those qualities, one or more inspired contributors made such an impact on the property that a legacy left upon it clearly defined a turning point in the road's outcome. For the Gulf, Mobile & Ohio, and predecessor Gulf, Mobile & Northern, that individual was incontrovertibly Isaac (Ike) Burton Tigrett. Not only was he a stable president for much of those dual lines' lives, he was well groomed for his responsibilities by early rail management experience.

Born September 15, 1879, at Friendship in rural west Tennessee, Tigrett — after graduating in 1898 from Union University at Jackson, Tennessee — had $800 to his name, harboring an appetite for banking. Renting a facility in Halls, a little burg near Jackson, he scribbled "Bank" on a window and formed a cashier's cage out of chicken wire. Patiently sitting in his cage every day Tigrett had to roost for a spell before his first patron appeared on the scene. He was really in business when that client deposited $50 with him. Although his commercial venture dawdled along, by one account "Tigrett's reputation as a man with a head for figures spread rapidly."[5] Within two years (1900) he was back in Jackson organizing the Union Bank and Trust Company. His peers elected him president of the Tennessee Bankers Association.

When some local capitalists rather impetuously agreed to create a 48-mile shortline railway that they would in due course dub the Birmingham & Northwestern Railroad (B&N), they appointed Tigrett as treasurer. (The road actually ran between Jackson and Dyersburg, Tennessee.) Tigrett intended to perform his duties for the road as a sideline to his banking trade but it didn't work out that way. Not only did he have charge of overseeing the money and paying the bills, his pledge brought him the obligation of figuring out how to raise the cash to keep the line operating. It was a blessing in disguise; it taught him many valuable lessons that were applicable down the way as his horizons in railroading broadened.

Tigrett accepted the B&N's presidency in 1911, and was elected a director of the struggling neighboring line, the Gulf, Mobile & Northern Railroad, a few years later. When nobody else could be found to manage the GM&N, he consented to become its president in 1919.

> The G.M. & N. was not much of a rail road. It did not go any place of industrial importance after it left Mobile and struck out into Mississippi & Tennessee. The roadbed was so bad that freight trains were often held to a top speed of 6 m.p.h....
>
> Ike Tigrett was never in any great hurry.
>
> He immensely enjoyed taking over bits & pieces of broken-down railroads in the Deep South, linking them together, and making them work for a profit.[6] The end product of this patient toil is the prosperous 1,970-mile Gulf, Mobile & Ohio Railroad Co., that links Mobile and New Orleans with East St. Louis....
>
> Ike Tigrett kept on buying up tottering railroads whenever he could get them at bottom prices, and used them to tap new sources of traffic for the G.M. & N. In 1933 he leased the New Orleans Great Northern Railway Co., which soon gave him a line into New Orleans and a chance to bid for export-import freight traffic. In 1940 Tigrett bought the Mobile & Ohio Railroad Co.
>
> That took him into East St. Louis. It also gave him an integrated system that became the current Gulf, Mobile & Ohio.[7]

Through the late 1930s, the Gulf, Mobile & Northern Railroad was controlled by the Chicago, Burlington & Quincy Railroad (CB&Q), which owned 27.7 percent of its stock.[8] (The CB&Q itself was controlled by the Great Northern and Northern Pacific railways.) Another 10 percent of the GM&N was owned by the St. Louis–San Francisco Railway (Frisco).[9] The Mobile & Ohio, meanwhile, had been in receivership since 1932. Southern Railway bought it in 1901, and still owned 94.4 percent of its stock.[10] While the Southern welcomed the proposed amalgamation, it pushed aside advances of the Frisco a few years before as that line sought to buy the Mobile & Ohio.[11] Intriguingly talks between the Frisco and GM&O in 1947, in regard to a merger of those lines potentially forming an 8,000-mile system linking the Great Lakes, the Gulf and the Southwest, broke down; the two sides decided to retain their independency.[12] The Gulf, Mobile & Ohio Railroad was — according to numerous observers —

created in 1938 "to put together two lines, the Gulf, Mobile & Northern Railroad and the Mobile & Ohio Railroad." The carriers formally merged in 1940. On that occasion a journalist reported:

> The setup will give modest, canny, homespun Ike Tigrett a chance to step up the $427,388 net profit his road made last year (M. & O. lost $440,924) to a respectable figure by getting a longer haul on a larger portion of the two lines' traffic. Already benefiting from the movement of industries to the South, he hopes to add more manufactured goods to the lumber, petroleum, bananas, etc. which are the standbys of his new road. Now 60, not old as railroad presidents go, he has been a railroad president longer than any other U.S. railroader except Baltimore & Ohio's venerable "Uncle Dan" Willard. He is also a pioneer of new railroading wrinkles.
>
> First to introduce streamliners to the South with the Rebels (New Orleans to Jackson, Tenn.), he went competitors one better by stocking his streamliners with smart, good-looking college girls—the U.S.'s first train hostesses.[13] Scheduled to pay for themselves in seven and a half years, the sleek, diesel-powered streamliners paid out in less than half that time. In 1936 President Tigrett formed Gulf Transport Co. to handle freight over a coordinated rail-highway system. To it he added a passenger service with tickets interchangeable between busses [*sic*] and trains. Says he: "We believe in hauling as far as we can by rail and then the rest of the way by highway."[14]

His may have been a small potatoes operation, but it was never bereft of innovative charm! In 1953, the year of Ike Tigrett's retirement as president, author James H. Lemly aptly credited him for his many accomplishments in the volume *The Gulf, Mobile, and Ohio: A Railroad That Had to Expand or Expire — A Dynamic History of the Tigrett Road.* Tigrett was GM&O's board chairman at the time of his death at 74 on May 2, 1954, in Northwood, Tennessee, a tiny community in west Tennessee. A small town in Dyer County near the rail baron's birthplace is today named Tigrett.

Despite the naming of one city in the taxonomy of Gulf, Mobile & Ohio, the railroad's headquarters was at Jackson, Tennessee. At its summit the line possessed 258 engines and 2,734 miles of track.[15]

The Gulf, Mobile & Ohio Railroad's last major increase, in 1947, occurred when the Alton Railroad, mentioned earlier, was purchased from the B&O and folded into the existing GM&O system. The expanded company was valued at $175 million.[16] That acquisition not only gave the GM&O access to downtown St. Louis but also to routes from the Gulf to Chicago and Kansas City, both major rail hubs. As the final critical piece of the line's geographical development, the Alton's history must not be missed.

The earliest antecedent of what was to become the Gulf, Mobile & Ohio Railroad — predating the Mobile & Ohio by a year — was the Alton & Sangamon Railroad (A&S). Launched when Alton, Illinois, businessman Captain Benjamin Godfrey (1794–1862) obtained a state charter in 1847, the A&S was completed in 1852.[17] It connected Alton, situated on the banks of the Mississippi River 27 miles north of St. Louis, with the state capital at Springfield. At the time Alton rivaled St. Louis as a great river port. Yet the river wasn't navigable beyond the falls up river from Alton for several months of the year. Captain Godfrey sought a reliable, direct transport connection with the middle and northern portions of the state. At about that time A&S nomenclature was altered to the Chicago & Mississippi Railroad (C&M), which would possibly infer that its course had been set for loftier horizons.

Construction to Bloomington was finished in 1853; the following year rails were extended to Joliet where a connection with the Chicago & Rock Island ferried passenger trains to the Windy City. For a short while they arrived and departed from the Illinois Central's downtown Chicago depot. When the Rock Island's LaSalle Street station was erected it became those travelers' destinations. The C&M was reorganized ca. 1855 and renamed the St. Louis, Alton & Chicago Railroad, which segued into the Chicago & Alton Railroad (C&A) ca. 1861.[18]

Leased in 1864, the Joliet & Chicago Railroad (J&C) gave the C&A access to joint-owned facilities with the Pittsburgh, Ft. Wayne & Chicago Railroad (eventually to be part of the Pennsylvania Railroad). Timothy Beach Blackstone (1829–1900), president of the J&C line beginning in 1861, was elected president of the C&A in 1864 and served to 1899. Born into affluence and remaining independently wealthy all his life, Blackstone's 35-year tenure with the C&A was marked by the fact he refused to accept a salary.[19] A design engineer earlier on several rail lines, he was mayor of La Salle, Illinois (1854-1855), and eventually founding president of the Chicago Union Stock Yards.

Under his leadership the C&A expanded massively through acquisitions, construction, purchases and perpetual lease agreements. In his years as president the C&A route essentially broadened to its present geography. Chief among that expansion were pivotal extensions to St. Louis in 1873 and Kansas City in 1879. After a long power struggle with New York rail baron E. H. Harriman (1848–1909), who headed a group of investors wanting to buy the C&A line in the late 19th century, Blackstone bowed out. Transferring his stock in the company,

he resigned its presidency on April 1, 1899, leaving Harriman and some might say "co-conspirators" to take control.[20] Subsequently acquired by the Baltimore & Ohio Railroad (B&O) in 1931, the C&A provided that company with a major trunk line, extending its reach from the East as far west as Kansas City, and as far south as St. Louis. During the years of B&O control lasting to May 31, 1947, the carrier was renamed the Alton Railroad Company.

Ike Tigrett, who presided over the Gulf, Mobile & Northern prior to the formation of the Gulf, Mobile & Ohio, was the first visionary in the South to make streamliners available to the region. He was also the first to put hostesses aboard his trains. By launching the *Rebel* between Jackson, Tennessee, and New Orleans in 1935, he got ahead of his southern brothers by a minimum of a quadrennial. Although the Seaboard Air Line's *Silver Meteor*, debuting in February 1939, is touted by rail historians as the breakthrough pacesetter in presenting streamliners to Dixie-land—followed closely by the Atlantic Coast Line's dual *Champions* that pre-

Four decades after Ike Tigrett introduced hostesses to the nation's passenger trains on Gulf, Mobile & Northern in the mid 1930s, this young lady was hired as a boarding rep for Auto Train Corporation. Amtrak hadn't yet acquired the lucrative Auto Train business when this shot was taken in April 1975 at Sanford, Florida, the route's southern terminus. The vehicle-toting passenger-hauler traveled to Lorton, Virginia, without intermediate stops. Lightweight consists included sleepers, diners, lounge- and dome-observation cars. Typically three GE U-36B locomotives pulled these trains (***courtesy Michael B. Robbins***).

miered in December 1939 — the dates don't lie. A couple of trainsets delivered in the summer of 1935 to the GM&N were "true streamliners," venerated rail scholars affirm.[21]

Possibly because the GM&N was such a minuscule system when compared to those high-visibility behemoths SAL and ACL, its inauguration of streamlining is downplayed by some authorities who have chronicled the industry. The *Rebel* was on the cutting edge of what numerous passenger lines would be adopting by the early 1950s, with most of them doing so in the 1940s. In the South the Gulf, Mobile & Northern's *Rebel*— retained by successor Gulf, Mobile & Ohio— was categorically the leader of the pack, the others' consists only following in its train! "No other Southern road has a better Confederate ancestry," affirmed one wag.[22]

> While this train may not be as well known as the *Super Chiefs* or *Empire Builders* it brought about two drastic upgrades to passenger rail operations. First, the original *Rebel* was a three-car streamlined "trainset," similar to that of the Burlington's famous *Zephyr 9900*. However, along with including more boxy streamlining than the *Zephyr*, the *Rebel* also had the ability to interchange or add cars (unlike the *Zephyr* and many other articulated, streamlined trainsets debuting around the country during that time which were rigid, semi-permanently coupled trains)....
>
> The original three-car *Rebel* streamliner was built by American Car & Foundry with the power car provided by the American Locomotive Company (Alco). While the train's initial route served Jackson, Tennessee and New Orleans, in 1942 it was stretched to St. Louis after the merger between the M&O and GM&N, and the trainsets were pulled off line in favor of true, streamlined passenger equipment.
>
> The new train featured a beautiful livery of red and silver with power provided by GE-Alco in the way of a DL-series, slant-nosed diesel locomotive.[23]

Fabricated by industrial stylist Otto Kuhler, the budding GM&N trainsets were made from high-strength lightweight Cor-Ten steel. Each consist included a baggage-power car, buffet-coach and sleeper-observation-lounge. Another coach was eventually added to support ridership between New Orleans and Jackson, Mississippi, where demands were profound. The *Rebel* entered regular service on July 29, 1935, sprinting over its appointed route overnight, creating the necessity for its sleeping car provisions. Of the nation's early streamliners, only the *Rebel* and two trains proffered by the Baltimore & Ohio Railroad (*Abraham Lincoln, Royal Blue*) avoided the costly mistake of the peer lines: contemporaries failed to create independent car consists and thereby negated what they could have realized in flexibility of rolling stock.[24]

Passengers took to the *Rebel* like fleas to a mongrel. Ridership for all of GM&N's passenger trains jumped from 379,442 in 1935, the year the *Rebel* was instituted, to 418,045 in 1936, a rise of more than 10 percent in one year. The GM&N attributed much of the patronage increase to the *Rebel*, its premier consists.[25] The *Rebel*'s sleeping cars were ventilated with "conditioned air," a newspaper account mused, which was "distributed through ducts in the permanent partitions between the sections." There were individual air currents for upper and lower berths. Adjustable spotlights were provided at every berth and seat, another innovation.[26]

In addition to its luxurious appointments, *Rebel* riders appreciated its fares, finding them at the same per-mile rate as those for all of GM&N's trains. "The little streamliners became a welcome fixture in the Deep South," one report gushed.[27] Not only that, they maintained an impressive safety record. The American Car and Foundry Company which built the *Rebels* revealed on June 21, 1938, that its first streamlined trains operating in Dixie had run a million miles over GM&N tracks: "No passenger suffered a consequential injury and no employe was hurt."[28] In commemorating that feat, the New Orleans Safety League awarded GM&N president Tigrett a silver plaque.

The GM&N instituted yet a third four-car trainset in 1938, at least a year before those celebrated SAL and ACL streamliner initiations rolled.[29] The newest *Rebel* raced along tracks linking Mobile and Union, Mississippi, where it connected with the original *Rebels* clipping along between Jackson, Tennessee, and New Orleans. Three years afterward, under the GM&O flag, the third *Rebel* trainset transferred to the opposite end of the line, adding service between Jackson and St. Louis in the pre–Alton era.

The legacy of the GM&O can be cited for a number of firsts beyond introducing stream-lining to the South.[30] The GM&O was the nation's first carrier to completely dieselize its motive power, receiving shipment of 35 new diesel engines in 1949.[31] By October 7, 1949, steam engines were history over its tracks.[32] Aside from those noteworthy innovations more occurred during the Chicago & Alton's watch. This was the antecedent nomenclature applied to the Alton Railroad, you recall.

For example in 1858, the first Pullman sleeper, the *Pioneer*, was built in the C&A's Bloom-ington, Illinois, shops under the direction of George Pullman.[33] His name was to be attached to those cars for nearly a century as he and others created a specialty trade in passenger railcar manufacture. The C&A was also the first carrier to provide an all-Pullman consist, launching a model that many other long-distance carriers copied. The initial railroad dining car, the *Delmonico*, was fabricated by the C&A, too. When reclining-seat chair-equipped cars appeared, the C&A introduced them to America's railroad travelers. During the 19th century one of the world's earliest steel bridges was constructed at Glasgow, Missouri, by the C&A.

The Chicago & Alton Railroad — an incredible precursor in the GM&O lineage while also a sometimes unheralded line, almost altogether so beyond the borders of Illinois and Missouri — was at the forefront of multiple innovations. Capturing the imagination of rail officials and the general public, the C&A's efforts remarkably improved rail travel, making the ride far more pleasant and comfortable than before. Until some C&A–instituted advance-ments (as well as those instituted by the GM&N) came along, rail travel was viewed by many as little more than a conveyance from Point A to Point B. That included mostly wooden cars and simple unadorned features with few amenities. While it kept pace with the rustic expe-rience that most Americans had always known, it wasn't much fun. The presentation of crea-ture comforts signaled a new day in rail transport, as those recounting the heritage of the GM&O proclaimed them to be among its most worthy contributions.

English poet and playwright Robert Browning (1812–1889) penned a line in *Rabbi Ben Ezra* that seems apropos to the Gulf, Mobile & Ohio and the forerunning Gulf, Mobile & Northern and Alton railroads: *We find great things are made of little things.* Applied in this instance, it is an understatement.

On August 10, 1972, the Illinois Central and Gulf, Mobile & Ohio railroads merged, put-ting their systems together to fashion a major 9,600-mile north-south compound that was identified for a while as the Illinois Central Gulf Railroad. And as is so often the case following amalgamations like this, a single partner inevitably becomes the dominant player while the other appears to take a back seat in succeeding transactions. It was certainly no different on this occasion. The IC, being the stronger, more powerful, more influential and financially stable of the pair, added to its prestige in those dimensions while substantially increasing its physical assets — enlarging control through the addition of more personnel, trackage, facilities, rolling stock, stakeholders and contractual agreements with clients and suppliers.

And as that was transpiring the GM&O's former base was eroding. The weaker road in the match-up was indisputably becoming the subservient carrier. The instantly identifiable red and maroon livery of GM&O rolling stock gradually gave way to the IC's habitual chocolate brown and orange hues with yellow trim. And because those partners had run lines between similar points over primarily paralleling tracks in the years they were fierce competitors, some changes were instituted for efficiency and economy's sake. It made good business sense, for instance, to disperse much of the Illinois Central Gulf's redundant trackage, thereby reducing personnel, facilities and equipment. By 1996, the bulk of those tracks were traded or sold to other carriers or abandoned altogether. Not surprisingly perhaps, most of those miles had prevailed under the GM&O banner in the period of dual operations. It didn't take rocket science to figure out that the light was being extinguished on much of the GM&O's former empire after its absorption into the larger railroad.

On February 11, 1998, the Illinois Central — which had dropped the word Gulf in its moniker and re-established itself by its former nomenclature — was purchased by the Canadian National Railway (CN). Integration of the IC's operations into the CN formally commenced July 1, 1999.

Concentrating now on passenger service on the Gulf, Mobile & Ohio, its premier trains embraced the *Rebel* taxonomy. There was the *Rebel* between New Orleans and St. Louis, which persisted to 1954; the *Gulf Coast Rebel* between Mobile and St. Louis, which ran to 1958 (a section to and from Montgomery connected with the mainline at Artesia, Mississippi); and the *Little Rebel* between Birmingham and St. Louis, which was discontinued in that same era.

Although the *Gulf Coast Rebel*, dubbed by many as the *Big Rebel*, was marketed as a streamliner, in the M&O years it really wasn't so. The Mobile & Ohio modernized old heavy-weight coaches and lounge-coaches at its Iselin Shops at Jackson, Tennessee. Concurrently it paid the Pullman Company to do the same with sleepers at its Chicagoland shops. Then the M&O put them together to allegedly offer streamlined equipment. It was something other lines were doing, too, but it certainly wasn't the captivatingly sleek, lightweight aluminum construct of which true streamliners were comprised.

Those cars exhibited tubed bodies with rounded edges instead of boxcar motifs. Those designs plus the lighter weight netted less wind resistance and translated into shorter travel times as they sped along at a much faster clip. But they were costly to buy. While the M&O sought to provide reliable and comfortable service, its *Gulf Coast Rebel* revealed that it was capable of cutting corners. It was also a lapse that the succeeding Gulf, Mobile & Ohio would rectify as soon as it could. One of the first things it could and would do is to return the conveyance to its Southern roots, too, over a more extensive route.

> The train operated daily on an overnight schedule between St. Louis and Mobile along the former–M&O route via Cairo, Illinois, Jackson, and Corinth and Meridian, Mississippi. Moving the *Gulf Coast Rebel* over the 648-mile run were new Alco-GE DL-series diesels. The chisel-nosed locomotives and their train wore the flashy silver-and-red scheme introduced by the original little Rebel trains of 1935 and 1937. In keeping with the *Rebel* tradition, the new big *Rebels* featured hostesses.
> In 1942, the early *Rebel* streamliners were removed from regional service, modified, and reconstituted as East St. Louis–New Orleans trains known simply as the *Rebel*. In this service, the trains operated overnight between New Orleans and Jackson and during the day between Jackson and St. Louis in both directions....
> Shortly after the merger [with the Alton, 1947], the railroad ordered new lightweight, streamline cars from American Car & Foundry, which permitted it to upgrade not only the *Gulf Coast Rebel* but the Chicago–St. Louis trains inherited from the Alton. These improvements included a through, lightweight sleeping car between Chicago and Mobile, southbound via the *Alton Limited* and *Gulf Coast Rebel* and northbound via the *Gulf Coast Rebel* and the streamliner *Abraham Lincoln*.[34]

From the Alton Railroad the GM&O multiplied its people-hauling commerce big time. There were seven daily consists plying the Alton route between Chicago and St. Louis. The *Abraham Lincoln*, *Alton Limited* and *Ann Rutledge* may be the best remembered of these trains. Other prominent passenger trains running over those tracks during the heyday of GM&O authority included the *Mail*, *Midnight Special* and *Prairie State Express*.

The *Lincoln* and *Rutledge* sobriquets remained well into the Amtrak epoch. With the state of Illinois underwriting most of Amtrak's "Lincoln Service" in 2010, a quartet of coach-

and-café car consists with business class service available to those willing to pay for it plied the tracks from St. Louis to Chicago every day. Scattered throughout the daytime hours at regular intervals— two in each direction in the morning and two moving each way in the late afternoon — they completed the 567-mile course in about five-and-a-half hours.

In the halcyon days a couple of added passenger trains from the Windy City turned off the mainline to traverse the route to Kansas City. Beyond that the *Night Hawk*, running between St. Louis and Kansas City, completed the GM&O's roster of best-known people-movers. All of these trains appeared in the line's striking livery of two-tone maroon-red with yellow trim. Simultaneously a handful of motortrain locals operated over GM&O's branch lines.

Although GM&O would run no more passenger trains south of St. Louis after 1958, eliminating the *Gulf Coast Rebel* to Mobile and Montgomery that year, a Bloomington–Chicago daily persisted to 1960. And the *Lincoln*, *Limited* and *Rutledge* rolled right along on their courses above Dixie, persisting under the GM&O flag until the inception of Amtrak in 1971. Whether this could be viewed as a clearly defined attribute may be debatable: the GM&O was among the first — and possibly was *the* first — rail carrier in Dixie to flee the people-hauling market. Most other lines would continue some, albeit reduced, passenger service in the primary territory until Amtrak took over most of that business on May 1, 1971. The *Rebels* were early casualties in no small measure due to superior, reliable and fast service offered by a couple of larger rivals that plied their own tracks between Chicago, St. Louis and New Orleans: the Illinois Central ran the *Panama Limited* and *City of New Orleans* while the Louisville & Nashville ran the *Humming Bird*, significantly reducing the potential market for the smaller GM&O.

Clearly reading the handwriting on the wall as the number of travelers moved closer and closer to extinction, the GM&O made a conscious business decision to focus its attention on the more lucrative rail transport segments: freight, mail and express. While the GM&N/GM&O had faithfully served traveling clientele for possibly four decades, it sharply reduced costs as it increased cargo capability. Although the mail traffic vanished before the end of the 1960s as the U.S. Postal Service transferred most of it to trucking firms, the carrier maintained shipping lanes between the Gulf and Great Lakes. In addition to numerous branch routes, its freight trains called at consequential cities between those bodies of water: Birmingham, Jackson (in two states), Kansas City, Memphis, Meridian, Montgomery, Paducah and Springfield.

The first line in the nation to dieselize its entire fleet with a forebear that inaugurated streamliners in the South, plus a passenger service that — while unusually brief — was superior to many peers, all were integral parts of the legacy of the Gulf, Mobile & Ohio Railroad. In many ways the antecedent carriers Gulf, Mobile & Northern and Chicago and Alton set the tone for creature comforts that the traveling public would ultimately encounter elsewhere. They introduced riders to onboard hostesses, all-Pullman consists, dining cars, improved air circulation systems and reclining-seat coaches. Offering upscale amenities at the same fares that less luxurious trainsets afforded must have spoken volumes to travelers: those carriers grasped their customers' plights— particularly during an epoch in which the nation was plunged into steep economic decline. Those lines comprehended the importance of building a loyal clientele that would keep coming back after the crisis had passed. The individuals who were ferrying those patrons back and forth across the mid–South and Midwest "got" what was transpiring among their neighbors. Even at reduced levels, their efforts were worthy of imitation by contemporaries.

8

ILLINOIS CENTRAL RAILROAD
First in Line to Land a Grant

The Illinois Central Railroad (IC), like many of its counterparts, holds a few momentous distinctions in the trade. It was the first line in America to be supported by a large (2.6 million acre) federal land grant following a provision signed into law by President Millard Fillmore in late 1850. Consequently that same model was pursued by other rail carriers, most notably the Central and Union Pacific companies, linking the nation with its first transcontinental system in 1869. The Illinois Central founded dozens of new towns in Illinois and made "colonization work"—attracting European and American settlers from elsewhere—a paramount objective of its corporate strategy.

Upon completion of IC's mainline within its home state in September 1856, the 705-mile road was the longest on the planet. Its "Chicago Branch" from Centralia (named after the carrier) to Lake Michigan opened in 1855, providing the sprawling Windy City with its "most important link" to the South. By 1985, that route formed the nucleus of most activity along the IC, overwhelmingly the focus compared with every other point served by the line. The IC played a pivotal role in funneling Federal troops and supplies southward during the War Between the States (1861–1865), keeping traffic flowing down the Mississippi River to the Gulf. A 1900 wreck on IC–owned rails lived in infamy, thanks to a ballad that reverberated in the annals of railway history.

Dubbing itself the *Main Line of Mid-America* as "the primary link between the Great Lakes and the Gulf of Mexico," IC supplied access to Dixie for Chicago products, populace and predilections. At the same time it was a foremost route north for millions transitioning in the "Great Migration" (ca. 1916–1930). It furthermore gained status as a major commuter system in and around Chicago.[1] Boasting 2,600 miles of track between Lake Michigan and the Gulf, from 1998 IC was a wholly owned subsidiary of Illinois Central Corporation, an ancillary of a transporter headquartered outside the United States, the Canadian National Railway Company. It is the only major rail carrier in America that, until 2001, operated under its own moniker, fundamentally doing so with little variance for 15 decades since its founding. (For a brief period beginning in 1972, the company was tagged Illinois Central Gulf Railroad. That happened when IC and Gulf, Mobile & Ohio Railroad fused their operations.)

The IC originated when the General Assembly of the state of Illinois authorized it in February 1851.[2] Illinois was the first to take advantage of the U.S. government's federal land grant proviso, supplying phenomenal help in realizing that objective. Congress gave Illinois 2,595,000 acres of public land in 1850, for constructing a railroad to extend from the southern terminus of the Illinois and Michigan Canal to a point near the junction of the Ohio and Mississippi rivers.[3] A branch running north-northeast off that line would reach Chicago. To complete the project, which ultimately cost $25 million and involved 10,000 workers between 1851 and 1856, the state tapped into the deep pockets of some well-heeled Dutch and English capitalists. In its most basic manifestation, the line they built connected an inland Chicago on the western shore of Lake Michigan with Cairo. The latter hamlet, at the confluence of the Mississippi and the Ohio, appeared to be sitting at the apex of shipping lanes to the world.

While the achievement hadn't come cheap, the road's intrinsic value couldn't possibly be measured by its upfront outlay. It would be serving as one of the Windy City's chief overland gateways for decades (centuries?) into the future. There could be no denying its import to the Midwestern economy. Even though the IC was acquired by a foreign carrier in the modern age, can there be any real doubt that the IC's functions, routes and franchise have remained critical to the financial welfare of Chicago and outlying region?

While only a footnote in history, it cannot be overlooked that Abraham Lincoln — on his way up — served the Illinois Central Railroad as a corporate lawyer, the railroad being one of his clients between 1853 and 1860. Those were the years immediately prior to Lincoln's presidential campaign and a foreboding era in the nation's existence leading to the Civil War. Although not a native of Illinois — he was born near Hodgenville, Kentucky — Lincoln nevertheless invested most of his adult life in Illinois (the state was later nicknamed "Land of Lincoln"). To have had such an imposing figure in its legacy must have been a feather in the cap of the Illinois Central. In at least one instance, however, the two had had their differences.

> Abraham Lincoln served the IC in a number of cases in the 1850's, and on one occasion presented the company with a bill for his fee of $2000. At that time George B. McClellan was vice-president in charge of operations. He looked at the bill with pretended astonishment. "Why, sir," he said to Attorney Lincoln, "this is as much as Daniel Webster himself would have charged. We cannot allow such a claim." Lincoln went away without his fee, but he sent in a new bill, this time for $5000, brought suit against the IC, and collected.[4]

Convinced of the railways' potential, nevertheless, Lincoln campaigned aboard trains, rode one to Washington, and authorized the first transcontinental rail line during his presidency.

On another front, overnight the Windy City became the IC's prime focal point with extensive freight, long-distance traveler and suburban commuter systems and facilities. By 1926, the railroad completed electrification of much of its suburban passenger service along the lakefront in Chicago. Connecting the suburbs with the urban center, that project is believed to be the largest Midwestern Class 1 rail system electrifying its lines, ultimately encompassing 155 miles. The tracks with stations along Michigan Avenue were distinct from the rails assigned to mainline passenger and freight trains.

The IC's premier passenger station was positioned in downtown Chicago. For many years Grand Central Depot filled that capacity located near Lake Michigan and slightly below the Chicago River. In the 1890s, that edifice was replaced with Central Station at 12th Street east of Michigan Avenue near Roosevelt Road. It served to 1971, the duration of IC's passenger-hauling age, and was razed once that ended. IC operated a gargantuan repair and maintenance facility, the Burnside Shops, on the city's south side at 95th and Cottage Grove. By the turn of the century that operation alone employed about 5,000 workmen.

Expansion was a byword in railroading in those days and the Illinois Central was no exception. Following the War Between the States the line progressed beyond its westernmost terminus at Galena, in the state's northwest corner. Crossing the Mississippi River, it entered Iowa at Dubuque (1867). By subsequently leasing the unfinished Dubuque & Sioux City Railroad, the IC extended its reach past Cedar Falls to Iowa Falls in the Hawkeye State's midsection. In 1869, tracks were completed to Sioux City on Iowa's western edge, a border it shared with Nebraska. In 1877, a branch accessed Sioux Falls, South Dakota. A stem at Fort Dodge, Iowa, eventually gave the IC access to Council Bluffs, Iowa, and Omaha, Nebraska (1899).

In the other direction, the Illinois Central — having, since 1856, relied on steamboats to stretch its grasp from Cairo, Illinois, to New Orleans—finally completed its mainline access the full extent of the trip (1882). That is, with the notable exception of the Ohio River crossing at Cairo; seven more years would pass before that connection was open. A traffic agreement with the New Orleans, Jackson & Great Northern Railroad allowed the IC to run trains as far south as Canton, Mississippi, in 1872.[5] In the same epoch the company gained trackage rights over the Mississippi Central Railway north to Jackson, Tennessee.

A new line, completed in 1873, linked Jackson with Cairo and superseded an agreement permitting the IC to travel over the Mobile & Ohio Railroad to Columbus, Kentucky. Transportation between Columbus and Cairo had been by riverboat. In 1874, the IC, principal bondholder of the other two lines, took them over and reorganized them as the New Orleans, St. Louis & Chicago Railroad. Three years hence the dual roads were restructured separately as the New Orleans, Jackson & Great Northern and the Central Mississippi railroads. They were eventually consolidated as the Chicago, St. Louis & New Orleans Railroad, a wholly owned subsidiary of the Illinois Central. Like most of the tracks in the South, the route from Cairo to New Orleans was constructed on a 5-foot gauge. The entire 550-mile route was converted to a standard 4-foot, 8.5-inch measure in a single day on July 29, 1881.

As with many similar railroad construction projects in the waning decades of the 19th century, the Illinois Central wasn't bereft of competition. As it sought to complete its mainline and acquire a handful of branch lines in Southern territory, some of its peers were doing the same.

> In the 1870s railroads began to penetrate the fertile Delta along the western edge of Mississippi. IC's entry was the Yazoo & Mississippi Valley Railroad, incorporated in 1882 to build a railroad westward from Jackson, Miss. Meanwhile, a rival route, the Louisville, New Orleans & Texas Railway, was under construction between Memphis and New Orleans via Vicksburg and Baton Rouge, west of the IC's main line. That line obtained the backing of C. P. Huntington, who saw the route as a connection between the Southern Pacific at New Orleans and his Chesapeake, Ohio & Southwestern at Memphis.[6] Huntington's forces completed the LNO&T in 1884 and then purchased the Mississippi & Tennessee Railroad, whose line from Grenada, Miss., to Memphis funneled traffic to IC.
>
> Saber rattling in the form of cancelled traffic agreements ensued, but Huntington's empire was in trouble. The IC purchased the LNO&T and the Mississippi & Tennessee and consolidated them with the Yazoo & Mississippi Valley. The acquisition not only increased significantly the IC's mileage, but also greatly expanded the IC's presence in the South. The southern lines were finally connected by rail to the northern part of the IC with the completion of the Ohio River bridge at Cairo in 1889. In 1893 IC purchased the Chesapeake, Ohio & Southwestern (Louisville to Memphis) and in 1895 built a line into St. Louis from the southeast.[7]

In the meantime the paralleling Louisville & Nashville Railroad (L&N) was to offer the IC competition in schlepping travelers and hauling freight between Chicago and New Orleans not only then but throughout much of the 20th century. Despite its attempts, comparatively speaking, in reality it may not have been all that much. The L&N focused its north-south passenger traffic east of the Illinois Central on a couple of strengths: reaching New Orleans from Cincinnati, a route fed by interline connections arriving from or passing through Baltimore, Charleston, Chicago, Columbus, Dayton, Detroit, Indianapolis, New York, Philadelphia, Pittsburgh, St. Louis, Toledo, Washington, and other places, and—of equal importance—transporting travelers from the Midwest (especially Chicago) to the southeast (Atlanta, Birmingham, Montgomery and all Florida points), deriving access to the Sunshine State via interline connections.

The L&N's longer route between Chicago and New Orleans (1,067 L&N miles vs. 926 IC miles) could be fixed among "secondary objectives." Riders between that pair of destinations normally made a seamless interline transition with the Chicago & Eastern Illinois Railroad at Evansville and from one L&N consist to another at Nashville as Pullmans were routinely shuffled in the night.[8] There were a few other options on L&N but all mandated greater distances. Make no mistake about the company, nevertheless; the L&N was an aggressive rival, gaining entry early into New Orleans (1880). As one of the prime end points of its mainline, the company worked judiciously, protectively, and continually not only to retain its investment there but also to generate new and expanded business, freight and passenger, for trains flowing into and out of the Crescent City.

A final word on the topic: not only did the IC possess the shorter route from Chicago to New Orleans, until 1969 and 1971— when the Louisville & Nashville purchased a couple of existing lines that extended its system all the way to Chicago— the IC had the sole advantage of maintaining all of the trackage it ran its trains over.[9] Twice blessed, the gods had surely smiled upon the Illinois Central in establishing that route.

The stories of railroads invariably include at least one financier-tycoon whose personal wealth and wisdom is unambiguously tied to the fortunes of one or more railroads during a given time frame. Sometimes, that's *many* railroads. For the Illinois Central, that individual was Edward Henry Harriman, whose visionary direction left an indelible mark on the IC in the final couple of decades of the 19th century and in the early years of the 20th. While he was never the line's president, Harriman held the purse strings for a while, effectually controlling a great deal of the line's protocol.

Harriman was a third generation American, the son of an Episcopalian minister whose great-grandfather emigrated from England in 1795. Born at Hempstead, New York, on February 25, 1848, his first line of work at age 14 was as an office boy on Wall Street. He eventually worked up to stockbroker and joined the New York Stock Exchange at 22 (1870). Biographer Maury Klein noted, "No one who sat on the exchange in the late 1800s could avoid involvement in railroad finance, and Harriman soon became associated with the nation's first big business." Klein continues:

> Harriman's early railroad involvement led to an association with Stuyvesant Fish [who was to be IC president from 1887 to 1906] and then to affiliation with the Illinois Central. [Harriman became a director of IC in 1883, and vice president four years later.] By the mid–1880s Harriman had thus begun to specialize in railroad securities without abandoning entirely other investment opportunities— a transition that reflected the growing financial specialization of the era. On the Illinois Central, Fish and Harriman enhanced an already prosperous railroad by improving the physical plant to enable the movement of larger volumes of traffic at lower per-unit cost. They also reorganized the managerial structure on the basis of decentralized operating divisions rather than centralized departments and insured that, in Harriman's words, "We should first adopt a plan & then make our officers fit into it as best we can, & not make a plan to fit our officers." ... Harriman was certainly not the first industry executive to think along those lines, and many of the policies for which he became famous were in reality derivative of Fish and others. However, Harriman did realize that the growth of giant railroad systems, increased competition, overbuilding, and growing traffic volumes, especially on western railroads, mandated the widespread application of these strategies.[10]

Growing conflicts with Fish led Harriman away from the Illinois Central and toward the Union Pacific (UP), where he became a director in 1897, chairman of the executive committee the following May, and president of the company in 1903.[11] He organized a syndicate to obtain the bankrupt UP and was successful in reversing the line's fortunes. By 1901, he acquired the Southern Pacific (SP) and was also its president (1901–1909). The IC, UP and SP formed the nucleus of the Harriman system, in theory a trio of separate corporate enterprises, yet demonstrating comparable organizational structures and philosophies. Such corresponding standardization and uniformity netted extensive economies of scale in purchasing and maintenance operations.

His success here did not insulate Harriman from trouble, however, and his latter years were debilitating both professionally and personally. One of Wall Street's grimmest financial setbacks resulted from an imbroglio involving the Great Northern Railroad's James J. Hill and Harriman. When those two rail magnates established a holding company for the Great Northern, Northern Pacific and Burlington roads in 1901, it became a lightning rod for increased public opposition to trusts. Publicly attacked by ex-pal President Theodore Roosevelt and former ally and IC president Stuyvesant Fish for some business practices, Harriman became an object of widespread ridicule.

The general public wasn't ready to admit that giant concentrations of capital were part of the American economy. Even the Interstate Commerce Commission launched an investigation into his activities. Exhausted, weakened and embattled, in the midst of the melee Harriman succumbed to stomach cancer on September 9, 1909, in Orange County, New York. He had played a significant role in the life of the Illinois Central Railroad — even purchased one of its important tributaries, the Central of Georgia Railway (CofG), in 1907, which passed into the hands of the IC following his death.

Harriman was one of the major players in railroading in the epoch in which he lived. At his death he controlled the CofG, IC, SP, UP, and St. Joseph & Grand Island Railroad, plus the Pacific Mail Steamship Company and the Wells Fargo Express Company.[12] Estimates of his estate, left altogether to his third wife, ranged between $200 million and $600 million, a remarkable haul in 1909. W. Averell Harriman (1891–1986), his son, followed in his father's footsteps in 1915, serving as chairman of the board of directors of both the Illinois Central and Union Pacific railroads (1932–1946). Active in Democratic politics, the younger Harriman was U.S. secretary of commerce from 1946 to 1948, governor of New York from 1954 to 1958, and a U.S. diplomat to Europe, the Far East and the Soviet Union. In 1956, he was an unsuccessful candidate for his party's nomination for president.

In the late 1880s under the leadership of E. H. Harriman the Illinois Central began expanding toward the west. The Chicago, Madison & Northern was incorporated in 1886 to build from Chicago to a connection with the IC's western line at Freeport, Illinois, then north to Madison and Dodgeville, Wisconsin.

On April 30, 1900, a fatal wreck on IC lines at Vaughan, Mississippi (sometimes spelled "Vaughn") — which otherwise likely would have been a nondescript footnote in the annals of railroad history — sprang to the nation's attention by way of a widely-acclaimed ballad.[13] Engineer John Luther "Casey" Jones (a nickname derived from his birthplace at Cayce, Kentucky) was at the throttle of a southbound mail that day, replacing a driver who didn't show up. As railway lore puts it, the 37-year-old Jones and fireman Sam Webb left Memphis 95 minutes behind schedule but made up time at dizzying speeds. Rounding a curve at Vaughan, Jones spied a freight that had pulled onto a siding but not far enough to clear the mainline and allow his fireball mail to pass. The brave engineer shouted for Webb to jump to safety, which he did as Jones braced himself for the collision that was inevitable.

After coworker Wallace Saunders, an engine wiper and Jones' pal, penned a folk song recounting his fate, the late IC engineer gained endemic immortality. It was, according to one wag, "the most popular railroad song ever written."[14] The incident was repeated through story and song, and people who hadn't known of the Illinois Central were aware of it forever thereafter.[15]

Jones had been a fireman on the Mobile & Ohio Railroad prior to joining the Illinois Central at Jackson, Tennessee, correctly guessing that he would have a better chance of promotion with the IC due to a shortage of engineers. He wasn't a "rounder" as one version of Saunders' song intimates. He neither smoked nor drank liquor nor caroused with women, and was described as "a devout Catholic family man." He is buried at Jackson, Tennessee.

Among observers of the death of engineer John Luther (Casey). Jones on April 30, 1956, at his Jackson, Tennessee, home were (left to right). Mayor George A. Smith; Sam Webb, Jones' fireman; Gov. Frank G. Clement; and Janie Jones, his widow. Jones died 56 years earlier on that date in the crash of a speeding Illinois Central mail in Mississippi, becoming a legend after his heroism was revealed in a ballad. His restored #382 steamer was moved beside his home and the ceremony used to signify a museum named for him, now the apex of a commercial enterprise (*courtesy Tennessee State Library and Archives*).

A bronze marker, since missing, commemorated the accident. It was unveiled at the crash site in 1953, an occasion attended by fireman Webb and Jones' widow, Janie, plus 3,000 onlookers. Mississippi officials opened a state park nearby named for Jones in 1980.[16]

In the meantime, Tennessee — where Jones lived at the time of his death — wasn't about to be outclassed by neighboring Mississippi. It cashed in on the nostalgic euphoria surrounding the legendary engineer by holding some ceremonies of its own. A restored steam engine 382 was placed beside Jones' Jackson residence. State and local dignitaries showed up to dedicate a museum adjacent to his home. Among participants in those April 30, 1956, festivities were Jones' wheelchair-bound widow, Janie, and the fireman who jumped to safety on his orders, Sam Webb.[17]

"Casey Jones is still perhaps the country's most famous railroad engineer," claims one storyteller.[18] Another, dubbing him "the most radiant of all American folk and ballad heroes," suggested: "When he wrecked the *Cannonball* that misty dawn at Vaughan, Mississippi, in 1900, Casey entered Valhalla still trailing intimations of the Illinois Central, a classic figure of tragedy who atoned for error with his own death while saving the lives of others."[19] It was a timeless railroad tale of a larger-than-life figure that persevered beyond anything most folks would have considered imaginable.

In the 20th century, the Illinois Central persisted in its appetite for expansion. An IC subsidiary, the Indianapolis Southern Railroad, finished a line from Effingham, Illinois, to the road's namesake city in 1906. Two years later the IC assembled a route largely with trackage rights from Fulton, Kentucky, to Birmingham, Alabama. From 1909 to 1942, the IC owned the Central of Georgia Railway, a prime connector between the lines serving the upper- and mid–South and Midwest and the north-south traffic linking the Northeast and Florida. In 1928, a cutoff line that avoided congestion at Cairo was built tying Edgewood, Illinois, with Fulton, Kentucky.

In the postwar era IC reduced its corporate structure by adding and deleting subsidiaries and adjacent short lines. The Gulf & Ship Island and Yazoo & Mississippi Valley railroads were absorbed into the IC route system in 1945 and 1946. Acting with the Rock Island Railroad in 1956, the IC bought the Waterloo, Cedar Falls & Northern Railroad, forming the Waterloo Railroad; a dozen years later the IC bought the Rock Island's interest in the Waterloo. The IC was on a purchasing roll by then, acquiring a handful of short lines, among them: Tremont & Gulf (1959), Peabody Short Line (1960, merged into IC in 1961), Louisiana Midland (1967, which regained its autonomy in 1974), and Tennessee Central (Hopkinsville, Kentucky–Nashville, Tennessee division in 1968).

While the late 1850s saw annual revenues of $2 million, three decades hence (1887) the IC touted 8,500 employees, 2,300 track miles and yearly income of $12 million.[20] Those figures substantially improved as time elapsed: in the peak workforce years of the 1920s, in excess of 70,000 labored for the Illinois Central while income netted $150 million annually. The Great Depression in the following decade, however, sharply reduced employment and revenue levels and the IC — like the rest of the trade — experienced continuing readjustments. Rising levels in freight, passengers and revenues during the Second World War weren't stable, unfortunately; high numbers of travelers evaporated everywhere in the postwar epoch, negatively affecting the bottom line. Increased highway and air travel was primarily blamed as an ongoing culprit.

By the 1960s, IC's workforce had solidified at about 20,000 with revenues topping $250 million. From that company's perspective and likely so on many other roads— with apologies to author Charles Dickens—"It was the best of times (for freight), it was the worst of times (for passenger revenues)."[21] That's not to imply that service declined on the IC, a hypothesis that will be substantiated shortly. But an era had arrived in which virtually all major carriers saw their accustomed numbers of boarding passengers start to dry up. This significantly affected income, number of employees, rolling stock, operating trackage and other dimensions of maintaining a profitable railroad.

In 1962, ownership of the company was transferred to a holding firm, Illinois Central Industries, which rapidly entered a variety of commercial interests (real estate development, industrial commodities, consumer goods). Thirteen years later (1975) the nomenclature was shortened to IC Industries; the passenger business had already been disposed of to Amtrak in 1971. On August 10, 1972, the enterprise merged with the Gulf, Mobile & Ohio Railroad (GM&O), reclassifying itself as the Illinois Central Gulf Railroad (ICG). The ICG owned almost 10,000 track miles.

> The mighty Illinois Central by the mid–1970s was a cog in a larger machine — one component in a merged railroad (Illinois Central Gulf) that itself was part of a giant conglomerate with interests in real estate (La Salle Properties), financial services (Benjamin Franklin Savings), consumer products (Midas muffler shops), and manufacturing (Waukesha Nuclear Castings). The railroad accounted for 31 percent of the income of parent IC Industries in 1973, a year when the ICG posted an all-time high revenue, thanks to strong grain, coal, and chemical traffic.
>
> Illinois Central Gulf was a transitional railroad, a type of railroad that would include the likes of Chessie System, Erie Lackawanna, Burlington Northern, and Penn Central. They were the

stepping stones between the famed railroads of the classic era and the megasystems of today. Transitional railroads were primarily created in a 10-year period between 1963 and 1972 by merging parallel networks, rather than those that connected end to end. The driving force behind this movement was the desire to rationalize systems by eliminating excess and duplicative trackage and facilities, thereby realizing significant cost savings.[22]

During the following decade, nonetheless, the line made a business decision to concentrate its efforts on its greatest potential geographic territorial strength, confirmed much earlier, between Chicago and the Gulf of Mexico—specifically with the port cities of New Orleans and Mobile. To do so the ICG reduced its trackage demonstrably, selling many of its routes that weren't focused on achieving that objective, relieving itself of nearly two-thirds of its mileage.[23] Most of its east-west lines were spun off while many redundant north-south lines that comprised much of the ex–GM&O were dispatched. Only the core north-south former IC main carried nationally significant volumes of traffic. Most other lines moved light densities over un-signaled, single-track secondaries and branch lines.

Other railroads bought most of those routes, including a trio of new systems: Chicago Central & Pacific Railroad; Chicago, Missouri & Western Railway; and Paducah & Louisville Railway. The "Gulf" designation was deleted from its legal nomenclature on February 29, 1988, returning the carrier to its original appellation: Illinois Central Railroad.

Speciously, an enduring Web site asserts more than once that the Illinois Central was one of "very few" rail systems serving markets that could be sited on a grid of chiefly north-south carriers rather than the "traditional east-west movements."[24] That avowal begs challenge. There can be little doubt that the cornucopia of predominantly east-west mainlines, a few of them traversing the Northeast and upper South, is (or was) profuse. Yet in the nation's eastern half there are (or were) as many or more mains among leading carriers that were pointed north and south as there were running east and west, to wit: Atlantic Coast Line; Carolina, Clinchfield & Ohio; Chicago & Eastern Illinois; Florida East Coast; Gulf, Mobile & Ohio; Illinois Central; Kansas City Southern; Monon; Seaboard Air Line; and Southern, all unambiguous examples. The IC appears to be in bountiful company as a longitudinal line, qualifying as a "traditional" road among its manifold peers.

The Illinois Central is something of an enigma among rail carriers. Here you had a Northern-based railroad characterized by name, headquarters, principals, revenues, and predominant facilities that was almost wholly dependent on its routes through Dixie for most of its business. Of the 926 route miles Amtrak plies today between Chicago and New Orleans, for example — nearly all of it over trackage nurtured by the Illinois Central once upon a time — only slightly more than a third of it is in Illinois, the rest in Dixie. The IC was reliant on Deep South connections that not only sparked its livelihood but contributed mightily to its home region's economy. A Yankee-headquartered road, IC's history and tradition were distinctly tied to the South, and perhaps even more so since the days of hauling passenger traffic slipped away.

In 1988, IC sold its Chicago commuter lines to Metropolitan Rail (Metra). The following year the road left IC Industries to become an independent railway known as Illinois Central Corporation. The new IC was bought by New York's Prospect Group. On February 11, 1998, Canadian National Railway Company acquired it for $2.4 billion.[25] That transaction signified "the last of the transitional railroads to disappear."[26] IC is now under the control of CN's holding enterprise, Grand Trunk Corporation.

> The IC sobriquet persisted until 2001, when the line's sesquicentennial was observed. After that its corporate identity gradually withered "through CN's maintenance and repainting programs."[27] On the sides of locomotive cabs one may still discover IC reporting marks and sub-lettering, although they are now painted into traditional CN hues.

The Illinois Central's mainline between Chicago and New Orleans as well as routes linking the Windy City with St. Louis, Sioux City and Omaha saw frequent passenger service in the halcyon days of train travel. Ferrying riders was heaviest at all times between its mainline destinations where its most famous "name" consists plied the tracks.

Foremost among them was the *Panama Limited*, a premier all-Pullman train running daily between Chicago, St. Louis and New Orleans. In its halcyon days this flagship operation was all about opulent travel for those who could afford its luxurious appointments, plush comfort and sumptuous service.

> The IC's *Panama Limited* was all about style and class. The train had been around since 1911, making it one of the oldest named trains in the country. However, like most passenger trains, the *Panama*'s iconic status was not achieved until the IC streamlined it in May of 1942. That spring when the train was re-inaugurated as a lightweight, streamlined operation ... it was bedecked in a beautiful livery of chocolate brown and red with yellow trim (another masterful artistic creation from the design team at EMD).
>
> The interior designs of the *Panama* were just as striking. Playing on Deep South and Cajun themes the train's entrées highlighted the finest of the region's cooking and lounge and parlor cars included bamboo furniture, floral patterned curtains, and squared etched glass on the windows.
>
> Two other attributes the *Panama Limited* became famous for was its ultra-fast schedule, as it was able to complete the journey between Chicago and New Orleans sometimes in as quick as just 16 hours, typically traveling at speeds of up to 100 mph (what allowed for such high speeds was the IC's main line between the two cities, which was very flat and straight); and two, its punctuality, as you hardly ever saw the *Panama*, or any of the IC's most important trains leaving even a few minutes late![28]

Upgraded with Vista-Dome sleeper-lounges in 1959, the *Panama Limited*'s high ridership levels persisted through the 1960s. The loss of Railway Post Office (RPO) business—a dynamic that hit all railways in the late 1960s when the U.S. Postal Service transferred the bulk of that work to truck transport—plus the rising costs of operating passenger trainsets, forced IC to downgrade its venerated *Panama Limited*. The flagship consist lost its all-Pullman status as the 1960s wore on. In 1967, IC combined it with the coach-only *Magnolia Star*. Despite that, it labored on through April 30, 1971, the day before Amtrak acquired IC's passenger service.

In the meantime IC fielded a second best-known passenger train along the same route, one whose moniker ultimately survived under the Amtrak banner. By 2010, it remained as a memento of the IC's rich heritage: *City of New Orleans*. If the *Panama Limited* was all about style and class, the *City of New Orleans* was about speed and comfort. Premiering as a streamliner in 1947, the *City* was bedecked in IC's striking livery of chocolate brown and red (or orange) with yellow trim, matching the *Panama*'s identifiable tints. Yet the *City*'s coach-only status made it more affordable to a greater number of patrons than its sister train.

It was (and is) the one of those two trains that's remembered today, not only thanks to Amtrak but in very large measure to a ballad penned by lyricist Steve Goodman. "The City of New Orleans" was recorded by Arlo Guthrie in 1972.[29] The enduring popularity of that folk song eventually persuaded Amtrak to drop the *Panama Limited* branding on its single passenger train after it had run between Chicago and New Orleans from 1971 to 1981. The *Panama* was replaced with the *City of New Orleans*. "In the day" under IC's watchful eye, the *City* plied those rails as a daytime-only operation in 16 hours and—running as "the train for everybody"—it included legions of station stops en route.

A modern Amtrak timetable reveals that the southbound *City*, now a coach-and-Pullman consist, leaves Chicago at 8 P.M. and arrives in New Orleans 19 and a half hours hence, at midafternoon the following day. Northbound, it leaves New Orleans at 1:45 P.M. and is due in Chicago the following morning after a 19 and a quarter hour trip. They don't make 'em like the used to any more!

Beginning in 1940, IC was responsible for ferrying the *City of Miami* from Chicago as far south as Birmingham on a vacillating pattern calling for travel every other day or three times a week. Though its crews left the train in Alabama, sometimes IC's head-end power and rolling stock persisted to Florida. That's captured in an artist's rendering of a typical tropical vista depicting IC 4000 leading a parade of *City* passenger cars down the line. The drawing appeared on posters, postcards and company literature marketing the Sunshine State and simultaneously one of IC's most venerated long-distance conveyances. Pullman-Standard fabricated the original *City*'s seven cars and the front-end power was furnished by a single 2000-hp EMD E6 (*courtesy Chuck Blardone*).

There were other trainsets delivering passengers along the Illinois Central route, of course. In addition to the *Magnolia Star*, which was united with the *Panama Limited* in 1967, other passenger consists plying the IC main included *The Creole* and *The Louisiane*. Meanwhile, the Illinois Central proffered the *Green Diamond* as its premier trainset operating between Chicago, Springfield and St. Louis. Other major runs included the *Hawkeye* from Chicago to Sioux City, Iowa, and the *City of Miami*, usually running every other day or three times weekly (the schedule fluctuated) between Chicago and its namesake city with sections bound from Jacksonville to St. Petersburg, Tampa and Sarasota. The *City of Miami* arrived at its southerly destinations via interline connections with the IC at Birmingham. There it transferred to the Central of Georgia (owned by the IC into the 1940s) with more transitions onto the Atlantic Coast Line at Albany, Georgia, and Florida East Coast at Jacksonville for the rest of the run.

In the great race among legacy carriers to be at the forefront of the cutting-edge streamliner movement of the mid thirties, Illinois Central introduced the *Green Diamond* in March 1936.[30] The company's time-honored emblem was a diamond, and the *Diamond Special* on the projected *Green Diamond*'s tracks between Chicago–Springfield–St. Louis was considered the route's "star." It would take something new to sway heads by creating excitement there, IC officials believed. Their answer was the *Green Diamond* in a striking two-tone emerald livery.

It looked different beyond its color scheme, however: the *Green Diamond*'s raised crew cab sat high above an ominous grilled nose. With four cars trailing that engine, its consist included a baggage-express-RPO, coach, coach-dinette, and dinette-kitchen-observation parlor car. Seating 100 in coach with 22 more in the parlor car (first class), the *Green Diamond* was the first standard-size diesel-powered streamliner on any U.S. railway. In April and May 1936, it was dispatched on a 7,000-mile journey through much of the nation's heartland during which more than 400,000 visitors had a chance to "ooohhh" and "aaahhh" as they sauntered through its Art Deco interior. Returning to work on its Chicago–St. Louis route on May 17, 1936, the *Green Diamond* made the 294-mile course in less than five hours each way, slightly under Amtrak's time today with the *Texas Eagle* over a 284-mile pathway.

There were yet more "name" trains on Illinois Central tracks: *Chickasaw, Daylight, Delta Express, Iowan, Irvin S. Cobb, Land O' Corn, Mid-American, Miss Lou, Night Diamond, Northern Express, Northwestern Limited, Planter, Seminole, Sinnissippi, Southern Express, Southwestern Limited* and *Sunchaser*. In all nearly three dozen identifiable trainsets ran over IC routes during the prime people-moving era of the late 19th century to mid 20th century.

The *Land O' Corn* was reflective of a handful of commuter-styled operations under Illinois Central auspices in the heyday of that mode of travel.[31] Early every morning it left Waterloo, Iowa, for a five-and-a-half-hour run to Chicago. Along its 275-mile course the consist, regularly comprised of three reclining-seat coaches and a café-lounge car, stopped at Dubuque, Iowa, and Galena, Freeport and Rockford, Illinois, plus almost a dozen lesser burgs before pulling into its ultimate destination near the banks of Lake Michigan. Outbound in the late afternoons, the *Corn* sported a full dining car as far west as Freeport, meeting the dinnertime crowd's demands.

Debuting in late 1941, the *Corn* was the IC's third streamliner (after the *Green Diamond* in 1936 and *City of Miami* in 1940). Then a self-propelled "Motorailer," it had a brief life in that incarnation. Less than four months later a fatal crash removed it from the line, then it was replaced by a steam-driven engine pulling a heavyweight consist. On February 12, 1947, it was reborn as a diesel-powered lightweight streamliner. After lots of tinkering and modifying, the *Land O' Corn* made its final run on August 4, 1967, having ferried tens of thousands of riders to and from Chicago in the dual decades it served.

For a while after 1971, Amtrak operated the *Shawnee* between Chicago and Carbondale, Illinois. In addition to the *City of New Orleans*, Amtrak runs dual all-coach consists with business class service available on that 310-mile stretch in the modern age. Each train normally makes it to its opposite station in five and a half hours. The *Saluki* departs from each end of the spectrum in the morning and arrives at its destination in early afternoon. The *Illini*, on the other hand, leaves those terminals in late afternoon and pulls into the appointed destinations late in the evening.

Today the old IC tracks—formerly transporting passengers, mail and freight—hauls only the latter. Cargo frequently includes chemicals (organic, inorganic, agricultural and others), coal, paper, grain and milled grain, intermodal trailers and containers bearing consumer commodities, lumber and other forest products, metals, and bulk commodities like sand, stone ores and coke. New Orleans and Mobile remain vital gateways for the flow of goods from the Midwest to the world. At the same time those port cities are crucial arrival points for commodities entering the country and bound for a vast region of the nation's midsection. There can be little doubt that the IC continues to affect the fortunes of the Prairie State and the Windy City just as it always has.

9

LOUISVILLE & NASHVILLE RAILROAD
A Tale of Two Cities Dispossessed

Louisville and Nashville Railroad timetables from the 1880s dubbed that road the "Great Thoroughfare between South and North ... without change and with speed unrivaled!" Only a few decades earlier a reality such as that would have appeared as little more than speculation. Consistent methods of moving people and goods in the mid–South always had been sorely lacking. And even the few that existed were sometimes cumbersome and unstable. Cities played one-upmanship with each other in their attempts to increase trade. Securing a dependable means of shipping would be a giant step in achieving that feat.

> For its own needs as well as its livelihood Louisville depended heavily upon the fickle waterways....
>
> Ambitious Louisvillians grappled with their transportation problem.... A road from Louisville to Nashville would free the Kentucky city from the tyranny of low water — during which times Nashville actually became a serious competitor as distributing center for the border region. A railroad would not only avert commercial isolation, it would also neutralize Nashville and steal a march on Cincinnati in the quest for southern markets....
>
> To survive Louisville needed to have a reliable connection to the interior. A road from Louisville to Nashville would be very expensive, risky, fraught with financial and engineering problems, and taxing upon the resources.... Regardless of the perils, several merchants, citizens, and editors understood clearly that the effort had to be made if Louisville wished to keep her future alive....
>
> Nashville interests responded to such pleas by proposing a [rail] line far enough north to penetrate the Louisville market without actually entering the city. Such a road would effectively isolate Louisville between Cincinnati north of the Ohio and Nashville south of the river....
>
> In short, the L & N Railroad was decidedly an offspring of the growing commercial rivalry between Louisville and Nashville.... Both towns saw the road as their chief weapon in the battle not only against each other but against such potential outsiders as Cincinnati, Chattanooga, Atlanta, Memphis, and even New Orleans.[1]

Granted a charter by the Commonwealth of Kentucky on March 5, 1850, the L&N was authorized "to build a line of railroad between Louisville and the Tennessee state line in the direction of Nashville." The Tennessee General Assembly, subsequently acting on December 4, 1851, sanctioned the new enterprise, empowering it to extend its tracks from the Tennessee line south to Nashville. "Born as a child of the commercial rivalry between Louisville and Nashville, the road's original route was plotted less by engineers than by the lottery of which towns cared to contribute to the construction of the line," a scholar affirmed.[2] "It was estimated ... that some 7,000 persons traveled annually between Louisville and Nashville, most of these making the trip by stagecoach, this costing the patron anywhere from $12 to $18."[3] In between the dates identified already, starting in July 1851, teams of appraisers launched the formidable task of determining a feasible route for the line. Within two years crews began clearing the terrain, working south from Louisville. Yet more than another two years elapsed before just eight miles of track were completed!

To celebrate that milestone, 300 Louisville travelers boarded a steam-powered consist on August 25, 1855, for the 16-mile round trip.[4] Whizzing along at a lightheaded 15 miles per hour, their journey reached its southernmost periphery in 27 minutes. But those trailblazers paused three times en route: once to take on water and twice to prod out of the way cows that were found loitering on the track.

The belated euphoria over finishing the first eight miles was indicative of just how slow the L&N's progress was. While construction crews met formidable odds as they reached and conquered Muldraugh's Hill (originally variously spelled Muldro and Muldrow and today known as Muldraugh Hill) north of Radcliff, they finally tunneled 1,986 feet through it at 135 feet beneath its summit.[5] By mid June 1858 — more than eight years after receiving their charter, seven years after starting surveys and five years after beginning construction — the first train rolled into Elizabethtown, only 42 miles south of Louisville! Not overlooking the

Adorning an extant 1905 L&N depot in Knoxville in 2007 is a stained glass window, a novelty that transcends time (*courtesy Michael C.R. Wall*).

excavation of the tunnel, which was formidable, by that time the building of the railroad was progressing at a snail's pace with just over eight miles of new track finished annually.[6]

Somebody must have lit a fire under the crews at that juncture. Twenty more miles were completed in the next six months. The following fall the line reached Bowling Green, not far from the Tennessee line. Things had really picked up steam by then; a true celebratory special consist rolled south from Louisville into Nashville on October 27, 1859.[7] Officials of the railroad and other prominent denizens from the environs of Louisville were aboard. A day later — having partied themselves out in the Tennessee capital — the Kentuckians returned to their home city. Not long afterward, on October 31, 1859, ongoing service commenced between the dual destinations.[8] Some $7 million had been expended to make it happen. Two daily (except Sunday) passenger trains connected the pair of municipalities forming the railroad's name; just one train linked them on Sunday. There was also a single scheduled freight train running on the route every day. Obviously there was greater interest — and market — in moving people instead of products in that era.

> Even before the main line to Nashville was completed, however, the L&N provided a local service of sorts, first from Louisville to Elizabethtown, Ky., then progressively southward to "end of track," with stage coaches conveying passengers around the uncompleted gaps in trackage.
> L&N's first public timetable advertised two trains each way making the 185-mile trip in about 9 hours. Then, on the eve of the Civil War in April 1861, through passenger service between Louisville and Memphis was inaugurated....
> Those new rail services offered obvious advantages to travelers in speed, convenience and dependability over competing stage lines and steamboats. The nine-hour Louisville–Nashville schedules were three times faster than those of the stages, which took 27 hours for the one-way

trip. Ads in 1861 Memphis newspapers declared that running times to Louisville — about 28 hours over the "new lines" — bettered the best river-packet timing between the two cities by 50 hours!

Of course on-train amenities offered passengers in the 1860s and 70s were spartan. Generous quantities of soot and cinders showered in through open windows, and dining service was virtually non-existent, except for whatever "vittles" the hardy traveler could carry or bolt down at infrequent meal stops. However, sleeping cars were introduced on the L&N as early as 1869, when "Rip Van Winkle" palace sleepers began operating between Louisville and Memphis and New Orleans. In the early 1880s, through service was established between Cincinnati and New Orleans, and two solid main line trains were running straight through, after 1886.[9]

Like other growing railroads of the 19th century, following the Civil War the L&N jumped into a rigorous expansion mode that persisted across three decades. From the War Between the States the L&N "emerged with the road intact, the treasury full, and an alert management eager to press its advantage over the prostrate roads of the defunct Confederacy."[10] The company accomplished some of its objectives by acquiring smaller railroads that could help it meet freight and passenger service requirements. Its new assets extended the L&N's reach beyond the namesake cities of Louisville and Nashville to Birmingham, Cincinnati, Evansville, Knoxville, Lexington, Memphis, Mobile, Montgomery, New Orleans, Pensacola and St. Louis.

After helping a couple of regional carriers — Memphis, Clarksville & Louisville, and Memphis & Ohio railroads — regain their business following track displacement in the Civil War, in 1869, the L&N supplemented its portfolio with both lines. Through train service that began in 1872, meanwhile, linked the Ohio Valley with Montgomery after more tracks were added south of Nashville. L&N leased the Nashville & Decatur (Alabama) and South & North Alabama railroads to accomplish it, finishing a track-building program in September 1872, begun by the latter carrier and tying Decatur to Montgomery. Birmingham, in the direct path that lay between them, dubbed the "Pittsburgh of the South" for its iron ore, coal and steel production, "came into being, largely as a result of the above acquisitions," proffered a source. "Over the decades, L&N played a prominent role in Birmingham's growth."[11] Much of the early trade in those industries was financed by the L&N. The railroad created a complex system that tapped into the plentiful natural deposits while serving a multiplicity of commercial developments in and near Birmingham.

Eight years after reaching Montgomery, L&N gained access to the imperative Gulf coast port cities of Mobile, New Orleans and Pensacola. That allowed the line to spread its trade beyond American shores by tapping into vast global markets. To accomplish all of this L&N acquired the 180-mile Mobile & Montgomery and 140-mile New Orleans & Mobile lines. It ran a connection to nearby Pensacola from a point 60 miles northeast of Mobile. Several smaller Mississippi ports were picked up in this expansion, including Biloxi, Gulfport and Pascagoula.

While all of this was transpiring, between 1879 and 1881, the L&N was also focusing attention at the other end of its route. By purchasing several short lines in Illinois, Indiana and Kentucky, it gained trackage leading to Evansville, St. Louis and the dynamic coal deposits in western Kentucky. When the Lebanon, Kentucky, branch line was extended southeast, Knoxville became an L&N destination with through train service between Louisville and Knoxville in 1883.

Meanwhile, by 1881, the Louisville, Cincinnati & Lexington Railroad joined the L&N in providing ties to Lexington and Covington, Kentucky, the latter hamlet only a few miles south of Cincinnati. The following year the L&N participated in crossing the Ohio River at Louisville with the debut of the first bridge of any kind there. This opened rail traffic to the promising markets in Northern and Midwestern states.

Back on the Gulf Coast, between 1881 and 1883, L&N extended its reach 160 miles eastward from Pensacola to join what would eventually be the Seaboard Air Line Railroad at Chatta-hoochee, in the Sunshine State's panhandle. The future SAL route continued eastward from Chattahoochee to Tallahassee and finally to the important north-south connections at Jacksonville near the Atlantic coast.

At about this same time some memorabilia emerged that was to remain as identifying symbols of the railroad for the rest of its life. The first, created in the South Louisville Shops by George Schumpp, was a highly recognizable logotype that applied the company's initials *L&N*. It began appearing as the insignia on timetables, advertising, promotional literature, tickets, stationery, signage and eventually the trains themselves, as well as the buildings owned by the line. The alphabet letters were displayed in white through a reverse process on a solid red rectangular background in bold block type. That was separated by a flourishing scripted ampersand and three thin horizontal white lines tying the elements together. At the request of general passenger agent C. P. Atmore in 1880, Schumpp submitted several designs for a permanent trademark. The latter man eventually earned the title of master painter for the railroad, and retired from it on July 1, 1929, after a half-century of service.

Also making its debut in the same epoch was the familiar motto that became emblazoned in many of the same places: *The Old Reliable*. The epithet is thought to have initially appeared in 1884 in an editorial penned by journalist R. M. Rawls for *The* (Athens) *Alabama Courier*. L&N officials subsequently adapted the maxim to a variety of applications. One of those consistent spots included the white cloths hanging over the tops of chairs in the coaches, giving the traveler sitting behind each one an in-your-face reminder of the logo and catchphrase *The Old Reliable*. On such occasions, as a patron looked at his watch and realized the train was running well behind schedule, one can only wonder: what must the passenger have pondered as he considered the meaning of that durable phrase?

In this same epoch the L&N's track was upgraded from iron to steel while the width of the tracks was modernized. A variety of gauges heretofore prevalent on L&N lines were discarded; a common denominator shared by other railway systems took their place, standardized at 4 feet 9 inches, allowing L&N consists to roll along unimpeded on other roads with similar widths, and vice versa.[12]

Much later the L&N adopted an emblematic royal blue hue for its livery. That coupled with *Louisville & Nashville* in gold script emblazoned on letterboards became an identifying company trademark. Following the Second World War, the *Humming Bird* and *Georgian* streamliners emerged exhibiting blue and silver coaches. The consists' trucks and other underbody gear were painted black while roofs were light gray. L&N sleepers, meanwhile, were often tinted in Tuscan red, a shade symbolizing the interline Pennsylvania Railroad that ferried those cars between Louisville and the Windy City. In the mid 1950s, the L&N and NC&StL color scheme was standardized on passenger cars to solid blue with gray roofs and letterboards bearing imitation gold striping in script type.

Access to the rich coal fields of southeastern Kentucky, Tennessee and Virginia was accomplished when the L&N bought the Kentucky Central's Covington–Winchester–Livingston route in 1891. A line from Pineville, Kentucky, in the heart of Appalachia, south through Middlesboro and into Tennessee turned northeast into the Old Dominion State, eventually terminating at Norton, Virginia, alongside large deposits of minerals.

From the mid 1850s onward company officers and their staffs were housed in several buildings in downtown Louisville, starting with a joint freight and passenger depot at 9th and Broadway in 1857. Not long afterward some offices moved to another structure at Main and Bullitt streets. In 1877, they shifted to a larger édifice at 2nd and Main streets. In 1902, in the same block in which the line's original station was situated, excavation began for an 11-story tower office building. In January 1907, a half-century after the first L&N facility

Ninth and Broadway in Louisville became synonymous with L&N as early as 1857, when the first enduring freight and passenger facility was erected at that corner. Two years passed before trains ran between L&N's namesake cities. As the line proliferated so did its general offices, spread over downtown Louisville. In 1907, this 11-story corporate headquarters opened on the same site that L&N initially occupied a half-century earlier. It remained the carrier's base until operations finally ceased more than eight decades later (*courtesy Erik Landrum*).

opened in that block, officers and employees transferred from 2nd and Main to spacious new quarters at 9th and Broadway. A matching annex was added in 1930. The company maintained a presence at that location to 1988.[13]

While all of the foundational development and acquisition was taking place during the L&N's early decades, two men born in the 19th century easily stood head and shoulders above all the others in cementing the operation on solid ground. One was Albert Fink; the other, Milton H. Smith. The contributions of both to the firm's future success deem them worthy of more than mere passing mention.

Born at Lauterbach, Germany, on October 27, 1827, and later earning an engineering degree there, at 22 Albert Fink migrated to Baltimore, Maryland. He was soon employed by the Baltimore & Ohio Railroad (B&O) as a draftsman, gaining prestige for his bridge-building blueprints. As the first of his profession in this country to craft a 200-foot span, he earned status with peers.[14] Fink's most impressive feat of the era was to design a bridge model that was to earn such acclaim it ultimately bore his name—the Fink Truss. He patented it and eventually realized significant revenue from its application in bridge, home and building construction. In 1852, the truss was used in the B&O viaduct at Fairmont, Virginia (now West Virginia) over the Monongahela River. On that occasion a trilogy of 305-foot arches combined to support the longest iron railroad trestle in America.[15]

Although he won multiple promotions with the B&O, Fink departed for Louisville in

1857, accepting the post of construction engineer proffered by the Louisville & Nashville Railroad. In that capacity he oversaw erection of a freight and passenger depot in 1858 while designing a soaring span over the Green River. The latter challenge was formidable: he fashioned the bridge over an extensive gorge in south central Kentucky — one of the railroad's few remaining physical hurdles in its charge to connect Nashville with Louisville. While all of this was transpiring, Fink fabricated and supervised the raising of a new courthouse in Louisville. In 1859, in addition to his engineering duties, he was given accountability for L&N machinery of all types. He was promoted to chief engineer the following year.

While a great deal of the L&N's physical assets were destroyed during the War Between the States, the company remained in business and occupied a strong financial posture following the war.[16] "It was ... largely Fink's ability to keep the road in operation that made the L&N the only Southern railroad to escape military seizure by the Union government during the war.... Fink and his men were doing as well or better with the harassed line than military railroaders could," one historiographer reported, adding: "The Union Government had begun to sense what the L&N could mean in waging war, so it ordered rolling stock from other roads delivered to the L&N."[17] Fink maintained "exceptional" records throughout the period and could be credited with much of the L&N's "good condition," another source allowed: "The company settled accounts with the government with little or no trouble, a feat that can not be said of many of its competitors."[18]

Named general superintendent of the railroad in 1865, Fink launched the task of rebuilding it materially and in other ways. For a decade he fostered business relations with rival railway systems. During that epoch he designed and built his most imposing legacy — bridging the one-mile gap over the Ohio River at Louisville, a span rising 400 feet above water connecting the city with southern Indiana. Fink incorporated the world's longest truss bridge in his plans.[19] In the meantime he was named vice-president in addition to general superintendent upon the death of an L&N president in 1869. Five years hence the *Railway Gazette* acknowledged that a cost analysis of transportation and freight rates completed by Fink netted "the fullest investigation into the cost of railroad transportation ever published in our country or language."[20]

With an eye toward commerce, the engineer-turned-administrator seized the opportunity to extend L&N's sphere of influence from Nashville to Montgomery. He accomplished it by successfully negotiating agreements with other railroads for use of their tracks in reaching Alabama's capital city. "To accomplish this required considerable financing which he [Fink] negotiated beyond the confines of American banking and through connections in England," noted one observer. "His insight into this financial activity proved successful when, during the 1873 panic, the Louisville and Nashville Railroad was able to maintain loan payments and escape the fate of bankruptcy."[21]

One historical account of the L&N intimated it was Fink's intent to retire at the young age of 47 when he resigned from the L&N in 1875. Whether it was so or not, his "retirement" didn't last long. While he kept a home in Louisville which he visited now and then, Fink reportedly left retirement twice — once to perform as first commissioner of a newly-organized Southern Railway and Steamship Association (1875–1877), and again to be the original commissioner of a newly-formed Trunk Line Association (1877–1889). The latter rate-setting agency was produced by a quartet of competing railroads that converged in the East: Baltimore & Ohio, Erie, New York Central, and Pennsylvania.[22] But stationed in New York City in 1887, in that job Fink was representing 40 of the largest U.S. transportation outfits and commanding a staff of hundreds.

His service was impressive: "No single man ever wielded so potent an influence directly upon the railway traffic of this country as did Albert Fink during a period of twelve years, beginning in 1877. In the last half of that period the pool organized and directed by him controlled the traffic operations of the Eastern lines. It was, in fact, the autocratic sway of that pool that led to the passage of the InterState Commerce act."[23] Fink's prior tenure with the L&N Railroad prepared him for his crowning achievement. During his later years he again served the L&N as a director. His death at Ossining, New York, on April 3, 1897, was followed by interment in his beloved Louisville.

The other pivotal L&N figure of the era, Milton Hannibal Smith, with more than three decades in the presidential suite, occupied it longer than anybody and thereby influenced the line much more than his counterparts. When Albert Fink was eight years old, Smith was born in Green County, New York, on September 12, 1836. He floundered for a while during a prolonged trial of adolescent searching. Smith tried teaching school in Chicago at 16, clerked in a grocery store after that, attended night classes at a St. Louis commercial college, and followed it on the road hawking school supplies in west Tennessee and north Mississippi.

Learning telegraphy on the side, at 23 he joined a regional telegraph firm. From 1861 to 1863, he was telegrapher for the Mississippi Central Railroad; the following two years he gained still more experience in multiple Southern cities working for U.S. military railroads. After a few months' service with a Louisville express company in 1865, Smith was offered a job by Albert Fink as Louisville freight agent with the L&N. The year was 1866. Smith accepted and put down roots: with time out as general freight agent for the Baltimore & Ohio Railroad (1878–1881) and three months as general agent for the Pennsylvania Railroad in the latter year, he spent the remainder of his life in Louisville with the L&N.[24]

Following the three-year sojourn away, Smith returned to the L&N as third vice president and traffic manager on January 1, 1882. After advancing to vice president he acceded to the presidency on June 11, 1884, filling that role until October 6, 1886, and returning to it March 9, 1891. He was president until his death at 84 in Louisville on February 22, 1921.[25] "Controversial yet purposeful, Smith shaped the L&N from a small regional carrier into one of America's major railroad systems," an authoritative informant maintained.[26]

A solidly historical account of the L&N cautioned against misconceptions about Smith adopted by some other scribes. Its author admitted that Smith was categorically linked to the L&N more emphatically than anybody was to any other rail line. Smith didn't, however, control the company, devise policy without help or dictate greater guiding principles. Some observers, said the academician, "mistakenly depicted Smith's presidency as one of an absolute monarch ruling over his private kingdom."[27] The account delineated further: "The effect of his 37-year presidency was to create the legend that Milton H. Smith ran the L & N Railroad — indeed that he *was* the L & N Railroad — and that he represented a last charming bastion of rugged individualism in the emerging corporate era."[28]

While the authority of his office, his persuasion, and utter willpower netted for him strong influence over operations, in financial matters Smith's "reign" was invariably held in check. "Put simply," that author certified, "Smith's policies often depended upon how much money he could get from his board, and he did not always get what he wanted."[29] The introspective examination visited that crushing limitation frequently, in fact. In a sweeping assessment, it reflected:

> Smith returned the management of the road from New York to Louisville and presided over the last golden age of L & N home rule. Under his leadership the company extended lines into the coal fields of eastern Kentucky and the mineral beds of northern Alabama. During the 1880s and 1890s the L & N built, leased, or absorbed more than fifty smaller roads. Then in 1902, through a convoluted sequence of Wall Street maneuvers, controlling interest in the L & N passed into the hands of another system, the Atlantic Coast Line. The swallower had itself been swallowed, but not fully digested.
>
> Despite this change of ownership, the L & N retained its separate identity as a system and

continued to expand under Smith. Between 1902 and 1921 its mileage rose from 3,327 to 5,041, most of it in the form of more feeder lines into untapped regions of Kentucky, Tennessee, and Alabama. The death of Smith in 1921 coincided with the opening of a new era.... The age of expansion had ended, never to return except in the form of mergers.[30]

The Atlantic Coast Line Railroad (ACL) purchased 51 percent of the L&N's stock in 1902.[31] That margin of control was maintained to 1945, when the ACL sold part of its holdings in the line, slashing its hegemony to 35 percent. That was subsequently reduced to a 33.8 percent stake. It remained such to 1971, when Seaboard Coast Line Industries, then-parent of the former ACL, bought 98 percent of L&N's stock.

The 1920s saw America utterly thriving. That decade witnessed an infusion of several new trains on the Louisville & Nashville Railroad just as similar activity was occurring elsewhere. Until that era the *New Orleans Limited*—which may be justifiably cited as the L&N's most enduring mainline passenger train—was, for decades, a veteran of the rails.[32] By 1922, the *Limited*'s schedule called for it to depart Cincinnati in early evening and arrive in New Orleans at about the same time the following evening. On the opposite run the *Limited* left the Crescent City in early morning with a late morning advent in Cincinnati the following day.

Traveling in both directions, this workhorse was scheduled into Nashville at roughly the same time as the Chicago–Atlanta–Florida *Dixie Limited*. For years a Chicago–New Orleans sleeper made a seamless transition between those trains at Nashville. In 1936, meanwhile, the *New Orleans Limited* was rebranded the *Azalean* and some newly air-conditioned coaches fabricated in L&N's South Louisville Shops were assigned to it. All overnight space on the *Azalean* was usually occupied, principally sold to passengers traveling to and from Cincinnati, Louisville, Nashville and Birmingham. The *Azalean* remained as an L&N mainstay to 1966.

Along the same Cincinnati–New Orleans route, the *Pan-American*—which quickly earned status as the Louisville & Nashville's flagship operation—debuted on December 5, 1921. With a 24-hour schedule, it covered the expanse between those two cities in slightly less time than any train before it ever had. *Pan-American* sections to Memphis and Pensacola were offered, too, the former breaking off the mainline at Bowling Green, Kentucky, while the latter left it at Flomaton, Alabama. Company literature touted: "Equipped with high-class all-steel coaches, chair cars, and sleepers ... and with our own dining cars offering meals of the highest class, the new train affords the traveling public a service superior to anything previously offered by the Old Reliable or its competitors."

Car-ending foyers were discarded on the train's diners to allow more travelers to eat concurrently. With new cars delivered by Pullman, in May 1925, the *Pan-American* became a sleeper-only consist providing 12-section (12 upper berths and 12 lower berths) and single drawing room sleepers, a 39-seat diner decked out in mahogany décor, a baggage club–library car, and a parlor-observation car on the end. The parlor-observation car boasted seating for 20 and a separate lounge for women. More deluxe features included maid and valet service, showers, radio with earphones—the first train anywhere so-equipped—and a choice of buffet and full dining service.

Baldwin mountain-type 4-8-2 steam engines easily powered the *Pan-American* over steeper grades. All of the train's amenities quickly crowned it L&N's premier passenger service, a reputation it maintained throughout its long life, even after some of the extras were amended or recalled.[33] Before long part of that jewel's journey was extended all the way to New York City. Through sleepers were transported beyond Cincinnati over the tracks of the Pennsylvania Railroad, with Pennsy and L&N exchanging those cars at Cincinnati.

For more than a decade starting August 15, 1933—as the *Pan-American* highballed south out of Nashville on weekday afternoons—a microphone alongside the L&N tracks beamed

Florida Surf, L&N private sleeping car 3448, built as car 251 for NC&StL by Pullman in 1954, shifted to L&N when NC&StL folded into it in 1957. The car sits on an SCL siding at St. Petersburg in 1974, owned at that time by two Tampa investors. The interior of the stainless steel conventional lightweight coach is peculiar: four roomettes, five bedrooms, one compartment, and four sections. Open sections were viewed as passé by then and may have been there because government workers traveled on its routes. The car is equipped with modern swing-hanger roller-bearing trucks (*courtesy Michael B. Robbins*).

the train's rushing din to the world. WSM Radio's 878-foot tower stood a few miles south of Nashville; that 50,000-watt broadcast powerhouse signified the *Pan-American*'s approach. Fan mail from every state in the union and numerous foreign countries persisted at a high level. It's the only known live broadcast of a passing train on a continuing basis. It all ended at last on June 2, 1945. A major factor in its demise was the loss of steam-driven engines, which were replaced by quieter, less enchanting diesel motive power, thereby canceling some of the listening public's fervor.

Meanwhile, the *Crescent Limited*— delivered by the Southern Railway from Washington, D.C., to Atlanta and the West Point Route from Atlanta to Montgomery — joined the L&N mainline in the latter city for the remaining stretch to New Orleans. A handful of seasonal trains also emerged to serve the gratifying Midwest-to-Florida circuit. They connected from far-flung northern outposts to L&N tracks at Cincinnati, Evansville, Louisville, Nashville and Birmingham. While less than 10 percent of L&N's business was generated in the people-moving sector, it nevertheless made an indelible impact on the bottom line.[34] A pattern was set that was to persist until the fading days of rail passenger service on freight-hauling roads. "L&N's dining car fare was well remembered," claimed one appraisal, "especially for the fresh Gulf Coast seafood gumbo and the Duncan Hines Kentucky Ham breakfasts."[35,36]

A major improvement in the postwar years included the extension of Centralized Traffic Control (CTC)—which had been introduced on a handful of active wartime routes—over hundreds of miles of main and crucial secondary tracks. CTC not only accelerated traffic but sometimes allowed second main tracks to be eliminated. Many of the cars that ran on these rails were either upgraded at the South Louisville Shops or replaced with new ones. A modernized fleet of passenger and freight carriers was the result as the L&N continued to emphasize efficiency, a quantity that had been a hallmark of Milton H. Smith's presidency in 1884–1886 and 1891–1921.

The milestone of L&N's century celebration on March 5, 1950, was marked with about 8,000 miles of track in use, including 4,780 miles or about 60 percent over mainline routes. The company owned 640 steam locomotives and 202 diesel units with 88 more of the latter variety already on order. L&N's inventory included 61,300 freight and 635 passenger cars with 6,950 total added cars on order. With 15,000 stockholders scattered across the 48 states, the line then employed 28,000 workers.[37]

One of the Louisville & Nashville Railroad's last major acquisitions—before the L&N itself finally lost its own identity on November 1, 1980, with the formation of the CSX Corporation—occurred August 30, 1957. The Nashville, Chattanooga & St. Louis Railway (NC&StL) was fully integrated into the system. The NC&StL was a strategically placed line with a history that went back even further than the L&N's. It began with a 151-mile antecedent route, the Nashville and Chattanooga Railway, in 1845.[38] A corporate relationship between the NC&StL and the L&N extended more than three-quarters of a century before the two lines joined their operations. In the late 1870s, with NC&StL president E. W. Cole trying to add extensive tracks across Illinois, Indiana and Kentucky, L&N stopped that cold. In 1880, L&N's retort was to purchase a majority of NC&StL stock. As a result the larger system took over the lines that NC&StL had bid for.

The 1957 merger was significant in that it was the first amalgamation of two major U.S. railroads in modern history, prompting a plethora of similar combinations that followed within the rail trade.[39] This fusion added 1,043 miles to L&N's routes, delivered direct lines between Nashville and Atlanta and Nashville and Memphis, and increased the L&N workforce by about 4,000, to approximately 25,000 employees. L&N became the third largest railroad in the South and the 16th largest in the nation as a result of that union.[40]

A contingent of scholarly railroad historians allowed that 62 percent of NC&StL's annual passenger revenues were generated by its "bridge" (or through) traffic.[41] The bulk could be attributed to trains running over its mainline between the Midwest, Atlanta and Florida. At 735 miles, *The Dixie Line* (which evolved into the NC&StL's enduring slogan) was the shortest, fastest, most direct route linking Chicago with Atlanta. In the halcyon days of U.S. rail passenger service from the late 19th century through the first half of the 20th, those tracks witnessed some of the heaviest tourist travel in the nation. The *Dixie Flyer* and *Dixie Limited*, NC&StL premier trains, were just two among a handful of "name" consists with *Dixie*-themed handles plying the course. You'll find more on the strategically-situated NC&StL in the succeeding chapter.

In June 1969, the L&N acquired the so-called "eastern" line of the former Chicago & Eastern Illinois Railroad (C&EI), adding 287 miles to the system. In doing so the L&N gained access to the gigantic Chicago gateway and market and offered shippers single-line service between the Great Lakes and the Central South, Gulf Coast and Southeast. Trains traveled from the Windy City to Louisville via Lafayette and Bloomington, Indiana.[42] Finally, on August 1, 1971, another 541 miles of trackage entered the L&N fold when it bought the Monon Railroad, thereby gaining a second route to Chicago.[43] Branches spread to the Indiana points of Indianapolis, French Lick and Michigan City.

With that last acquisition the L&N reached 6,574 route miles spread across 13 states: Alabama, Florida, Georgia, Illinois, Indiana, Kentucky, Louisiana, Mississippi, Missouri, North Carolina, Ohio, Tennessee, and Virginia. Just a trio of those states accounted for nearly three-fifths of the L&N's trackage at its peak in 1971: Kentucky, 28 percent (1,800 miles); Alabama, 17 percent (1,100 miles); and Tennessee, 14 percent (900 miles).[44]

After the Atlantic Coast Line and Seaboard Air Line railroads merged to form the Seaboard Coast Line (SCL), the "Family Lines System" was designated with the L&N (previously owned by the ACL and then SCL) added to the mix. In November 1971, Seaboard Coast Line Industries increased its holdings in L&N stock from 33 to 98 percent, giving it virtually total control.[45] While the L&N headquarters remained in Louisville, officers presided over fewer and fewer functions: "The once mighty L & N system had become in effect a subsidiary in a larger entity."[46]

Despite the lack of creature comforts that the traveling public experienced in the early days of L&N, all that began to change as a new century approached. Timetables of the 1880s and 1890s strutted: "The through-car service of the L&N is unsurpassed by any line in the South. Sleepers are the latest model Pullman vestibuled buffet cars, and coaches are equipped with all modern improvements." In 1886, L&N offered sleeping car service between St. Louis and Nashville. Six years beyond it that train was extended over NC&StL and other routes to Jacksonville. It was dubbed the *Dixie Flyer*, an enduring moniker that was immortalized over the decades. By 1908, the *Flyer* was running every day between the Windy City and Jacksonville.

Before continuing, let's interrupt the progression of "name" trains to explore the realizations of some of the creature comforts experienced by Louisville and Nashville travelers. The dining car, for instance, was—comparatively speaking—a rather late arrival on L&N routes. A dining car department with Superintendent L. M. Hill, formerly of the Chicago & Eastern Illinois Railroad, was added to the headquarters staff in 1901. That occurred after similar appointments were made by some other Class 1 rail lines.[47] That year (1901) the Pullman Company sold a trio of wood-fabricated dining cars to L&N that were placed in regular service in October. Steel-constructed dining cars that rapidly became the norm were introduced on L&N routes as early as 1914. With a steward, two cooks and three waiters onboard each of the original dining cars, 56,908 meals were served by L&N's staff in the first year of operation, increasing the bottom line by $47,425 — typically less than 84 cents per meal.

Until then L&N passengers customarily purchased most of their food en route in restaurants at scheduled station stops. Time was included in travel schedules for this purpose. Despite the proliferating number of dining cars, the practice of allowing patrons to de-board to eat and re-board to travel persisted as late as the 1940s, although it was diminishing as time elapsed. In a few cases prior to the inception of the dining cars in the rolling stock, onboard meals were provided to Pullman passengers. L&N and interline partners worked especially hard to keep meal prices down.

> The L&N and NC&StL dining car departments prided themselves on buying only the best grade of food supplies. No consideration was ever given to second grade foods even though such use would have reduced annual losses incurred in dining car operations. The two departments insisted that passengers be served generous portions, that perishable foods were fresh and that ample supplies of all foods and equipment always be on hand for their cars. During one month in 1942, L&N's dining car department purchased 7,000 lbs. of butter, 10,000 dozen eggs, 20,000 loaves of bread and 104,000 lbs. of meat![48]

As time went on the dining experience was upgraded. In one modernization of L&N diners in 1956-1957, onboard kitchens were equipped with gas ranges and mechanical refrigeration. Until then coal-burning ranges and charcoal-burning coffee urns were in use. An assessment of the company's food service, based on data in 1963, noted that — on heavy runs — the dining car crew might include as many as nine employees: steward, chef, two cooks, pantry man, and four waiters.[49]

In the matter of overnight travel accommodations, on September 2, 1864, John B. Anderson & Company contracted with the Louisville & Nashville Railroad to operate sleeping cars on its routes. That contract was later shifted to Paine Harris & Company, which was superseded by one with Pullman Southern Car Company on June 19, 1872. Pullman was to have exclusive drawing room, parlor and sleeping car privileges on L&N to 1887.[50] Before the time was up, however, Pullman Southern Car Company was integrated into Pullman Palace Car Company (1882), which was succeeded by Pullman Company (1899). Pullman continued to operate nearly all sleeping cars on American railroads until 1949, when the Interstate Commerce Commission intervened. Pullman continued manufacturing sleeping cars but the operation of those cars over rail lines was separated and distributed to the railroads.

On July 1, 1949, L&N began running 57 conventional-weight sleeping cars acquired from the Pullman enterprise, just as other Class 1 railroads were doing.[51] From then on L&N staffed and maintained its own sleeping car service. Twenty-two lightweight sleepers were added by L&N in 1953. Each contained six sections (six upper berths and six lower berths), four double bedrooms and six roomettes. L&N's acquisition of the Nashville, Chattanooga & St. Louis Railway (1957) added three more lightweight sleepers to its inventory.

The *Chicago & Florida Limited* arrived in December 1901, a precedent-setting winter-season train. A pundit observed that it was "the first of a succession of elegantly equipped and appointed 'named' trains" connecting the Midwest with Florida's beaches and resorts and running beside the Alabama and Mississippi Gulf Coast. Along its 32-hour trek between the Windy City and St. Augustine, its southern terminus, the *Limited* proffered "wide vestibules, steam heat, gas lights, and dining car service" to pamper those patrons on their excursions. Many more passenger trains would follow in the *Limited*'s stead. The success of the *Dixie Flyer*, plus an NC&StL sleeper, the *Quickstep*, rolling over tracks linking Nashville and Atlanta — plus the Florida resort boom — had all played a monumental role in the debut of the *Chicago & Florida Limited*.

The *South Atlantic Limited*, which premiered over the L&N's Cincinnati–Knoxville–Atlanta route in 1909, increased ridership between the Southeast and Florida. With through sleeping car connections from Lexington and Louisville and widely touted "electric lighted" passenger cars, the consist contributed heavily to growing service over L&N's "second" mainline. By 1915, the train was renamed the *Southland*. It was also forwarding through Pullmans between Chicago and strategic points on both coasts of the Sunshine State, a much larger enterprise than when it debuted.

Although the Louisville & Nashville Railroad had less opportunity than some other lines to run commuter trains due to fewer metropolitan centers it could serve, in a few cases it successfully carried riders to and from work every day. A couple of them are worth noting. One, the *Danville Flyer*, will be recounted later at the sequential spot it occupied in evolving L&N history.

From the 1920s to the 1960s, however, L&N was involved in daily commuter service connecting the Mississippi Gulf Coast with New Orleans. In fact, for a long while two such trains ran weekdays over an 83-mile route between Ocean Springs, Mississippi, and the Crescent City. A lack of highways linking some of the smaller burgs as well as a convenient train schedule figured prominently in the dual trains' durability. The second train was dropped in the mid 1950s, but the other persisted. Early each morning except Sunday it ran westward on a 2-hour 25-minute course to New Orleans. Six late afternoons weekly it ran eastward out of the Crescent City over the same route.

The one-way fare in 1951 was $2.08 for the full distance. But travelers could purchase a 10-trip ticket for $14.58 ($1.46 per trip) or a 46-trip ticket for $32.99 (less than 72 cents per trip). Reduced fares were available for shorter distances, of course. The route was trimmed to end at Pass Christian, Mississippi, later in the 1950s. With automobile and bus service overtaking commuter rail, the latter was finally withdrawn in the summer of 1965—a pleasant memory for patrons who may have participated in it for decades.

The first one-night-out train between Chicago and Miami, the seasonal *Dixieland*, premiered in January 1936. Leaving Chicago early in the morning, the coach-and-Pullman consist arrived in Miami on the following evening, 32 hours after its departure—the first train to traverse that route in so brief a span. The interline *Dixieland* operated via Evansville, Nashville, Atlanta and Jacksonville over rails of the Chicago & Eastern Illinois; L&N; NC&StL; Atlanta, Birmingham & Coast; and Florida East Coast roads.

In the early 1930s, as passenger rail took a nosedive when the effects of the Great Depression lingered, an innovative L&N and four smaller southeastern railroads instituted an experiment to attract more people to their trains.[52] Beginning April 1, 1933, they sharply slashed fares and eliminated surcharges for Pullman passengers, reducing overall sleeping-car rates by a third. Patronage showed an immediate upward tick. When fares were cut still more on December 1, 1933, more and more people returned to the rails. Still other reductions were implemented as late as June 1, 1939. The maneuvers were a persuasive argument that L&N officials were in tune with the times. Obviously they were willing to make adjustments to meet the abilities of their potential clientele to pay while simultaneously providing a service to satisfy the needs of those travelers.

Air conditioning was introduced to L&N passengers in May 1934. The new creature comfort initially was limited to a handful of Pullman cars and eight dining cars. The overnight sensation, however, earned such quick acclaim that a host of coaches, dining cars and Pullmans running over L&N routes were air-conditioned during the following three years. With the exception of a few local trains, by July 1937, virtually all of the company's mainline rolling stock was cooled throughout. Although it cost L&N more than a million dollars to implement it in about 150 coaches and dining cars, the conversion "paid dividends in the form of a satisfied and comfortable traveling public," a source insisted.

How many freight trains can you think of that were assigned names? The L&N was among the railroads that boasted one. The *Silver Bullet*, inaugurated in autumn 1938, sped manufactured goods, raw materials and other commodities between Cincinnati, Louisville, Nashville, Birmingham and Montgomery to the port cities of Pensacola, Mobile and New Orleans. Departing Covington, Kentucky—opposite Cincinnati on the Ohio River's southern banks—at 5:15 P.M., by dawn of the second morning its freight was deposited at terminals along the Gulf, ready for reloading onto ships destined for the world. Priority was given the *Silver Bullet* that shrunk an unnamed predecessor train's time by 10 and a half hours. Coupled with the morning delivery schedule—which was adjusted to meet freight receivers' needs—in practice, it saved shippers 24 hours. Heretofore the train's coastal arrival was late in the afternoon, leaving those hauls unloaded until the following day. The *Silver Bullet* made the L&N even more competitive by responding to the needs of freight traffic customers.

Near the end of 1940, two crack streamliners between Chicago and Miami appeared on L&N tracks making such striking impressions that they are remembered today by many railfans who rode them. The *Dixie Flagler* debuted on December 17 and the *South Wind* two days later. Both were slated initially for winter runs only. The traveling public embraced them from the start, however, enough so that they were retained as year-round operations. While the pair emerged as coach-only consists, they were soon rebranded as coach-and-Pullman trains. Interline partners, including L&N, all agreed to maintain meal prices at affordable levels. On either train travelers paid 50 cents for breakfasts and 60 cents for lunches and dinners. While that lasted those riders were treated to a "value menu" (a term we often see in some restaurants now) that encompassed everything those diners had to offer. What a deal!

The *Flagler* left Chicago for Evansville, where it was handed over to L&N crews steering it to Nashville. The *Wind* traveled from Chicago to Louisville with L&N crews operating it between Louisville and Montgomery. The L&N equipped the *Wind* with a super-tank proffering a 27.5-ton coal capacity plus 20,000 gallons of water. This "camel's hump" allowed the streamliner to run without stopping between Louisville and Nashville and again between Nashville and Birmingham. At the time the 205-mile leg between Nashville and Birmingham was the longest non-stop coal-powered run in the U.S.[53] The *Dixie Flagler* remained in service to 1954, succeeded by the *Dixieland*, which persisted to 1957. The *South Wind*, on the other hand, retained a colorful history under that moniker to 1971, when it was renamed the *Floridian*. It stopped running in 1979, almost four decades after its launch.

America's inaugural postwar lightweight streamliners, the *Humming Bird* and *Georgian*, went into service in November 1946. Contest winners for naming them were picked from nearly 300,000 entries representing a wide spectrum of the general public.[54]

The former train took flight on the Cincinnati–New Orleans mainline while the latter navigated the tracks between originations at Chicago and St. Louis (combined at Evansville) and Atlanta. The overnight popularity of the *Humming Bird* can be seen in some revealing statistics: by the close of 1947 — its first full year of operation — it had carried more than 275,000 passengers. That averages to a minimum of 753 travelers per day for a year or 377 per train, one train running daily in each direction.

Amtrak's ***Floridian*** is led by SDP40F 645 on August 4, 1979, pausing at Decatur, Alabama, on its northerly trek to Nashville, Louisville and Chicago terminus. Two Florida-originating sections (Miami, Tampa). fused at Jacksonville prior to 645's stops at Montgomery and Birmingham. This train, until 1971 known as the *South Wind*, dates from December 19, 1940, alternating departure days then with the *Dixie Flagler*, a pair traveling contrary routes (***courtesy Jay T. Thomson***).

While it appears to be rolling down the tracks, a stationary L&N passenger consist led by EMD E-8 796 rests on a siding at Bowling Green, Kentucky's Historic Railpark on May 4, 2009. The streamliner's front end power that plied L&N's popular routes from 1951 to 1971 exhibits a blue-and-cream livery for which the carrier is well remembered (*courtesy Clyde Woodruff*).

Market forecasts for the *Georgian* proved higher than that train was able to deliver during its earliest months. It turned out that St. Louis as a Midwestern terminus wasn't as much in demand as it had been initially projected. But when, in June 1948, the train was rerouted to add separate sections beyond Evansville that continued on to Chicago *and* St. Louis, it gained the right impetus to turn into a winner.

One of the great recollections of the halcyon days of American passenger railroading emerged out of the legendary *Humming Bird* and *Georgian* operations. The schedules of those four consists, two northbound and two southbound, were eventually tightly synchronized at the point where they crossed paths at Nashville. In so doing, the passengers in certain sleeping cars (and possibly coaches, too) on one train could be seamlessly switched to another. In theory and in practice, their directions were thus altered overnight.

A 1958 timetable confirms: The southbound *Humming Bird* departed Cincinnati at 7:05 P.M. and rested at Nashville from 1:10 to 1:30 A.M. before continuing to New Orleans for a 3:30 P.M. arrival. The southbound *Georgian*, meanwhile, left Chicago at 3:45 P.M. and paused in Nashville from 1:05 to 1:30 A.M. Then it continued to Atlanta, arriving at 8:45 A.M. Now focus on the critical minutes shortly after 1 A.M.: One or more sleeping car(s) on the Cincinnati–New Orleans route might be diverted at Nashville to Atlanta as its final destination. At the same time one or more sleeping cars on the Chicago–Atlanta run might be redirected there to New Orleans.

It normally worked like a charm, and the same way in the other direction: The *Georgian* left Atlanta at 5:45 P.M., stopped in Nashville from 10:53 to 11:30 P.M., and was in Chicago at 9:05 A.M. Conversely the *Humming Bird* was out of New Orleans at 9:30 A.M., into Nashville at 10:53 P.M., and on its way at 11:50 P.M. with arrival in Cincinnati at 7:00 A.M. Thus, the Atlanta–Chicago consist could lose one or more cars to Cincinnati at Nashville while the New Orleans–Cincinnati train might lose one or more cars to Chicago.

Many factors came into play to make all of this work. For one of those trains to arrive very late in Nashville was simply not an option. It also took a skilled local staff to accomplish those maneuvers in the briefest timeframe. L&N stationed dependable crews at Nashville who anticipated their nightly rituals and carried them out with dispatch. The seven-night-a-week contrivance executed there marked some of the most highly coordinated nocturnal passenger exchanges in the country, and it persisted for many years.

Despite the *Pan-American*'s fanciful reputation as the L&N's flagship consist, at its inception in 1946, the *Humming Bird*'s 19-hour tear over the 922-mile route from Cincinnati to New Orleans put it well ahead of its more famous rival. Its thrust could be attributed to several factors that hastened the journey: use of diesel motive power, a fixed lightweight consist, an embargo on checked baggage, and briefer depot stopovers. At its premier a quarter-century earlier, the steam-driven heavyweight *Pan-American* required 24 hours to make the trip — although at that time it was still the fastest train ever to traverse the route.

A cadre of railroad historians offered an insightful summary of the L&N's passenger equipment — and management's operating philosophy — over the years.[55] A few excerpts follow:

> L&N's management could be proactive when necessary, with perhaps its finest hour the bold and early postwar inauguration of fast-schedule lightweight service on the *Humming Bird* and *Georgian* in 1946. But more typically, its moves were conservative, as older cars were rebuilt ... or reactive, as with near-grudging participation in the 1949 *Crescent* upgrade.
>
> Despite these conservative leanings, the L&N purchased 614 passenger cars between 1913 and 1969, and rostered another 92 through the LH&StL (1929) and NC&StL (1957) mergers. At the 1946 zenith of L&N passenger-miles, 587 were in service, and even as late as 1961, a fleet of 387 passenger cars burnished L&N's rails.
>
> While most passenger car types were represented in the roster, the fleet showed strong biases vs. what was typical on other roads. Heavyweight cars predominated on the L&N. In 1950, L&N's fleet was 7% lightweight vs. the industry average of 18%.... This ... was offset by L&N's skills in rebuilding aging heavyweights to lightweight standards, a specialty matched by only a few other roads.... Rebuilt heavyweights proved able substitutes for the more costly light-weights.... The sourcing of L&N's fleet presented yet another unusual bias, as four-fifths of L&N's non-wooden and non-sleeping cars would be built by ACF[56] — at best a minority builder on most other roads. The proximity of key ACF manufacturing facilities to L&N's routes undoubtedly helped cement this relationship, and many of L&N's heavyweights were built at ACF's Jeffersonville, Ind., plant just across the Ohio River from L&N's Louisville headquarters.

The number of passengers riding American rails during the years of the Second World War escalated tremendously nearly everywhere. A lot of this pertained to military travel, of course. In comparison to the post–Depression era, the flood of added bodies was good news to rail operators and the rail workforce. Although highways and airways would attract fickle travelers in significant numbers by the early 1950s, people flocked to trains from the late 1930s to the mid 1940s, a cause to celebrate. The L&N hauled its share of travelers in that time and maybe then some. In 1939, for instance, 3,202,442 patrons boarded L&N trains. Just five years hence, at the peak of the world's conflict in 1944, a recorded 12,440,022 travelers climbed aboard L&N cars, an appreciable 288 percent increase in five years. In the same time frame L&N reduced its number of passenger cars from 704 at the end of 1939 to 589 at the close of 1944.[57] Talk about sardine cans! Most of those trains were full up!

The impressive increase in travelers (and their commensurate revenues) fell sharply across America following the war. By 1950, as the L&N marked its centennial, just 2,624,736 people responded to a conductor's cry of "All aboard!" on the line's routes. In 1958, the figure had diminished to 1,097, 384; another 58 percent of paying customers— and merely a remnant of what was there in the mid 1940s— had vanished so far in that decade.[58] The days in which the freight-dominant railroads, including L&N, could profitably sustain passenger traffic were surely numbered. It was just a matter of time. Somebody had to figure out what was going to happen to those travelers next.

In the decade of the 1950s, the decreasing patronage on many L&N trains—mostly locals, but a few celebrated streamliners also—resulted in discontinuing 74 passenger trains and passenger service on 34 mixed trains (passenger-freight combos). Those reductions saved the railroad $5.7 million annually and let it focus on improving equipment and service on the remainder of its runs. Twenty-two lightweight sleeping cars exhibiting the latest innovations in rail travel were added to the *Flamingo, Georgian, Humming Bird, Pan-American* and *South Wind* trainsets. Before long another lightweight sleeper, plus 13 lightweight coaches, made their way on to these consists, significantly upgrading the rolling stock.

One of the last faces to guide the Louisville & Nashville Railroad arrived on the scene in the mid 1950s, William H. Kendall. Born March 24, 1910, at Somerville, Massachusetts, he was a veteran of no less than four railroads at 44 when he joined the L&N. A third-generation railroader whose grandfather was a Vermont station agent and whose dad was an Association of American Railroads official, Kendall's debut on the rails began early. He worked on the Ann Arbor Railroad during high school summer vacations in the 1920s. After graduating with an engineering degree from Dartmouth College in 1933, he joined the Pennsylvania Railroad as assistant track supervisor. Kendall moved on to the Atlantic Coast Line Railroad before transferring, in 1949, to the Clinchfield Railroad as general manager. Five years hence he joined the L&N as assistant to the president. In 1957, Kendall was elevated to the posts of vice president, general manager and director.

Elected L&N president on April 1, 1959, Kendall presided over what had by then become the second largest railroad in the South.[59] It was a road that could be primarily designated a bituminous coal-hauling workhorse and not a whole lot else. While the L&N continued a heavy investment in the passenger side of its business, diminishing effects resulted in more than nine-tenths of its revenues being derived then from its freight commerce. Operating revenues produced $227 million and profits of $13,244,000 in 1958, with only a fraction of that resulting from people-moving.[60]

Kendall remained on board through the transition in 1970-1971 into the hands of Seaboard Coast Line Industries, Inc. That conglomerate was a holding company formed in 1967 to oversee the merger of the Atlantic Coast Line and Seaboard Air Line railroads (combined as Seaboard Coast Line Railroad). On February 21, 1972, Kendall became vice chairman of the holding company. He retired in 1975, and lived in Louisville until shortly before his death at Jacksonville, Florida, on March 31, 1989.

Prime F. Osborn 3d succeeded Kendall as L&N president in 1972. Since 1969, Osborn had been president of Seaboard Coast Line Industries. He became the final L&N chief executive as the company joined with the SCL and other railroads to form the CSX Corporation in 1980. Born at Greensboro, Alabama, in 1915, Osborn earned a law degree from the University of Alabama before becoming that state's assistant state attorney general.[61] Following his release from the Army in the Second World War, he returned to civilian life as a staff attorney for the Gulf, Mobile and Ohio Railroad at Mobile. In 1951, Osborn joined the Louisville & Nashville Railroad in Louisville as general solicitor. He shifted to the Atlantic Coast Line Railroad at Wilmington, North Carolina, in 1957, taking a post as vice president and general counsel. He was one of the architects of the complex amalgamation of the ACL and the Seaboard Air Line Railroad that formed the Seaboard Coast Line Railroad in 1967. Osborn ascended to Seaboard Industries' presidency a couple of years later. After serving L&N as president (1972–1980) he became chairman of CSX Corporation, overseeing the L&N, SCL, Chessie System and a few other rail lines. He retired in 1982, succumbing to death at his Jacksonville home on January 4, 1986.

As the 1960s came on the L&N's well-patronized passenger services began to unravel noticeably. Through sleeping cars from New York to Nashville that the *Pan-American* had

L&N's South Louisville Shops was the line's chief maintenance and conversion facility. At this massive center, locomotives, freight and passenger cars were restored to running standards, retooled and rebuilt as needs modified. While light maintenance could be processed at distant points, L&N handled most major overhauls and extensive repairs here. A transfer table between shop structures is vital to operations. Similar to a railroad turntable but unable to turn equipment, the table's single-track length allows perpendicular shifts. The track serves a shed with stalls for multiple locomotives and rolling stock, greatly reducing space required for movement with lots of points (*courtesy John Landrum*).

exchanged with the Pennsylvania Railroad at Cincinnati were discontinued in 1964. The following year the same train's Bowling Green–Memphis section was abandoned. L&N was tightening its belt to cope with the downward spiral in rail travel that was affecting all U.S. carriers. Counter-lounge cars, rebuilt in the South Louisville Shops, replaced diner-lounge cars on the *Pan-American* in 1965. It was an obvious trend of the times. A once proud tradition was showing visible signs of tarnishing.

In 1966, the *Azalean* made its final run. That train had antecedents in the *New Orleans Limited*, whose history extended all the way back to the 1800s, making it — you may recall — L&N's longest-running passenger train. The *Limited* was renamed *Azalean* in 1936. For several years before it folded it operated at a much slower pace over the Cincinnati–New Orleans route than its respected tradition had witnessed in the glory days. Its ominous death did nothing to allay the gathering clouds hovering above frequent railway travelers. Other casualties followed that same year.

The durable *Dixie Flyer*, running over Chicago–Evansville–Nashville–Atlanta tracks, also disappeared in 1966. Also that year in another cost-cutting retrenchment, L&N combined the *Humming Bird* with the *Crescent* between Montgomery and New Orleans. A federal decision saw Railway Post Office cars disappear from the *Humming Bird*'s consist in 1967. They were realigned with aircraft and truck transport, putting further pressure on the railroads as a reliable source of revenue vanished into thin air. The same thing happened on the *Pan-American* in 1968. A similar source of dependable income dried up at about the same time when REA Express shifted its loads from railways to highways, eating further into rail's bottom lines.

The Chicago & Eastern Illinois Railroad deleted its Chicago–Evansville portion of the *Georgian* route in February 1968, leaving that carriage as a St. Louis–Atlanta only train. You will recall that this was unsuccessful at the *Georgian*'s inception in 1946, and that adding Chicago as an alternative destination raised the train's viability with travelers incredibly. A second adverse byproduct of the decision to drop the Chicago section occurred as the *Humming Bird* and *Georgian*'s schedules could no longer make simplified passenger exchanges workable at Nashville.

By spring 1969, in the waning days of American rail passenger service, just a quartet of people-moving consists persisted over the routes of the Louisville & Nashville Railroad. They included the *Gulf Wind* between New Orleans and Jacksonville; *Pan-American* between Cincinnati and New Orleans; and *South Wind* between Chicago and Jacksonville, with split sections seamlessly traveling from Jacksonville to Miami and Florida west coast points (the aforementioned streamliners ran daily offering sleeper and coach service); plus a daily unnamed all-coach train between St. Louis and Atlanta. When the public voiced its concern that passengers were being severely penalized by the railroad at the expense of freight traffic, L&N president William H. Kendall had a ready answer for them: "With diminishing patronage ... railroads were forced to take steps to reduce some services to offset revenue losses while continuing enough service to accommodate remaining passengers. The public ... often overlooked what railroads actually did to woo patronage well before they had to initiate service reductions."

Some tinkering with trains and schedules continued as the era of the freight-driven passenger service neared its end before Amtrak assumed it on May 1, 1971. When Penn Central discontinued sleepers over its part of the *South Wind* route between Louisville and Chicago in November 1970, L&N rescheduled the *Pan-American* to provide sleeping accommodations for both routes between Louisville and Montgomery while reducing its costs at the same time. Although L&N and Seaboard Coast Line attempted to maintain longstanding Chicago to Florida service at acceptable levels, without the Chicago to Louisville through sleepers continuing south, the route's popularity took a definite hit.

On the positive side, however, L&N's purchase of the eastern line of the Chicago & Eastern Illinois Railroad produced the *Danville Flyer*. This daily commuter train over a 123-mile stretch between Danville and Chicago offered travelers coach and buffet-lounge accommodations and proved popular in getting patrons to and from their bedroom communities and jobs in the big city. L&N, you may recall, had many years of experience with a commuter line it operated along the Mississippi Gulf coast to New Orleans.

In a tribute to L&N's passenger service and the people who provided it, a deputation of L&N admirers penned these lines:

> L&N passenger service by 1971 was but a pale reflection of what had been offered in 1940, or even 1961. But patrons then as now fondly remembered L&N for its clean, courteous and dependable service and the superb meals served in its dining cars. Recognition surely must go to countless men and women, living and deceased, who, over the years, gave life and purpose to this railroad's passenger service. Over telephones, at ticket and baggage counters, on trains, in dining cars and sleepers and in many other places little observed by the public, these employees served patrons ably and well and caused praise to be heaped on L&N passenger train travel.[62]

The humble beginnings of Amtrak are recorded in greater detail in a later chapter. For a while, the *South Wind* (renamed *Floridian* in November 1971) was the only traditional passenger train operating under that aegis over L&N rails. A Midwest *Auto Train*, begun in May 1974 between Louisville and Sanford, Florida, persisted to 1976, when Amtrak mixed that operation with the *Floridian*. An *Auto Train* running between Louisville and Florida on an

On its way out of Louisville in August 1971, the *South Wind*, recently acquired by Amtrak, passes L&N's extensive South Louisville Shops southbound over L&N trackage to Montgomery. There it will take SCL rails to Jacksonville, where it will divide — one section persisting to Tampa and one to Miami. Its journey began at Chicago over PRR and then moved onto L&N's newly-purchased Monon route before reaching Louisville. Led by two L&N E-units, it rolled through an era when the freight-only lines still provided motive power, preceding Amtrak's purchase of its own diesels and branding. *South Wind's* revered handle would be altered soon to *Floridian,* long before the train was suspended in 1979 (*courtesy Jay T. Thomson*).

erratic schedule (sometimes tri-weekly, twice weekly or weekly) never produced the results its sponsors anticipated and the service was deleted in late 1977. The *Floridian,* meanwhile, continued to October 9, 1979, when Amtrak pulled it from the schedule, citing insufficient support. Its cancellation marked the first time in 120 years that regularly scheduled passenger service wasn't offered somewhere on an L&N route.

A handful of reprieves, nonetheless — some of them less than impressive — was instituted over the next couple of decades. On October 1, 1980, the *Hoosier State* began running over L&N trackage between Crawfordsville and Maynard, Indiana, using other lines to extend service to Indianapolis and Chicago. The train persisted until it fell under the ax of budgetary cutbacks in September 1995. Furthermore in the 1980s, Amtrak transferred its tri-weekly Chicago–Washington, D.C., *Cardinal* to the Monon (L&N) route between Crawfordsville and Maynard. During the 1984 World's Fair in New Orleans, the *Gulf Breeze* operated over the L&N line between Mobile and the Crescent City from April to the following winter. In the late 1980s, Amtrak restored daytime coach service from Mobile to connect with the *Crescent* in Birmingham. The *Crescent* ran daily between New Orleans and New York City. In some 1995 cost-cutting measures the Mobile–Birmingham service was also eliminated.

The mainline routes of most of the major roads running across the South in the 19th and 20th centuries — the heyday of passenger service — are still in demand now. Although Amtrak offers infinitely reduced numbers of trains when compared with the freight-dominant railways it replaced, every major north-south route in Dixie is currently supplied by Amtrak

In January 1973, a trio of Auto Train U36B units (4008, 4007 and 4009) performed test runs over L&N tracks from Louisville to Sanford, Florida. A proposed route via South Etowah, Tennessee, shown here, was later rejected in favor of one through Nashville (*courtesy Jay T. Thomson*).

with one glaring exception: there is no passenger service over the Louisville & Nashville mains. David P. Morgan, who held the venerable pen of *Trains* magazine editor from 1952 to 1987, pontificated that the Louisville & Nashville Railroad was the "least recognized" member of the prestigious breed of leading U.S. railway systems.[63] Was he right? Looking at Amtrak's map today suggests that he may very well have been.

A string of thriving strategically situated mid-sized cities in the nation's interior have been left dispossessed of any railway passenger service. They include Chattanooga, Evansville, Knoxville, Lexington, Louisville, Mobile, Montgomery and Nashville. It's as if the ex-pivotal routes between Chicago, Cincinnati and other Midwest centers and the cities of Atlanta, the Florida points on both coasts and New Orleans don't matter any longer — and haven't mattered in more than three decades.

> Many years ago, the fine singer Jean Ritchie recorded a song called "The L & N Don't Stop Here Anymore," which mourned the passing of a played-out coal mining town. It is a beautiful and nostalgic song, and today it rings true in quite another way. The system of railroads built and acquired by the L & N over the years continues to operate and do a thriving business. The tracks and all their appurtenances are still there, but they have long since lost their original identity and become synonymous components. The railroad still serves most of the same cities and towns, but the L & N don't stop there anymore.[64]

In a very real sense it's a travesty that consumers across a vast region of the nation's hinterland have been thereby disenfranchised, particularly at a time when mass transit has acquired a far greater magnitude in the nation's psyche. To restore it will require large subsidies from the federal transportation budget and participating state and local government coffers. That could provide sound infrastructure, reliable rolling stock, concerned management, proper scheduling, sufficient marketing and other factors to insure success. Given that, routes extending southward from the Great Lakes to the Gulf and Florida's beckoning resorts could

In its heyday this depot on L&N's main in the south central Alabama hamlet of Greenville saw locals board for Montgomery, Birmingham and Atlanta above it and Mobile, Pensacola and New Orleans below it. Later, when Amtrak assumed passenger traffic, the Greenville station prospered again. From the late 1980s to 1995, travelers caught the *Gulf Breeze* here running from Mobile to Birmingham, linking with the *Crescent* (New Orleans–New York) at Birmingham. The photograph is dated June 13, 1995, at the end of the era (*courtesy Clyde Woodruff*).

once again become reality — just like those trains that never quit radiating southward daily on a handful of routes from Washington, D.C., and Chicago (in other directions).

As the 21st century approached, Amtrak attempted to partially plug the gap between them by running daily sleepers and coaches from Chicago to Louisville. The *Kentucky Cardinal* was unsuccessful in drawing a steady clientele, however. Its quick demise could be heavily attributed to bad track between Indianapolis and Louisville. That portion of the trip could be covered by automobile in less than two hours while the faltering roadbed netted a 30 mile-per-hour limit by rail equaling a five-hour journey between Indianapolis and Louisville. With several more hours en route to Chicago the journey was far too unwieldy to sustain most people's interest.

The hole in the schedule from the Great Lakes to the Gulf with through service to Florida's resorts remains unplugged. It probably should be one of the earliest oversights addressed by Amtrak officials as they seek to supply needs that presently exist in the nation's heartland.[65] For cities like Louisville and Nashville, with metropolitan statistical populations between 1.2 and 1.5 million each at the close of 2007, it's a particularly cruel turn. Here are municipalities for whom one of the nation's leading Class 1 rail carriers was named — one of the few classic fallen flags whose original moniker was never altered in 13 decades at a time that millions traveled its strategic routes. It's unthinkable now that both namesake cities remain disconnected from passenger rail service, and have been almost totally disenfranchised since 1979.

Is this not an idea whose time has come?

10

NASHVILLE, CHATTANOOGA
& ST. LOUIS RAILWAY
Short Route from the Great Lakes to Florida

The narrative of the Nashville, Chattanooga & St. Louis Railway (NC&StL) is intertwined with that of the Louisville & Nashville Railroad (L&N) to such an extent that — to a novice railfan — there might appear little to distinguish the separate components of that duo at a mere cursory glance. Rest assured, however, that each line was decidedly conspicuous in its own right. While the pair of Class 1 railroads eventually merged — setting up the initial union of two major U.S. roads in modern history while triggering multiple additional combinations of other roads that soon followed — both commercial enterprises brought laudable assets to the blend.[1] While the pair was a business partnership that worked in tandem throughout their long histories, the twin roads may have performed even more judiciously once they were administered under the same roof.

The union, in 1957, established a rail line that instantly achieved status as the third most extensive in the South.[2] Within two years the amalgamation moved up that conspicuous ladder to command the second spot among all Southern roads.[3] The sum of its parts working cohesively together was impressive in its ability to supply the demands of clientele throughout the mid–South. As the previous chapter hints, the combined L&N and NC&StL responded well to the transportation needs of both freight and passenger traffic between the key markets it filled.

By any account the NC&StL could be labeled a "bridge" carrier, plying most of its noteworthy trains over what came to be widely known as "The Dixie Line." The company's enduring slogan was emblematic of a 735-mile main that extended from Memphis to Atlanta in the decades before unification. With a branch reaching as far north as Paducah, Kentucky, the NC&StL joined lines tying colossal Midwest metropolises like Chicago and St. Louis to prominent southeastern targets far beyond the southern end of its route.[4] The latter destinations weren't limited to but included Florida resorts on both coasts. The NC&StL's strategic geographical location gave it a commanding advantage in serving communities separated by wide distances. At the same time the line generated local traffic of its own, rolling over some of the most heavily traveled tourist tracks in America.

And it did so with panache, with an eye firmly fixed on creature comforts. The NC&StL was duly signified with an earned reputation for providing distinctive travel service that its recurring patrons came to expect: steady, first class, commensurate with larger lines that carried passenger cars from the ends of its mainline to markets in widely diverse territories. NC&StL invariably proved it was up to the challenges, earning the reputation of a reliably stable transporter for decades.

The tale of this tactically situated line predates that of its bigger brother, the L&N, by a few years. The L&N was chartered by the Commonwealth of Kentucky on March 5, 1850. But railroad promoters in Tennessee and Georgia were already at work well before then. The NC&StL's earliest forebear was the Western & Atlantic Railway (W&A), organized in 1836 by the state of Georgia.[5] There can be no question that the W&A was imperative to the eventual success of the NC&StL as the latter sought a route into the key Atlanta market.

Probably no ancestor superseded the 151-mile Nashville & Chattanooga Railway (N&C), chartered in December 1845, in importance to this mix. As the first rail line to flourish in the Volunteer State, the N&C fashioned the earliest trackage linking the Cumberland and Tennessee rivers. It was to ultimately be the NC&StL's most heavily traveled route, including passenger service between the namesake cities and beyond: its stems extended to hamlets like Sparta and Pikeville, Tennessee; to Huntsville, Attalla and Gadsden, Alabama; and — with interline connections at Chattanooga — it offered continuing service to Knoxville, Johnson City and Bristol, Tennessee.

More than eight years transpired before the finished line of the Nashville and Chattanooga Railway became reality. For the first time farmers and suppliers could readily access dependable transportation for their agricultural crops that were raised in middle Tennessee's fertile soil. As a result they could reach the infinite markets that beckoned beyond the cargo ships that docked along the Atlantic seaboard.

Thinking ahead and envisioning an even larger prominence for their road than purely regional status, the Nashville and Chattanooga's backers expected to one day extend their railroad well beyond its then-limited confines. Hoping to reach more distant interior turf and the potential for commercial development it proffered, they anticipated a rail system tying crucial Midwestern and Ohio Valley markets to the mounting Southeast. The fact that their road ultimately became a conduit in the process was immaterial to them; their intent was resolute and was eventually realized as the business coup they had long intended.

In 1846, the chief engineer of the Georgia Railroad, John Edgar Thomson, was hired by the N&C to ride on horseback on a trek between those namesake cities. He was given authority to survey and essentially situate the route that was, in due course, to connect those dual municipalities. In his path stood the formidable elevations of the Highland Rim and the Cumberland Plateau, which challenged him but weren't insurmountable. He would find a way to negotiate them. Among his recommendations, Thompson urged that a 2,228-foot tunnel be bored through the Cumberland Mountains near Cowan, Tennessee, and not many miles north of the Alabama state line. Thompson's design was adopted and the challenging tunneling project was launched in the spring of 1849. It would take two years to complete — readied well before the tracks reached it, by the way. Upon its completion that tunnel was widely considered to be one of the engineering marvels of its time.

In December 1850, meanwhile, the N&C's first locomotive was delivered to the road's headquarters at Nashville. In April of the following year — with nine miles of track already completed — the Nashville and Chattanooga sent its first train from the capital city to Antioch (which is today a Nashville suburb). Tracks were readied as far as Murfreesboro in July 1851, a distance of 31 miles southeast of Nashville. As the work progressed a couple of new towns sprang up along the railway's route. Included were Tullahoma in Coffee County and Estill Springs in Franklin County.

By the following spring (1852) tracks had been laid to Decherd, 82 miles from Nashville. At that juncture stagecoaches were meeting the trains to transport continuing travelers to Huntsville, Alabama. There riders transferred to Tennessee River steamers for the final leg of their journeys into Chattanooga. When the tracks were extended another 40 miles beyond Decherd to Bridgeport, Alabama — with rails situated by the banks of the Tennessee River — one step in the convoluted transit process, the stagecoach, could be eliminated. Steamers ferried passengers the remaining 29 miles to Chattanooga. The end was in sight! Finally, by early 1854, the 151 miles of track had been laid and opened at last between Nashville and Chattanooga.

The completed road might be a curious one to anyone studying a map of the route. Even though both Nashville and Chattanooga are major Tennessee cities, the mainline descends into a second state — and not into Georgia, whose southern border the Chattanooga city limits rest hard against. Because of the Appalachian mountainous chain that encompasses the municipality, trailblazing horseback rider John Thompson found an easier — if not meandering — route into town. His course negotiated fewer and easier summits than the most direct path. For a few miles his circuitous itinerary carried him and his mount into neighboring northeastern Alabama before it turned northward into the Volunteer State for a gallop directly into Chattanooga.[6]

When the Nashville and Chattanooga Railway was completed to the latter town, it was connected with the Georgia-owned Western & Atlantic Railway (W&A). Having been surveyed in the 1830s—the decade in which America's railroads were inaugurated—the W&A built northward during the 1840s from what was to become Atlanta. By 1850, trackage arrived in Chattanooga. In June 1854, the Nashville and Chattanooga Railway promoted passenger service that extended all the way to the Atlantic seaboard cities of Savannah and Charleston. The route to the coast relied on a handful of cooperating rail systems operating beyond Nashville and Chattanooga by way of Atlanta.

In the meantime an extension at the other end of the N&C's mainline would soon be available, too, witnessing continuous traffic to Louisville. Tracks of the Louisville & Nashville Railroad were open for daily runs in October 1859. Gradually America's interior was becoming accessible to more extensive national and international travel. In the decade of the 1850s, N&C was already on a course toward becoming a conduit (bridge) taking people on journeys that were to stretch well beyond the ends of its line.

In this same epoch yet another precursor of the NC&StL Railway emerged, in the form of the Nashville & Northwestern Railway (N&N). Established in 1852, it began what turned into a 16-year construction undertaking. Ultimately it connected the Volunteer State capital with the Mississippi River, 168 miles west at Hickman, Kentucky.

Let us digress for a moment. Parenthetically, you might note the multiple occasions when waterways came into play in determining a railroad's decisions about routing and terminations for its tracks. This was done with good reason. At this time navigable channels still offered the nation's principal method of moving goods and throngs across great expanses of territory. Roads were often nonexistent or extremely mediocre. Sometimes they existed as little more than pathways. Invariably they were subject to nature's whims. Gasoline-powered conveyances (cars, trucks, etc.) were a half-century away from reality and many more years would lapse before they reached the common man in productive quantities. Foot, horseback and stagecoach were still the prime means of most individuals' travel. Each required significant time, patience and even courage in some situations when contemplating especially lengthy and arduous treks.

For obvious reasons, then, it's clear why those early railroad developers were mindful of the major navigable rivers, lakes and oceans that were nearest them. They attempted to link their systems to water routes whenever possible for they didn't have a whole lot of other options, especially as they tried to reach shipping channels that were linked to the outside world. Those connections moved people, raw materials and finished goods to distant places nationally and internationally. They were often considered a godsend by local railway interests.

Returning to the story, the Nashville & Northwestern began construction at Hickman at the farthest end of its planned course in west Tennessee. It arrived at Union City in 1855. Six years later it was extended to McKenzie. At that juncture the War Between the States interrupted. Not only did the project experience delays, what had already been completed suffered extensive damage principally at the hands of Union General William T. Sherman. He gave orders to his Northern troops to "destroy virtually every physical asset" that the militia encountered on a tumultuous rampage to the sea at Savannah, Georgia.

The N&C, too, was vital to both the Union and Confederate forces and randomly pressed into service at sundry times in supplying both armies. The line was attacked, sabotaged, damaged and repaired on numerous occasions by the opposing mercenaries. Furthermore, the devastation hit several Georgia roads including the Western & Atlantic. It was not until 1868 — three years beyond the close of the divisional conflict — that passengers could finally board a train in Nashville and ride unhindered to the end of the N&N line on the Mississippi River at Hickman. Little by little the pieces that were to contribute strategic components to the NC&StL were falling into place.

Yet another key division of that future achievement was a line that extended through rail travel to Memphis. By utilizing the Louisville & Nashville's Memphis branch from McKenzie to Memphis, the Nashville and Chattanooga Railway offered continuous passenger service between Nashville and Memphis. That changed in 1920. Most travelers between Nashville and Memphis were then rerouted through Bruceton and Jackson, replacing a shift to the L&N's Louisville–Bowling Green–Memphis tracks at McKenzie.[7]

In 1870, the N&C began operating the N&N under lease, and two years hence it formally acquired that road. N&C also gained connections with a precursor of the Illinois Central Railroad at Martin, Tennessee, and the Mobile & Ohio Railroad (later Gulf, Mobile & Ohio) at Union City, Tennessee, which were to figure prominently in the assets of the NC&StL. The following year (1873), the Nashville and Chattanooga's directors revised the road's nomenclature to signify it with the much more encompassing brand Nashville, Chattanooga & St. Louis Railway. Backers envisioned a 319-mile mainline between Hickman and Chattanooga eventually linking St. Louis—situated above Hickman on the Mississippi River—with Nashville, Chattanooga, Atlanta and even beyond.

Still more daring moves were taking place. In 1879, the NC&StL bought into an uncompleted Owensboro & Nashville Railway in the Bluegrass State. At about the same time it took an interest in the Illinois and Indiana segments of the St. Louis & Southeastern Railway. That line joined East St. Louis, Illinois, on the eastern banks of the Mississippi River, with Evansville. "The threat was too much for the Louisville & Nashville, with its own aspirations of growth," noted one wag.[8] Sensing eminent risk to its expansion plans, the L&N responded swiftly.

In 1879, the L&N purchased a line extending from Evansville to Nashville. The St. Louis & Southeastern Railway had opened the tracks only a few years before. The following year (1880) L&N went still further in halting any grand schemes that a visibly competitive NC&StL might be harboring: it bought controlling interest in its Nashville-based rival. While L&N permitted the ambitious, older, and perhaps not-as-well-financed NC&StL to maintain its offices and shops in Nashville, there could be no debate about which line was the child and which was the parent in that relationship. The all-encompassing decisions about the NC&StL's destiny henceforth would be announced in Louisville.

That "separation" arrangement remained in force for 77 years, until the L&N fully integrated the NC&StL into its corporate structure. At that juncture (1957) it replaced the moniker and "The Dixie Line" motto with L&N's "The Old Reliable." The headquarters building in Nashville was closed and the administrative staff shifted to Louisville, integrating another 4,000 people into L&N's workforce of approximately 21,000. By then, of course, the heyday of passenger traffic had passed. Despite that fact, L&N would remain active in the people-moving business until Amtrak took over its final train on May 1, 1971.

After L&N bought NC&StL in 1880, another decade elapsed before the combo finally reached the imposing market of metropolitan Atlanta, where numerous rail lines already terminated.[9] At the other end of the NC&StL spectrum, meanwhile, L&N leased its own interests in a couple of rail connections west of Nashville to NC&StL in 1896: Paducah, Tennessee & Alabama Railway and Tennessee Midland Railway. Converging at Lexington, Tennessee, those twin lines formed a strategic 230-mile route connecting Paducah with Memphis. Overseen by NC&StL, this opportunity opened a valuable course to transport people and products from the Ohio River area of far west Kentucky to the extensive rail carriers operating from Memphis in southerly and southwesterly directions. Some of those were bound for New Orleans and other key coastal destinations.

As the rest of the 19th century played out, branch lines sprang up in the NC&StL domain in Tennessee and north Alabama. By 1905, with 1,100 route miles in its portfolio, the NC&StL had extended its trackage as far as it would ever go.[10] In 1900, the L&N and NC&StL formed Nashville Terminals to build Union Station, which opened in September of that year. Nashville Terminals furthermore designed the local rail traffic flow that existed in the city until the L&N's Radnor Yard was expanded in the early 1950s.

In the late 1890s and early 1900s, meanwhile, under the prodding of Major W. L. Danley, NC&StL general passenger agent, the line turned a spotlight on improving personal rail transportation. Heaviest emphasis was given the Midwest-to-Florida route which, from the NC&StL's stance, showed the most potential as a prime moneymaker. Marketing began with the *Dixie Flyer*, a Nashville–Atlanta consist in 1892, with through sleeping car service continuing to Jacksonville over cooperating roads' tracks.[11] Danley touted "The Lookout Mountain Route" as he urged impending patrons to view "the mountains of Tennessee and Georgia and the Battlefields of the Civil War" on their way to and from Florida's beaches and their Midwestern domiciles.

The Chicago & Eastern Illinois (C&EI), Illinois Central (IC) and L&N railroads stood to gain significant business by attracting the *Dixie Flyer* to their systems. All of them lobbied heavily to continue the passenger train to Chicago at the far western reaches of NC&StL tracks. IC was the first to get the nod, originating separate sections in Chicago and St. Louis that were ultimately combined on their way south.

By 1901, the *Chicago & Florida Limited* was nevertheless substantially abridging that trip. It cut the time that the *Dixie Flyer* spent in transit by discovering a shorter (and thereby, faster) route via C&EI to Evansville, L&N to Nashville, and NC&StL to Atlanta before other carriers forwarded it to the Sunshine State. During its 32-hour journey between the Windy City and a southernmost terminus at St. Augustine, the *Limited* proffered "wide vestibules, steam heat, gas lights, and dining car service" to indulge riders who were fortunate enough to be aboard. The success of the *Dixie Flyer*, plus an NC&StL sleeper, the *Quickstep*, rolling over the NC&StL main linking Nashville and Atlanta — along with the Florida resort boom — figured prominently in the premier of the *Chicago & Florida Limited*.

A fleet of Midwest-to-Florida trains alongside the *Dixie Flyer* emerged over the NC&StL's mainline in the 1920s, including the *Dixie Limited* and a handful of winter season consists. The Central of Georgia Railway (CofG) eagerly awaited the expanding business it was to pick up at the lower end of the NC&StL's tracks. CofG, another "bridge" operator, was responsible for ferrying those interline trains to the hands of other railways— its most frequent partner being the Atlantic Coast Line Railroad. ACL maintained extensive service to both Florida coasts as well as its interior.

In the second and third decades of the 20th century, L&N focused on significantly improving its depots through refurbishments, remodelings or replacements. New stations were erected at Atlanta, Bruceton, Chattanooga and Memphis. In 1923, an eight-story headquarters edifice was erected in Nashville at 10th and Broadway, cattycornered to Union Station. It replaced a smaller administrative office building that had been in use since 1881.

Starting in 1940, NC&StL launched a systemwide upgrade of its rolling stock and facilities to bring them up to contemporary standards. In the mid 1950s, new yards were jointly completed with L&N at Nashville (Radnor) and Atlanta (Hills Park, later renamed Tilford). Meanwhile, in the decade of the 1940s, NC&StL began converting steam-driven locomotives to more efficient, faster diesel models—for both freight and passenger hauling. The first lightweight streamliner, the *Georgian*, appeared on NC&StL rails in 1946. It became a workhorse that for years ferried tens of thousands of travelers up and down the mainline between Nashville and Atlanta.

The following year (1947) the *City of Memphis*, also a streamliner, traversed the NC&StL rails between Nashville and Memphis. With upgraded Centralized Traffic Control and an extensive reduction of curves and grades realized throughout the system, NC&StL decreased travel times by speeding passenger trains along while concurrently enhancing safety precautions. The steam-powered *City of Memphis* routinely made its 239-mile trek with six intermediate stops at speeds averaging 47.8 miles an hour. It finished the trip in five hours, whereas the shortest span for previous trainsets over that course had been six hours and 50 minutes. By 1953, all NC&StL steam locomotives were converted to diesels.

> The merger of NC&StL into Louisville & Nashville in 1957 was long anticipated.... What with the competitive climate the rail industry faced after World War II, the economies of a single system made good sense. Initially, opposition to the merger came from NC&StL stockholders and the city of Nashville and led to lengthy hearings by the ICC. In promoting the merger, Louisville & Nashville emphasized again the benefits a stronger, unified company could bring to passengers, shippers, employees and the region as a whole.[12]

The summons for merger had, of course, been issued more than three-quarters of a century earlier when the L&N bought majority stock in its smaller rival. The union of the two simply hadn't been executed to its fullest extent. The Interstate Commerce Commission ruled in Louisville & Nashville's favor on August 30, 1957, and the dual lines thereafter were fully combined.

Modern historians have, in some cases surprisingly, felt it their duty to vilify the actions of the L&N as they revealed more details about those transactions, to wit:

> The Louisville and Nashville Railroad, an aggressive, potential competitor of the NC&StL, gained controlling interest in it in 1880 with a hostile stock takeover that created massive civic rancor between the cities of Nashville and Louisville....
> The L&N, itself controlled by the Atlantic Coast Line Railroad [beginning in 1902] in the same fashion that the L&N controlled the NC&StL, was merged in to the Seaboard System Railroad, and then into the CSX freight rail conglomerate, which continues to use the original NC&StL tracks between Nashville, Chattanooga and Atlanta.[13]
> The railroad became a victim of a vicious takeover by the Louisville & Nashville Railroad in 1880 (the two railroads were bitter rivals), an act which resulted in significant distrust towards the L&N by the cities of Nashville and Louisville for some time.[14]

While it may seem a "vicious takeover" to some today, when one considers that the L&N dealt the NC&StL a fairly objective hand for 77 years, the "takeover" doesn't appear quite as sadistic as those words might lead us to believe. Until 1957, the NC&StL was left with its own corporate offices, shops and management team in place, along with its name, insignia and slogan. Outwardly it appeared to the public as if it was a separate operation. Thus "vicious takeover" and "a hostile stock takeover" coupled with "massive civic rancor" by "bitter rivals" resulting in "significant distrust" seems, under the circumstances—at least on the surface—

In late 1940, this streamlined Pacific 277 supplied motive power for two popular Budd-light passenger trains under L&N control. They were the *Dixie Flagler* and *South Wind*, which operated on alternating days and routes between dual Florida coasts and Chicago. The pair was under L&N auspices between Atlanta and Evansville (*Flagler*) and between Montgomery and Louisville (*Wind*). Debuting as seasonal only, the duo was so acclaimed by travelers that they became mainstays, persisting all year for years. The *South Wind* lasted past Amtrak's arrival in 1971, in fact (*courtesy Chuck Blardone*).

to be possibly misplaced assumptions. A handful of texts issued in the last couple of decades don't suggest those harsh realities to any real extent. Common sense hints that some of those sources either simply might have misunderstood the situation or perhaps magnified its gravity, for reasons unknown, beyond what actually transpired.

A NC&StL Preservation Society, formed in 2001, fosters interest in the historic rail system today. Its prime exhibit is the line's final remaining steam engine, No. 576, donated to the city of Nashville by NC&StL in 1953. The black J3-57 class 4-8-4 locomotive, manufactured in 1942 by ALCO and originally branded a Yellow Jacket, is on public display under a trainshed erected especially for it in Nashville's Centennial Park off West End Avenue.

A host of trains with the "Dixie" labeling may have been responsible for the NC&StL gaining the sobriquet of "The Dixie Line." Certainly the aphorism and the fact that the *Dixie Flagler, Dixie Flyer, Dixie Limited, Dixieland* and similarly-themed trainsets regularly plied its mainline made indelible impressions on the traveling public. "The Dixie Line" became a persuasive sales tool that NC&StL extensively capitalized on in its marketing efforts, as it repetitiously touted "the shortest route between the Great Lakes and Florida."

The splendid *Dixie Flagler* initially appeared on December 17, 1940, running between Chicago and Miami every third day, alternating days with two other superb trains on different routes. At its start the *Flagler*— named after Florida East Coast Railway (FEC) developer Henry Morrison Flagler, over whose tracks it proceeded from Jacksonville to Miami — was considered a winter-only run. Yet it became such an overnight hit the *Flagler* was retained for year-round service. And although it debuted as a coach-only consist the train soon added Pullmans, which had the effect of significantly raising its stature with the traveling public. The southbound *Flagler* arrived in Nashville via L&N from Evansville and before that C&EI trackage from the Windy City. It continued making the journey into 1954.

Premiering in January 1936, the seasonal *Dixieland* both preceded and superseded the *Dixie Flagler*. It began nearly five years before its sibling and lasted three years beyond it to 1957. The coach-Pullman *Dixieland* was the first one-night-out train linking Chicago and Miami, departing the Windy City early one morning and arriving in Miami the following evening. It was also the first to traverse the whole route in as little as 32 hours. The *Dixieland* ran via Evansville, Nashville, Atlanta and Jacksonville over the tracks of a half-dozen interline partners: C&EI, L&N, NC&StL, Atlanta Birmingham & Coast, ACL, and FEC.

Timing harshly governed the *Flagler* and *Dixieland*. The pair was run against the clock. Only two stops—five minutes at Chattanooga and a conditional stop at Tullahoma—were listed in timetables appearing for both trains prior to 1942. The *Dixieland*, pulled by steam power over the 286-mile Nashville–Atlanta portion, made the journey in six and a half hours, averaging 43 miles an hour over grade that rose and fell by two percent. The lightweight *Flagler* on the other hand raced between Nashville and Atlanta in slightly more than six hours, a rather astonishing achievement, yet one that would eventually be eclipsed.

The *Dixie Limited* was still another "name" train pressed into service on the acclaimed Chicago–Atlanta–Florida route. Its inaugural was celebrated in the 1920s. Along with the *Dixie Flyer*, the duo provided NC&StL's foremost trainsets in that epoch. For years the *Limited*'s arrivals and departures at Nashville were timed to coincide with the north-south *New Orleans Limited*. The latter was the L&N's most durable mainline passenger consist, sprinting nightly between Cincinnati, Louisville, Nashville, Birmingham, Montgomery and New Orleans. At Nashville, both *Limited*s seamlessly exchanged sleeping cars, allowing some of their travelers to proceed in opposite directions from those that their originating locomotives would have taken them. Riders on the *Dixie Limited* might be transferred to the *New Orleans Limited* while Cincinnati-boarding passengers might be switched to the *Dixie Limited*, then heading for Florida resorts.

The better known *Dixie Flyer*, previously mentioned, also made its first trip in the 1920s. In either direction the *Flyer*'s originating two-night run between Chicago and Jacksonville netted a scenic daylight excursion through middle and east Tennessee and north Georgia. Northbound the L&N provided crews from Nashville to Evansville plus a section continuing on to St. Louis. The C&EI took over a section that traversed the tracks from Evansville to Chicago.

In the Great Depression period the southbound *Flyer* and *Limited* were joined with the *Southland* and *Flamingo*— also interline trains plying other routes to Atlanta — on their dash between Atlanta and both Florida coasts. As the Central of Georgia handled those trips south of Atlanta, it was necessary for *Flyer* and *Limited* passengers to transfer depots in Atlanta. NC&StL, L&N and Georgia Railway called at Union Station; nearby Terminal Station served Central of Georgia, Atlanta & West Point, Seaboard Air Line, Southern and a few smaller lines.

There were lots more unnamed passenger trains in NC&StL's collection, some of them serving larger cities, some branch line communities only, some with complete consists, others as mixed runs (including freight, mail and passengers). Yet there were also some added "name" trains. The *Lookout* left Chattanooga every morning for Nashville, returning in the late afternoon. Another, the *Volunteer*, provided one of three daily round-trips offered between Memphis and Nashville.

Although the *Dixie Flyer* might have been certified as the NC&StL's flagship conveyance for the 1920s, 1930s and early 1940s, by the late 1940s it was outclassed by the newer lightweight *Georgian* streamliner.[15] Entering the competition in November 1946, the *Georgian* boasted no checked baggage, which aided its crews in moving the train at a speedier clip. Its consists included a quartet of Pullmans—three running between Chicago and Atlanta plus another between St. Louis and Atlanta; a similar quantity of reserved-seat coaches; dual dining cars between Chicago–Atlanta and St. Louis–Evansville; and a club-lounge car between Chicago–Atlanta. Compared with the *Flyer*'s pair of Pullmans (Chicago–Jacksonville, St. Louis–Nashville); unreserved coaches between Chicago–Jacksonville, St. Louis–Evansville and Jacksonville–Miami; and dining cars operating from Evansville–Atlanta and Jacksonville–Miami, well — there really was no comparison. The *Georgian* was superior to the *Flyer* in every way.

For many years the *Humming Bird*, another streamliner introduced at the same time as the *Georgian* and running over the L&N's north-south main, had consequential bearing on the *Georgian*'s timing. With the *Humming Bird* traveling between Cincinnati and New Orleans and the *Georgian* between Chicago, St. Louis and Atlanta, the two trains' schedules were adjusted in order for sleeping car passengers to be rerouted during overnight meetings in Nashville as the pair crossed paths. The same kinds of exchanges had long been practiced at Nashville with previous trains, at least as early as the 1920s. As already noted the *Dixie Limited* operated between Chicago and St. Louis, Atlanta and Florida and the *New Orleans Limited* ran between Cincinnati and the Crescent City. Both seamlessly transferred sleeping car occupants overnight at Nashville.

You will recall that in the track race between Atlanta and Nashville, by the early 1940s, the steam-driven *Dixieland*— impressively running that distance in six and a half hours— and the lightweight *Dixie Flagler*— operating at a pace just over six hours— were setting new speed records. Now what's a record without a challenger? And a new victor? While the *Flagler* typically plied the course over extensive mountainous terrain at an incredible 43 miles per hour, an upstart *Georgian*— the first trainset with diesel power on the *Dixie Line*— shattered the *Flagler*'s striking performance. At 48 miles an hour it plied those tracks in six hours flat. And it never slowed down after leaving Nashville, continuing at a stupefying gait to St. Louis. In those days from start to finish the *Georgian*'s 609-mile trip between Atlanta and St. Louis was routinely completed in 13 hours, a never-before-witnessed triumph.[16]

While the *Dixie Flyer*'s ancestry dated to 1886, it was withdrawn in 1966. The *Georgian*, on the other hand, persisted on the infamous route to the spring of 1969, when time finally caught up with it. It was the last of the great "name" passenger trains to vacate the long-established *Dixie Line*, having outlived every other consist that figured into casting NC&StL's durable motto.

On May 1, 1971, when Amtrak assumed most of the nation's rail passenger service, the last surviving train plying that route — a nameless lackluster consist running between St. Louis and Atlanta — vanished. Shorn of sleepers, diners and lounges, its schedule had paradoxically continued to match that of the glorious *Georgian* in far better days. With that final train's demise, an inglorious end transpired to a fabulous epoch of travel along a spectacularly scenic route through "the mountains of Tennessee and Georgia and the Battlefields of the Civil War."

11

NORFOLK & WESTERN RAILWAY
The Last Steam Road in America

The Norfolk & Western Railway (N&W) may be best remembered as another of the bituminous (soft) coal-haulers that plied the Appalachian Mountains. Those carriers earned the bulk of their revenues by ferrying millions of tons of black diamonds from their natural habitats to ships docked at multiple inland and coastal ports. From there the precious cargo was transported over waterways to national and international destinations. The Chesapeake & Ohio (C&O), Clinchfield (CRR), Virginian (VGN) and other lines joined N&W in making their living principally from this trade.

N&W maintained only a handful of passenger trains in the 20th century. Its concentration there could seldom be considered much of anything but unpretentious. In addition to its significant commitment to coal traffic, another explanation for the road's reluctance to invest inordinate sums in people-moving is that there were relatively few travelers living within its service field. The pool from which it could draw potential patronage remained, frankly, incredibly small.[1] For that reason alone, most of the passengers who rode over N&W tracks were aboard long-distance trains that operated under the joint auspices of several common carriers. Examples of this pattern will be explored in greater depth presently.

> The Norfolk & Western Railway was a unique operation of modest proportions that achieved recognition beyond contemporary railroads of similar size. In actuality, Norfolk & Western had two differing styles. Before 1964, it was a coal hauler known for its excellent financial performance, and which operated arguably the finest fleet of steam motive power at the head of long coal trains. The routine tonnage carried on these trains would be considered records elsewhere. Changes began first with dieselization and then merger with Virginian Railway in the late 1950s. In 1964 Norfolk & Western leased, merged with, or purchased several other railroads to expand its operation, becoming a major Midwestern carrier. As such it operated routes from Norfolk VA and Buffalo NY to Chicago IL and St. Louis and Kansas City MO.[2]

But its humble origins would belie whatever acclamation it ultimately achieved after more than 200 railroad mergers transpiring over 150 years. It started as the Norfolk and Western Railroad before falling into bankruptcy and, in 1896, emerging as the "Railway" of the same destinations. It dates to 1836, when the Commonwealth of Virginia granted a charter to a company labeling itself City Point Railroad.[3] Its mission was to construct a rail line joining the central Virginia towns of Petersburg and City Point (later renamed Hopewell). The two were only nine miles apart but with overland travel limited to foot, horseback and buckboard, a more modern (easier, faster, reliable) means of transportation was sought. With the spate of railroads surfacing in America in the decade of the 1830s, Virginians intended to be at the forefront of the breakthrough. They were already experimenting elsewhere with the prospect of establishing rail lines in sundry locations.

In 1847, the City Point Railroad was reorganized, purchased by the City of Petersburg and renamed the Appomattox Railroad.[4] Seven years hence, in 1854 — then much too small to be advantageous in the larger world as a stand-alone system, a world in which competition for rail services was rapidly expanding — the Appomattox was acquired by the Southside Railroad (SRR). The latter enterprise was chartered in 1846. With its construction launched in 1849, it was completed five years later. In 1852, two years before it was finished, the SRR was connected with the Richmond and Danville Railroad at Burkesville, appreciably widening its reach beyond its immediate surroundings. Southside joined Petersburg with the farming lands south and west of that town as it rolled along to Lynchburg. From City Point to Lynchburg, its trackage extended 141 miles. In buying the Appomattox (formerly City Point), incidentally — the original wedge of the eventual Norfolk & Western Railway — Southside gained access to a site on a navigable portion of the James River, a crucial dynamic. This central Virginia waterway flowed to the banks of City Point.

The War Between the States (1861–1865) had a major impact on Southside Railroad, just as it did on many other Southern rail carriers. SRR was vital to the Confederate States of America, as Richmond was that body's capital. Beyond the lines of battle until the war's final year, the principal damage Southside suffered was the financial weakness caused by Confederate compensation policies and currency.[5] In the war's ending year considerable physical impairment was inflicted by both sides in the fight, continuing until the conflict ended in April 1865. The final battles occurred near Appomattox Station on the Southside Railroad at Appomattox Courthouse. Ironically, in 1864-1865, the nine-mile Appomattox Railroad portion was of great value to Union troops during a siege at Petersburg. General Ulysses S. Grant used the road to move men and material from the port at City Point to territory south and east of Petersburg. By then that section of the route was being run by the U.S. Military Railroad, which took over many of the Union-captured lines.

Realizing the growing importance of expanding, in 1870, a trio of nearby rail carriers formed a coalition. Operating under the nomenclature Atlantic, Mississippi & Ohio Railroad (AM&O), the Norfolk & Petersburg, Southside, and Virginia & Tennessee railroads cast their lots together. The blended company covered 408 miles between Norfolk and Bristol, Virginia/Tennessee, with every intention of expanding westward. Spearheading the venture was Major General William Mahone (1826–1895), who sequentially presided over all three roads in the order named during the period 1858 to 1870. Although the AM&O initially performed well, in due course an 1873 panic that swept the nation threw it into receivership.

At a foreclosure auction sale in 1881, for $8.6 million, Clarence H. Clark and Associates, Philadelphia financiers with strong ties to the powerful Pennsylvania Railroad, bought the majority of AM&O stock.[6] Those securities soon passed into the larger road's hands. Mahone, who had been running the line before it fell on hard times, was out.[7] Pennsy controlled the Shenandoah Valley Railroad then being built, running to and from the Potomac River. On the lookout for a southern extension, its owner believed AM&O fit the bill.

In the meantime, possibly as a throwback to an 1850s charter sought by some Norfolkians, in May 1881, AM&O was renamed Norfolk & Western Railroad. When it was again sold under foreclosure 15 years hence it was to reopen September 24, 1896, as Norfolk & Western *Railway*.[8] That remained its moniker throughout its years as an independent carrier. The Virginia junction selected by rail officials for the connection between the Shenandoah Valley and Norfolk & Western was dubbed Big Lick. Sitting on the banks of the Roanoke River, in time Big Lick would be renamed Roanoke and would become the base of operations for N&W for the majority of its life.

N&W by the way, perhaps surprisingly given its overarching reputation as a coal carrier, largely transported agricultural commodities in its earliest days. But Frederick J. Kimball, a civil engineer and partner in owner C. H. Clark's firm and recently named first vice president of N&W, soon led the system into a new absorption.[9] Personally exhibiting an acute fascination with geology, he turned the road's economic focus to the Pocahontas coalfields in western Virginia and southern West Virginia: "He knew the practical value of coal to industry both in America and England, and he knew how to 'prospect' for it. After seeing for himself the thick seam exposed on the east slope of Flattop Mountain near the Virginia–West Virginia border, he directed construction of what would become the main line of the N&W toward the rugged highlands."[10]

"Organized primarily to develop coal, iron and other resources, and especially attracted by the discovery of good coal near the site of present-day Pocahontas, Virginia, the N&W began its existence by the purchase of the proposed New River Railroad."[11] Pocahontas, incidentally, would figure into the sobriquets applied to a couple of crack N&W passenger trains in the succeeding century, to be encountered later.

The New River Railroad had obtained a Virginia charter in 1872, intending to run tracks into the interior of the rich coal fields. After N&W bought the unfinished line, it installed Fred Kimball as president, rerouted it and relentlessly persisted in securing land in the geographical zone surrounding Pocahontas. As soon as tracks were completed, on March 12, 1883, the first carloads of Pocahontas coal departed for Norfolk's port.[12] On May 2, 1883, the new N&W route from New River, Virginia, to Bluefield, West Virginia, was opened to traffic. Coal transported to Norfolk quickly became N&W's prime commodity, leading to immense wealth and profitability.[13] Kimball became president of the whole N&W system, overseeing its further expansion.

In 1885, a cluster of diminutive mining companies occupying about 400,000 acres of bituminous coal reserves formed the coalfields' largest landowning alliance, the Philadelphia-based Flat-Top Coal and Land Association. Norfolk & Western Railway later purchased that fraternity, reorganized it and renamed it Pocahontas Coal and Coke Company. It was subsequently designated Pocahontas Land Corporation and remains a subsidiary of today's Norfolk Southern Railroad.

A litany of further developments — including extensions, additions of branch lines, etc., including numerous acquisitions by lease and by purchase — occurred over the next couple of decades. By the time of Kimball's demise in 1903, N&W had achieved the basic route structure it employed for the next six decades.[14] The road ultimately reached not only Virginia and West Virginia but North Carolina, Tennessee, Maryland and Ohio. Its easternmost point was Norfolk and Virginia's Tidewater Basin (Newport News, Portsmouth, and others); its northernmost summit was Hagerstown, Maryland, in the East and Columbus, Ohio, in the Midwest; its southernmost tracks extended to Winston-Salem and Durham, North Carolina; and its westernmost route terminated at Cincinnati, Ohio. Hardly more than 2,000 miles altogether — a rather succinct system by competing Class 1 railroad standards — nevertheless N&W "easily made up for this by its strategic location in Appalachian coal country."[15]

In its latter decades N&W fostered a few more strategic acquisitions through mergers. The first, with the Virginian Railway (VGN), occurred in 1959. That line had built a "Mountains to Sea" road from southern West Virginia coal fields to a port near Norfolk at Sewell's Point in the Hampton Roads harbor.

> They accomplished this right under the noses of the pre-existing and much bigger C&O and N&W railroads and their leaders by forming two small intrastate railroads, Deepwater Railway, in West Virginia, and Tidewater Railway in Virginia. Once right-of-way and land acquisitions had been secured, the two small railroads were merged in 1907 to form the Virginian Railway....
> Mark Twain spoke at the dedication of the new railroad in Norfolk....
> For 50 years, the Virginian Railway enjoyed a more modern pathway built to the highest standards, providing major competition for coal traffic to its larger neighboring railroads, the C&O [Chesapeake & Ohio] and N&W. The 600-mile VGN followed [co-founder Henry] Rogers' philosophy throughout its profitable history, earning the nickname "Richest Little Railroad in the World."[16]

In addition to its acquisition of the Virginian, N&W gained the Nickel Plate and the Wabash roads through 1962 mergers. N&W took over the Delaware & Hudson and Erie Lackawanna, also, as part of a 1964 merger pact, including them under the company name Dereco. That holding was eventually disposed of when N&W's parent, the Pennsylvania, was required to divest itself of the N&W in 1964, prior to its own disastrous merger with the New York Central.[17]

The end of the Norfolk & Western Railway began to emerge in 1980, when it and the Southern Railway — two major Class 1 roads headquartered in the mid Atlantic region — were dwarfed by a gigantic CSX Transportation system. CSX was formed by the unification of the former Seaboard Coast Line, Louisville & Nashville, Chesapeake & Ohio, Baltimore & Ohio, Western Maryland and a few smaller lines under one umbrella, overwhelming all the rivals in the region. In order to survive in a highly competitive business climate, N&W and Southern joined forces under the Norfolk Southern Corporation handle with headquarters established in Norfolk.

> The Norfolk and Western Railway's merger with the Southern Railway in 1982 was quite fitting due to both railroads' similar style of operation: extremely efficient and well managed....
> Aside from the N&W's astronomical earnings derived from hauling coal, the railroad was also successful because of its sound financial practices. First and foremost the railroad always made sure its physical plant was in top-notch condition, pouring millions annually into maintenance programs. Likewise the N&W was meticulous about keeping its locomotive fleet and equipment in good running order.[18]

N&W exuded something else. It was a tight knit family to thousands of workers who were loyal to it almost to a fault. Dissatisfied to depend on it solely for their livelihoods, many sacrificed for it, revering it as an institution worthy of respect, frequently fostered by the competence and care exhibited by the company's executive authorities. In such a capacity in the 1950s, R. H. Smith inspired his coworkers. "He came up through the ranks and was knowledgeable but unpretentious. Even as president of the railroad he maintained his office on the second floor of the corporate offices rather than the favored top floor so that he could observe his beloved railroad more closely."[19] In a published volume of black-and-white photography depicting N&W and its successor road over a four-decade timeframe (1955–1995), freelance shutterbug O. Winston Link attests:

> "With his [Smith's] blessing, I was able to do anything I needed to have done to get the picture I had planned. I was never refused and I was never kept waiting when I wanted to see him. He was always kind, considerate, and understanding. I never knew what word he passed down the line, but it seemed to me that he gave me 2,300 miles of track, 450 steam locomotives and all the employees of the N&W to help me get the job done. He was what I like to regard as a true American and his personality was reflected in every employee I met in those years."[20]

In spite of its phenomenal success in hauling coal, and its moderate asset in moving people, Norfolk & Western was known for something more. A great deal more, in fact. In its mammoth Roanoke Shops, N&W became legendary throughout the trade for fabricating steam locomotives in-house. While the practice of railways manufacturing their own engines was common in Great Britain — sometimes English railroads hired contractors to custom-build motive power to their specifications — the practice was rare in the United States. Thousands of craftsmen employed by the Roanoke Shops, nevertheless, made, serviced and repaired locomotives as well as other forms of rolling stock. The Roanoke Shops produced a trio of engine types that gained widespread notoriety: Classes A, J, and Y6.

> Designed, built and maintained by N&W personnel, these three types made the company known industry-wide for its excellence in steam power. N&W's commitment to steam power was due in part to its investment in the manufacturing capacity and human resources to build

and operate steam locomotives, and partially due to the major commodity it hauled, coal. In 1960 ... N&W was the last major railroad in the United States to convert from steam to diesel-electric motive power. Even after manufacturing steam locomotives ended, the Roanoke Shops continued to build and repair other forms of rolling stock, work which continued under N&W successor, Norfolk Southern, in the early 21st century.[21]

Passenger service on the N&W, as already noted, was minimal when compared to some of the larger horizontal rail lines connecting the East with the Midwest (e.g., Baltimore & Ohio, Chesapeake & Ohio, New York Central, Pennsylvania). N&W launched a laconic handful of people-movers which traversed the mostly double-mainline tracks linking Norfolk and Cincinnati.

> When one thinks of passenger trains on the Pocahontas roads, he thinks of the scheduled named trains mostly, because railroads spent money and effort advertising them. But there were the locals, all with numbers, assigned regular crews and listed in public timetables, that ran to obscure places and made no money for the roads but which were provided for the convenience of coal operators and coal and railroad company employees before good roads came to the mountains. Often the locals enabled mountain youth to attend high school.[22]

There were, indeed, lots of reasons for people to ride trains. And some of them hardly involved great distances on those journeys. The locals were often equipped with air-conditioned coaches that traveled to secondary mainline terminals like Durham and Winston-Salem in the upper Piedmont region of North Carolina and Norton in far southwestern Virginia. There were provisions for travelers that extended from mainlines to virtually every branch line's limit — sometimes including mixed trains that combined freight and passenger loads.

N&W's flagship transport was the *Powhatan Arrow* which, with its sister train *Pocahontas*, purveyed a Native American theme. The *Arrow*'s maiden voyage on April 28, 1946, occurred after a "name the train" contest produced over 140,000 entries and a Dry Branch, Virginia, winner. Initially driven by streamlined Class J 4-8-4 steam engines crafted in the renowned Roanoke Shops, its consists composed of coaches, diner, and a tavern-lounge observation car transported its human cargo typically 15,000 miles per month and an estimated three million miles across a span of 23 years. A contemporary observer covering the railroad industry described the Class J engines as "the most beautiful Northern Type steam locomotives to ever be streamlined."[23] Other historians noted, "Once west of the flat Dismal Swamp area of eastern Virginia, the *Arrow*'s route was anything but arrow straight: N&W's main line snaked its way through the Blue Ridge Mountains and rugged Appalachian scenery, providing *Arrow* riders with a constantly changing panorama.... The *Arrow*'s daily passing no doubt flashed optimism at residents trapped in the countless impoverished coal-mining communities lining the N&W main."[24] Still other rail historians issued this disclaimer: "Why, the N&W reasoned, just because Welch, West Virginia, didn't have the population of a Cleveland or a Chicago was no reason its citizens should have to depart in less luxury when it came time to take a trip!"[25]

With the middle segment of its route ascending and descending scores of precipitous mountain inclines, the train averaged 43 miles an hour over a 677-mile course. In spite of that, the train ran the route from start to finish in a single day, without the necessity of providing Pullmans in its consists. A 1950 timetable, for example, reveals that the westbound run departed Norfolk at 7:25 A.M. and —18 stops later (the last three at varied Cincinnati stations)— pulled into Cincinnati's Union Terminal at 11:05 P.M., all times Eastern. The eastbound *Arrow* left Cincinnati's Union Terminal at 8:20 A.M. and arrived in Norfolk at 11:50 P.M. The daytime trip in both directions crossed the picturesque slopes of western Virginia and West Virginia.

N&W demonstrated a cool belief in its ability to arrive at its stations on time with its

Norfolk & Western Class J 4-8-4 steam engines like 611 were among the most acclaimed fabrications of N&W's Roanoke Shops back in the day. Shown on April 3, 1993, at Chattanooga, it had hauled some excursion railfans from Birmingham before returning them to their starting point. The trip was sponsored by N&W heir Norfolk Southern (*courtesy Clyde Woodruff*).

flagship train. For instance, both the eastbound *Arrow* and an Atlantic Coast Line connection at Petersburg, Virginia, were scheduled to depart Petersburg on their disparate routes at 10:25 P.M. That vote of confidence was modified by the fact the ACL train was the last of the day to traverse the Petersburg–Richmond course: anybody who missed the ACL waited through the night or found another method of getting to Richmond. The *Arrow's* schedule was later amended radically. In 1967, that premier train was turned into an overnight operation in both directions between Norfolk and Roanoke with daylight service west of Roanoke.

Long before this, Norfolk & Western ordered 10 coaches, each seating 56 patrons, from Pullman-Standard in April 1946, the month in which it inaugurated streamlined passenger trains. The new smooth-sided lightweight coaches sported a striking livery of Tuscan red and black with gold trim. Upon their arrival in 1949, some of the new coaches were assigned to the *Powhatan Arrow* while the remainder went to its sister trainsets, the *Pocahontas*, plying the same route. In the early 1950s, the cars' lettering and striping was repainted in imitation gold with roofs and trucks in black. Following the Wabash merger in the mid 1960s, N&W altered those hues once more to consists transporting passengers in blue and yellow liveries.

The flagship *Arrow* pursued a route that nearly paralleled the Chesapeake & Ohio's (C&O) acclaimed *George Washington* flagship train. The *GW* ran daily between Newport News and Cincinnati through areas that were better inhabited, giving it a decided edge over the *Arrow*. As the 1960s waned, ridership diminished on most passenger trains, including on this pair of rivals. By 1969, the *Arrow* was but a shadow of its former glory, offering just a couple of coaches and a diner that ran between Roanoke and Williamson, West Virginia. When the U.S. Postal Service transferred its mail-hauling from trains to trucks in that era, N&W requested that the Interstate Commerce Commission (ICC) allow it to discontinue the *Powhatan Arrow*.

The very same N&W Class J 611 is off on another excursion, this one from Greensboro, North Carolina, to Covington, in southwestern Virginia's hilly terrain. "Not sure why I love these pix from the train," the photographer allowed. "Something about the train ride, the motion, easier pace, and when you get the right setup, a cool railroading picture. Double track crossing a river, mountains on both sides and a big steam engine in front with a clean stack — what else do you need on a sunny, beautiful day?" It works for us (*courtesy Jay Miller*).

The ICC did so in spring 1969, stipulating that N&W must upgrade and retain the *Pocahontas*. The *Arrow* made its final trip on May 23, 1969, and the *Pocahontas* received the *Arrow*'s Vista-Dome car and some other cosmetic improvements.[26]

N&W's last regularly scheduled passenger train, the *Pocahontas*, persisted until Amtrak acquired most of the nation's rail travel service on May 1, 1971.[27] As the *Arrow* hadn't survived until Amtrak came into being, it wasn't retained, although it likely wouldn't have been kept anyway. The *Cardinal*, fostered by the C&O, served more populous municipalities in essentially the same territory. The *Cardinal* continued under Amtrak and operates in the present day.

Those famous Class J 4-8-4s powering the *Powhatan Arrow* did the same for N&W's other prominent "name" trains, the *Pocahontas* and *Cavalier*, plying the same east-west route, as well as Southern Railway's *Tennessean* between Lynchburg, Virginia, and Bristol, Tennessee. The *Pocahontas* premiered in 1926, while the *Cavalier* debuted a year later.[28] Not until the late 1950s did N&W begin to replace its steam-driven locomotives with EMD E-series diesel power. As already observed, N&W was the last major Class 1 railroad to totally dieselize, in 1960.

In addition to its operation of a trio of crack trains on the Norfolk–Cincinnati route — *Cavalier*, *Pocahontas* and *Powhatan Arrow* — N&W was responsible for ferrying several imposing 20th century interline consists over portions of its tracks every day. Between Lynchburg and Bristol it handled the *Birmingham Special*, *Pelican* and *Tennessean* in conjunction with the Pennsylvania Railroad and Southern Railway. The first of those ran between New York City and Birmingham; the second, between New York and New Orleans; and the third, between New York and Memphis. On yet another route, between Norfolk and Petersburg, N&W carried the *Cannon Ball*, which continued north to New York via tracks of the Atlantic Coast Line, the Richmond, Fredericksburg & Potomac, and the Pennsylvania roads.

More than anything else Norfolk & Western Railway was widely branded as a coal-hauler of superior demarcation. It furthermore invested heavily in designing and manufacturing its own engines and rolling stock, a near-oddity in the railroad industry. In doing that it became the last major U.S. railroad to convert from mainstay steam to diesel motive power. Fortunate to be run by leaders whose oversight gave prominence to detail and whose genuine care was exhibited routinely, N&W was liberally blessed from a human resources stance.

And finally, in its own limited way, the line fielded a small handful of passenger consists that shuttled travelers back and forth across scenic mountain vistas in the heyday of rail travel. From the Ohio River to the Atlantic Ocean, and in many places in between, denizens counted on the N&W to help them get where they were going—and, sometimes—to keep them connected to the outside world. N&W wasn't a large operation in transporting riders. But it was dependable, outwardly caring, comfortable, and possibly even contagious, as it supplied an optimistic spirit to the riders who lived beside its tracks.

12

ST. LOUIS–SAN FRANCISCO RAILWAY
Unfilled Destiny

Of nine states—Alabama, Arkansas, Florida, Kansas, Mississippi, Missouri, Oklahoma, Tennessee and Texas—in which the St. Louis–San Francisco Railway (SLSF) operated, a line more commonly branded the "Frisco," five of them are geographically sited in the Old South. Small portions of trackage ran through a trio of Southern states—Florida, Mississippi and Tennessee—and Memphis was an imposing gateway in the SSW system. Yet at its peak the bulk of Frisco's routes were concentrated in a half-dozen *other* states—Alabama, Arkansas, Kansas, Missouri, Oklahoma and Texas. Of that group only Alabama and Arkansas truly qualify for inclusion in this text.

The Frisco was unique by multiple gauges: it never got within 1,500 miles of one of its namesake endpoints, although its intent from the start was to stretch to the West Coast. While it performed adequately in the territory served, its misnomer in identification was a permanent reminder of its destiny that forever went unrealized.

About half of the top dozen passenger consists in Frisco's inventory dipped into Dixie. Yet not all could be measured as stand-alone Frisco routes—some required interline connections to arrive at their destinations. And unlike nearly every major carrier headlining a chapter in this text, at one of Frisco's prime Southern hubs—Memphis—from the 1940s to the 1960s, through chair car (coach) travelers aboard one of its crack streamliners found it necessary to detrain and re-board another car in order to leave town. It was a fairly startling, perhaps unnerving, circumstance that generally distinguished Frisco from many other carriers in the region. This specific situation will be explored more in depth a little later.

Incorporated in Missouri as the St. Louis and San Francisco Railway on September 7, 1876, the line's origins were drawn from the Central and Missouri divisions of the Atlantic and Pacific Railroad (A&P), another overly ambitious road that also came up short. The A&P was chartered by an act of the U.S. Congress on July 27, 1866. It was to run westward from Springfield, Missouri, across Native American Territory, roughly along the 35th parallel to San Francisco. That didn't happen precisely as envisioned.

A&P had a precursor, too: the Pacific Railroad, authorized by the Missouri General Assembly on March 3, 1849. It aimed to run tracks across the center of the Show-Me State between St. Louis and a point south of Kansas City. Three years hence, in December 1852, when federal public land grants were made available to Missouri for a couple of intrastate rail lines, a Southwest Branch below the Osage River was added. Originating at Franklin (now Pacific) on the Pacific Railroad's main, that stem persisted on a west-southwesterly course, reaching Rolla by 1860, about 77 miles from its starting point.[1] There construction languished; an incomplete 12-mile addition leading to Arlington, Missouri, was held in abeyance after the War Between the States bankrupted the company with bonds in default.

Following the conflict in March 1866, the state seized the road and completed it to Arlington. Missouri sold it three months afterward for $1.3 million to one-time presidential candidate, military tactician, and subsequent Arizona territorial governor John C. Fremont (1813–1890). The original Pacific Railroad, authorized in 1849, wasn't put on the market, however. In time it was to emerge as the Missouri Pacific Railroad. By September 1866, Fremont altered the nomenclature of the Southwest Branch to Southwest Pacific Railroad. A month before, the U.S. Congress designated Fremont and a few partners as recipients of federal land grants, charged with developing a rail line from Springfield to the Pacific Ocean. A connecting shoot was to extend from Van Buren, Arkansas.

Operating under the banner of Atlantic & Pacific Railroad in early 1867, the Fremont group also defaulted on payments. Missouri once again stepped into the fray to salvage the noble transcontinental effort. Successor South Pacific Railroad, which acquired the assets in July 1868, vanished almost as quickly as Fremont and company had; in October 1870, a second reincarnation under the Atlantic & Pacific appellation took over. That followed the pattern of previous owners, its Missouri Division (extending from Franklin to Seneca, Missouri, the latter burg on the Oklahoma border) falling into receivership in November 1875. A lease of the Pacific (later Missouri Pacific) Railroad signed in June 1872 was terminated.

In September 1876, A&P incorporated the St. Louis–San Francisco Railway, acquiring the property of the Missouri Division and leasing the Central Division (Seneca to Vinita, Oklahoma). Not long afterward some of the newly-formed outfit's workforce derived the "Frisco" branding and coonskin insignia that readily passed muster with the line's management. Those dual identifications were symbols of the system from that time forward. By 1883, SSW opened a direct extension from Franklin to St. Louis: it wouldn't rely on Missouri Pacific for trackage to that key terminus any longer.

The copious undertakings and foibles of the diverse railways and rail barons that were tied to the progression to the Far West nets some charismatic reading.[2] But it isn't germane to our chronicle of passenger train service that played out in the Southeastern United States. At this juncture therefore it is fundamentally dispatched to other sources. We'll deliberate expressly on the outgrowth of the St. Louis–San Francisco Railway instead.[3]

In 1890, SSW — which forged a pact with the Atchison, Topeka & Santa Fe Railroad (AT&SF) in January 1880 — was acquired by AT&SF. Following a nationwide financial panic both companies entered into receivership in December 1893. On June 29, 1896, St. Louis and San Francisco Railroad (renamed from the earlier *Railway*) was incorporated. By December 1897, SSW regained its independence. Under foreclosure proceedings it purchased the Central Division while A&P, still operating until then, disappeared forever.

SSW again went bankrupt and reorganized on August 24, 1916, regaining its original label: St. Louis–San Francisco *Railway*. The rebranding stuck throughout its independent existence until its acquisition November 21, 1980, by the Burlington Northern Railroad (BN).[4] "The reason the BN chose the Frisco was because the railroad gave the BN a much more diversified traffic base," affirmed one source, "and extended it into the southeastern regions of Memphis, Arkansas, Mississippi, Alabama, and the Gulf Coast."[5] If that presumption is correct then the South played a pivotal role in the folding of the resilient Frisco as an independent player among the rail traffic suppliers in Middle America.

Fifteen years hence BN combined with Santa Fe Railroad to become the Burlington Northern Santa Fe Railroad (BNSF). In between 1916 and 1980, meanwhile, Frisco had lots of time to do its stuff, making notable strides over 5,000 miles of tracks in Midwest and South Central transportation. In so doing it left an indelible mark upon the trade, the region, and the people it served.

The St Louis–San Francisco Railway, known as the Frisco, was a dominant railroad ... primarily in Missouri, Arkansas, Oklahoma, and Kansas. It played an important role in the lives of people all along the rails. The Frisco had acquired rights of way through much of the region and had an interest in the development of that land, which would eventually bring people to an area, people who would use the services of the railroad. Many of the towns began initially as a result of a depot or station needed by the Frisco for fuel and water. The population also expanded along the railroad as a result of the opportunities for employment it provided....

For many years the Frisco provided a primary link between small towns in the South and Midwest to the rest of the country.[6]

Just as it did with competitors, the 1930s Great Depression wreaked havoc on Frisco, being clearly responsible for sharp declines in revenues derived from passengers, freight, mail and express traffic. Like many of its peers, the company again fell into receivership, with Frisco's plight extending some 15 years from 1932 to 1947. While no major abandonments occurred prior to 1940, shippers' and travelers' growing reliance on highway and air transport in the postwar epoch resulted in substantial reductions in passenger service. Several branch lines were also shut down.

During its halcyon days the St. Louis–San Francisco Railway sustained two main routes. One ran between St. Louis and Oklahoma City via Tulsa. The other, of special interest, persevered from Kansas City to Birmingham via Memphis. The pair crossed at Springfield, Missouri, where the company maintained its principal repair, assembly and refurbishing shops. Not only that, its operational headquarters was housed at Springfield along with numerous supporting units of diverse persuasions. Frisco's impact on the local community as the region's largest employer cannot be minimized.

Beyond those mainlines SSW operated a handful of subordinate routes, mostly for freight traffic, and most eluding the territory that is the focus of this text. There was a road between St. Louis and River Junction, Arkansas, for instance, leading to nearby Memphis by joining the Kansas City–Birmingham main. A southerly course off that route near the Mississippi–Alabama border was split into diverse Gulf Coast destinations—one proceeded to Mobile while the other linked to Pensacola. Yet another road persisted from Monett, Missouri, through western Arkansas to Paris, Texas.

Of its most celebrated name trains Frisco's sumptuous *Texas Special*—jointly operated with the Missouri–Kansas–Texas Railroad (MKT or Katy) between St. Louis and San Antonio from March 1917 to January 1959—was considered its most impressive. Said one flowery piece of promotional copy: "Chair cars [coaches] between St. Louis and Texas have the famed 'Sleepy Hollow' seats providing head-to-toe luxury ... a marvel seat that lets the entire body relax ... at no extra fare!" While that train operated on tracks outside the parameters of the Southeast, as the dominant player in the Frisco system it would be unthinkable to gloss over its impact on passenger service. Some of its travelers included transferring passengers at St. Louis who arrived from or departed to the Deep South on other trains.

Katy originated the *Texas Special* between St. Louis and San Antonio in 1915. Frisco signed on within a couple of years, March 4, 1917, sending the train along its route to Vinita, Oklahoma. There the *Special* was handed over to Katy for the remainder of the journey, a total of 982 miles between terminal cities. Leaving Vinita, the *Special* called at Muskogee, McAlester and Durant, Oklahoma, before entering the Lone Star State for Denison. There it was subdivided into a trio of sections—one bound for Wichita Falls, one for Fort Worth, and one for San Antonio. The latter covered the largest territory, making the most intermediate stops including Dallas, Waco and Austin before reaching its southernmost endpoint.

The *Special* was the flagship passenger trainset of both Frisco and Katy systems. Pulled by steam engines for three decades, it was upgraded to faster, more efficient, more comfortable dieselized streamliner status in 1947.[7] Its cars were constructed in Pullman-Standard's Chicago shops. One of the nation's most profitable people-movers, the *Special* flaunted cosmetic stainless steel corrugations with striking hues: red roofs and pier panels, maroon shirts and silver trucks. Frisco and Katy initially outfitted a streamliner each with both trainsets comprised of 14 cars: seven sleepers, a trio of coaches, coach-buffet-lounge car, diner, Railway Post Office–baggage car, and an observation car (either sleeper-lounge-observation or buffet-lounge-observation).

As the *Special*'s popularity grew, so did its consist, at times increasing to 20 cars in each direction. Demand eventually necessitated a third trainset, which was added from refurbished heavyweight cars. Its consist included multiple 12-section single drawing-room sleepers plus a coach-buffet car and a diner car. The passenger units in that version of the *Texas Special* could be recognized by a red and silver paint scheme offset by shadow striping.

A 1948 timetable exhibits through sleeping cars of the *Texas Special* transported over Baltimore & Ohio Railroad tracks between Washington, D.C. and St. Louis. They departed the former city at 6:30 P.M. and arrived in the latter at 1:20 P.M. the following day. There was a second train making a seamless interline transition in St. Louis, too. It left New York City at 7:35 P.M. over Pennsylvania Railroad tracks, due in St. Louis at 3 P.M. the next day. The connecting Frisco–Katy consist departed St. Louis at 5:30 P.M. and was expected in San Antonio at 2:45 P.M. a day later.

The northbound train left San Antonio at 12:01 P.M. and was due in St. Louis the next day at 8:30 A.M. Connecting trains departed St. Louis at 9:45 A.M. for New York, arriving the following morning at 7:25 A.M.; and 9:55 A.M. for Washington, getting there at 7:40 A.M. the next day. The distance from Washington to San Antonio was 1, 864 miles and from New York 2,032 miles.

The *Texas Special* joint operation created one of the shortest routes linking some of the Lone Star State's financial centers with those in the East. Frisco's involvement in the revered train persisted through January 5, 1959, when the company withdrew as a partner in the operation. There is a story behind that momentous decision, as in many cases involving passenger rail service.

> In the mid–1950s the Katy was taken over by a conglomerate whose focus was freight train profits; they showed little interest in properly maintaining the track and equipment to operate a comfortable passenger streamliner. Trains would run late and passengers soon were finding alternative transportation. By 1959 conditions had deteriorated so much on the Katy lines that Frisco pulled out of the venture. This meant Katy had to move the northern terminus of the *Texas Special* from St. Louis to Kansas City, Missouri. In 1964 *Texas Special* service was discontinued south of Dallas, Texas. The last *Texas Special* ran on July 1, 1965.[8]

So special was the *Special* that it gained status as a designer archetype in model railroading. A second passenger train, in the meantime, the *Bluebonnet*, plied the same tracks from St. Louis to San Antonio between December 11, 1927, and May 1, 1948. Yet it missed the panache of the *Texas Special*; while for two decades it faithfully schlepped travelers back and forth between its termini under steam power, the *Bluebonnet* was still "the other train" on the route, and never achieved the spectacular status of its older sister.

Worthy of note is the fact that — when the Frisco purchased E7 diesel locomotives and Pullman cars for the *Texas Special* in 1947 — in that same order it received similar engines and passenger cars for the *Meteor*. A section of that daily train ran between Fort Smith, Arkansas, and St. Louis.[9] The *Special* and the *Meteor*, both diesel-powered streamliners as of May 14, 1948, shared an uncommonly distinctive red and silver livery.[10]

Of particular interest to Southeastern travelers is the *Kansas City–Florida Special*, which operated daily with interline connections at Birmingham between its named city and Jacksonville; the *Memphian*, from St. Louis to Memphis; the *Meteor*, between St. Louis and dual endpoints at Fort Smith, Arkansas, and Oklahoma City (and not to be confused with the

Seaboard Air Line's and now Amtrak's *Silver Meteor* running between New York City and Miami); the *Southland*, between Kansas City and Birmingham; and the *Sunnyland*, with termini at Kansas City and St. Louis and trains going to the opposite dual cities of Atlanta and Pensacola, with north-south routes crossing at Memphis.[11] Timetables for most of these trains are available from the summer of 1957. By that juncture the Pensacola passenger consist had been deleted from the schedule.

As noted previously, at one of Frisco's prime Dixieland hubs—Memphis—continuing travelers aboard one train, the *Sunnyland*, a daily consist running between Kansas City, St. Louis and Atlanta (the Birmingham–Atlanta portion was over a Southern Railway route) were required to leave their originating Frisco cars for reassignment to separate Frisco cars at Memphis.[12] This occurred in both directions on this train, no matter if one traveled in a coach or sleeper. (The single sleeper ran between Memphis and Atlanta exclusively.)

Losing the more profitable revenue that could have been generated by continuing the sleeper between Memphis and Kansas City or St. Louis, Frisco instead ended it in Tennessee. That caused everybody going beyond Memphis to scramble to gather belongings, detrain, wait, reboard, and resettle in new quarters. It was a disconcerting maneuver for years that inconvenienced all patrons equally.[13] Most carriers normally handled such exchanges more efficiently during passenger rail's heyday. Frisco, for whatever its reasons, opted to downgrade this particular trainset.

The southbound *Sunnyland* departed Kansas City at 8:15 A.M. In between Kansas City and Atlanta the train called at a handful of intermediate stops, among them Springfield, Missouri; Jonesboro, Arkansas; Memphis; Tupelo, Mississippi; and Birmingham. Sleeper and coach passengers joining the trip at Memphis could occupy their space as early as 9:30 P.M., 20 minutes before the riders from Kansas City were scheduled to arrive and do the same—and an hour before they all left Memphis at 10:30 P.M.

The "new" consist was due in Birmingham at 7 A.M. the following day. Twenty-five minutes later it departed Birmingham over Southern Railway trackage, making it to Atlanta by 1:10 P.M. Curiously, most express contracts on that route were held by the Seaboard Air Line Railroad (SAL).[14] While passengers generally traveled over Southern rails between Birmingham and Atlanta, a second train for express traffic operated over SAL rails. Departing Birmingham at 7:40 A.M., it too arrived in Atlanta at 1:10 P.M.

On the return trip the *Sunnyland* left Atlanta at 4:15 P.M., was in Birmingham at 8 P.M. and out at 9:45 P.M. (The SAL express train didn't leave Atlanta until 5:10 P.M., however; it arrived in Birmingham at 8:25.) At 6:15 A.M. the next day the Sunnyland was in Memphis, where it was split into dual segments. Sleeping car customers getting off in Memphis could occupy their space until 8 A.M., that car being moved to a side rail. Not so for the folks who continued beyond Memphis in either sleeping car or coaches. Theirs was a rude awakening as they changed cars for a 7:30 A.M. departure for Kansas City. The *Sunnyland* was due there at 8:40 that evening.

In addition to all of the above, there was the connecting *Sunnyland* of sorts operating between St. Louis and Memphis. "Of sorts" means that it offered a single unreserved seat, reclining chair car sans sleeper, diner and lounge car. Box lunches were available en route for purchase at Chaffee, Missouri. This section was marked by lengthy layovers at Memphis, too, especially remembered by those catching the southbound *Sunnyland* from Kansas City. The train left St. Louis at 8:40 A.M. and was in Memphis at 5:15 P.M. for a 10:30 P.M. departure for Birmingham and Atlanta. On the return trip, which met the northbound *Sunnyland* arriving in Memphis at 6:15 A.M., the St. Louis section left at 7:40 A.M. It was due to reach its St. Louis termination at 3:35 P.M.

At a later date the *Sunnyland* proffered a buffet car between Memphis and St. Louis and a diner between Birmingham and Atlanta. By the early 1950s, however, the meal service was reduced to a combination dinette-coach on the Birmingham–Atlanta segment, with no onboard food service provided elsewhere. It was a sure sign of the changing fortunes and diminishing values in some pockets of rail travel that were to gradually become much more pervasive.

Despite whatever disillusionment may have prevailed with the *Sunnyland*, it was nevertheless the catalyst for composer Walter Davis' "Railroad Man Blues" back in the day. One of a growing lot of rail-themed tunes, Davis' lyrics lament: "*Sunnyland* that runs on the Frisco line ... stole that girl of mine."

Unquestionably the better-equipped, more widely celebrated and geographically-enveloping train on the mainline, meanwhile, was the *Kansas City–Florida Special*. It included a pair of sleepers running between Kansas City and Jacksonville. One of those included 14 roomettes and four double-bedrooms while the other boasted 10 sections, two double-bedrooms and a single compartment. There were separate dining and lounge cars in the consist from Kansas City to Atlanta and from Jacksonville to Miami (the latter extension was provided by the Florida East Coast Railway). Deluxe reclining chair cars plied the rails from Kansas City to Jacksonville and between Jacksonville and Miami. Without regard to accommodations, a change in venue was mandated at Jacksonville for all continuing passengers. The Frisco ferried the travelers from Kansas City to Birmingham while Southern Railway carried them through Atlanta to Jacksonville. Those continuing on to Miami made an intermediate stop at West Palm Beach.

The southbound train left Kansas City daily at 11:25 P.M., although sleeping car riders could board as early as 10 P.M. The *KC–Florida Special* made the same stops as its sister train, the *Sunnyland*, as far as Atlanta. It reached Jacksonville the second morning of the trip at 7:30 A.M. After changing cars, ongoing passengers left Jacksonville 50 minutes later and were due in Miami that day at 3:40 P.M. The northbound journey left Miami at 12:40 P.M., arrived in Jacksonville at 8:40 P.M. for a 40-minute layover, and returned to Kansas City on the second morning at 7:30 A.M.

Yet another Frisco passenger train operating much of its short route in Dixie, the *Memphian*, an overnight reclining chair car consist (no sleepers) left St. Louis at 11:15 P.M., arriving Memphis at 7:15 A.M. (Parenthetically, might that consist have been the inspiration for the country music hit *Take That Night Train to Memphis* recorded by Roy Acuff, Dolly Parton and others, and a 1946 B-film in which Acuff and company starred? It meets the criteria, but so do those of the IC and NC&StL lines, among several.) Passengers continuing south to Birmingham and beyond transferred to the *Kansas City–Florida Special* which departed Memphis at 10:25 A.M.

Northbound, travelers arrived into Memphis from Birmingham and points south at 6:45 P.M. Following an extended layover they left Memphis at 11:15 P.M. and were in St. Louis at 7:37 A.M. the following morning.

There was yet one more Frisco train on the mainline running daily between Kansas City and Birmingham, the *Southland*. Ultimately it became the system's last passenger operation, making its final run on December 9, 1967. For many years Frisco had been eliminating the people-movers, unable to stem the tide of rising costs and fading patronage. Its *Bluebonnet* from St. Louis to San Antonio vanished nearly two decades before this while Frisco withdrew its four-decade participation in the flagship *Texas Special* almost a decade back. In the mid 1940s, the *Southland* ferried 450 people daily along its route. As the end approached it typically carried 29 riders and had lost $950,000 in 1966, pretty compelling reasons to pull the plug. A 34-year rail buffet car veteran who worked that final trip on the *Southland*, Charles D. Ross of St. Louis, recalled far more buoyant times[15]:

Back in those days the dining car was considered the acme of service.... Every train that went out had a diner. There'd be a dining car steward all decked out in a spotless uniform, five or six waiters and four cooks. We could serve 48 passengers at a time.

Everything was immaculate. The table service was silver, not that silver-plate stuff but the solid thing. Everybody liked the coffee. It was the best in the world and we served it from silver pots. The cuisine was superb, equal to the best hotels and restaurants. Passengers considered the dining car meal the height of the trip.[16]

With the departure of its last passenger consist, Frisco became one of a handful of influential carriers with operations in the Southeast that threw in the towel before any rescue could be formulated and implemented. Amtrak was the rescuer but it didn't acquire the faltering passenger business until May 1, 1971. Some communities were thus left without adequate provisions for the traveling public for more than three years.

The final passenger train out of town was much more than a mere sentimental journey. It was also unmistakably the end of an era.

13

SEABOARD AIR LINE RAILROAD
The Train of Tomorrow

During the Victorian Era, which was roughly equated with the reign of Queen Victoria on Great Britain's throne from 1837 to 1901, more than a handful of American railroads added the idiom "Air Line" to their legal nomenclature. The last residual carrier doing so was the Seaboard Air Line Railroad (SAL). With the SAL, nevertheless, the reference was marked by greater endurance than most, for it surfaced virtually in the War Between the States epoch (1861–1865). During that period people began referencing the Seaboard & Roanoke Railroad (SAR) by that soon-to-be formalized brand. Yet neither the SAR nor SAL nor any of their similarly labeled equivalents were ever into flying—at least, not off terra firma. Seaboard began showcasing the "Air Line" handle long before aircraft were invented and, in fact, while "Orville and Wilbur Wright still dangled from their mother's knee."[1] In retrospect, the reference to "Air Line" implied, with obvious exaggeration, that those roads purveyed routes straight as an arrow, capable of reducing travel time from Point A to Point B to absolute minimums. In this circumstance we see that taking editorial license—when it could be persuasively applied as a marketing tool—wasn't limited solely to the modern age.

Although a number of railroad historians have mistakenly cited Seaboard as the first railroad to run streamlined trains along Southeastern tracks, it was merely the first "legacy" carrier to do so. Copying the model of a precedent-setting Gulf, Mobile & Northern Railroad (GM&N)—a comparatively minor-league though highly innovative peer—SAL simply led the pack of enduring trunk lines.[2] In early 1939, a quadrennial after GM&N's pioneering development, SAL launched streamlined equipment on its rails, heralded for getting a jump on its competition. Despite the accomplishment, the trade viewed the SAL as a "weak line wedged between two stronger rivals." Nevertheless, during the 1920s, SAL was particularly profitable.[3] Subsequent optimism led to overexpansion during the 1930s Great Depression era, resulting in bankruptcy. But in the postwar season of the latter 1940s, SAL soared, becoming "a strong and profitable mainstay of the South's transportation system."[4]

Seaboard's earliest antecedent was the Portsmouth & Roanoke Railroad (P&R). Chartered in 1832 to link Portsmouth, Virginia, with Weldon, North Carolina, 79 miles distant, construction began the following year.[5] Heading in a southwesterly direction from Portsmouth, the line reached Suffolk, Virginia, in July 1834, brushing the western rim of the Great Dismal Swamp.

Premiering without any engines to tug its loads, in the earliest days the P&R ran two daily round-trips along the route with crudely-fabricated wooden coaches pulled by literal horse power.[6] In every sense it was a glorified stagecoach system over an improved roadbed that made the trip less jarring and faster than comparable travel over conventional dirt pathways exhibiting muddy ruts when it rained, unremitting stones and uneven surfaces aplenty. The one-way ride on the P&R between Portsmouth and Suffolk cost a dollar, and a round-trip on the same day could be had for 50 cents more. For anybody who could amass the cash, it was the most luxurious mode of travel available between those two points in the summer of 1834.

A sizeable upgrade in service was on its way, however. On September 4 of that year a packet schooner delivered a four-wheel, five-ton steam engine named the *John Barnett* to Portsmouth from its Philadelphia manufacturing site.[7] A short time beyond, that engine replaced the literal horsepower with the figurative kind between Portsmouth and Suffolk. Moving at 15 miles an hour, the steam-driven train traversed the route in 75 minutes.[8] Most of those denizens had never witnessed anything like it. Within two years the line was open all the way to Weldon.[9]

Unfortunately for the early zealots who invested in that fledgling enterprise, some deficiencies sprouted that couldn't be readily overcome. Perhaps a workforce incapable of grasping the challenge was hired to cultivate the roadbed and secure the tracks. Perhaps too much haste to complete it quickly resulted in short-cuts with receding consequences. Perhaps cost-cutting measures in construction overrode common sense. Perhaps all of these and more played a part in the debilitating misfortunes that eventually materialized in the line's physical condition. Whatever the root causes, it wasn't long before the fact that the railway had been poorly built surfaced. To satisfy its outstanding creditors, in 1843, the original forerunner of the Seaboard Railroad went on the auction block.

Three years hence the Seaboard & Roanoke Railroad (a different moniker) emerged out of that debacle.[10] Its new owners set about rebuilding the railway's first 61 miles from Portsmouth to the Virginia–North Carolina border. A second outfit, calling itself the Roanoke Railroad, rebuilt the remaining 18 miles of the route from the state line to Weldon. In three more years (1849), the latter results were absorbed by the S&R, with the full Portsmouth-Weldon route reopened to vastly improved standards by 1851. In the latter half of the 19th century, strategic acquisitions, interline connections and additional construction increased the S&R's mileage as well as broadened its influence in generous proportions.

The Raleigh & Gaston Railroad (R&G), for example — incorporated in 1835, completed in 1840, with tracks linking those Tar Heel towns some 85 miles apart (Gaston's name was eventually altered to Thelma) — extended its line to Weldon. It joined the Seaboard & Roanoke there in 1853. North Carolina commodities could, for the very first time, transfer seamlessly from the state capital to ports around Norfolk for dispatch to Baltimore, Philadelphia, New York and other American metropolises as well as to the European continent.[11]

In 1871, R&G increased its portfolio by adding the Raleigh & Augusta Air-Line Railroad (note the use of "Air Line" jargon).[12] Raleigh & Augusta had debuted that same year as the Chatham Railroad and was building, but had not yet finished, a 98-mile route south of Raleigh to Hamlet, North Carolina. It finally reached Hamlet in 1877, joining the Carolina Central Railway there (to be presented momentarily) in ferrying traffic east and west.

A brief introspective into Hamlet will be invaluable to our understanding of later developments in SAL traffic patterns. Hamlet, in the wilds of Richmond County sited hard against the North Carolina border with South Carolina, was in due course one of the most — if not *the* most — exalted junctions on the future Seaboard Air Line Railroad. Through Hamlet all of SAL's mainline traffic passed. A nondescript backwater in its earliest days, in the glory years Hamlet exhibited SAL trackage that ultimately headed into no fewer than five tactical directions. Over the years it became to Seaboard what nearby Florence, South Carolina, became to rival Atlantic Coast Line, whose north-south main plus three other major routes convened at that strategic junction.

Hamlet and Florence boasted extensive shops for their respective lines, too, where thousands of SAL workers kept the trains running. While Hamlet was a tiny, appropriately dubbed,

Hamlet, North Carolina, wasn't merely a one-railway town: to SAL, it was not *just* the area's largest employer, for it controlled much of the physical aspects of the carrier's total operations along the Eastern seaboard. An early postcard by Frank Marchant includes SAL's grand depot in the middle of nowhere. Beside it resides a magnificent Seaboard Air Line Hotel. Do you get a glimmer of Hamlet's strategic worth to SAL? (*courtesy North Carolina State Archives*).

seemingly insignificant burg in the pre–SAL era, its moniker was to eventually begat misnomer. To SAL, it controlled everything passing through its portals—freight, mail, express and passengers—and very possibly to a greater extent than anywhere else on the line except maybe Jacksonville.

In November 1881 (some reporters say 1883), the Seaboard & Roanoke Railroad gained control of the Carolina Central Railroad (CCR), an imposing east-west Tar Heel State route with a colorful past.[13] The CCR's humble beginnings date to 1857, when a precursor Wilmington, Charlotte, and Rutherfordton Railroad was created. That line would ultimately link Rutherfordton in North Carolina's Appalachian foothills with Charlotte in the south central Piedmont district and Wilmington on the Cape Fear River, emptying in the nearby Atlantic Ocean.

It was a 267-mile route (plus eight more miles of short branches near its western end) playing heavily into freight and human cargo over an eventual Seaboard Air Line Railroad. By the time the Wilmington, Charlotte, and Rutherfordton was reorganized as the CCR on April 10, 1873, however, trackage from Wilmington had only reached Charlotte and not much farther. It wouldn't arrive at Shelby, North Carolina, until 1884, the year following its transfer to the Seaboard & Roanoke. And the "end of the line" at Rutherfordton wouldn't be met until 1887, some three decades after the original Wilmington, Charlotte, and Rutherfordton set out to get there! By then, of course, the S&R had been operating the line for several years.

During this same time a Philadelphia rail magnate, John Moncure Robinson, scion of a potent clan dominating multiple Virginia and North Carolina railroads, presided over several of those lines. Among them: Raleigh & Gaston and its subsidiary (Raleigh & Augusta Air-Line); Richmond, Fredericksburg & Potomac (running north-south between Richmond, Virginia, and Washington, D.C.); and Seaboard & Roanoke and its subsidiary (Carolina Central).

John M. Robinson was born in "The City of Brotherly Love" on October 22, 1835.[14] Following his formal education that included Virginia Military Institute, Lawrence Scientific School and Harvard University, he became a civil engineer for Washington Turnpike Company. Though a native Yankee, Robinson served in the Confederacy's engineering corps during the War Between the States earning the rank of colonel. Following that he joined the Seaboard & Roanoke road as superintendent. He was also managing director of the Baltimore Steamship Company (Bay Line), assuming its presidency in 1867. He was president of the Old Dominion and Albemarle Steamship companies later and subsequently gained the presidency of the various Seaboard railroads.

Before it ran its first train, the Georgia, Carolina, and Northern Railway (GC&N), organized in 1888, was leased for life by the Seaboard & Roanoke and the Raleigh & Gaston railroads.[15] With just 15 miles of its 268-mile route in North Carolina (from Monroe, east of Charlotte on the Carolina Central Railway line, to the South Carolina border by way of Waxhaw), in 1900, the GC&N was to become the Atlanta Division of the Seaboard Air Line.[16] The route to Atlanta was completed in 1892.

The Seaboard Air-Line System came into being on August 1, 1893, as five separate companies with tracks extending from Portsmouth through the Carolinas to Atlanta without legal implications united under that banner.[17] The five, in order of their sequential appearance, sometimes under diverse appellations, included the Seaboard & Roanoke (1832), Raleigh & Gaston (1835), Carolina Central (1857), Raleigh & Augusta Air-Line (1871), and Georgia, Carolina & Northern (1888). Without lawful sanction, the "system" set traffic policies among its member roads while attempting to increase freight and passenger revenues for all.

At the same time it was doing business by rail, the Seaboard alliance was operating transport commerce on water. It controlled a steamboat fleet owned by the Baltimore Steam Packet Company, plying sundry channels serving Baltimore, Norfolk, Old Point Comfort and Portsmouth. Concurrently, just as a few other independent railroads were doing, Seaboard & Roanoke owned some stock in the Old Dominion Steamship Company. That outfit's vessels allowed the Seaboard Air-Line System to have ready access to the port of New York City.

The same year that Seaboard Air-Line System was organized, John M. Robinson, president of most of those lines, died in Baltimore on February 14, 1893. For a few years Richard Curzon Hoffman (July 13, 1839–January 21, 1926, a native Baltimorean who also died there) replaced Robinson as president of the Seaboard & Roanoke.[18] But it was the next man in the line of progression that is remembered as the unequivocal "father of the Seaboard." Hoffman's successor, John Skelton Williams, completed expansion of the Seaboard Air-Line System and oversaw the creation of the Seaboard Air Line Railroad.

He was born in Powhatan County, Virginia, July 6, 1865, and was distantly related to Martha Washington. Williams' nativity occurred only a few weeks after General Robert E. Lee surrendered at Appomattox Court House, Virginia, to General Ulysses S. Grant, formally ending the four-year War Between the States. Educated in private schools in Richmond, he briefly studied law at the University of Virginia before quitting at 18 to join his dad's banking firm. In that era he published a guide for financial investors that earned him widespread acclaim.

Williams and associates—including the banking firms of John L. Williams & Sons of Richmond and Middendorf, Oliver & Company of Baltimore—financed some electric streetcar ventures and banking projects in Virginia and South Carolina before focusing on railroad banking in 1895. The collaborators bought controlling interest in the Savannah, Americus & Montgomery Railroad.[19] They quickly set about reorganizing the 263-mile road that connected Lyons, a tiny village in rural southeastern Georgia, with Montgomery, Alabama, that state's capital. With John Skelton Williams, then 30, as president, the entity progressed under the revised sobriquet Georgia & Alabama Railway.

In the following year (1896), through some hard-nosed negotiating with the Central of Georgia Railway (CofG), young Williams snagged a prize that was to pay dividends in perpetuity. He threatened CofG officials, telling them he would lay his own parallel tracks from Lyons to the key port city of Savannah, 17 miles east, if they did not help him. Under duress they reluctantly agreed to lease some unused trackage to the Georgia & Alabama Railway that the CofG owned which linked those two towns. Gaining that, Williams had unimpeded access to the Atlantic Ocean from Alabama's state capital, 280 miles inland from the coast. It was but a solo exhibition of the man's intensity and tenacity for getting his way and set a pattern that would be revisited.

   The Georgia & Alabama styled itself as "The Savannah Short Line," and advertised that it possessed the shortest route between Savannah and both Columbus and Montgomery. Its daily passenger train between Savannah and Montgomery featured a buffet parlor car. By 1899 the G&A, along with the Florida Central & Peninsular, was listed as a part of the Seaboard Air Line in the *Official Guide*. It was formally operated as a part of the new Seaboard Air Line from July 1, 1900, and was officially purchased by the SAL on February 20, 1902. At the time it began operation by the Seaboard, the G&A owned 448 miles of track and some 39 locomotives.[20]

In 1897, meanwhile, Williams jockeyed into position with backers of a projected Richmond, Petersburg and Carolina Railroad (RP&C), heir to the Virginia & Carolina Railroad incorporated in 1882. Working alongside his Middendorf, Oliver & Company colleagues who helped him acquire the Savannah, Americus & Montgomery road, in December 1898, Williams maneuvered a takeover of the RP&C. By then he had attained controlling interest in the nonbinding Seaboard Air-Line System. His star was rapidly rising among a mere handful of Southern railway tycoons.

   Without resting on any laurels, in February 1899, Williams and his cohorts became majority owners in the 940-mile Florida Central & Peninsular Railroad (FC&P). The outfit operated within Florida, Georgia and South Carolina, having grown from legions of ancestor lines. Its earliest forbear, the Tallahassee Railroad, was chartered 65 years before (1834). The FC&P would supply the rising Seaboard Air Line Railroad with some valuable routes, linking Columbia, South Carolina, with Jacksonville, Florida, via Savannah; Waldo, in central Florida, with Tampa; plus several more key Sunshine State connections.

   To anybody looking on, it must have been obvious that the strategic parts necessary for a long-distance carrier were rapidly falling into place like dominoes. Eight months after gaining control of the FC&P, Williams and his Baltimore buddies were the principal stockholders in a railway enterprise comprised of 18 diverse companies extending their collective tracks 2,600 miles. Those private firms had been operated under a trio of pluralistic ensembles: the Seaboard Air-Line System, Georgia & Alabama Railway, and Florida Central & Peninsular Railroad. To join that trilogy without delay, the new owners laid about 200 more miles of track to form a unified system. Securing Hamlet to Columbia was a top priority because, until that was completed, everything south of Hamlet was disengaged from that north of it.

   When the project was totally finished in 1900, John Skelton Williams, at 34, presided over a mainline that extended from Richmond to Tampa, a distance of 850 miles. Not only that, he could chuckle out loud as he realized that the SAL had trimmed 79 miles off the route of his chief competitor, the Atlantic Coast Line Railroad, between Richmond and Tampa. Shaving those miles, theoretically at least, was to make freight and passenger travel a little quicker via the SAL. This became a valid selling point to travelers and shippers in a hurry. In the meantime Williams' grasp had exceeded his reach.

   John Skelton Williams realized that direct rail service through the Washington, D. C., gateway to the Northeast would be essential if his company was to successfully compete with the Atlantic Coast Line Railroad and the Southern Railway. Of course the ACL had no intention of allowing the Seaboard to gain access to its traffic in the Northeast. The Richmond, Fredericksburg and Potomac Railroad, at that time controlled by the ACL, initially refused to work out satisfactory arrangements to handle Seaboard traffic north of Richmond. Those companies felt quite secure in their position [on] account [of] the long-time provisions contained in the RF&P's charter which provided that the General Assembly would not permit another railroad to be built parallel to the RF&P.

However, both the RF&P and the ACL underestimated Williams' influence in the Commonwealth of Virginia. Using the same tactic that he had employed with the Central of Georgia when he sought entry into Savannah, Williams threatened to extend the trackage of the Seaboard through Richmond to Washington. When Williams was granted a charter by act of the Virginia General Assembly on March 3, 1900, to build a new railroad between Richmond and Washington and the Legislature coupled to this franchise the condition that the incorporators of the new railroad could purchase the State's interest in the RF&P's common stock, the RF&P and the ACL quickly acquiesced in an agreement for the interchange of SAL traffic at Richmond.[21]

The Richmond, Petersburg & Carolina Railroad's nomenclature was fixed as the Seaboard Air Line Railway on April 10, 1900. On May 30 of that year a couple of unique passenger trains left Richmond for Tampa over the just opened tracks of the SAL. Railroad executives, public officials, journalists and business leaders filled those cars for a 1,700-mile round-trip inspection journey down the SAL's mainline. Aboard was a red-coated 32-piece brass band drawn from the Portsmouth Shops which struck up rousing tunes en route at each stop. During those encounters mayors and other local dignitaries read proclamations and bestowed posies and mementoes on Seaboard president Williams. A prearranged steamboat tour carried the guests across Tampa Bay at the end of the line. The travelers were feted with a luncheon during which Williams lauded the fact SAL was "owned in the South and did not owe one cent to a financial institution north of Baltimore."[22] While that would change three years hence, it was well received by a crowd that was proud of its Southern, albeit unabashedly provincial, heritage.

When those pioneering journeymen returned to Richmond on June 2, a "Golden Spike Ceremony" marked the official launch of the Seaboard Air Line Railway. A 14-course celebratory banquet that evening at the Hotel Jefferson was presided over by Virginia Governor James H. Tyler. During a series of speeches Williams' earlier theme was reiterated: SAL was "a Southern system, created by Southern enterprise and Southern money against the machinations of Wall Street, manned by Southern men, devoted to the upbringing of Southern cities, [and] the prosperity of Southern states."[23] While the coalition of the Confederacy was 35 years in the past, unassailable allegiance remained of paramount substance to these Dixieland entrepreneurs![24]

An "equal share" pact controlling traffic over the existing "Richmond–Washington Line" (RF&P and Washington Southern) was signed by officials of six railway carriers on July 1, 1901. The half-dozen lines shared equally in owning the New Jersey–based Richmond-Washington Company, which oversaw the operations and maintenance. Their federation was comprised of the Atlantic Coast Line, Baltimore & Ohio, Chesapeake & Ohio, Pennsylvania, Seaboard Air Line, and Southern.

In the first couple of decades of the 20th century, SAL continued expanding while experiencing its initial receivership and reorganization. John Skelton Williams lost control of his beloved Seaboard during this time. In 1904, the line was extended from Atlanta to Birmingham, opening access to vast coal and iron ore resources in central Alabama.[25] Birmingham provided a link to the St. Louis–San Francisco Railway (Frisco), allowing the dual roads to promote the shortest route from the Midwest to the eastern seaboard for transporting Midwestern grain. The Frisco connection also provided the Seaboard with a route for through-train passenger cars from New York to Memphis via Washington, Richmond, Raleigh, Hamlet, Monroe, Athens, Atlanta, Birmingham and Tupelo.[26]

There were other improvements in SAL holdings elsewhere. None superseded the achievements in the Sunshine State, offering many promises of future development. There the railroad entered into contract with the Florida West Shore Railway (FWS) in 1903, becoming the "preferred connection" of that enterprise. Within a half-dozen years FWS would be absorbed into the Seaboard system. Only a short time before their affiliation in 1903, FWS had expanded from the Manatee River to Sarasota, Fruitville and Bradenton. As a result SAL was handed access to enormous untapped territory where fruits and vegetables were harvested, to be shipped to distant points. SAL provided the means. After 1909, the line was extended south to Venice and north to Inverness and Hernando, in the state's interior above Tampa. The southern route would impact the tourist industry with Venice, directly on the Gulf Coast, becoming a regular terminus for several passenger trains.

SAL opened avenues to south Florida phosphate mines when it bought a handful of short lines in that area (including the Plant City, Arcadia & Gulf, and Charlotte Harbor & Northern railroads). By 1909, SAL debuted its own port at Tampa, capable of transferring lumber, coal, phosphate and other reserves to waiting cargo ships.

While all of the growth and expansion indicated positive signs on SAL's horizons, undermining it in the same period were economic reverses, a political power struggle, disillusionment and reorganization. Although this was shaping the line for its halcyon passenger days of the 20th century, those were yet a few decades away. A change in leadership resulted after John Skelton Williams borrowed capital to finance the Birmingham extension. He got his money from a man who caused him a great deal of trouble previously, Thomas Fortune Ryan. Students of SAL history have speculated about Williams' decision, apparently without discovering a satisfactory answer for the selection of Ryan.[27] Was there no one else he could turn

Occupying SCL tracks between Tampa and Bradenton, the southbound *American Freedom Train* in red, white and blue hues crosses a trestle into the latter Florida city in 1976. Exhibiting historic artifacts and documents in its lengthy consist, the *AFT* passes through a bascule bridge opened for large craft and sailboat clearance. The oil-burning Northern type 4-8-4 steam engine 4449 leading its way was fabricated in the 1940s at Lima Locomotive Works. Note the salt water barnacles on pilings supporting the trestle (*courtesy Michael B. Robbins*).

to? A major stockholder in the Seaboard & Roanoke Railroad (a moniker dating to 1846, you recall), Ryan emphatically opposed the SAL's creation. But once he had furnished SAL's coffers with substantial infusions of cash, the railroad's management — perhaps with little choice — found itself taking him rather seriously.[28]

In a few months Ryan and some comrades dislodged Williams from the presidency and wrested control of the SAL. In 1904, realizing his contributions to the line were over, a disillusioned, resentful Williams — along with the Baltimore financiers that helped him — sold their SAL stock. Williams resigned from the board of directors. For the rest of his life he apparently remained an arch enemy of SAL leadership.

Having earned a reputation as a financier, publicist and railroad builder, following his death in Richmond on November 4, 1926, Williams was remembered as a public servant in Woodrow Wilson's presidency. He was appointed assistant secretary of the treasury in 1913, and promoted the following year to comptroller of the currency, a post he held to 1921. At the same time Williams was on the advisory board of the Interstate Commerce Commission, focused on railway, steamship and telegraph properties. Controversy stirred about him routinely and some detractors doggedly fought his rise during the Wilson administration. Williams' embattled SAL years were two decades in his past but a penchant for confrontations characterized his life.

In an unsettling period following Williams' departure from SAL, the portal to the president's suite hardly swung shut as a trio of bench-warmers passed through it in a single year. By 1908, SAL went into bankruptcy, coming out the following year. The line regrouped and achieved stability and prosperity under S. Davies Warfield, a successor whose influence was extensive. The Baltimore native helped John Skelton Williams create SAL in its formative days. After being chairman of the receivers in 1908-1909, this intrepid, dynamic entrepreneurial financier was elected chairman of the board of directors in 1912. He transferred to the SAL president's office in 1918, and served until his death in October 1927, maintaining the aggressive expansion policy that characterized the company's early history. "The eventual physical property of the modern day Seaboard was shaped during Warfield's administration," one assessment correctly noted.

Solomon Davies Warfield was born September 4, 1859, at Baltimore, the place of his death on October 24, 1927. The lifelong bachelor amassed a residue of about $4 million, most of it going to launch a home for elderly dependent women at his country estate in Baltimore County following his death. In addition to his SAL interests, Warfield was president at the same time of Baltimore's Continental Trust Company and Baltimore Steam Packet Company (Old Bay Line). He held directorships with Maryland Casualty and New York Life Insurance companies. The son of a prominent Maryland family, Warfield devoted his early career to financial and manufacturing concerns. From 1804 to 1905, he was Baltimore's U.S. postmaster.

He manifested a great interest in Dixie throughout his life, considered himself a Southerner (his slave-holding family resided in Maryland, above the renowned Mason-Dixon Line), and gave liberally to Southern arts and munificent causes while playing a large hand in developing Florida, devoting special attention to the Everglades district. At his passing Warfield's attorney acknowledged that his client "showed undying love and affection for the South, his sincere interest in its development and his entire confidence in its future."[29] Warfield himself once said, "The Seaboard Air Line Railway, capable as I believe it is, of doing a great constructive work in the upbuilding of the South, presented to me, a Southern-born man, a field for useful work, with an outlet for the sentiment I feel both for the South and for that railroad."[30]

In 1915, the Seaboard Air Line Railway and the Carolina, Atlantic and Western Railway that operated in the two Carolinas merged to create the Seaboard Air Line Railway Company. One of the significant alterations this union provided was a second SAL mainline between Hamlet, North Carolina, and Savannah, Georgia. The new route was dubbed by insiders the "East Carolina Line." The established main took a southwesterly course before turning south-southeast between Hamlet and Savannah. On the way there it encompassed places like Cheraw, McBee, Camden, Columbia (the Palmetto State capital), Denmark and Fairfax, all in South Carolina. Conversely, the newer route swung southeasterly from Hamlet toward the coast before hugging the shoreline to Savannah. On its way traffic encountered places like Dillon, Poston, Andrews, Charleston (the state's major Atlantic port city) and Wiggins.

The traditional course via Columbia, where most of Seaboard's travelers journeyed (and some Amtrak patrons ride today), is 247 miles between Hamlet and Savannah. The "East Carolina Line" via Charleston, on the contrary, is 263 miles.[31] For reference, the mainline of the Atlantic Coast Line Railroad passed through Pembroke, North Carolina, not many miles east of Hamlet, to Savannah while pursuing a north-south course between the SAL's left and right mainlines. The ACL distance from Pembroke to Savannah is 263 miles. Although it isn't a precise comparison (more like apples to oranges), it's evident the trio of routes is in fairly close proximity to one another distance-wise. Many of today's Amtrak passengers pass over the former ACL (now CSX) tracks between their Northeast and Florida destinations.

> As the decade of the 1920s began, S. Davies Warfield was firmly of the opinion that the only way the Seaboard could gain a competitive edge on its rivals [Atlantic Coast Line, Florida East Coast, Southern] was to further expand its position in the State of Florida.... Boldly, he proposed that the Seaboard ... build a cross-state railroad connecting the East and West Coasts of Florida.
> Beginning in 1924, the SAL built a 204-mile extension from its Jacksonville–Tampa main line at Coleman to West Palm Beach. When opened on January 21, 1925, it gave Florida its first cross-state railroad. The following year, the SAL extended the main line from West Palm Beach to Miami on the East Coast and to St. Petersburg, the Pinellas Peninsula, Fort Myers and Naples on the West Coast. This gave the Seaboard not only two main lines, one down the East Coast to Miami and one down the West Coast to Tampa and Fort Myers, but also a line of railroad across the state connecting those magical cities. In January 1927, these lines were officially opened.[32]

A devastating hurricane subsequently curtailed Florida's land boom, devaluing property in the areas in which SAL had just expanded. On top of it, Davies Warfield died the year his Florida extension was done. The South's economy was in recession and SAL's financial picture was shattered. Into this abyss stepped the youngest president of a major U.S. railroad, Legh Richmond Powell, Jr., at 43, with daunting tasks before him. Davies Warfield had hand-picked Powell, trained him, mentored him and even left a stipulation in his will that Powell should follow him.

Born in Seaboard's original home town of Portsmouth, Virginia, on March 10, 1884, in 1902, at the age of 18, young Powell joined the railroad as a clerk for the auditor of passenger accounts. His dedication and ability served him well as he eventually climbed the proverbial corporate stairs. In 1918, he was elected vice president and controller. "Powell's intimate knowledge of the Seaboard, especially of its finances, enabled him to pilot the company through difficult times and groom it into one of the most efficiently operated railroads in the country," attested one wag.

By leasing the Georgia, Florida and Alabama Railway in 1928, Powell led SAL to create a new gateway for western traffic between the Florida panhandle and Montgomery, Alabama. But SAL's expansionist policies didn't come without a price, and especially in an epoch in which revenues radically shrank from the Florida real estate collapse and intense competition from rival railroads. That same year (1928) SAL submitted a voluntary reorganization plan to stockholders and investors. Not long afterward, in October 1929, the nation's economy collapsed in the stock market crash precipitating the Great Depression. Things could hardly have been worse. On December 23, 1930, SAL was forced into receivership a second time, extending to 1946. Powell was appointed by a U.S. District Court as one of two receivers for the troubled line throughout that prolonged era.

The Depression itself had a devastating effect on SAL, just as it did on virtually all U.S. railroads. The collapse of the Florida real estate boom in spring 1927 already netted a 20 percent decrease in Seaboard passenger revenues from the previous year.[33] The Depression brought only more misery, each year getting progressively worse. Another 20 percent revenue loss occurred in 1930, then 25 percent in 1931, 35 percent in 1932, and more than 50 percent of pre–Depression receipts in 1933, the peak of the decline. Yet by significantly lowering rail fares while totally equipping a trio of its major passenger trains with air conditioning in 1934 (the first road in the South doing that), SAL saw travelers coming back on board. In a dramatic shift, income from passengers increased 44 percent that year over 1933, with riders increasing by an aggregate 64 percent.

By instituting sound financial policies and preparing the line to become a high-achiever in the railroad industry once it was out of receivership, SAL officials did themselves a favor. Over 400 miles of unprofitable branch lines were abandoned while economical gas-electric passenger trains replaced costly steam-powered locals. Meanwhile, SAL continued to improve services. In 1933, its crack passenger train, the *Orange Blossom Special*, was air-conditioned. The same train witnessed the premier of diesel-electric engines in the Southeast when its motive power was upgraded in 1938.

With the inauguration of the *Silver Meteor* on February 2, 1939, between New York and separate sections below Jacksonville running to Miami and Tampa–St. Petersburg, SAL was truly at the forefront of innovators blazing trails, assuredly so in the South. SAL wasn't the initial Dixieland carrier to offer streamlined equipment, but the *Meteor's* meteoric rise ushered in one of the most triumphant rail passenger renaissances in the nation: the Florida streamliner.

On the side a conservative, watchful ACL sat, hesitant to buy into the lightweight stream-liner phenomenon until it saw the overwhelming outburst of public fawning over the SAL's *Meteor*. For one thing, that equipment required a huge upfront cash outlay, although those trainsets could be operated much more efficiently and inexpensively than heavyweight consists. They were also faster and signaled "modern" instead of "outmoded." Reacting swiftly, in June 1939, ACL placed an order with manufacturer Budd Corporation for four streamliner sets. In the interim the *Meteor* took off to wild abandon literally and figuratively, grossing $8 million-plus in 1944 — more than the whole SAL operation lost in receivership in 1933.[34] Suddenly perennial underdog SAL had found a way to eclipse its most enduring rival, if only for a little while.

ACL didn't get "on the road" with its own streamliners until December 1, 1939. But it decided to go Seaboard one better by introducing not merely one but two of the newfangled trains on the same day. Calling them the *East Coast Champion* and the *West Coast Champion*, ACL ran them not as detached sections — as the SAL was doing with its *Silver Meteor* — but as actual separate trains between New York and Miami and New York and Jacksonville. From the latter municipality ACL consists departed over diverse routes to either Tampa or St. Petersburg.

"In the post-war years, the Seaboard finally fulfilled the dreams of John Skelton Williams and S. Davies Warfield to become one of the premier railroads in the Southeastern section of the country," a railway historian acknowledged. "It enjoyed a particularly outstanding repu-tation for the excellence of its passenger service, especially for the service and accommodations on its famous silver fleet of streamliners."[35]

> The South boomed after World War II. For generations following the devastation of the Civil War, the region had been an economic backwater, somnolent and impoverished. Now, after decades of anticipation, a "New South" was emerging at last. Population grew rapidly and new industry poured in. Expansion in South Florida and around Atlanta was especially phenomenal.

As the South prospered so did the Seaboard. In 1947, revenue freight tonnage reached 35,261,000 tons, higher than the wartime peak established in 1943. And it continued to grow, reaching 43,000,000 tons in 1951 and 51,000,000 in 1959. Seaboard had managed to lose money in 1945, the final year of the war, but it was the last year the railroad would ever sustain a loss. Net income increased from slightly over $6 million in 1947 to almost $21 million in 1953.[36]

Some of those figures would soon be dwarfed, as the Seaboard continued to thrive.[37] The line's revenue freight tonnage in 1966, for instance, nearly reached 62 million. That year SAL transported more passengers, too, than it had in any of the eight previous years, another indicator of the system's vibrancy, even at that late date.

The Seaboard mainline was squeezed between a couple of larger and stronger rival companies: the Atlantic Coast Line was chiefly to its east while the Southern Railway was principally to its west. SAL operated at a competitive disadvantage, for the others had more favorable rights of way in many cases. In the late 19th and early 20th centuries, some of affluent financier J. P. Morgan's dealings intertwined with those of ACL and Southern. This was apt to result in cooperation between those two behemoths at the expense of competing rail giants. ACL and Southern, for example, jointly owned the Chesapeake Steamship Company which contended with SAL's Old Bay Line on Chesapeake Bay. ACL provided trackage rights to Southern leading to both Jacksonville and Portsmouth, competing again with SAL.

Between the Midwest and Florida SAL again found itself disenfranchised. Southern operated its own route between Cincinnati and Florida. ACL schlepped riders and cargo between a handful of Alabama and Georgia points and the Sunshine State. Those routes extended to Chicago, Cincinnati, St. Louis or Detroit via one or two interline connections. SAL, on the other hand, which possessed only limited northwest-southeast service (handling none beyond Atlanta and Birmingham), relied on a patchwork of interline linkages. They involved having passengers physically transfer companies en route on occasions, and sometimes terminals, too. And even between Alabama, Georgia and Florida, SAL's routes were usually longer to the same destinations.

Another disadvantage was the fact Seaboard was a predominantly single-track line as opposed to mostly double-track by its major competitors (ACL, FEC, Southern). That translated into frequent slows-downs and, therefore, lengthened trips as trains pulled off onto sidings to allow others to pass. Fewer than 100 miles of the SAL system had been converted to double-tracking by its final few years as an independent road.[38]

That's not to say SAL was inevitably the underdog. It was the only railroad in Florida to possess its own lines connecting the Atlantic and Gulf coasts. It maintained the only direct line across that state heading due west from the pivotal Jacksonville gateway—it connected at River Junction (now Chattahoochee) with the Louisville & Nashville Railroad to New Orleans. In different eras, first the Southern Pacific, later Amtrak, ran the only legitimate transcontinental passenger trains across America along this route (from New Orleans to Los Angeles coupled with the New Orleans–Jacksonville L&N/SAL segment). Seaboard also called at a number of cities that parallel rival ACL's mainline missed, among them Raleigh and Pinehurst, North Carolina; Camden and Columbia, South Carolina; and some smaller communities from Virginia to Florida. Of the half-dozen states in which ACL and SAL operated, ACL tracks reached four state capitals (one on the mainline) while SAL entered all six (three on its north-south mainline).

After nearly a half-century of service to the company, Legh Powell retired from the SAL presidency in 1952. His was a distinguished career and proved he was the man for the job when he assumed operations under disastrous conditions in 1927, a situation that only got infinitely worse before at last turning around. His death at 85, on October 14, 1969, occurred at Norfolk.

SCL Maintenance of Way dining car 765384 rests in Chattanooga in November 1983. It may have been previously owned by ancestor SAL. Many large railroads had these cars in their track and facilities upkeep inventories. Care for crews was vital to adequately prepare for the passage of passenger and freight trains on mainlines and secondary routes (*courtesy Jay T. Thomson*).

On a pretty day in 1950, ACL 864 ferries passengers along one of its routes near Florence, South Carolina. From Florence, home of a major shop facility, ACL trains radiated in assorted directions — south to Charleston, east to Wilmington, north to Fayetteville, west to Columbia and Augusta, and northwest freight traffic to Winston-Salem. Florence is strategically situated for the many services it performs (*courtesy North Carolina State Archives*).

Raleigh was one of a half-dozen state capitals where SAL passenger trains called. Three, including Raleigh, were on SAL's north-south main. Here a crowd awaits the return of a conductor (car attendant now). on June 20, 1951, at the SAL depot there. The boarding passengers are so conservatively attired, a trait of that day, it's unfeasible to determine if they are Florida-bound or heading north. "Seaboard Station," where the photograph was made, received trains from 1942 to 1986, and was later converted into Raleigh's only downtown shopping center (*courtesy North Carolina State Archives*).

Powell was succeeded by John W. Smith, final president of the Seaboard Air Line, who oversaw the transition to its next phase. Powell's predecessor (S. Davies Warfield) and successor (Smith) both hailed from Baltimore. Smith was born July 20, 1900, the month following the Seaboard's formal premiere. And like Powell, Smith came up through the SAL ranks, joining its engineering department in Norfolk in 1925, having graduated from the University of Maryland three years earlier. Shortly afterward he was dispatched to Florida as a construction engineer on a new SAL extension being built from West Palm Beach through Miami to Homestead. When that job was done at the end of 1926, he moved to the operating department before becoming administrative vice-president under Powell in 1951.

Upgrading and modernizing equipment and facilities characterized much of his presidency. But the thing for which Smith is best remembered is bringing about a merger with the SAL's most durable rival, the Atlantic Coast Line Railroad (ACL). Exploratory discussions regarding that possibility began a decade before it became fact. As early as 1957, shortly after William Thomas Rice, president of the Richmond, Fredericksburg & Potomac Railroad, was elected to the presidency of the ACL, talks began. Both camps investigated the effects of operating those parallel lines that served the same territory in the same six states under unilateral management. Not only could efficiencies and improved productivity result, they theorized, in an era in which freight, mail and people traffic was turning to highways and airways in greater numbers than ever witnessed, it seemed prudent to seriously consider combining the operations. Another reason unification might be worthwhile was to fend off any potential aggressors who could seek to control them from afar. For all of these reasons and others, SAL's Smith and ACL's Rice took painstaking, deliberate steps to carefully study — to get it right — and to lay the groundwork for a future amalgamation.

In its heyday SAL maintained two parallel platforms on opposite sides of its mainline at Plant City, Florida. The low-level access on the right is for passengers while the higher-level facing one is for freight. The joint passenger station served ACL trains at its far end where ACL's east-west main crossed SAL's at a diamond. The carriers merged to form SCL a few years before this 1974 photograph. The track links Tampa (ahead) with Jacksonville (*courtesy Michael B. Robbins*).

An SCL Maintenance of Way work train sits on a siding at Wildwood, Florida, in 1975. When ACL rebuilt these cars it installed straight equalized six-wheel trucks with SKF roller bearings and turtle-back roofs with squared-off ends to match newer lightweight cars. There's totally new side plating with new doors and windows plus other mechanical improvements. The first heavyweight car appears to be an ex–ACL Emerson Shops rebuilt RPO. The middle car seems to be a galley car for work train food service. The last car resembles an old Pullman for MOW crews' sleeping quarters (*courtesy Michael B. Robbins*).

Common methods of turning engines around include roundhouses and a wye. Railways applied wyes not just to turn locomotives but whole trains to head them in opposite directions. Wyes were rife at passenger stations with stub-end rails. As seen in this upper eastern North Carolina SAL layout, a wye is composed of a three-sided pattern (note the freight on the wye's distant leg). After a train pulls forward far enough, it backs into a second leg of the triangle, then pulls forward in the third leg, reversing its arrival path. Some Dixie terminals featured wyes for part or all tracks, including Atlanta Terminal Station, Jacksonville, New Orleans and Tampa (*courtesy Jay Miller*).

There was substantial resistance to the proposed merger from multiple railroads that competed in the region, however. Their arguments would have to be addressed by the Interstate Commerce Commission (ICC) before any final verdict could be rendered. Florida East Coast, for example, had much to lose if its chief connector to the north, ACL — on whom it depended for most of the trains traveling its coastal route between Jacksonville and Miami — were to be realigned with its prime intrastate challenger, SAL. SAL, of course, arrived in Miami over its own trackage, the only other long distance carrier to do so.[39]

Given the prospects of an overwhelming presence in their back yards, other campers along the ACL and SAL routes weren't happy either. The Central of Georgia contended that it would be surrounded by the new line if those companies merged. Three other systems — Gulf, Mobile & Ohio, Illinois Central, and Southern — complained about the control of formidable competitor Louisville & Nashville that a united entity would wield. ACL was already a major shareowner of L&N stock. IC and Southern lobbied independently that they should be allowed to buy ACL's interest in L&N. Furthermore, Southern maintained that — if it was to remain competitive against an ACL-SAL mélange — as a condition of approval to that fusion, the ICC should require the new firm to sell to Southern one of its existing lines between Savannah and Tampa via Jacksonville.

By way of information, although Atlantic Coast Line and Seaboard Air Line were analogous in many ways, ACL was considerably larger.[40] It owned 5,700 miles of track to SAL's

4,100, which was actually about 72 percent of ACL's routes. In reality, however, Coast Line controlled 12,000 miles, reducing SAL's percentage to about a third by comparison. Included was a third interest that ACL held in the 6,000-mile Louisville & Nashville Railroad (L&N) predominating in Kentucky, Tennessee and Alabama, plus a trio of lines jointly owned by ACL and L&N: Clinchfield, Georgia, and West Point Route (the latter a combined Atlanta & West Point and Western Railway of Alabama). Comparing operating revenues for 1965, these totaled $201 million (ACL) vs. $181 million (SAL). Net income that year was $18 million (ACL) vs. $16 million (SAL).

By a 9–2 vote, the ICC endorsed joining the dual railroads on December 2, 1963. While both partners were making money, the margin of commissioners believed that neither line was making fair returns on its investment. The squabble over lopsided competition to be anticipated by pooling those resources evidently didn't sufficiently impress the ICC members. Whether to allow merger of a couple of rivals that already dominated the territory and think it in the public interest to do so figured prominently into the two "no" votes in the ICC's rendering.

Nevertheless it still wasn't a done deal; the wrangling persisted for another couple of years. The ICC's decision was appealed to the federal courts with the U.S. District Court for Florida's Middle District finally setting it aside and sending it back to the ICC for further consideration. Ultimately the U.S. Supreme Court, replying on December 22, 1965, vacated the District Court's act, in effect giving final approval to the applicants' request.

The union was consummated a year and a half beyond, on July 1, 1967. The new alliance, in an obvious attempt to say it all, was branded with the archaic terminology of Seaboard Coast Line Railroad Company.[41] The former SAL's John W. Smith became chairman of the board and CEO of the newly formed parent firm while ex–ACL executive leader William Thomas Rice became president. Six months hence the CEO duties shifted from Smith to Rice. Smith remained as chairman until his retirement in 1970. He died at 71 two years later in May 1972 in Richmond.

A Seaboard biographer shared some personal thoughts on the transition from SAL to SCL. One senses the dismay of an admiring railfan in contemplating what used to be.[42]

> The new railroad was predominantly under the influence of former Coast Line people. Even though it was officially headquartered in Richmond, most of its general offices remained in Jacksonville, the location of ACL's main offices.... The new railroad adopted ACL's uninspired black color scheme for its locomotives. Even its cabooses were painted Coast Line orange instead of Seaboard's traditional red....
>
> Some lines were soon abandoned in favor of alternative former ACL lines. The most notable were ... between Charleston and Savannah and most of the line from the Chattahoochee River to Montgomery, Ala. Subsequently, all or part of several other major Seaboard mainlines have been scrapped, including ... between Richmond and Raleigh, Atlanta and Birmingham, and Savannah and Jacksonville.... The line between West Palm Beach and Miami was sold in 1988.... While some former Seaboard lines are still heavily used for freight traffic, only a shadow of the old SAL remains....
>
> The Seaboard Air Line is now but a small part of CSX transportation. CSX is a truly massive amalgamation of rail lines. It extends from Philadelphia to New Orleans and from Chicago to South Florida.... CSX Corp. owns ships, barge lines and vast real estate interests, as well as railroads. Seaboard's name has disappeared and it may now just be a drop in the conglomerate bucket, but at least it accounts for the "S" in CSX. That's more than Coast Line, B&O or L&N could say.

William Thomas Rice was around for the next merger, taking an active hand in designing and implementing the launch of CSX Transportation in November 1980. Joining with the Seaboard Coast Line were numerous former flags (some having fallen much earlier) including the Baltimore & Ohio; Chesapeake & Ohio; Clinchfield; Louisville & Nashville; Monon;

Nashville, Chattanooga & St. Louis; Western Maryland; and others.[43] At the turn of the 21st century CSX was to be one of but a handful of major American Class 1 rail lines still operating in a highly competitive environment.

The Seaboard Air Line's headquarters was spread across as many as a quartet of office buildings in Norfolk and Portsmouth, Virginia, in the years between 1900 and 1958. But on August 22, 1958, a new consolidated general office building opened in Richmond, that city's largest office facility with 315,000 square feet of space covering eight floors on West Broad Street. When SAL and ACL merged into SCL, most of the line was consolidated into the ACL headquarters edifice in Jacksonville, Florida.

In a postscript to the years of independent SAL service, another of its historians laments[44]:

> The Seaboard Coast Line was created by the merger of two roads with parallel routes and 75 common points. Since the majority of the economics were to be achieved by the consolidation of functions and elimination of duplicate routes, it was inevitable that this merger would result in some substantial retirements on the former properties. Unfortunately for admirers of the Seaboard, the majority of lines and facilities abandoned happened to be on the former SAL. In the years since 1967, either all or substantial portions of the former SAL lines between Richmond and Raleigh, Atlanta and Birmingham, Savannah and Jacksonville, Charleston and Savannah, and the Chattahoochee River and Montgomery have been retired and taken up for scrap.
>
> But if the Seaboard is gone, it certainly is not forgotten. Its legacy lives on in those segments of the road that still form a vital part of the CSX Transportation system and in its many innovations that endure as an ingredient of today's modern railroads. And it still lives on in the hearts of those admirers who came to know that "The Route of Courteous Service" was more than just another company slogan. It really was the way the Seaboard Air Line did business.

A couple of things are worth mentioning in regard to routes before exploring the Seaboard's venerated passenger service. First, as already observed, most travelers heading south aboard SAL trains departed the crucial gateway at Hamlet, North Carolina, for Savannah on a course that carried them through Cheraw, McBee, Camden, Columbia, Denmark and Fairfax, South Carolina. In the meantime the "East Carolina Line" to Savannah via Dillon, Poston, Charleston and Wiggins was almost exclusively (but not entirely) relegated to freight traffic.

Second, in 1925, SAL opened a 204-mile enlargement of its mainline from Coleman, Florida, to West Palm Beach, which was increased another 70 miles to Miami two years afterward. Not only did this link both Florida coasts by rail but it opened the southeast Sunshine State shores to continuous tracks owned by a single operator that reached Richmond, connecting with eastern trunk lines to myriad destinations. With that background consider the little burg of Wildwood, not quite five miles north of Coleman, where the new addition tied into the SAL main between Jacksonville and Tampa–St. Petersburg. Wildwood—lying 127 miles below Jacksonville in Florida's northeast quadrant—soon became analogous to Hamlet. Through it passed the preponderance of SAL's north-south trains.[45]

At the central junction at Wildwood many passenger trains paused while some of their cars were shifted behind locomotives heading southwest to Tampa, Sarasota, Venice, Boca Grande or Fort Myers, or southeast to West Palm Beach, Delray Beach, Fort Lauderdale, Hollywood and Miami. Trains from those destinations moved through the same process at Wildwood before realignment into single consists bound for Jacksonville and points north. While it wasn't "just like Hamlet," after Jacksonville—the busiest point in the SAL system—Wildwood may have witnessed as much physical maneuvering in a day's time as occurred anywhere on Seaboard tracks.

Until that extension to southeast Florida was completed, whatever SAL passenger trains arrived in the Gold Coast of Florida did so by way of the Florida East Coast Railway (FEC). Its line skirted the ocean from Jacksonville to Miami and saw dozens of trains bearing FEC,

ACL and SAL insignia on its route daily. Unlike the SAL, the ACL was never able to establish its own independent main to Miami, though its reasons for not doing so even now aren't absolutely clear. It was a concern that perennially rankled many ACL officials. Meanwhile, until disaster struck the FEC in early 1963, only SAL possessed an exclusive portal into and out of the enormously popular gentle-breeze, warm-climate playgrounds along the southeast Florida beaches. As a result ACL trains shifted to some of Seaboard's trackage. You may anticipate reading more on that topic a little later.

In the years preceding the opening of the Coleman–Gold Coast extension, the *Seaboard Fast Mail* ran over the SAL mainline between Richmond and Tampa. Seamless connections to New York were provided by the Richmond, Fredericksburg & Potomac (Richmond–Washington) and Pennsylvania (Washington–New York) railroads. Simultaneously, a quartet of passenger consists plied SAL routes from New York to both Florida coasts in those same years. On their southbound treks they all were divided at Jacksonville: one section continued over the SAL main to Tampa, St. Petersburg, Sarasota and Venice while the other section moved along FEC trackage to West Palm Beach, Fort Lauderdale and Miami. That foursome included the *Florida-Cuba Special* (reclassified as the *Carolina-Florida Special* later), the *Seaboard Florida Limited* (an all-Pullman winter consist), the *Floridian* and the *All Florida Special*.[46,47] Before 1925, SAL sent no fewer than five New York–Florida trainsets down its mainline every day in winter with four of them running year-round.

Historically one of the most imposing Seaboard passenger trains—returned to the public spotlight by country singer Johnny Cash after a few decades in the shadows—was the *Orange Blossom Special*. Launched on November 21, 1925, within a brief span it was widely recognized as a premier method of travel between New York and both Florida coasts and in between. To project a status that became legendary, according to one account, "The train's personnel were specially selected and at one time a daily report of the *Special*'s performance, occupancy and noteworthy passengers was submitted to Seaboard's president. The emphasis was on comfort and the train included such amenities as a barber, a lady's maid, and shower baths." Valet service and dining cars featuring exquisite cuisine were among its celebrated traditions. The *Special* was air conditioned throughout in 1934, one of the earliest U.S. trains to add that sumptuous amenity. It also christened the Seaboard's new route from Coleman to West Palm Beach (and later, Miami), a genuine piece of marketing grandeur.

The *Orange Blossom Special* was dieselized on December 15, 1938, the first in the Southeast to gain that distinction, too, making it much faster than the steam-powered engines it replaced. In addition to a Boston–Miami sleeper, its east coast section boasted a buffet-club-library car and a buffet-lounge-recreation car plus a diner. That section bypassed both Savannah and Jacksonville in a drive to reach its destinations in the quickest time.

In January 1940, the east coast section departed New York's Pennsylvania Station at 1:20 P.M. and was due in Miami, 1,162 miles distant, the following day at 3:35 P.M. The trip took 14 and a quarter hours (compared to 26 and a quarter hours three years before under steam power with unlimited stops). Northbound the *Special* left Miami at 1:10 P.M. and was in New York at 3:30 P.M. the next day.

A southbound west coast section, running over a 1,021-mile route to Tampa and St. Petersburg with stops at Savannah and Jacksonville, left New York at 1:30 P.M. It arrived in Tampa at 1:15 P.M. the following day and St. Petersburg at 3 P.M. Heading north the train left St. Petersburg at 1:15 P.M., Tampa at 2:55 P.M. and was in New York at 3 P.M. the next day.

Seaboard publicists continued to cash in on the *Orange Blossom Special*'s notoriety throughout its long life, even though it was eventually superseded by another introduction as the line's flagship product. In its February 1, 1953, timetable, nevertheless, the SAL proudly hawked its durable streamliner thusly:

Once again it's
Orange Blossom Time

THE ORANGE BLOSSOM SPECIAL, Seaboard's all-Pullman attractively-styled Winter Season train, has long been a favorite with discriminating travelers between the East and Florida resorts, its name a symbol of gracious traveling.

While the larger types of private rooms are featured on the ORANGE BLOSSOM, a wide variety of Pullman accommodations are to be found throughout its hospitable interiors. Ample provisions for relaxation and recreation are available in spacious lounges. Dining car meals are prepared with your fullest enjoyment in mind ... and always you are surrounded by the attentive but unobtrusive service for which Seaboard is famous. In short.... A train you will remember with pleasure, and one you will wish to use again and again.

To insure your obtaining the accommodations you desire, we suggest making your ORANGE BLOSSOM reservations as far in advance as possible.

The Route of *Courteous Service*

Despite being replaced by the luster of streamliners to the SAL system as time went on, the *Orange Blossom Special* retained much of its eminence. The Seaboard finally dispatched it to the great rail yard in the sky at the close of the four-month 1952-1953 winter season. One wag labeled that final departure "the saddest cut of all." At its end the *Blossom*'s 15-car consist between New York and Miami included two dining cars, two Pullman buffet-lounge cars, two through Boston–Miami Pullmans, two Washington–Miami Pullmans, and seven New York–Miami Pullmans. Yet it lost out to the competition, a flashy winter-season all-Pullman streamliner, the *Florida Special*, fostered by ACL between the same pair of cities. Never reequipped, the heavyweight *Orange Blossom Special* was no match for its sleeker, swifter opponent in the "now" generation. An SAL chronicler mourned its passing.[48]

> The *Orange Blossom Special* had indeed been "special." Before the arrival of the "Silver" streamliners, it had been the one really outstanding train in an otherwise mediocre fleet. In its heyday it was unquestionably one of the finest trains in the nation.... Years later, in 1982, Seaboard System revived the name for a crack freight train, a redball from Florida to the Northeast devoted, naturally, to the transportation of citrus fruit. And the freight was worthy of its heritage. At the time, it was the fastest long-distance freight train in the United States.

In May 1926, Seaboard added a new train, the *Southerner*, on its route between New York and Sebring, a popular tourist Mecca lying in the heart of central Florida 233 miles south of Jacksonville and 103 miles northwest of West Palm Beach. A connection journeyed between Jacksonville and Tampa–St. Pete. This *Southerner*, by the way, shouldn't be confused with a venerated streamliner of the same sobriquet operated by Southern Railway between Washington and New Orleans in the 1940s, 1950s and 1960s, one of that line's premier consists.

A couple of clever railroad scribes described the phase into Dixie streamliners.[49]

> The Florida trains had a unique charm of their own. Winter-weary southbound passengers seemed to undergo a metamorphosis as soon as they stepped on board. Hanging up coats they'd no longer need, Florida-bound riders settled in for the fast overnight run to tropical paradise. On board there was the wonderful experience of dinner in the diner ... while passengers stared out at the frigid winterscape they were leaving behind. The cozy confines of a sleeping-car room with starched, clean linens turned down for the night invited sleep as the Carolinas slid by in darkness. The next morning one awoke to sunshine streaming through the window as his or her train rocketed along through Florida orange groves. Following a breakfast of fresh-brewed coffee and ham and scrambled eggs highlighted by such exotica as orange or grapefruit marmalade, passengers began arriving at their various destinations ... delighting in ... unaccustomed warmth.

The SAL's new flagship train produced a model that was to characterize the company's streamliner passenger service for the remainder of the firm's existence — with consists molded of lightweight stainless steel. The first of the line, dubbed the *Silver Meteor*, was introduced as the "Train of Tomorrow" (which rightfully, it was) to a groundswell of wild approbation

Ever wonder what a largely southern consist looks like north of the Mason-Dixon Line? SAL's #58 *Silver Meteor*, originating at Miami and St. Petersburg, crosses over at the Baldwin (Pennsylvania) tower en route to New York on July 28, 1965. Electrified at Washington, D.C., it's pulled by GG1 4852 ever since RF&P — which took control from SAL at Richmond — parked its diesel. In this photograph operating as PRR #114, the train looks different than it did in Dixie. For one thing, the catenary creates an absolutely distinct environment (*courtesy Chuck Blardone*).

at the 1939 New York World's Fair, creating a stir that spilled out to other parts of the industry.[50] So fascinated was the traveling public with it, in fact, that nearly every trip was operated at full capacity. While originally expected to run to and from Miami and St. Petersburg every third day, in 10 months following its debut the *Meteor* was racing to both Florida coasts every day. Noticeably moved by all of this was the ACL, as previously noted, which — until the *Meteor* premiered — sat silently on the sidelines of the streamliner innovation. Patiently it observed until it could no longer ignore what its chief opponent was about. A normally conformist ACL would answer the call before the year was out, and do so with a still greater flourish by introducing a pair of *Champion*s to Florida-bound travelers.

The *Silver Meteor*'s inaugural run, on February 2, 1939, brought out the best that SAL could muster, securing its place in the one-upmanship game for a while. Like the *Orange Blossom Special*, the *Meteor* also skipped Savannah and Jacksonville, displaying greater exclusivity than that shown by its older sister: it made no revenue stops in the 767 miles between Richmond and Wildwood. At that juncture a coaches-only section veered off to Tampa, St. Petersburg, Sarasota and Venice. Early in the game the diesel-powered *Meteor* plied the New York–Miami route in both directions in 24 hours, start to finish. Averaging 48.4 miles per hour, it accomplished that feat despite half-a-dozen stops before reaching SAL tracks at Richmond and five more between Wildwood and Miami.

The flagship train's early consists included an observation-lounge-coach, diner, tavern-coach, baggage-dormitory coach, and three all-chair reserved seat coaches. As demand increased, the number of coaches and sleepers was amplified to meet the growing needs. Following a trend established by the airlines, there was a stewardess-nurse aboard every *Meteor* plus a traveling passenger agent to assist patrons. It was one of the earliest trains in the country to offer those specialized services.

In early 1953 — then making revenue stops between Richmond and Miami at Raleigh,

Columbia, Savannah, Thalmann, Jacksonville, Baldwin, Waldo, Ocala, and 11 more cities from Wildwood to Miami — the *Meteor* still completed the route in 25 and a half hours. It left New York at 2:25 P.M. for arrivals in Tampa at 1:10 P.M. the following day, St. Petersburg at 2:55 and Miami at 3:55. Yet another section proceeded from Tampa to Bradenton, Sarasota and Venice. Northbound it left Miami at 9 A.M., St. Petersburg at 9:45 and Tampa at 11:30. Following the rendezvous at Wildwood, the train pulled into New York's Pennsylvania Station at 10:25 A.M. the next morning.

Today the *Meteor* appellation survives, along with a second train (*Silver Star*) in Amtrak's portfolio. Those two supply the passenger carrier's Northeast-Florida service on routes that formerly witnessed nearly a score of daily runs. In the contemporary era the *Meteor* operates with reserved seat coaches, Viewliner sleeping cars and a full service dining car principally over ACL trackage to Auburndale, Florida, continuing beyond over the SAL mainline. After leaving New York in mid afternoon, its present route includes Richmond, Florence, Charleston, Savannah, Jacksonville, Orlando, Lakeland, Winter Haven, West Palm Beach, Fort Lauderdale, Hollywood and Miami with arrival at its southern terminus in early evening of the following day. The *Meteor* departs Miami in early morning for arrival in New York the next day at midday.

Seaboard's involvement in passenger service to and from the Midwest was always minimal, mostly limited to a few through Pullmans forwarded by Southern Railway. SAL's most noteworthy contribution in the heyday of rail travel was the *Florida Sunbeam*, a winter season limited. From 1936 to 1949, that trainset operating between Cincinnati and Florida succeeded an earlier venture, the *Suwannee River Special*, abandoned in the Great Depression epoch. The *Sunbeam* carried through sleeping cars from Detroit, Cleveland, Chicago and Toledo, relinquished at Cincinnati by the New York Central. Running over Southern tracks from Ohio, the southbound *Sunbeam* transitioned to SAL at Hampton, Florida; that was a junction on the Jacksonville–Wildwood main 33 miles below Baldwin. The train proceeded to both Sunshine State coasts. While dieselized by other carriers in the 1940s, the *Sunbeam* was powered by steam engines on SAL.

The SAL main saw many more passenger consists during the halcyon era of train travel. Among them:

• *Southern States Special* between New York and St. Petersburg with a Wildwood–Miami connection, a precursor to the *Silver Meteor*. This train was renamed the *Sun Queen* in December 1941, and was run independently of the *Cotton States Special* north of Hamlet. Eventually its route was reduced, terminating in Tampa instead of St. Pete, although it was restored to St. Pete for a brief while in 1948–1949. Oddly, SAL encountered a sizeable hurdle in picking a permanent moniker for the *Southern States Special/Sun Queen*. In May 1947, it was rechristened *Camellia*; in December 1948, its appellation was *Sunland*. For much of its existence, under whatever handle it went, this train was responsible for ferrying the *Silver Comet*'s Portsmouth–Atlanta sleeper and coach between Norlina (above Raleigh) and Hamlet, North Carolina, in both directions.

As time progressed the *Sunland* was steadily devalued, eventually becoming little more than a mail and express run. It was terminated northbound at Washington in 1952, included no sleeping cars south of Jacksonville, and lost its dining and lounge cars in 1955. A Wildwood–Miami train, which did not connect with the Washington–Tampa consist, ran exclusively during the winter season some years. The *Sunland* persisted through the 1960s; by then whatever promise it exhibited at its start was long gone, only a figment of its former self.

• *Cotton States Special* between New York and Birmingham via Hamlet and Atlanta, traveling in conjunction with the *Southern States Special* between New York–Hamlet to December 1941.

• *Robert E. Lee* between Washington and Memphis via Hamlet, Atlanta and Birmingham, running over Frisco tracks from Birmingham to Memphis. On May 18, 1947, this train was renamed the *Cotton Blossom*. In 1949, it was downgraded; its dining and sleeping cars were removed from the consists. Beginning then its run terminated at Atlanta, a separate numbered trainset running between Atlanta and Birmingham. Restored to operate from Washington to Birmingham in 1952, the service was soon diminished again, leaving it a nameless passenger-mail-express run. Other changes subsequently were instituted; however, only the southbound consist persisted on the whole route after the 1967 merger.

• *New York–Florida Limited* between New York and Miami. At Jacksonville, a section turned off the mainline and headed west to River Junction, where it was handed to L&N for the remainder of the trek to New Orleans. On the SAL main, meanwhile, cross-state Pullman cars from Tampa to West Lake Wales connected at the latter for Miami or New York. The cross-state overnight tie vanished in April 1953, although coach service remained for a while between Miami and Tampa. Ironically the *Limited* moved at a slower pace than its peers, requiring two nights and a day to make the journey between northern and southern hubs.

In December 1941, the *Limited* was labeled the *Palmland*, a branding that lasted to 1967. The *Palmland* flaunted a complex consist: there was a dining car in its 97-mile lineup between Raleigh and Hamlet (sumptuous eating in so short a span that it gave unique meaning to the expression "fast food"). A converted coach turned into a grill car replaced the diner as the train plied the 386 miles from Hamlet to Jacksonville; with a sole attendant, it was equipped with a lunch counter, the only trainset on the system with that rather clumsy layout. The *Palmland*'s short run from Tampa to St. Petersburg ended February 11, 1951, leaving St. Pete served by just two trains: the all-year-long *Silver Meteor* and a winter season *Silver Star*.

An era of dramatic change pervaded Seaboard's passenger service during the late 1940s and early 1950s. Lightweight stainless steel streamliners powered by diesel locomotives were suddenly "in" as SAL (and a whole lot of other lines) pushed their longstanding heavyweight steam-driven consists "out." Although equipment was ordered in 1946, the manufacturer didn't deliver new sleepers until 1949; hence SAL and multiple peer roads ran with conventional heavyweight Pullmans longer than they preferred. A trio of new arrivals on SAL routes surfaced on the winning strength of the *Silver Meteor*, which was upgraded. Debuting were the *Silver Star* running from New York to multiple Florida terminals, the *Silver Comet* from New York to Birmingham and the *Gulf Wind* from Jacksonville to River Junction, Florida, where it seamlessly transferred to Louisville & Nashville for continuation to New Orleans.

The *Silver Star* premiered as a winter-only train in 1946; by 1949, it was traveling year-round. Like its sister *Meteor*, the crack streamliner bypassed Savannah and Jacksonville in both directions and bore a stewardess-nurse and traveling passenger agent on its Miami–New York run. As standard procedure, a section peeled off at Wildwood ferrying passengers to multiple Gulf Coast cities and resorts that included Bradenton, Sarasota, Venice and Boca Grande. By the early 1950s, the *Star* made the trip from New York to Miami in about 25 hours, to Tampa in about 22 hours and St. Petersburg in 24 hours.

Like the *Meteor*, its name has persisted into the present era of Amtrak where — at this writing — it remains a cornerstone of the contemporary carrier's Northeast-Florida service. The daily *Star* flaunts reserved seat coaches and is equipped with Viewliner sleeping cars and a full meal service dining car. Its route demonstrates an affinity for the former Seaboard line in deference to the companion *Meteor* which favors the ACL to Auburndale, Florida. Today's *Silver Star* departs New York's Pennsylvania Station in late morning for a run through the usual Northeastern megalopolises before entering the South. It calls at Richmond, Raleigh, Hamlet, Columbia, Savannah, Jacksonville, Orlando and Lakeland. Making a 31-mile run

Running at speed after stopping at Lakeland, Florida, on May 5, 2007, Amtrak's 181 *Silver Star* is bound for Tampa, 31 miles west, where it will back into Union Station. Pulling forward to proceed, the *Star* will retrace its route to Lakeland before turning south to Miami or north to New York. Another passenger route — SAL's main via Ocala to Tampa — was forsaken by Amtrak a few years ago, netting the back-and-forth Lakeland digression (*courtesy Michael B. Robbins*).

from Lakeland to Tampa, where it arrives at midday (on the day after leaving New York), it returns to Lakeland from Tampa for continuation to Winter Haven, West Palm Beach, Fort Lauderdale, Hollywood and Miami with arrival in early evening. In the opposite direction the *Star* departs Miami at midday, leaves Tampa in late afternoon and arrives in New York late the following day.

Premiering on May 18, 1947, the *Silver Comet* replaced the *Cotton States Special* between New York and Birmingham. In addition, SAL operated a sleeper and a coach between Atlanta and Hamlet that continued in another consist to Portsmouth via Norlina, North Carolina, 59 miles above Raleigh. Like its silver sisters, the *Comet* came complete with reserved coach seating plus a nurse and a passenger agent. Leaving New York at midday, it was normally in Atlanta early the following morning and Birmingham by mid to late morning. Returning, it departed Birmingham in early afternoon, Atlanta in early evening and arrived in New York early the next afternoon.

On July 31, 1949, the *Gulf Wind* — virtually the only SAL streamliner that wasn't "silver" — made its maiden run, departing Jacksonville for New Orleans. It was handed over to L&N 208 miles west at River Junction (now Chattahoochee, renamed for the waterway alongside it). Carrying through coaches between Jacksonville and New Orleans, most of the *Wind*'s cars featured L&N's traditional dark blue hue. There was an exception, however: a fashionable stainless steel five double-bedroom observation lounge was in its consist. For many years, too, SAL included a heavyweight dining car between Jacksonville and the state capital at Tallahassee, 43 miles east of River Junction. With the dawn of the *Gulf Wind*, another train already traversing that route, the *New Orleans–Florida Limited*, was relegated to a nameless local from Jacksonville to Flomaton, Alabama, where it connected to other trains on L&N's mainline.

In addition to its "name trains," Seaboard operated a handful of numbered but unnamed all-coach consists that ran on branch or second mains. Those submerged conveyances were pushed to the latter pages of SAL timetables yet were vital to a dependent traveling sector. Typical among them was daily service provided between Charlotte and Wilmington, North Carolina, between Hamlet, North Carolina, and Savannah, Georgia, via Charleston, South Carolina, between Norlina, North Carolina, and Portsmouth, Virginia (one consist on this line was eventually named *Tidewater* in the 1950s), and between Savannah and Montgomery, Alabama. Those trains usually crossed paths with one or more mainline limiteds at Hamlet or Savannah.

In addition to these operations, SAL timetables published data about extensions beyond its lines through other transport carriers. There was bus service on Greyhound Lines, Queen City Coach Company and Tamiami Trail Tours over multiple routes: Jacksonville–Orlando, Ocala–Orlando, Jacksonville–St. Petersburg, Charlotte–Wilmington, Tampa–Venice, and Miami–Key West.

The Baltimore Steam Packet Company offered steamship connections (Norfolk–Baltimore and Norfolk–Washington); the Peninsular & Occidental Steamship Company did the same (Miami–Havana); the Dominican Republic Steamship Line answered the call (Miami–Nassau); an unspecified yacht service delivered continuing SAL passengers between Boca Grande and Useppa Island in the Gulf of Mexico; and a ferry service was provided across the Elizabeth River between Portsmouth and Norfolk.

There was also synchronized air service scheduling with Pan American Airways, National Airlines, British Overseas Airways and Guest Airways linking Miami with Havana, Nassau and Mexico City. Ground transportation met trains arriving at Thalmann, Georgia, hauling travelers to resorts at Brunswick, Sea Island and Jekyll Island. Seaboard Air Line patrons had a lot of options for getting where they wanted to go.

Across a dozen years between 1947 and 1959, SAL's riders thinned from 2.2 million to 894,000. The impact was ameliorated by a rise in the length of the average trip over that period, from 315 miles to 498 miles, helping the bottom line. After 1959, SAL passenger numbers stabilized and never fell below 900,000 in a subsequent year.[51]

On January 23, 1963, Seaboard's passenger service was surprised when the Florida East Coast Railway — which, beyond its own trains, forwarded ACL consists between Jacksonville and Miami — experienced the start of a prolonged labor stoppage. A trio of Coast Line trainsets abruptly transferred to ACL-SAL routing south of Jacksonville to get to their final destination. ACL's west coast mainline called at Palatka, Sanford, Orlando, Kissimmee, Haines City, Lakeland and Plant City before reaching Tampa. SAL's mainline to Miami intersected with ACL trackage at tiny Auburndale, between Haines City and Lakeland, a regular stop for Seaboard but not Coast Line.

When the FEC course hugging the Atlantic shore wasn't available any longer, Miami-bound ACL trains plied the ACL Jacksonville–Tampa main to Auburndale. There they turned onto the SAL main and proceeded 220 more miles to Miami. As they did so they encountered many SAL passenger consists along the way. The FEC strike continued for many years, thus the SAL-ACL arrangement persisted, setting a precedent that remains unbroken as of 2010 (47 years and counting). The Jacksonville–Auburndale–Miami route lasted not merely until Amtrak took over passenger traffic on May 1, 1971: Amtrak has since run its *Silver Meteor*, *Silver Star* and a few other trains since withdrawn over that route to the Gold Coast. Who

In what would have been an oddity much earlier, ACL 6 with EMD 4040 on point (A-B configuration), northbound *City of Miami*, passes the SAL station at West Lake Wales, Florida. It's 1963, the year some unions struck FEC, which had schlepped ACL's passengers since the previous century to and from destinations south of Jacksonville (not including Florida's west coast). That disruption caused ACL and SAL, archrivals for passenger and freight patronage, to share SAL's main south of Auburndale. That's where it intersected with ACL's Tampa main from Jacksonville. The pattern is still followed by Amtrak today (*photograph by David W. Salter, courtesy Chuck Blardone*).

In 1974, Amtrak's *Silver Star* passes Auburndale, Florida, a prime crossing for ACL and SAL more than a decade earlier. Led by a trio of EMD E8s, the *Star* will pass over the old ACL east-west mainline diamond momentarily. The main is straight for miles here and high speed occurs on joined rail, welded track not yet having been installed. In 1963, after several unions struck FEC, which schlepped ACL travelers to Miami since the previous century, ACL went checkbook in hand to competitor SAL. They signed a pact allowing ACL trains to join SAL rails at Auburndale for 220 miles to Miami. The pattern persists today (*courtesy Michael B. Robbins*).

would have dreamed that a 1963 strike could determine which way the traffic flows this late in the game?

The Seaboard maintained its high standards of service even as revenues derived from it consistently diminished, thanks largely to highways and airways steadily siphoning off America's rail passengers in the 1950s and 1960s. While some of its people-movers were discontinued or downgraded (including reduced frequencies and diners and sleepers removed), SAL — at the time of the merger with ACL (1967) — was still running four daily trains over its Northeast-Florida main plus three to Atlanta and the *Gulf Wind* on the Jacksonville–New Orleans route. There was little there to suggest that SAL's traditional devotion to superior passenger service was about to be abandoned. It wasn't: it continued under the SCL banner to the Amtrak era. "The extent of Seaboard's commitment to quality passenger service may be gauged by the fact that it bought 20 new passenger locomotives in 1964 ... and picked up 36 lightweight cars from the FEC in 1965," observed one historian.[52]

In many ways a formidable Seaboard operation played the underdog in an ongoing rivalry in delivering frozen Northern denizens to warm Southern climes. Despite its perceptual reduction to second-class status by some, SAL's service usually prevailed as first-class, responding well in a highly competitive environment. The line's early introduction of streamlined trains to Dixie among the region's "legacy" carriers opened doors for a revolution in transportation styles and led to an epoch in which Seaboard had little reason to offer apologies to anybody.

14

SOUTHERN RAILWAY
Crescent Rolls

"The Southern Serves the South" was an epithet emblazoned on literature, advertising, freight cars and signage identifying the Southern Railway (SOU) system for decades. That aphorism may embrace the rails of Dixie better than any road's motto.[1] Other leading lines with north-south route structures in the East didn't enter their own territory (roll onto their own trackage) until they arrived at Richmond, Virginia, 114 miles south of the nation's capital. Just 8.2 miles below Washington's Union Station, however, after crossing the Potomac River into neighboring Virginia, Southern's trains were on Southern rails from Alexandria south.[2] And throughout its life as an independent line SOU was headquartered just above that terminus point in the city of Washington at 15th and K Street NW.

Through passenger consists trekked to New York City after an interline connection with the Pennsylvania Railroad. Southern's main out of Washington–Alexandria persisted 1,154 miles to New Orleans via Charlotte, Atlanta and Birmingham. The line was double-tracked the full 638 miles between Washington and Atlanta. And while some other prestigious roads in the Southeast confined their commerce to a half-dozen states or less, Southern's far-flung operations embraced more than a dozen with a few outside the customary Southeast: Alabama, Florida, Georgia, Illinois, Indiana, Kentucky, Louisiana, Mississippi, Missouri, North Carolina, Ohio, South Carolina, Tennessee and Virginia.

Although SOU was always a teeming freight carrier, during its heyday it was also heavily invested in passenger transport, as much or more than any road in Dixie. Upon reflection, "The Southern Serves the South" is a descriptive branding for the system's diversified functions in the region in which it was concentrated — and where it made not only a significant contribution but a difference to the patrons it satisfied.

The SOU's beginnings date back to 1827, the year that the South Carolina Canal and Railroad Company (SCC&R), oldest ancestor of Southern Railway, was organized.[3] Within three years the firm took possession of a steam engine crafted for it at a cost of $4,000 in the shops of the West Point Foundry Association beside the banks of New York City's North (Hudson) River. Its designers established that it should be able to pull as many as 50 people at a momentum of 15 to 20 miles an hour. Without any tracks nearby to test it, however, those fabricators couldn't be absolutely positive about just how reliably that engine would perform to their estimates. The readied locomotive was floated by barge down the North River to the Atlantic Ocean and thence southward to the coastal city of Charleston.

On Christmas Day, December 25, 1830, the SCC&R demonstrated the capability of its newfangled power source. Labeling the wood-burning engine the *Best Friend of Charleston*, that holiday it pulled a flatcar with three men and a flag-covered cannon aboard, the gents repeatedly firing the cannon in celebratory elation. Also in the consist (if that's a proper designate for that early period) were a couple of attached wagons. They bore in excess of 140

Doesn't it look real? Imagine that you can see the radiant green and gold livery! Actually it's part of the moving exhibition at the North Carolina Transportation Museum at Spencer captured on June 13, 2009. An eyewitness allowed: "You could almost believe it was in the 60s and Southern still existed and they still had passenger trains rumbling along in the green grass of summer." What a perfectly blissful thought! (*courtesy Jay Miller*).

A dirty Southern Railway E8 6912 and three mates bring the *Crescent* into Washington, D.C., in 1976, the year of the country's bicentennial celebration (note the placard saluting Dixie signers of the *Declaration of Independence*). Still running its own passenger consists in an Amtrak epoch, Southern sends its locomotives to be serviced at nearby Ivy City yard. Amtrak operates these trains between Washington and New York (*courtesy Michael B. Robbins*).

denizens, mostly sophisticates from the South Carolina Low Country. Six miles of rail had been laid. Off into the wilds of the Palmetto State charged that giddy, ecstatic contingent, deftly defying the manufacturer's presumption of 50 riders.

The train had success written all over it from that very first day. Three weeks afterward, on January 15, 1831, the *Best Friend of Charleston* supplied continuous trips to anybody desiring to get from one end of its six-mile terminus to the other. And it did so at an average speed of 25 miles an hour, improving on the builder's projected, seemingly conservative gait. *Best Friend* was certified, as Southern Railway officials and their successors were fond of insisting, as "the nation's first scheduled passenger service to be pulled regularly by a steam locomotive." In effect it was America's original ongoing engine-driven people-mover on land.

It persisted unabated for six months until a boiler explosion on June 7, 1831, fueled by a negligent fireman, turned deadly. It killed not only the laborer but the engine, too. The powers behind the SCC&R would not be thwarted, however; they salvaged what they could of it, had it rebuilt and — by early 1831 — the reconditioned engine, then running under the appellation *Phoenix*, rolled over the same rails once again pulling passenger cars. That year (1831) a second locomotive, the *South Carolina*, was added to SCC&R's expanding inventory setting a precedent in diversification. By 1834, the company added a third engine, *Native*, to its pool, that one built by SCC&R's own qualified craftsmen.

A year earlier, meanwhile, in October 1833, the company finished laying some 136 miles of track from the port city of Charleston to the inland community of Hamburg, South Carolina. That placed the line at the forefront of all others in yet another dimension: the longest continuous trackage on earth. In addition the SCC&R was the first road to transport U.S. troops and mail.[4] All of these feathers were added to the cap that Southern Railway would eventually wear (and hype).

Altogether there were nearly 150 forebears in the ancestral lineage of the Southern Railway system according to its contemporary historical association.[5] As rail fever struck other states in Dixie, networks gradually spread across a wider terrain and ultimately beyond the mountain ranges as westward habitation proliferated. While the railroad movement would come to a grinding halt during the War Between the States (1861–1865), once that ended interest picked right back up again. The South was an integral part of this growing relevance, as this volume has repeatedly testified.

Southern Railway was formally established in 1894. It resulted when two regional systems that had fallen on hard times blended their operations to form a larger amalgamation with the ability to withstand the financial hazards both were up against. One was the strapped Richmond & Danville Railroad (R&D), the other the East Tennessee, Virginia & Georgia Railroad (ETV&G). There were plenty of deceptive machinations transpiring behind the scenes, too, that factored into this deal. They involved roads linked to the Richmond and West Point Terminal Railway and Warehouse Company and infused a complex state of affairs with extensive intrigue. While the tale makes for fascinating investigation, it won't be dealt with in detail here.[6]

Over the years the R&D and ETV&G acquired tracks from many smaller or more distant carriers, yet they were unable to make a "go" of it independently. From its start the newly combined venture accessed 4,500 miles of rail. While Southern Railway owned about two-thirds of that outright, the residue was available through leases, agreements and control of stock. Speculating on 2,500 more miles of Central of Georgia rails the company was to rule, *The New York Times* observed in 1894: "This system will practically gridiron the Southern and Southeastern States."[7] A map of the territory affirms that the newspaper's assessment was likely on target.

Among the individuals playing large hands at the initiation of Southern Railway, none is more relevant than eminent financier John Pierpont Morgan (1837–1913). His name is linked with the early days of several major railroads, so he looms large in the pages of this text. He grew to dominate two U.S. industries: consolidation of Eastern railroads, and formation of the United States Steel Corporation (1901). His New York City firm, Drexel, Morgan & Company — later known as J. P. Morgan & Company — was considered by many analysts to be the foremost corporate banking house of the late 19th century.

In 1892, a contingent of railway securities holders requested Morgan to craft a plan for a unified system. The Terminal Company, the R&D, the ETV&G and the Central of Georgia were all in receivership. Morgan championed a "blind pool" concept to distribute equity and anguish among the securities-holders. Many months passed until he was able to inaugurate the Southern Railway Company on July 1, 1894, comprised of 4,400 miles of tracks.[8]

Its first president, Samuel Spencer, a Drexel, Morgan rail authority, had worked on the reorganization plan from its start. Born March 2, 1847, at Columbus, Georgia, Spencer was in the Confederate army during the Civil War. Earning degrees from the universities of Georgia (1867) and Virginia (1869), he entered rail service as a surveyor for the Savannah & Memphis line. Departing that road in 1872, Spencer affiliated with the New Jersey Southern Railroad. The following year he joined the Baltimore & Ohio Railroad (B&O). Spencer was named superintendent of the Virginia Midland Railroad in 1877, and general superintendent of the Long Island Railroad (LIRR) the following year. There he met J. P. Morgan, who held a large portion of LIRR's securities.

By 1879, Spencer returned to the B&O as assistant to the president. In less than a decade he rose to vice president and finally president in December 1887. But that lasted just over a year: B&O directors were convinced he was a deputy for Morgan, who gave them cause to believe he was trying to wrest the B&O from them and add it to his growing holdings. Spencer was fired but almost immediately hired by Drexel, Morgan & Company as its rail specialist. By 1890, he was a partner in the firm. Two years later he was given substantial authority for the reorganization of the systems that were present at the Southern Railway's birth.

> Spencer proved up to the job. He was a shrewd manager and made sound financial decisions on behalf of the Morgan bank, which was still its parent company. From 1894 until his death a dozen years later, the system's mileage increased from 4,391 to 7,515 miles of lines, and the number of passengers carried from 3.4 million to more than 11 million; its freight tonnage also quadrupled. Earnings, not surprisingly, rose at a corresponding rate, from $17 million to $53 million.[9]

At 59 Spencer died in a pre-dawn collision of two trains near Lawyers, Virginia, on November 29, 1906. The town of Spencer, North Carolina, was named for him while he was still alive. For several decades it was the site of the Spencer Shops, Southern Railway's mammoth railroad-car repair facility.

Ultimately SOU's trackage was to balloon to more than 10,000 miles through acquisitions, purchases, lease agreements, stock control and construction of new rail.[10] On June 18, 1953, Southern became the first Class 1 U.S. freight road to totally convert from steam-driven engines to diesel-electric motive power, yet another key bragging right.[11] Conversely and paradoxically, in 1960, Norfolk & Western Railway — with which Southern was to be enduringly linked in time — was the last Class 1 U.S. freight road to banish steam altogether as its motive power and adopt diesel engines throughout its system.

As the transport environment shifted, in 1980, the Interstate Commerce Commission allowed a couple of major rival rail systems in the East — Chessie and Seaboard Coast Line — to unify their operations, creating CSX Transportation. To effectively compete against that powerhouse, Norfolk & Western Railway and Southern Railway determined that their best chance for survival was to also integrate. There will be more exploration into this action subsequently.

Back in the day SOU became legendary in an industry that recognized superior talent. "The railroad's famous green paint scheme was fitting ... as it became the most respected and arguably the best managed railroad of its day before it disappeared into a merger," a contemporary Web site dedicated to all American railroads claims.[12] One of its longstanding catchphrases, "Southern Gives a Green Light to Innovation," was, many railfans believe, more than a mere slogan.

Beyond double-tracking many of its routes, netting safer operations and swifter movement, plus dieselizing the fleet to attain better results, Southern was one of the first Class 1 roads to implement fresh technologies to improve efficiencies. Adding Centralized Traffic Control early throughout much of its system is a typical example. For more than half of the 20th century, SOU was also recognized by the industry for maintaining a first-class passenger operation. "Southern took great pride in its passenger fleet believing in the highest quality service and keeping trains clean and on time," one assessment professes.[13]

One of the bright gems among American ballad lore revolves around a legendary, larger-than-life figure who piloted a Southern mail train that led to his death and immortality.[14]

> The flashing green and gold livery of the Southern Railway and its reputation at the turn of the century as a fast-operating line ... gave birth in 1903 to the ballad which, next to "Casey Jones," must rank as the foremost railroading contribution to American folklore. On September 27 of that year, the Southern's train No. 97, *The Fast Mail*, with Engineer Joseph A. Broady at the throttle, was an hour late out of Monroe, Virginia, and Broady promised, as the song later had it, "to put her into Spencer on time." Spencer was the next stop, 166 miles down the line. Two firemen were pouring on the coal as the Southern's engine No. 1102 hit the curve leading into Stillhouse Trestle, high above Cherrystone Creek at Danville, at a highly accelerated speed, although probably not the ninety miles an hour of the subsequent ballad. The train climbed the rails and leaped a full hundred feet clear of the trestle before crashing in the creek bed.... Five cars followed and burst into flames, and the dead numbered thirteen, including Engineer Broady. The song, written shortly afterward by a local hillbilly named Dave George told the story [the authorship was disputed]:
>
> > He was going down hill at ninety miles an hour
> > When the whistle broke into a scream.
> > He was found in the wreck with his hand on the throttle,
> > A-scalded to death with the steam.[15]

Unlike many of its peer people-movers in American rail transportation, when stream-lining was introduced to motive power and passenger consists in the mid 1930s, Southern Railway hung back. As more and more rivals bit the bullet (translate: spent the money) to embrace this expensive transition to streamlined equipment, SOU officials dug their heels in deeper. Nevertheless, claimed one scholar, the innovation of streamlining proved to be "the single most successful improvement in attracting passengers to the rails." That modernization in the South arrived on the undersized, almost otherwise negligible Gulf, Mobile & Northern (GM&N) road at the start of the craze in mid 1935. GM&N, a forebear of better known successor Gulf, Mobile & Ohio Railroad, broke new ground running its *Rebel* streamliners between the company's headquarters at Jackson, Tennessee, and New Orleans.

In 1939, SOU's two biggest competitors on money-making North-South routes launched their own imaginative versions of streamline travel. Each displayed riveting lightweight-tube aluminum cars complete with every available amenity for passenger comfort en route known to man. Seaboard Air Line's (SAL) *Silver Meteor*, the first of those, originated in New York over other carriers' tracks, made a seamless connection with SAL in Richmond, and continued south with sections to Miami and Tampa–St. Petersburg. Atlantic Coast Line (ACL) responded with a pair of *Champion*s. The East Coast version from New York went to Miami while a West Coast rendering plied the tracks to Tampa. All of these trains not only made a stunning hit with riders but an equally big splash in the pages of print media.

Despite mounting evidence that, more than anything else, streamlining was drawing patrons back to the rails—people whose travel aspirations had diminished or evaporated in the wake of the devastating economic plummeting in the 1930s—a very conservative Southern Railway refused to purchase new rolling stock. Instead it focused on reduced coach fares, air-conditioned heavyweight cars and diesels added to local short-haul trains. This helped attract some customers and retain others. But none of it created the excitement that the rival lines were enjoying with their streamlined equipment.

In the end it took the inhabitants of Atlanta, Georgia, to begin to persuade Southern officials to think differently.

> Railroad and industrial center of the South, served by over 100 passenger trains daily, but no streamliners, Atlanta was a proud city unwilling to take a back seat in anything. Thanks to an *Atlanta Journal* editorial one Sunday in March 1940, residents discovered over toast and coffee that their city was somehow not reaching its potential, in part because it was unserved by light-weight trains. A series of other well-researched articles followed.... Before long local civic groups had stirred from their slumber and began asking tough questions of both the Southern and the L&N who, at first, held firm on the issue—streamliners were not under consideration. Later, while Southern sulked, L&N had a change of heart.... L&N would operate a Florida streamliner, the *Dixie Flagler*, through Atlanta every third day beginning in December 1940. Atlanta had its first lightweight train.[16]

While Atlanta's unrest got the ball rolling, the euphoria emanating from SAL's and ACL's conversion to streamliners was so loud it could be heard all the way from their paralleling surfside routes to the SOU corporate suites in downtown Washington. It was evident that they'd be a fool to ignore the success that almost every other prestigious carrier was realizing from converting to streamlining. Thus, in October 1940, SOU revealed it had purchased five diesel locomotives and 44 streamlined cars with which it would outfit two distinct trains. The *Southerner* was to run daily starting March 31, 1941, between New York and New Orleans over a route that included Charlotte, Atlanta and Birmingham. The *Tennessean* would operate daily between Washington and Memphis via Bristol, Knoxville and Chattanooga. Sleepers would be added on two legs, Bristol–Nashville, and Chattanooga–Memphis.

Although some stalwarts have insisted that the *Crescent* was Southern's "finest passenger train"—the flagship consist in the SOU stash—the *Southerner* can easily claim parity to the lofty status conferred on her older sister. And in one significant way it outperformed the old girl by lengthening its trip 212 miles at one end of its route. During the postwar period the *Crescent* was re-equipped to create a third streamliner in Southern's inventory.

In their halcyon days the *Southerner* and the *Crescent* ran between New York and New Orleans every day over separate courses from Atlanta to the Crescent City. The *Crescent* left the Georgia capital on the West Point Route, schlepping travelers to a seamless interline link with the Louisville & Nashville Railroad (L&N) at Montgomery. For the remainder of the trip the *Crescent* plied the L&N main. The *Southerner*, in the meantime, stayed on SOU rails for the duration of its journey. It headed west from Atlanta to Birmingham, turning southwest to call at Meridian and Hattiesburg, Mississippi, before reaching the end of the line.

The storied history of the *Crescent* encompasses 88 years of passenger transport under the flags of a Southern predecessor and SOU. Add to it another three decades under the over-sight of Amtrak's watchful eye (through 2009) and you have a train with a heritage dating no less than 118 years. The *Crescent*'s origins are rooted in the era of the Richmond & Danville Railroad (R&D), one of dual organisms that were welded into SOU at its start. In 1891, three years before SOU evolved, the tracks between Washington and New Orleans hadn't been com-bined into a synchronized system in any formal way. Over the rails of the Atlanta & West Point, Western Railway of Alabama and Louisville & Nashville, the R&D then ran a train dubbed the *Washington & Southwestern Vestibule Limited*.

The *Tennessean,* shown near Greeneville in upper east Tennessee on July 11, 1941, is one of two stream-liners Southern Railway inaugurated a few months before. The consist, with sleepers on part of its route, departed Washington daily for the Volunteer State, calling at Bristol, Knoxville, Chattanooga and Memphis and at a Nashville connection (*courtesy Tennessee State Library and Archives*).

To announce the train's impending start, company literature glorified it with flowery phrasing, giving it the full treatment: "The management of the leading Southern System — The Richmond & Danville Railroad Company — has determined to inaugurate a service second to none in completeness and elegance of detail, combining the highest degree of speed consistent with safety, and providing the latest and best facilities for the comfort and enjoyment of its patrons."

This train, nevertheless, did have something new to offer. The vestibule in the title demonstrated a widely promoted advance in passenger-car concepts — a practical yet stunning innovation in railway amenities for that era. For one of the first times riders could walk from one car to another without encountering the outside elements, passing instead through enclosed "corridors" between cars. And although *Washington & Southwestern Vestibule Limited* was longer than the name of most trains in subsequent years, that wasn't out of character for 19th century consists.

In 1893, the *Vestibule* was marketed as "A magnificent train of Pullman Vestibuled Palaces, consisting of Drawing-room, Dining, Sleeping and Library cars of the latest and most magnificent and luxurious designs, built expressly for this service, and run daily." Southern Railway, at its formal organization in 1894, altered the *Vestibule*'s label to *Washington & Southwestern Limited* when it ran southbound and to *New York Limited* in the opposite direction. A single name, *New York & New Orleans Limited,* was implemented in 1906. At the same time the train was equipped with Pullman service only and observation and club cars were added to its consist.

Receiving new equipment for it in 1925, the company marked that milestone by assigning

In Jones County, Mississippi, Amtrak's southbound *Crescent* crosses Little Rocky Creek on its way to New Orleans on July 21, 1991. One of Amtrak's long-distance mainstays since 1979 and of Southern Railway before that, the *Crescent* has a storied history. Passenger service predates Southern's formation by three years, to 1891, when Richmond & Danville ran the *Washington & Southwestern Vestibule Limited* along rails of myriad carriers to reach the Big Easy. Under several handles the *Crescent* stems from this train, still running a dozen decades after its inception (*courtesy Clyde Woodruff*).

a more contemporary moniker to its oldest passenger train. It altered the appellation to *Crescent Limited* to call attention to the refurbishment. For the first time in the South a fee was added to the standard fare for riding this train resulting from the "superior facilities" it proffered. The extra charge was $5.00. It was a pattern that was soon instituted by other lines on their premier trains.

The following year (1926) the carrier's Class Ps-4 Pacifics (4-6-2) became the *Crescent Limited's* power source, presumed by one verdict "the most beautiful steam locomotive ever built."[17] The *Crescent Limited* brandished hues of Virginia green and gold with silver trim. Those tints were thereafter symbolic of Southern Railway. That livery — plus advertising, timetables and other company literature, signage, etc. — turned into a staple of the Southern stable. Other personalized touches became hallmarks of SOU, too. Included were brass candlesticks on the smoke box and spread eagles in bronze. They survived until the diesel age.

The *Crescent Limited's* appellation was deleted in 1934 and operated with coaches in its consist merely as trains 37 (southbound) and 38 (northbound). The modified name of *Crescent* returned in 1938. Three years later (1941) the Pacifics were replaced by streamlined EMD E6A diesel locomotives. It would take eight more years (1949) before the whole train's conversion to lightweight streamlined cars matching its modern engines was implemented. It was also re-converted to an all-Pullman consist then, although in 1956, coaches returned running between New York and Charlotte. (The coach section continued from Charlotte to Columbia, South Carolina, and finally to Augusta, Georgia.) In the meantime, in 1951, SOU upgraded the company's entire passenger locomotive fleet to EMD E8As.

In the streamliner epoch the *Crescent*'s consist included a mixed sleeper-observation car featuring extra-large windows with elevated seats facing outward so travelers could watch the scenery as it flashed by. This was an early rendition of the "sightseer lounge cars" (observation cars, really) that Amtrak currently includes in its Superliner trains between the Midwest and West and along the West Coast.[18] Another new feature, also still in use by Amtrak, was the introduction of master bedrooms (designated "deluxe" in present lingo), large enough to sleep three and containing private showers.

In the post-steam halcyon days of U.S. rail travel, the *Crescent* "All-Pullman Train" as far as Atlanta touted a radio-equipped Pullman club car, a diner on the full New York–New Orleans route, and a mixed bag of 10 sleepers (featuring sections, double bedrooms, drawing rooms and compartments)—between varied pairs of cities (New York–New Orleans, New York–Atlanta, Washington–Atlanta, Washington–New Orleans). Coaches were added on the 493 miles between Atlanta and New Orleans.

On the other hand the *Southerner* was a streamlined coach train at the time. It carried a diner, mixed passenger-baggage car, partitioned coach (where the races were cordoned off from each other, a widely practiced custom — see Chapter 15) and four more coaches. At the rear of the train was a rounded-end radio-equipped tavern-observation car. With the exception of a single coach between New York and Atlanta, all of the cars ran the full distance.

The streamlined *Southerner* appeared on New York–New Orleans tracks for the first time in 1941.[19] "Regarded by the Southern as just as luxurious as the *Crescent*," the *Southerner* proffered a line-up that was similar to that on the older train: reclining-seat coaches, diner, sleeper-lounges, sleeping cars and a sleeper-observation car at the rear.[20] It, too, had extra-large windows with elevated seats that faced outward while its master bedrooms—large enough to

In the late 1940s, heavyweight Pullman cars were reflective of the inventory of Southern Railway and more long-distance passenger lines. *Lake Pearl*, car 2422, was billed as 10-1-2 containing 10 sections (upper and lower berths), a single drawing room and dual compartments. By mid 20th century almost all serious rivals made the switch to streamliners if they could afford to. Berths were out while compartments and bedrooms were in. Highly desirable lightweight aluminum models then in vogue offered a speedier, flashier way to travel — much more hip, comfortable and enviable (*courtesy Chuck Blardone*).

accommodate a trio—also had private showers. Those deluxe bedroom-shower combinations were rare in postwar America: only the two Southern trains and the Pennsylvania Railroad's flagship *Broadway Limited* could boast of them.

Much had changed in the ebb and flow of declining passenger service as the 1950s progressed. By the early 1960s both premier trains had segued into multiple reclining-seat coaches, a dining car and a variety of sleeping car patterns (with roomettes and double bedrooms). Additionally the *Southerner* was equipped with a tavern lounge car between Washington and Atlanta while the L&N furnished the *Crescent* with a dining-lounge car from Mobile to New Orleans.

In the heyday of both trains in 1947, the *Crescent* trekked its 1,131-mile path from the Big Apple to the Big Easy with 33 scheduled intermediate stops in 30 hours 35 minutes. Thirteen years later, with passenger traffic on the skids, the southbound trek with 41 scheduled intermediate stops could be completed in 31 hours five minutes, only a half-hour longer with eight more stops. On the opposite route in 1947, the southbound *Southerner* ran its 1,154-mile course between New York and New Orleans (23 miles further than the *Crescent* route) with 28 intermediate stops in 29 hours 58 minutes—37 minutes quicker than the *Crescent* but with 13 fewer stops. In 1960, the *Southerner* made 32 scheduled stops (four more than before) in 29 hours 55 minutes (three minutes less) on its southbound journey.

For a couple of decades, from the 1940s to the 1960s, the *Crescent* was vaunted for legendary on-time service. As noted the *Southerner* was already running from Boston to New Orleans. Part of this was under Penn Central Railroad auspices and without the shift in terminals required earlier in New York City. The *Southerner* lost its separate identity in 1970. That year the *Crescent* and the *Southerner* were blended into the *Southern Crescent* and adopted the full *Southerner* route of 1,611 miles from Boston to New Orleans by way of Birmingham instead of Montgomery.

As the most enduring SOU consist still rolling at that juncture, the *Crescent* would ultimately earn the extraordinary distinction of being the last privately operated streamlined passenger train in America. When Amtrak began running that traffic for America's railroads on May 1, 1971, a minuscule handful of Class 1 roads persisted in what they had been doing: transferring travelers from place to place independently over their own lines. Southern Railway may have been the largest of those persevering people-movers. Reducing its portfolio to a mere trio, SOU included the longrunning *Southern Crescent* among them. Amtrak would retain the simplified *Crescent* nomenclature once it took over the train.

Daily for nearly eight more years Southern operated it between Washington and Atlanta, extending it three times weekly to New Orleans.[21] It handed over the throttles to Amtrak in early 1979. Amtrak continues to run the *Crescent* between New York and New Orleans daily. As this is written the schedule calls for 30 hours 18 minutes southbound and 29 hours 52 minutes northbound with 31 scheduled intermediate stops in both directions. The contemporary consist includes coaches, sleeping cars, diner and lounge car. A noticeable difference then and now is that today's *Crescent* follows the route of the *Southerner* to New Orleans via Birmingham, Meridian and Hattiesburg, and not its longstanding path through Montgomery, Mobile and a handful of Mississippi coastal resorts.

There were numerous other worthy trains in Southern's inventory which deserve attention. Many plied some of those same mainline rails, including—from New York to New Orleans—the *Piedmont Limited* and the *Washington–Atlanta–New Orleans Express* following the *Crescent* route to their destination. Then there was the *Peach Queen* which operated daily between New York and Atlanta. Several other trains ran on portions of the SOU main before turning to other destinations.

Multiple consists out of Washington followed the mainline 173 miles to Lynchburg, Vir-

Tennessee hosted a year-long festival dubbed Homecoming '86 that year. Pulled by dual re-numbered Southern FP7As in the carrier's classic green, white and gold livery, a celebration train crisscrossed the Volunteer State all year whipping up enthusiasm for the commemoration. The governor, event officials and other dignitaries were aboard. In May 1986, the special consist has just left Cleveland, Tennessee, on the next leg of its merry-making (*courtesy Jay T. Thomson*).

ginia. They rolled onto Norfolk & Western Railway tracks there, where they advanced in a southwesterly direction via Roanoke to Bristol, Virginia–Tennessee. From the latter city they proceeded once more onto Southern rails. The *Birmingham Special*, its terminus or origination in that Alabama city, also dispatched a section sprinting from Chattanooga to Memphis.

The *Tennessean*— after passing through Knoxville and Chattanooga —continued to Memphis by way of Huntsville, Decatur and Sheffield–Tuscumbia, Alabama, and Corinth, Mississippi. A connecting train over the Nashville, Chattanooga & St. Louis Railway departed Chattanooga for Nashville, thus encompassing the Volunteer State's four largest metropolitan centers. Leaving Chattanooga, the *Pelican* persevered to Birmingham, Meridian, Hattiesburg and New Orleans. At Meridian travelers could go west to Shreveport, Louisiana, via the Illinois Central Railroad.

There were still other passenger services partially dependent upon Southern's main out of the nation's capital in the glory days of 20th century rail travel. The *Augusta Special* followed that route 378 miles to Charlotte before heading due south to Columbia, South Carolina, and Augusta, Georgia. The *Asheville Special* turned west at mile marker 284, Greensboro, North Carolina, for a trek to Winston-Salem en route to its namesake mountain burg.

Southern wasn't wholly dependent upon trains running to and from Washington by any means. Rail biographer Tom Murray pointed out that the system's principal passenger routes could be visualized as a large "X" on a map of the nation's Eastern third.[22] One axis ran from Washington to New Orleans while the other ran from Cincinnati to Jacksonville. The two crossed in Atlanta. For all of its dependence upon the nation's capital for so many of its functions, including but not limited to it as its base of operations, Southern maintained a heavy investment in its Midwest terminus of Cincinnati "where the river winds, 'tween the Mason and the Dixon line."

With New York Central connections originating in Chicago, Cleveland, Detroit and St. Louis, from Cincinnati SOU dispatched the *Carolina Special* (to Asheville with dual sections persisting to Charleston, South Carolina, and Goldsboro, North Carolina). It sent the *Ponce de Leon* and the *Royal Palm* from Cincinnati to Jacksonville with Florida East Coast and Seaboard Air Line connections awaiting it to take travelers on to Miami and Tampa. On another major route in that direction Southern operated a portion of the *Kansas City–Florida Special* with dual sections originating in Kansas City and St. Louis. At Birmingham, arriving on Frisco tracks, the train was handed over to SOU, which took it via Atlanta to Jacksonville with links there to both Florida coasts.

Then there was the Cincinnati–New Orleans traffic, competing with the paralleling Louisville & Nashville's trains over its mainline. The Queen & Crescent Route — one of the systems acquired by Southern in its formative years, named for the endpoint cities of Cincinnati (Queen City) and New Orleans (Crescent City) — saw the *Cincinnati & New Orleans Special* traverse its course. Southern persisted in the practice under that moniker through the 1940s. But by mid 20th century the company viewed its route as largely supplying shorter markets like Cincinnati–Chattanooga, Chattanooga–Birmingham and Birmingham–New Orleans. At that point it dropped the *Cincinnati & New Orleans Special* label to offer two unnamed trains daily between Cincinnati and New Orleans over its own rails. One of those trains was joined en route at Danville, Kentucky, by a Louisville section. At Chattanooga that train linked with the *Birmingham Special* and continued south to Birmingham.

While these were some of Southern's key people-movers back in the day, they were but the tip of the iceberg. SOU operated an extraordinary number of secondary routes. A handful of overnight sleeping-car lines tied several city pairs together that normally might not be deemed financially rewarding, but most of which proved sound business decisions. Among them: Atlanta–Brunswick, Georgia; Atlanta–Columbia, South Carolina; Asheville–Jacksonville; Columbia–Louisville; and Charlotte–Richmond, Virginia. There were several more. In addition SOU sustained passenger traffic over many other lines, like Birmingham–Mobile; Birmingham–Columbus, Mississippi; Marion, North Carolina–Rock Hill, South Carolina; and many others.

One of the services touted quite heavily for decades in Southern timetables was its arrangement with the Pennsylvania, West Point Route, Louisville & Nashville and Southern Pacific roads netting "Coast to Coast Service" along the popular "Sunset Route." Southern's literature extolled it as "The Most Interesting Trans-Continental Route via Atlanta, Montgomery, New Orleans, Houston, San Antonio, El Paso and Tucson." Taking advantage of SOU's *Crescent* and *Piedmont Limited* runs in each direction (which plied Pennsylvania tracks between Washington and New York), trains joined the Southern Pacific's (SP) rails at New Orleans once a week, traveling to Los Angeles with connections to San Francisco.

In 1954, a typical westbound schedule called for New York departure Sunday at 2 P.M. Eastern Time on the *Crescent* with arrival in New Orleans at 6:45 P.M. Central Time on Monday. Passengers boarded the SP's *Sunset Limited* there, leaving at 11:45 P.M., pulling into Los Angeles at 4:15 P.M. Pacific Time on Wednesday. The connection left at 8 P.M. for arrival into San Francisco at 8 A.M. on Thursday. While it took almost four days for those travelers to cross the country, anyone selecting the route probably could verify the unparalleled scenic wonders floating by those big picture windows.

"In 1964 Southern still had a fleet of 36 daily passenger trains and one mail train," wrote rail historian Ralph Ward.[23] "Those trains varied from the usually all-streamlined, always on time *Crescent* and *Southerner* to the locals which ran with mostly heavyweight equipment and whose timekeeping was highly variable."

Within three years after maintaining those 36 daily passenger consists, about seven out of 10 weren't operating any longer. A mere 10 trains were still running in 1967. And the days of most of them were numbered. SOU president Dennis William (Bill) Brosnan saw the finality of transporting travelers rapidly approaching and was jubilantly buoyed. Prosperity, he reflected, was couched in hauling freight, not people. Given the "track" record (pun debatable) of most Class 1 roads in the 1960s, who might sensibly differ on that issue? Brosnan was on an unswerving tear to reduce and finally eliminate all passenger service on Southern routes. While he called the shots from February 1, 1962, to November 28, 1967, he had been allowed to oversee a great deal of the company in the previous decade. Under ex-president Harry A. DeButts, who was CEO from January 1, 1952, to January 31, 1962, Brosnan virtually had carte blanche to meddle as he wished in his roles as VP–operations and executive vice president.[24]

Born April 14, 1903, at Albany, Georgia, Brosnan earned a bachelor's degree in civil engineering from Georgia Tech in 1923.[25] After working for the Georgia Highway Department three years, his railroad career began in 1926, as a student apprentice and track laborer in Macon. Progressively and aggressively he climbed the corporate ladder. He was appointed general manager of the Southern Railway System in 1947. Brosnan became vice president for operations in 1952 and executive VP in 1960. In 1963, the year following his ascendancy to the SOU presidency, he received a trio of signal honors: for "having done the most for the railroad industry," readers of the trade periodical *Modern Railroads* selected him as "Railroad Man of the Year"; in recognition of "his outstanding contribution as a salesman of the free enterprise system," Sales and Marketing Executives International named him National Salesman of the Year; for "outstanding contributions to industry and to the public," Phi Sigma Kappa fraternity chose him Phi Sig of the Year.

Brosnan was credited with bringing about major reforms through centralization, automation, rail welding, centralized wheel and axle maintenance. He instituted computerization for manifold purposes including tracking locations of all Southern freight cars at a given time, an innovation believed to have saved the road $8 million annually. He installed hot-box detectors on rolling stock. He also found ways to perform the work of 300 new diesels (at $160,000 each) that were about to be ordered by doing more with 84 new diesels instead, saving nearly $34.6 million. To attract furniture and grain shippers, he had special freight cars designed to reduce damage to furniture en route and new grain cars implemented that could double previous shipment sizes.

Leaving the SOU presidency, Brosnan was chairman to March 1976, and he stayed on the board until 1983. In retirement he lived in Asheville, North Carolina, still serving on the boards of several organizations, both commercial and fraternal. Brosnan died June 14, 1985, in Asheville.

During Brosnan's presidency and with his blessing, SOU lawyers worked at a feverish pitch in their relentless efforts to convince state regulatory bodies and Interstate Commerce Commission members to curtail passenger trains. "Remnants of former interstate trains continued to run on an intrastate basis," historian Tom Murray affirmed, "essentially from nowhere to nowhere, until the evidence was overwhelming that a train's operating expenses far outweighed any public benefit that it might be providing."[26]

Of the 10 SOU daily consists still plying the rails at Brosnan's earlier-than-planned retirement (1967), a half-dozen departed Washington's Union Station for Southeastern targets. Included, with their destinations in parentheses, were: the *Crescent* and *Southerner* (New Orleans), *Peach Queen* (Atlanta), *Piedmont Limited* (its name truly apropos then, cut from its past New Orleans terminus to Salisbury, North Carolina, shaving 797 miles off its previous 1,131-mile run), *Birmingham Special* (Birmingham via N&W through Lynchburg), and *Pelican* (New Orleans via N&W through Lynchburg).

Beyond those six was the *Asheville Special*, its route reduced from New York–Greens-

boro–Asheville to Asheville–Greensboro; *Carolina Special,* formerly Cincinnati–Charleston/
Goldsboro, shrunk to Cincinnati–Columbia/Greensboro with sections still splitting at
Asheville; *Royal Palm,* formerly a premier train bathed in luxury and ferrying patrons from
Cincinnati to Miami/St. Petersburg, diminished then to Cincinnati–Valdosta, Georgia, and —
by year's end — only as far as Cincinnati–Atlanta (sans diner, with box meals brought aboard
in both directions at Somerset, Kentucky, and Chattanooga); and the *Tennessean,* previously
New York–Chattanooga–Memphis, condensed to Chattanooga–Memphis. If anybody wondered about the fate of rail passenger service in America by Class 1 predominantly freight carriers, Southern's arrival and departure billboards were fairly convincing displays: the old
system was irretrievably broken, then only a figment of its former self.

Brosnan's hand-picked successor, W. Graham Claytor, Jr., a Washington lawyer, had a sunnier
disposition when it came to passenger railroading. A review by railway historiographer Richard
Saunders of the early days following the change of command is cautiously optimistic: "It was
Graham Claytor's task to build on the technological excellence begun by Brosnan, but also to
end Brosnan's reign of terror and restore the Southern's relations with the rest of the industry.
Brosnan died in 1985, a deeply flawed genius but one who had changed railroading forever."[27]

William Graham Claytor, Jr., was born March 14, 1912, in Roanoke, Virginia. A railfan
in boyhood, he shared that obsession with a younger sibling Bob (Robert B. Claytor), who
became president of the Norfolk & Western Railway (N&W) in 1981. Southern Railway and
N&W merged the next year.[28] Bob Claytor was that amalgamated line's inaugural chairman
and CEO. In Roanoke, the Claytor siblings— both of whom died in 1994 — are now subjects
of a semi-permanent exhibit at the Virginia Museum of Transportation.[29]

From the University of Virginia, Graham Claytor earned a bachelor's degree (1933), and
from Harvard University, a law degree (1936). He was president of the *Harvard Law Review.*
In 1938, he joined the law firm of Covington & Burling in the nation's capital, with which he
was identified to 1967, and again from 1981 to 1982.[30]

Bill Brosnan recruited Claytor to Southern Railway as vice president in 1963. In what
turned out to be a stroke of genius, Brosnan picked SOU's next executive leader. Although
few may have deduced it at the start, a gifted Claytor was able to turn inspired visualizations
into myriad productive achievements for the company. His management style was generally
celebrated. He was effective in repairing human relations that had suffered misfortune in the
years before he reached the presidential suite. The accolades he collected over a 14-year period
with SOU are impressive. During his presidency *Dun's Review* named Southern one of America's best managed enterprises, crediting "a savvy and far-sighted top management" with creating "a trim, tough, up-to-date railroad." And that platform was merely laying the
groundwork for his next acts to follow, which will be addressed momentarily.

Anticipating Amtrak's assumption of the lion's share of the nation's rail passenger service
on May 1, 1971, Claytor reasoned that Southern didn't have to "sign up" for any relief. (Note
the marked difference in his style and that of Brosnan.) "We could afford to keep our primary
train and made it the finest in the country," Claytor determined. "If we turned the *Crescent*
over to Amtrak, I knew what would happen. It would go to hell, very fast."[31]

The *Southern Crescent*—formed earlier by combining the celebrated *Southerner* with the
legendary *Crescent* into a single streamlined flagship consist operating between Boston and
New Orleans— would be maintained. For a while it ran to Birmingham daily and three days
a week along the *Southerner's* old route to New Orleans. It was later trimmed to daily to
Atlanta and three days weekly beyond. One review, obviously from a gastronomic disciple,
observed that — even in that late era — "Meals in the diner meant muffins baked fresh on the
car for breakfast and Southern's savory fried chicken for dinner." There was no shortchanging
there; no slouching allowed. "The SR maintained its Southern Crescent in the grand manner,"

acknowledged that source.[32] The renowned train was finally relinquished to Amtrak on January 31, 1979, which rebranded it the *Crescent*.

In the meantime a pair of Southern's familiar and enduring consists plied a few more tracks to haul travelers to and fro. The *Asheville Special* (Asheville–Greensboro) and the *Piedmont Limited* (Washington–Salisbury, North Carolina) persisted for a while. The *Special* exited the timetable, by then a mere folder, on August 8, 1975. The *Piedmont* lasted to 1976.

Not merely parenthetically, for more than a decade SOU's identifying green-and-gold F8 passenger diesels had lost their luster. Extending from the DeButts–Brosnan years as far back as 1958, the strikingly distinctive colors applied to the upfront power units had been replaced by steam era black. Claytor was unhappy. To signify what he perceived as perhaps something of a renaissance in public transit, in 1972 — in what may have been an act of love — he directed that the road's few remaining passenger locomotives be restored to their earlier livery brilliance. Even in that early Amtrak epoch, when it might have made little difference to most travelers what the engines that Southern was running looked like, it was important to the line's president. He called for something dynamic and memorable. Self-respect was worth a great deal, so his action insinuated, even for a railroad.

Over the years Southern had acquired power over scores of less prominent rail systems. Aside from a plethora of short lines and other secondary roads there were several Class 1 carriers within its pool. None was unimportant; but among SOU's most valued properties, especially beyond the prime of golden age travel by rail — and possibly its most prized extension — was the Central of Georgia Railway (CofG) added in 1963. The transaction regarding it is detailed briefly in Chapter 4. Lamentably it wasn't a gratifying outcome to some members of the board and staff of CofG, indisputably due to the way it was handled by SOU president Bill Brosnan. On the first day of the acquisition he dismissed 1,500 CofG hires plus the chairman of CofG's board, who had crossed swords with him in the past. While CofG prevailed under its own sobriquet and joined Amtrak as that agency opened for business, it was reduced, some would argue, to a minion in a slaveholding camp. Resentment abounded among some of the former line's staunchest supporters.

There is more to the story of W. Graham Claytor, Jr., SOU president from 1967 to 1976, when he assumed the chairmanship, that bears repeating. Retiring at 65 in 1977, Claytor wasn't idle very long. Appointed by President Jimmy Carter, he was U.S. secretary of the Navy between 1977 and 1979. In the latter year he served as acting U.S. secretary of transportation. Also from 1979 to 1981, he was U.S. deputy secretary of defense. But he still wasn't done yet. In one sense, he had really just begun. Do you recall his perceived anti–Amtrak stance in 1971? Some pundits viewed him as unimpressed by that emerging enterprise. He would have a change of heart as the years advanced. Claytor, seeking a new challenge at age 70 (1982), was in the right place at the right time.

> At Amtrak's birth in 1971, Mr. Claytor was president of Southern Railway ... and one of Amtrak's most vocal critics. Perhaps that is why Democrat Claytor was acceptable to the Reagan White House. Recalls President Reagan's first Transportation Secretary, Drew Lewis: "We had to get somebody to run Amtrak. I sent Graham's somebody over to the White House and it got turned down by the President's advisers: Lynn Nofsinger, Jim Baker, and Ed Meese.
> "I said, 'Okay, guys, you find somebody better to run Amtrak, and I'll take them, but you can't turn the guy down just because he's a Democrat. Democrats and Republicans can run railroads.'"
> Claytor brilliantly demonstrated that Lewis's faith was not misplaced. During the 11 Claytor years, Amtrak reduced its need for federal operating subsidies by more than 40%.[33]

By the time Claytor retired from Amtrak in 1993, fares and other revenues covered 80 percent of the company's expenses, up from 42 percent in 1980.[34] He died only a short time after leaving Amtrak, at 82, on May 14, 1994, at Bradenton, Florida. The cavernous hall at Washington's Union Station was dubbed "Claytor Concourse" by Amtrak's board of directors for his efforts in restoring that historic venue. To honor his memory, in late 1994, *Railway Age* established the W. Graham Claytor, Jr. Award for Distinguished Service to Passenger Transportation. In succeeding years that honor recognized astute individuals for their winning contributions. In *The Amtrak Story*, Frank N. Wilner obsessed:

> His love of railroads and, most assuredly, divine providence, delivered Graham Claytor to America's railroad industry—first to Southern Railway; then to Amtrak.
> Those who knew this considerate, enduring, dignified Virginia gentleman; those who took his instruction; and those who grasped his wisdom, are fortunate indeed....
> Let the record show for eternity—for it cannot be contradicted by evidence—that Amtrak survived, that Amtrak is, and that Amtrak will be because of William Graham Claytor, Jr.

One of the last big acquisitions by Southern Railway in its latter days under that exclusive imprint was that of the original Norfolk Southern Railway (NS) on January 1, 1974. NS operated 622 route miles between Norfolk and Charlotte with stems to Virginia Beach, Virginia; Fayetteville, New Bern and multiple phosphate-mining centers of Beaufort County, North Carolina. Combined with Southern-owned Carolina & Northwestern Railroad (C&N) on that occasion, the NS & C&N operated for a while under NS nomenclature. When SOU merged with the Norfolk & Western Railway (N&W) in 1982, the NS subsidiary was renamed Carolina & Northwestern, freeing Norfolk Southern as a moniker for a newly-created outfit embracing SOU and N&W rail systems.

Amtrak EMD E8 217 has just arrived at the St. Petersburg station one day in 1974 with a three-car consist in tow. A switch engine will haul the train to the railroad yard for service and maintenance. This view is west to the station, tracks and platforms. Built by ACL, the facility opened in 1963. Following ACL's merger with SAL in 1967 the new tenant here was SCL (*courtesy Michael B. Robbins*).

Both lines were competitively beset after a handful of leading freight carriers in the East (among them a couple of old SOU competitors—Seaboard Coast Line and ancillary Louisville & Nashville) formed CSX. This was a behemoth freight system with many thousands of route miles situated in SOU and N&W territory, now unified under a single umbrella. Unable to miss the handwriting on the wall that this portended for their futures, to avoid loss of revenues, prestige and possibly their whole businesses, the outsiders agreed to mingle their diverse operations in a new bloc. The resulting alliance was named Norfolk Southern Corporation, a holding company, based in Norfolk. On December 31, 1990, the line was renamed Norfolk Southern Railway. At that juncture control of the Norfolk & Western Railway transferred from the holding company to Norfolk Southern Railway.

The venture grew appreciably on June 1, 1999, by acquiring 58 percent of Conrail's 11,000-mile routes (Northeastern railway systems that were dominated by the former Pennsylvania and New York Central railroads, fallen flags that had worn a Penn Central label in their latter days). Norfolk Southern was to be largely identified as a key Eastern U.S. transporter of domestic and export coal, mined mainly in Kentucky, Pennsylvania, Tennessee, Virginia and West Virginia. The line now owns and operates 21,300 track miles in 22 states with hubs at Harrisburg, Pennsylvania; Chicago; and Atlanta.

Measured by revenues since earned, of the nine Class 1 freight railroads operating within the United States in 2007 (the most recent year for which data is available at this writing), Norfolk Southern Corporation earned $9,432,000, good enough for third place following Union Pacific ($16,249,000) and BNSF ($15,909,000). NS's nearest rival, in fourth place, was CSX Transportation ($9,039,000).[35] The legacy of the former Norfolk & Western and Southern Railway systems remains strong, viably entrenched among the freight traffic leaders in America. It's part of a heritage that organizationally began in 1894, with its earliest forebear traceable all the way back to 1827.

Although passenger-hauling over those tracks under a Southern Railway banner vanished more than three decades ago (1979), when the *Crescent* rolls today under its Amtrak auspices, riders traverse the same mainline rails where "The Southern Serves the South" embraced a venerated tradition of exquisite travel. And if it's possible, perhaps somewhere out there a larger-than-life figure of W. Graham Claytor, Jr., is observing those Norfolk Southern and Amtrak operations—working in tandem on the same mainline. And quite possibly he's smiling … broadly.

III

The Human Dimension

15

SEGREGATION AND PREJUDICE
Jim Crow, Colored Coaches and "Ladies' Cars"

As we have observed consistently, travel by train — especially in the first half of the 20th century — had a whole lot going for it. Beyond all of the keepsake recollections that can be detailed, nonetheless, for some Americans riding the rails in a significant portion of the period under scrutiny, it wasn't as we have described. Some of the attributes of railroading that others highly prized were noticeably missing in their journeys over the rails.

As it turned out, discrimination in mass transit was but one faction of a far larger motif of isolationism in this country. In the sphere of transportation, it was dated to the early decades of the 19th century. Its zenith occurred in the ensuing century with its derivatives commonplace into the 1960s and 1970s. Its repercussions, however, stayed long after the legal force to abolish bigotry's tentacles was in place. While the tools were then available, the reality is that something that pervasive just doesn't evaporate overnight.

The so-called Jim Crow laws prevented Negroes (now African Americans or blacks) from enjoying the full benefits of rail travel which were guaranteed to other journeymen.[1] In 1908, a regional survey of the "color line" by journalist Ray S. Baker revealed, "No other point of race contact is so much and so bitterly discussed among Negroes as the Jim Crow car." It remained valid three dozen years afterward when, in a 1944 study, Swedish sociologist Gunnar Myrdal found "The Jim Crow car is resented more bitterly among Negroes than most other forms of segregation." Although the problem was rooted in inequitable practices displayed throughout the country in earlier decades, for a century its most pronounced incursions prevailed across the South.

Long before that time, prejudicial stigmas toward people of color proliferated in many areas regardless of geographic district. "There was no place in the United States that allowed African Americans to travel in the same class as white people," one academician professed. "Slave owners traveling with their slaves were able to travel in first class but free African Americans were forced to travel in second-class cars."[2]

In Boston, to mention one, in the 15-year period following 1830, discrimination against Negroes aboard public transit systems was stridently enforced. Prejudicial behavior was customary in that epoch in the passenger cars of the Eastern Railroad Company of Massachusetts. Abolitionist Charles Lennox Redmond delivered numerous addresses throughout the commonwealth then calling for recognition of the rights of all citizens everywhere, regardless of "complexion, or any other physical peculiarity or conformation."

Railroad executives argued that all Massachusetts corporations had been granted the power to make "reasonable and proper" by-laws for the management of their business, and "the established usage and the public sentiment of this community authorize a separation of the blacks and whites in public places...."

Through constant campaigning the abolitionists got their desired result. In 1842, a joint legislative committee ... reported that the railroad restrictions violated African Americans' rights as citizens, conflicted with the state constitution, and "would be an insult to any white man." The committee recommended a bill [to] prohibit ... distinctions in accommodations because of descent, sect, or color....

    The growing impact of public opinion, and the threat of legislative action prompted the railroad companies to abandon segregation.[3]

At least so in Massachusetts. A joint special committee proposed legislation guaranteeing equal rights in rail accommodations to colored persons. The Massachusetts Senate and House of Representatives subsequently passed such a bill in 1843:

> Sec. 1. No rail corporation shall, by themselves, their directors, or other, make or establish by-law or regulation, which shall make any distinction, or give a preference in accommodation to any one or more persons over other, on account of descent, sect, or color.
>
> Sec. 2. Any officer or servant of any rail-road corporation, who shall assault any person for the purpose of depriving him of his right or privilege, in any car or other rail-road accommodation, on account of descent, sect, or color ... shall be punished by imprisonment in the county jail not less than six days, or by fine not less than ten dollars; and shall also be answerable to the person assaulted....

Not all segregated transportation in the commonwealth was halted by this measure, however. A magazine article the following year observed that railroad executives believed public sentiment demanded "separate cars for Negroes," pointing out blacks could "stand on the platforms of any cars."[4] After a black woman was removed from a "white" car, a judge alleged Negroes that were "sober, well-behaved, and free from disease" couldn't be denied rights enjoyed by whites on public conveyances.

For a while Philadelphia Negroes fared no better than those in Massachusetts. After streetcars were introduced there in 1858, people of color were permitted to ride only on the front platforms even in inclement weather. Think of the monstrously cold winters! Some protested and a local newspaper revealed that the city was the only metropolitan area in the North that kept Negroes from riding inside public conveyances. This, of course, had a negative bearing on those patrons' capacities for traveling some distance from the city center where less expensive and better housing possibilities existed, creating a double whammy. Limited behavior like this persisted for nearly a decade until 1867. That year the Pennsylvania legislature passed a measure outlawing segregation in public conveyances.

In another illustration when two freedmen attempted to purchase tickets for a sleeping car operating between Washington, D.C., and New York City, "white passengers said they would leave the car if the Negroes were admitted."[5] The black riders were turned away. On a separate occasion a Negro in Baltimore tried to buy a ticket to ride inside a railway car but was banished instead "to the front platform where colored persons were allowed to ride."[6] Such instances were common in the 1800s throughout the Northeast.

It is duly noted — although we hear and read much that is disparaging to a segregated South in the 20th century, reviling the region for having a lock on the arena — that in truth much of the country advocated and practiced racial discrimination. As a potent outcome of social custom, prejudice gradually seeped into numerous facets of everyday life including commercial transactions. It should come as no surprise then that as public transit — local and long distance — was embedded within the American fabric, discriminatory practices evolved into some its most characteristic traits. For most citizens, distinguishing between the races was a natural, accepted way of life no matter where it was evidenced.

For segregation to stick, however, it had to intrude into the simplest everyday activity such as taking a drink of water in public places. Hence, in railroad stations one could find dual drinking fountains, usually side-by-side: one was labeled "Colored" and one was marked "White." There were also divided waiting rooms, separate waiting areas alongside the tracks and on platforms, designated rest rooms, and distinct sections of lunch counters—if Negroes were permitted to purchase food at all.[7] As the years roll along now it may seem unthinkable that skin tone could have been the basis for dividing Americans to the degree it did. It was so and travel by rail reflected, exacerbated and perpetuated established practices in countless realms of life.

New York City native Jim McFarland, born in 1944, emanated from a clan that arrived in the Big Apple from the Deep South some years before. His grandma had grown up in Dixie before moving North. Every summer it was a family ritual for her to take Jim and his brother on a train trip to visit their Southern kin. They did this from the time Jim was four until he turned 11. McFarland's story, recalled as an adult remembering his childhood experiences, might be typical of scads of black youngsters with similar incidents from their excursions down to Dixie.[8]

> In those days, the trip presented drastic changes that let McFarland know he was far from New York. The switch began, he said ... when their train reached Washington.
>
> "When we got to D.C.," McFarland recalled, "we would get out of an integrated car and we'd go into an all-colored car.
>
> "I thought this was the greatest thing that could ever happen," McFarland says. "Because now I'm in a car with all my people. They've got the brown paper bags with the greasy chicken, and the sandwiches. We're having a good time."
>
> But on the following stops, McFarland often had trouble with the divided bathrooms. He was too young to read "White" and "Colored" well. "Use the one with the 'C' on it," his grandmother would tell him....
>
> When he got back to New York, McFarland's friends would ask him, "What was the South about?"
>
> "Them brothers got it going on in the South," he would answer. "We got our own bathroom. We got our own water fountain."
>
> McFarland's grandmother never let on to the details of the situation.... But he found out on his own about segregation, and the feelings behind it.
>
> That was when he was 11—and when McFarland told his grandmother, "I don't want to go to the South any more."

Below the Mason-Dixon Line that's how pronounced segregation was in the halcyon days of rail travel.

> Segregated transit was a special concern in Virginia, which served as a gateway for south-bound bus and railway passengers. Crossing into the Old Dominion from the District of Columbia, which had no Jim Crow restrictions, or from Maryland, which, unlike Virginia, limited its segregationist mandate to local and intrastate passengers, could be a jarring and bewildering experience for travelers unfamiliar with the complexities of border-state life. This was an old problem, dating back at least a half century, but the number of violations and interracial incidents involving interstate passengers ... multiplied ... especially since the outbreak of World War II.[9]

Before the War Between the States (1861–1865), in the South little need existed to separate the blacks and whites because all but about five percent of blacks were slaves. New laws passed in the postwar era, commonly known as the Black Codes, set undisputed boundaries for Negroes who, by then, were free for the first time.

In the contemporary age, a respected Southern-based intellectual fount observed that the Black Codes "rigidly controlled and managed the lives of black citizens ... they foreshadowed the social and geographic control that full-scale segregation would bring."[10] Their directives applied to schools, theaters, taverns and numerous other public places frequented by both races.

In 1866, seizing upon an opportunity to remake the South, the U.S. Congress responded forcefully. The Republican Party, organized by anti-slavery activists in the early 1850s, pushed to include Negroes in society, a sharp contrast from the blacks' past. Heretofore strong Dem-ocratically-controlled Southern legislatures—which had made new state laws to the con-trary—acquiesced for a time. Most of the new anti-black legislation was repealed.

During the final couple of decades of the 19th century, many Negroes enjoyed the rights granted in the 13th, 14th and 15th amendments to the U.S. Constitution. For eight years, they were also protected by the Civil Rights Act of March 1, 1875. The latter was passed by the U.S. Congress and signed into law on that date by President U.S. Grant. It guaranteed all citizens without distinction by race, color, or previous condition of servitude were entitled to similar treatment in "public accommodations" (e.g., lodging, public conveyances, and amusement palaces). As a result blacks and whites rode together in the same railway cars, ate in the same restaurants and used the same public facilities, although they did not interact as equals. That was about to change altogether.

All of that was reversed beginning in 1877. Democratic majorities, which were weakened for a brief spell, gained renewed strength and with that renewed zeal. They put shackles, at least figuratively so, on Negroes, in doing so interrupting reconstruction advancement. This had a destructive effect on people of color. In many places they could no longer hold political office, they lost their right to vote and their participation as equal members of society was voided. Disenfranchisement and segregation were the dual chief objectives of new legislation that threw cold water on the freedoms they had so recently won.

The contempt and disrespect by which people of color were treated in some quarters is exemplified by their status in railway servitude. A published article at the turn of the 20th century portraying the Southern Railway shops at Spencer, North Carolina, is telling: "No mechanical device has been installed for handling coal and ashes, as colored labor is very cheap in the South."[11]

The right to vote was discouraged, principally by assessing poll taxes—fees levied at voting booths that most Negroes didn't possess, and therefore couldn't hand over; and by lit-eracy tests. Teaching Negroes was illegal and most adult blacks were ex-slaves and illiterate. It was difficult for them to comprehend and properly respond to questions that were simple for most whites to answer. Meanwhile, in reaching their other aim — segregation — lawmakers designated that schools and other public facilities, including public transit, weren't to be mutually shared by the races.

All of this had telling effects on race relations across the South.[12] While 130,344 Negroes were registered to vote in Louisiana in 1896, that number diminished to just 5,320 by the early 1900s. It resulted largely from a newly-drafted state constitution discouraging blacks from exercising their entitlement. In Alabama, also at the start of the 20th century, 3,000 of 180,000 Negroes (about 1.67 percent) of voting age were registered. As time progressed, the states carried their discrimination habits into the classroom, amusement venues and a pro-fusion of select social practices.[13]

State courts and then the U.S. Supreme Court, in the 1883 case *Pace v. Alabama*, indicated that such laws were permissible. Facilitating all of this going on in the states, the U.S. Supreme Court determined that Congress had "no power to prevent private acts of discrimination." Legal challenges to segregated transportation increased, and Negroes sought to enforce their legal rights under congressional legislation. The federal government meanwhile demonstrated loss of will to enforce equality.

The U.S. Supreme Court considered the landmark case of *Plessy v. Ferguson* in 1896, in which mixed-race plaintiff Homer Plessy challenged Louisiana's 1890 law mandating separate accommodations for black and white passengers in railway cars. The high court's decision handed the segregationists exactly what they were in search of and issued a demoralizing set-back to abolitionists that was to hold sway for more than half a century. Subsequent enactments built on that ruling. In 1926, the high court decreed that individuals could decide privately not to rent or sell properties to Negroes, following in that blueprint.

The panel struck down the Civil Rights Act of 1875 in 1883. Many of its tenets wouldn't reappear until successive jurists adopted the Civil Rights Act of 1964, the Voting Rights Act of 1965, and the Fair Housing Act of 1968. From that time forward federal power was applied in governing interstate commerce. The panelists reinforced their public transportation stance in *Plessy v. Ferguson* (1896), reaffirming a Louisiana law authorizing separate but equal accommodations for the dual races on intrastate railroads. The ruling provided a legal underpinning for many more social actions by state and local authorities in which blacks and whites were kept apart. Not until May 31, 1954, when the court ruled in the case of *Brown v. Board of Education*, did it overturn *Plessy v. Ferguson*, declaring that separate but equal was unconstitutional.[14] On that occasion, 63 years after the protracted episode began, and 29 years following his death, a civil disobedient Homer Plessy finally won.

In *Plessy v. Ferguson* a handful of New Orleans black professionals labeling themselves the Citizens' Committee to Test the Constitutionality of the Separate Car Law (or more simply, Comité des Citoyens) ventured an experiment challenging the Louisiana Separate Car Act (1890).

> In 1892, with a new year, a full war chest, a clear position, and lawyers at the ready, the Comité des Citoyens prepared to challenge the interstate aspects of the Separate Car Act. Could the state regulate people traveling from, say, Florida to Texas, passing through Louisiana? Or could they regulate someone departing in Louisiana to a state outside the state's jurisdiction? ...
>
> On February 24, 1892, the Comité des Citoyens acted. Its operatives provided the musician son of Rodolphe Desdunes, Daniel Desdunes, with a first-class ticket. At 8 A.M. that morning, the younger Desdunes made his way to the L&N Depot on Canal Street and took a seat in a whites-only car bound for Mobile, Alabama. But he got no further than the two miles it took to get to the corner of Elysian Fields and North Claiborne Avenues. Here, the conductor stopped the train. Private detectives hired by the Comité des Citoyens got on board and arrested Daniel Desdunes. They booked him with violating the Separate Car Act. Comité des Citoyens treasurer Paul Bonseigneur arrived at the precinct station to have the thirty-year-old younger Desdunes released on a surety bond....
>
> By June 1892, the Comité des Citoyens readied themselves to move forward on the intrastate portion of the act, knowing this could be the toughest legal nut to crack. Now came Homer Plessy's turn to ride the train.[15]

Born March 17, 1863, a Creole mixed-blood New Orleans native whose lighter skin tone allowed him to be accepted as white in some situations, Plessy was arrested on June 7, 1892. The faction's lawyer, Albion Tourgée, was spokesman for the Comité des Citoyens in the inquiry that followed the arrest: a Louisiana district court had already declared that forced segregation in railroad cars traveling between states was unconstitutional. Once it had that verdict, the Comité des Citoyens was now assessing the constitutionality of segregation on railroad cars running within a single state. It teamed with a railway conductor and a private detective to hinder the multiracial Plessy until his arrest. With Plessy having obviously violated the ruling, Tourgée's strategy was to question the law's ambiguity.

The Separate Car Act that Homer Plessy defied marked the beginning of a saga that persisted for decades and adversely and directly affected the lives of hundreds of thousands of human beings. And its inception can be traced to the events that transpired on another rail car deep in the heart of Dixie: "On Tuesday evening, a Negro named Plessy was arrested by Private Detective Cain on the East Louisiana train and locked up for violating section 2 of act 111 of 1890, relative to separate coaches.... He waved examination yesterday before Recorder Moulin and was sent before the criminal court under $500.00 bond."[16]

As written, the part (Section 2, Act 111) of the Separate Car Act passed by the 1890 Louisiana legislature and breached by Plessy read:

The officers of passenger trains shall have power and are hereby required to assign each passenger to the coach or compartment used for the race to which such passenger belongs; any person insisting on going into a coach or compartment to which by race he does not belong, shall be liable to a fine of Twenty-Five Dollars or in lieu thereof to imprisonment for a period of not more [than] twenty days in the Parish Prison.

It should be noted parenthetically that the Separate Car Act was not looked upon with favor by many of the railroads any more than it was by black Americans.[17] The carriers incurred considerable added expense once they were ordered to provide dissimilar space (cars or split cars) for the dual ethnic groups. Beyond presenting policing and enforcement issues involving train personnel, sometimes the designated space for one party went empty or was only partially required. This constraint had the negative effect of reducing operating efficiencies on several fronts.

The presiding judge in the Plessy infraction was John Howard Ferguson (1838–1915). Born at Martha's Vineyard, Massachusetts, in his 20s he studied law in Boston and hung out his shingle there in 1863. Sensing greater opportunity in a defeated South following the Civil War, Ferguson soon resettled in New Orleans, where he spent the remainder of his life, initially as a civil lawyer. For a year, in 1877–1878, his family's Democratic Party credentials propelled him into the state legislature. In 1891, Ferguson became a defense attorney in criminal court, revealing nothing of a racially-oriented agenda that would surface later.

The Louisiana district court, presided over by Ferguson, ruled that a state possessed constitutional powers to regulate railway companies operating solely within its borders. It declared that the Louisiana Separate Car Act was indeed lawful. On November 18, 1892, Ferguson's decision stated:

> There is no pretense that he [Plessy] was not provided with equal accommodations with the white passengers. He was simply deprived of the liberty of doing as he pleased, and of violating a penal statute with impunity.... The railway company was blameless in the matter. The ticket purchased by the defendant was not used simply because the defendant refused to ride in the car, or compartment, to which he was assigned by the conductor, without a valid reason for said refusal, and insisted on going into a coach in which by race he did not belong.[18]

In 1893, the Comité des Citoyens appealed the verdict to the state Supreme Court and three years hence to the U.S. Supreme Court. Both times Tourgée pled the case arguing that Plessy was denied equal protection under the 14th Amendment. The 13th Amendment was also violated, said the contingent's attorney, when "the essential features of slavery" were perpetuated.

> Eight of the nine justices were unconvinced by Tourgée's arguments, and ruled that neither the Thirteenth nor Fourteenth Amendment was applicable.... The majority opinion delivered by Henry Billings Brown, attacked the Thirteenth Amendment claims by distinguishing between political and social equality. According to this distinction, blacks and whites were politically equal (in the sense that they had the same political rights) but socially unequal (blacks were not as socially advanced as whites):
> "Legislation is powerless to eradicate racial instincts or to abolish distinctions based on physical differences, and the attempt to do so can only result in accentuating the differences of the present situation. If the civil and political rights of both races be equal, one cannot be inferior to the other civilly or politically. If one race be inferior to the other socially, the Constitution of the United States cannot put them on the same plane."
> The majority also attacked Tourgée's Fourteenth Amendment claims by arguing that enforced separation does not "stamp" blacks with the badge of inferiority, because both blacks and whites were treated equally under the law — in the sense that whites were forbidden to sit in a railroad car designated for blacks. In his famous dissenting opinion, John Marshall Harlan attacked the constitutionality of the Louisiana law and argued that while the law may appear to treat blacks and whites equally, "every one knows that the statute in question had its origin in the purpose, not so much to exclude white persons from railroad cars occupied by blacks, as to exclude colored people from coaches occupied by or assigned to white persons."[19]

Justice Harlan's line of reasoning admonished: "There is in this country no superior, dominant, ruling class of citizens. There is no caste here. Our Constitution is color-blind, and neither knows nor tolerates classes among citizens. In respect to civil rights, all citizens are equal before the law. The humblest is the peer of the most powerful." While all of this seems sycophantic to Harlan for his singular open-mindedness on the issue, it can be noted: "Within a couple of years, Justice Harland began voting in favor of the type of segregation laws he so vigorously opposed in the Plessy case."[20]

Harlan's argument on this occasion, however, was brushed aside by the majority on the court. The rendering in *Plessy v. Ferguson* was the organizing legal justification — the rallying cry — for racial segregation during all those years that followed. It formed the underpinnings of a glut of ensuing acts that involved public transportation and so many more facets impinging in its strain. The ruling left the South in a state of perpetual racial division for a minimum of six decades and possibly more. And while the region implemented discriminatory practices, it did so under absolute federal authority that granted the subjugation of one people by another. In supplying not merely tacit approval but legal standing for those proceedings, the high court rendered its endorsement of what occurred.

Before dismissing Homer Plessy, wouldn't you like to know what became of him? On January 11, 1897, four and a half years after he was arrested for sitting in the wrong railway car, he pleaded guilty to violating the Separate Car Act. Thereupon he paid a $25 fine and evaporated into obscurity. "Louisiana's insistence on trying Plessy after all that time only hinted at the fanaticism with which the South would apply the 'separate but equal' principle," proffered one of the phenomenon's scholars.[21] After Plessey's notoriety subsided he faded into the shadows, returning to his longtime occupation as a cobbler, never more to be civil disobedient. Alternately he worked as a laborer, warehouseman and clerk before collecting for black-owned People's Life Insurance Company beginning in 1910. He never left the downtown neighborhoods of the Crescent City as his permanent place of residence. In a peripheral role he was vice president of the Société des Francs Amis, one of the more durable local Creole organizations that harkened back to the antebellum period. Plessy died in his native city on March 1, 1825, at 61.

Now would it be possible to establish that Americans universally — as opposed to purely Southerners — bear some weight in what transpired in Dixie in the years between 1896 and 1954 and possibly beyond? While the laws permitting segregation gave the geographical district a black eye from which it is yet to fully recover, those instigations were legally protected by a cluster that represents Everyman. In that sense it would seem that the nation is to blame for the realities of what many consider to be an ignoble era.

By the time the United States became embroiled in the Second World War in 1941, the South had long been a fully segregated society. Schools, restaurants, hotels, train cars, waiting rooms, elevators, public restrooms, colleges, hospitals, banks, cemeteries, theaters, swimming pools, drinking fountains, picnic areas, beaches, parks, prisons and churches were all separate: most were designated wholly or in part for blacks or whites exclusively, but never for both ethnic groups to occupy the same space at the same time. A blend of ridicule and humiliation, dismal economic opportunities and segregated education for their children drove legions of Negroes to flee the territory during the Jim Crow epoch.

Tens of thousands departed the only homes they had ever known, many boarding segregated rail cars in their attempts to distance themselves from the past. Seeking improved standards of living as well as hoping to experience a measure of personal dignity, those comrades pursued their fortunes in a fundamentally industrialized North. Many lived out their existences there, never to permanently return to areas with warmer climes, diversified occupational possibilities and a radically altered social environment. In Dixie, as time moved on and the influence of the hard-liners faded, an atmosphere of racial discord that persisted for two centuries was gradually replaced by one of growing acceptance nearly everywhere.

In the South in particular, railway cars had been an early target for establishing the building blocks of segregation. In the late 1870s and the 1880s, railroads began to gravitate away from a perk they had trumpeted in appealing to women: for a good while on some of their premier trains, certain roads reserved one or more passenger cars exclusively for ladies traveling alone or in small contingents with other women. It was a practice that attracted some in the segment to patronize the railroads. On the New Albany & Salem route, for instance, the last car on the train was dubbed the "Ladies' Car."[22] One historian, describing the arrangement, observed: "Into this no male dared enter unless accompanied by a woman, who might or might not be a lady. All other males had to sit in the smoker, whether or not they smoked."[23] There is more commentary on this topic in the succeeding chapter (16) on creature comforts.

But the ritual of a private distaff conveyance diminished and finally ceased altogether after railway magnates chose or were forced to invoke segregation policies. Instead of specifying certain cars for feminine riders as they had done heretofore, trains suddenly designated cars or portions of them divided by screens for their white-only or black-only passengers. Streetcars (and later, city buses) did the same in many communities, displaying signage reading "White" and "Colored" in disparate parts of those transit forms.[24]

As all of this became widespread, manifold states and municipalities in Dixie implemented new laws mandating racial segregation on trains passing through their jurisdictions. The die cast a dark shadow upon a region and a people that was already trying men's souls, whatever the degree of pigment in their skin.

Copious examples of this discrimination on the rails abound. Negroes riding the Atlantic Coast Line's (ACL) dual flagship streamliners *East Coast Champion* and *West Coast Champion*, for instance, were separated by a "colored" coach in each train's daily consist. Actually, it wasn't even a whole car. The company inserted a combination baggage-coach in the unenviable spot directly behind the diesel engine. That placement was branded not only by increased noise and stench but also by a generally perceived bumpier ride than in the cars situated further back in the convoy. (On earlier trains in the steam-engine era, the soot was also complimentary.)

Blacks could visit the dining car, too, yet they were cordoned off from other patrons. They were seated at a couple of appointed tables in a less desirable location adjacent to the kitchen which, at times, was distinguished by lots of noise and unpleasant odors. Negroes were alienated from other diners by a curtain. People of color were also invariably barred from the Pullmans and from the inviting (except to blacks) curved-end deep-window observation-tavern-lounge cars at the rear of certain premier trains.[25] Even after the Interstate Commerce Commission, the U.S. courts and President Harry S Truman issued a proclamation (in 1948) banning segregation in rail dining cars, practices like these persisted on multiple roads. The "colored" coaches on the *Champion*s weren't retired until 1957, just one example among many.[26]

ACL wasn't totally indifferent to the plight of its dark-skinned riders, nonetheless. In one expression in 1949, which may have been indicative of the road's actual position on the matter, ACL president Champ Davis reprimanded L. S. Jeffords, vice-president and general manager. His comments pertained to an "unfortunate and unnecessary incident" wherein a "colored" coach wasn't sufficiently air conditioned. In addition to their entitlement to equal accommodations, said Davis in a letter, Negroes' patronage aboard ACL trains was "much more consistent" than whites'. It behooved the line to deplore such conditions and avoid replications. About that time ACL posted sizeable notices within its "colored" coaches thanking Negroes for their business. Not only did it seem the right thing to do, it could possibly increase that segment of travelers if they felt genuinely appreciated.

Still other examples proliferated, reminiscent of the disenfranchisement that policies separating the races generated. The *Southerner*, for one, also appearing in the streamliner epoch, which challenged Southern Railway's flagship consist the *Crescent* as that road's foremost train, was equipped with a split coach. There the races encountered physical barriers, insuring their inability to interact. On that luxury conveyance sleepers and a rounded-end radio-equipped tavern-observation car at the rear of the consist were off-limits to people of color. In the dining car meanwhile practices similar to those observed by Atlantic Coast Line and other long-haul carriers prevailed.

"The obvious differences between white and black railway cars were well known; indeed, the only similarity was that they were both headed in the same direction," claimed one exponent of mixing the races.[27] That scholar's observations are tinged with symbolism:

> Most trains would not admit black passengers to Pullman sleeping cars, dining cars, or club cars. When baggage and mail cars were added behind the locomotive, a Jim Crow car invariably followed (or was de facto half of the baggage car). Its dingy interior, lack of heat or carpeting, and filthy toilet were a far cry from the quality coaches designated for whites. Nor was there complete racial separation, since whites who smoked or drank, as well as shackled prisoners accompanied by guards, were routinely found in the Jim Crow car....
>
> When the Negroes ... were excluded by law from decent accommodations on railroad cars, they could sense that they would lose other rights, too, from voting and jury service to decent schools and medical care. The white elite was turning citizenship into a privilege of a private club, with membership open only to those without a "drop of black blood."[28]

Now, for a moment, consider one possibility in all of this: were the railway coaches and passengers within them that made their way through Dixie differentiated by race because the rail barons or management desired it? Or is it just possible, and maybe even logical, that — to comply with the dictates of local community, municipality and state enactments which, of course, didn't affect every track collectively — it was simply easier to separate the races for an entire trip than to do so intermittently as needed? Doesn't that make better sense than immobilizing a train in order to repetitiously play fruit basket turnover now and then?

Segregated consists might not have been the will or even the ultimate decision of the railway tycoons after all; they could have been the result of cooperative ventures involving local standards and practices that were acceptable to judicial authorities and ascribed to legal statutes then implemented by state and local law enforcement. In such cases, for the railroads to have responded otherwise would have run them afoul of official ordinances mandating segregation. That would have most probably jeopardized their ability to run trains along certain routes.

Historians generally have been quick to paint pictures of this phenomenon which leave some readers solely condemning the railroads for instigating all of the discriminatory practices in transportation that existed between the races. But is that fair? Those divided and assigned cars, just as the separate waiting rooms and drinking fountains at stations and depots, may well have been at the hands of local ordinances more than at the pleasure of the railroads. It would appear from this distance to be a rap that can be shared equally by manifold sources and not merely the railroads.

Today, of course, there is no legal discrimination between ethnic sects journeying on the rails in America. It's a far cry from what peoples of multiple persuasions experienced in earlier generations. Bigotry, discrimination and segregation are out. Acceptance and cohesiveness are in. People of color sit where they please in coaches, diners, sleepers and lounge cars. Divided waiting rooms and separate drinking fountains are long gone. The changes in railway travel were among early evidences — and particularly so among people inhabiting the modern South — that a new day had dawned. In the new South an about-face turned foes to friends. With people of all persuasions riding together, it's a lifestyle that their forebears could never have begun to contemplate.

16

AMENITIES AND APPOINTMENTS
Club Car, Parlor Car, Dining Car, Pullman

For a long while creature comforts — those satisfying attributes that ostensibly can make or break a journey — have been among the indispensables sought by most Americans on the road, their mode of transit notwithstanding. This applies to ordinary citizens as well as those with discriminating tastes who are classically symbolized by finesse and culture. The latter group is often willing to pay a little more to achieve better treatment in getting from here to there. To tell the truth, nevertheless, universally as a people we like to be pampered. When our needs are pleasingly met we may recall our travel escapades with fondness. Conversely, when our expectations go unrealized, our appraisal may not be signified in terms of endearment.

By the start of the 20th century Americans were exposed to numerous advancements in physical movement from place to place that hadn't been available at the inception of trains in this country seven decades before. As time elapsed there were many improvements. In the receding decades of the 19th century — as human ingenuity combined with technological developments and mechanical inventions — new doors opened for vastly upgraded equipment and services. Primitive styles of mass transit offering little more than rough seats mixed with meal stops or box lunches gradually were replaced by upgraded features in more inviting surroundings. By then rail passengers were finding their mode of travel not only a means of getting to a destination but allowing them to enjoy the ride to some degree at last. The novel perfections implemented over time turned trips into something rewarding while concurrently filling a practical need.

All of it established a discernible shift in train travel. For the first time it evolved into a lot more than simply hauling people from one place to another. As modernization was instituted the emphasis in rail transit broadened: physical amenities appealing to travelers' sensibilities became a focus of those journeys, many for the first time. The leading long-haul carriers encountered keen competition in the industry. To maintain parity and gain competitive advantage no major road could afford to allow its rivals to surpass it by simply ignoring new innovations. The effect of all of this was to turn the rails into an even more accommodating form of transportation. Not only did it evolve into more pleasant trips, it infused them with a magnificent level of services never previously encountered in this country. Adding intrinsic values had the net effect of making expeditions more pleasant, restful and memorable.

The South was a major beneficiary of these advancements. Not only did trains originating in the metropolitan districts of the Northeast and Midwest that trekked to Dixie destinations exhibit many new enhancements, so did the carriers with routes running altogether below the Mason-Dixon Line. The enhancements generated a win-win reaction: the passengers aboard those trains not only reaped the rewards but this also provided a windfall to the railroads that adopted those advancements.

The inaugural run of the *Florida Arrow* on January 2, 1936, witnesses a congenial crowd in the observation car. The *Arrow* is ready to roll out of Chicago where the passenger train will access Pennsylvania tracks to Louisville, L&N rails to Montgomery, and ACL routes to Florida (*courtesy Chuck Blardone*).

Return for a moment to the early days of travel by rail in this country. Aboard the *Best Friend of Charleston* in 1830, passengers could anticipate what has been described as open-sided "wagons" pulled on tracks by a hissing steam-driven locomotive belching hot ashes, vapors and soot on the patrons seated behind it. All of this as it reached a precedent-setting top speed of 25 miles an hour, hardly a comfort zone by any measure! When the boiler blew six months into that gig, rail travel on the Charleston & Hamburg temporarily halted. It wasn't resumed until a new engine was created, with the first one returned to service following repairs and reformatting with a new boiler.

From earlier mentions you may recall that the operator, SCC&R, was the first road in the U.S. offering regularly scheduled passenger service powered by steam engines.[1] In that regard the South pioneered in human transit on the tracks. But did we say *primitive*? While much of the experimental phase was implemented by trial and error, it seems like *primordial*, *archaic*, *primeval* and *prehistoric* might be terms more properly evocative of the circumstance. Certainly any thought of travel inducements for the patrons paying the freight (now there's an anomaly!) hadn't been seriously considered at the time. It was just enough to get the folks from Point A to Point B, a concept that overwhelmingly persisted for more than three decades virtually everywhere.

Riding the rails was launched in nothing more than open wagons pulled by horses, then by steam engines. (The latter had to have been the first upgrade!) As time went on enclosed conveyances made their way onto the tracks. They offered protection to patrons from the elements (rain, sleet, snow, cold, heat), and from the spewing cinders and other residue generated by the locomotives as well as flying insects and whatever else might be headed for riders. At the same time the enclosures supplied a greater sense of security. All of this was fundamental in the evolving modern rail coach.

Beyond supplying it in its most elementary forms, seating was given little thought during these incubatory years of rail travel. Club or parlor cars added a distinct touch of elegance later, perhaps even opulence with their marvelously adorned luxury chairs lining colossal picture windows. Improvement in standard coach seating, however, didn't start to reach its zenith until the streamliners arrived in the mid 1930s. From then on some premier trains introduced new levels of deluxe: large, well-padded cloth-covered reclining seat coaches appeared, some requiring booking reserved space before boarding. Set in rows with dual chairs on each side of the aisle, not only did their seats tilt back, they were equipped with footrests, generous legroom between rows, separate lighting for day and night travel, air conditioning and heating, luggage racks above the seats, dual restrooms in each car, and large windows allowing riders to suck in the magnificent panorama passing by their vantage points. All of these features became standard equipment on many trains in time, particularly on those of the long distance variety. With that the common man came to experience a degree of opulence never known in transit accommodations.

Before getting to that point, however, the railroads had to confront a very real problem. Here's a single example of how a complex and perplexing dilemma was finally resolved with doses of ingenuity. For a while patrons were confined to single cars because there was no easy or reliably safe method of crossing platforms between cars while the train was in motion. Nor was there a way to protect riders from the elements while transitioning from one car to another. As sleepers, diners and club cars were added to the coach consists, the need for a type of secure shielded passageway became vital. "An act which passengers had always been cautioned against, and forbidden to undertake — the crossing of platforms while the train is in motion — now became necessary," a historian noted.[2]

As early as 1852 and 1855, patents were recorded for canvas diaphragms that could connect the cars.[3] But after flawed trials on Connecticut's Naugatuck Railroad between 1857 and 1861, those unworkable designs were discarded. Other entrepreneurs addressed the issue but experienced similarly unacceptable outcomes with their models. A couple of decades passed after the canvas rendering without sufficiently meeting the need.

Nevertheless in 1880, movement between moving railroad cars was enhanced after an elastic diaphragm was added to both ends of the cars. Coupling them together netted an enclosed passageway that permitted relatively easy and safe negotiation in the interim of space between lurching coaches. Until then, according to one prognosticator, those crossings were "not for the young, the old, or the fainthearted."

Six years later, in 1886, rail car designer-fabricator George Mortimer Pullman (1831–1897) — who, as early as 1858, had been attracted to the challenges proffered by the physical conditions of train travel from the riders' perspective — pondered how to perfect the connectional system.[4] His ideas encompassed a "continuous trains" hypothesis that would allow provisional flexibility during the motion of the train while it was rounding curves. Pullman's theory netted what became known as the "vestibuled" train.[5] In a summary originally released in 1888, his new innovation, patented only a year earlier, was heralded thusly[6]:

> This invention ... succeeded not only in supplying the means of constructing a perfectly enclosed vestibule of handsome architectural appearance between the cars, but it accomplished what is even still more important, the introduction of a safety appliance more valuable than any yet devised for the protection of human life in case of collisions. The elastic diaphragms which are attached to the ends of the cars have steel frames, the faces ... of which are pressed firmly against each other by powerful spiral springs, which create a friction upon the faces of the frames, hold them firmly in position, prevent the oscillation of the cars, and furnish a buffer extending from the platform to the roof which precludes the possibility of one platform "riding" the other and producing telescoping in case of collision.... With a free circulation of air throughout the train, the cars opening into each other ... this train is the acme of safe and luxurious travel. An ordinary passenger travels in as princely a style in these cars as any crowned head in Europe in a royal special train.

One of the earliest examples of its application, stridently promoted by mentioning the new form in the moniker of an 1891 debuting palatial train, was the *Washington & Southwestern Vestibule Limited*.[7] It ran along tracks of the Richmond, Fredericksburg & Potomac, the Richmond & Danville, Atlanta & West Point, Western Railway of Alabama and Louisville & Nashville between the nation's capital and New Orleans, a route soon to be incorporated into portions of the mainline of the Southern Railway established in 1894. The vestibuled cars were instantly gratifying to the patrons privileged to ride in them. Replicas were liberally adopted by other lines that realized the advantages of the sheltering between cars which turned a once harrowing experience into a protected, reasonably secure environment.

Later innovators built upon Pullman's model and those of other engineers, modifying and improving those designs. Their accomplishments evolved into the enclosed accordion-style pass-through-door version that was put into widespread use in the 20th and 21st centuries and which may be found aboard Amtrak coaches today.

One of the big issues in creature comforts encountered by rail car manufacturers after those open-sided conveyances were enclosed was to settle on acceptable methods of warming and, later, cooling them. In regard to the latter, that was done by opening the windows until experimentations with air conditioning trains occurred around 1930. The result was climate-controlled cars later in that decade. And when dieselized streamliners began to arrive, AC consists were a part of the package, taking riders to new levels of comfort.

But the matter of heating those cars in a safe, reliable, sufficient manner presented formidable challenges. If a railroad, even one traversing the generally warmer South, was to attract a dependable crowd, adequate temperature ranges within those consists was obligatory. Many methods were tested: included were a stove sitting in the middle of a car (a most dangerous scheme) plus many experiments with heated water and vapors piped into a car or beneath its floorboard, some attempting to capture and redistribute steam thrown off by the early engines.

> The heating of cars was not successfully accomplished till a method was devised for circulating hot water through pipes running near the floor.... The loss of human life from the destruction of trains by fires originating from stoves aroused such a feeling throughout the country that legisla-

tures of many States ... passed laws ... prohibiting the use of stoves, and the railway managers [devised] plans for heating the trains with steam furnished from the boiler of the locomotive.[8]

Café, club, dome, library, lounge, observation, parlor, recreation, tavern and similarly ascribed cars, and any combination thereof, began to proliferate on leading trains, especially those covering considerable distances. In the early decades of rail travel men (but not women) could drink and smoke there. In the 19th century those multi-use domains were often equipped with hairdressing and barber salons while some boasted book shelves and organs that especially appealed to sophisticated travelers. The frills in most of the versatile cars, beyond plush seating, included newspapers, magazines, and often beverages and snacks for purchase. In the 20th century many were radio-equipped, another advantage doubling as a marketing tool.

In the streamliner era glassy lightweight rounded-end lounge-observation cars brought up the rear of a few key trains. From the inception of those tube-like aluminum carriages in the South the dual *Champion*s of the Atlantic Coast Line, the *Silver Meteor* of the Seaboard Air Line, and the *Southerner* and later the *Crescent* of Southern Railway sported those innovations. At its launch in 1939, the *Meteor* was one of the first trains in the country with two specialized staffers on board for the express purpose of meeting every patron's whim: there was a stewardess-nurse and a traveling passenger agent.[9] The concept met with instant acclaim and was soon copied by other carriers. That notion enjoyed a very long run: more than six decades hence, at the start of the 21st century, Amtrak was still including an agent labeled "passenger service representative" who assisted riders and train crew members with numerous concerns on some of its key long-distance trainsets. (The PSRs were also among the first staffers to be dismissed when belt-tightening occurred at Amtrak.)

In the streamliner epoch on some of the premier trains like #6 *City of Miami*, a glassy lightweight rounded-end tavern-observation car brings up the rear of the consist. At Vero Beach, Florida, the *City* plies along FEC rails in December 1954. It will move onto ACL tracks at Jacksonville for the run to Richmond, where it will be intercepted by RF&P. PRR will take it on the final link from Washington to New York City (*photograph by Peter C. McLachlan, courtesy Richard C. Beall*).

One of the intriguing variations in passenger conveyances during the early decades of train travel, especially in Dixie, was the designation of a single car (or portion of a car) exclusively (on some occasions) for women. The arrangement appealed to a woman who might be traveling unaccompanied, or to small groups preferring disbarment of a general population of males. Recalling the environment of the 19th century that precipitated that circumstance, one wag — originally acknowledging it in the 20th century — advanced a few notions of what the situation was like.[10]

> The early American was a gregarious fellow, and in spite of all warnings he liked to travel through the train and inquire into the business of his fellow passengers.
>
> He was also an inveterate tobacco-chewer with habits, when so engaged, that were obnoxious to the lady passengers, so that some of the best trains were shortly carrying ladies' cars, reserved for women and any men who might be traveling with them. In these cars all the latest comforts and conveniences were to be found, and as early as August, 1838, maid service was available.... In the ladies' car tobacco-chewing and smoking were strictly prohibited ... but in the other cars life was free and easy....
>
> The use of a special car for women, however, seems to have been confined chiefly to the railroads operating in the South, or running into the South, for *Holly's Railroad Advocate* of September 20, 1856, in commenting on the practice, said: "The New York Central commenced but soon discontinued the arrangement so much in vogue in the South, of setting the bachelors in a separate car. Probably too much space was lost, as two cars half filled had to be carried, often where one would answer if the passengers were allowed to choose their own seats. Ladies' cars are barbarisms. There is no more seclusion, nor safety against tobacco indecencies, where a lady journeys with married gentlemen or gallants, than where she may chance to have the company of bachelors or stray benedicts."

In a similar vein an Englishman, touring the United States by rail and reporting his travels in a treatise published in 1869, recalled his observations and experiences on a sleeper between Louisville and

Here's what folks saw who were privileged to lounge in one of the tavern-observation cars in the 1950s. This car, **Saint Lucie Sound**, is typical of the creature comforts offered by the prestigious long-distance carriers. The cars were usually staffed with bartenders or other service personnel. The smoke stands were a sign of the times (**photograph by Peter C. McLachlan, courtesy Richard C. Beall**).

Memphis: "There is a partition at the head and foot, and curtain in front, to render the whole as private as such a place can be made. To the south of the Ohio [River] the gentlemen's portion of the sleeping-cars is divided by a curtain from the remainder, which is appropriated to the ladies or to 'couples,' and a separate dressing-room is provided at each end. In the North this luxury is dispensed with, and ladies have to take their turn with the lords of the creation."[11]

In the late 1870s and the 1880s, the railroads in Dixie drifted away from the practice of providing a car or section of their trains purely for women. The ladies' car disappeared not so much for efficiency's sake as to implement yet a new variant. From the late 19th century to the mid 20th century, segregation infiltrated many of the consists crossing the South, including leading and secondary runs. As a result mixed races within the coaches simply weren't seen. Riders were categorized ethnically and assigned to certain cars while they were forbidden to enter others. This division dispelled the carriers' ability to parcel out discernible space any longer in which members of a single gender could congregate. The ladies' car had been a marketing ploy that attracted some travelers. By and large, however, it faded from the scene in the late 19th century, just as the racially-conspicuous car replacing it would do a few decades in the future.

In 1873, yet another Englishman who toured America by rail published his impressions of trackside life.[12] Citing some of the creature comforts and disturbances travelers encountered (some of which exist on Amtrak in modern America), he surfaced the matter of vendors passing freely through cars with their wares, relentlessly hawking unquenchable deals. Some reading this will recall the newsboys and sandwich-coffee-cola peddlers who sustained that tradition in the heyday of passenger rail traffic in the first half of the last century.

> I traveled in the *Lightning Express* from Nashville to Memphis in the Autumn of 1860.... The cars ... contain from forty to fifty passengers. The seats, holding two persons each, are ranged in rows down each side of the car, with a path for the conductor and itinerant salesmen down the middle. The seats have low backs which are sometimes padded with velvet or on the poorer lines with carpet or leather. The floors are always carpeted or matted and the windows generally have Venetian blinds and shutters for the night or for the severe cold weather.... On most lines, especially in the South, a Negro boy or girl comes around every half hour and offers a glass of water from the cool, gurgling jug.
>
> The conductor ... works in and out through the doors at either end that lead from one car to another and this perpetual slamming of the fore door and aft door is a special irritation, particularly when one wants to get to sleep.... The brakeman, sometimes a great laughing Negro in the far South, stands outside the car door on the platform where men go to smoke.... This is not the smokers' special stand and perch as there is always a smoking-car to every train and a ladies' car where no smoking is allowed. The smoking-car is small, with seats running all around, and there is a table in the middle on which the newsboy generally spreads his store of intellectual sophistry. It is the den from which he emerges to deliver his five-cent oracles.
>
> No want can arise in the traveler's mind that there is not some one in the train ready to administer to. Every town you pass pelts you with its daily papers. If you stop for ten minutes at a central station a quack is sure to come into the car and inform everyone that the Dead Shot Worm Candy is now selling at twenty-five cents the packet, that Vestris's Bloom, the finest cosmetic in the known world, is to be had for a half dollar the quarter pound, or that Knickerbocker's Corn Exterminator makes life's path easy at a dime the ounce packet. Presently you fall asleep and awaken covered with a heavy snow of handbills about Harper's reprints and Peterson's unscrupulous robberies from English authors. Anon, a huge fellow with enormous apples, two cents each, peaches in their season, hickory nuts, pecans or maple sugar cakes. To them succeed sellers of ivory combs, parched corn and packets of mixed sweetmeats.

Turning to rail diners and sleepers, George M. Pullman, Webster Wagner (New York Central), G. B. Gates (Lake Shore), Edward Collings Knight (Baltimore & Ohio, Camden & Amboy), T. T. Woodruff (Terre Haute & Alton), William D'Alton Mann (independent) and multiple lesser names began producing daytime coaches that could be converted for nocturnal rest. Some extended their proficiency to also design parlor and dining cars. Unapologetically these early fabricators were fixed on brassy, garish, tawdry, ornate styles, particularly so in the opening years of their craft. Everything then reflected the Brits' Victorian Era (1837–1901). Handiwork was bathed in plush, damask, paneled wood, and an incessant reliance upon mirrors augmented with silver-plated cuspidors. The result was "a true horror on wheels that caught the fancy of the mass of new *eleganti* who were just emerging from the log-cabin era and were likely to confuse elaborateness with beauty, whether in a house design by M. Mansard or a railroad coach by G. Pullman."[13]

Although those entrepreneurs staunchly defended their individual turf, stubbornly clashing with one another by cheating, lying, bribing, gouging and committing perjury to gain advantage in attaining their ambitious goals, nonetheless they radically improved rail travel in the steam-powered age. The conveyances were safer than they had ever been and more comfortably so by 1870.[14] The achievements of the pioneers made the cars running behind the engines infinitely more pleasant and satisfying to an ever-enlarging mass of beneficiaries.

In spite of the concerted efforts of multiple competing manufacturers of rail cars in meeting those travelers' needs, in the end a single name outlasted all the others: Pullman. His tale of personal achievement in overtaking every rival within 30 years—either by running them out of business or buying their enterprises and absorbing them into his own—is riveting, resulting in enticing accounts of American entrepreneurship which are recorded in copious texts.

> No matter what you might say about George Pullman, he and his men were always just a little in advance of their competition. Pullman adopted kerosene lamps ahead of almost everyone. He introduced to America the brilliant Pintsch light from Europe, for many years thereafter the standard illumination in all railroad passenger cars. When the electric light was ready, Pullman adopted it, just as he did a succession of constantly improving generators. Pullman probably was the first to introduce bed linen to the rails, linen changed every day....
> Pullman washrooms and toilets grew in elegance and ingenuity.... Any inventor of gadgets or designer of new furnishings went to Pullman with them, and anyone who had something really new and good to offer was given a hearing.[15]

By the final decade of the 19th century the Pullman Company had very little competition—and none threatening its domination of the trade. For many years on any given night more people slept in Pullman car berths—typically 100,000 guests in 10,000 sleepers during its 1920s peak—than in the beds of the world's largest hotel chains. Pullman could be certified as the nation's undisputed "innkeeper."[16] By then the original "berths" that consisted of double facing seats for daytime carriage and were converted to curtained-off lower-and-upper beds for nocturnal rest (commonly called "sections") branched into fancier digs.

In the streamliner epoch there were drawing rooms, compartments, single and double bedrooms, roomettes and the like, giving those willing to pay for them more space and indulgences as well as greater privacy than they had been accustomed to.[17] In the fanciest of the modular designs on some leading trains, private bath and shower facilities were also available. Pullman branded the upgrades "luxury for the middle class."

Not only did Pullman design and manufacture sleeping and dining cars, he staffed them with his own forces. He relieved the railroads of that obligation by supplying well-trained attendants offering sterling service in a controlled environment. Following the War Between the States, Pullman went to the South on recruitment trips, engaging "the best and brightest former slaves to work on these rolling five-star hotels, men who had already been trained to perform the service duties he required."[18] He solicited Negroes in search of improved standards of living, many of them newly freed men who owned no land or shelter and had no incomes

The zenith of luxury, comfort and privacy was to arrive in one's own private rail car. There was more of it than you might think. FEC "official" car 95 about 1959, for example, routinely appeared on the stub tracks at the south side of FEC's Miami passenger station. Notice the shades pulled at the windows. Owners took advantage of Florida's magnetic field while operating out of their own "hotel." Private cars belonging to millionaires and dignitaries routinely appeared on these tracks (*photograph by Fred Carnes, courtesy Richard C. Beall*).

and little or no responsibility. Though his work involved serving affluent and middle-class whites, Pullman helped create the first black middle class in America with some of the best jobs they could find.[19] "Despite the degradation and continuing exploitation of these porters, who had to make beds, mend clothes, and shine shoes, they took their new paid positions with pride and dignity."[20]

As a consequence Pullman passengers were transported in beds of ease to virtually any part of the country in cars of uniform construction, equipped for day and night travel while served and protected by employees of Pullman, not of the railroads. The safety, comfort and convenience of those patrons were the sole focus of Pullman's stable of onboard attendants.

For it Pullman, the founder, reaped enormous profits. Desiring more and more for himself, nevertheless, he became a tyrannical dictator to thousands of minions, extracting his pound of flesh through unreasonable fees from estimates of up to 20,000 workers who resided at his Pullman, Illinois, municipality south of Chicago.[21] Following a national depression in 1893, Pullman reduced the wages he paid his helpers but not the monthly rent those workers owed him for their housing.[22] While many merely tolerated his imperial style, others rebelled and, in 1894, struck the company. Reports of the numbers vary but some accounts acknowledge that 34 people died in rioting that ensued at the Pullman plant. The U.S. Army was summoned to restore order and some individuals were jailed as a result of that melee.[23]

Subsequently Pullman, the inventive genius of promise who had become a benevolent father figure to many, greatly beloved on earlier occasions, lost what he had gained with some of his subordinates. His name instead was linked with industrial tyranny.[24] When he died at 66 in 1897, he was resented and, sadly so, maybe hated by more individuals than those who had been awed by the brilliance of his magnificent obsession. His grave at Graceland Cemetery in Chicago was dug quite deep and reinforced with concrete and steel. Some of his ex-employees, it was feared, might attempt to desecrate his body.[25]

Most of Pullman's tryouts with new innovations had been conducted on the Chicago & Alton Railroad (C&A). One wag referred to C&A as "the guinea-pig route for all of Pullman's experiments." Do you recall that C&A was a key precursor of the Gulf, Mobile & Ohio Railroad? Pullman's inaugural sleeper, the *Pioneer*, came to life in the C&A's shops in Bloomington, Illinois.

A half-dozen years afterward, the *President*, his first "hotel" car, was rolled out and pressed into service.[26] That model was a kitchen-equipped sleeper with clientele served meals on small tables placed at their seats at appropriate times and then removed. A 6 × 3-foot kitchen was flanked by a pantry and wine closet. The menu included ham at 40 cents and steak and potatoes at 60 cents. A downside to the sleeper-kitchen was food odors wafting intermittently throughout the car, including times when the passengers retired to snooze. The solution to that problem resulted in a car solely for cooking and eating. Pullman created the *Delmonico* diner in 1868. It, too, ran along the rails of the Chicago & Alton.

Pullman's advancements met with general favor among travelers but rival lines were slow to copy them due to heavy investments in building, staffing and running those specialized conveyances. "In all the years that dining cars have operated, right up to the present, they've always lost money," noted one surveyor in the 21st century. So the competition refused to play for a while, unwilling to part with the cash when most other carriers also skipped those extras. Ultimately "railroad companies came to believe that diners were a requirement of first-class service, however, and a way to make their own trains stand out."[27] Long-distance carriers eventually reached the universal affirmation: "What passengers remembered most about their train trip was the dining experience."[28]

In Dixie, in the halcyon days of rail travel as elsewhere, those companies capitalized on several regional preferences. Country ham, bacon, sausage, eggs, grits, biscuits and gravy, toast and honey, or — if one preferred — railroad French toast, pancakes or waffles, plus fruit, coffee and freshly-squeezed orange or grapefruit juice were mainstays of the abundant breakfasts on Southern rails. Mack Gordon said it ably in the immortal words to *Chattanooga Choo Choo*: "Dinner in the diner ... nothing could be finer ... than to have your ham an' eggs in Carolina...."

Below the Mason-Dixon Line, other meals frequently highlighted local delicacies like Virginia ("city") ham, New Orleans shrimp Creole, just-caught Florida fish in bountiful varieties, fried chicken and barbecue from the Carolinas to the Mississippi. The peanut soup in Seaboard's diners became a staple of the diets of many who sampled it en route to their destinations. All of the cuisine was served in generous portions on china plates and in bowls and cups alongside silver flatware and genuine glassware. Entrees were accompanied by fresh vegetables (corn, peas, turnips, potatoes, okra, beans, etc.), salads (mixed greens, fresh fruit, coleslaw, gelatin, etc.), cornbread, fluffy biscuits made from scratch and real butter, and a profusion of desserts (think piping hot blackberry or peach cobbler in season à la mode), sometimes with a dozen or more choices. Nothing really was any finer, whatever the selections. It underscored once more that Southerners took a backseat to no one when it came to cuisine!

In the meantime "the government had long since told the Pullman people they were a horrid monopoly and must sell either their business of manufacturing cars or their business of operating them. Pullman [the company] chose to sell the latter. The sale to a group of railroads, made in 1945, was approved by the government in 1947."[29] Nearly all of Pullman's lightweight sleepers plus many of its heavyweight cars were dispatched to 57 railroads on whose tracks they had been running. Railroad-owned cars were then leased back to Pullman. In most other respects the contracts between the carriers and Pullman remained very close to what they had been.[30]

The Pullman Company persisted in fabricating those cars until it, too, finally reached the end of the line. After a century of service, on December 31, 1968, the venerable old firm shut its (vestibule) doors forever. In so doing it withdrew the name that had been synonymous with *sleeping car* for so long and transferred that identification to a more generic term (*sleeping car* or *sleeper*), one commonly employed by Amtrak today.

The tangible, corporal, physical assets—including the rolling stock, tracks and station facilities—were critical to the comfort, safety and security of travelers. The owners-administrators of trains trekking across Southeastern routes were also cognizant of a large number of intangible, subtle, obscure, perhaps at times subliminal factors that bore some accountability for guaranteeing continued patronage from a loyal clientele.

Beyond the on-board and depot service issues which remained elevated in their minds, the stewards of Dixie's railroads were also focused on a plethora of supplementary matters: ongoing emphasis on safety concerns; eye appeal — the sleek, modern, attractive, clean trainsets of the streamliner epoch were literal shining examples; keeping trips short, an aspect accomplished with fast lightweight consists, use of direct routes, curtailing wait times at stations, diminishing or eliminating changes between trains en route, and double-tracking to reduce pulling off on sidetracks to allow other trains to pass; maintaining seamless transitions between carriers so continuing passengers could access multiple carriers without exiting their original cars; and adding schedule frequencies on popular routes, running manifold sections of a train in peak periods and seasons.

A contemporary scholar, citing a lapse in the industry a century ago in an opposite corner of the country, shared this introspective[31]:

> Only one railway, the Vanderbilts' New York Central Railroad, came directly into Manhattan, and that from upstate. The New York Central ran down the east bank of the Hudson River, across the narrow Harlem River, and into the heart of Gotham. For many decades, sole ownership of this wonderful monopoly had made the Vanderbilts America's richest family, notorious for their churlish indifference to the well-being of their road's passengers. The late, large William H. Vanderbilt — his mausoleum still guarded by Pinkertons around the clock against grave robbers — had summed it up neatly with his infamously imperious, "Let the public be damned."

Can you imagine those words cascading from the lips of most of those overseers who cared for the image and responsibility of the rail systems in Dixie in the time they were privileged to lead them? In addition to making their lines successful, keeping the patrons happy was of paramount importance to Atlantic Coast Line's Champ Davis, to Gulf, Mobile & Ohio's Ike Tigrett, to Seaboard's Davies Warfield and Southern's Graham Claytor and their contemporaries. On their watch indelible marks were made on passenger transport. Those principals turned journeys through the Southland into pleasurable escapes for millions of satisfied customers and their performances just may have been a fundamental reason why so many kept coming back for more.

17

PORTALS TO THE WORLD
Early Waiting Rooms

By one estimate, about 140,000 train stations of varying persuasions opened in America's cities, towns and rural backwaters during the eight decades that elapsed from 1850 to 1930.[1] In spite of the fact a high percentage of those were replacement facilities—built to reinstate depots lost to fires, floods and other natural disasters, plus some restored after inadequate and often dilapidated structures were deemed unsatisfactory or unsafe and, as a result, had been torn down, plus some which were modernized through replacements—nevertheless an average of 1,750 "new" terminals appeared annually across that four-score-years timeframe. "No other type of building was given such a world-wide incidence so rapidly," one report qualified. "Despite the vast numbers of stations built in so many environments, they were all united by function."[2]

Some larger municipalities erected three or more railway edifices on the same site. As those urban centers flourished, local city fathers arrived at a common understanding that one way to extend the sphere of influence of their metropolitan districts was to enlarge the area's railway terminal while capitalizing on the prospects for its grandeur. After all, it was here that the public regularly gathered to come and go—whether they were actually leaving town or not. In the early days of railroading in most places the depot was the true "community hall," an assembling point where townsfolk met to exchange the news.

Just what comprises a railway station? Surprisingly, there is more than one simplistic response.

Florida East Coast Railway author-railfan Seth Bramson conjectures the answer lies in *any facility listed in a railroad timetable, regardless of type or construction ... providing at least a paved or planked platform from which to board a passenger train.* And transport specialist Kevin Holland is even more specific in his sweeping assessment: *A station can be as minimalistic as a sign on a post and a simple cinder platform, without the comfort of even a rudimentary depot building.* While a widespread perception exists that a depot is where travelers buy tickets and sit in a waiting room until time for the train has been called, that's obviously an outmoded theory.

> Many "stations" never had a place to buy a ticket, wait for a train, or provided a place where passengers were allowed to board....
>
> The depot is the building designed to accommodate passengers, freight, or both. In small depots the handling of this cargo, human and otherwise, was often combined. However, "main track" stations often had separate depots for freight and passengers.
>
> Sometimes depots or "train order offices" were built in places where there were neither passengers or freight business, just to have an operator or telegrapher present to pass along train orders. These places could be extremely isolated and remote. Depot historian Henry Bender says, "the depot customarily served two major functions—it helped operate the railroad by coordinating train movements, and it promoted the company's business by selling tickets. There were several ancillary functions too: serving as agencies for railway express, Western Union telegraph services, and others.[3]

Back in the day when freight railroads operated the nation's passenger trains, here's what the fireman was seeing out his window approaching the platform at Daytona Beach, Florida's depot from the south. He's aboard E7 1010 — train 6, the *City of Miami* — in this April 7, 1960, view. A "window seat" does make a difference in one's perspective, doesn't it? (***photograph by Frank Gregg, courtesy Richard C. Beall***).

Somewhere between all of these rather conflicting interpretations a railway passenger depot would seem to be as much or as little as is required — possibly a majestic structure of imposing design, but it could be nothing more than an appointed place where travelers gather to board the train and disperse after leaving it. Does that about sum it up? It allows a lot of latitude in what one finds along the tracks, and particularly on routes dominated by secondary and local passenger trains. "The most striking thing about the railway station," one source proffers, "is its remarkable diversity."[4] And while the breadth of wide-ranging possibilities is dramatically evidenced across the South, it shouldn't be misconstrued that Dixie cornered that market. The prolific variety in stopping places was prevalent throughout the nation.

The metropolitan centers, as one example of the diversity, proudly exhibited grand high-ceilinged halls in stately edifices that often displayed architectural treasures: Greek Revival columns, Romanesque domes and arches, Mission Revival covered colonnades, Victorian bay windows, Beaux Arts forms that combined a myriad of features under one roof, and dissimilar styles. Many stations dating from the 19th century reflected the structural design of the period, majestic in scale and size.

> At its most basic level, the railway station was the nineteenth century's distinctive contribution to architectural forms. It combined within itself in eloquent reflection of the age which produced it both a daring and innovative modernity.... The modernity came in the technological skill which went into the production of the train-sheds, the great single- and double-span roofs, for which unsung engineers solved complex structural problems of weight and distribution with breath-taking brilliance and boldly utilized the new materials, iron and glass, to construct the naves and transepts of the cathedral stations.[5]

At first glance this former depot appears situated in the little town of Florist. The moniker in reality identifies the private business operating there in the upper central South Carolina hamlet of Kershaw, a flag stop for Southern Railway back in the day. Built in 1926 and sold to new owners about 1945, the depot's bay window gave its telegraph operator an unobstructed view of what was coming down the track, typical of southern stations constructed in that era. Today the Lancaster & Chester freight shortline leases the track from Norfolk Southern (*courtesy Jay Miller*).

The result added to a city's prestige just as it did to that of the railroads that built them. And as the trains sped along the tracks to the hinterlands, the splendor of the spectacular terminals, stations and depots that could be observed in the metroplexes was progressively reduced.

In smaller burgs, with fewer passenger consists passing through, presumably generating fewer boardings and deboardings, the grandiose shrines of steam (and later, destinations of diesels) in the bigger cities were almost nonexistent. Instead those trains paused at more modest, serviceable structures where efficiency and practicality were emphasized. Travelers encountered simple brick, concrete, stucco and wood frame buildings that were most often locally designed and constructed. With few frills, they accommodated the basic needs of the townspeople and those living in the surrounding districts.

In some places, especially during the initial decades of railroading, the facilities as such were, as noted already, virtually non-existent: there might be a primitive shelter or trainshed and possibly only a platform available. In the earliest instances a marked "stop" might be there, perhaps a sign on a post and maybe not even that—but no waiting room, no shelter, and no platform. There a train momentarily paused to let travelers off or take more on. It was virtually a glorified tram or bus stop. Given that perspective, the maxim *you've come a long way, baby* seems profoundly appropriate when applied in today's railway environment.

As time passed these stops became more elaborate by adding wood, stone or concrete platforms alongside the tracks to assist riders in accessing trains easily and safely. Little by little more augmentations occurred: enhanced platforms with wood coverings (simplistic trainsheds) for protection from the elements, benches for seating, and gas lamps for lighting at night. Then small ticket booths staffed by railroad personnel appeared on the scene.

As the sensibilities of the carriers increased toward the plight of their clientele, some of the outdoor "waiting rooms" were enclosed. And a few more creature comforts and conveniences were added to the mix: larger waiting areas with adequate seating provisions, restrooms, drinking fountains, fireplaces with chimneys, baggage handling services, arrivals boards, and so forth. As rudimentary styles gave way to more sophisticated models, those facilities were equipped with improved lighting and furnishings, banks of ticket windows, luggage carts, snack stands, vending machines, dining rooms, news stands, shoeshine stands, retail shops, taverns, central heat and air conditioning, ticket kiosks, tract racks, and other innovative accoutrements designed to make waiting a pleasant experience.

Beyond all of this, many of the complexes erected in metropolitan centers in the early years of the 20th century—depots, stations and terminals—were architectural gems. Those magnificent temples of trains with their grand lobbies suffused in stunning high-ceilinged splendor were fronted with exteriors in a wide range of unparalleled structural designs. Their appearances gave local communities some incredibly bold artistic treasures. And while a few of these imposing edifices persist as calling places for passenger trains in contemporary times, most do not.

Some have been razed since the Gilded Age of train travel ended. Some have made successful transitions to adaptive reuse by public and private organizations and are currently occupied by chambers of commerce, museums, governmental agencies, libraries, offices, restaurants, and a diverse assortment of retail vendors and sundry commercial ventures. Some languish unobtrusively, unattended, deteriorating and virtually forgotten, likely awaiting visits by the wrecking ball and the bulldozer if no rescue arrives in time.

"Beautiful" is a term that comes to mind when considering the Spanish design of FEC's Hollywood, Florida, station in the late 1950s. Numerous railway facilities constructed in the early decades of the 20th century embodied territorial customs of local districts through their architecture (*photograph by Fred Carnes, courtesy Richard C. Beall*).

One source concerned about the lapse of attention to these shrines of the past in so many municipalities laments: "Almost like a rite of passage, cities across the country embraced the era of Interstates, Big Macs, and suburban sprawl by tearing down their train depots.... But time and experience are showing that train stations are vital organs in a healthy city, and removing them deadens the entire organism. The lesson is especially stark at the moment, as cities around the country face the challenge of rebuilding the infrastructure for regional high speed rail networks.... One lesson of this legacy is that what replaces a well designed and centrally located rail depot is rarely of equal worth to the city."

In the modern age as newer structures supplant those demolished or shunted aside in an economically-driven environment, a wave of stark utilitarian designs has come into vogue. Another historian encapsulates: "Stations built more recently often have a similar feel to airports, with a cold and plain abstract style."

Many of these are transitioning into intermodal facilities, supplying their communities with transportation hubs for a multiplicity of conveyances: intercity, light rail and commuter trains; intercity and local transit buses; trolleys; taxicab fleets; rental car agencies; bicycles and whatever other forms of wheeled passage may be added. Increasingly planned complexes are expectantly awaiting the arrival of rapid railway systems which could be just over the horizon. As these are implemented, a new phase of moving the masses will evolve. For a host of factors a dependency on rail travel will almost certainly return, integrated into a complex of mass transit options that keep the nation moving.

What was the significance of the passenger train waiting area in the old South? Without any doubt it was the focal point for generations of local denizens, not only for gathering to bid "good-by" to someone departing on a journey, or to receive and embrace someone returning from a trip, but for swapping information and exchanging gossip about the community and its people. In no other provision did a cross-section of a town's locals come together so often to trade tales and share their good fortune as well as their adversity.

> In many American communities the railroad depot was the most important building in town. More than the court house, the school, the hospital, or the mansion on the hill, the depot touched the lives of people in the community. It was the portal to the rest of the world.... It took whatever you had to sell off to market, it brought back whatever you wanted to buy. Everything that was important to a community — people, information, products, coin of the realm — came and went through America's railroad depots.[6]

"It is mainly the human interest to be found in and about a railway station which is the secret of its fascination," observed historian James Scott.[7] In many hamlets this general assembly venue persisted for decades, a genuine byproduct of the depot's reason for existence.

In that day the railway station also functioned much as an international airport does now, for it was a link to the country and the world. "In its most basic function," insists Kevin Holland, "a railroad station is a gateway to the village, town, or city in which it stands."[8] Its connectivity to other depots in every corner of the country, and in so many places in between, erased the physical gaps that had heretofore separated America until those stations emerged on the national landscape.

While this treatise offers only a mild introduction to the railway depots, stations and terminals that supplied the spot where rail riders began and ended their journeys aboard rail passenger consists, it's obviously just the tip of the iceberg. Be informed, nonetheless, that some absorbing tales filled with provocative anecdotes of a few of the leading passenger facilities serving the routes of Dixie's major carriers are to be found in the pithy narratives at the back of this volume in Appendix E. While not every town is included by any stretch of the imagination, a representative group of more than 50 of those with influential passenger operations in the yesterdays of our lives — and in some cases, in the todays of our lives — await.

As "the most important building in town" according to railway chroniclers Hans and April Halberstadt, these pivotal palaces and wayside waits have been chronicled in historical vignettes to offer some fascinating insights to supplement discoveries already made about passenger railroading in the South. The gathering places for arrivals and departures were, for many years in hundreds of Southern communities, our uncontested portals to the world.

IV

Present and Future

18

PASSENGERS WANTED
Railroads in Decline and the Advent of Amtrak

Beginning in the postwar epoch of the 1940s, a handful of forces were at work precipitating the decline of the railroads as the paramount system of mass transportation in America. Historians have pinned the causes for the rails' rejection commonly on one or two circumstances. In reality, however, a plethora of dynamics shaped the collapse of the industry and its inability to satisfactorily cope alongside some swiftly mounting alternatives. Gathering steam as it raced downhill, the rail industry saw the domestic travel preferences of shippers and passengers alike shift unhesitatingly to newer modes of transit.

From the middle of the 20th century and for a couple of decades thereafter, the railroads— until then at the forefront of moving people and goods in the U.S.— were displaced, unrepentantly shunted to the back of the line to "let a winner lead the way." Only, in this instance, there were several victors that overtook the original means of unifying the vast geographical expanses of space lying from border to border. The railroads had performed their task well, contributing significantly to populating thousands of miles of heretofore undeveloped territory within the nation's interior.

A few stats from that juncture will confirm how inexorably regressive the shifting tide was for the railroads at mid century. After that, some classic reasons for the pummeling they took will be enumerated.

• In the dual decades between 1896 and 1916, U.S. travel by train tripled. Four years hence, in 1920, moving people by rail attained a new zenith as 1.2 billion people navigated the tracks to their destinations. As automobile ownership escalated in the 1920s, however, that pinnacle eroded. By the close of the decade one in five patrons that had been aboard trains at the start of the 1920s was covering great distances by car, an omen of things to come.[1] While a net gain of 38 percent in rail travel transpired between 1933 and 1939, the tangible passenger total at the end of the 1930s was short of six million, less than half of what it was just two decades earlier.[2]

• Freight trains ferried 77 percent of the nation's goods in 1916. By 1980, they transported a mere 35 percent, a figure that rose slightly to 38 percent in 2005.[3]

• In the 1920s, more than 20,000 passenger trains were running on American tracks. Four decades later that number had tumbled to 500.[4]

• During the Second World War, a peak period due to the military's heavy reliance on rail to move troops and equipment, the nation's tracks accounted for 67 million passenger miles (i.e., converts to one passenger transported one mile). In 1970, the year Congress authorized Amtrak, railways carried people 6.2 million miles, a 90 percent reduction from the earlier plateau. Airplanes traveled in excess of 100 million passenger miles as intercity buses supplied an extra 25 million passenger miles. By 2005, air carriers accounted for nearly 584 million

On July 2, 1976, a quartet of fairly new Amtrak EMD SDP40F locomotives wait for assignment in the yard at Ivy City's locomotive service facility in Washington, D.C. Any or all may soon be southbound (*courtesy Michael B. Robbins*).

passenger miles, buses another 163 million, and intercity rail including Amtrak just 5.3 million.[5]

• Between 1946 and 1964, rail patronage levels in this country slumped 61.3 percent, from 770 million riders to 298 million.[6]

• In the 1950s, almost one-fourth of all U.S. passenger train routes, 53,416 miles, was eliminated from service. Passenger train consists were simultaneously cut from 43,585 to 28,396 cars, a rolling stock reduction of 34 percent in a single decade.[7] At the start of the same decade passenger revenue — 20 percent of freight income in 1920 — fell to 10 percent.[8]

There were multiple conditions that emerged in that era which prevented the railroads from remaining at the top of their game, particularly when it came to transporting passengers to the degree to which they had long been accustomed. A few have been alluded to in the figures from the descent. All of the following situations, nevertheless, impacted that outcome.

The advent of the automobile had a devastating effect on passenger trains as it ushered in the age of mobility to the American populace. By the 1920s, the Lincoln Highway and further primitive auto trails that were exploited in the opening years of the 20th century were replaced by a more resilient and expanded national highway system. Consumers with sufficient resources responded by purchasing personal conveyances to travel those new roads. Single-lane thoroughfares on heavily traveled routes were sometimes replaced by dual lanes. The automobile and its counterpart, the truck, were upgraded during the postwar period with incredible power and complemented by accouterments unthinkable.

By then a revitalized national economy provided many citizens with good-paying jobs, security and discretionary funds for what earlier had been unaffordable for most — a private means of long-distance transportation. And to top it off in 1956, President Dwight D. Eisenhower announced the creation of an interstate system of superhighways to not only speed surface travel but to make it safer and more hassle-free. Much of mass transit, including moving people and products, was securely in the clutches of the purveyors of asphalt and concrete.

Motor freight captured a significant portion of the less-than-carload business in transferring natural resources, raw materials, and finished products. Especially on shorter routes, trucks frequently provided a degree of mobility, flexibility and speed that was difficult for cargo-haulers to equal over the tracks. As railroads' bread-and-butter trade, when freight suffered, the implications were often there for reduced passenger service.

At the same time all of this was happening, commercial air carriers were transforming into a foremost brigade of people-movers. This segment had been siphoning off small numbers of rail riders for years, but not with the spectacular splash it was poised to make in the 1950s. As jet propulsion was introduced to the general aviation industry, the time and cost of long-distance trips were dramatically abridged. In particular business travelers took advantage of this phenomenon, many of them instantly shifting their allegiance to air and away from ground transport.

As their passenger clientele steadily eroded, the rail carriers found little incentive to make costly capital investments in improving tracks, signaling, depots, trestles and other structures. Some maintenance was held to meeting minimum requirements. The federal government was already committed to a $41 billion outlay for building the interstate highway system. In the same epoch the feds and many states and local municipalities were increasing their financial commitments to airport upgrades and related new construction projects.

By 1958, with 96 percent of intercity travel in the U.S. provided by a form other than rail, the railroads simply weren't interested in applying their lucrative freight traffic revenues to similar support for passenger rail.[9] In practice, that service competed with systems that were already receiving an influx of tax dollars from myriad sources, a grossly unfair advantage as the rail carriers viewed it.

There were yet other forces hindering the railroads in turning their people-moving into money-making endeavors. The federal government imposed a 15 percent excise tax on train travelers during the Second World War to depress civilian rail trips in an era of military conflict. Slightly reduced in 1954, the tax wasn't eliminated in total until 1962, some 17 years after the last battle ended. It hardly encouraged more riders to choose travel by train, and

One 1975 afternoon the Amtrak passenger station at St. Petersburg was busy with two trains at the platform. The combination passenger and freight facility was built for ACL and opened in 1963. SCL operated the station from 1967 to 1971 after ACL and SAL combined operations. The tavern-observation car on the left brings up the rear of the recently arrived *Champion* while EMD SDP40F 546 will lead the departing *Floridian* on the inner track. Note that turnouts or switches at this station are manually operated (*courtesy Michael B. Robbins*).

was a detriment to the railroads in marketing their wares. Meanwhile, increased municipal property taxes imposed on local railway facilities (stations, storage and maintenance facilities, etc.) were often applied by small towns to subsidize new airports for their communities.

The reduction in passenger business was scarcely an enticement for the railroads to upgrade their services like providing greater frequencies, sufficient staff to meet travelers' needs at depots and onboard trains, and rolling stock that in the past included diners, sleepers, observation, dome, lounge, café, and tavern cars. In more and more cases fewer and fewer amenities appeared. Instead carriers met basic Interstate Commerce Commission (ICC)– imposed obligations while removing the frills that patrons had come to expect. In the process much of the joy of going by train diminished. Rail travel instead ceased to be either luxurious or convenient and even those who loved journeying by rail were clearly relying on it less and less.

Adding to the industry's outwardly blatant and growing disregard for passenger contentment, as the late 1960s approached the railroads still didn't accept major credit cards for payment of travel and services rendered on its trains.[10] It was unthinkable in an era in which credit was widely accepted almost everywhere by major common carriers. At the same time the railroads dug their own graves by shunning professional travel agents, turning away potential allies rather than enlisting them to produce greater patronage for unfilled trains. Meanwhile antiquated railroad work policies prevailed; those outdated rules reflected century-old conditions netting astronomical crew costs. The most modern rolling stock was generally one or two decades old. More often than not major maintenance procedures were deferred to save money in the short term. None of it made for better traveling experiences for passengers, of course — it didn't bring more in nor did it bring more back.

The feds delivered yet another stinging blow to passenger service when, in 1967, it withdrew its money-making mail service from the trains, transferring it to motor freight carriers and airlines. Even the railways that had been willing to lose money to continue running passenger trains couldn't afford to do so any longer once the mail subsidy was gone. Passenger trains were dying by the carload, and if they were to survive in any form, government intervention was necessary for a rescue.

An overriding factor was the government's blatant disregard for the railroads as expressed through heavy-handed regulation of the industry. Forced to continue providing minimal passenger service into territories that could no longer sustain it, let alone make that provision reasonably justified, the railroads saw the profits they made from hauling cargo drained. At the forefront of all of this bureaucracy was the Interstate Commerce Commission, a vanguard agency charged with a federal mandate to set and administer railroad policies. Behind the commission stood members of Congress, whose key interest seemed to be in keeping handfuls of voters satiated in their home districts. One method was by supplying passenger trains to geographic areas with very few inhabitants in order to connect them with the outside world.

For a long while the railroads' pleas to the ICC to allow them to eliminate specific trains or routes, lay off workers, raise or lower freight charges or completely abandon service fell on deaf ears. Not until the 1960s and 1970s did the swell of protests from within the industry rise to epic proportions. It was so universally deafening, in fact, the ICC could no longer ignore them. In response to the crisis the bureaucrats permitted great railway names to vanish altogether. Scores of legendary trains were allowed to die while service on many lines was extensively trimmed. It was a foretaste of things to come.

"If a single individual can be called the father of Amtrak," claims a contemporary source, "it's probably Anthony Haswell."[11] In 1967, attorney Haswell founded and was elected first executive director of a public rail preservation lobby and support faction known as the National Association of Railroad Passengers. In June 1969, Colorado Senator Gordon Allot maneuvered a piece of legislation through Congress that was bent on retaining the nation's passenger trains. With Haswell agitating, the media reporting and the government inquiring, much of it due to Allot's measure, a new method was proffered for providing travel by train in America.

After a task force appointed by the Federal Railroad Administration evaluated the current climate, the U.S. Department of Transportation produced a written procedure, made public on January 18, 1970, that was to evolve into Amtrak. A contingent of historians metaphorically cited Amtrak as "a fragile phoenix of intercity rail service rising from the ashes of the languishing streamliners of the private railroads."[12] It sounded good. But its roadbed has been anything but smooth — indeed — it has been rocky most of the way.

On May 1, 1970, precisely a year before its full execution, the Rail Passenger Service Act of 1970 was introduced to Congress. It established the National Railroad Passenger Corporation (NRPC), initially shortened to *Railpax* and later to *Amtrak*, a quasi-government agency directed to run the nation's passenger trains. (*Amtrak* is a contraction of *America* and *track*.)

The fact that the powerful Penn Central Railroad filed for bankruptcy on June 21, 1970, didn't in any measurable way hinder Amtrak's chances of creation. If anything it hastened its formation. On February 1, 1968, the Penn Central had become an amalgamation of the New York Central and Pennsylvania roads, adding the New York, New Haven & Hartford Railway to its mix later that year. Yet the PC was visibly unable to make it financially after two years under its newly burnished trainshed.

Many realized the projected loss of this dominant passenger and freight hauler in the Northeast and parts of the Midwest could spell big trouble for the whole nation. For one thing the travel plans of millions would be interrupted and very possibly curtailed without its presence. Even more disastrous would be its effect on shippers and related trades with livelihoods dependent on Penn Central's existence. Conrail was later formed to care for the cargo traffic. And for the travelers, wasn't all that talk about Amtrak surfacing at a most propitious moment?

Not everybody was happy about it, however.

A General Electric–powered P42DC leads Amtrak's #9, the *Crescent*, north from New Orleans into Laurel, Mississippi, on June 18, 2009. On a hot, cloudless summer day the engine's radiant blue-silver hues contrast brilliantly with the stainless steel passenger coaches that follow (*courtesy Clyde Woodruff*).

Many Washington insiders, including President Nixon and his aides, viewed the corporation as a face-saving way for the President and Congress to give passenger trains the one "last hurrah" demanded by the public, but expected that the NRPC would quietly disappear as a result of disinterest within a few years of its creation. However, while Amtrak's political and financial support has often been shaky, popular and political support for Amtrak has allowed it to survive long past its expected lifetime.[13]

The Rail Passenger Service Act signed into law by a hesitant President Richard M. Nixon took place on October 30, 1970. The NRPC would assume the passenger operations of any qualifying U.S. railroad desiring to be relieved of that duty effective May 1, 1971. Nixon acceded to the company's formation with the proviso that it be put to death after a couple of years.[14] A Republican loyalist, Roger Lewis, was appointed Amtrak's first president. Although the back room shenanigans hadn't yet come to light, Lewis was to implement the accord that the railroads had secretly forged with the White House.

That era's Amtrak spokesperson Bruce Heard subsequently acknowledged, "The only good thing to say about Roger is he failed to make Amtrak fail."[15] Rather than killing the agency, Lewis foolhardily or inadvertently helped it gain traction and persist. The ruse earned credibility when Louis W. Menk, chairman of the Burlington Northern Railroad, was enraged after Amtrak's mismanagement was exposed in a 1974 *Fortune* article. Off the record he bitterly protested that the account was "undermining [our] scheme to kill off the company."[16]

> The Rail Passenger Service Act of 1970 left railroads free to choose whether to join in the new quasi-public passenger initiative or not. Those that opted out ... were not eligible to go before the ICC with any further petitions to discontinue passenger trains until 1975. The twenty carriers that did choose to participate were required to invest a sum in the new venture. Such payments would constitute the rail industry's dowry to marry off their equivalent of an old maid, their aging and unattractive passenger trains. This amount was to be "computed by one of three formulas, whichever was most favorable to the railroad: (1) 50 percent of the fully allocated passenger deficits of the railroad for 1969; (2) 100 percent of the avoidable loss for all intercity rail passenger service operated by the railroad during 1969; (3) 200 percent of the avoidable loss for the intercity rail passenger service operated in 1969 by the railroad over routes between points chosen for the basic system...."
>
> Their initial investment ... could be paid either in cash, in kind through the transfer of passenger cars and locomotives, or by a credit against the fees that the new enterprise would pay to run passenger trains over these carriers' tracks.... They ... received the choice of taking common stock in Amtrak, or obtaining a one-time tax deduction for this expense.... The greatest return on their investment ... was the long awaited opportunity for a complete exit from the passenger business.[17]

With 20 private roads joining Amtrak by start day, only a half-dozen that were eligible to participate demurred. For their own reasons they continued to run their own trains instead of handing them over to this fledgling untried operator. Included in that assemblage were the Chicago, Rock Island & Pacific; Chicago South Shore & South Bend; Denver & Rio Grande Western; Georgia; Reading; and Southern. The tracks of both the Georgia and the Southern roads were, of course, predominantly or altogether in Dixie.

On May 6, 1983, the mixed train operated by then-owner Seaboard System over the Georgia Railroad made its final sprint between Atlanta and Augusta. To maintain that commitment for a dozen years following Amtrak's inception was an extensive stretch for such limited service. On the surface at least the operators seemed utterly dedicated to the people of Augusta and those in the bucolic countryside along the way. In reality, however, there may have been a less noble incentive for their gesture. By supplying mixed train service over its entire mainline the Georgia Railroad enjoyed a tariff reduction and did not fancy a loss of that tax benefit.[18]

Since 1845, trains plying the 171-mile Atlanta–Augusta route had made profound contributions to the lives of rural Georgians trekking to and from the state capital. Business opportunities, shopping experiences, entertainment venues, relatives, friends and acquaintances awaited them in Atlanta as those denizens left their homes in the small burgs dotting the eastern environs of the Peach State. And when, after 138 years, that tradition was irretrievably broken, no replacement appeared on the horizon for a durably acclaimed service whose time had manifestly passed.

Southern Railway, on the other hand, opted to continue running its *Southern Crescent* between New Orleans and Washington, with an extension over the tracks of other carriers to New York and Boston. It did alter the lower terminus from New Orleans to Atlanta four days each week while persisting to the Crescent City the other three days.

In addition, two other less notable but longstanding passenger monikers fostered by SOU continued to ply the tracks, although in significantly reduced runs from their glory days. Each was pegged to Tar Heel towns. The *Asheville Special* made the daily run to 1975 between its namesake mountain Mecca and Greensboro. And the *Piedmont Limited* then aptly named for its acute condensation dashed to 1976 between Salisbury and the nation's capital.

When Southern finally bowed out of the passenger business on February 1, 1979, Amtrak abridged SOU's final consist's nomenclature to *Crescent*. It also restored that train's daily endpoint at New Orleans. Complete with coaches, sleepers, diner and lounge car, the *Crescent* in the modern age still makes the same journey every day via Hattiesburg, Meridian, Birmingham, Atlanta, Greenville, Charlotte, Greensboro, Lynchburg, Charlottesville and Washington. It's one of only a few precious premier trains that Amtrak still operates in the South that hark back to the halcyon days of rail travel.

Even that wasn't always secure nonetheless. About the time Amtrak took over the *Crescent*, a drastic cost-cutting proposal by Secretary of Transportation Brock Adams called for a greatly

Amtrak's *Crescent* #828 takes the curve that intersects State School Road just below Ellisville, Mississippi, on a pleasant May 1994 afternoon. The passenger consist is bound for New Orleans 138 miles away. Ellisville is situated between Hattiesburg and Meridian on ex–Southern Railway's main (*courtesy Clyde Woodruff*).

SDP40F 608 leads Amtrak's *Floridian* northbound on July 5, 1978, sitting on the west side of Union Station in Nashville prior to departure. The 20-month-old passenger train replaced the *South Wind* that had plied those tracks since 1940. The *Floridian*'s tenure didn't compare with its ancient ancestor; in 15 more months, on October 9, 1979, it too was history (*courtesy Jay T. Thomson*).

reduced passenger rail network. It was his intent to delete 43 percent of Amtrak's route mileage. Included on his list were the *Floridian* linking major Florida points and Chicago (via Montgomery, Birmingham, Nashville and Louisville), the *Crescent*, multiple Western routes, and most local traffic. While the *Floridian*, the *Hilltopper* (trans–West Virginia service via the Norfolk & Western mainline), and several more legendary consists beyond the South were sacrificed — a 16 percent reduction in Amtrak mileage — there was marked congressional pressure for sustaining the *Crescent*. It was finally removed from the chopping block.

To be sure, the greatest debacle from a Southerner's viewpoint was the undoing of the *Floridian*. That took away the only single-train service connecting the mid and upper South with both Florida and the Midwest. It's a glaring void in Amtrak's map that has been allowed to persist for more than three decades. There are no announced plans at this writing for restoring that precise route leaving dozens of municipalities in Dixie, including some very large ones, without any passenger rail.

The score of roads signing up with Amtrak to unload their passenger services in 1971 included the Atchison, Topeka & Santa Fe; Baltimore & Ohio (no service until September 8, 1971, when the *West Virginian* debuted); Burlington Northern; Central of Georgia (no service ever under Amtrak); Chesapeake & Ohio; Chicago, Milwaukee, St. Paul & Pacific; Chicago & North Western (no service under Amtrak); Delaware & Hudson (no service until August 6, 1974, when the *Adirondack* debuted); Grand Trunk Western (no service until September 15, 1974, when the *Blue Water Limited* debuted); Gulf, Mobile & Ohio; Illinois Central; Louisville & Nashville; Missouri Pacific; Norfolk & Western (no service until March 25, 1975, when the *Mountaineer* debuted); Northwestern Pacific (no service under Amtrak); Penn Central; Richmond, Fredericksburg & Potomac; Seaboard Coast Line; Southern Pacific; and Union Pacific.

Although half of those carriers ran some portion or all of their routes on Dixie rails, at Amtrak's inaugural there were just six (Chesapeake & Ohio; Illinois Central; Louisville & Nashville; Richmond, Fredericksburg & Potomac; Seaboard Coast Line; and Southern Pacific) transporting Amtrak trains to their destinations through the South. Within a brief while two were added to that fold (Baltimore & Ohio; Norfolk & Western). In the meantime Gulf, Mobile & Ohio fostered a special circumstance. While GM&O was a Southern-based carrier, it shut down all of its passenger service south of St. Louis in 1958. Ironically it no longer transported passenger trains in Dixie where the vast majority of its roadbed lay, concentrating on Illinois and Missouri travelers alone.

All of this transition turned Amtrak into a colorful array of mismatched rolling stock on opening day and for some time thereafter, looking like anything but a cohesive unit. The new carrier exhibited a hodgepodge of styles, sizes, hues, and car configurations, with a surfeit of oddities within consists bearing the names of their former owners. Not until Amtrak received delivery of 600 Amfleet and Amfleet II cars and 284 Superliners—including locomotives, coaches, lounges, sleepers and diners in varied combinations—did it begin to resemble an authentic railway carrier.[19] That didn't happen until the mid to late 1970s. In the meantime the early 1970s was indeed a fascinating time for railfans and train-watchers in this country.

At Amtrak's premier three out of five U.S. passenger trains were eliminated and as time progressed still more disappeared from the roadbeds and timetables.[20] Current Amtrak routes in the Northeast Corridor are difficult to quantify because the bulk of those trains do not operate every day. The same is true of the California trains under the San Joaquin, Capitol Corridor, and Pacific Surfliner banners. Many run on designated days, e.g., Monday through Friday, weekends, Saturdays only, Sundays only, holidays and special occasions. Recently deleted from Amtrak's published schedules although available online are manifests for Acela Express and Northeast Regional trains.

With the coastal exceptions, the remainder of the country is fairly simple to tabulate. In Amtrak data available at the time of this writing that extends to spring 2010, there are just 49 identifiable passenger trains exclusive of those in the previously mentioned coastal regions. Most of them operate seven days a week although one runs six days weekly and another couple roll three days a week. That 49 might be tripled or quadrupled when the unrecognized coastal consists are added to the mix. Whatever the total, it's still a far cry from what it was in the era in which Amtrak inherited America's passenger rail system. In 1970, the total U.S. passenger trains were about 500, down from 20,000-plus in 1930. If today's Amtrak is doing anything at all it's unequivocally following a longstanding precedent.

As mandated by Congress, at the outset Amtrak was to satisfy a trio of quests[21]: (1) To operate rail passenger service on a for-profit basis. (2) To use innovative operating and marketing concepts to fully develop the potential of modern railway passenger service to meet intercity transportation needs. (3) To provide a modern, efficient intercity rail passenger service. Prior to its inception Congress authorized operational grants of $40 million and loan guarantees for new equipment of $100 million. Direct funding was to persist for two years tops by which time the corporation was to be totally self-supporting.

The presumption of a collective congressional body was that within a short while Amtrak would be self-sufficient. Instead of needing federal subsidies to pay its bills, the lawmakers convinced themselves—and openly doted on a "done deal"—that the new agency soon would be making money. Things don't work out the way they are envisioned sometimes. The possibility of breaking even, let alone gleaning any revenue, was remote. Anybody who knows minimally about railway passenger transportation, as only a portion of Congress appears to have learned even now, realizes that may be purely wishful thinking.

There have been few times in history when any intercity rail passenger operation in the world has been profitable, even with respect to only its operating costs, and passenger trains have never brought in enough revenue to pay their infrastructure costs. Even highly efficient private-sector railroads such as the Norfolk and Western Railway could not earn a profit, or even recover operating expenses for passenger service. The concept of Amtrak as a for-profit business was fatally flawed before the first passenger boarded.[22]

A few highlights of Amtrak's years of service indicate not every ride has been a smooth one along the crossties. In 1983, Amtrak adjusted from a supervisory function to one of ownership of rail services by employing crews and centralizing reservations. Given some extraordinary revenues generated by 1994, that year Congress insisted the firm must become a self-sufficient operation. Only three years later, conversely, Amtrak was on the brink of bankruptcy. Three years after that (2000), it premiered the Acela regional passenger service connecting Boston and Washington, D.C. It avoided insolvency just three years afterward when Congress promised it $2 billion annually for the next half-dozen years (2004–2010). Today Amtrak accounts for just two tenths of one percent of America's transportation trade, or as many think "hardly enough for anyone to take seriously."[23]

Operationally the ride on Amtrak's watch has been a roller coaster with incessant ups and downs. A fairly significant contingent of individuals has held the capacity of president and chief executive officer in less than four decades. That certainly hints at an atmosphere that is politically charged. Actually, that's a perpetuating tradition, both internally and externally.

In the first arena board members have frequently found themselves working on a different page from the organization's hired executive leadership. The priorities, goals, methods, and decisions of the two have been so far apart and the tensions so great that on multiple occasions leaders of the agency were canned or forced to resign. In a few cases temporary appointees have filled this pivotal slot.

Externally, meanwhile, throughout Amtrak's relatively brief history some members of Congress have sought to manipulate it for their own purposes. By law they have controlled

During 1974, the Miami-originated section of Amtrak's *Floridian* awaits the arrival of the west coast section at Auburndale, Florida. The pair will be joined for the remainder of the trip to Chicago. The lead locomotive is a Burlington EMD E8 followed by an Amtrak painted E8. The switching moves to get this train in proper order in Auburndale will be performed by the locomotive on the west coast section. The train is running on the ex–SAL main in Florida while traveling under SCL control (*courtesy Michael B. Robbins*).

its purse strings, yet routinely held the quasi-federal agency hostage over operating subsidies used to underwrite equipment purchases, maintain rolling stock and facilities, and literally to just keep the lights on, in order to perform. A contemporary historian and once-spokesman for the U.S. Office of Management and Budget put it this way: "So long as Amtrak is forced to go hat in hand to Congress as an annual supplicant rather than being a routine part of the funding process it will never be truly viable. Piecemeal appropriations of that sort rarely sustain a program, and they often die or are cut below subsistence level when times are tough and budgets slim. Amtrak's annual funding should be included in each year's budget like funds for highways, air, and water transport."[24]

Assessing the then-current status of Amtrak two decades ago, an informed author who invested his professional career in diverse aspects of transportation could have just as easily been writing in the modern epoch: "Amtrak has a hard time overcoming its stigma as a loser, particularly when federal partisans repeatedly moan about Amtrak's 'subsidy' while referring to federal aid to aviation and highways as an 'investment.' Such prejudiced treatment often causes uninformed people to call for an end to Amtrak, but these same people would never think of calling for an 'end to highways' or an 'end to aviation.'"[25]

There have been times when Amtrak's fate literally hung in the balance as more than one U.S. president (Reagan, Bush 1, Bush 2) called for reducing its annual allocation to zero. Additionally there were several transportation secretaries who persistently recommended drastic service cutbacks. Sometimes the passenger hauler's financial receipts were trimmed as a result of those efforts, certainly the intent of those behind the measures.

The attacks have been sources of constant upheaval and have probably contributed to the perception of a "lack of vision" at the top by some of the agency leaders. Surely they must have frequently wondered about the size of their next subsidy — and on rare occasions, whether anything would be coming their way. The Obama administration seems to have given a reprieve to those fears, although the adjudicators have yet to render a final verdict because the outcome isn't yet clear. Nonetheless there must have been some euphoria along with optimism within the higher echelons at Amtrak when the previous administration departed. It's a matter of public record that Amtrak fared poorly during much of their time in office.

Looking beyond the money, on occasions Congress has attempted to influence policies, routes, service frequencies, and other matters of import. Worse, at times there have been some who have given the impression they would be just as happy if Amtrak went away forever — except they were wise enough to realize that if that happened on their watch it would provoke a serious backlash from disgruntled voters who would call them out for it. Despite the turmoil and chaotic environment, Amtrak has continued to function, albeit not always to the satisfaction of its board, nor to the executive and legislative branches of government, or to the general public, its clientele. There is no perfect system, of course, and Amtrak is living proof.

The author would like to take some space to mention a few personal observations about traveling aboard Amtrak trains. Annually my wife and I have boarded one or two long-distance Amtrak trains over the last 15 years. In that time we have been on virtually every major route once and on some multiple times, and at least one cross-country run a half-dozen times or more. Over the years we have learned what to anticipate and what not to foresee.

We've expected to meet some pretty amazing and wonderful people from all over the country and from other lands and have never been disappointed. On occasions our conversations have led to follow-up communications after our trips have ended. We're constantly amused when travelers unaccustomed to Amtrak's "open seating" dining policy — a throwback to the railroads of earlier days in which many people got acquainted with their travel-mates by eating at the same table. Some don't do well with this, and we take it as a personal challenge to peel back the shells if only during a single brief encounter. In all but a few cases, even the most reserved have risen to the occasion.

There's a two-pronged theme in our travels aboard Amtrak, at least so in the 21st century: (a) we aren't in a hurry to get somewhere (if we were, we would take another form of transportation), and (b) we accept the system's warts and all, knowing perfection is not merely elusive, it doesn't exist.

That means we know in advance that the chinaware on which we will be served is closer to Chinet (a high quality paper plate, mind you, yet a far cry from those porcelain jobs embossed with a railroad name, logo and color scheme in the halcyon days). We know they'll predictably run out of what we most want to consume before our destination is in sight. The heat and air conditioning will likely be either too hot or too cold for some travelers. The connecting doors between the deluxe sleeping compartments will rattle all night (this is a given that will never be permanently fixed though it can sometimes be toned down with the right paper wedge). Some toilets won't work properly (if at all). If patrons want to keep their luggage within easy reach they'll have to pack lightly and tightly before boarding or it won't fit the minuscule space they have been assigned, particularly in the sleepers. Most riders probably will be unable to hear the announcements transmitted throughout the train; it's a result of the nearby public address speakers not working properly. And after one has experienced stuff like this a few times, if he keeps coming back for more, he has obviously reached a point where a few minor inconveniences will be offset by the absolute joys he has encountered in traveling by train.

For this rider, that includes many things. Beyond all of the new acquaintances and hearing the fascinating tales about their pilgrimages in life, there are the enormous picture windows to observe passing vistas through. As America rolls by, somebody else will be doing the driving, leaving you free to soak it all in. There are long uninterrupted periods at one's seat, sleeping compartment or lounge space for reading, conversation, or listening to portable sound devices. Walking the full length of the train is one of our exercises. Invariably we discover some of the train's hidden secrets on a pass-through while at the same time we meet up with still other intriguing travelers. Some people can get lots of business done while on a train, too, including paperwork, through interactive media and interrelating with other businesspeople aboard their consist. The delights of train travel seem to know no end!

Although I could tell many stories about our trips with Amtrak, I'll forgo that to merely explain that — unlike most travelers' concepts of applying a conveyance to get to a particular spot so a vacation may begin — *the train is our vacation*. While we often disembark at an appointed place, and may remain there one, two or three days, just as often we may roll into a town and catch another train heading elsewhere. At times we have even hopped off one train and onto another, returning to our original point of embarkation. Although it may sound far-fetched it's in style with *why* we ride trains: to experience (enjoy) all that comprises travel by train. For us, the destination doesn't really matter; the real doing is in the *delivery*.

In spite of so many positive things that may be said about Amtrak's performance, to be objective, it definitely has its detractors. Some of those are outside the halls where the laws are made and the fates are sealed. A very vocal arbiter almost relentlessly on Amtrak's case is the United Rail Passenger Alliance, Inc. (URPA), an independent advocacy group branding itself "America's foremost passenger rail policy institute." Until 2010, URPA was headquartered in Jacksonville, a stronghold hardly new to the annals of American railroading. Indeed, the price of admission to Florida by rail has traditionally been nothing less than a glance at its enormous yard, if not a station stopover, and possibly a change of trains at Jacksonville. URPA isn't a membership alliance and doesn't accept funding from "outside sources" (whatever that means). Through its web site, nevertheless, URPA senses its obligation not only to unearth but to report the flaws it perceives in Amtrak's operations. This it does dutifully and regularly, to wit:

> Here's the pertinent question: Is Amtrak really interested in being a successful company?
>
> Amtrak doesn't seem interested in route or frequency expansion, Amtrak doesn't seem interested in drawing new passengers, and Amtrak doesn't seem interested in cultivating new friends.
>
> All Amtrak seems interested in doing is keeping a company going which constantly has to feed at the various public troughs on the federal level and in several of the united states.... [The latter reference is to a handful of routes heavily-funded by individual state governments.]
>
> Nobody wants to— or seems capable of—coming up with a realistic business plan calling for expansion, growth, and prosperity. All we see is the same song on a different page; more highly expensive, low revenue short distance corridors which are designed to financially fail.
>
> Substantial new equipment orders seem to be an elusive myth; existing passenger cars continue to deteriorate and become less reliable.
>
> Amtrak was a huge beneficiary of free stimulus money, and lots of projects were funded that needed to get done, but very few of those projects will actually produce any new revenue outside of the small number of out of service passenger cars and locomotives which will be put back into service.
>
> So, the question remains, is Amtrak as a corporate culture interested in being a success?
>
> The obvious answer is no. The anguish is Amtrak has such huge potential, but no desire to fulfill that potential. What a waste.[26]

Sometimes the rhetoric is even more intimidating. Without identifying its source, URPA released an open letter to Amtrak it received which was also shared with more than 30 state passenger rail associations. "The natives are definitely restless, and the Army seems to be close to being in a state of agitated rebellion," URPA commented. Here's an abbreviated rendering of the letter's salient points.[27]

> For the last 30 years Amtrak's "business plan" has been: "If anybody wants us to run trains we'll run them — just bring a check." Outside of the Northeast Corridor, this message has been directed solely to state governments and has resulted in the addition of primarily intra-state trains. There has been no acknowledgment of any interstate route obligations beyond what Amtrak inherited from the private railroads....
>
> When the ARRA funds suddenly became available in 2009, Amtrak didn't even have a wish list ready and is only now belatedly beginning to talk about a large-scale acquisition program. Amtrak needs to get started on that list now. But, it must do more than propose an order for cars or locomotives. Priority should also be given to route planning and expansion. It should develop a real vision for expansion of the current Amtrak system, laying the foundation for a truly national network....
>
> Amtrak needs to evangelize governors, mayors, chambers of commerce, major colleges and universities and regional economic-development authorities about the good news robust train service can bring. It must champion trains nationally and regionally and lobby Congress for a national budget sufficient to support multi-state route expansions. It must court Congress, the Obama Administration, states, local leaders and others to promote its own survival and prosperity by developing plans for expansion that do not depend solely on the largesse of state legislatures. If Amtrak fails to do this, its relevance will continue to be a question in the minds of many....
>
> We in the advocacy community have supported and defended Amtrak over the decades, but that support is conditional. If Amtrak wants our continued support, it will have to change, and soon. Amtrak must embrace the future, and if that means separating itself from those who feel comfortable only with the past, so be it. Nothing less will be acceptable. We are committed to the creation of a truly national rail passenger system by all possible means, whether it's through Amtrak or some other approach.
>
> The time to build a national passenger-rail system is now and Amtrak must become proactive and forward-thinking or risk its own demise.

Is URPA rendering a disservice to the nationwide railroad passenger carrier? Possibly. On the other hand it points out shortcomings the public doesn't read about in the press releases generated by Amtrak publicists nor from the pro–Amtrak National Association of Railroad Passengers. That group's paid-up members qualify for a 10 percent fare reduction in Amtrak coach car portage (though it doesn't apply to sleeping car accommodations and dining and lounge car tabs). Of course, by surfacing those blemishes, URPA puts the glare of the spotlight on them in order for them to be properly addressed.

Plenty of other assessments appear in print, in publications and online. A rather large proportion of the commentaries are quick to point out Amtrak's alleged Achilles' heel.

> The American passenger rail — once a model around the globe — is now something of an odd-ball novelty, a political boondoggle to some, a colossal transit failure to others. The author James Howard Kunstler likes to say that American trains "would be the laughing stock of Bulgaria." ...
>
> The reasons for Amtrak's bad reputation are totally damning — its service is neither practical nor reliable. Impractical because most of the time, it's cheaper and faster to drive or fly. Unreliable because more often than not, the trains are really, really late. There are stories of 12-hour delays on routes that would take six hours to drive; of breakdowns in the desert; of five-hour unexplained standstills in upstate New York. Then there's the mother of all Amtrak horror stories: a *California Zephyr* that stopped dead on its tracks for two full days, victim of both an "act of God" (as corporate legalese wisely defines a landslide on the tracks) and gross staffing negligence....
>
> Amtrak faces an interesting challenge — to capture the nostalgic romance of the rails while offering a service fit for the 21st century.... Delays are a fact of life on Amtrak — a symptom of a system that's been on life support since birth.[28]

There are still others who sometimes differ with Amtrak and offer pertinent observations. In a summary of the company's current status and projected outlook, a popular railroad fanzine noted[29]:

> Amtrak has never been a success. "It has simply never had a strategic plan or a vision that it could sell. So it is simply reacting to whatever its banker, Congress, wants at the moment," says [James W.] McClellan, a retired senior vice president of Norfolk Southern. Thus, Amtrak is a shadow of what it should be....
>
> Many of the company's 1,500 cars are ancient and cry for replacement. Some older equipment is falling apart. When it rains, for instance, water pours through the vents on long-distance coaches and showers the passengers.... Because the fleet lacks back-up equipment, one minor repair job on a car can delay the entire train....
>
> Passengers complain that a number of its hourly employees give the impression they are merely there to put in time until retirement.... Congress, which is prone to interfering with operations, sometimes makes it all the more difficult to deliver quality service. Diners and café cars, for instance, are under-manned because of a congressional limit on staffing.
>
> Despite all that, Amtrak serves its customers pretty well. Its engine crews are experienced and dedicated. Most of the employees passengers deal with, from ticket agents to conductors and dining car waiters, are friendly and helpful. But there are serious gaps, and they need to be plugged. Quality lacks the consistency passengers get from an airline like Southwest or the standards their parents enjoyed when passenger trains were run by private railroads.

The beat goes on. While the trains continue to roll, the lack of permanent leadership with strategic vision for the future and a plan to reach it, plus trust in that effort by board members, removing the meddling hand of Congress, and including passenger rail service in an assured adequate funding proviso may be key ingredients that are missing in Amtrak's operations today. As of this writing, methods of fixing them haven't been publicly announced, if indeed they are in the offing. None surfaced in 1971 either. The implications of the necessity of change are everywhere. It would seem that how to go about making them happen hasn't been sufficiently addressed for the long haul.

"Washington's procrastination is partly due to the fact that too few organized groups speak up for Amtrak," said one transportation insider. "The National Association of Railroad Passengers and a few rail labor unions have nowhere near the clout that the dozens of aviation

Lots of progressive changes were witnessed at Lakeland, Florida, after this 1975 photograph. Except for platforms and canopy sheds, the old station was demolished, superseded by a new downtown Amtrak terminal. Track owner CSX installed welded rail on the east-west mainline between Tampa and Jacksonville. You'll not see a Railway Express truck (left) nearby either. On an overcast day a trio of EMD E-8 diesel electrics leads Amtrak's *Champion* consist of 11 cars netting a lot of brake smoke. Running on the ex–ACL main, then owned by survivor SCL, the *Champion* will meet up with the *Silver Meteor* from Miami and thence be reclassified as *Silver Meteor/Champion* (*courtesy Michael B. Robbins*).

and highway groups wield in favor of their government-supported programs."[30] Who could argue with that? Passenger rail traffic, once at the forefront of the industry, was shunted to stepchild status a half-century ago. Its wants and needs are passed over now as stronger voices consume the larger shares of the pie.

In the South as elsewhere Amtrak is missing lots of urban centers and smaller communities that might be well served with an opportunity for regularly scheduled passenger trains. Of course, the funding has to be there to provide the equipment, facilities and personnel. And maybe before that, a long-range blueprint has to precede the capital.

By early 2010, two Southern states, North Carolina and Virginia, were among 15 whose departments of transportation are working with (not against) Amtrak to prop up passenger services within their borders to benefit both business and leisure travelers. (Others: California, Illinois, Maine, Michigan, Missouri, New York, Oklahoma, Oregon, Pennsylvania, Texas, Vermont, Washington, and Wisconsin.) As these resourceful developments relieve congestion while delivering patrons at predetermined times and places, they do so swiftly, safely, comfortably, and at an affordable fare — often in the heart of urban centers. They are surely setting the stage for the next wave of intercity rail: high speed systems.

In a state-by-state examination of present Amtrak circumstances, Appendix C at the back of this volume reveals some of the conspicuous gaps in service to Dixie taxpayers in the corporation's current model.

Was consolidation a good thing? Or, in the intervening years, have we broached the possibility of the American traveler being conned? The jury may not be finished deliberating that. As things stand now there could be compelling evidence for rendering a decision in either direction. And even if the most serious problems *can* be fixed, don't lose sight of the fact that it's up to somebody else to throw Amtrak a green light before it can proceed down the track.

Finally, will it always be the case that it's Amtrak running the nation's passenger rail system? Is Amtrak the sole logical choice to man the throttles? Or will other private operators acquire a piece of the action — and possibly replace Amtrak altogether? On occasion, as we have intimated, there has been talk of it and a move afoot to turn threats into realities. There's even been a hint now and then that some of the freight railroads might add passenger-hauling to their services. Sound far-fetched? In all likelihood all it would take would be a nod from Congress, provided that body felt an alternative plan was superior to Amtrak.

How would riders fare under a new regime? There is no telling, of course. One strong advantage any substitutes would have is a whole lot of history that wasn't there for Amtrak at its inception. Over the long haul it's probably unwise to bet the rent that Amtrak alone will be running the trains that ferry Americans to their destinations perpetually. Nothing lasts forever. The freight railroads prior to the 1970s are pretty convincing examples.

19

ON THE FAST TRACK
The Anticipation of High Speed Rail

There's a new streak on the drawing boards for America's passenger trains. And eventually, its presence is going to be felt in the Deep South. When high speed rail (HSR) is totally realized in this nation we'll see consists filled with travelers not merely running or even sprinting toward their destinations but whizzing by in flashes of sound and light, making travel by train even more alluring than most Americans can begin to conceive of now. While it won't happen overnight, the wheels are already in motion for a start-up date within our lifetimes — and completion of a nationwide system within the lifetimes of anybody born after the golden age of rail travel split. As more people attain a forward vision, and conditions in mass transit continue to deteriorate, an enormous outcry for full steam ahead on HSR will be heard across the land (not literally for steam, of course, but maybe electrification or another green-friendly power source!).

Before probing into this topic further here's a question for you that sooner or later surfaces in comparable discussions and by implication tends to cast the nation in a rather pale light: How did the Japanese and Europeans get so far ahead of us in developing HSR transit? The first HSR line began operating October 1, 1964, between Tokyo and Osaka. Since then numerous routes have been added to their systems while extensive networks have proliferated in several industrialized nations. Was somebody asleep at the switch?

Short Answer: In Europe and Japan, rebuilding the railways was viewed as of paramount importance to densely populated areas following the devastation of homelands that occurred during the Second World War. In the meantime in the United States, constructing a massive national interstate highway system along with newer, larger and more modernized airports in local communities rose to the forefront. At the same time urban mass transport was generally eschewed.

Railways were the first form of land mass transportation. In 1896, that was followed by the development of the "horseless carriage" by former steam-engine repairman Henry Ford. His efforts, combined with the experiments of an array of like-minded inventors, evolved into the gasoline-powered engine that netted the automobile.[1] The young entrepreneur was to successfully and mightily impact a budding industry when he established the Ford Motor Company in Detroit on June 16, 1903. Even though the passenger train would not reach its zenith until the 1920s, it was evident fairly early to rational observers that the motor vehicle's quick rise in mobility, availability, affordability and reliability was to validate a form of transport that would eventually surpass the train in popularity. As a result, in due course it was to gain an effective monopoly on land-based travel.

In their attempts to recapture some of the clientele that had vanished from their passenger consists in the interim, in the mid 1930s, the railroads of Europe and the United States implemented streamlined trains. One of those trains' compelling attractions was an ability to sustain high speeds. With an average gait of 80 miles an hour, they attained a top speed of more than 100 miles an hour.

In 1957, Tokyo's Odakyu Electric Railway put into service the Romancecar 3999 SE running 90 miles an hour, setting a new world record for a narrow gauge train. Closely watching this unfold, Japanese designers and operators were persuaded by that success that they could safely and dependably develop still faster trains to run over standard gauge tracks. The concept of high speed railways yielded a potential solution to overcrowded trains on the conventional tracks between Osaka and Tokyo. With no other prospect in sight for relief, it was surely an idea whose time had come. A modern educator proclaimed, "It was the first time that a railroad organization had presented a vision running counter to the conventional postwar wisdom that the trains' obsolete technology was propelling them into a state of terminal industrial decline."[2]

In April 1959, construction of the world's first contemporary high volume high speed train, Japan's Tōkaidō Shinkansen, got underway. When finished, comprised of a dozen cars, its official launch in October 1964 established a new record in rapid transit. With a normal operating speed of 130 miles per hour on the 342-mile Osaka–Kyoto–Nagoya–Tokyo route, it traveled faster than man had ever achieved on land in any sustained mass transit attempt.

The Japanese were on to something and their European contemporaries were busy taking notes. In June 1965, HSR was inaugurated on the continent at Munich during an International Transport Fair. There DB Class 103 hauled 347 exhibition trains between Munich and Augsburg at 125 miles per hour. In the thinking of many observers, "slow trains" had been superseded by something far grander than anything previously contemplated.

As others developed consequential passenger rail programs to transport large throngs of people over sundry distances, rightly or wrongly, America committed its resources to other equally demanding priorities. And now time has caught up with us. The literal cost of operating our selections has risen to new highs while a general alarm over their cost to the environment is soaring. Our inability to transfer large masses of people swiftly, economically and simultaneously is stifled by inefficiency and waste. As congestion, delays and safety concerns rise to epic proportions, America has little alternative but to join others in a commitment to world-class rail transit. High speed rail provides an inherent solution to multifaceted problems; and the necessity for implementing it is becoming abundantly clear. We must follow the examples set by others once again in solving a dynamic that is spinning beyond our ability to control. One Amtrak critic states, "In earlier eras, we used the British-born steam locomotive to conquer time and distance; we copied Italian architecture in planning some of our biggest train stations; we studied French aerodynamic theories in developing our airplanes; and we modified German rocket designs in our space program. Why shouldn't we take advantage of foreign technology now to conquer pollution and gridlock?"[3]

Myriad definitions have been assigned to high speed rail by as many sources. While all of them seem to agree that it operates "significantly faster than normal speed of rail traffic," not all purveyors of such data have settled on an exact pace qualifying that designation. The European Union, for instance, sets HSR at 125 miles per hour "and faster, depending on whether the track is upgraded or new."[4] The U.S. Federal Railroad Administration puts it "above 90 miles per hour."[5] That's in keeping with today's Acela Express passenger trains running over predominantly Amtrak-owned rails between Boston and Washington, D.C.[6] (By employing tilting trains on existing tracks, at spots Acela achieves speeds up to 150 miles per hour.) The advocacy group High Speed Rail USA,[7] meanwhile, quantifies the velocity of HSR as "at least 150 miles per hour" and maintains that "current projects worldwide use 220 miles per hour as a contemporary benchmark."[8] The International Union of Railways sets HSR at services which "regularly operate at or above 250 kilometers [about 159 miles an hour] on new tracks, or 200 kilometers [about 124 miles an hour] on existing tracks."[9]

The numbers plainly fall all over the place. What can be said definitively is that those speeds are customarily faster than the typical Amtrak train traveling in open countryside in most places today. Even consists rolling along straight, prolonged rural stretches of flat land unencumbered by other trains, trestles or grade crossings don't proceed at the gait envisioned for future American rail travelers. Indeed, in the era of HSR, it will be an exciting time to be alive!

There are some common denominators among the preponderance of HSR systems in operation today and among those under consideration for us. Most are electrically-driven by way of overhead lines. But this isn't automatic, not a central or restrictive feature. There are still other modes of propulsion: a couple of leaders among them include more powerful — and thereby faster — diesel locomotives, and magnetic levitation (maglev). In the latter instance basic principles of magnets are harnessed to supplant steel wheels and tracks while trains glide (or float) over guideways at very high speeds.[10]

A classic trait of HSR is the application of uninterrupted welded rail to decrease track vibration and inconsistency between rail segments. It allows trains to pass at speeds above 125 miles an hour. The fundamental limiting dynamic in a train's speed appears to be curve radius. In patterns designed for other countries, the possibility of derailment is generally given a higher priority than passenger comfort, which impacts velocity.

While there are a few rare exceptions, zero tolerance for grade crossings is a near-universal rule that operators of the globe's HSR systems follow. Although high speed rail trains can travel on standard tracks, in the United States the Federal Railroad Administration has ruled that trains proceeding faster than 125 miles per hour must operate on tracks with no grade crossings, meaning no intersections with public roadways.

Critic Joe Vranich asks, "When will the United States elect a president of either party who can provide the leadership needed to untangle our clogged roads and crowded skies? ... Where is the visionary American who, when elected president, will finally declare — for the first time in our nation's history — that 'America will have a passenger train network second to none.'"[11]

Candidate Barack Obama, on a campaign stop in Miami in the summer of 2008, enthused: "We'll invest in ... high speed rails because I don't want to see the fastest train in the world built halfway around the world in Shanghai. I want to see it built right here in the United States of America."[12] Not long after he began serving as the nation's chief executive, Obama affirmed[13]: "There's no reason why we can't do this. This is America. There's no reason why the future of travel should lie somewhere else beyond our borders. Building a new system of high speed rail in America will be faster, cheaper and easier than building more freeways or adding to an already overburdened aviation system. And everybody stands to benefit."

Could it be? Do you think? Among a few more pressing priorities — and clearly from a railfan's point of view — could Obama have been elected to high office "for such a time as this"?[14] In announcing his proposal for a new national HSR network on April 16, 2009, the president outlined 10 potential high speed intercity corridors for federal funding: California, Pacific Northwest, Midwest, Southeast, Gulf Coast, South Central, Pennsylvania, Florida, New York, and New England. Each is a territory of between 100 and 600 miles and he purports that some trains will journey over their routes at a velocity in excess of 150 miles an hour.

"My high speed rail proposal will lead to innovations that change the way we travel in America," said Obama. "We must start developing clean, energy-efficient transportation that will define our regions for centuries to come."[15] His plan would be marginally paid for through an $8 billion appropriation earmarked for rail service improvements in a 2009 $787 billion stimulus plan. Obama proposed another $5 billion HSR investment over five years beginning with the 2010 federal budget. Of the initial 10 high speed corridors envisaged by President Obama, half are in geographical regions embracing the South either heavily or lightly:

(1) *Midwest*— Although the Midwest Corridor only brushes Dixie, nevertheless it restores passenger service to a major metropolitan center disenfranchised for most of the last three decades: Louisville. The route north from the River City via Indianapolis terminates in Chicago, where there are planned links to and from the Windy City on four more HSR lines plus multiple conventional routes.

(2) *Southeast*— This segment anticipates embracing a trio of directions. The lengthiest of the three encounters seven Dixie states and parallels portions of the itineraries of a half-dozen existing trains: *Carolinian, Crescent, Palmetto, Piedmont, Silver Meteor,* and *Silver Star*. In essence it follows the *Carolinian* from New York to Charlotte by Richmond and Raleigh. Overlapping the *Crescent* route between Greensboro and Charlotte and adopting it for the remainder of the journey, the line persists southwest of the Queen City to Greenville, Atlanta, Birmingham and Meridian on its way to New Orleans. It's in the HSR Gulf Coast corridor when it arrives in the Crescent City. A second Southeast division follows the *Silver Star* pathway from New York to Jacksonville via Raleigh (where it proceeds due south) to Columbia and Savannah en route. A third fragment restores service from Atlanta to the Atlantic coast through Macon. At Jesup, Georgia, it links with the HSR route cited above (New York–Jacksonville), where trains turn north (to Savannah) or south (to Jacksonville).

(3) *Gulf Coast*— Already mentioned in connection with the Southeast sector where the *Crescent* route terminates in New Orleans, this region proposes one more HSR line. Running east to west it extends from Mobile through New Orleans to Houston. Unless the *Sunset Limited* conventional train is restored east of New Orleans— a matter pending as this is written — HSR would be the only service along the upper Gulf Coast east of the Crescent City.

(4) *South Central*— This projection is shaped like a "Y" with the bottom portion extending from San Antonio northward to Dallas–Fort Worth. At that juncture the two upper prongs are divided. One goes north to Oklahoma City and Tulsa while the other goes east, entering Dixie at Texarkana before proceeding to a Little Rock terminus.

(5) *Florida*— This is one of the simpler ideals, connecting Tampa and Miami through Orlando. Much of the route appears to duplicate the present lower end of the *Silver Star* course, although the trip to Orlando isn't the most direct path for anybody traveling between the other two municipalities. HSR will almost assuredly make it viable.

Not all those campaigning for high speed rail in this country are in accord with this approach in implementing it, however. The "grassroots movement of concerned citizens" operating under the handle High Speed Rail USA isn't happy about the plans to expand HSR piecemeal, preferring instead "bold new fast lines" to supplement existing trackage.[16]

> We applaud the Department of Transportation's leadership on high speed rail in America. However, we think the current federal vision is too incremental and therefore will take too long to reach the truly state-of-the-art passenger service which has been accomplished in several other countries already. Instead, we support the second approach, for building the infrastructure for 220 mph trains on separate dedicated tracks. California is leading the way in this initiative, and we call on the rest of the country to follow.

If the legislative and executive branches of government believe HSR to be beneficial, "We can have high speed trains operating ... by 2015 and a full national system by 2030," High Speed Rail USA leaders proclaimed in 2009. Calling for "a complete national system similar to the U.S. interstate highway system," the faction urged beginning with the most congested corridors and eventually connecting them nationwide. In theory the idea doesn't seem vastly different from the 10 high speed corridors proposed by President Obama.

High Speed Rail USA also elucidates on the setup for running the system once it's done: "The ideal situation would be to have the U.S. government own the right-of-way, track infrastructure and stations. Private companies, then, would operate trains with a franchise license from the government."[17] It cites the example of the aviation industry where local governments own and operate airports and runways, the FAA and TSA regulate traffic, and private enterprises own and run the aircraft.

To an abundance of skeptics who maintain that trains will travel empty along high speed passageways, there is historic evidence signifying otherwise, a contemporary travel journalist maintains. His notions, on the surface, at least, seem sensible and may hold genuine merit.[18]

> Since Amtrak beefed up its service in the Northeast corridor with the launch of the high speed Acela trains, their market share has grown fourfold, from 12% just a few years ago to more than 50% of the air/rail market in the Northeast Corridor today....
>
> Of all the money-losing routes on the Amtrak network, the Northeast corridor is the one exception and a similar high speed service in the most populous state on the other side of the country would likely garner the same effect, relieving much of the congestion on the roads and in the skies that are the bane of California.
>
> High speed rail is not for long distance travel. High speed rail works well with segments of 250 to 500 miles where the two to four hour train ride rivals the total time of air travel, including the trip to the airport and all that time waiting around....
>
> If high speed rail is implemented correctly, as has been done in many European countries with rail lines running right into airport terminals, transfer from plane to train will be seamless and render the need for flights of less than 500 miles unnecessary in most cases.
>
> The fuel and emissions savings of electrified rail lines would be enormous and the productivity gains amassed from unclogging our skies and highways would be substantial if such a national high speed rail network could be implemented and fully integrated with the existing air transport system.

There are many city pair combinations of interest to Southern travelers that are about 250 to 500 miles distant from one another. This is optimally advantageous to HSR according to the observations just stated. Applying the incremental HSR system proposed by the administration, whisking passengers by rail could easily rival air time in these examples (with commensurate highway miles in parentheses): Atlanta–Raleigh (352), Savannah–Richmond (430), Richmond–Charlotte (246), Atlanta–New Orleans (429), Birmingham–Jacksonville (375), Mobile–Houston (440), Louisville–Chicago (272), Meridian–Greenville, South Carolina (401), Columbia–Washington, D.C. (404), Greensboro–New York (451).

If the proposed high speed rail plan is accomplished, both leisure and business travelers in Dixie will fare well under it. This covers when it is completed in segments and ultimately when its varied components are connected in a national blueprint linking all the corners of America. There are also some glaring holes in the original projection which are, despite a severe shortage of funding, disturbing nevertheless.

Tampa, Orlando and Miami—linked by HSR—are a unit unto themselves while Jacksonville—just 120 surface miles north of Orlando—is the terminus for an East Coast route that extends 1,024 miles from Boston and abruptly quits! To leave those three lower Sunshine State destinations simply dangling out there is unthinkable and demands an early fix. It may be advantageous to many Floridians as it is. But it's not to most tourists and commercial interests that will undoubtedly effect a resurgence unseen in Florida traffic in a while.

Tennessee is liberated, having no projected HSR service. Once more no Amtrak train comes within three hours of the state capital at Nashville, a metropolitan services district with 1.5 million citizens. Birmingham, three hours south, and Louisville, three hours north, are on proposed HSR lines. Omitting Nashville is a colossal oversight that demands rethinking.

Memphis, too, has been overlooked in plans for debuting HSR. While Memphis has a conventional Amtrak train, this influential center could be linked to a planned HSR route at Little Rock, New Orleans or Birmingham.

There is no east-west HSR corridor planned across the mountainous terrain separating Virginia/North Carolina from West Virginia/Kentucky. The difficulty and expense as well as low population density may prevent this from happening in the foreseeable future. Based on numbers alone, when the time comes to pursue it, there's probably a greater likelihood of a northerly route over the hills. Possibly Pittsburgh–Cincinnati–St. Louis will get the nod and become the best those living farther south can anticipate.

The Nashville omission could be corrected and a route over the mountains regained if the HSR line from Chicago to Louisville is extended to Nashville and Chattanooga and ultimately to Atlanta. There it could link with continuous service to Jacksonville (and, hopefully, Orlando, Tampa and Miami); and to Birmingham, New Orleans, Mobile and Houston. All it takes is sufficient capital!

You may recall *The Lone Ranger*'s interlocutor prevailed on devoted radio and television aficionados to "return with us now to those thrilling days of yesteryear" at the start of the Champion of Justice's airtime adventures. The future could be just as exciting for high speed rail enthusiasts in their day. Their unbridled anticipation may leap as high as the great horse Silver. This time, however, it will be an *iron* horse — a *Sliver Streak* — that's imminent, blazing new trails while crossing immense expanses of terrain in record-setting time.

20

PROGRESSIVE SOUTHERN MUNICIPALITIES
Urban and Intercity Mass Transit

Pretend we are playing *Jeopardy*. The category selected is *Local Mass Rail Transportation*.

The answer to this chapter's leading question is: *In Dixie, they exhibited the tenacity to put pedal to the metal to solve wide-ranging concerns for present and future generations.*

The question is: *What do Atlanta, Charlotte, Fort Lauderdale, Jacksonville, Little Rock, Memphis, Miami, Nashville, New Orleans, Norfolk, Orlando, Savannah, Tampa, the northern counties of Virginia, and West Palm Beach all have in common?*

In a broad sweep of mass transportation tied to indigenous communities, this handful of Southern metropolitan centers has already demonstrated the backbone required to get the job done. Not content to merely comprehend disquieting projections for their fate if left unattended, or even to draft carefully reasoned plans for cracking those challenges without successfully bringing them to fruition, a few thus far have acted on their discoveries in responsible fashion.

Through comprehensive transportation discussions and studies, they have brought many parties to the table to air the challenges they face. Some of their basic concerns invariably relate to the matters of increasing congestion, costs and funding, creating operational efficiencies, and the environment. Their actions—and the support of a majority of the people within their districts—have been able to point the way toward implementing solutions for the synchronized movement of large numbers of people through innovative rail systems. Each city has been able to garner enough progressive voters who were sufficiently troubled by local transit issues to cause them to move forward with plans that could supply present and long-range benefits.

While many American municipalities have mass transit systems up and running or nearing completion instead of in vague or even in meticulous phases on drawing boards for instituting "some day," a handful of Southern conurbations have turned dreams into reality. In Dixie, they are leading the way for an anticipated influx of analogous concepts. Still more systems now in exploratory phases are expected to be activated, too, within a myriad of Southern metropolises before the 2020s are history.

A series of complex constraints often limits, sometimes insurmountably, a community's enthusiasm for passenger rail and must be doggedly pursued by enlightened community leaders. Included is widespread hesitancy by an often fickle public which has to be properly educated to a point of conviction and a vision that becomes a passion. There usually are political implications and potential fallout associated with those decisions. Funding is of paramount importance—sometimes, once a community is "sold" on an idea, how to pay for it becomes the single greatest deterrent in its realization. There are other issues that complicate its execution: the selection of routes, acquiring rights-of-way, ecological impact, safety hazards, ongoing operational requirements, physical facilities, choices of rolling stock — all are matters of consequence that must be weighed deliberately. It's never simple to start up a mass transit system. And possessing winning advocates and persuasive leadership has often been a key to turning a program into one celebrated by a local community.

Parenthetically, a succinct overview of the record of city rail transit services in this nation will illuminate how far we've come. At the same time it offers us a foundation for where we are now and where we appear to be headed.

As communities across the nation grew at random paces into urbanized centers, some type of infrastructure for hauling their residents from place to place became highly desirable, eventually even obligatory. Mass local transit was born. Most cities embraced some kind of process that involved vehicles on rails. The most distinguishing feature separating the sundry processes that evolved was their power source. Some cities applied steam or cable to drive their vehicles. Steam, of course, exhibited the debilitating traits of loud blasts accompanied by rumbling clatter. There was also unending pollution as witnessed in the soot, thick smoke, and vapors it produced. (While this concern would be more disturbing to modern generations, steam engines nevertheless left a calling card wherever they went and were judged unwelcome by many. And because these conveyances ran almost exclusively within urbanized centers and rather frequently, they were of greater concern to local residents than their sibling intercity steam-powered trains.) In addition, steam and cable both earned a reputation for persistent maintenance issues that seldom could be solved for the long term.

In the 19th century especially, the majority of American cities didn't rely solely on steam or cable to haul people. They depended on horsepower to do the trick. Some of those communities extended their lines to envelop outlying districts. The range and pace of the routes was restricted to the endurance and velocity of the animals pressed into service. This form of power displayed other extenuating circumstances. When an epizootic epidemic swept the nation in 1872, for a while nearly every North American city was deprived of mass transportation.

To diminish such disparities in the future, local leaders began to quest for alternative methods of transferring people across short and longer distances as cities began to grow and burgeon. Early experiments with battery-powered conveyances on rails failed. The introduction of the generator, however, led to the electrification of streetcars. This upsurge in technology was to reach its zenith in the interurban, to be contemplated momentarily.

Every metroplex identified in the *Jeopardy* answer earlier in this chapter is now either operating one or more forms of passenger rail traffic within its jurisdiction or is in an advanced developmental stage for its realization within the foreseeable future. As a result the individual and collective achievements have become inspirations to neighboring communities with similar intents that have not yet reached their exalted plateaus, and where denizens sometimes enviously observe what others have already been able to achieve.

What types of mass passenger rail transportation currently exist or are about to be discharged in municipalities below the Mason-Dixon Line? There is no less than a trio of prospering systems that can be fairly easily separated by a few central differences: interurban, commuter, and light rail. An examination of that threesome is basic to considering the progress presently in the works.

Interurban rail, by definition, is a type of electric passenger railroad that enjoyed almost universal popularity in North American cities during the first three decades of the 20th century. Until the early 1920s, most roadways were unpaved and could become virtually impassable during wet weather. Most travel was by water vessels of many types or on land via a handful of methods: on foot, horseback (in earlier days perhaps even in crude oxcarts pulled by teams of oxen), by buckboard, carriage, cart, or wagon.

The interurban, first introduced in this country in 1893 in far flung geographical zones (Portland, Oregon and Sandusky, Ohio), offered a new reliable, resilient, and relaxed method of travel. When getting there is half the fun, the interurban proved it was up to a challenge. At the same time, on occasions, it even transported small cargoes like crops and dairy goods from farms to towns. Especially was this true in the epoch before trucks were widely used for transferring commodities of many types.

A couple of passenger rail scholars, George Hilton and John Due, among the form's leading observers, are usually cited for providing the most sweeping assessment of an interurban. A half-century ago the pair claimed an interurban shared all or most of a quartet of attributes: it runs on electric power; it is primarily a passenger service; its equipment is heavier and faster than urban streetcars; and it proceeds on street trackage within cities but on roadside tracks or private rights-of-way in rural areas.[1]

> The interurbans seemed to fill a travel void for much of America. Aside from what slow, infrequent, grimy local passenger service might be available from the steam railroads, rural America was pretty well restricted to whatever lay within horse and buggy range. The interurbans were bright and clean, stopped almost everywhere, and ran far more frequently than the steam trains, for one car made a train. Once in town the cars usually operated through the streets and went right downtown. They were almost always cheaper than steam trains, too.
> Rails could connect cities to their suburbs. Extended further they could service rural communities, making regular travel to "the city" reasonable.[2]

While exceptions to every rule may be found, an interurban is usually differentiated from streetcars by being fully enclosed, partially enclosed, or convertible. A streetcar, on the other hand, typically operates as an open-air conveyance. The earliest interurban coaches were denoted by very large arch windows on all-wooden coaches. Because they had a tendency to "telescope" in wrecks (a large number of injuries and deaths resulted), after 1915, only steel cars were manufactured by several of the country's foremost fabricators. Steel-constructed interurbans were less vulnerable to the threat of fire and, perhaps surprisingly, were lighter and thereby faster. Contrary to commonly held notions, there were interurban models that actually achieved speeds above 90 miles an hour. Competing directly with nearby steam railroads in diverse places, they offered more frequent service, lower fares, and more periodic stops—often at a specific home, farm or other specific site on request. And at their peak, 1916, they plied nearly 16,000 miles of track within the United States.[3]

Hail to the interurbans! Considering what had preceded them, they were contemporary Cadillacs in a flivver age!

How did they work? In general, their technology lay somewhere between a streetcar line and a full-scale railroad. Overhead wire, simply strung, was the power source of the majority. On heavily trafficked high speed lines, catenaries, a more complex wiring system, was present. In either case, a trolley pole or pantograph transferred voltage from the wire to the locomotive pulling an interurban freight or passenger car. Some interurbans directed electricity to the trains by way of a third rail. Current ran parallel to and outside the rails when on private rights-of-way. Elsewhere an overhead supply was tapped, especially in built-up districts. Power was shifted to the train using a "shoe" attached to the locomotive or car.

What was once typified as interurban rail is now classified as one or the other of the two more passenger rail systems under consideration within this chapter that are found in municipalities today—commuter rail and light rail. Depending on the form it applies, that could include urban streetcar lines. It may be difficult to demarcate interurban rail precisely due to the fact it often encompasses multiple categories. Some streetcar systems partially evolved into interurbans with extensions or acquisitions, for example. Some others effectively became light rail carriers with no street running at all. In still more cases, as an interurban's passenger traffic diminished, cargo displaced it and may have, ultimately, become its sole purpose for remaining in business.

Interurbans required significant operating capital to sustain relatively large workforces. They needed large sums to acquire and maintain rolling stock, to provide upkeep for tracks, and to keep repair shops functioning. In a good year an interurban easily could be bankrupt and in receivership. A washed out trestle, a collision, an inferno, work stoppage, or clash with a municipality over track issues, taxes, or franchise fees could lead an already stressed carrier into insolvency.

By the opening of the 1920s, the commercial sector known as interurbans stood on the threshold of overwhelming regression whether anybody had yet recognized it. During the decade that followed an expanding segment of citizens owning personal vehicles augmented by state construction of hard-wearing roads crept onto the interurban's turf: all of it cut deeply into the transit business on which interurbans had thrived and even been an effective monopoly in most municipalities of any credible size.

The final nail in the coffin for most electrified local transportation systems was the Great Depression. In the early 1930s, it was driving interurbans rapidly into bankruptcy. Before that decade ended the interurban was dead in many places and on life support in others. Only a handful of systems hung on to the 1950s, with fewer still running into the 1960s, primarily confined to Northern and Pacific coast megalopolises. One source inferred the consequences were crushing: "The demise of the interurban in the middle of the twentieth century set the United States behind every other major country in terms of rail infrastructure."[4] The day of the interurban appeared to be over forever.

But appearances can be deceiving.

As the Great American Pastime maintains, "The game ain't over till it's over." To almost everyone's surprise, interurbans began making a comeback in a contemporary America. While few historic interurban lines are still operated in their original form of a century ago, a number of more recently constructed transit lines could be considered interurbans by Hilton and Due's standards delineated already. According to one modern source, a half-dozen cities in the U.S. presently maintain atypical "interurban style street-running" freight trains. Three of them are in the South. All are in Georgia, in the cities of Albany, Augusta, and Columbus. The spirit of the interurban has been renewed in the light rail movement of recent decades, to be examined shortly.

The defining characteristics of commuter rail on the other hand might sound very familiar, particularly as they relate to interurbans. One assessment clarifies commuter rail as providing common carrier passenger travel along railway tracks with scheduled service on fixed routes on a non-reservation basis. Its riders normally journey relatively short distances between a central business district and one or more contiguous suburbs.

Unlike light rail, which most often is powered by electricity supplied by overhead wires or a third rail running alongside the tracks, in most cases commuter rail draws energy from another source. A majority of its networks rely on diesel-electric or electric locomotives. Leading manufacturers of diesel-electrics model their designs on EMD F40PH and F59PHI blueprints. In some situations self-contained units replace or supplement these engines.

To be impartial, there are places—notably in a few megalopolises above the Mason-Dixon Line—where electric power is supplied to these trains or single units in much the same fashion as with interurbans. The rewards from it include faster acceleration, diminished noise, and reduced air-quality concerns. Powering commuter rail by electric lines or rails is more common in Europe than it is in North America, nevertheless.

Beyond this dissimilarity, Hilton and Due affirm that interurbans characteristically run many of their lines on street trackage. As a rule, commuter rail doesn't do so, another striking difference in the two systems. Commuter rail isn't designed to stop as frequently as interurbans either; it certainly doesn't stop by personal request as in the case of some interurbans! Nor does it maintain a sustained frequency throughout the day in many places that is so typical of interurbans. Commuter lines may operate only at peak times, perhaps during morning and evening rush hours. Where that pattern is in effect, service may be limited to a round-trip configuration — inbound in the morning, outbound in the evening.

Operators may sell weekly or monthly passes or other multi-trip tickets at reduced fares. To enhance its effectiveness and accessibility, commuter rail frequently connects to metro train and bus services along its routes and at a network's endpoints. Commuter trains may be operated by a cab car at one end that remotely controls the locomotive to avert turning the train around at a route's end, a push-pull schematic. Most commuter systems are authorized by government bureaus or quasi-government agencies. Some share tracks or rights-of-way with Amtrak, freight trains and other commuter services.

It's significant to note that what is commonly referred to as commuter rail routinely serves other purposes in addition to ferrying workforces to and from jobs. Students—particularly those in colleges, skill and technical schools, adult night programs, academies and private institutions— may be counted among their most loyal clientele. As people take advantage of leisure opportunities, it's sometimes less expensive, faster, and stress-reducing to access a venue by mass transit — without the necessity for finding a place to stash a personal vehicle during that period. Sporting events, trade shows, theaters, concerts and other entertainment draws, plus recreational and weekend getaway enticements increase ridership on commuter rail.

In the Gilded Age of intercity passenger rail travel in America there were some splendid examples of commuter service then in daily practice.

One of the most enduring in the South was operated by Louisville & Nashville Railroad between a handful of hamlets along the Mississippi Gulf Coast and New Orleans. In an experiment that persisted from the 1920s to the 1960s, L&N supplied one or two weekday commuter consists plying an 83-mile course between Ocean Springs, Mississippi, and the Crescent City. Its westbound itinerary included stops at Biloxi, Edgewater Park, Mississippi City, Gulfport, Long Beach, Pass Christian, Bay St. Louis, and Waveland, all in the Magnolia State. Convenient schedules and — early on — a lack of modern highways figured substantially in the dual trains' popularity and resiliency. One of the two trains was scrubbed in the mid 1950s. Early each morning except Sunday the surviving all-coach consist departed Ocean Springs at 6:20 A.M. and arrived in New Orleans at 8:40 A.M. Six afternoons a week it left the Crescent City at 5:15 P.M. and was back in Crescent Springs at 7:35 P.M.

The one-way fare in 1951 was $2.08 for the full distance. But travelers could purchase a 10-trip ticket for $14.58 ($1.46 per trip) or a 46-trip ticket for $32.99 (less than 72 cents per trip). Reduced fares were available for shorter distances. Late in the 1950s, the route's itinerary was trimmed to 57 miles, originating and terminating at Pass Christian. With automobiles setting a new pace in travel and bus service demonstrably vying for the same sector, L&N's ability to turn a profit eroded. In the summer of 1965, after four decades of hauling Mississippians to and from jobs and schools and shopping ventures and other appointments in New Orleans, those scenic trips beside the sea came to an end.

But Louisville & Nashville wasn't to be out of the commuter business for long, however. It simply shifted its focus elsewhere. On June 6, 1969, L&N bought the 206-mile Woodland Junction, Illinois–Evansville, Indiana, leg of the Chicago & Eastern Illinois Railroad. The parent carrier simultaneously gained trackage rights north of Woodland Junction to Chicago. In so doing L&N also picked up C&EI's *Danville Flyer*, a daily commuter train running between Danville, Illinois, and the Windy City.

Departing early mornings out of Danville and late afternoons out of Chicago, the *Flyer* made multiple stops along a 123-mile stretch of mostly rural farmland and suburban homes and businesses. Travelers were offered coach and buffet-lounge accommodations. A crowd of recurring customers who depended on the *Flyer* to ferry them between hinterland bedroom communities and their jobs in the distant city generally gave the service high marks. And while its assumption by L&N came late in the day of passenger and commuter rail, the company was a well practiced servant of the form.

There are several more examples of commuter rail that operated within the territorial confines of Dixie during the heyday of rail travel.

In 1918, Southern Railway constructed a second Atlanta depot on its north-south mainline expressly for the purpose of growing a commuter business that would appeal to local residents living in the fashionable suburbs north of the city. Who could have thought then that Southern's small Brookwood Station (more widely known as the Peachtree Station in later years because of its abutment to Atlanta's renowned Peachtree Street) would now be the only surviving passenger terminal in town? ("Terminal" can be loosely applied here, considering it is but a minuscule imitation of two spectacular, once proud facilities—Terminal and Union stations—that operated downtown and were razed long ago.) Back in the day not only did the Peachtree Station usher laborers 4.2 miles into and out of the city center, it offered convenient access to nearby residents traveling much longer distances, too.

Florida East Coast Railway erected a second station to serve greater Miami, which shared a similar outcome with that of Atlanta. After a pervasive strike halted FEC operations in the early 1960s, responding in haste, Miami officials bulldozed an imposing end-of-the-line passenger terminal downtown. When passenger rail service was restored by court order between 1965 and 1968, FEC had but one place for its trains to reach a finish line: a small, less-than-commodious depot it had built in 1955 in North Miami. Although city leaders balked, it proffered the only "Welcome to Miami" greeting train travelers were to receive in those years in a metroplex capitalizing on tourist dollars. The little out-of-the-way depot had—much like Atlanta's Peachtree Station—been a jumping off spot for northside residents traveling to and from occupations nearer FEC's final stop between 1955 and 1963. While it was a short hop, it proffered all of the obvious advantages that commuter rail riders enjoyed in longer-distance markets.

Washington, D.C., heavily benefited from a multiplicity of mass transit systems ferrying workers to and from the city. Tens of thousands traveled from the northern suburbs of Virginia, both then and now. In the modern epoch, with proliferating commuter services, many times they now reside much farther away.

Finally, from a passenger standpoint, the interurban Piedmont & Northern Railroad could probably be considered as much commuter rail as anything else. Its North Carolina division ran up to eight passenger cars daily in each direction between Gastonia and Charlotte, a distance of about 25 miles. From 1910 to 1951, the carrier transported riders on a route laden with small town stops. Included were two stations at Charlotte—one downtown and one on the city's northwest fringe at suburban Thrift. P&N also ran extra trains at peak hours, suggesting its caretakers were responsive to the needs of a significant commuting sector.

There are other examples of commuter rail across Dixie. Perceptions that rail transit commuters are people working in offices and factories and for big retailers only in the North are limiting views. In the backyards of the South during the first half of the 20th century, thousands of employees relied on commuter rail to get to work. While the numbers were fewer than in an industrialized North, Southern riders were as dependent on this service as those to be found everywhere else.

Light rail is the last of the three forms for detailed exploration. Categorized as a specific species of passenger rail, it was so designated by the U.S. Urban Mass Transportation Administration (predecessor of the present Federal Transportation Administration) nearly four decades ago (1972). In its initial application it was used to brand streetcar transformations occurring in the United States and Europe. Some federal officials at that time preferred the idiom *city rail* to the one adopted. Their opposition was ultimately silenced. Here are its characteristic attributes:

Light is employed in the sense of "intended for light loads and fast movement" as opposed to physical weight. Vehicles often weigh more than those on professed heavy rail systems. The investment in infrastructure is normally lighter than that comprising a heavy rail system, however. The American Public Transportation Association defines light rail thus: "An electric railway with a 'light volume' traffic capacity compared to heavy rail. Light rail may use shared or exclusive rights-of-way, high or low platform loading and multi-car trains or single cars." Some diesel-powered transit nevertheless dubs itself light rail (there are current examples in New Jersey and Ottawa, Canada). In traditional transit terminology, however, these might be best labeled commuter rail or branch lines or interurbans. If electrified, they would unmistakably be termed interurbans.

The English long ago implemented the phrase *light railway* to denote operations carried out under less demanding regulations using lightweight gear at speeds lower than those on mainline railroads. *Light rail*, a generic international English designation for these types of rail systems, essentially means the same thing throughout the Anglo-sphere.[5]

The origins of modern light rail technology are believed to be primarily vested in German experimentation. Following the Second World War, Germany retained its streetcar networks and developed them into light rail systems (*stadtbahnen*). Most medium-sized German cities (with the notable exception of Hamburg) sustain light rail networks. Writing in 1962, transport researcher Dean Quinby separated historic streetcar systems from their modern light rail counterparts.[6] He cited several newer features that are present in light rail: they have an ability to haul more travelers than streetcars; their looks typically resemble conventional trains in that two or more coaches are linked together instead of a solo car running independently; more doorways permit greater use of available space; and they run faster and generate less noise than streetcars.

> Quinby discerned two attributes common to most of the rebuilding efforts that together constituted ... the emergence of a new transit concept. One was capacity enhancement with emphasis on larger cars, operation of cars in trains, and much greater door capacity with new fare systems to make use of that capacity. The result was that for the first time surface transit could engorge and disgorge large volumes of passengers at intermediate stops quickly. The other was speed enhancement, achieved through traffic engineering and light infrastructure investments with short applications of heavy infrastructure investment in critical areas.[7]

Sixteen years elapsed following Quinby's evaluation before a North American light rail system was in operation at Edmonton, Alberta, Canada (1978). Today, more than three decades afterwards, no fewer than 30 U.S. light rail networks are up and running. More are planned.

Most were built on standard gauge. Older standard gauge vehicles couldn't negotiate the sharp turns as easily as those constructed on narrow gauge layouts. Modern light rail systems achieve tighter turning radii, nonetheless, by including articulated cars (those with a pivot or hinge connection) that allows them to negotiate hard curves. One of the clear advantages is in using standard railway maintenance apparatus in deference to custom-built paraphernalia. There's no issue with standard gauge light rail vehicles moving over tracks bearing mostly freight traffic either. And with accessibility legislation requiring lower floors, there's another plus offered by standard gauge that isn't available in most narrow-gauge networks.

Light rail and high speed rail (see Chapter 19) may be plainly differentiated in no less than two observable ways: how they look and where they run. Light rail usually produces a narrower car body than that typically offered in high speed rail situations where most coaches are unequivocally larger. In addition, light rail's articulated properties, absent in high speed rail, allow the trains to be turned on a dime in comparison to the quarter or half-dollar required by high speed rail. That's due to a larger radius prompted by the bigger cars.

Finally, light rail can run in mixed traffic while high speed cannot. High speed is often traveling much faster than the prevailing traffic around it. If it was moving alongside automobiles, trucks, vans, motorcycles, etc. and through the intersections they use, that would create the potential for perilous outcomes. Another safety issue preventing high speed from running in the street is the presence of an electrified third rail many times. Light rail's ability to run its trains down existing thoroughfares, on the other hand, may diminish or altogether eliminate costly projects like constructing elevated and subway fragments. Those pricey consequences are part of doing business in high speed rail with little alternative for reaching "the other side."

There is yet another discernible factor separating the two networks that isn't always witnessed by passengers. While high speed rail may run unattended with automatic train operation (ATO) in place, there is no substitute for having a train operator present in light rail situations. That individual is the key element for maintaining a protected network. Without an operator physically present, nobody would be there to stop the train if an automobile veered off in front of it on a roadway that both are negotiating. The train's operator must be qualified to deal with almost any type of emergency, in fact. Light rail and ATO systems—like texting and driving—simply don't mix.

In addition to these varied forms of local transit over multiple types of imposed trackage systems, there are yet other mass rail transit layouts currently in operation in Southern cities as well as the rest of the United States. They include traditional and heritage trolleys (both sometimes dubbed streetcars) and automated people mover systems. One source observes that *trolley* is the preferred application in the eastern United States with *streetcar* more prevalent in the West and across Canada. Of the systems presently operating in Dixie, *streetcar* holds an edge, however.

Traditional trolleys are usually older, slower-moving wheeled vehicles running on rails and are commonly propelled by electricity. Their power may be collected from an underground conductor, an overhead wire, or a third rail transmitted to the vehicle's motor.

Heritage trolleys are often newer vehicles or may be refurbished traditional trolley models exhibiting a unique distinguishing trait separating them from their early 20th century precursors: their décor and other trappings are designed as a throwback to the vintage cars operating in American cities 50 or 100 years ago. Modernized with conveniences, they may be air-conditioned, provide improved seating and lighting and other features that their counterparts didn't. In displaying a semblance of historic authenticity, these replications add ambience and character to their locations. In every case, however, they are genuine rail lines and not buses passing themselves off as streetcars. The latter breed—a cheaper imitation that may be found in profusion today in large, medium and smaller cities in the South as well as elsewhere—may be mistakenly referred to as *trolleys*. A bus by any other name is, for sure, still a bus.

Automated people mover systems embrace at least four varieties of technologies: monorail, duorail, automated guideway transit, or maglev. Propulsion may be driven by conventional onboard electric motors, linear motors, or cable traction. Several of these innovative techniques are in operation in the South today. Most are typically identified with airports, theme parks, and downtown commercial districts serving workforces, shoppers, tourists, entertainment and sporting venues.

Returning to those Southern cities mentioned much earlier that have already realized, or are about to instigate, visionary local programs in rail transit, their projects—and those of a few more places in Dixie—are detailed in Appendix I (the letter I) at the end of this volume.

The bottom line in all of this is that some progressive urban centers in the South are acting responsibly about their present and future needs. A growing trend is seeing the execution of new methods of transferring large numbers of people safely, swiftly, economically, comfortably, conveniently and with as little negative impact on their surroundings as can be mustered. There is plenty of opportunity for others to join them lest their economies fade into needless decline, a handicap that can be partially offset by making adequate provisions in the arena of public transport. If communities are to avoid falling behind their peers they must not be caught napping or wringing their hands or failing to take sensible action.

All of the models presented here are shortlines that are going someplace. Before the train leaves the station, however, it's time for more municipalities to hop aboard.

APPENDICES

A: *Glossary*

ACF: American Car and Foundry, railcar fabricator once based at St. Charles, Missouri, near St. Louis.

ALCO (American Locomotive Company): A major fabricator of American steam and diesel-electric locomotives based in Schenectady, New York, from the latter years of the 19th century to 1969.

Amfleet: Starting in 1975, single-level passenger equipment delivered to Amtrak by the Budd Company of Philadelphia.

ashcat: Locomotive fireman; also known as *bake head, bell ringer, blackie, diamond cracker, dust-raiser,* and a plethora of added designations.

automated people mover system: Applies monorail, duorail, automated guideway transit, and maglev technologies in local travel; may be powered by onboard electric motors, linear motors, or cable traction.

bad order: Nonworking car or engine often designated a *cripple*; it must be marked at night by a blue light when people are working around it.

baggage car: Car for passenger luggage, packages, small parcels. In early railroading, staffers handled baggage from the car; later much of it was mechanized. In the Amtrak era baggage handling on trains is done by car attendants and patrons while a few handlers still work in large terminals.

ballast: Crushed stone or gravel underlying and supporting the track.

ballast scorcher: High-speed engineer.

ball of fire: Fast run.

barn: Locomotive roundhouse named after the structure where streetcars were stored.

baron: A wealthy businessman who bought and financed the construction, implementation and consolidation of U.S. railways (1800s, early 1900s).

beat 'er on the back: Make fast time; work an engine at full stroke.

beehive: Railroad yard office.

big boys: Exclusive trains for officials.

Big E: Engineer, derived from the large initial on affiliation pins of the Brotherhood of Locomotive Engineers.

Big O (Big Ox): Conductor, named for the first initial in the Order of Railway Conductors.

black hole: Tunnel.

boiler: Large metal drum on a steam locomotive holding water converted to steam for power.

bootlegger: Train that runs over more than one railroad.

boxcar tourist: Hobo or tramp.

brains (brainless wonder, the brains): Conductor.

brakeman: Trainman whose duties include coupling and uncoupling cars, throwing switches, inspecting brakes, and generally protecting the train.

branch: Feeder line to mainline, usually with light track and small trains.

brass buttons: Passenger conductor on railway or streetcar line.

brass collar (brass hat): Railroad official (usually conductor) wearing gold-braided collar and brass plate on his cap.

bridge route: A connecting railroad between other carriers' lines that ferries more passenger or freight traffic on its tracks than it generates.

Budd: Philadelphia's E. G. Budd Manufacturing Company, a world-class fabricator of lightweight streamlined cars in the 20th century.

buffet-lounge: A lounge car featuring a counter for serving snacks and refreshments.

bullpen: Crew room.

bumper: Anything to stop a car from rolling off the end of a track.

business car: A railroad-owned passenger car for railroad executives' use.

bust up a cut: Separating cars in a consist, removing some reaching their destination while sending others to through trains.

caller: An employee who announces trains or summons crews for trains.

calliope: Steam engine.

273

canned: Removed from service.

captain (skipper): Conductor.

car inspector: With hotbox detectors and diverse apparatus, he or she walks the train at intervals, visually and electronically checking brakes and other gear in all weather before a train's journey begins or resumes.

carrying green: Train exhibiting green flags by day or green lights by night that indicates a second section is following closely. *Carrying white* in the same manner signifies an extra train.

carrying the mail: Bringing train orders.

Casey Jones: Any engineer but particularly a fast one, named after John Luther (Casey) Jones.

Catenary: An elaborate wiring scheme above trains, interurbans, streetcars and trolleys powered by electrical current; voltage is conveyed to the train through an attached pantograph or pole.

clerestory: Outside wall of a room or building rising above an adjoining roof containing windows, a common trait of late 19th and early 20th century railroad trainsheds.

coach: Any passenger car yet theoretically limited to one with rows of seats in a common area supplying "coach class" or comparably identified seating.

coke: Early steam locomotives relied on this type of coal as fuel.

combine: A blended passenger coach and baggage car.

commuter rail: Common carrier passenger travel along railway tracks with scheduled service on fixed routes on a non-reservation basis; usually relies on diesel-electric or electric locomotives for power.

conductor (big ox, brass hat, captain): Crewman in charge of the train and its staff, responsible for orders, proper car handling, safety of passengers and freight, schedules, tickets. In a figurative sense, he or she "drives the train," feeding instructions to the engineer maneuvering the throttle.

consist: The order and number of cars that make up a train. (Note: *First syllable is emphasized ... CONsist.*)

cornfield meet: Head-on wreck.

counting the ties: Reducing speed.

couplers: Devices connecting cars and engines. Automatic couplers fasten when pushed together and disengage when levers on car sides are tripped.

CTC (Centralized Traffic Control): Major railroads' system using telephone lines to transfer data to wayside and control signals.

current: On a multi-track mainline, a common traffic course.

cushions: Cars in passenger consists that don't haul travelers (e.g., baggage, express, mail cars).

cut: Block of cars; to make a cut, uncouple.

days: Demerits; 90 "days" accumulation is normally cause for dismissal.

deadhead: A nonpaying passenger; a railroad employee riding on a pass; an engine hauled "dead" on a train.

deboard: Action by passengers leaving a train.

dehorn: To demote; remove one's authority.

derail: To run off the track; to protect the mainline by sending (derailing) one or more cars onto a side track.

diamond: Grade crossing where two railroad tracks intersect.

die on the law: To leave a train, replaced by another crew, when the allowable ceiling of lawful work hours is reached after one's shift begins.

diesel: An internal-combustion engine that burns crude fuel oil without aid of spark plugs; fuel oil is injected into the cylinder's compression chamber and ignited by compressed air.

diesel-electric engine: Locomotive burning diesel fuel that generates electric power required to run the engine.

ding-dong (doodlebug): Gas or gas-electric coach, usually appearing on small roads or branch lines not large enough to support regular trains; the sound of its bell precipitated its moniker.

dining car: Car composed of a restaurant, kitchen, and pantry.

dispatcher: One who routes trains, determines where they are to encounter other trains, issues orders, and maintains awareness of speed restrictions.

dogcatchers: Crew dispatched to relieve another overtaken by law (*dog law, hog law, pure-food law*) limiting number of work hours.

dome car: Exhibiting a bubble-like glass extension on top, this coach offers unrivaled views in upstairs seating, although available seating is sometimes limited.

dorm car: Rail car for long-distance passenger train personnel, exclusive of engineer and conductor, who are restricted to maximum work hour limits.

double bedroom: Private room in sleeping car for two occupants, with two chairs or a chair and sofa by day and two fold-down beds at night.

double-header: Train pulled by dual engines.

drag: Heavy or slow freight train.

drink: Water for locomotive.

drone cage: Private car.

drop (flying switch): Moving cars to the opposite end of the engine by uncoupling them, speeding up the engine and running over a switch, throwing the switch to permit the cars to go onto other track.

drunkard: Late Saturday night passenger train.

ducats: Passenger conductor's hat checks.

dude: Passenger conductor.

easy sign: Signal indicating a train is to proceed slowly.

electric engine: Locomotive run on volts from electric cable or third rail.

Electro-Motive (EMC, EMD): The chief fabricator of U.S. diesel-electric streamliner power cars and passenger locomotives from 1934 to the 1990s; initially Cleveland, Ohio–based Electro-Motive Corporation, in 1941, EMC merged with Winton Engine Company, folded into Electro-Motive Division of General Motors Corporation in La-Grange, Illinois.

engineer (eagle eye, hogger, hoghead): Second to conductor in accountability on a train's crew; the locomotive's physical operator.

express train: Fast passenger train making only limited stops.

extra: A train that isn't listed in a timetable; working jobs left undone by others; a section of track that skirts another.

extra board: Record of crew members performing added duties.

firebox: Metal box behind steam locomotive's boiler where fuel burns.

fireman (fire boy, tallow pot): Aide to engineer helping scrutinize signals; on coal-burning locomotives, chief duty to move tons of wood or coal from tender to firebox while sustaining fire and boiler pressure.

flagman: Rear brakeman, also rear man.

flimsy: Train order, called that due to its appearance on lightweight stock — originally on onionskin paper to facilitate producing carbon copies.

fog: Steam.

foreign car: Car running over any railroad besides the one that owns it.

freight cars: Cargo-haulers in sundry formats (e.g., box, flat, gondola, hopper, refrigerator, tank, etc.).

front-end power: Engine(s) supplying force that pulls a consist.

gauge: Size of track measured between insides of rails.

girl (old girl): Term of sentiment for steam engine; as a ship, "she" not "it."

glass cars: Passenger cars.

glimmer: Locomotive headlamp.

glory road: Term of affection for railroad.

goat: Switch engine for transferring cars to other locations in a station or rail yard or on siding.

god of iron: Massive, potent locomotive.

grabber: Passenger train conductor, grabs tickets.

grade: Inclination of rail section (1 percent grade means a rise of 1 foot per 100 feet).

grade crossing: Intersection of a railroad and public road or where two rail lines meet at the same level.

grass wagon: Tourist car.

harness: Uniforms of passenger train personnel.

hayburner: Coal or oil lamp, commonly used as a train signal before battery- and electric-powered light.

head-end cars: Cars hauling baggage, mail, or express; most often appear in a consist between locomotives and passenger-carrying cars.

head-end power (HEP): Electricity for a train's lighting, heating, and air conditioning produced by diesel engines on a locomotive.

headhouse: A railway depot structure that contains passenger waiting area, support facilities and offices.

head in: Meeting another train by taking a side-track.

head man: Chief brakeman.

heavyweight: Heavy all-steel construction passenger car, standard in First World War era; typically riding on heavy-duty six-wheel trucks; riveted sides, square windows, clerestory roof (short windows the car top length).

HEP (head end power): Electricity supplied a passenger train by locomotive, derived from main engine or smaller diesel engine within locomotive.

heritage trolley (or) streetcar: New or refurbished rail car with décor recapturing vintage models of long ago; updated with modern conveniences, adding ambience and character to local transit systems.

high ball: Being cleared to go, given authority to proceed or take off.

highball artist: An engineer who's recognized for running fast.

high iron: Mainline or high-speed track, laid with heavier rail than that on unimportant branches or passing track or spurs.

high liner: Fast mainline passenger train.

high speed rail: A system of trains running notably faster than most rail traffic, ranging 90 to 220 miles an hour; often electrified, has continuous welded rail, almost no grade crossings, and travel dedicated rights-of-way.

high wheeler: Fast passenger train; also passenger train engine.

hog law: Federal law limiting number of hours within a 24-hour period that a railroad employee may be on the job.

hold 'em (big hole 'em, plug 'em): Emergency directive to stop.

holding her against the brass: Running electric car at full speed.

hole: Passing track where one train pulls onto it to meet another.

Hours of Service Law (hog law): Federal regulation mandating train personnel can only be on duty 12 hours at a stretch; specific provisions for time off in an effort to curtail fatigue.

HSR (High Speed Rail): Travel assigned from 90 to 220 miles an hour by a wide variety of sources, with little tolerance for grade crossings.

hump: Artificial knoll at end of classification yard over which cars are pushed so they roll on their own momentum to separate tracks; also summit of a hill division or top of a prominent grade.

interurban: A type of electrified railroad introduced in the U.S. in 1893, it was widely accepted in hauling passengers and limited freight in early decades of the next century; heavier and faster than streetcars, it runs on city streets and occupies its own right-of-way outside urban territory.

in the hole: On a siding; also lower berth of a sleeping car section (sections prevalent mid 1800s to mid 1900s).

iron (rail): Track; *single iron* is single track.

iron horse: Slang for *locomotive*.

jitney: Four-wheel electric truck toting baggage in a depot, station or terminal.

junk pile: Ancient locomotive still in service.

knock her in the head: Slow down.

layover: Waiting time between two connecting trains.

lift transportation: Collect passenger tickets.

light rail: With cars often weighing more than heavy rail system cars, its infrastructure outlay is normally lighter, its load lighter and speed faster; most networks derive power from electrification while a few use diesels.

lightweight car: Aerodynamically designed rail passenger conveyance that is streamlined with rounded edges and fabricated of light metals or alloys, typically stainless steel or (less commonly) aluminum; the net result is a sleek, modern manifestation moving swiftly along the tracks.

limited: A fast train making a restricted number of stops.

liner: Passenger train.

link (cross-over): A train crossing between two parallel tracks.

lizard scorcher: Chef in dining car.

locomotive (engine): Self-propelled vehicle that pulls or pushes cars, mostly steam-driven, to mid 1900s, after which diesel power dominated.

mainline: The principal track(s) of a railway company, frequently linking two or more important metropolitan areas.

marker: Red light at train's rear to protect it and denote a train is complete.

master mind: An official.

matching dials: Comparing time.

meet order: Train order designating a precise point where two or more trains will meet on a single track, one on a *siding*, another on *high iron*.

mileage hog: Conductor or engineer, paid by miles traveled, and resented by junior workers when one applies seniority to gain best runs.

mixed train: Consist combining freight and passenger cars.

monkey: Caught away from their destination, when a train crew is on duty enough hours to reach federal guideline limits, *the monkey gets them* and they must stop and wait for a fresh crew to arrive to replace them.

monkey money: Traveler riding gratis possesses this "pass."

MOW (maintenance of way): Sleeping and dining cars and even whole trainsets for railway road crews.

mule skinner: Driver of a mule cart, primitive form of trains on rails.

name trains: Venerated above trains with mere numbers, at times these passenger consists were awarded "premier" status with priority over numbered "locals"; in vogue mainly in the epoch of private railroads.

narrow gauge: Distance between inner surfaces of the rails on "narrow gauge" railway lines was typically two or three feet.

news butcher: Peddler selling newspapers, magazines, cards, candy, fruit, crackers, sodas and other wares in passenger trains.

nickel grabber: Streetcar conductor.

observation cars: Rounded end-of-train cars in streamliner era, some with dome sections, allowing receding countryside view; squared-end heavyweight observation car might have sheltered "back porch" platform where riders collected; on Midwest–West Coast runs now Amtrak's double-decker Superliner lounge cars, glassed on three sides with seats facing out, are often identified as "observation cars" by travelers, not a misnomer.

old hand (old head): Seasoned railroader, often one with lots of seniority.

on the advertised (on the card, on the cat hop): Right on time or according to schedule.

on the law: Reference to Hours of Service Law pertaining to work time limits and required rest hours for conductor and engineer.

open the gate: To switch a train on or off a siding; *close the gate* is to secure the switch after the train passes it.

orders: Given to every conductor and engineer, contains release form giving a train authority to proceed, temporary bulletins for each subdivision to be entered including slow orders, work foremen and any other notices.

out: When a trainman is at a point other than home terminal, he or she is *out*.

over the knoll: Getting up a hill.

paddle wheel: Narrow-gauge engine with driving boxes outside its wheels.

pair of pliers: Conductor's punch.

pantograph: Metal frame atop an electric locomotive that receives voltage from cables above the track to power the engine.

passenger cars: Any cars carrying human travelers—club cars, coaches, diners, dome cars, observation cars, parlor cars, tavern cars, etc.

pax: Passenger.

peaked end (pointed end, sharp end): Head end of a train.

peanut roaster: Small steam engine.

pig: Locomotive.

plug: "One-horse" passenger train; locals identified at times as *plug runs*.

plush run: Passenger train.

porter: Most often Pullman Company staffer; helped riders with luggage and located their seats or reserved sleeping quarters.

pound her: To push a locomotive to fullest capability.

power car: Diesel or electric engine forever linked to passenger carriage set.

puller: Switch engine hauling cars from one yard to another at one depot; also operator of electric truck transporting baggage and mail at a depot.

Pullman: A sleeping car manufactured, operated and staffed by Pullman Company of Chicago. After a federal crackdown on its monopoly of the market, Pullman shed operational activities in 1947, persisting as prime maker of sleeping cars. For a century, until the last rolled off the assembly line in 1968, Pullman was seen as the epitome of sleeping car perfection.

pull the calf's tail: Yank the whistle cord.

quill: Whistle (especially used in Dixie).

rail: Parallel lengths of steel, iron, or wood on which a train's wheels roll.

railfan: A railroad hobbyist.

rattle her hocks: Get speed out of an engine.

receivership: A business managed by a receiver in bankruptcy procedures.

red board (red eye): Stop signal; *red eye* is also liquor.

redcap: Station porter.

restricted speed: 20 mph or less; allows train to stop within half vision range of stop signal, train, track worker, or unsafe situation.

roadbed: Base coating of fill sustaining track form (ballast, rail, ties, etc.).

road hog: Any large motor vehicle on a highway, particularly intercity trucks and buses which cut into rail passenger and freight revenue.

rolling stock: Passenger or freight cars plus locomotives.

roomette: Celebrated sleeping-car space with door, for one or two persons (one ca. 1942–1956), offering clothes locker, toilet and sink, dual facing chairs making into bed at night, second bed folded from wall; an upgrade from *sections* with curtained upper and lower berths and end-of-car toilet.

roundhouse: Normally built in an arc over the fan of tracks radiating from a turntable, it's a shed where locomotives are serviced, lightly maintained, and stored when out of use.

route mileage: Geographical distance traveled from point to point (not including sidings, yards, extra track, etc.).

RPO (Railway Post Office): U.S. Postal Service sorted mail en route in this car to late 1960s, after which operations mostly shifted from rail to truck.

run: A trainman's work assignment is on a particular "run."

rust pile: Ancient locomotive.

saw by: Slow, complex operation as one train passes another on single track while one is on siding too short for the whole train; *saw by* applies to any move through switches to facilitate one train passing another.

seat hog: Traveler in car or depot taking more than one seat spreading bags, packages, and food over adjacent space as other patrons are left to stand.

section: Two single facing seats in sleeping car converted to upper and lower berths at night, cordoned off by heavy curtains; toilets are at end of car.

shoe: A device on a train or car powered by a third rail that makes contact with that rail, supplying electricity to the vehicle to make it run.

shops: A railroad facility where locomotives, cars, and other apparatus are fabricated, repaired and maintained.

siding (the hole): Side rail connected to main rail by switches at both ends that provide a place for trains to meet or pass one another.

sightseer lounge: Amtrak double-deck Superliner car appearing on the *Coast Starlight* and four routes between the Pacific and New Orleans and Chicago. Some seats swivel while all face glass sides that nearly reach the floor. Glass persists on the ceiling with unobstructed panoramic views.

sleeper: Passenger car with seats converted to beds at night; usually offers multiple floor plan configurations with varying accommodation grades.

smart aleck: Passenger conductor.

snoozer: Sleeping car.

soft bellies: Wooden frame cars.

spur: Side rail connected to main rail at only one end providing a place for loading or storing cars.

standard gauge: Distance between inner surfaces of the rails, widely accepted at 4 feet $8^1/_2$ inches by 1870s.

station master: Overseer of passenger depot; responsible for proper consist makeup within allotted time; may also sell tickets.

steam engine: Wood-, coal-, or oil-burning locomotive that — given water — produces steam to propel the engine forward and backward.

stove: Steam engine.

streamliner: Introduced in 1934, smooth and efficient lightweight train that moves rapidly. (See lightweight car.)

stub-end depot: A terminal at which tracks abruptly cease instead of passing through; requires trains to pull forward and back out or — using a wye — to back into the station in order to be headed forward at departure.

superliner: Bi-level passenger car on most Amtrak runs in West since 1979.

switch: Moveable track part letting trains be diverted to different route.

TA: Coach, sleeping car, or train attendant.

tender: Vehicle behind a steam locomotive toting fuel and water.

third rail: Ground rail supplying electricity (direct current mostly) to some electric trains, placed alongside or between the rails of a railway track.

31 order: Train order requiring signature on receipt; train stops to pick it up.

three-bagger: Train requiring trio of engines to pull or push it.

ties: Rails are spiked to these crosspieces for support.

tin lizard: Streamlined train.

track: Fixed path along which trains run including roadbed, ties, rail.

traditional trolley (or) streetcar: Usually older, slower-moving wheeled vehicle on rails, commonly propelled by electricity.

train: In theory a cluster of cars powered by a locomotive approved to run on some portion of a railroad; any other grouping is a "string" or "cut" of cars.

trainman: A member of a train crew supervised by a conductor; trainmen and conductors may be of either gender in the modern age.

trainshed: A open-sided structure built for shelter usually found paralleling the tracks at a depot; it shields passengers and railroad employees from the elements along with luggage, freight and equipment, especially helpful as trains are loaded and unloaded.

transcontinental train: By strict definition, train running coast-to-coast, e.g., Atlantic to Pacific. One train met the criteria in history of U.S. passenger service, Amtrak's *Sunset Limited*, from Miami/Orlando to Los Angeles, 1993–2005, when Hurricane Katrina intervened and damaged tracks in the Gulf Coast area.

trestle: A braced framework of timbers, piles or steel for carrying a railroad or road over a depression.

trolley pole: A connecting rod that transfers electricity from an overhead wire to power a trolley or streetcar.

truck: The rotating wheel-axle-frame assembly beneath dual ends of a car or locomotive, wheels guided along rails by a lip or flange cast on inner edges.

turntable: Rarely used now, apparatus normally found in a roundhouse to turn engines onto different tracks — includes a moveable bridge mounted in a pit and powered to revolve 360 degrees.

varnish: Originally certified wooden passenger cars with high-gloss varnish coats; still applied today to passenger cars and equipment.

viewliner: Single-level sleeping car launched in 1996; used on Amtrak long-distance runs passing into tunnels to Manhattan in New York City.

vista dome: Car with standard roof height but a raised glass-enclosed upper level seating area with nearly 360-degree views mainly built by Budd Company but generically applied to dome cars of multiple manufacturers.

wye: Triangular arrangement of track employed in reversing direction of consists by backing them into one leg of the triangle, then going forward down the other leg.

yard: System of tracks spread across many acres where trains are made up or taken apart, serviced, and freight cars loaded and sorted.

zoo keeper: Gate tender at a passenger depot.

B: *Additional Passenger Lines*

This appendix introduces 13 more passenger lines that also ran below the Mason-Dixon Line.

Baltimore & Ohio Railroad
Clinchfield Railroad
Georgia Railroad
Kansas City Southern Railway
Missouri Pacific Railroad
Norfolk Southern Railway
Pennsylvania Railroad
Piedmont & Northern Railroad
Richmond, Fredericksburg & Potomac Railroad
Rock Island Railroad
Southern Pacific Railroad
Tennessee Central Railway
Virginian Railway

Baltimore & Ohio Railroad

Formed: February 21, 1827
Headquarters: Baltimore, Maryland
Précis: Founding brothers Evan and Philip Thomas persuaded enough Baltimoreans to invest in running horse-drawn or wind-powered rail cars on a narrow gauge track to launch the B&O. The siblings' idea for a line from Baltimore to "some suitable city upon the Ohio River" was predicated on accessing an agriculturally rich Ohio Valley and feeding a rapidly escalating East Coast populace faced with mounting food shortages. Converting meanwhile to steam-driven locomotives, it took the B&O 25 years (1852) to lay tracks to the Ohio at Wheeling, West Virginia. Local lines gave it connections to Cincinnati, Cleveland, Columbus, Detroit, Indianapolis, Louisville, St. Louis, and Springfield. People-hauling was secondary but a sterling attribute. By 1860, West Virginia and Ohio coal produced a third of its revenues.
  Mileage: 6,350
  Mainlines: Jersey City, New Jersey (with bus extension to Manhattan) via Philadelphia, Baltimore, and Washington, D.C., to Cumberland, Maryland, and across West Virginia (Grafton, Clarksburg, Parkersburg, with stems to Charleston and Kenova) en route to Cincinnati and St. Louis, and from Cumberland through Pittsburgh to Chicago
  Name Trains: *Abraham Lincoln, Capitol Limited, Diplomat, National Limited, Royal Blue, Shenandoah*
  Logo: U.S. capitol dome in circle
  Dominant Colors: Blue and gray with black and gold trim
  Mottos: *Linking 13 Great States with the Nation, The Royal Blue Line*
  Passenger Service End: April 30, 1971
  Disposition: From the 1930s to the 1970s, the B&O had financial trouble. Except for prosperity during the Second World War epoch (1939–1945), track mileage and profits declined while inflation and strong union demands escalated labor costs. Between 1932 and 1952, no dividends were paid on B&O's common stock. In the mid 1950s, the line petitioned public service commissions in New York and Maryland to suspend service between Baltimore and New York due to "enormous deficits" on the route. As the carrier continued losing money it sought a financially sound rival with which to merge. After receiving permission from the Interstate Commerce Commission, the Chesapeake & Ohio Railway took control of the B&O on February 4, 1963, and the pair was renamed Chessie System in 1972. To gain access to the booming southeastern U.S. those operators merged with Seaboard Coastline Industries, Inc., then the eighth largest railroad in the country, in 1982. Chessie System and Sea-board formed CSX Corporation, a holding company controlling one of the nation's largest rail systems. Like B&O in 1860, in a short while CSX Corporation earned a third of its revenue hauling coal.

Clinchfield Railroad

Formed: 1909
Headquarters: Johnson City, Tennessee
Précis: The Clinchfield is widely cited as a coal-hauling freight line. Cargo was its bread and butter, yet in its steam-powered days it carried people, too, an often missed fact. In 1835, South Carolina Senator John C. Calhoun foresaw a rail linkage between the Atlantic Ocean at Charleston and the Ohio River at Cincinnati, both strategic market waterways. After seven decades, when others failed to realize the dream, an enterprising George L. Carter and some cohorts did. Traversing the Blue Ridge Mountains was an arduous task, boring through 18 tunnels. Their scheme was touted as "the costliest railroad in America" and "the engineering wonder of the 20th century." In 1909, the Carolina, Clinchfield, & Ohio Railway chugged from Spartanburg, South Carolina, north to Marion, North Carolina, and Erwin, Tennessee, terminating at Dante, Virginia. By 1915, it persisted past Dante to Elkhorn, Kentucky, schlepping travelers from Elkhorn to Spartanburg, and connecting them to other routes at either end. As a throwback to that time, promoters subsequently offered widely advertised seasonal excursions over the line. When ownership changed in 1925, the moniker was reduced to Clinchfield, and the workhorse refocused on profitability, taking Kentucky coal to the southern Piedmont as its chief motivation. Despite that emphasis passenger service persisted to the mid 1950s. Initially there were two trains in each direction daily, a service reduced to one daily in the early 1930s. During the final two years of transporting people, a single train trekked in one direction one day and on the opposite course the next.
  Route Mileage: 277
  Mainline: Spartanburg, South Carolina, to Elkhorn, Kentucky
  Name Trains: Numbered trains
  Logo: Circle bearing Clinchfield Railroad in yellow reversed through grey at top and bottom respectively, separated by a train with diesel engines at either end pulling a banner in the middle reading Quick Service — Short Route between the Central West and Southeast
  Dominant Colors: Grey and yellow
  Motto: *Quick Service — Short Route between the Central West and Southeast*
  Passenger Service End: 1954
  Disposition: The carrier was leased to the At-

The ex–Clinchfield Railroad passenger station at Erwin, Tennessee, as of this date — November 11, 2006 — has been adapted as a public library. An active, busy CSX rail yard exists behind the facility (*courtesy Michael B. Robbins*).

lantic Coast Line and Louisville & Nashville railroads for 999 years in 1925. The new owners organized the Clinchfield Railroad Company, which ran the route independently of them for 57 years, although it wore Family Lines logo and paint in its latter free years. The autonomy vanished as L&N and ACL survivor Seaboard Coast Line became Seaboard System (1982) and CSX Transportation (1986).

Georgia Railroad

Formed: December 21, 1833

Headquarters: Athens, Georgia (1833); Augusta, Georgia (1840)

Précis: In 1833, James Camak led a cluster of Athenians to invest in a rail line linking their hamlet with Augusta. When, three years hence, a lateral banking venture overtook haulage by producing greater revenues, Georgia Railroad Company altered its appellation to Georgia Railroad & Banking Company. The 39-mile road completed in 1841 linked endpoints with horses pulling cars along tracks. Steam-driven locomotives replaced the livestock in 1847. By 1840, meanwhile, ownership was wrested from the Athenians and shifted into the hands of Augustans. Notably the then-prospering venture built a 171-mile mainline from Augusta to the state capital at Atlanta (1845). Travelers relied on it heavily to access both cities. The route became crucial to a through line linking Charleston and Memphis. In 1878, Georgia Railroad acquired a stem to Macon off its main. With subsequent investments in the Atlanta & West Point Railroad and Western Railway of Alabama, the carrier morphed into a vibrant regional system extending the breadth of the Peach State to Montgomery, state capital of neighboring Alabama, and beyond to Selma.

Route Mileage: 525

Mainline: Augusta to Atlanta

Name Trains: *Georgia Cannonball*

Logo: Wheel (truck) assembly linking name and that of two partner carriers

Dominant Colors: Unknown

Motto: *Safety — Courtesy — Service*

Passenger Service End: Georgia Railroad's charter specified daily except Sunday passenger service. Attorneys counseled management to provide it on all routes to escape a charter violation. It may have left it the final carrier to run mixed (freight-passenger) trains in the 48 contiguous states well into the Amtrak epoch.

Disposition: In 1881, Georgia Railroad was leased for 99 years to William M. Wadley, Central of Georgia Railway president, who assigned it jointly to CofG and Louisville & Nashville Railroad. In 1898, financially strapped CofG sold its half-interest to L&N, which reassigned that half to Atlantic Coast Line Railroad (1899). In three years ACL controlled L&N (1902). Maintaining its separate identity, Georgia Railroad was touted as a unit of the "Family Lines System" after 1972. The carrier folded into Seaboard Coast Line Industries, Inc., a decade hence, netting CSX Transportation in 1986. Georgia Railroad & Banking Company, meanwhile, is today in real estate development, owning many properties along its ex-rail lines.

Kansas City Southern Railway

Formed: 1897

Headquarters: Kansas City, Missouri

Précis: The KCS originated with the Kansas City Suburban Belt Railway in 1887. Visionary Arthur E. Stilwell had still bolder dreams—a north-south route to the Gulf of Mexico to haul grain, coal, lumber, and more minerals. His Kansas City, Pittsburg & Gulf Railroad connected Kansas City with Port Arthur, Texas, in 1897, with the name altered to Kansas City Southern Railway by 1900. When KCS bought the Louisiana & Arkansas Railway (1939), it gained links with New Orleans and Dallas and from Shreveport to Minden, Louisiana, and Hope, Arkansas. KCS ran a luxury consist daily between Kansas City and New Orleans (1940–1969) as part of its passenger traffic. In the post-travelers' era, it acquired MidSouth Rail Corporation, extending its reach to Meridian, Mississippi; Tuscaloosa and Birmingham, Alabama; and Counce, Tennessee, with trackage rights to Gulfport, Mississippi (1994). The next year KCS entered a pact with a Mexican operator that led to a wholly-owned ancillary, Kansas City Southern de Mexico (2005). A line from Kansas City to East St. Louis, Illinois, was added in 2001, and KCS took a half-interest in the Panama Canal Railway Company (2002).

Route Mileage: 6,000 (including 2,700 outside the U.S.)

Mainlines: Kansas City to Port Arthur, Texas, and New Orleans to Dallas, the pair crossing at Shreveport, providing a choice of directions

Name Trains: *Flying Crow, Hustler, Shreveporter, Southern Belle*

Logo: Eight-sided shield bearing company name and colors

Dominant Colors: Red and white

Mottos: *Route of the Flying Crow, Route of the Southern Belle*

Passenger Service End: November 2, 1969

Disposition: "The people of KCS wear labels such as 'scrappy,' 'ambitious,' 'entrepreneurial' and 'independent' like badges of honor," KCS publicists profess. Sidestepping formidable odds, the non-conventional bit player among massive Class 1 carriers savors its independency, demonstrating so frequently.

Missouri Pacific Railroad

Formed: March 12, 1849

Headquarters: St. Louis, Missouri

Précis: Pacific Railroad (original name) was chartered to "extend from St. Louis via Jefferson City to the western boundary of Missouri and thence to the Pacific Ocean." Through mergers, acquisitions, purchases and extended trackage rights it spread to a dozen states. Financial distress in 1872 netted restructuring and new taxonomy—Missouri Pacific (MoPac). Between 1892 and 1910, MoPac added Arkansas and Louisiana routes. In 1924, Gulf Coast Lines joined it providing a presence from the Rio Grande to the Mississippi and spawning passenger traffic from New Orleans to Houston. Some key freight terminals in Dixie were Baton Rouge, Little Rock, Memphis, New Orleans, Shreveport, and Texarkana. In 1976, the huge Texas & Pacific and Chicago & Eastern Illinois systems were folded into MoPac, extending its identity from Chicago to the far Southwest. The line refocused on "total transportation" in 1961, offering shippers multiple choices. Piggyback and containerized traffic, intermodal distribution centers and two trucking outfits augmented the mix.

Route Mileage: 12,000

Mainline: St. Louis to Kansas City, Missouri

Name Trains: *Delta Eagle, Houstonian, Missouri River Eagle, Orleanean, Ozarker, Rainbow Special, Southern Scenic, Sunshine Special, Texan, Texas Eagle*

Logo: Red circular seal with block name in white superimposed over tracks and crossties

Dominant Colors: Red, white and blue

Motto: *Route of the Eagles*

Passenger Service End: April 30, 1971

Disposition: In 1959, a holding company in cement fabrication that controlled auxiliaries producing and transmitting natural gas, Mississippi River Corporation, began buying MoPac stock. It gained voting control in 1962. Missouri Pacific Railroad merged into longtime arch-rival Union Pacific Railroad on January 1, 1997, with UPRR being the surviving corporation.

Norfolk Southern Railway

Formed: January 20, 1870

Headquarters: Norfolk, Virginia; Raleigh, North Carolina (from September 29, 1961)

Précis: The earliest antecedent of the original Norfolk Southern Railway—not to be mistaken for a Class 1 freight carrier formed by Norfolk & Western and Southern railways in 1982—was the Elizabeth City & Norfolk Railroad. A decade lapsed before construction began; its first revenue run on a 46-mile course was May 26, 1881. To embrace a southerly extension, its taxonomy was altered to Norfolk Southern Railroad on February 1, 1883. In receivership thrice (1889–1891, 1908–1910, 1932–1942), NS emerged stronger each time. Between 1889 and 1906, it expanded through mergers and acquisitions, gaining the Albemarle & Pantego; Norfolk, Virginia Beach & Southern; Chesapeake Transit; Washington & Plymouth; and four more short rail lines to create a route from Norfolk to Raleigh with stems to 10 nearby burgs. A nine-mile ferry at Albemarle Sound was the bane of otherwise unbroken track. That was remedied January 1, 1910, when the first train ran over a five-mile wooden trestle. In 1911, NS bought the Raleigh, Charlotte & Southern Railroad and four lesser carriers to gain access to a half-dozen Tar Heel cities. On December 1, 1913, its first train departed the state's largest metroplex, Charlotte, on a 622-mile main to Norfolk. Leasing the Durham & South Carolina Railroad on May 27, 1920, NS reached its trackage summit. In a final reorganization, its appellation was changed to Norfolk Southern Railway on January 21, 1942.

Route Mileage: 942

Mainline: Charlotte to Norfolk via Raleigh

Name Trains: *Carolina Golfer* (SAL all–Pullman consist with its last six miles on NS tracks to Pinehurst), *Midnight Express* (Raleigh–Norfolk)

Logo: Oval with *NS* in large caps in horizontal stripe center, *Norfolk Southern* above it, *Railway Co.* below it

Dominant Colors: Red and white

Motto: *East Carolina Dispatch*

Passenger Service End: January 31, 1948

Disposition: On January 1, 1974, NS was one of the final big buys by Southern Railway. Joined with Southern-owned Carolina & Northwestern Railroad, NS & C&N operated briefly under the NS handle. When SOU merged with Norfolk & Western Railway in 1982, the ancillary was relabeled Carolina & Northwestern Railway to free Norfolk Southern as a moniker for the new business that welded SOU and N&W rail systems.

Pennsylvania Railroad

Formed: April 13, 1846

Headquarters: Philadelphia, Pennsylvania

Précis: Although it would touch only the upper fringes of Dixie at Louisville, Norfolk (by steamer), Wheeling, and a few hamlets in the Virginias, the Pennsylvania directly affected most rail travelers between the Northeast and Southeast. Over its tracks a majority of consists from south Atlantic coastal states persisted above Washington, D.C. At the capital multiple lines converged with the Pennsy to finish the trek to Baltimore, Wilmington, Philadelphia, Newark and New York City. Thwarted in attempts to lay track in 1812, the "father of American railways" John Stevens didn't quit. After more failures, in the early 1830s, he put together a mix of rails and canals to connect Philadelphia with Harrisburg. But it took him to 1846 to get a state

Would you like the combo? Running north as PRR 126 at Baldwin, Pennsylvania, on September 7, 1965, this GG1 4933-led passenger consist began life many miles south. As the *Pelican*, SOU 42, part of it originated at Chattanooga. As the *Palmetto*, ACL 78, part commenced at Augusta. At Washington, D.C., the pair joined PRR's *Legislator* to form the trio combo *Legislator/Pelican/Palmetto* for the balance of the trek to New York City (*courtesy Chuck Blardone*).

charter, assigned under the Pennsylvania Railroad handle. In six years rails extended the breadth of the Keystone State to Pittsburgh (1852), providing an express link to an indispensable Ohio River channel, superhighway to the West. For a while the carrier was one of the nation's most powerful rail systems reaching far flung locales like Buffalo, Chicago, Cincinnati, Cleveland, Detroit, Indianapolis, Mackinaw City, New York City, Peoria, Rochester, and St. Louis.

Route Mileage: 12,000

Mainlines: New York City to Washington, D.C., via Philadelphia, with extensions via Pittsburgh to Chicago and St. Louis

Name Trains: *Broadway Limited, Cincinnati Limited, Colonial, Delmarva Express, Federal Express, Northern Arrow, South Wind*

Logo: Interlocking PRR buff-colored block letters on red emblem with buff striping just inside the edge

Dominant Colors: Red and buff (or white)

Mottos: *Standard Railroad of the World, Serving the Nation, Don't Stand Me Still!*

Passenger Service End: April 30, 1971

Disposition: Many saw the 1964 dismantling of New York's famed palace of grandeur, Pennsylvania Station, as symbolic of the decline and fall of a once great road. With ridership in decline, fortunes evaporating and onerous federal policies keeping unprofitable routes alive while favoring highway and airway lobbies, railroads were in a bad way. In 1968, two archenemies, Pennsy and New York Central, formed Penn Central which lost $2.8 million that year. PC declared bankruptcy after losing $325 million in 1970. On November 9, 1975, Conrail was derived from the tatters of Pennsy, New York Central, Lehigh Valley, Reading, Erie Lackawanna, and more. On June 1, 1999, Norfolk Southern and CSX acquired Conrail, NS gaining the largest share of Pennsy's ex-mainline.

Piedmont & Northern Railroad

Formed: 1909

Headquarters: Charlotte, North Carolina

Précis: When Southern Power and Utilities Company VP William Lee States proposed the firm expand into "an electrically powered interurban railway system linking the major cities of the Piedmont Carolinas," president James B. Duke liked it enough to give States carte blanche. Named the line's president, States led his agency to construct the road in two sections—from Charlotte west to Gastonia, North Carolina, and a longer run from Greenwood, South Carolina, north to Spartanburg via Greenville. A third section, never built, would have connected the segments and been part of a

master plan to extend the line southward to Atlanta and northward to Winston-Salem and Washington, D.C. It likely would have happened if an insistent Southern Railway hadn't arm-twisted the Interstate Commerce Commission, which denied P&N's application — even to hook its disjointed system together. P&N nevertheless hauled unfathomable tons of coal, cotton, paper, merchandise, fertilizer, grain, oil, gasoline and textiles along its routes. One of its mainstays on both segments was passengers, running up to eight trains in each direction daily, gradually paring to three or four.

Route Mileage: 150

Mainlines: Charlotte to Gastonia, North Carolina; Spartanburg to Greenwood, South Carolina

Name Trains: Numbered trains

Logo: White circle with Piedmont and Northern Lines at the top and The Great Electric System of the South at the bottom; separated from the words by a thin black circle, the center displayed a three-pronged voltage bolt

Dominant Colors: Black and white

Mottos: *Service with Courtesy, The Great Electric System of the South*

Passenger Service End: 1951

Disposition: When the electric locomotives competing against steam engines were all replaced with diesel power by 1954, some of the electrics were shipped to South America while others were scrapped. On July 1, 1969, P&N's operations were merged into the Seaboard Coast Line Railroad, ending P&N's service as a separate entity six decades after its conception.

Richmond, Fredericksburg & Potomac Railroad

Formed: February 25, 1834

Headquarters: Richmond, Virginia

Précis: The Richmond, Fredericksburg & Potomac Railroad bridge line retained a business identity and management cluster, yet wasn't autonomous for most of its life. It was the property of a half-dozen large carriers instead. Built to link Richmond, Virginia, with the Potomac River, it reached Quantico in 1842. Connecting with a trio of isolated lines it breached the gap to Washington, D.C., on the Potomac's north bank. The RF&P and Washington Southern Railway formed the Richmond-Washington Company on September 5, 1901. Operators included the rail systems Atlantic Coast Line, Baltimore & Ohio, Chesapeake & Ohio, Pennsylvania, Seaboard Air Line, and Southern. RF&P connected with almost every key northeastern and southeastern railroad, a geographic benefit that made it highly valuable. It carried an astonishing volume of passenger and freight traffic on heavy railed, thick ballasted double track. In the heyday of travel by train RF&P's consists north of Richmond's Broad Street Station were so frequent they were said to resemble streetcar movements. In the Second World War more than 100 such trains plied those tracks daily.

Route Mileage: 150

Mainline: Richmond to Washington, D.C.

Name Trains: Dozens of passenger consists of RF&P's six owner lines

Logo: Within a circle with full name of line in small caps at circle edge and 1834 at bottom of circle, an inner circle separates a tight RF&P in an uneven line with letters in bold caps, ampersand squeezed in below raised F and P

Dominant Colors: Blue and gray

Motto: *Capital Cities Route, Linking North and South*

Passenger Service End: Amtrak continues ferrying some of what the freight railroads discontinued

Disposition: Following multiple mergers the RF&P was acquired in total by CSX Transportation in 1991. CSX is the operating railroad of CSX Corporation, created in 1987 by the amalgamation of the Chessie and Seaboard systems. That pair was partially formed by joining the B&O, C&O, ACL, and SAL. After CSX acquired two-thirds of RF&P, Norfolk Southern Railway (SOU descendant) and Conrail (PRR heir) relinquished their RF&P interests.

Rock Island Railroad

Formed: February 27, 1847

Headquarters: Chicago, Illinois

Précis: When James Grant set plans in motion for a rail link between the Mississippi River port of Rock Island and the Illinois & Michigan Canal in LaSalle, Illinois, the Rock Island & LaSalle Railroad stood on the precipice of much more. Chicago was the terminus of the renamed Chicago & Rock Island Railroad in 1852. Through circuitous routing that fledgling system ultimately reached Dallas, Denver, El Paso, Houston, Minneapolis, St. Louis, and Waterloo. While the Rock Island hauled heavy tonnage over its freight rails through Arkansas and Louisiana, in the passenger arena a major consist trekked over Dixie tracks: the *Choctaw Rocket*, a daily prestige run, navigated the 761-mile Rock Island line from Memphis to Amarillo via Little Rock. Downgraded to secondary status in 1952, it chugged on as the *Choctaw Rockette*; the train was finally humiliated as unnamed #23–#24 in 1964, persisting to 1967. Undaunted, the carrier was one of six (others: Chicago South Shore & South Bend;

Denver & Rio Grande Western; Georgia; Reading; and Southern) to offer limited travel by train after Amtrak assumed most U.S. passenger service in 1971.

Route Mileage: Almost 8,000

Mainlines: Chicago to El Paso via St. Louis, Kansas City, and Tucumcari, New Mexico; Memphis to Tucumcari via Little Rock, Oklahoma City, and Amarillo; Chicago/St. Louis to Minneapolis

Name Trains: *Choctaw Rocket* (*Rockette*), *Corn Belt Rocket*, *Golden State Limited*, *Rocky Mountain Rocket* (later *Cornhusker*), *Twin Star Rocket*

Logo: Shield with white lettering reversed through red for edging border and reading Rock Island System within the border

Dominant Colors: Red and white (black and white where red wasn't available)

Motto: *The Road of Planned Progress ... Geared to the Nation's Future*

Passenger Service End: November 10, 1967 (Memphis–Little Rock–Amarillo)

Disposition: From the early 1980s, Canadian Pacific Rail helped a struggling Rock Island with loans, repaid by track sell-offs and CP's use of Rock Island rails. New alliances were forged with Southern Pacific, CP, Kansas City Southern and New York Central to boost bridge traffic and on-line industries. The Chicago, Rock Island & Pacific Railroad (full name) is now a key gateway to Los Angeles for eastern railroads and the same at Gulf ports for Midwest and Canadian carriers.

Southern Pacific Railroad

Formed: December 2, 1865

Headquarters: San Francisco, California

Précis: Big Four rail magnates Collis P. Huntington, Mark Hopkins, Leland Stanford, and Charles Crocker bought the promising Southern Pacific in 1868, just three years after Timothy Phelps and other enterprising capitalists launched it. Acquiring the Central Pacific Railroad and some profitable locomotive fabricators in 1870, SP was well positioned to put a stamp on the industry coast-to-coast. It linked Los Angeles and San Francisco by rail in 1876, and opened a second transcontinental route January 12, 1883. By 1932, it controlled the St. Louis–Southwestern Railway's mainline from St. Louis to Dallas with stems to Memphis and Shreveport. SP's greatest Dixie impact was its line between New Orleans and the West, a workhouse freight route to and from Gulf and Mississippi River ports. From 1893, the *Sunset Limited* ferried legions of travelers between the bayous and Pacific. With cars upgraded from wood to steel in 1924, and dieselized in 1950, it was purely sumptuous splendor on wheels.

Route Mileage: 9,000

Mainline: San Francisco to New Orleans via Los Angeles, El Paso and Houston

Name Trains: *Arizona Limited, City of San Francisco, Coast Daylight, Del Monte (Express), Golden State (Limited), Overland Limited, Starlight*

Logo: Blue and white circle with tracks protruding from center yellow sunburst; words in white reversed through blue reading Southern Pacific Lines

Dominant Colors: Blue and White

Mottos: *The Sunset Route, Route of the Daylights*

Passenger Service End: April 30, 1971

Disposition: Despite efforts to retain the Southern Pacific appellation, it faded. The Interstate Commerce Commission faulted conditions of a merger of SP and Santa Fe roads in 1984. The ICC sanctioned Santa Fe Pacific Corporation as a new name, deleting "Southern." When Rio Grande Industries bought the outfit October 13, 1988, it reinstituted "Southern Pacific." After Rio Grande fell on hard times, Union Pacific Railroad swept in, bought it (1996), and "Southern Pacific" vanished perhaps forever.

Tennessee Central Railway

Formed: June 1897

Headquarters: Nashville, Tennessee

Précis: Formed out of an uncompleted route, the Tennessee Central Railway led by Jere Baxter capitalized on precursor Alexander Crawford's work in launching the Nashville & Knoxville Railroad in March 1884. Even before it reached Nashville in April 1902, Baxter had already turned the attention west of town, reaching Ashland City 18 months hence. In four more months TC was extended to Hopkinsville, Kentucky, 95 miles northwest of Nashville, connecting there with the Illinois Central Railroad. The same year (1904) its eastern terminus moved to Harriman, Tennessee, gaining a crucial connection with Southern Railway to Knoxville there.

Route Mileage: 300

Mainline: Hopkinsville, Kentucky, to Harriman, Tennessee, via Nashville

Name Trains: Trains were generally numbered rather than named

Logo: Circle with interlocking initials TC inside thin circle in white, all reversed through black background

Dominant Colors: Black and white

Mottos: *The Nashville Route, The Route of Personal Service*

Passenger Service End: 1930 (Nashville–Hopkinsville), 1955 (Nashville–Harriman)

Disposition: Financial clouds hung forebodingly over the Tennessee Central following the Second World War. In spite of them, the Little Train That Could chugged along until it could withstand nothing more. In the mid 1950s, it borrowed nearly $5 million from the feds' Reconstruction Finance Corporation to improve rights-of-way. While that kept

Outside Nashville & Eastern's shops and offices at Lebanon, Tennessee, an ex–Broadway Dinner Train plies the tracks on December 6, 2008. Running in push-pull mode, it's now a tourist train for the Tennessee Central Railway Museum. Led by TCRX E8A 6902 with a lengthy rail heritage followed by TCRX F7B, at its opposite end is another F7B and F40PHR. Broadway Dinner Train, meanwhile, runs out of Nashville on a 1904 TC route (*courtesy Robert W. Thomson*).

the TC operating, the money wasn't repaid. In 1968, TC was bankrupt and $10 million in debt. Its tracks were sold to the Illinois Central (Nashville–Hopkinsville route), Louisville & Nashville (Nashville–Crossville), and Southern Railway (Crossville–Harriman). With equipment and property divided and sold, TC quietly passed from the scene on August 31, 1968.

Virginian Railway

Formed: April 15, 1907
Headquarters: Norfolk, Virginia
Précis: The Virginian was surely industrialist-philanthropist Henry Huttleston Rogers' zenith in a career in which the wealthy oilman multiplied his fortune by investing in minerals and mainlines. As sole financier, he sank $40 million into the Virginian to take advantage of West Virginia coal mining. His route from Deepwater to Tidewater led to ships that sailed the world. Zillions of tons of "black gold" rewarded Rogers handsomely, supplying 90 percent of the firm's haulage. By the 1930s, the Virginian's steam locomotives were among the planet's biggest, its engines on a 134-mile electrified segment that was the globe's most powerful, and its dock-loading capacity at Hampton Roads hit 10,800 tons an hour. From the coal fields to the Atlantic, its route was shortest, its grades easiest and its operating ratio lowest of any major U.S. carrier. The Virginian also ran a modest passenger service along its mainline and on some key stems. By 1935, that was reduced to "one antiquated train" said a reporter, adding: "If regulatory bodies would consent, even that train would not run." By then the line earned less than one percent of its revenues in passenger, mail and express arenas. When highways improved after the Second World War, its final people-mover disappeared.

Route Mileage: 600
Mainlines: Deepwater, West Virginia, to Norfolk, Virginia, via Roanoke
Name Trains: Numbered consists
Logo: Circle with Virginian at top and Railway at bottom separated by VGN; reversed through black in yellow with circle rings above and below words
Dominant Colors: Black and yellow
Motto: *Richest Little Railroad in the World*
Passenger Service End: Late 1940s
Disposition: The Virginian was merged into the Norfolk & Western Railway, a longtime bituminous coal-hauling rival, in 1959. The combination is said to be the start of a "modern era of major railroad mergers as the ICC came to accept that railroads needed to be able to compete successfully against other modes of transport rather than just against each other."

C: Amtrak

When a register of the 75 most-populous cities in the nation was compiled in 2009, drawn from mid-year 2008 U.S. Census Bureau figures, 62 metropolises were missing from the dozen states that are incorporated within the pages of this volume. (A dozen cities are in California while Texas accounts for another nine.) Just 13 of these municipalities are in Dixie. To some readers this may come as a revelation. In conjunction with it, perusing the 13 may offer a few eye-popping surprises. The data is based on findings surrounding those jurisdictions' effective corporate service limits and doesn't include any expanded or peripheral Metropolitan Statistical Areas. Ranked Dixie urban centers on the list of the topmost 75, along with their 2008 populations, are:

13	Jacksonville, Florida	807,815
18	Charlotte, North Carolina	687,456
19	Memphis, Tennessee	669,651
26	Nashville, Tennessee	596,462
30	Louisville, Kentucky	557,224
33	Atlanta, Georgia	537,958

42	Virginia Beach, Virginia	433,746
43	Miami, Florida	413,201
45	Raleigh, North Carolina	392,552
53	Tampa, Florida	340,882
59	New Orleans, Louisiana	311,853
65	Lexington, Kentucky	282,114
75	Greensboro, North Carolina	250,642

Of the 13 dominant metropolises below the Mason-Dixon Line, Amtrak passenger trains call at a station within 25 miles of all but three of the conurbations: Nashville, the nation's 26th largest city; Louisville, 30th; and Lexington, 65th. As this is prepared in late 2009, the remaining cities have access to at least one long-distance Amtrak train, most with daily service. Seven — Jacksonville, Charlotte, Virginia Beach, Miami, Raleigh, New Orleans, and Greensboro — are favored with multiple Amtrak arrivals every day.

Unrelated to this, although not inconsequential, there is no Amtrak passenger train service currently offered to five of Dixie's 12 state capitals: Alabama (Montgomery), Florida (Tallahassee), Kentucky

(Frankfort), Louisiana (Baton Rouge), and Tennessee (Nashville).

The table herewith provides a fuller picture of Amtrak's present service to Southern cities. It's based on the U.S. Census Bureau figures for July 1, 2008, the most current data available at the time this text is prepared. It embraces Amtrak's passenger train service in the dozen Southern states comprising this tome's concentration, including all of the cities with populations of 50,000 or more. Of 698 urban centers in the United States meeting that criteria on the date specified, 140 (20 percent or one in five) are situated in Dixie.

The compendium distinguishes which have access to an Amtrak rail station within 25 miles of their geographical location and which do not. The symbol (•) signifies no Amtrak passenger train service within a 25-mile radius. The symbol (‡) denotes a flag stop, meaning the train stops only on signal or advance notice to the conductor. Other symbols pertaining to specific situations in a few states are explained at the end of each list.

Alabama

Scheduled passenger train stops in Alabama:
Anniston, Birmingham, Tuscaloosa.

Auburn •	Huntsville •
Birmingham	Mobile •
Decatur •	Montgomery •
Dothan •	Tuscaloosa
Hoover (Birmingham)	

Arkansas

Scheduled passenger train stops in Arkansas:
Arkadelphia ‡, Little Rock, Malvern ‡, Walnut Ridge.

Conway (Little Rock)	North Little Rock
Fayetteville •	(Little Rock)
Fort Smith •	Pine Bluff •
Jonesboro (Walnut Ridge)	Rogers •
Little Rock	Springdale •

Florida

Scheduled passenger train stops in Florida:
Deerfield Beach, DeLand, Delray Beach, Fort Lauderdale, Hollywood, Jacksonville, Kissimmee, Lakeland, Miami, Okeechobee, Orlando, Palatka, Sanford, Sebring, Tampa, West Palm Beach, Winter Haven, Winter Park.

Boca Raton	Clearwater (Tampa)
(Deerfield Beach)	Coconut Creek
Boynton Beach	(Deerfield Beach)
(Delray Beach)	Coral Springs
Bradenton • § ¶	(Deerfield Beach)
Cape Coral •	North Port •
Davie (Hollywood)	Ocala • #
Daytona Beach	Orlando
(DeLand)	Palm Bay •
Deerfield Beach	Palm Coast •
Delray Beach	Pembroke Pines
Deltona (DeLand)	(Hollywood)
Fort Lauderdale	Pensacola •
Fort Myers • § ¶	Plantation
Gainesville • #	(F. Lauderdale)
Hialeah (Miami)	Pompano Beach
Hollywood	(Deerfield Beach)
Homestead (Miami)	Port Orange
Jacksonville	(DeLand)
Kissimmee	Port St. Lucie •
Lakeland ¶	St. Petersburg
Largo (Tampa)	(Tampa) § ¶
Lauderhill	Sanford (DeLand)
(F. Lauderdale)	Sarasota • § ¶
Margate	Sunrise
(Deerfield Beach)	(F. Lauderdale)
Melbourne •	Tallahassee •
Miami	Tampa ¶
Miami Beach	Wellington
Miami Gardens	(W. Palm Beach)
Miramar	·Weston
(Hollywood)	(F. Lauderdale)
North Miami	West Palm Beach
(Hollywood)	

 # Daily Thruway Motorcoach service is provided between Jacksonville and Lakeland, connecting with the Silver Star in both directions.

§ These cities are linked to the Silver Star daily at Tampa via Thruway Motorcoach service.

¶ These cities are linked to the Silver Meteor daily at Orlando via Thruway Motorcoach service.

Georgia

Scheduled passenger train stops in Georgia:
Atlanta, Gainesville, Jesup, Savannah, Toccoa ‡.

Albany •	Macon •
Athens •	Marietta (Atlanta)
Atlanta	Roswell (Atlanta)
Augusta •	Sandy Springs
Columbus •	(Atlanta)
Johns Creek	Savannah
(Atlanta)	Warner Robins*

Kentucky

Scheduled passenger train stops in Kentucky:
Ashland, Fulton ‡, Maysville, South Portsmouth/South Shore.

Bowling Green •	Louisville • #
Lexington •	Owensboro •

 # Daily Thruway Motorcoach service is provided between Louisville and Chicago.

Louisiana

Scheduled passenger train stops in Louisiana:
Hammond, Lafayette, Lake Charles, New Iberia ‡,
New Orleans, Schriever ‡, Slidell ‡.

Baton Rouge • #	Lake Charles
Bossier City • #	Monroe •
Kenner (New Orleans)	New Orleans
Lafayette	Shreveport • #

*# Daily Thruway Motorcoach service is provided be-
tween Baton Rouge and New Orleans, connecting with
the* Sunset Limited *and* City of New Orleans *but not
the* Crescent. *Similar service is provided between Shreveport (near Bossier City) and Longview, Texas, connecting
with the* Texas Eagle.

Mississippi

Scheduled passenger train stops in Mississippi:
Brookhaven ‡, Greenwood, Hattiesburg, Hazlehurst
‡, Jackson, Laurel, McComb ‡, Meridian, Picayune,
Yazoo City ‡.

Gulfport •	Jackson
Hattiesburg	

North Carolina

**Scheduled passenger train stops in North Car-
olina:** Burlington, Cary, Charlotte, Durham, Fayetteville, Gastonia, Greensboro, Hamlet, High Point,
Kannapolis, Raleigh, Rocky Mount, Salisbury,
Selma/Smithfield, Southern Pines, Wilson.

Asheville •	Greensboro
Burlington	Greenville •
Cary	High Point
Chapel Hill (Durham)	Jacksonville •
Charlotte	Raleigh
Concord (Kannapolis)	Rocky Mount
Durham	Wilmington •
Fayetteville	Winston-Salem
Gastonia	(High Point) #

*# Twice daily Thruway Motorcoach service is provided
between Winston-Salem and High Point, connecting at
the latter city with the* Carolinian *and* Piedmont *in both
directions.*

South Carolina

**Scheduled passenger train stops in South Car-
olina:** Camden, Charleston, Clemson, Columbia,
Denmark, Dillon, Florence, Greenville, Kingstree,
Spartanburg, Yemassee.

Charleston	North Charleston
Columbia	(Charleston)
Greenville	Rock Hill (Charlotte)
Mount Pleasant	
(Charleston)	

Tennessee

Scheduled passenger train stops in Tennessee:
Memphis, Newbern/Dyersburg ‡.

Chattanooga •	Knoxville •
Clarksville •	Memphis
Franklin •	Murfreesboro •
Jackson •	Nashville •
Johnson City •	

Virginia

Scheduled passenger train stops in Virginia:
Alexandria, Ashland, Charlottesville, Clifton Forge,
Culpeper, Danville, Franconia/Springfield, Freder-
icksburg, Lynchburg, Manassas, Newport News,
Petersburg, Quantico, Richmond, Staunton, Wil-
liamsburg, Woodbridge.

Alexandria	Portsmouth
Arlington (Alexandria)	(Newport News)
Chesapeake	Richmond
(Newport News)	Roanoke •
Hampton	Suffolk
(Newport News)	(Newport News)
Lynchburg	Virginia Beach
Newport News	(Newport News)
Norfolk	
(Newport News)	

West Virginia

**Scheduled passenger train stops in West Vir-
ginia:** Alderson ‡, Charleston, Hinton, Huntington,
Montgomery, Prince, Thurmond ‡.

Charleston

A modern Web site offers a separate study of
large U.S. cities where Amtrak service is noticeably
absent: http://en.wikipedia.org/wiki/List_of_ma
jor_cities_in_U.S._lacking_Amtrak_service. Data
was amassed by an independent researcher and encompasses not only residents within city limits but
regional business centers as well. Presumably the
territory approximates each city's Metropolitan
Statistical Area. Findings support many already
presented. Five American megaplexes, for instance — each with more than a million inhabitants
in their retail-commercial districts — aren't served
by Amtrak trains: Phoenix, Arizona, with a metro
population of 4.2 million; Las Vegas, Nevada, 1.8
million; Columbus, Ohio, 1.7 million; Nashville,
Tennessee, 1.5 million; and Louisville, Kentucky,
1.2 million. The latter two are, of course, in Dixie.

The most stunning revelation of the inquiry,
nevertheless, is that — of 63 U.S. metropolitan centers with at least 100,000 denizens having no Amtrak rail service — a disproportionate 27 (43 percent) are situated below the Mason-Dixon Line.

They aren't in less densely populated Western territories where one might anticipate finding them. In addition to 22 cities already on the earlier state lists (above), five more Dixie megaplexes can be added that never hear the shrill of a passenger train whistle: Florence/Muscle Shoals, Alabama; Myrtle Beach, South Carolina; Tri-Cities, Tennessee; Tupelo, Mississippi; and Wheeling, West Virginia. It's a reality that's conceivably tough for a Southern railfan to digest.

D: Museums and Exhibitions (by State)

Here you will find a representative sampling of the numerous museums and exhibitions in the South pertaining to railroads, some housing artifacts, photographs, model train layouts, tools and a wide range of supplementary memorabilia. Many of these collections are displayed in vintage turn-of-the-century depots, stations and terminals that have been painstakingly refurbished to their original forms and furnished with period pieces by volunteers committed to preserving the past.

You'll also find a representative number of excursion trains, dinner trains, drama/comedy/mystery/music trains, scenic trains and the like; railway gift shops; hotels, restaurants and resorts with railroad themes; restored locomotives (steam, diesel and diesel-electric) and a plethora of rolling stock (passenger coaches, dining cars, sleepers, baggage cars, dome cars, tavern-lounge cars, observation cars, office cars, freight cars, cabooses, etc.); and a mixture of railroad equipment.

It isn't an exhaustive list—for indeed, there are hundreds of railroad "museums" across Dixie (even though some may be nominal collections in vintage cabooses, those old relics parked on a siding, for example).

A disclaimer is in order: when this material was gathered in 2009, the schedules, hours, services, fares, telephone numbers and addresses were believed to be correct. Any part of that may have changed.

Before presenting the list, the author offers a few personal reflections about these modern quests with the rails of yesteryear.

I would be remiss in leading you to think I've experienced many of these outfits personally. I have not. Most of what I'm sharing has come through research.

Those exhibits that I have visited verified and enlivened my research. Beyond those generalizations, I submit that modern interpretation of the realities of the Southern railroads differs significantly from the historical perspective.

At one Dixieland exhibit, for instance, sweeping calligraphy on a descriptive board informs visitors that—while the railroads maintained separate passenger cars for the dual races in *other* parts of the country (italics mine)—this was not the practice in the South where skin tones didn't prevent patrons from sitting together. Anyone who has to any degree studied trains running below the Mason-Dixon Line from the latter decades of the 19th century through the early decades of the 20th knows differently: the opposite is true. Contradicting that very statement, not five yards distant within the walls of the depot where that sign is displayed is another reading "Colored Waiting Room" at the portal to that distinct provision.

Along the way I've ridden a few excursion trains and had dinner aboard one. That experience was so elegant it reminded me of nothing I had ever witnessed in the day of ACL, L&N, SAL or Southern dining cars or of the china-plate Amtrak service that's gone forever. The ambience was unparalleled, while the food was exquisite and the service superb. I've also spent a night at a railroad hotel, one converted from one of the more infamous historic depots of yesteryear. To a railfan, what could compare?

These attractions draw people of wide-ranging interests. Aside from the lifelong railfans, as well as those eager to "remember when" by visiting a vintage train or museum—there are also the younger generations who pass through the doors. Many are school-age children (by the bus-loads they arrive!) and their knowledge of the past is extensively broadened through their visits. Americana as they never experienced it is on display!

Alabama

HEART OF DIXIE RAILROAD MUSEUM— Calera

The Calera & Shelby Railroad (C&S) operates on a portion of ex–Louisville & Nashville Railroad (L&N) tracks established by the L&N as an Alabama mineral branch line in 1891. Historically the stem was responsible for hauling zillions of tons of raw materials from nearby quarries to steel mill furnaces in that burgeoning industry in Birmingham. The city was branded "The Pittsburgh of the South" for its heavy investment in the trade.

Today the C&S offers hour-long excursion trips aboard passenger cars fabricated between 1910 and

1955, and pulled by first generation diesel electric locomotives. Passengers board at a refurbished turn-of-the-century depot and ride through picturesque Shelby County forests to Springs Junction, then return to the Calera station over the same route.

Cited as the "official" railroad museum for the state of Alabama, Heart of Dixie exhibits artifacts and other train memorabilia in the restored depot. There is a railway gift shop, too. In a rail yard outdoors visitors inspect several pieces of rolling stock (locomotives and cars) and railway equipment. Fares are modestly priced, children's rates based on age, while higher-priced rides with limited availability are offered in locomotives and cabooses.

The Shelby & Southern Railroad, meanwhile, a two-foot narrow gauge fire-breathing steam locomotive, pulls families (most often) on quarter-hour adventures through the museum's grounds. This little engine that could formerly ferried visitors through Birmingham Zoo property. Fares are kept low to attract riders. On both train routes anyone two and under rides free.

The museum's usual operating schedule is Tuesday through Saturday, 9 A.M. to 4 P.M., from mid March through mid December. It's also open Sundays on specified occasions (e.g. Easter, Steam Days, Father's Day, Halloween, Christmas, and similar events).

Of special interest to historians and railway addicts is the W. A. Boone Memorial Railroad Library. It's a storehouse of railroad print including art, books, periodicals and sundry materials. The library is housed separately in the Woodlawn Depot. The Heart of Dixie Museum acquired that facility in 2000, transporting it to its own site for library use. Operating hours, independent of the museum itself, are 10 A.M. to 4 P.M. Thursday and Saturday.

The Heart of Dixie Railroad Museum is a nonprofit, all-volunteer organization and proceeds from sales and donations are channeled into its operations, preservation and restoration of equipment. Fares in 2009 for the one-hour Calera & Shelby ride were $12 for adults, $8 for children 2–11, $30 in the locomotive cab and $20 in the caboose. The quarter-hour Shelby & Southern fare, regardless of age for 2 and above, was $3. For detailed information about excursion dates and times, which vary widely, contact the museum at Box 727, Calera, AL 35040, visit it at 1919 9th Street, Calera, telephone (205) 668-3435 or (800) 943-4490, or go online to http://www.hodrrm.org.

NORTH ALABAMA RAILROAD MUSEUM, INC.— Huntsville

In the latter decades of the 19th century, Chase Nurseries rose to some prominence, eventually becoming a leader in its industry. When a Chase sibling traveled by rail through northeastern Alabama in the 1880s, he was impressed that it offered an excellent growing season as well as railway traffic in four directions, of consequence to shippers. Early in the 20th century, Chase bought some property there and erected a small depot. The community, northeast and adjacent to Huntsville, applied his name as its location. In 1937, the Chase clan replaced the original fixture with a new depot, now the centerpiece of the North Alabama Railroad Museum, Inc. (NARM). In recent decades the all-volunteer outfit signed a long-term lease with Madison County to maintain the depot. NARM's purpose is to preserve and enhance the railroadiana of north Alabama and south central Tennessee.

In the early 1990s, NARM secured a five-mile section of track that originally was on a branch of the Nashville, Chattanooga & St. Louis Railway, later absorbed by the Louisville & Nashville Railroad (now CSX Corporation). Train rides over the route (full round-trip 10 miles) are available on certain Saturdays plus annual holiday runs at Easter, Mother's Day, Father's Day, Halloween, Christmas, and other occasions. The line is named the Mercury and Chase Railroad after a couple of stations along the way.

The passenger train is but a portion of NARM's offerings. Volunteers are customarily present on Wednesdays and Saturdays between 9 A.M. and 2 P.M. to answer questions and process train ticket requests. The museum in the Chase Depot is open every day between 9 A.M. and 4 P.M. all year long and at other times by special appointment. Visitors examine, film and photograph historic rail equipment. They can take a self-guided tour any time or a guided tour on train days. Fees are nominal — and none for the self-guided tour although the museum welcomes donations.

Patrons can inspect several pieces of rolling stock: a Railway Post Office car, heavyweight day coach, 1914 diner, Pullman sleeper, and Southern Railway caboose. The building itself is touted as "the smallest union depot in the country." During the heyday of passenger rail traffic, two lines passed within a few feet of the tiny station: Southern Railway (now part of Norfolk Southern Railroad) generated major traffic through Chase on its Chattanooga–Memphis route. The NC&StL (later L&N) ran a connection past Chase north to the mainline at Dechard, Tennessee, and south to Gadsden, Alabama, facilitated by a ferry on the Tennessee River between Hobbs Island and Guntersville that breached a gap where no rail existed.

NARM's street address is 694 Chase Road, Huntsville, Alabama; its mailing address is Box 4163, Huntsville, AL 35815-4163; telephone (256) 851-6276; with details about the museum, train schedule, rates, etc., on its Web site: http://www.northalabamarailroadmuseum.com/welcome.htm.

STEVENSON RAILROAD DEPOT MUSEUM — Stevenson

Exhibiting history pertaining to Stevenson's participation in the War Between the States, this attraction rests between the tracks of a couple of railroads of the past: Nashville & Chattanooga and Memphis & Charleston. Those lines met at a single depot built around 1852, the antecedent of the present station where the museum is located, erected in 1872. The original may have met its fate during the Civil War.

The contemporary museum's focus goes well beyond railroading's past, nonetheless. It includes artifacts that pertain to Native American and pioneer life, the Civil War, plus more recent historical events. The facility is included on the National Register of Historic Places.

While a "Depot Days" festival is scheduled every June in Stevenson, its name might be misleading to the more obsessive, passionate railfan. The special occasion simply embraces a whole lot more than mere railways. In what appears to be a bow to publicity, a source acknowledges: "The celebration includes many different aspects of the southern town's culture and celebrates the great things that Stevenson represents. The week-long celebration is concluded with a parade, a day full of activities, and a street dance in the middle of Downtown Stevenson."

The museum, at 207 West Main Street, maintains a mailing address of Box 894, Stevenson, AL 35772, telephone (256) 437-3012, and a Web site at http://www.stevensondepotmuseum.com/. Currently the structure is open from 8 A.M. to 4 P.M. Monday through Friday.

Arkansas

ARKANSAS & MISSOURI RAILROAD EXCURSIONS — Fort Smith, Springdale, Van Buren, Winslow

From an operator's stance the greatest thing about this railway passenger road is the income it generates, which is icing on the cake to subsidize its main revenue-producer: freight. The 140-mile Arkansas & Missouri Railroad (A&M), acquired from the Burlington Northern Railroad in 1986, is one of a handful of U.S. lines with freight and passenger service still coexisting. Collaborating with a trio of Class 1 rail interchanges (Burlington Northern Santa Fe, Kansas City Southern, Union Pacific), the Class 3 Arkansas & Missouri Railroad hauls goods of 150-plus permanent customers to and from regional, national and international points. The tariffs for passenger excursions are steep nevertheless, reminding railfans it's a for-profit enterprise.

Running along a scenic corridor between Fort Smith, Arkansas, and Monett, Missouri, the A&M traverses the mountains and valleys of northwestern Arkansas ("The Natural State"). Over trestles with distant views and through a quarter-mile tunnel, the journey ferries patrons to the top of the picturesque Boston Mountains of the Ozark Range and down to the Arkansas River Basin. Trip lengths vary seasonally and multiple classes of service are offered. At least one all-day excursion calls for a three-hour layover at Van Buren so riders can peruse the historic town and buy lunch while there. Special trips are added to the schedule for certain holidays and other occasional observances and events.

The A&M may be contacted at 107 North Commercial Street, Springdale, AR 72764; telephone (800) 687-8600 or (501) 751-8600; and its schedule and pricing data are available at http://www.arkansasmissouri-rr.com/.

ARKANSAS RAILROAD MUSEUM — Pine Bluff

A contemporary Web site ostensibly unrelated to the Arkansas Railroad Museum considers it "an upper-level railroad preservation facility." Operated by the Cotton Belt Rail Historical Society volunteers, the attraction is open Monday through Saturday from 9 A.M. to 3 P.M. and on Sunday afternoon by appointment. Railfans love it when endeavors like this proffer no admission fee, yet a monetary gift is anticipated from every visitor. "Cotton Belt Route," incidentally, was the popular common name of the St. Louis–Southwestern Railway (SSW) back in the day.

A collection of railroad equipment is on display at the Pine Bluff venue at 1700 Port Road. It includes a steam locomotive fabricated at the line's Pine Bluff shops in 1942. That engine saw a dozen years of active service before diesels overtook it. More than a score of vintage rolling stock are on display, most open for inspection ("the centerpiece of the museum," claims another Web site). A handful of cabooses are of special interest. "The variety of ages gives a good retrospective on the evolution of technology," a source observed. There are dual steam locomotives, multiple diesels, a myriad of added cars, and sundry pieces of equipment that include a seldom seen snow plow.

The museum's allure extends to a plethora of railroad artifacts—historical items from carriers traversing the tracks of "The Natural State" being particularly emphasized—and a full scale replica of a railway station's interior. There's also a railroad gift emporium. Situated in the SSW's chief steam locomotive shops built between 1882 and 1894, the museum prevails where construction, repairs and refurbishing occurred for many decades. The property, now owned by successor Union Pacific Railroad, is leased to the city of Pine Bluff.

A Railroadiana Model Train Exposition is conducted by the society at the museum the first Sat-

American Locomotive Company fabricated this steamer as a coal-burner in 1904, later retrofitted with an oil-burning engine. With an international ambience in its storied past, the 2-6-0 locomotive plied tracks beside the Panama Canal before pulling excursion trains at Eureka Springs, Arkansas. It's just returned from a single-car dinner trip on June 7, 1997, here (*courtesy Clyde Woodruff*).

urday of April every year unless that weekend is Easter. When that happens, it's set for a different date. The organization may be reached by telephone at (870) 535-8819 or contacted by e-mail at arkr-rmus@seark.net or on the Web at http://www.geo cities.com/TheTropics/8199/cb819.html. The Cotton Belt Rail Historical Society publishes a quarterly newsletter.

EUREKA SPRINGS & NORTH ARKANSAS RAILWAY — Eureka Springs

Established in 1981, this for-profit passenger tourist railway runs along 2.5 miles of restored track right-of-way. The route was once owned by the Arkansas & Ozarks Railway Company, the final embodiment of the North Arkansas Line. The original was chartered at the site in 1882 as the Eureka Springs Railway, continuing from that hamlet to Seligman, Missouri. The road's history can be traced through a succession of rail carriers: St. Louis & North Arkansas (1899), Missouri & North Arkansas (1906), Missouri & Arkansas (1935), and Arkansas & Ozarks (1949), ending with the latter in 1961. At its peak the North Arkansas Line reached 360 miles between Helena, Arkansas, and Joplin, Missouri. In addition, the Eureka Springs depot, constructed in 1913, is a repository for scores of railroadiana items.

"Rain or shine," this attraction's promotions reveal, you'll be taken on "a nostalgic 4.5-mile ride through the hills of the Ozarks" aboard the Eureka Springs & North Arkansas Railway's excursion. Running April through October daily except Sunday and

Monday (as well as Sundays on Memorial Day and Labor Day weekends), 45-minute trips depart four times daily, subject to passenger minimums. Adult fares ($12 in 2009) are knocked down to half that for kids ages 4 to 10 and free to younger children when accompanied by an adult. An hour-long lunch train at noon and an hour-and-a-half dinner train at 5 P.M. plow the same course. Web site reviews submitted by tourists who have taken these trips appear to contrast markedly with one another.

Visitors to the Eureka Springs property witness numerous exhibits that include a restored turntable, handcar, vintage locomotives and rolling stock, and an automobile outfitted for rail travel. There's a gift shop inside the depot, too. Located at 299 North Main Street, the adventure maintains a mailing address of Box 310, Eureka Springs, AR 72632, telephone (479) 253-9623, and Web address www.esnarailway.com/.

Florida

CENTRAL FLORIDA RAILROAD MUSEUM — Winter Garden

The Tavares & Gulf Railroad (T&G) depot at Winter Garden, built in 1913, is the site of the Central Florida Railroad Museum. Back in the day the T&G interchanged with the Seaboard Air Line Railroad (SAL) at Tavares and the Atlantic Coast Line Railroad (ACL) at Winter Garden. After the SAL purchased the T&G in 1926, the smaller carrier continued to be identified under its own taxonomy.

The appellation persisted until the T&G was ultimately absorbed into the Seaboard Coast Line Railroad (SCL) in 1969, following a merger of the ACL and SAL two years earlier. The depot continued to provide an office for an SCL freight agent to 1978.

During the transitions the Central Florida Chapter of the National Railway Historical Society was organized in 1970. In 1979, the non-profit group bought the depot from SCL and began restoring it to its original specifications. The museum at 101 South Boyd Street in Winter Garden is currently open daily from 1 to 5 P.M. It exhibits artifacts pertaining to central Florida railroad history. A large collection of dining car china and silver service is of particular interest to many railfans. A Clinchfield Railroad caboose and tri-head interlocking signal from the ACL-SAL junction at Plant City, Florida, is displayed outside the depot-museum.

The Central Florida Chapter occasionally offers railroad excursions in conjunction with Florida Rail Adventures at Eustis, Florida. The chapter may be accessed at telephone (407) 656-0559 or Web address http://www.cfcnrhs.org/. Its meetings, the second Monday of each month at 7 P.M. at the depot, are open to the public.

DAVID BROWNING RAILROAD MUSEUM — Palatka

The David Browning Railroad Museum houses a model train layout depicting rail traffic in and around Palatka, Florida, during the era's halcyon days. This 30 × 25-foot room is part of a larger preservation operation staged by the Palatka Railroad Preservation Society since 1993. Artifacts are exhibited in a historic joint railway depot built by the Atlantic Coast Line Railroad to serve its trains and those of partner Florida East Coast Railway. Today the facility serves two Amtrak trains (*Silver Meteor, Silver Star*) passing through Palatka daily between south Florida and the Northeast. It's also on the National Register of Historic Places.

A section of the depot is reserved for the "Railrodeo" created by Irvin P. Saylor, billed as the "World's Largest Mobile HO Scale Model Railroad" since it began touring the East Coast in 1975. Each October the museum presents a two-day Railfest that draws many people to renew their ties with railroading of the past or to cultivate a new interest in the field. At the same time it exposes the purposes and accomplishments of the operation's volunteers to a wider audience. There is no admission charge and free parking is available for the Railfest as well viewing the museum any time.

The museum, on Palatka's Reid Street in the station at 220 North 11th Street, may be contacted at (386) 328-0305, or online at http://www.railsof palatka.org.

FLORIDA GULF COAST RAILROAD MUSEUM — Parrish

In 1903, the Seaboard Air Line Railroad (SAL) began operating a subsidiary, the Florida & West Indies Railroad and Steamship Company, along the Gulf coast. Two years afterward this ancillary unit became the SAL's Sarasota Branch. For the first time Tampa was connected with some of the rising coastal tourist cities below it including Bradenton, Sarasota and Venice. Today along a half-dozen miles of ex–SAL track in Manatee County the Florida Gulf Coast Railroad Museum —founded in 1981— runs a heritage excursion railroad. The weekend trips have been available since 1992. There are also special occasions announced throughout the year. In addition the line's caboose is available for chartering small private parties and the whole train may be chartered for larger family and corporate events.

The attraction's "Be the Engineer" program appeals to many who travel great distances for a shot at literally driving the train. Candidates take a training course and then control the 1,500-horsepower locomotive for an hour. The museum allows those who are qualified (age 18 and above, who possess a valid driver's license and are physically capable of climbing into the engine cab) to run the train, clang the bell, and blow the whistle on an authentic locomotive.

The museum is open every Saturday and Sunday excluding a two-week break at Christmas and New Year's Day. The train runs rain-or-shine on a 13-mile 90-minute course. The current round-trip schedule calls for departures from Parrish at 11 A.M. and 2 P.M. The museum at 12210 83rd Street East, Parrish, may be contacted at mailing address Box 355, Parrish, FL 34219, telephone (877) 869-0800 or (941) 776-0906, or Web site address http://www. frrm.org/. Museum admission in 2009 was $10 for adults, $6 for children, and excursion train rides were $20 for adults, $16 for children.

FLORIDA RAIL ADVENTURES — Eustis

One of Florida Rail Adventures' most recently advertised draws is visitors can "ride Florida's Movie Train behind our 1907 Baldwin steam engine as featured in the movie hit *3:10 to Yuma*." That alone separates the excursion headquartered in Eustis from its competitors, all of whom constantly seek a larger share of the pie. Like some others this attraction offers a murder mystery express (Thursday and Friday, 6 P.M.), a dinner train (Saturday, 6 P.M.), plus seasonal and children's specials. At times multiple trains run throughout the day on Saturday and on Sunday through Wednesday nights. The *Mt. Dora Meteor*, departing from Mt. Dora, Florida, operates with multiple trains daily Wednesday through Sunday.

Current schedules are posted at the attraction's Web site at http://railflorida.com/. Rail Florida Adventures is located at 51 West Magnolia Avenue, Eustis, FL 32726, telephone (352) 589-4300. Ticket office hours are daily except Sunday from 10 A.M. to noon and 1 to 4 P.M.

GOLD COAST RAILROAD MUSEUM — Miami

In 1957, a handful of Miamians dedicated themselves to attempting to preserve some of Florida's history that was rapidly slipping away. Together they established the non-profit Gold Coast Railroad Museum. They were fortunate to acquire some abandoned property of the Naval Air Station at Richmond, which — with three miles of tracks — evolved into an ideal spot for exhibiting a railway collection.

The centerpiece of that collection is unquestionably the Ferdinand Magellan presidential rail car, the only such train fabricated in the 20th century (1928, Pullman Company). Refurbished in 1942, it transported U.S. chief executives Franklin D. Roosevelt, Harry S Truman, Dwight D. Eisenhower, and — during whistle-stop campaigning — Ronald Reagan. Ceiling escape hatches in the observation room and the presidential bathroom invariably fascinate tourists. Yet another important "find" in Gold Coast's collection of more than vintage engines, dining, sleeping and vista cars sitting on a half-mile of track is Florida East Coast Railway steam locomotive #153. This is the engine sent to fetch the stranded rescue train that encountered the devastating hurricane in the Keys in September 1935, the disaster ending the Overseas Railroad of the Florida East Coast Railway.

Patrons can hop aboard coaches, locomotive cabs and narrow gauge track for weekend train rides. Fares are reasonably priced. Numerous special events are also scheduled constantly, particularly appealing to families with young children. A schedule of these events is available on the attraction's Web site normally several weeks in advance. Of particular interest is a model railroad exhibit featuring multiple gauges of model trains and a "hands on" model railroad exhibit that draws juveniles. The property is also available for private parties, personal and business gatherings, group tours and field trips.

Located at 12450 S.W. 152nd Street, Miami, FL 33177-1402, the Gold Coast Railroad Museum may be contacted by telephone at (888) 608-7246 or (305) 253-0063 or online at http://www.gcrm.org/. Operating hours, except for major U.S. holidays, are currently 10 A.M. to 4 P.M. Tuesday, Wednesday and Friday; 10 A.M. to 7 P.M. Thursday; and 11 A.M. to 4 P.M. Saturday and Sunday. The attraction is closed Monday except on specified holidays. "Though this line is a fun place to visit," advises a cautionary source, "the tour won't take long. We recommend combining this outing with Miami MetroZoo (they're adjacent to each other)."

HENRY MORRISON FLAGLER MUSEUM — Palm Beach

Whitehall, the extravagant Palm Beach mansion of Henry Morrison Flagler, founder of the Florida East Coast Railway, was presented to his third bride in 1902. Today it is the centerpiece of the museum bearing his name. The splendid white-columned edifice was, according to *The New York Herald*, "more wonderful than any palace in Europe, grander and more magnificent than any other private dwelling in the world." With 22 bathrooms, electric lighting, central heating and a telephone system, it could be considered overindulgent even for the Gilded Age.

Today Whitehall is a National Landmark and a public house museum visited by legions from around the globe. "It stands as a monument to a time when the American character we celebrate was born from a unique series of events that came together in history only one time and in only one place — here, in America," said a Web site extolling its virtues. "Florida could not have hoped for a more appropriate or impressive place as its first museum."

Railfans should understand that while it honors rail baron Flagler, the passion of those behind the contemporary museum is to preserve and exhibit the art collectibles and ornate furnishings Flagler gathered throughout the world for his "world-class" home. His private rail car added to the grounds in 1959 notwithstanding — the one in which he regularly inspected progress on the Key West extension — visitors chiefly view his objects d'art instead of railway artifacts.

Museum admission in 2009 was $15 for adults, $8 for ages 13–18, and $3 for ages 6–12. In addition, a Gilded Age lunch served on the premises between late November and early April followed a set menu at $33 for the Museum's non-members. The hours of operation are Sunday noon to 5 P.M. and Tuesday through Saturday 10 A.M. to 5 P.M. Located at One Whitehall Way, the museum may be contacted by mail at Box 969, Palm Beach, FL 33480, at (561) 655-2833, by fax at (561) 655-2826, or online at http://www.flaglermuseum.us/html.

SEMINOLE GULF RAILWAY — Fort Myers

The 118-mile Seminole Gulf Railway is southwest Florida's only freight rail line. It extends from a connection with the national rail system at Arcadia and links North Naples, Oneco (Bradenton) and Sarasota. Some of the Arcadia route dates to 1885, offering a colorful history of successive multiple carriers across the decades: Florida Southern, Plant System, Atlantic Coast Line, Fort Myers Southern, Seaboard Air Line, Seaboard Coast Line, and CSX Transportation. Buying its routes from CSX in November 1987, Seminole Gulf assumed the freight traffic. By January 1991, Seminole was also running a dinner train as well as daytime excursion trains out of Railhead Park in North Naples. Not long afterward passenger traffic transferred to a new Colonial Station in Fort Myers.

Hallmarks of the excursion operation include comical murder mysteries, dinner train specials, educational daytime trips and festive holiday affairs. Recurring clientele commonly recognize the attraction as "The Murder Mystery Dinner Train." On those excursions up to 200 guests can be seated in a quartet of reconditioned cars fabricated in the 1930s and 1940s. On some of the other excursion trains there is a narrated tour covering the region's history, animals and plant life as the train passes spectacular foliage and seascapes. The company claims to have carried more than 450,000 patrons on its excursions since 1991, making it one of the larger operations of its kind in the South.

Evening dinner trains include a five-course meal and a 3.5-hour journey. Midday dinner trains include a 2-hour 45-minute trip. In 2009, fares for Seminole's plethora of tourist excursions, including many especially designed for children, ranged between $12 and $125 per person. Reviews at varied Web sites are prolific and tend to be weighted on the positive side, some stating they are satisfied recurring customers.

Seminole Gulf Railway's address is 4110 Centerpointe Drive, Suite 207, Fort Myers, FL 33916, telephone (239) 275-6060, fax (239) 275-0581, and on the Web at http://www.semgulf.com.

SOUTH FLORIDA RAILWAY MUSEUM — Deerfield Beach

This attraction's dual intent is to "chronicle the history of south Florida as related to the railroads that brought commerce and development to the area and to educate the general population." It's fulfilling this mission by focusing on the 1940s, 1950s and 1960s through displays of artifacts plus a model railroad exhibit that depicts the region in that period. Located at 1300 West Hillsboro Boulevard in Deerfield Beach, the museum is housed in the Seaboard Air Line Railroad depot constructed in 1926 to compete with the Florida East Coast Railway. The attraction may be reached at telephone (954) 698-6620, and Web address http://southflorida.metromix.com/arts-culture/history/south-florida-railway-museum-deerfield-beach/125360/content.

WEST FLORIDA RAILROAD MUSEUM — Milton

In the period 1881–1883, the Pensacola & Atlantic Railroad (P&A) was constructed in the Florida panhandle. In May 1883, it connected its namesake city with the Florida Central and Western Railroad (FC&W) at River Junction, Florida. The FC&W was to eventually become the Seaboard Air Line Railroad while River Junction was renamed Chattahoochee. On July 1, 1885, the P&A ceased operations altogether as an independent carrier by being folded into an expanding Louisville & Nashville Railroad (L&N). The L&N had backed the P&A financially during its construction phase. That bigger carrier had a spur off its mainline between Cincinnati and New Orleans at Flomaton, Alabama, which ran to Pensacola. Through the extension there, via the P&A route, passengers and freight were seamlessly transported between L&N's northern and southern extremities and Jacksonville with the River Junction connection.

All this traffic across the panhandle came and went through Milton, where the West Florida Railroad Museum was established more than a century later. At its 1920s peak, Milton's passenger service claimed six daily trains. The museum's physical site at 5003 Henry Street is in the joint freight-passenger railway station built in 1907–1909 by L&N. That's the same site as the original P&A depot constructed in 1882. Closed in 1973, the L&N station was purchased by the Santa Rosa Historical Society and partially restored with a 1976 bicentennial grant. The restoration wasn't finished, however, until after the museum opened there in 1989. Several vintage pieces of rolling stock are on display along with a couple of outbuildings. The depot itself includes a plethora of artifacts from the L&N, Frisco and other lines. There is also an HO model layout on the museum property for viewing during regular operating hours.

On the National Register of Historic Places since 1982, the Milton depot is owned by the Santa Rosa group and leased to the museum that is staffed by volunteers. The attraction and a model railroad gift shop are open Fridays and Saturdays between 10 A.M. and 3 P.M. and at other times by appointment. The museum may be contacted at Box 770, Milton, FL 32572, by telephone at (850) 623-3645, by e-mail at conductor@wfrm.org, and on the Web at http://www.wfrm.org/wfrmmain.html.

Georgia

SAVANNAH HISTORY MUSEUM and ROUNDHOUSE RAILROAD MUSEUM — Savannah

The Coastal Heritage Society maintains not only a museum at the Central of Georgia Railway (CofG) passenger station at 303 Martin Luther King Jr. Boulevard in Savannah, it operates adjacent rail shops of that line at 601 West Harris Street. The latter is a National Historic Landmark. Visitors enter the roundhouse museum (the station itself is a sales shop) where tickets may be purchased to examine outdoor facilities and equipment. Tickets also entitle holders to ride in an open-air coach a distance of about two miles round trip as a narrator contributes background history and answers questions.

The complex of 13 railroading structures, still

standing, comprising the CofG headquarters shops, includes an operational roundhouse and turntable which slowly spins passengers on their journey, a thrill for many visitors. Society publicists claim it is the nation's "oldest and most complete antebellum railroad repair facility in existence." Several pieces of vintage rolling stock, including a 1890 steam locomotive, along with some antique machinery are on display. Hours the museum and shops are open are not always the same, thus those planning trips here should inquire in advance. The Savannah History Museum may be reached by telephone at (912) 651-6825 or fax (912) 651-6827

while the Roundhouse Railroad Museum may be contacted at (912) 651-6823 or fax (912) 651-3194. The Coastal Heritage Society runs them both and may be accessed on the Web at http://www.chsgeorgia.org/.

SOUTHERN MUSEUM OF CIVIL WAR AND LOCOMOTIVE HISTORY— Kennesaw

This collection of artifacts, rolling stock, Civil War memorabilia and a video depicting the Great Locomotive Chase features the distinguished *General* steam locomotive in the renowned chase. In 1862, during the War Between the States, the *General* and

Imagine the stories this small light Pacific could tell if only it could talk! Photographed between Cary and Research Triangle Park, North Carolina, it's on a fan trip originating in Atlanta this late 1980s day. Savannah & Atlanta rails never went to Atlanta in the halcyon days, by the way. Its mainline from the coast ended at Camak, Georgia, where its trains joined Georgia Railroad's main — which did go to Atlanta west and Augusta east. As for 750 here, it could mesmerize patrons of the 1980s just as it had years earlier (*courtesy Jay Miller*).

Most of Southern's active E-units were amassed at Atlanta's downtown Pegram Shops on March 26, 1978, including E8As 6913, 6906 and 6901. Two of those survive to the modern age: 6913 went for restoration at Southern Appalachian Railroad Museum, Oak Ridge, Tennessee; 6901 is exhibited at Southeastern Railway Museum, Duluth, Georgia. And the Atlanta facilities? Shops, adjacent yard and an unseen turntable reportedly are still there (*courtesy Jay T. Thomson*).

its tender were stolen by Union troops, followed by the famous chase by Confederates through north Georgia to recover their property. The perpetrators who were caught were hanged. Today the locomotive and tender are exhibited not more than a hundred yards from the site where the chase began.

Admission prices in 2009 were $7.50 for adults and $5.50 for children 4–12, with free admittance for those younger than 4. The museum is open Monday through Saturday from 9:30 A.M. to 5 P.M. and closed on major U.S. holidays. Located at 2829 Cherokee Street, Kennesaw, the attraction may be reached at (770) 427-2117 or Web site address http://www.southernmuseum.org/.

SOUTHEASTERN RAILWAY MUSEUM — Duluth

With more than 90 pieces of rolling stock, many of them available to visitors to climb aboard, and spread over a 12-acre tract, this is arguably one of the largest outdoor rail collections in Dixie. Inventory includes a commissary car, library car, steam and diesel locomotives, wood cars, coaches, Pullman sleepers, private cars and a club car. In 1966, Southern Railway transferred the land for the museum. On it rests a half-mile of standard gauge loop track along with six yard tracks, a shop and a 7.5-inch gauge rail system. On-site train rides aboard restored cabooses or converted open-air freight cars, subject to crew and equipment availability, are scheduled when weather permits.

Trains are alternately powered by steam and diesel engines. Group tours can be arranged for schools, day cares, scout troops and fraternal groups. The site, including picnic facilities, may be rented for business, club, family or social gatherings. The attraction's full season runs from April through December, open Thursday, Friday and Saturday from 10 A.M. to 5 P.M. In January, February and March, it's open those same hours Saturday only. The grounds are closed on major holidays. Contact the Southeastern Railway Museum at Box 1267, Duluth, GA 30136, telephone (770) 476-2013, and Web address http://www.southeasternrailwaymuseum.org.

Kentucky

BIG SOUTH FORK SCENIC RAILWAY — Stearns

Among the provisions entrepreneur-industrialist Justus S. Stearns established in southern Kentucky starting in 1902, in addition to the Stearns Coal & Lumber Company, and a town named for him, was the Kentucky & Tennessee Railway (K&T). Stearns operated 12 steam locomotives over the 25-mile line extending into the Big South Fork River Valley hauling timber, coal, supplies and workers em-ployed by his multiple ventures. The K&T also ferried passengers through the mountainous region. Several Stearns mines closed in the 1950s and passenger service was eliminated then. Ownership shifted to another commercial enterprise in 1976, and subsequently to national and private owner-operators. In the modern age the McCreary County Heritage Foundation, Inc., emphasizes the history of the town, its industries and rail roots through varied exhibitions.

A 16-mile round-trip excursion descends 600 feet into the gorge before reaching the end of the line at Blue Heron Coal Mining Camp, a National Park Service interpretive site. Rail tickets entitle holders to enter the McCreary County Museum in Stearns in addition to the journey by train. Fares (2009 prices) between April and October are $18 for adults, $9 for children 3–12. In November prices are reduced to $15 and $7.50. Cab rides in a diesel-electric locomotive are $35 any time. There are also special event trains such as Mother's, Father's and Grandparents' days, Halloween and Christmas. A Saturday Pass ($25/$15), Rail and Canoe Package ($50) and Caboose Rentals ($240) are additional options. Hours vary by seasons.

The Big South Fork Scenic Railway at 100 Henderson Street may be contacted at Box 368, Stearns, KY 42647, telephone (800) 462-5664 or (606) 376-5330, and online at http://www.bsfsry.com.

BLUEGRASS RAILROAD MUSEUM — Versailles

Bluegrass Railroad Museum is a private enterprise launched in 1976, at 175 Beasley Drive, Versailles, in the heart of Bluegrass Country. While the museum grounds are open all year, a gift shop and an exhibition car are open from mid May through October. Gift shop hours are 12:30 to 4 P.M.

Built in 1889 by the Louisville Southern Railroad, those rails today are witness to modern excursion trips over the same route that eventually formed a portion of the Monon Railroad. Trains run seasonally on Saturdays and Sundays at 2 P.M. Halfway through their trip passengers disembark to walk a short distance to view "Young's High Bridge," a strategic trestle constructed in 1888. A century later (1988), the museum bought the segment of the route on which those trains operate today.

Adult ticket fares are $10 in 2009, and $25 for locomotive cab rides. Fares for children age 2 to 12 are $8, with those under 2 free. Discounts are available to seniors and groups. Private parties may rent the whole train, too. A plethora of special excursions, many tied to seasonal and holiday events, are scheduled throughout the year.

The Bluegrass Railroad Museum may be reached at Box 27, Versailles, KY 40383, by telephone at (800) 755-2476 or (859) 873-2476, or at Web address http://www.bgrm.org/.

HISTORIC RAILPARK TRAIN MUSEUM —
Bowling Green

On the outside of this historic Louisville & Nashville Railroad (L&N) depot at Bowling Green patrons get a hands-on feel for vintage rolling stock. A walk-through tour conducted by a guide carries one into an authentic Pullman sleeper, Duncan Hines dining car, caboose, Railway Post Office, and railway presidential office car. There's also a restored streamlined diesel engine parked along the tracks. The depot itself, completed in October 1925, was the second L&N station to serve Bowling Green, continuing to do so to 1979. After abandonment and housing a branch of the city library, the structure was refurbished by volunteers and turned into the Railpark.

Inside the museum visitors are treated to a working model railroad layout, a railway-theme gift shop and artifacts and photographs depicting life on the L&N during its heyday. Some of the exhibits are interactive. The original mosaic tile floor and a few early furnishings remain. Included within the structure is the original 18-seat "Colored Waiting Room" just as it was then, separated by walls from the larger space assigned to others. On the second level, which houses many of the exhibits, there's a small theater that perennially screens railway films, the majority of them pertaining to the L&N and Illinois Central. Tickets to the museum, theater, model railroad and guided tour at $10 for adults in 2009, seem fair for the value rendered. There are also many special events (speakers, celebrations, dramas, storytelling, children's and seasonal activities) scheduled on an ongoing basis at the Railpark.

The museum is open daily every day between May 1 and September 30, and every day except Monday the rest of the year. Located at 401 Kentucky Street, the Railpark may be contacted at telephone (270) 745-7317 or online at http://www.his toricrailpark.com.

KENTUCKY RAILROAD MUSEUM — New Haven

In a modern depot replicating the original at 136 South Main Street in New Haven, visitors discover 4,000-square-feet of artifacts depicting the history of Kentucky railroading. Outside the facility are more than 50 pieces of rolling stock with 10 locomotives — some in storage or under restoration — with many on display. Steam and diesel locomotives alternate pulling excursion trains over 1857 Louisville & Nashville Railroad trackage. The 90-minue 22-mile route traverses the scenic Rolling Fork River Valley between New Haven and Boston, Kentucky. There are special excursions tied to an-

For 113 years many passenger trains included Railroad Post Office cars in their consists, like L&N 1107 at the Historic Railpark Train Museum at Bowling Green, Kentucky, in May 2007. These fixtures on American railways were staffed by U.S. Postal Service workers. Withdrawing them in the late 1960s — transferring mail to trucks and aircraft — was another nail in the coffins of passenger lines that had lost riders and revenues for years (*courtesy Clyde Woodruff*).

nual occasions, too: Rolling Fork Iron Horse Festival, Kentucky Bourbon Festival, Murder Mystery Weekend, Halloween, and Christmas. Charters are available for private parties.

A wide variety of operational days, fares and excursion types is available so it's best to contact the museum in advance of any planned outing. The attraction can be accessed at Box 240, New Haven, KY 40051-0240, telephone (800) 272-0152, or online at http://www.kyrail.org/.

MY OLD KENTUCKY DINNER TRAIN — Bardstown

My Old Kentucky Dinner Train begins and ends in the historic city that is the site of My Old Kentucky Home State Park with a summer outdoor musical production named for the song. The train's excursion concentrates on what it does best, nevertheless: feeding patrons in stylish surroundings reminiscent of vintage railroad dining. Running over an 1850s 20-mile shortline that originally was the Bardstown stem of the Louisville & Nashville Railroad (which connected to the L&N mainline at Bardstown Junction), the dinner train premiered in 1988. A year earlier the private enterprise that owned it launched freight haulage through that forested territory.

The dinner train is headquartered in an 1860 depot that has seen more than its share of wear. Listed in the National Register of Historic Places and the last "drylaid" limestone depot in the Commonwealth of Kentucky, part of the facility has survived a couple of devastating fires. If one examines the ceiling and beams carefully, evidence of those catastrophes may still be detected. While some of the structure was rebuilt, altering its image considerably, there are portions of the original that remain virtually unscathed and as they were a sesquicentennial ago.

The food and the service on the dinner (and lunch!) trains are generally applauded by patrons. It may be the setting itself, however, they acclaim the most. Dual diesel locomotives pull a trio of refurbished dining cars (two of which started their lives as other types). The ambience is immediate, as patrons are seated in cars with polished mahogany walls, brass fixtures, specially designed sodium vapor lights and historic artifacts. Dubbed by one rail historian "one of the most popular" dinner train excursions in the U.S., the two-hour journey is a pleasant encounter with other guests while being served efficiently and elegantly.

Many of its trips depend on demand so it's best to contact the attraction in advance of any planned trip to determine schedule and reserve space. The luncheon journey in 2009 is $60 for adults ($35 for children) and the dinner trip is $75 ($45 for children) with murder mystery excursions $98 for adults ($58 for children) and a variety of special meal packages for two ranging between $150 and $320. Located at 602 North Third Street in Bardstown, the attraction may be contacted at telephone (502) 348-7300, and Web site http://www.rjcorman.com/dinnertrain.html.

RAILWAY EXPOSITION COMPANY MUSEUM — Covington

On weekend afternoons from May through October this outdoor collection of more than 50 restored rail cars and a quartet of locomotives is on display for public inspection via guided tours. While not all the pieces are available for viewing, enough are to make it a charming walk down memory lane at a reasonable fee. The dining cars in this exhibition are also available for rent for private and commercial gatherings.

More information is available from the company, located at 315 West Southern Avenue, Covington. The mailing address is Box 15065, Covington, KY 41015-0065, or telephone (859) 491-7245.

Louisiana

DeQUINCY RAILROAD MUSEUM — DeQuincy

This museum is housed in the 1923 Kansas City Southern Railroad restored Mission Revival depot at 400 Lake Charles Avenue. It displays numerous artifacts and memorabilia relating to rail travel in the past. Outside its walls visitors encounter a 1913 steam locomotive, a 1929 caboose, and a 1947 passenger coach. Annually on the second weekend of April the city stages a DeQuincy Railroad Days Festival, drawing onlookers far and wide to commemorate the local heritage of its tracks. Open year-round and free — although contributions are welcome — the museum's hours are 8 A.M. to 5 P.M. Monday through Friday and 1 to 5 P.M. weekends. It's closed New Year's Day, Thanksgiving and Christmas. More information is available at telephone (337) 786-2823.

LOUISIANA STATE RAILROAD MUSEUM — Gretna

Situated in the brick Gretna depot erected in 1905 by the Texas & Pacific Railroad, the Louisiana State Railroad Museum at Huey P. Long and Fourth streets houses a collection of vintage rail memorabilia inside and outside the station. The museum is linked with a red caboose parked behind Gretna's Southern Pacific Railroad depot under auspices of the Gretna Historical Society, too. The museum may be contacted at City of Gretna, Box 404, Gretna, LA 70054, telephone (888) 4-GRETNA or (504) 363-1580.

Mississippi

CASEY JONES RAILROAD MUSEUM STATE PARK — Vaughan

On April 30, 1900, engineer John Luther ("Casey") Jones, 37 (nicknamed for his birthplace at Cayce, Kentucky), was at the throttle of an Illinois Central Railroad southbound fireball mail as it neared Vaughan, Mississippi. Running decidedly late, the train raced at dizzying speeds as it rounded a curve and slammed into a parked freight that hadn't pulled far enough onto a siding to clear the mainline. Jones died in the crash and was immortalized forever in a folk song penned by Wallace Saunders. It made Jones a martyred hero, leading some historians to dub him "the world's most famous railroad engineer."

The state park named after him sports a museum less than a mile from the accident site. Housed in a railway depot that originally served trains calling at Pickens, Mississippi, the museum includes not only memorabilia pertaining to the Jones saga, it depicts the historic significance of the rails in Mississippi, too. A steam locomotive built in 1923 rests on a siding adjacent to the depot-museum, representative of an era long past and a monument to Jones' passion for railroading.

The park is open all year, as is the museum. A slight fee is assessed visitors to the latter. More information may be available from the Division of Parks and Recreation, Mississippi Department of Wildlife, Fisheries and Parks, Box 451, Jackson, MS 39205-0451.

McCOMB RAILROAD MUSEUM — McComb

With a collection of more than 1,400 cataloged artifacts and a restored locomotive and several intriguing railcars outside the depot, publicists for McComb Railroad Museum tout it as "the best rail museum south of Chicago" and "one of the South's best preserved collections of railroad history." The competition might argue differently but the Web site cites as one reason for its claims "the passion that railroad retirees still have for the preservation of railroad history," hinting that their dedication puts McComb a cut above others doing similar work. Whether so or not, the facility is a team effort.

When the Illinois Central Railroad (IC) shops at McComb closed in 1987, Edwin Etheridge's 45-year career ended with the IC, the last of them as final shop superintendent. But that visionary saved hundreds of pieces of memorabilia, intending to launch a museum preserving the history of the rails in southwest Mississippi. Possibly the centerpiece was to be (and is) the shop's whistle, which blew at the start and close of work and the lunch period every day.

After several false starts, and the state's renovation of the 1901 depot in 1998, everything came together for the station to become the ideal spot for a McComb Railroad Museum. While some of the structure was reserved for the Pike County Chamber of Commerce and Industrial Development Foundation, the old baggage room off the waiting area was converted into a repository-exhibition venue for artifacts. Volunteers were enlisted to catalog and display the materials.

Today Amtrak also calls at the station on its daily north-south *City of New Orleans* journey between the Crescent City and Chicago. Located at 108 North Railroad Boulevard, the museum's mailing address is Box 7220, McComb, MS 39649-7220, telephone (601) 684-2291, and Web site address http://www.mcrrmuseum.com/.

North Carolina

FLOYD McEACHERN HISTORICAL TRAIN MUSEUM — Dillsboro

For several decades railfan Floyd McEachern collected and refurbished artifacts and equipment pertaining to the railroads. His exhibits, including more than 3,000 pieces from his own collection and those of others, cover every detail of steam railroad history. An "O" gauge track layout allows a huge model train to operate as part of the museum. There is a small entrance fee and the season is limited to April through December offering daily hours.

Located at 1 Front Street, the attraction may be contacted at Box 180, Dillsboro, NC 28725, telephone (704) 586-4085, or fax (704) 586-8806.

GREAT SMOKY MOUNTAINS RAILROAD — Bryson City

This attraction has been ferrying riders through this scenic range since mid 1988, traversing a section of track opened in 1891. Launched in the 1840s, the Western North Carolina Railroad was later acquired by Southern Railway. It operated trains on the route to 1982, when Southern merged with the Chessie System to form Norfolk Southern Railroad. That line ultimately abandoned 67 miles of track between Dillsboro and Murphy, North Carolina. After the North Carolina Department of Transportation purchased it in 1988, it leased the tracks to Great Smoky Mountain Railway, Inc. This assured that freight traffic would persist and passenger traffic would be implemented again via excursion travel. Excursion trains now operate between Dillsboro and Andrews, east of Murphy.

A mixture of diesel-electrics and steam locomotives supply the front-end power required to haul patrons in refurbished coaches by the Cherokee Indian Reservation, picturesque cascading waterfalls, the Appalachian Trail and Great Smoky Mountains National Park. In addition to "regular" excursions,

There's nothing like being behind a steam locomotive on a railfan excursion. In this case, it's Southern Railway's 2-8-2 722 in the mid 1970s. On a morning cool enough to show steam exhaust from far back in the consist we see not merely steam but Atlanta's skyline in the distant haze. Alas, Southern's heirs subsequently got out of the steam fan-trip arena, selling the apparatus to service and restore steamers. But alas again, at the start of 2010, engine 722 was reportedly being restored at Dillsboro, North Carolina, by volunteers at Great Smoky Mountains Railroad. Time lives on! (*courtesy Jay Miller*).

County." On display are photographs, maps, exhibits and a model HO railroad layout.

The attraction is financed in a peculiar yet ingenious way: the bulk of its resources are derived from The Grab Thrift and Gift Shop, a retail store selling clothing, school uniforms, household articles and furniture at reduced prices. It's an all-volunteer operation in business since January 2008. As a non-profit agency, the emporium benefits those making charitable donations by offering a tax deduction for merchandise gifts or cash.

Until recent years the museum was housed at Hamlet's former Victorian-styled SAL depot at 2 West Main Street built in 1900. Numerous rail passenger stations maintain a claim to fame that's touted proudly in their advertising and promotion. This one, on the list of National Historic Landmarks, alleges it is "the most photographed station in the eastern United States."

There is no admission fee to visit the National Railroad Museum and Hall of Fame at its new site. Although regular hours are Sunday 1 to 4 P.M. and Saturday 11 A.M. to 4 P.M., the outfit opens its doors any day of the week by appointment. It may be contacted at its mailing address at Box 1583, Hamlet, NC 28345, by telephone at (910) 582-2383, or on the Web at http://nationalrrmuseum.tripod.com/.

a number of specialty offerings are scheduled throughout the year (such as rafting and railing combinations, mystery theater dinner trains, children's and seasonal events). The operation has amassed more than 7,000 Lionel train engines, cars and accessories for one of the nation's largest exhibitions with dual running model train layouts.

Hours and fees vary by trips selected. For more information contact the railroad at 226 Everett Street, Bryson City, NC 28713, telephone (800) 872-4681 or (828) 586-8811, or on the Web at http://www.gsmr.com.

NATIONAL RAILROAD MUSEUM AND HALL OF FAME — Hamlet

The National Railroad Museum and Hall of Fame is located at 120 East Spring Street in Hamlet. At its zenith Hamlet was a major north-south, east-west junction of the Seaboard Air Line Railroad (SAL). Most of the families in Hamlet in the heyday of passenger railroading earned their livelihoods from the shops of the SAL, where one or more family members labored. Opened in 1976, the museum offers "a source of entertainment as well as a place for learning about the history of railroading, the history of Hamlet and the history of Richmond

NORTH CAROLINA TRANSPORTATION MUSEUM — Spencer

"The South's Largest Transportation Museum," this one bills itself, situated at the historic Spencer Shops. Spencer was once Southern Railway's largest steam locomotive servicing facility, employing more than 2,500 at its peak. Both the town and the town's largest industry were named after Samuel Spencer, first president of the impervious road. When Southern discontinued its Spencer operations in the late 1970s—having been diminishing in size for three decades—local preservationists launched a campaign to save those historic facilities and turn them into a transportation museum.

Baldwin Locomotive Works fabricated ACL 1031 in June 1913, one of 25 that ACL ordered. Serving mostly around Fayetteville, Rocky Mount and Wilmington, North Carolina, sporadically it turned up anywhere between Jacksonville and Richmond. In the 1950s, 1031 was a mainstay of East Carolina at Tarboro and then Virginia & Carolina Southern at Lumberton. It retired in 1959, idling behind the Florence, South Carolina, depot near ACL's massive rail yard. The City of Florence donated it to the Spencer museum in 1994, where it received a cosmetic restoration to a 1940s look. It's on the turntable on June 13, 2009, soon to be coupled and pushed by a waiting Navy switcher (*courtesy Jay Miller*).

A Norfolk Southern business car is included in the rolling stock exhibited at the North Carolina Train Museum on June 13, 2009, during the facility's annual Railroad Days. "It must have tons of wax," a visitor observed of its shiny slick finish (*courtesy Jay Miller*).

With the help of legislators and a gift of the deed to four acres of that strategic site (presented by Southern Railway to the North Carolina governor in 1977), the prospective museum took a giant leap forward. Two years hence Southern donated another 53 acres, including several structures. By 1983, under the watchful eye of the state Department of Cultural Resources, the initial exhibitions opened in the Spencer Shops at 411 South Salisbury Avenue. By the late 1990s, more than $2 million in rare transportation artifacts were acquired, restored and displayed. The attraction's mission is "to preserve and interpret the history of transportation in North Carolina and to present this history in a manner that allows visitors to enjoy their experience as well as learn from it."

Tours of the site are provided in refurbished coaches pulled by steam or diesel engines. On exhibit is a Model T Ford depot hack, an RFD mail wagon, a steam engine and several pieces of vintage rolling stock, including locomotives and passenger cars. Entrance fees are nominal and schedules vary by seasons and days of the week. For specific information it's best to contact the museum at Box 44, Spencer, NC 28159, telephone (704) 636-2889, fax (704) 639-1881, or its Web site address, http://www.nctrans.org.

The most unique part of the North Carolina Transportation Museum's operation, nevertheless, is a wide variety of excursions that go well beyond the property where they begin and end. Especially in demand are trips to distant locales such as Charlottesville, Virginia, and Asheville, North Carolina, and other picturesque destinations. These daytime features sell out early and may include meals at each passenger's option. They normally begin above $100 and may range to $300 per person in premium-seating dome cars (about four classes of seating are provided). Contact the museum for details. It may very well be "The South's Largest Transportation Museum" based on the variety of opportunities it offers.

WILMINGTON RAILROAD MUSEUM — Wilmington

Visitors to this museum recapture part of the past in railroading when they board a steam locomotive or a bright red caboose. They also view extensive photographic exhibitions and other railroad artifacts with extremes like a 150-ton locomotive and a conductor's 4-ounce timepiece.

This has long been a railroad town, having been home to the Wilmington & Weldon Railroad (W&W) chartered in 1834 and debuting in 1840. The W&W is said to have been "the longest rail line in the world" at the time, linking South to North with 161 miles of track. Mergers and monikers altered the W&W over the years, eventually folding into the Atlantic Coast Line Railroad (ACL) around the turn of the century. ACL based its headquarters operations at Wilmington, adding substantially to its significance as a railway municipality.

The museum is open year-round. For information about hours contact the Wilmington Railroad Museum Foundation at 501 Nutt Street, Wilmington, NC 28401, telephone (910) 763-2634.

South Carolina

BRANCHVILLE RAILROAD SHRINE AND MUSEUM — Branchville

This arresting facility is situated at the crossing of the world's first railway intersect. Branchville was on the route of the globe's longest railroad in 1833, a stop on the 136-mile Charleston–Hamburg route (the latter town, in Aiken County, is no longer in existence). Branchville became the initial rail junction a few years hence when tracks between it and Columbia were laid. After a fire nearly destroyed the historic depot in 1995, it was restored to its earlier condition and turned into a railroad museum.

The most important exhibition in the attraction's collection is clearly a model depicting the *Best Friend of Charleston*, the first American passenger-toting steam locomotive that moved travelers along the line between Charleston and Hamburg. A source correctly suggests, "It was the start of a transportation transformation in the United States."

The museum, at 7505 Freedom Road in Branchville (29702), is in an 1877 depot serving Southern Railway during the heyday of travel by train. Admission to the museum is free and it's open daily from 9 A.M. to 5 P.M. but closed on major holidays. Tours of the structure may be scheduled by appointment. Call the town hall at telephone (803) 274-8820.

SOUTH CAROLINA RAILROAD MUSEUM — Winnsboro

"Preservation and interpretation of railroading in South Carolina" is the mission of this attraction. An extensive inventory of rolling stock and excursion rides are hallmarks of its growing collection of railroad memorabilia. Begun in 1973, the museum's inventory includes a great many locomotives, passenger cars, freight cars, cabooses, and maintenance of way equipment. Excursions, operating schedules and fares vary widely. Located at 110 Industrial Park Road, Winnsboro, SC 2910, the attraction may be reached at its mailing address, Box 7246, Columbia, SC 29202-7246, or telephone (803) 635-9893, by e-mail at info@scrm.org, or Web site http://www.scrm.org/main.asp.

Tennessee

BROADWAY DINNER TRAIN — Nashville

Following a Tennessee Central Railway route opened in 1904, the Broadway Dinner Train departs from Riverfront Depot at the foot of Broadway in Nashville along the banks of the Cumberland River. The precise address is 108 First Avenue, South, Nashville, TN 37201. Traveling about 35 miles round trip and powered by a 1952 diesel engine, the train carries diners to Old Hickory, Tennessee, northeast of town, an area populated by mansions of some of Music City's most celebrated country music stars. The excursion's consist includes not only several dining cars but also a dome lounge and a tavern-observation car. Entertainment is provided in the dome lounge while a four-course meal with choice of entrees is served during the 2.5-hour trip.

For more information and reservations, which are strongly recommended, contact the attraction at the street address above or telephone (800) 274-8010 or (615) 254-8000.

CHATTANOOGA CHOO CHOO HOLIDAY INN — Chattanooga

For a price one can sleep in one of several refurbished parlor cars resting on tracks outside Terminal Station in downtown Chattanooga. Completed in 1909, the station is situated near the Tennessee River at 1400 Market Street. If you can obtain enough ambience by merely looking at those cars from the outside, however, for a relatively modest fee you can stay in a conventional Holiday Inn room adjacent to the depot with more traditional trappings. Either way you'll experience the ecstasy of checking in at the contemporary "ticket window" front desk in the terminal's grand hall. And you may be treated to a charmingly polished experience in the dining area of that hall. A superbly attired wait staff offering impeccable service and selections from a railroad menu reminiscent of those days of yore will likely meet your every whim.

This hotel captures the imagination of the passionate railfan. It is arguably one of Dixie's most readily recognized landmarks, made famous by the lilting rhythm and lyrics of "The Chattanooga Choo Choo," sung or played by hosts of recording artists back in the day.

For reservations, call (800) TRACK29 (872-2529) or (423) 266-5000, or go to Web site http://www.choochoo.com/. And if the idea of spending the night in one of those parlor cars won't let you go, you probably should make your reservations early. Those rooms are often spoken for well in advance, particularly during commemorative occasions and on lots of weekends.

COWAN RAILROAD MUSEUM — Cowan

It took three years for the Nashville, Chattanooga & St. Louis Railway (NC&StL) — successor to the Nashville & Chattanooga Railway — to complete the job started in 1849, boring a tunnel through the Cumberland Mountains two miles southeast of Cowan. Once it was done and the tracks were laid through it, it was possible to take a rail journey all the way to Nashville from Cowan and travel south beyond that little burg. While a primitive depot was placed in Cowan by the NC&StL, when the city outgrew it, a new frame depot was added in 1904. By then the line was owned by the Louisville & Nashville Railroad, although the NC&StL was allowed to continue operating as an independent carrier, retaining separate identity until 1957.

Today that 1904 depot at 108 Front Street still stands housing the Cowan Railroad Museum within its walls. Most of the attraction's 1000 artifacts depict railroading in and around Cowan. Exhibits include figures in period attire, photographs, tools, documents, maps, and out-of-print railroad volumes. There is a railroad gift shop, and model trains of many persuasions are on display.

Outside the depot in a landscaped park, visitors observe a full-size train including a steam locomotive, flat car and wooden caboose with bay window. There is also a diesel switch engine owned by the museum. Noting that a steady entourage of freight traffic passes by regularly, museum publicists aver: "One can now climb into the Depot's observation tower and while away the afternoon watching current day operations of big-time railroading complete with monster Diesel pusher engines working southbound on about half the trains as they attack the grade approaching the distant tunnel. On a cool day, you can hear the engines as they work echo off the face of the mountain two miles distant and more than 200 feet higher up. It is AWESOME to even the most casual observer!"

Volunteers man the museum from May through October on Sundays between 1 and 4 P.M. and Mondays, Thursdays, Fridays and Saturdays between 10 A.M. and 4 P.M. There is no admission fee although donations are welcome. Contact the museum at Box 53, Cowan, TN 37318-0053, telephone (931) 967-3078, or Web site http://www.cowanrailroad museum.org/.

HISTORIC CASEY JONES HOME & RAILROAD MUSEUM — Jackson

A larger Casey Jones "village" is made up of the Casey Jones Home & Railroad Museum and several retail enterprises embrace a mercantile emporium and dining facilities. All of it revolves around the life of the brave Illinois Central engineer immortalized in a popular ballad following his death in a rail crash April 30, 1900, at Vaughan, Mississippi.

Tours include a short motion picture on the life and death of the famous engineer, a scale model of the wreck, a replica of the engine and coal car Jones guided on his final run, a horse-drawn hearse that ferried him to his grave, a detailed model train exhibit inside a 1890s baggage car, and Jones' own residence displaying memorabilia and period furniture. An 8,000-square-foot depot addition completed in 2009 provides more space for displaying the museum's growing exhibitions.

Open daily, the attraction's hours are 8 A.M. to 9 P.M. March through December and 9 A.M. to 5 P.M. January and February. It may be one of the best bargains in the South for such operations—Casey Jones' admission fee is $6.50 for adults, $4.50 for ages 6–12 (2009 prices). More data is available from The Historic Casey Jones Home and Railroad Museum at 30 Casey Jones Lane, Jackson, TN 38305, telephone (877) 700-7942 or (731) 668-1222, e-mail at caseyjonesmuseum@gmail.com, and online at http://www.caseyjones.com.

L&N DEPOT AND RAILROAD MUSEUM—Etowah

"Growing Up with the L&N—Life and Times in a Railroad Town" is the heart and soul of this museum dedicated to the experiences of Etowah's people in the halcyon days of rail travel. The city now owns the 15-room bi-level Victorian station accommodating the museum along with a visitor center and art gallery. Built in 1906 by the Louisville & Nashville Railroad, for a long time this station was the L&N's Atlanta Division headquarters. Two world wars, a 1922 national shopman's strike, the Great Depression and other events with far-ranging implications impinging on this small community are depicted in the exhibits of photographs and artifacts on display. A classic caboose rests outside the depot.

The attraction is closed Mondays and major holidays but open year-round Sundays 1 to 4 P.M. and Tuesdays through Saturdays 9 A.M. to 4:30 P.M. While there is no charge to visit, donations are welcomed. The museum, at 727 Tennessee Avenue, may be reached at Box 390, Etowah, TN 37331, telephone (423) 263-7840, or online at http://www.tell iquah.com/etowah.htm.

TENNESSEE VALLEY RAILROAD—Chattanooga

Hailed as "the largest *operating* historic railroad in the South," the Tennessee Valley follows the right-of-way of the East Tennessee & Georgia Railroad most of the way. That's a celebrated line that was critical during the War Between the States. The attraction dates to 1961, when a coterie of Chattanooga-area preservation-minded citizens pooled their efforts to focus on maintaining and running steam engines that hauled passengers.

Today travelers may board at either end of the line—Grand Junction, sporting a replica of the Tuscumbia, Alabama, 1888 depot, out of which the

At Cambria, Tennessee, northeast of Chattanooga, on October 28, 2009, Southern Railway coach 1037 lumbers down the line on its way to become part of Tennessee Valley Railroad Museum's tourist trains. The passenger car is pushed along by unseen CSX B40-8s 5962 and 5968, both of which earlier served in Norfolk Southern and Clinchfield inventories (*courtesy Jay T. Thomson*).

After Central of Georgia combined seven roads to form Savannah & Western in 1888, Baldwin Locomotive Works built this Class E 4-4-0 for S&W (1891). When S&W and CofG fused in 1895, the engine was assigned number 1587, altered to 1581 in 1912. It was finally designated 349 in 1926. Subsequently pulling tourists aboard Stone Mountain Railroad trains, it's now exhibited at Chattanooga's Tennessee Valley Railroad Museum (*courtesy Clyde Woodruff*).

On a 1970s fan trip, Southern Railway 630 is serviced at Macon, Georgia, before returning passengers to Atlanta, its point of origin for this outing. The steam locomotive is preserved at Chattanooga's Tennessee Valley Railroad Museum, a railfan's paradise for perusing engines of the steam epoch as well as more historic rolling stock, all patiently restored by volunteers (*courtesy Jay Miller*).

original Tennessee Valley Railroad ran; or East Chattanooga, with a modest wood frame structure akin to an 1890s epoch station. There are numerous exhibits at East Chattanooga as well as a backshop where heavy rail maintenance and restoration is ongoing. Guided tours through vintage railcars, included with tickets, are offered at both ends. At Grand Junction, the main entrance to the attraction, there's also an audiovisual presentation, exhibits, tours of a repair shop, plus a dining room and gift shop.

The road's season runs from March through December — daily through October, then weekends in November and December. Depots are usually open by 9:30 A.M., a half-hour before the first trains depart on the 55-minute six-mile-round-trip Missionary Ridge Local run. Tickets are $8 for adults, $4 for children ages 3–12, with higher fares for upgraded seating (2009 prices). There are also longer excursions at scheduled times to Chickamauga, Hiawassee and Copperhill, the latter two departing from Etowah, Tennessee. More information is available from Tennessee Valley Railroad at 4119 Cromwell Road, Chattanooga, TN 37421-2119, telephone (423) 894-8028, or Web site address http://www.tvrail.com.

UNION STATION — Nashville

Nashville's historic Union Station at 1001 Broadway opened in 1900. For 75 years it served passenger trains. In 1986, the imposing facility, refurbished and its upstairs floors remodeled, witnessed the opening of Union Station Hotel. Run by another operator then, it has been a Wyndham Hotels property in recent years. In the cavernous main hall that once was a waiting room, patrons are fed in a white-tablecloth dining room served by bustling waiters reminiscent of traveling days. Much of the structure's traditional ambience remains, right down to the vintage arrivals and departures board, a backdrop to the hotel's front desk. A preponderance of guest rooms (formerly railway offices) open onto the original balcony for several floors overlooking the former waiting room. One sleeps well here. Despite the lack of motion, the bedrooms are still above the tracks that lie in Nashville's infamous railroad gulch. For information, contact the hotel at telephone (615) 726-1001 or go on the Web to http://www.unionstation hotelnashville.com.

Virginia

OLD DOMINION RAILWAY MUSEUM — Richmond

The Old Dominion Chapter of the National Railway Historical Society maintains the purpose "to educate members of the public to the basic role of transportation in building and maintaining American society through the establishment and maintenance of a museum and library for public display and study." It accomplishes that mission by interpreting "the social and economic impact that the area railroads and their employees had, and continue to have, on the Richmond area and its citizens."

Situated in an express car (through summer 2009) donated by the Richmond, Fredericksburg and Potomac Railroad, the chapter's operations have been carried out at 102 Hull Street in South Richmond next to the ex–Southern Railway passenger station. The museum-library is open Saturdays from 11 A.M. to 4 P.M. and Sundays from 1 to 4 P.M. While there is no admission fee, donations are encouraged.

Southern Railway transferred the Hull Street Station to the chapter for its permanent home. The organization has since bought the land on which the station rests and temporarily closed the operation in September 2009 for conversion to the museum and library. That was expected to be completed in early 2010.

For more information about the museum and library, contact it at Box 8583, Richmond, VA 23226, telephone (804) 233-6237, or on the Web at http://www.odcnrhs.org/Museum.htm.

VIRGINIA MUSEUM OF TRANSPORTATION — Roanoke

The casual visitor to the Old Dominion State's official transportation museum — designated such by the commonwealth's general assembly — will encounter nearly five dozen pieces of railway transportation history. The Virginia Museum of Transportation at Roanoke, opened in 1986, built upon an earlier Roanoke Transportation Museum (1963–1985) that was effectively washed away in a flood along with most of its collection and facility.

Reopening in a new location under a new moniker, the current attraction includes not only all that rolling stock and equipment but some permanent exhibitions among "indoor" displays: African-American Heritage on the Norfolk & Western Railroad, 1930–1970, is one; another is Big Lick — a replica of a 1930s era small town train depot complete with bona fide artifacts like telegraphy apparatus and freight scales; plus many more temporary exhibitions.

The museum is open Sundays from 1 to 5 P.M., Mondays through Saturdays from 10 A.M. to 5 P.M., and closed most major U.S. holidays as well as certain holiday eves. The 2009 admission prices were $8 for adults, $6 for children ages 3–11, and free to those under 3. The Virginia Museum of Transportation at 303 Norfolk Avenue in Roanoke

A workhorse that's seen lots of service powering excursion trains since it was at the head end of N&W passenger consists, Class J 611 idles in Virginia in the mid 1980s where it has taken a load of Tar Heel day-trippers. Don't let two tenders fool you: in the steam age, these engines — needing tons of water — had regular water stops. On a fan outing, with no water stops en route, the auxiliary tender holding water only moves the train from Point A to B where the engine is serviced with coal and water before its return to Point A (*courtesy Jay Miller*).

(24016) may be telephoned at (540) 342-5670. Its Web address is http://www.info@vmt.org.

West Virginia

CASS SCENIC RAILROAD STATE PARK — Cass

The last 11 miles of a 3,000-mile logging rail line — in 1911, the Mountain State led the nation in miles dedicated to that purpose — persist within the confines of Cass State Park and the hamlet from which it draws its name. Completed in 1902, those tracks in the contemporary age have been adapted to hauling riders instead: today steam locomotives pull logging flatcars that have been converted to modern passenger coaches for excursions through the park.

An eight-mile 90-minute round-trip to Whittaker Station costs $17–$20 per adult traveler and $12–$15 for children (highest fares on weekends). The 22-mile 4.5-hour round-trip to Bald Knob costs $23–$26 per adult traveler and $16–$19 for children (highest fares on weekends). Tickets include entrance to Cass Showcase orientation film,

Wildlife Museum, and Historical Museum. There are dinner trains by reservation only with a variety of prices depending upon occasion and season. All rates were in effect in 2009.

Contact the park at Box 107, Cass, WV 24927, telephone (800) CALL WVA or (304) 456-4300, or e-mail at cassrailroad@wvdnr.gov, or go to the Web at http://www.cassrailroad.com.

HUNTINGTON RAILROAD MUSEUM — Huntington

Collis Potter Huntington, for whom the city and museum were named, was a wealthy entrepreneur-rail magnate whose stamp on the Chesapeake & Ohio Railroad in this territory was powerful. Huntington ultimately had a hand in the Central Pacific Railroad, supplying some of the route for the first transcontinental road in the late 1860s. The West Virginia city named for him, meanwhile, was home to many of his railroad workers who constructed the C&O through rugged, challenging and often difficult mountainous terrain.

Today the Huntington Railroad Museum is but a segment of a multi-part attraction under auspices of the Collis P. Huntington Railroad Historical Society. Included are the museum plus a handful of train excursions. Several pieces of rolling stock comprise the outdoor museum for visitor inspection.

While there are no ongoing scheduled trips, excursions traverse the tracks regularly. To be aware of what's currently available contact the society at Box 451, Kenova, WV 25530-0451, telephone (800) 553-6108 or (304) 453-1641, or on the Web at http://www.museumsofwv.org/museum.cfm?Museum=42.

POTOMAC EAGLE SCENIC RAILWAY—
Romney

From mid–May through October, this weekend tourist train runs diesel-powered passenger excursions from the Wappocomo Station a mile north of Romney. Each three-hour trip is narrated through picturesque mountain terrain. Saturday evening dinner trains and journeys on special occasions are scattered throughout the schedule. Times and costs vary so it's best to contact the railway in advance at Box 657, Romney, WV 26757, telephone (304) 424-0736, or online at http://www.potomaceagle.info.

E: Terminals (by State)

This appendix offers a sampling of past, present and future railway terminals in Southern cities from small to large. More than 50 municipalities are included. In some cases the history of a given community has been provided, particularly when a city and the railroads' impact on it are so closely intertwined they cannot be readily separated.

For a prelude to these vignettes, see Chapter 17.

Alabama

ANNISTON

Anniston, with iron ore smelting as its draw in the Civil War era, owes its name to the rails. Settled in 1872, and chartered as a private venture by Woodstock Iron Company in 1879, it was dubbed "Annie's Town" ("Annis-ton") after Annie Scott Tyler. Her spouse, Alfred L. Tyler, builder and president of an early rail line through the area, gave her moniker to the community. Anniston prospered as iron and steel manufacturing took advantage of the region's ample deposits of iron ore and coal. Rail access helped to make Anniston the state's fifth largest city from the 1890s to the 1950s.

In 1925, Milo R. Hanker erected the brick classical revival edifice serving as Southern Railway's depot, still operational. The facility was added to the National Register of Historic Places in 1994. When Norfolk Southern Railway sold it to the city for $55,000 in 2001, Anniston launched an enduring restoration. Tapping $430,000 in state and federal transportation grants thus far, the overhaul was scheduled for the finish line in 2009. The structure's future is expected to be multi-purposeful, serving not only Amtrak but with quarters for intercity buses and local taxis.

While the Anniston passenger station at 126 West 4th Street no longer maintains any rail staff, a guardian unlocks the waiting room as Amtrak's *Crescent* from New York to New Orleans is due (southbound in mid morning, northbound in mid afternoon). Although ticketing and baggage services aren't offered, in Amtrak's fiscal year 2008, Anniston handled 5,181 riders (14 daily) and revenues there reached $431,163.

BIRMINGHAM

In Birmingham's earliest railroad days, trains arrived and departed under a few uninspired wood frame canopies sheltering modest platforms. Not until April 1, 1887, when the Louisville & Nashville Railroad (L&N) opened Union Station on the site of the first hotel — the 37-room wood fabricated Relay House on 19th Street near Morris Avenue — did the city manifest a real depot. L&N played a key role in the city's development, taking infinite interest in abundant iron ore, coal and limestone deposits in the area. L&N also capitalized on steel production that evolved out of it.

Located on Morris Avenue at 20th Street, the city's first rail facility cost $134,163 to build (almost $3.2 million in 2008 figures) and welcomed 18 trains daily at its inception. Not only did L&N stop in but also Alabama Great Southern Railroad and Georgia Pacific Railway (a Southern Railway ancestor). That trio soon expanded by collecting under its shed the Atlanta, Birmingham & Atlantic Railway, Birmingham Mineral Railroad, Central of Georgia Railway, Kansas City, Memphis & Birmingham Railroad, and Southern Railway.

That huge shed, incidentally, spanning several tracks at grade level, was dismantled in the early 1930s, obliging a downtown grade separation project favored by the city. A perilous crossing on a major downtown thoroughfare was overcome by

When the traffic could no longer justify Birmingham's palatial Terminal Station, the *Crescent* called at multiple subsequent facilities, each invariably diminished from its forerunner in status and size. On May 28, 1979, after Southern Railway transferred *Crescent*'s control to Amtrak on February 1, 1979, the prestigious train waits in Birmingham. It's led by Southern E8A 6901, 6905 and an unidentified Amtrak E8 or E9 unit. While the *Crescent* persisted as a premier train, many of the depots it visited paled to their precursors (*courtesy Jay T. Thomson*).

raising the tracks above grade level and permitting an underpass at 20th Avenue North. The Atlanta, Birmingham & Coast Railroad (ex–ABA) moved its passenger operations in tandem to the west end's Elyton Yard. From that time onward L&N was Union Station's lone occupant, long hailed by locals as "the L&N Station."

The pioneering farm settlement of Elyton preceded the town established in 1871; Birmingham was named after an English industrial behemoth. Properties near a planned crossing of the Alabama & Chattanooga and South & North Alabama railroads were sold to attract more settlers. Throughout the first half of the 20th century the city was a natural resources leviathan of the American South.

In the interim, meanwhile, the state's largest metropolis reveled in a spectacular railroad temple so enormous that for a while it dwarfed every other transit center in Dixie. Construction of the $3 million ($71.3 million today) multi-block 5th and 6th century Byzantine edifice was finished in 1909. It touted 10 parallel tracks and drew a half-dozen rail lines. Into Birmingham's Terminal Station rolled consists of all the carriers calling at Union Station except L&N and ABA. The new palace of grandeur saw 54 trains arriving every day at its summit (1943). The number fell to seven daily in 1969, prompting city fathers to bulldoze the magnificent architectural trophy. Their intent was to erect a federal building on the site. But after Terminal Station was flattened, the Red Mountain Expressway connecting downtown to Interstates 20 and 59 filled that spot.

Facing similar realities of diminishing returns

(and arrivals!) a few years earlier, L&N's operations were radically downsized in 1960. The company closed its fading 73-year-old Union Station and transferred its modest trade to a less imposing structure one block west. Yet another underpass was added at 19th Street. The facade of L&N's dual-story edifice indulged a large tile mosaic mural exhibiting locomotives of the past. Passengers collected in a small well-lit air-conditioned lobby inside. The shift in sites must have prompted the wrecking-ball fate that befell the once proud, palatial Terminal Station.

When Southern Railway transferred the *Crescent* to Amtrak on January 31, 1979, it also relinquished to Amtrak the task of operating Birmingham's second L&N station. That traffic was soon consolidated in yet a smaller office adjacent to the tracks at 18th Street North, a portion of the final L&N passenger facility still branded "the L&N station" by a few locals. In 2010, the *Crescent* called at a nondescript passenger waiting room at 1819 Morris Avenue in downtown Birmingham's south side on daily runs to and from New Orleans and New York. With an elevated platform situated above the station and 18th Street, the unadorned facility imparts minimal effort. For anybody who remembers, of course, it doesn't begin to typify the graceful charm of Union Station (1887–1960) or the majestic elegance of Terminal Station (1909–1969).

A total of 32,733 people (90 daily) boarded or left passenger trains at Birmingham in Amtrak's fiscal year 2008, a 20 percent rise over the previous year. The company generated revenues there of $2,041,643 in 2007 (latest released data).

A long-planned intermodal transportation complex is in the works with completion presently targeted for 2012. Amtrak, Greyhound, local transit services and airport bus shuttles will be accessed there.

MONTGOMERY

The Montgomery Visitor Center, on the second floor of Union Station in Alabama's capital, resides in an edifice of arresting scope. With a loft above it and a gargantuan trainshed behind it — the latter cited as a "Monument of Historic Importance" — the triple-story testament to high-beam, brick-interior waiting rooms is representative of the late Victorian period. Once dubbed the "Showplace of Alabama," Union Station was built by the Louisville & Nashville Railroad (L&N) and detailed by architect Benjamin Boswell Smith. It opened for business on May 6, 1898, serving L&N and trains of five other carriers: Atlantic Coast Line, Central of Georgia, Mobile & Ohio, Seaboard Air Line and Western Railway of Alabama.

Facing north at 300 Water Street opposite Lee Street, back in the day the stately structure beckoned travelers in an inviting manner. Patrons rode up to grandiose front doors on horseback, buckboard, buggy, carriage, wagon or motorcar. Descending under a canopy, they entered the mammoth hall to transact their business at a bank of ticket windows and then await the departure or arrival of their trains. They sprawled in rows of wooden benches with backs and armrests, typical of myriad railway lobbies. The dual rows of benches held up to 10 people, five on each side facing opposite directions. The high-ceilinged classic hall's outsized space left generous room for travelers to interact with one another and move freely.

With the public's fickle allegiance to rail transportation shifting to highways and airways in the 1960s, one wag, recalling those days in Montgomery, allowed "the station was hardly used anymore." While Union Station still served trains of the L&N and Southern Railway in that decade, it was running on borrowed time. Once Amtrak acquired the remnants of passenger service from Southern Railway in early 1979, the facility was shuttered after the last train left town.

Reconfigured for commercial and office space in 1982-1983, the old depot was the site of Bludau's Restaurant by January 1, 1990. Later added to a massive downtown development project fronting the Alabama River, Union Station became part of an "Old Alabama Town" assemblage of 50 painstakingly restored structures. Self-guided walking tours now encompass buildings reminiscent of pioneer days: taverns, one-room schools, cotton gins, grist mills, blacksmith shops, antebellum townhouses and slave quarters are stops along the zone's route.

The former rail facility morphed into a new generation once the city acquired it in the late 20th century. On February 8, 1999, Union Station reopened not merely as headquarters of the Montgomery Convention and Visitor Bureau but also as a distinctive concert venue. As one of the remaining city rail complexes in the South spared the wrecking ball so far, Union Station is a stately monument to the anticipation those citadels provoked.

MOBILE

Shortly after the turn of the century in 1905-1906, the Mobile & Ohio Railroad constructed a striking railway center in downtown Mobile, the line's operational hub. Draftsman P. Thorton Mayre created the fortress-like three-story Spanish Colonial Revival depot at 110 Beauregard Street near the intersection of Water Street. With 16 large arch passageways along its front façade and a grand interior rotunda topped with a sky-lighted dome and characteristically Spanish red tile roof, the edifice is riveting. Erected at a cost of $575,000 ($13.6 million in 2008 dollars), it was then commonly known as Union Station. It also served trains of the New Orleans, Mobile & Chattanooga Railway, Southern Railway (which controlled the M&O from 1901–1940), and a few smaller carriers. The Mobile & Ohio combined with other roads in 1940 to form the Gulf, Mobile & Ohio Railroad with headquarters in Jackson, Tennessee. The teeming Mobile complex remained the line's southeastern terminus.

When passenger service ended, the railroad vacated its grand square-block Gulf, Mobile & Ohio station in 1986. Sitting idle for several years, the property was saved from the wrecking ball when the city of Mobile purchased it. Following a $19 million makeover and upgrade — including new HVAC, mechanical and electrical systems — the facility has become a sterling model of adaptive reuse. Platforms and space where tracks once were offer a bus station and parking today. Union Station itself was transformed into multiple commercial and retail enterprises, the largest the command post of Metro Transit Authority (MTA), the city's bus service. Although the city intends to retain about 6,200-square-feet of the property's 64,000-foot floor space for the MTA, it recently touted the remainder to prospective single clients as permanent lessees. If that happens it could secure the structure's presence for many years.

Another local depot that didn't fare as well served the Louisville & Nashville Railroad (L&N). There were actually two L&N stations that met their demise in the popularly recognized "Azalea City." Opened in the late 19th century or early 20th at the foot of Government Street, the first sheltered some of L&N's tracks with a massive trainshed. A parallel road behind the terminal with tracks on both sides allowed travelers and greeters in motorcars to park beside the trains and board or welcome arriving parties instead of waiting inside the station.

In the shifting tides of reduced passenger service, L&N razed the building when a smaller replacement was readied on the same spot in 1956. In a foretaste of things to come, the proxy was but a shell of its former self. Bereft of the bustle of swarms that kept the old station thriving, the unadorned exterior of the stepchild portended what was inside: an uninspired "room" of minimal proportions surrounded by contemporary plastic chairs and a couple of holdover benches. No arches, no high ceilings, no classic railroad trappings, all virtually belying the fact it was a waiting room for trains. Keep in mind this was the 1950s, not the 1990s.

This second L&N depot served Mobile as long as the trains came and ultimately passed into the hands of Seaboard Coast Line Railroad's "Family Lines System" (which embraced L&N and several more carriers) in 1967. In May 1971, Amtrak's assumption of rail passenger service left Mobile with a dwindling bare-bones operation, for Amtrak had less money to play with. A couple of things transpired on its watch, however, that made indelible marks on rail service there.

In 1993, Amtrak experienced its worst fatal disaster just outside Mobile, near Chickasaw, Alabama. That night 47 riders on the *Sunset Limited* (Los Angeles–Orlando) who had just left Mobile heading east lost their lives as another 103 were injured. The train plunged off a trestle into a river after a barge on the river struck a support beam and dislodged it. In August 2005, Hurricane Katrina struck the Gulf coast, severely damaging CSX tracks used by the *Sunset Limited* and flooding the Mobile station. Service east of New Orleans ended and was never restored, though the tracks were reinstated within a short while. CSX, which owned the ex–L&N property in Mobile, sold it to a developer in 2006; the following year the station was razed and a parking lot replaced it. "Mobile's history with trains has been dicey," interpretively observed a journalist.

Mobile railfans and those nearby who would benefit by a return of passenger trains are optimistic that Congress will offer a green signal to Amtrak's intent to resume service in the region in the near future. Multiple plans linking the city to New Orleans and perhaps Jacksonville were advanced in mid 2009. If that should happen, Amtrak will open yet another small depot to process local travelers.

TUSCALOOSA

The nondescript station situated a mile south of downtown Tuscaloosa occupies the turf at 2105 Greensboro Avenue close to where it intersects with Hargrove Road. Built in the late 1800s by British-owned Alabama Great Southern Railroad, it served a handful of Southern Railway passenger and freight trains during most of its history. Today the property is owned by Southern successor Norfolk Southern Railway (NS) which maintains a freight operation there. Amtrak, assuming responsibility for the *Crescent* passenger train (New York–New Orleans) from Southern Railway in 1979, runs the train along NS rails daily, once in each direction.

In 2008, a correspondent for *The Tuscaloosa News* paid a visit to the depot and issued an indictment that might be duplicated in many other places: "Tall weeds covered the sign on the south side of the building identifying it as the station." Parking was so limited, when a train arrived, automobiles blocked one another. Some patrons interviewed hinted that conditions inside the depot were "unsanitary" with restrooms "not in great condition." More signs of neglect included stains on the ceiling from a leaky roof and spider webs on windows in a hallway. "Many who use the train station say they hope ... owners will clean up and maintain the station's facilities, while others say they have abandoned hope of that and are uncomfortable while in the waiting area," the reporter concluded.

In fiscal year 2008, Amtrak served 10,030 travelers at Tuscaloosa, a daily average of about 27 riders, and a 24 percent increase over the previous year. Ticket revenues in 2008 generated $696,454.

Tuscaloosa is a comparatively small town (81,000 residents in a recent year), its principal claim to fame being the main campus of the University of Alabama. In the heyday of rail travel, nevertheless, the Louisville & Nashville Railroad operated a second depot there. While it hasn't served trains for years it still stands, most recently housing a local commercial enterprise.

Arkansas

FORT SMITH

While trains stopped at outposts earlier at Fort Smith — the second largest city in Arkansas, hard by the state's boundary with Oklahoma — the first structure that could be classified as a true passenger station opened its doors April 29, 1897. That day the Arkansas Central Railroad (AC), a line eventually extending east 47 miles to Paris, Arkansas, welcomed riders at Arkansas Central Garrison Avenue Station. It was a facility shared with the St. Louis, Iron Mountain & Southern Railway (SLIMS), controlled by the St. Louis–San Francisco Railway (Frisco). In an interesting twist SLIMS acquired AC by 1901.

A handful of added depots premiered in this relatively tiny burg in the same epoch. Formed January 25, 1899, the Fort Smith & Western Railroad Company launched its own station at 10th and Garrison. On December 9, 1903, the Frisco line initiated a passenger terminal on Garrison Avenue (possibly the 1897 AC-SLIMS fixture refurbished and expanded); this one included provisions for Frisco's Central Division headquarters. Yet another rail station was added in 1903 when the Midland Valley Railroad unveiled its separate depot. (Midland Valley was bought by Texas & Pacific Railway in 1964, after which its trains no longer visited Fort Smith. Its depot wasn't razed until 1995, however.)

A point worth noting is that — within a six-year span (1897–1903) — the little hamlet of Fort Smith witnessed construction of no fewer than three and maybe four individual depots within its town limits. Several implications stem from it. Not only is the independence of the early railroads exhibited, reliance by the local community upon trains for passenger and freight hauling is evident. The rails' significance to the larger region is also underscored. Carriers saw potential in the area as numerous small lines joined at these depots, gambling their routes on Fort Smith in individual quests to secure their own futures.

The Garrison Avenue Station met the largest of these early carriers' (Frisco's) requirements until May 1, 1912. That day Union Depot (subsequently branded Union Station)—jointly owned by Kansas City Southern Railway (KCS) and SL–SF (Frisco)—was christened on Rogers Avenue. The tenants' passenger trains called at Union Station a long while. On August 31, 1941, KCS ran its final consist out of there. KCS returned in another capacity when — in 1965 — it built a bus passenger terminal and package freight office in the city.

Frisco lingered at Union Station another seven years after KCS' departure, finally retreating to its original eight-columned stately two-story Garrison Avenue Station on June 30, 1948. It remained "put" until its last SL–SF passenger train pulled out of Fort Smith on September 18, 1965. While freight traffic persisted, the break signaled the end of a love affair Frisco maintained with Fort Smith travelers dating back three generations. Union Station was demolished in July 1966, clearing the path for a new convention center.

LITTLE ROCK

In the halcyon days of rail transportation in America, Pulaski County, Arkansas, encompassing the state's capital, lay claim to a handful of premier passenger facilities, among them: Choctaw Route Station at 1010 East Third Street, 1899, featuring intricate terra cotta details; MoPac Station (aka Union Station) at 1400 West Markham Street and Victory Street, 1921, a rambling Romanesque bas-

tion that replaced an earlier terminal destroyed by fire; and Rock Island Argenta Depot at Fourth and Hazel Streets in adjacent North Little Rock, 1913, exhibiting Mediterranean style architecture. The three survivors are included on the National Register of Historic Places.

A deteriorating depot in Little Rock proper, the Choctaw Route Station saw trains traveling east to Memphis and west to El Reno, Oklahoma, and Tucumcari, New Mexico. Built by the Choctaw, Oklahoma & Gulf Railroad (CO&G), the facility is the only CO&G terminal between Memphis and Oklahoma still standing. In a hostile takeover by the Rock Island System in 1904, the CO&G lost its independence. Passenger service ended on the Choctaw mainline on November 10, 1967. Thirteen years hence the Rock Island Railroad also ceased operations. In the meantime the 16,500-square-foot depot saw a progression of new owners: *The Arkansas Gazette* was first followed by a lengthy period of abandonment, then Spaghetti Warehouse restaurant (1990–1996), The Edge nightclub (1996-1997), and the City of Little Rock (1999–present) initially using it for sundry activities. In 2002, following a charitable trust donation that provided a $4 million building makeover, the William J. Clinton Foundation leased the property from the city. A once proud depot that was lying dormant, virtually forgotten, and overrun with wildly advancing shrubs—seemingly, a prime candidate for the wrecking ball — was not only rescued but infused with new life. This appears to have assured its future.

Choctaw Station was transformed into the University of Arkansas Clinton School of Public Service, the first U.S. institution given to that pursuit. It contains dual classrooms, library, common room and staff provisions on the main floor and upstairs space for an office for the former president and the Clinton Foundation. The facility was integrated into the adjacent 148,000-square-foot Clinton Presidential Library complex. Nearby, the Choctaw-Rock Island bridge over the Arkansas River is part of a pedestrian river trail planned for bikers and hikers. That link encompasses an allusion to a catchphrase from Clinton's 1996 re-election drive: *Building a Bridge to the 21st Century*.

Elsewhere back in the day Little Rock's commanding MoPac Station was a southern terminus for a handful of premier Missouri Pacific trains running to opposite points at Kansas City and St. Louis. That depot also saw lots of traffic as a key stop along routes linking those cities with San Antonio and New Orleans passing through Little Rock. The edifice was designed by MoPac chief architect E. M. Tucker, who performed the same service in Texarkana later in the decade. At one time Ripley's *Believe It or Not* acclaimed the Little

Rock structure "the largest train station in the nation served by only one railroad." Sold by Missouri Pacific Railroad Company on April 27, 1973, the 110,000-square-foot complex brought a purchase price of $923,000.

Today Amtrak's *Texas Eagle* calls at (MoPac) Union Station twice daily on its trek between Chicago and San Antonio, pursuing much of the course MoPac trains traipsed almost a century ago (1915). Situated midway between the Arkansas River and state capitol, Union Station affords unobstructed views of the capitol's dome on a hillside to the south as trains enter the terminal. In fiscal year 2008, some 19,724 riders got on or off the *Texas Eagle* in Little Rock or 54 per day while local sales contributed $1,573,621 to Amtrak's bottom line. Local ridership improved 21 percent over a year earlier.

TEXARKANA

"If there ever was a railroad town, Texarkana would be it" begins a treatise on a modern Web site. "The city was founded by railroad companies." In 1873, the Texas & Pacific Railroad constructed a line from Dallas to Texarkana: "At the end of their line, they built a town, Texarkana, Texas." The following year the Cairo & Fulton Railroad launched trackage from St. Louis to Texarkana: "At the end of their line, they built a town, Texarkana, Arkansas." In 1876, the U.S. Congress mandated that a depot in Texarkana must straddle the state line. A dozen years afterward (1888) the Missouri Pacific Railroad (MoPac), which superseded the Cairo & Fulton, and the Texas & Pacific joined forces in a station erected precisely on the border separating the states.

The 100 East Front Street facility they built was long and low. At least 20 wood posts along the front propped up a covered walkway running the full length of the building. The frame structure paralleled the tracks alongside the depot's façade. The whole affair proffered a throwback to a western town general store, bank, delicatessen, or blacksmith shop, ostensibly straight out of TV's *Gunsmoke*. Of course it wasn't far removed from that environment by time or place. Although provisions for a restaurant were incorporated in the station's design, the intervention of the Great Depression prevented it from happening. A snack bar and newsstand sufficed.

A decade following the station's opening the Cotton Belt Railway brought its tracks to Texarkana and moved into the station as a tenant. Appropriating serious funding to upgrade the facility, five years hence the Cotton Belt became a partner with the other roads in owning it. By 1920, local inhabitants envisioned the next step in meeting their city's transportation needs, a new station. The trio

of carriers already there plus a new one, Kansas City Southern Railway, erected a 67,000-square-foot tri-level Union Station on the site of the old one at a cost of $1,667,000, officially opening April 17, 1930.

Designed by E. M. Tucker, MoPac's chief architect — who had drawn details for the Little Rock MoPac (Union) Station in 1921— the new grand Renaissance revival facility, similar to Texarkana's downtown post office, was built by Stewart-McGehee Construction Company of Little Rock. Tucker's concept projected five bays centered on the Arkansas–Texas state line. The central bay projected forward with each side wing stepping progressively down and back. A unique feature was the inclusion of a seam allowing up to eight inches of expansion in length during the summer, returning to its original size in winter. And the elusive restaurant that had missed out the first time around was there.

MoPac and Texas & Pacific, carriers with the most passenger trains calling at Union Station, managed to operate through the facility without backup movements. Cotton Belt and Kansas City Southern required backup moves to access the station.

A private realtor in Texarkana purchased the structure in 2003, calling it "a venue ripe for multi-use entertainment options." In *The Texarkana Gazette* the new owner said he saw "adaptive reuse as one of the ways to reinvent downtown, taking historical structures and spaces and reshaping them for the future." The depot contained 8,000-square-feet of unfinished office space on its upper level. At the time he bought it the new landlord was convinced "Union Station was the cornerstone of our community's economic prosperity, if not the cornerstone from the region's prosperity."

When Amtrak acquired the *Texas Eagle* from MoPac in 1971, it required but a small front corner of massive Union Station for its operations. The train runs daily in both directions between Chicago and San Antonio, stopping briefly in Texarkana en route. In fiscal year 2008, Texarkana generated 6,972 patrons for or from the *Eagle*, roughly 19 riders per day, a gain of 21 percent over a year.

"Although the Arkansas–Texas border bisects the center of the structure, the current Amtrak waiting room and ticket office is located in a former Railway Express Agency office on the Arkansas side of the structure," a contemporary source recently noted. "When Amtrak's *Texas Eagle* is stopped in Texarkana, the west end of the train is in Texas, and the east end of the train is in Arkansas." Yet another informant lamented not long ago, "Most of the building is in desperate need of restoration." It's an impression that isn't confined to Texarkana.

Florida

JACKSONVILLE

New Orleans, Richmond and other rail centers notwithstanding, back in the day Jacksonville was the colossus of Southeastern passenger trains. Every route except one eventually encountered the unofficial "Welcome to Florida" station. Save for a handful of mid 20th century streamliners that bypassed the "Gateway City," few traveling south, north, northwest or west missed it. Before that majestic apex complex opened in 1919, a profusion of lesser facilities prevailed.

Jacksonville's foray into depots occurred in 1858-1859, early in the evolution of railroads. The Florida, Atlantic & Gulf Central Railroad (FA&GC) erected a covered platform, small waiting room and blacksmith shop. It was archaic by future standards in an area that could be deemed frontier. With about 2,500 inhabitants at the Civil War's outbreak (1861), Jax was the state's third "metropolis" (after Key West and Pensacola). After the war the FA&GC improved its image by constructing a bigger enclosed wooden terminal. Beside the St. Johns River at the base of Julia Street the carrier made innovative use of space: some tracks and warehouses were elevated on pilings, extending over the water (perchance railways' initial "air rights"?). By 1881, this structure became the city's original Union Station after the Waycross Short Line Railway reached Jax and sent its trains there.

Other stations appeared. The area's first "decent" depot, insisted a source, was built by the Savannah, Florida & Western Railway (SF&W) on the north bank of the St. Johns River (1883). "Plain-looking on the outside" with a conforming design, even so it embraced essentials for that era: restrooms, café, and a caretaker tending an "elegantly furnished ladies waiting room with an ornate fireplace." When the Jacksonville, Tampa & Key West Railway (JT&KW) came to town the next year (1884) the SF&W depot modified into a Union Station, too. Both carriers were forerunners of the Atlantic Coast Line Railroad (ACL) founded in 1900.

In the meantime the Florida Central & Peninsular Railroad, a precursor of the Seaboard Air Line Railroad, constructed another depot at the foot of Hogan Street three blocks east of the SF&W/ JT&KW Union Station. These facilities exhibited a strong advantage by securing spots alongside riverbanks. For some years— until tracks were laid south of town — steamboats ferried travelers going to destinations below Jax.

After the Jacksonville & Southwestern Railway, yet another ACL ancestor, established a depot along the water's edge on East Bay Street at Catherine Street, trouble brewed. The Atlantic, Valdosta & Western Railway (AV&W), operating its own depot next door to that one, liked the J&S terminal much better and asked to participate. Turned down, AV&W went to court, which ruled in its favor.

There were still other serviceable yet unadorned terminals springing up at Jax and a handful of neighbor burbs opposite the St. Johns— in Arlington, Burnside, Mayport, Pablo and South Jacksonville. Believed to serve only briefly, they left sim-

Southbound 5 *City of Miami* awaits departure from the Jacksonville terminal in this scene about 1960. It's led by a trio of FEC E-units, 1033, 1053, and 103. Arriving in Jacksonville from Richmond over ACL trackage, #5 will access its namesake city on FEC rails 366 miles south seven hours after departure. The originating consist will be reduced, meanwhile, as sections break off for two more destinations — St. Petersburg and Sarasota (***photograph by Fred Carnes, courtesy Richard C. Beall***).

On a sunny afternoon in 1973, Amtrak's *Floridian* is ready to depart Jacksonville to continue its trip to Chicago via Montgomery, Birmingham, Nashville and Louisville. The 10-car lightweight passenger train includes a dome coach in its consist and is powered by dual EMD E8s. The tall building at right is SCL's headquarters, now CSX's. The station's roof is poking above the train to the left. There are many tracks with long platforms here because in the heyday more than 100 trains daily, often including more than 20 cars, called here. Closed in 1974, the station is the Prime F. Osborn III Convention Center now. Amtrak relocated to a smaller depot northwest of the city (*courtesy Michael B. Robbins*).

ilar impressions, details likely lost to history. Some may have been little more than ticket stands or windows by the tracks. The Florida East Coast and Georgia Southern & Florida railways both built separate depots in Jax. At the turn of the century there may have been as many as a dozen train "stations" competing for business in Duval County (Jax).

Seeing an opening for himself and the road he owned (Florida East Coast), in 1893, enterprising rail magnate Henry M. Flagler formed the Jacksonville Terminal Company and became its president. Five lines drawn to Flagler's pursuit erected a rambling Union Depot at Bay and Stuart streets near the water, the fourth one in Jax. Opened February 4, 1895, and completed January 15, 1897, Flagler Depot (a nickname the locals gave it) included a 1,000 by 150-foot trainshed ("the longest in the world," local dailies asserted). In 1912, the classic Spanish mission structure saw 92 trains come and go daily on a dozen tracks as Jacksonvillians — realizing their depot was sadly overtaxed — called for a larger one.

The city fathers wanted to relocate Union Station between Adams and Forsyth streets west of Myrtle Avenue. But the rail tycoons prevailed, contending a shift from the Flagler site would be costly due to the loss of yards and enclosures. The mammoth trainshed was demolished to make way for a new edifice a block west of the existing terminal. Most of the old facility was left intact, supplying a baggage room and offices. An 11-cubicle roundhouse and 115-car coach yard facilitated equipment servicing. The yard processed up to 210 trains per day.

By then several owners of the Jacksonville Terminal Company had changed names and upgraded operations. Joint ownership included the Atlantic Coast Line, Florida East Coast and Seaboard Air Line roads, each one holding a 25 percent interest. The remaining quarter was divided evenly between Southern Railway and its Georgia, Southern & Florida ancillary.

In 1916, Jacksonville Terminal Company engaged New York City draftsman Kenneth M. Murcheson to craft the city's fifth Union Station, one that would impress on millions of arriving visitors that they were "Where Florida Begins," another of Jax's slogans. Copying Manhattan's expansive Pennsylvania Station waiting room in a pared down version, Murcheson was inspired by "lines and dimensions of the majestic ancient Roman baths of Caracalla, Titus and Diocletion." Those baths featuring central halls were noted as "temples of space and light" and the Jax terminal followed suit. Construction, delayed by the First World War, began April 1, 1918. It included a 180-foot façade of 14 Doric columns, each weighing 45 tons and rising 42 feet, at the entrance offering a classic colonnade of splendid proportions. All who passed through those portals were dwarfed by it.

A barrel-vaulted ceiling framing enormous arched windows soared cathedral-like 75 feet above the main room's marble floor. In unexpected places there was stained glass in spheres and stripes. An elegant restaurant flanked by snack bars, newsstands, barbershop, floral shop, gift shops, pharmacy and sundry other retailers completed the public space in the great hall. Ornamental iron

The enduring FEC passenger station in Miami serving travelers from 1912 to 1963 was at 200 NW 1st Avenue. Look just above the white structure labeled "Florida East Coast Ry. Passenger Station"— it's the imposing facility in the center. It received trains from Jacksonville and beyond in the heyday as well as from Key West from 1912 to 1935. A consist adjacent to the station in this ca. 1930s illustration is ready for departure north (*photograph by Al Perez, courtesy Cal Winter*).

gates leading to the trains dominated the concourse beyond the waiting room.

Attesting to Jax's geographical site, on opening day, November 17, 1919, the $3.5 million ($43.2 million in 2008 figures) Union Station processed 20,000 travelers and 110 trains. At its summit a quarter-century hence (1944), Jax might see 100,000 civilians and servicemen come and go on a busy day. No other Southern terminal except Atlanta could boast anything like it. In the heyday of rail travel, an eyewitness declared: "The volume of seasonal traffic is enormous. Trains tend to arrive [in Jacksonville] in batches—a half dozen or more. Worse, in peak season, each 'train' may have ... a half-dozen consists arriving, one after another at short intervals.... Traffic follows a unique pattern. Trains arrive from several points north, northwest and west with sleepers bound for various destinations on both coasts. Each arriving train has to be broken up and the cars shuffled into new consists gently as they are occupied."

The final train left the terminal on January 3, 1974. Up to 15 million people had passed through that facility annually. After 54 years of continuous

service it was then to experience a checkered existence of neglect. For years it languished, forgotten, left to the impulses of delinquents and drifters degrading its façade. When promoters found little success in turning it into an entertainment venue or renting it to retailers, it filled with sporadic flea markets and bazaars. All of that belied the splendor of its architecture and superlative traditions.

Just when it seemed Union Station was a sure candidate for the wrecking ball, some local civic and commercial leaders partnered with the city to rescue it. The year was 1982. On October 17, 1986, the Prime F. Osborn III Convention Center, occupying the former Union Station at 1000 Water Street, opened as Jax's premier convention center. Osborn, an ex–CSX chairman who steered the rescue squad, was lauded by city officials for his civic-mindedness. While there are few cues today of the structure's heritage, some original gates and train signs are preserved in pre-function areas where the trains backed into the station.

In the meantime the passenger trains transferred to a modest depot at 3570 Clifford Lane on the northwest side of town. This Amtrak Station was situated on the old ACL's mainline. No longer did trains intersect numerous city streets, travel extra miles downtown or lose more time backing into the station. As of 2010, Amtrak's *Silver Meteor* and *Silver Star* call there twice daily on their treks between New York and south Florida. While the *Auto Train* passes through daily between Lorton, Virginia, and Sanford, Florida, it doesn't stop. A move is afoot to restore daily service through Jax linking New Orleans and Orlando that existed until Hurricane Katrina interrupted it in August 2005.

While Jax now sees but an infinitesimal fraction of the passenger traffic it enjoyed in the halcyon days, to shivering southbound riders seeking a place in the sun it remains an undisputed gateway. In fiscal year 2008, some 61,758 travelers (169 daily) boarded or left Amtrak trains in Jax, up 6.9 percent in a year. Sanford, Orlando, Tampa, Miami and Jacksonville (in that order) led Amtrak's Florida travel in 2008. A historian noted only 15 percent of rail riders arriving in Jax get off there. For the South's largest metropolis with a resident populace of 808,000 (2008 U.S. Census Bureau figures) it's clear the magnetism of other destinations is still pulling patrons through Jacksonville.

MIAMI

At the figurative and literal end of the line, Miami might never have hit the big time had someone not kept on tracking. Henry M. Flagler's Florida East Coast Railway (FEC) put the outpost at Biscayne Bay on the proverbial map. In doing so any notion the subtropics were swamps with profusions of wild foliage, crawling creatures and mosquito-infested jungles marked by erratic, powerful storms was radically altered. Once Flagler entered the settlement of Fort Dallas (later renamed Miami) in 1896, rail-laying crews in tow, the future was assured. Overnight a village of 300 swelled to 1,500, a 400 percent increase, as word of a charmed oasis warmed by gentle breezes and brushed by white silver sands got out. To make it even better it was at last readily accessible by land.

The first FEC depot was little more than a platform and shelter in Miami at the intersection of Flagler Street and NW 1st Avenue. It was superseded by a wooden station "uptown" at the corner of Biscayne Boulevard and NE 6th Street. But the Florida East Coast's more memorable terminal was at 200 NW 1st Avenue, built in 1912. That edifice served FEC trains until an ugly, destructively deadly strike occurred against the line beginning January 23, 1963, halting traffic forevermore to that depot. While limited passenger service was restored by court order from 1965 to 1968, acting in haste Miami civic leaders bulldozed the longstanding FEC terminal before 1963 was out.

With no place to go and under orders to resume,

the FEC brought its trains south from Jacksonville to a small station it had staffed since 1955 in North Miami. It was located at the junction of NE 16th Avenue and 129th Street. Far from ideal, it nevertheless sufficed, filling in until the state Public Service Commission allowed the FEC to suspend hauling travelers.

Through the years the FEC sustained an agreement with the Atlantic Coast Line Railroad (ACL) to transfer riders to and from FEC's Miami-bound trains at Jacksonville, ACL's east coast terminus. That changed in 1963. ACL joined ranks with its oft bitter rival, the Seaboard Air Line Railroad (SAL), for the final two-thirds of its trek down the Florida peninsula. SAL was "the other guy" in Miami, extending its tracks there in January 1927. It originally constructed a depot at Flagler Street and LeJeune Road (now 42nd Avenue). SAL subsequently opened at 2210 NW 7th Avenue in a facility that obliged ACL trains from 1963. The merged operations of the dual carriers—as the Seaboard Coast Line Railroad—came and went there as of 1967. The station was demolished in 1980.

Some Miamians familiar with both FEC and SAL terminals, assessing the latter depot on modern Web sites, have been less than charitable, to wit: "The station had a rundown appearance and looked like something from a Third World country." Another: "The building appeared to be more than it was. It was wooden covered with stucco. Years of water leaks and uncertain maintenance resulted in it being ready to collapse. The location resulted in high operating costs—trains had to be backed out of the station and taken several miles away to be serviced; long trains blocked city streets resulting in doubling trains on the platform tracks, all requiring services of switchers and crews meaning a lot of money. In the 1960s it [the depot] was dingy and appeared to need a good stiff cleaning. The wood wasn't equal to that used in the FEC station and it slowly succumbed to a humid climate." Yet another: "The trip from Hialeah south to the station was S-L-O-W. Whatever its virtues architecturally (which were few) SAL's station in Miami and its poor location [were] never remotely adequate or worthy of the railroad's boldness in building to the southeast coast in the first place. SAL's apologetic, back-door entrance into Miami made clear to all that by the time the railroad finally reached town the Florida land boom had crashed."

"Amtrak certainly wasn't about to pay a lot of money to fix the building, nor was it willing to live with the added operational costs" that were in the SAL/ACL/SCL terminal, an observer noted. After Amtrak acquired passenger service May 1, 1971, it looked for a new location as a southern terminus. It found an ideal one in North Miami in 1978. Its

During the halcyon days of railway travel the Miami FEC passenger station was an extremely busy place, substantiated by this December 22, 1954, image (*courtesy Richard C. Beall*).

Another view of the crowd at the Miami FEC station on December 22, 1954, confirms how busy it was until other forms swamped rail as the nation's means of long-distance travel (*courtesy Richard C. Beall*).

modern station there was erected at the south end of the CSX (SCL) freight yard at 8303 NW 37th Avenue and NW 83rd Street. Today that depot receives two Amtrak trains, *Silver Meteor* and *Silver Star*, daily. In fiscal year 2008 Amtrak boarded or detrained 80,348 passengers (220 daily) in Miami, an 18.8 percent increase in one year. The company's 2008 Miami revenues topped $5.8 million.

An intermodal center in unincorporated Miami situated just east of the airport is expected to partially open in 2011 and be fully functioning in 2012. Miami Central Station will combine Amtrak, Tri-Rail commuter trains, Metrorail rapid transit, Greyhound, Metrobus, airport people-mover, shuttles, courtesy buses and vans and taxis.

ORLANDO

No fewer than five depots served Orlando after it was incorporated in July 1875, three sequentially occupying the same spot. The first, a wooden structure at 76 Church Street built by the South Florida Railroad (SF) when it came to town October 2, 1880, connected with nearby Sanford. SF took over the charter of the Lake Monroe and Orlando Railroad in 1874, and then joined the Plant System in 1883. Among Plant's manifold routes was a vital one linking Orlando and Tampa, appreciably adding to successor Atlantic Coast Line Railroad (founded in 1900). In 1890, rail baron Henry B. Plant replaced the wooden depot in Orlando with one of brick veneer. Even that was to be upgraded after his death a few years later (June 23, 1899).

The third in the string of stations on the site at Depot Place and West Church Street was finished in 1900. It was fabricated of brick too, yet distinguished by late Victorian architecture. A complicated roof line of the bi-level terminal extended over porches on the ground level on both front and back sides. Designed by draftsman T. B. Cotter, the ACL facility was modified in the 1920s, with its slate roof replaced by tin. Eyebrow-shaped roof dormer windows were replaced by triangular-shaped gable windows. The structure was added to the U.S. National Register of Historic Places on April 22, 1976. In the next decade (1980s) what had gone around came around: the roof was returned to original red, silver and gray slate and the gables were replaced by eyebrow dormers.

A passenger depot from 1900 to 1926, the building was a ticket outlet and freight station from 1926 to 1972. An ensuing Church Street Station commercial development is well known in the region though it has spent a topsy-turvy existence at times, shut down at one point for several years. The complex housed retail operations of varied persuasions and simultaneously was an entertainment venue while changing ownership frequently.

A fourth station in Orlando, owned by Seaboard Air Line Railroad at 61 West Central Boulevard, was wedged between Garland and Orange avenues just two blocks north of Church Street. Until the merger of SAL and ACL in 1967, after which the resulting Seaboard Coast Line Railroad operated out of ACL digs, SAL was relatively small potatoes in Orlando. In the heyday of passenger rail traffic it withdrew altogether from transitioning people by train to and from Orlando. Instead it dispatched Florida Greyhound Lines buses to fetch and deliver them. As the mid 20th century arrived, those travelers connected with SAL trains at Ocala for west coast Florida points and Jacksonville for interstate destinations.

Orlando's prominent passenger carrier, ACL, departed its Church Street dwelling in 1926, entering a more impressive Spanish style terminal at 1400 Sligh Boulevard, Orlando's fifth. "Seaboard Coast Line" brandishing is still stenciled into that structure's white portico façade above its tri-arches today. Provisions within are sobering and austere though serviceable. In 2008, a local resident used a Web site to disparage the facility as "a rotting train station in complete disrepair." He cited paint peeling, broken windows, rusted gutters, termite damage, wood rot and lack of pay phones in his complaint. Faulting poor housekeeping, this was harmful to the city's image as a tourist Mecca, he allowed. Like many depots Orlando's is owned by a host railroad (in this case, CSX) while Amtrak — which runs the trains and sells the tickets — has little responsibility for the physical plants in which it is simply a lessee.

With 147,491 Amtrak passengers in fiscal year 2008 (404 average daily) alighting from and boarding the *Silver Meteor* and *Silver Star* — both Miami–New York trains — Orlando is Florida's second most popular rail destination. That's a 13.9 percent rise in a year. It's a distant second to the Auto Train terminus at Sanford with 234,839 users in 2008 (643 per day). Orlando contributed $11.8 million to Amtrak's bottom line in 2008.

A projected SunRail commuter transport system initially linking four central Florida counties with rapid transit is expected to include the Orlando Amtrak station on its route. Given a green light by the Florida legislature and signed into law by the state's governor in December 2009, the historic bill covers SunRail, Tri-Rail (in southeast Florida), and plans for high speed rail linking Tampa and Miami.

PENSACOLA

After receiving a charter to operate in 1850, it took the Louisville & Nashville Railroad (L&N) three decades to reach the port cities of Mobile, New Orleans and Pensacola (1880). With its mainline finally complete L&N could tap into the vast trading resources beyond U.S. shores as people, products and raw materials were ferried through seaside terminals. L&N's foothold in Pensacola, the Sunshine State's westernmost city, required a wait stop for passenger traffic, yet its early form is elusive. It was likely a modest, nearly obscure attempt. Though it may have been primitive, that wouldn't have been out of character for depots of the 19th century in out-of-the-way places.

L&N still may have been in pioneer mode in the century's fading years but management wanted to grow a business in Pensacola. It ordered a fancy station to demonstrate its resolve. The bi-level wood-frame depot at the northwest corner of Wright and Tarragona streets (the latter then identified as Railroad Street) was but a few blocks north of Tarragona Wharf on Pensacola Bay. L&N tracks ran to it and out over the water to facilitate the loading and unloading of steamers. The passenger depot, meanwhile, virtually filled the block it fronted. A tower stood at one end, rising three levels above the second floor. And the second story was outfitted with an exterior balcony that extended all the way around the building's perimeter. That early L&N depot must have been an awesome sight to local denizens at the turn of the century, a stunning structure on Pensacola's downtown skyline.

But L&N wasn't done with Pensacola by any means. In 1912, at 239 North Alcaniz Street, the carrier opened a brand new station that in every measurable way superseded its presence a few blocks away. Yet it's what has become of this building in "The City of Five Flags" (for the governments of Spain, France, Great Britain, the Confederacy, and the United States, all of which flew banners there) in the years after passenger trains left town that makes it particularly compelling to railfans today. In what is one of the most ingenious developments in the post-passenger epoch, that 1912 station is now the unique portal of one of Pensacola's most prestigious lodging properties. The final passenger train rolled out of the station April 30, 1971. Now the facility, still on its original site, fronts the 15-story glass-tower Crowne Plaza Pensacola Grand Hotel (originally Pensacola Grand Hotel) behind it at 200 East Gregory Street. This L&N depot went on the U.S. National Register of Historic Places in 1979.

Through a concerted and meticulous preservation effort, almost all of the station's original Spanish mission design was retained. It's notably spiked with traces of Italianate and decidedly influenced by Prairie School architectural élan. Refurbished in 1984, the ornate structure was connected with the hotel tower offering 210 sleeping quarters. The stellar bi-level depot includes the hotel's main lobby, lounge, dining room ("1912 The Restaurant"), spa, gift shop, "The L&N Lobby Bar," conference space and a grand ballroom. Promotion proudly elicits: "Our reception area is a delight! It's actually the historic L&N Train Depot built in 1912 and filled with antiques and other authentic period fixtures. It's a lobby not to be hurried through, but a wealth of memories meant for a leisurely tour."

Our own inspection of this facility in 2009 sup-

In 1975, a pair of Amtrak EMD E8 locomotives wait with consists in the ex–ACL yard then operated by SCL at St. Petersburg. Of special interest to railfans is a second E8 locomotive behind 218: it's a former IC engine still wearing its brown and orange livery. Until Amtrak bought new equipment, for a while it relied on what had been used by the freight lines. Behind the locomotives at left and unseen rests railroad shop buildings (*courtesy Michael B. Robbins*).

ports the advertising. The original brick walls on the outside surround interior tile floors nearly a century old. Soft shades of brown complement the bricks offset by tan, beige and white hues. Behind the ticket windows one can occupy the hotel's business center or a private sitting room. Vintage tapestries and chandeliers adorn the spacious lobby (ex-waiting room) while a quartet of center brick columns still supports the upper level. There's a large railroad clock reminiscent of the era. Comfortable plush seating invites guests to linger in the lobby (the wood benches are gone). Coffee tables and a magnificent grand piano are modern treatments that increase the ambience in the historic hall. Arriving guests drive over a red brick road to pull up to a marquee-covered entrance, the kind that dramatically announced great theaters in the past. This is a venue not to be missed — a former rail terminal making a sterling contribution to the commercial enterprise that owns it. It's also one of the better examples of adaptive reuse of an out-of-service depot to be found anywhere in the South.

After the St. Louis–San Francisco Railway (commonly known as the Frisco line) lost its route to New Orleans before 1920, it sought another shipping outlet to the Gulf of Mexico. In July 1925, the company bought the Muscle Shoals, Birmingham and Pensacola Railroad that connected Pensacola with the little hamlet of Kimbrough, Alabama, 143 miles above the seaport city. When new tracks linking Kimbrough to Frisco's mainline at Memphis were completed in July 1928, the carrier's aspirations for a route to sea once again came to fruition. Pensacola was particularly desirable as a freight gateway to international commerce. Although by the mid 1950s Frisco's passenger station located near the Pensacola Naval Air Station no longer saw travelers arrive, the depot remained intact until it was razed in 1970.

In 1993, Amtrak agreed to extend the route of the *Sunset Limited* running between Los Angeles and New Orleans to the east of the latter city, making it the only true transcontinental line by reaching Jacksonville, Orlando and initially, Miami. Amtrak needed a station in Pensacola to host the tri-weekly passenger consist. It was able to lease a building at 980 East Heinberg Street just east of the downtown historic district, a lease it may still hold. Hurricane Katrina's visit to the Gulf Coast in late August 2005 nevertheless curtailed the passenger line from operating east of New Orleans. There have been solo and collective efforts since calling for restoration of the full route. Congress must approve capital for it if it is to happen. If so it will take Amtrak a while to amass sufficient rolling stock, equipment, stations and personnel, and to coordinate marketing efforts. Hope springs eternal among the panhandle's patient railfans.

ST. PETERSBURG

The tracks around Old Tampa Bay were extended into Pinellas County in the final decades of the 19th century. Pushing past Tarpon Springs and Clearwater in the early months of 1888, by May 1 the narrow gauge Orange Belt Railway opened to the end of the central west coast Florida peninsula dominated by St. Petersburg. Reorganized as the Sanford and St. Petersburg Railroad in 1893, a 152-mile mainline connecting the pair of towns, the company embraced the Plant System two years hence which promptly standard-gauged it. The route was absorbed into the budding Atlantic Coast Line Railroad (ACL) in 1902, following rail magnate Henry B. Plant's death (1899).

While rails were laid to move fruits and vegetables from the St. Petersburg wharf to Northern markets, the Orange Belt and successors supplied winter passenger requests for excursions between St. Pete and Tarpon Springs. As more tourists arrived the need for a launch pad was evident. Late in the century a charming Victorian station was erected in downtown St. Pete. It was just above a 2000-foot rail pier that jutted into Tampa Bay where the contents of incoming ships were unloaded onto freight cars. The passenger terminal on Railroad Avenue was situated between 3rd and 4th streets and flanked by a smaller freight depot to the station's immediate left.

In the opening decades of the 20th century the traveling public demand escalated. In the 1920s, ACL improved on the original facility with a commodious Mediterranean depot at the corner of 1st Avenue South and 2nd Street. A unique feature of this structure was a floodlight atop a reverse-shape "L" wood pole, its light blanketing one end of the building and tracks. A frame shed covered a walkway that extended beyond the station beside a trio of parallel tracks. ACL relied on this depot until 1963. It was dismantled then, although in succeeding years the next-door freight depot was pressed into service for offices, a flea market, a feed store, an import and antique concern, and a warehouse.

In the meantime a potential competitor, the Tampa & Gulf Coast Railway (T&GC) commencing in 1913, planned to extend its tracks from Tarpon Springs to St. Pete. The line began at a junction with the Tampa Northern Railroad above the Hillsborough River near Lutz in Hillsborough County. From there it proceeded westerly to Tarpon Springs, Port Richey and Clearwater. Applying to the City of St. Petersburg for permission to create a southern terminus in that town, T&GC met spirited protests from ACL, which then owned the rival line that controlled that market for more than a quarter-century. The St. Pete city fathers nevertheless wisely put the issue to a public referendum and the outcome was decidedly in favor of a second railway.

On an overcast, rainy 1974 day, Amtrak's *Champion* has left the St. Petersburg passenger station heading north on SCL rails, passing the ex–ACL yard limit sign and milepost 895. A quartet of EMD E-units, possibly all E-8As, lead a train that will call at Clearwater, Tampa, Lakeland, Orlando, Jacksonville and smaller burgs before departing the Sunshine State for New York. A dormitory-baggage car behind the motive power precedes heritage passenger cars. Steam produced by generators for the heritage fleet is escaping as the lead engine approaches the U.S. 19 (34th Street). overpass (*courtesy Michael B. Robbins*).

By September 22, 1914, T&GC opened a route down the peninsula's extreme west side that carried it to Bay Pines, Pasadena and Gulfport before reaching St. Pete. The original T&GC brick depot was set at 2nd Avenue South and 9th Street. A freight depot opened two years hence, on September 13, 1926, and remained in business to 1967. In the meantime Tampa & Gulf Coast was leased by the Seaboard Air Line Railroad (SAL) in 1927, which also acquired the St. Pete facilities. With those secure footholds the two main contenders for Florida passenger traffic were ready to battle one another on the state's Gulf Coast.

While St. Petersburg welcomed both railroads within its borders between 1888 and 1914, by the Second World War it was pushing them out. As more and more people settled in "The City of the Green Bench" (a reference to scads of outdoor emerald settees that a local drug mercantiler added to downtown sidewalks), demand for commercial space reached premium levels. The land the railroads occupied was valuable. Both ACL and SAL were asked to move their operations away from the downtown district. By 1959, ACL relocated its passenger depot to 34th Street North and 38th Avenue.

The SAL followed suit, moving to 34th Street North between 7th and 8th avenues North in a structure exhibiting masonry vernacular architecture.

Eventually the trains quit arriving in St. Petersburg altogether, ceasing their western journeys at Tampa in the pre–Amtrak epoch of the 1960s. Buses were dispatched with St. Pete passengers at that juncture, a motif pursued by Amtrak today. Following a million-dollar renovation, the SAL depot was occupied by a local business. The facility was added to the local Historic Register in 1993.

In recent years the city purchased a two-mile ex-SAL corridor to extend an already extant 34-mile fitness trail from Tarpon Springs to downtown St. Pete. It passes the historic Seaboard Coast Line depot after traversing eight towns and several waterways, connecting multiple state and local parks. About a million visitors bike, run or walk the trail annually.

TALLAHASSEE

Erected in 1858, the depot that continued to serve the Sunshine State's capital city when Hurricane Katrina curtailed Amtrak service through the area in August 2005 is one of the South's most enduring stations. Located at 918-½ Railroad Avenue, it exhibits a second level added to the utilitarian, nondescript and fairly unadorned structure in 1885. It was placed on the U.S. National Register of Historic Places on December 30, 1997.

The facility wasn't pressed into service continuously, however. A separate nearby terminal also on Railroad Avenue was utilized in subsequent decades by various carriers during passenger rail's heyday. It served successors Jacksonville, Pensacola and Mobile, the Seaboard Air Line and Seaboard Coast Line railroads. When Amtrak acquired the service on May 1, 1971, it no longer hauled travelers through Tallahassee, shutting down the depot. Reviving that passenger service in 1993—the *Sunset Limited* route from Los Angeles–New Orleans was initially expanded to Miami and later trimmed to an Orlando terminus—Amtrak welcomed the train three times weekly in the smaller 1858 Tallahassee structure. It likely served the Tallahassee St. Marks Railroad Company, too, originally a 20-mile mule-driven line chartered in 1835. In the 1850s, that company converted its wooden rails to steel and replaced donkey power with steam engines. It was a logical time (1858) to erect the longstanding depot.

There is currently speculation travelers may once again pull up to its covered platform. Congress is considering three proposals by Amtrak for restoring passenger trains between New Orleans and Orlando. A source points out: "Re-establishing the *Sunset Limited* would take a minimum of 20 months from the date funding is made available.... Two options are about four years away from implementation because purchase of additional equipment would be required." If local residents are to again board the trains there, it appears they might not be doing so any time in the short term.

TAMPA

The dual-story brick edifice at 601 Nebraska Avenue in downtown Tampa tenders a lengthy, proud and illustrious heritage. It's a terminal which contemporary railfans include among the jeweled treasures that their quests to reinstate the past have accorded. Prospering in the halcyon days of railroad travel and falling into decay and disrepute in the years beyond, the facility's earlier glories are recalled following a literal rescue, renaissance and restoration resulting from the dedicated efforts of many.

Designed by architect J. F. Leitner of the W. C. Hobbs Company, Tampa Union Station—proffering classic Italian Renaissance Revival architecture—first opened its doors May 15, 1912. Its construction satisfied a great need for a central gathering place for travelers boarding and leaving trains of a trio of carriers: Atlantic Coast Line (ACL), Seaboard Air Line (SAL) and Tampa Northern railroads. (The latter, a 49-mile line north to Lutz and Brooksville, was bought by SAL that year; in 1913, SAL absorbed the Tampa & Gulf Coast Railroad with tracks from Lutz—15 miles above Tampa—to the mounting coastal tourist Meccas of Tarpon Springs, Clearwater and St. Petersburg, with St. Pete also signified as a key freight rail port.) On June 5, 1974, the Tampa depot was added to the U.S. National Register of Historic Places.

The oblong terminal faces south with acreage

Equipped with heritage passenger cars, Amtrak's ***Champion*** backs down stub-end tracks at Tampa's Union Station in 1974. The conductor or trainman at the end of the last car has the air control whistle in his hand to warn people the train is backing. In his left hand he seems to have a communications radio. He's aboard what may be an ex–SAL dormitory-baggage car. SCL controls trackage formerly operated by ACL and SAL. Block signals and manual switches for turnouts are in place near the terminal (***courtesy Michael B. Robbins***).

Manifold cities and communities along the Sunshine State's eastern shore still pay tribute for their existence to rail tycoon Henry M. Flagler, who literally put them on the map. Today while his endeavors may not be as renowned as they once were, his impact remains visible at **West Palm Beach. At Whitehall**, his 55-room, 60,000-square-foot mansion erected in 1902, Flagler lived in sumptuous grandeur. There he moved pieces of a vast rail, hotel, shipping and real estate empire like pawns on a chess board. In its glory days following his death the *Dixie Flagler* between Miami and Chicago was one of the most discernible tokens of the Flagler legacy (*courtesy Chuck Blardone*).

that provides a separate baggage-handling building behind Union Station's right end now used as a private commercial enterprise. Nine stub-end tracks from the north, complemented by paralleling platform sheds, lead toward back doors on either end of the depot. Gently sloping concrete inclines allow patrons to descend from either of dual back doors to the concrete platforms. A high shed covers the full area to the rear of the depot. A through-track platform also exists to one side of the station. It served trains running through Tampa to and from Clearwater and St. Petersburg.

It's inside Union Station that today's travelers may truly appreciate "how things used to be," nevertheless. A handful of oversized archetypical railway benches grace magnificent marble floors under ceilings two stories high and separated by expansive arched windows at the front. With a ticket window to the left and restrooms and vending machines to the right, the grand hall's vast open spread permits even muted conversations to be magnified, particularly if few people are present, another symbol of depots of the Gilded Age.

Although Tampa Union Station remains fairly quiet now during most of its hours of operation, in the hour or so before Amtrak's *Silver Star* arrives twice daily activity noticeably escalates, rising from a stir to an intensive fever pitch that erupts into a

crescendo of commotion and commensurate din as the train appears. The *Silver Star* runs between New York and Miami, traveling beyond the northern extremities of Tampa's stub-end tracks before backing into Union Station. It's reminiscent of ACL and SAL trains of yesteryear that moved similarly, whether bound for Florida west coast or east coast resorts or a Northeastern or Midwestern metropolis. Though multiple Florida Gulf coast cities received heavy tourist traffic back in the day, Tampa Union Station remained the major Gulf Coast hub of rivals ACL and SAL. Rail service to Clearwater, Fort Myers, Naples, St. Pete, Sarasota and intermediate destinations was eventually replaced by connecting bus service from Tampa Union Station. It's a system that's still in effect under the Amtrak regime.

Tampa operations contributed $5.4 million to Amtrak's 2008 fiscal year balance sheet by processing 100,119 (274 daily) passengers that year. Only two cities, Sanford (the Auto Train termination depot) and Orlando, regularly receive and board more passengers in the Sunshine State.

The restoration phase of Tampa Union Station occurred following years of structural deterioration and finally closing the facility in 1984. For 14 years the terminal's operations were reduced to a prefabricated provision alongside track platforms, allowing Amtrak to continue serving Florida's west coast. In 1991, Tampa Union Station Preservation & Redevelopment, Inc., a non-profit entity, was assigned control of the property's restoration by CSX Transportation, corporate descendent of the original railway owners. The local group acquired grants from the Florida Department of Transportation and the City of Tampa, plus a loan sans interest from the National Trust for Historic Preservation, and contributions from thousands of interested citizens and groups. In all more than $4 million was amassed to apply toward restoring the revered historic landmark. After refurbishing was complete the city held a grand reopening ceremony on May 30, 1998, a party that drew 12,000 admirers. Once again Union Station served the patrons of Amtrak, this time inside an application of grandeur that hadn't been witnessed by locals in a very long while. CSX transferred the station's title to the City of Tampa, also in 1998.

In September 2008, a subsequent private donor cluster, Community Foundation of Tampa Bay — formed in conjunction with the City of Tampa and the Florida Coalition of Rail Passengers — instituted an endowment for perpetual care and upkeep of Tampa Union Station. The income generated by that source is transferred to the city to help underwrite maintenance of Union Station in an effort to prevent a reoccurrence of the earlier deterioration.

Is there a new station in Tampa's future? In August 2009, *Trains* magazine's Web site quoted a Tampa source stating that projected high speed trains wouldn't use historic Union Station. They will "stop at a new station on property where a county jail used to sit," it reported. The concept suggests the *Silver Star* and similar "conventional trains" would continue to call at Union Station while buses or light rail transfer travelers between terminals. A Friends of Tampa Union Station rep called the plan "very shortsighted" while a Tampa transit manager urged the state to rely on Union Station for future high speed activity. At this writing the issue remains unsettled.

WEST PALM BEACH

When Henry Flagler pushed his Florida East Coast Railway (FEC) into Palm Beach County in 1894 — having headed south a half-dozen years earlier after buying the Jacksonville, St. Augustine & Halifax River Railway — it seemed he could now rest, having crossed a logical finish line in reaching sparse inhabitants of the outposts staked along the ocean's shoreline. That assumption, of course, was to be amended twice with Flagler extending his rails to Miami (1896) and Key West (1912). His earliest stopping place in Palm Beach may have been little more than a covered platform adjacent to a rail yard used for turning rolling stock northward toward

Jacksonville. Flagler built magnificent luxury hotels in the area for wealthy Northern tourists arriving on his trains so they could pass the winters in warm tropical climes.

Those efforts notwithstanding, the most enduring and striking railway facility in that vicinity was erected in 1925. That year the Seaboard Air Line Railroad completed a Mission Spanish Revival structure at 201 South Tamarind Avenue south of First Street (Banyan Boulevard). Designed by L. Philips Clarke of the local architecture firm Harvey & Clarke, it opened for business January 25, 1925. Nearly a half-century afterward it was listed on the National Register of Historic Places on June 19, 1973.

Still in use and branded the West Palm Beach Intermodal Terminal in the modern age, it now witnesses the arrival of two daily New York–Miami trains (*Silver Meteor* and *Silver Star*); Tri-Rail commuters which have since 1989 ferried passengers multiple times daily to Fort Lauderdale, Miami and other southeast Florida coastal communities; Greyhound, Palm Tran and city transit buses; and taxis. Beyond the usual terminal vendors, a small restaurant was incorporated into the complex May 14, 2008.

Amtrak's dual trains through West Palm Beach added $3.6 million to the company's bottom line in fiscal year 2008. With 52,249 individuals getting on or off there that year (averaging 143 patrons per day), West Palm Beach is Amtrak's sixth business-generating market in Florida following Sanford, Orlando, Tampa, Miami and Jacksonville in that order.

Georgia

ATLANTA

Like so many Southern cities Atlanta's inception is traced to the rails. Unlike the others, however, it was to be the colossus of transportation — so then, so now, transport being "the catalyst for Atlanta's growth and economic vitality," a modern Web site attests. Reportedly 325 passenger trains visited Atlanta every day in the 1920s, and more than 100 daily in the 1950s. *Atlanta* was preceded by a trio of monikers: In the War of 1812, the first white settlement, *Fort Peachtree*, surfaced on the banks of the Chattahoochee River near the Cherokee village of Standing Peachtree. In 1936, laborers assembled to build a state-owned Western & Atlantic Railroad (W&A), dubbing their commune *Terminus*. As the little village spread from the depot it was relabeled *Marthasville* (1843) for Governor Wilson Lumpkin's daughter Martha. Two years hence army engineer Steve Long, who chose the route W&A pursued to link the sea and the mountains, gave the city its lasting sobriquet. Long proposed a feminine derivative of "Atlantic" as a new handle to signify the town's expansion instead of the more rural form in use; *Atlanta* stuck. Not only did the rails influence the appellations, the city's very raison d'être was tied to the tracks. As a true child of the railroads, Atlanta was the nation's first major landlocked city.

The environs of Atlanta were to host more depots than any other Dixie metroplex. First in that lineage was the W&A waiting room adjacent to today's Underground Atlanta. That provision at Central Avenue and Alabama Street is long gone although the W&A's zero mile marker is still visible at the lower level of a restored Georgia Railroad freight facility at 65 Martin Luther King Jr. Drive SE. Surprisingly adorned with French doors and delicate fanlights, the freight depot is now the site of manifold weddings, receptions and other formal affairs. When the state General Assembly convenes the site hosts legislative functions galore — parties, teas, receptions, brunches, luncheons, banquets. It's an inducement that an edifice with a venerated heritage seldom goes out of style.

Over the years the same district witnessed a trio of successive structures branded "Union Station." The first, erected in 1853, occupied the block now bounded by Central Avenue and Alabama, Pryor and Wall streets, presently adjacent to Underground Atlanta. Called the "passenger depot" at its opening, its tag was altered to "car shed" later. Designed by civil engineer E. A. Vincent, the massive brick edifice boasted 18 grand archway openings on either side with two parallel tracks running through the oblong depot and multiple rails alongside it. This initial Union Depot hosted a quartet of carriers: Atlanta & West Point Railroad, Georgia Railroad, Macon & Western Railroad, and W&A. It was a model for the main depot of the Stone Mountain (Ga.) Park Scenic Railroad.

This voluminous "car shed" built in 1853 likely would have supplied the needs of Atlanta's increasing rail lines for decades had the Civil War — and, specifically, General William Tecumseh Sherman and his troops then on their infamous "March to the Sea" — not intervened. It was Sherman's intent to obliterate whatever was in his path that could be used by the Confederates to advantage. One of his prime targets was the city's Union Station, rapidly reduced to rubble in 1864. Seven years elapsed before a second Union Station opened (1871) on the same site, bounded by the same streets. Atlanta architect Max Corput fashioned it as a commodious facility to serve a thriving community. This second in the trilogy served the trains of Atlanta, Birm-

Southern Railway's prestigious lightweight *Crescent* streamliner arrives at the carrier's Brookwood Station (identified by many as Peachtree Station). in Atlanta. Southern's operations shifted from Terminal Station downtown to Brookwood in 1970, although this suburban facility had been a regular stop on the mainline since opening in 1918. It is still the place where the *Crescent* calls today, and under Amtrak auspices since 1979 (*courtesy Chuck Blardone*).

ingham & Coast Railroad, Georgia Railroad, and Nashville, Chattanooga & St. Louis Railway. This depot persisted nearly six decades until a replacement was readied in 1930. The site of the 1853 and 1871 versions is currently the home of a parking garage.

During the 1890s, incidentally, a half-dozen rail companies joined the quartet already operating in the city, bolstering Atlanta's radiating lines to 10 by the turn of the century. Included were five divisions of the Southern Railway System underscoring the Peach State capital's status as Dixie's rail center, W. T. Sherman notwithstanding.

Atlanta's third and final Union Station (1930) was constructed above the tracks running between the viaducts demarcating Forsyth and Spring streets. Four column pairs defended the entrance to its dual-story central hall. The great foyer was flanked on either side by single-story wings. Trains of the Atlantic Coast Line (successor to the Atlanta, Birmingham & Coast), Georgia, Louisville & Nashville, and Nashville, Chattanooga & St. Louis railroads called there. The facility was razed in 1972. Georgia Railroad, the only Union Station line still operating a daily passenger consist (to Augusta), while not joining Amtrak, transferred its operations to its Atlanta freight depot. Although construction of Underground Atlanta and MARTA's (Metropolitan Atlanta Rapid Transit Authority) commuter rapid rail system almost wholly annihilated the site, platform remnants are still viewed behind *The Atlanta Journal-Constitution* building at 72 Marietta Street NW. (The newspaper is relocating to suburban Dunwoody in 2010.)

In spite of the fact there were three stations by the nomenclature "Union" in the city and each was grander than its predecessor, few Atlantans living in the Gilded Age could be convinced that any approached the city's Terminal Station in pure majestic stateliness. This sphere of palatial splendor opened May 3, 1905, at the northwest corner of Madison Avenue (now Spring Street) and Mitchell Street. It was conceived by District of Columbia architect P. Thornton Marye and constructed by Atlanta contractors Gude & Walker at a cost of $1.6 million ($37.9 million in 2008). The four-story Renaissance revival Terminal Station was an imposing edifice marked by even higher twin towers near opposing ends of the gargantuan structure. It was the home of Atlanta & West Point; Atlanta, Birmingham & Atlantic (later Atlanta, Birmingham & Coast); Central of Georgia; Seaboard Air Line; and Southern Railway systems. (Except for ABA/ABC — acquired by the Atlantic Coast Line — and SAL, Southern eventually controlled the remainder of this business.)

A mammoth trainshed behind Terminal Station persisted to 1925, and then was torn away. The upper belfries of the twin towers were also deleted. Southern Railway's Atlanta headquarters was next door at 99 Spring Street and serviced subsequent rail owner Norfolk Southern Railway. The last train rolled from Terminal Station in June 1970. Two of Southern's remaining trio of passenger consists serving Atlanta (*Piedmont* and *Southern Crescent*) called only at the northside Peachtree Station. The third, ancillary Central of Georgia's *Nancy Hanks*, operated out of a small freight facility on Spring Street. In 1972, Terminal Station was razed to make way for the Richard B. Russell Federal Building (1980). A bronze statue of Southern's first president, native Georgian Samuel Spencer (1947–1906), once graced a prominent green space fronting Terminal Station. Now surrounded by skyscrapers and whizzing vehicle traffic, the statue currently rests on a concrete rostrum in a petite plaza where Peachtree and West Peachtree streets split.

Southern Railway was still running passenger consists when Terminal Station closed in 1970, doing so until 1979, when it handed them over to Amtrak. As already noted the *Crescent* (New York–New Orleans), a Southern flagship operated by Amtrak today, paused at Southern's Brookwood Station (often referred to locally as Peachtree Station). That depot is at 1688 Peachtree Street NW where it intersects Deering Road between Buckhead and Midtown. Built in 1918 in the Brookwood Hills district on Atlanta's fashionable north side, the facility originally was a commuter stop. It ushered workers into and out of the city on Southern's Washington mainline while providing more convenient access to nearby residents traveling further.

The rectangular Renaissance structure designed by foremost neoclassical draftsman Neel Reid of Hentz, Reid & Adler architectural firm exhibits a graceful façade of arched doorways and columns. A contemporary Web site purports that the building "lures not only those forever caught by the romance of train travel but also those who love architectural gems." The Brookwood Station's classic wooden benches, marble floors, vaulted ceiling and globe lights gleam following a half-million-dollar renovation for the 1996 Olympics. A windowed waiting area provides stunning views of Atlanta's magnificent downtown skyline.

Brookwood Station sits above a trio of rail tracks far below, accessible by a single elevator or a lengthy covered staircase that hugs an inordinately steep outdoor embankment. The bustling passenger traffic sustained today was never envisioned, of course, almost a century ago. Parking is at a premium, a precious few vehicles squeezing into the depot's lot. In fiscal year 2008, Amtrak boarded or detrained 101,084 patrons at Brookwood Station, 277 travelers on average per day. They furnished $9.7 million to Amtrak's revenues that year.

Since the start of the 21st century numerous proposals have been floated for a downtown multimodal passenger terminal near Atlanta's conjectural center at Five Points. While it will include Amtrak, MARTA commuter rail and buses, intercity buses, taxis, shuttles and other forms of ground transport, denizens have been negligent in getting their act together. As progressive as Atlanta is, it seems quaint that in this instance so far unification has been elusive.

Today more than 50 depots are extant in Atlanta's 28-county metropolitan area that fed trains to and from Terminal Station and the Union stations. Most now function in unrelated capacities. A half-dozen in suburban Atlanta are typical: Decatur — Georgia Railroad's 1871 depot at 303 East Howard Avenue at Candler Street near Agnes Scott College was repositioned further from the tracks before renovation as a Cajun restaurant; Emory — a café occupies the Seaboard Air Line's brick facility at 662 Asbury Circle, built in 1916 to serve Emory University; Hapeville — the 1890 Central of Georgia depot at 620 South Central Avenue housed a history-transportation museum most recently; Marietta — another visitor center occupies the Nashville, Chattanooga & St. Louis station at 4 Depot Street NE; Norcross — still another café serves patrons at a station built by Southern Railroad in 1909 at 40 South Peachtree Street, this one jammed with railway memorabilia; and Stone Mountain — a granite depot at 922 Main Street, now the village's City Hall, built in the 1850s and added to in 1914.

AUGUSTA

For all but the first seven years of its life, the Georgia Railroad (1833–1983) was headquartered at Augusta. During that time passenger trains trekked daily between Augusta and the state capital at Atlanta. The town's first depot, perhaps little more than a sheltered platform or a rustic waiting room, belonged to the Georgia line. The company dramatically improved on its effort about 1870 when it constructed the city's initial Union Station. That facility served a handful of short lines radiating from Augusta. The long curved-roof brick structure was highlighted by myriad deep arching windows and doorways. It was the first depot in Augusta to be cited for acquiring absolute command of the turf it occupied.

Even though it was the city's original Union Station, it didn't stand alone: some other lines had already developed their own separate facilities. Not much is left in the way of physical evidence of any of them, however. The single exception — and it isn't much — is from the South Carolina Railroad's depot dating from the 1850s. Situated at the corner of Fifth and Reynolds streets, parts of that building still stand beside today's CSX tracks. In the years

between then and now the structure became Southern Railway's freight depot. Southern absorbed the vintage Palmetto State carrier, as it did so many other shortline operators in the region. In 2006, a $450,000 state transportation grant was awarded to renovate the dilapidated historic facility sometimes identified as "Reynolds Street Depot."

The Charlotte, Columbia & Augusta Railroad (1869–1894), another of the many later acquired by Southern Railway, maintained its own station in Augusta's downtown, too. Coupled with CC&A's freight yards, its passenger facility occupied the block bounded by Fenwick, Fifth, Washington, and Watkins streets. Still another early Augusta depot was opened by the Augusta, Gibson & Sandersville Railroad (1884–1934), renamed Augusta Southern Railway in 1893. It, too, was eventually bought by Southern. Before that, the outfit maintained its headquarters, passenger waiting room and repair shops on the banks of the Savannah River in Augusta. The precise location is between the railroad bridge and freight shops previously denoted, in time owned by Southern Railway.

The culmination of all of this train activity in Augusta, however, was ultimately expressed in the erection of a second, much more magnificent Union Station. Completed in 1903, its location at Barrett Square about five blocks from the riverfront attracted all the carriers. Designed by Frank Pierce Milburn (1868–1926), an energetic New South architect who also drew plans for Savannah's Union Station and many more, the Spanish Renaissance complex was of utterly majestic proportions. Set under a cathedral dome, its spacious dual-level central gathering hall was the centerpiece of a stately facility whose extensive left and right single-story units completed a picture of formidable dominion. A mammoth trainshed at the rear ran the length of the station, and Georgia Railroad's freight depot was situated behind Union Station, too.

This important terminal served a half-dozen railroads back in the day: Atlantic Coast Line, Central of Georgia, Charleston & Western Carolina, Georgia, Georgia & Florida, and Southern. When Seaboard Coast Line (a line partially developed from ACL in 1967) sent its last train out of Augusta on April 7, 1968, Union Station officially ceased operations. That structure was another victim of the wrecking ball in 1972. Reminiscing on its era in a 2009 blog, a historian opined: "You emerged from it [Union Station] into Barrett Plaza, a park-square that remains — although fenced off from the taxpayers — in front of the refurbished federal courthouse at Telfair and Eighth streets.... It must have been a sight because the station was frequently featured in post cards." The city's primary U.S. Post Office subsequently occupied its address on Walker Street between Eighth Street and James Brown

Boulevard. Today various government facilities dot the area that once bustled with train travelers.

As Georgia's second largest city, Augusta and its prideful civic leadership have disdained the fact that many smaller communities have better surface transport. While a multimodal center to handle Amtrak and Greyhound and other people-mover systems has been bantered about for years, putting all the parts together to make it happen has eluded city planners. Amtrak hasn't signed to provide rail service from the city to a logical connection (possibly Atlanta, Savannah, or Columbia, S.C.). Requests for an Amtrak Thruway bus to Columbia linking with the *Silver Star* (daily from Miami to New York) have been repeatedly thwarted. Overwhelmed by similar requests, by early 2010, Amtrak hadn't given Augustans any news they've waited more than a decade for.

COLUMBUS

Union Station was erected in 1901 in the original city's eastern perimeter at 1200 Sixth Avenue where it intersected with 12th Street. Locals commonly dubbed the facility "Sixth Avenue Station." For seven decades, until rail passenger service ceased to Columbus in 1971, Union Station received trains of the Central of Georgia, Seaboard Air Line and Southern roads. Drawn in Second Empire style by the Atlanta architectural firm Bruce and Morgan, its brick exterior is earmarked by deep arched windows on twin floors. A sheltered portico distinguished by matching arched walkways covers the main entrance where patrons were unloaded and loaded to and from their travels. Originally the drive-through typically saw horse-drawn buckboards and covered wagons pulling up to the doors, subsequently replaced by motorized vehicles in later years.

When it opened in 1901, the terminal featured a large curved-roof trainshed attached to the rear. The shed was similar to those adorning multiple major Georgia depots, including those in Atlanta, Augusta, Macon, Savannah and West Point. After the passenger trains quit arriving, Union Station languished for a while. It was added to the National Register of Historic Places in 1980, yet four years hence it appeared vulnerable to demolition. The edifice was nevertheless spared by a quartet of parties working conjunctively — Historic Columbus Foundation, Southern Railway System, Consolidated Government of Columbus, and numerous supportive denizens. Ultimately rehabilitated, the ex-depot was given a new lease on life, finally becoming the venue of the Greater Columbus Chamber of Commerce.

MACON

In 1843, the Central of Georgia Railway (CofG) reached the fringes of Macon — then one of its state's most populous cities — with trackage from Savannah. But eight more years passed before the route from the sea crossed the Ocmulgee River after a trestle was completed, allowing CofG to arrive in downtown Macon proper. Linking with the Macon & Western Railroad there, for the first time a rail connection from Atlanta to Savannah was opened, a route extending 221 miles. While Macon became CofG's most prominent intermediary city, data about the facility that served its passengers in the incubatory years is scarce. We know CofG traveled down the east side of Fifth Street to Union Depot while another carrier — Georgia Southern & Florida — plied the rails on the west side of Fifth to the station at Plum Street. Those two carriers merged yards well before Southern Railway arrived in town, which most likely was the late 1890s. Early in the 20th century, that trio joined their passenger operations in a celebrated new facility.

Until then Southern Railway passengers came and went from the line's depot at the corner of Ocmulgee and Fifth streets (now Riverside Drive and Martin Luther King Jr. Boulevard). That dual-level frame facility was marked by a three-story tower and an overhanging roof below the second story windows. The overhang was wrapped around the structure and offered some protection to bystanders from nature's elements. There was no trainshed at the time — only two exposed tracks behind the station. Just beyond the Southern depot CofG trains avoided Southern's rails by traversing a bridge over them, thereby eliminating a grade crossing.

A contemporary Peach State railway Web site alleges Macon's Terminal Station, erected at the foot of Cherry Street four blocks north of Plum in 1916, is now "Georgia's grandest surviving railroad station." Within a decade the Beaux Arts facility exhibiting arches and columns so proudly was handling 100 train arrivals and departures daily. Nearly all represented the Central of Georgia, Georgia Southern & Florida, and Southern Railway systems which together built it. Passengers accessed the train platforms by way of a tunnel beneath the tracks.

The tri-level depot was designed by architect Alfred Fellheimer (1875–1959) whose handiwork along with that of some partners may be seen also in the Buffalo and Cincinnati terminals. Four stone eagles rest atop a like number of columns beside the main entrance to the Macon facility. Above it a striking two-story-tall arched window beckons patrons. To the far left of the immense edifice lies a separate yet irrefutably disproportionate entryway to a colored waiting room. While the doorway is arched, it is nevertheless diminishing in comparison to the façade's balance. It seems an afterthought almost tacked on to the far side. Despite that the style and material are of similar quality to that marking the gateway at the structure's center. Macon wasn't alone in the practice of dual accesses. The distinction is a reminder of a time when division typified customs and interaction of the races was held to a minimum.

For several years following its 1975 closing, Terminal Station stood in limbo and encroaching disarray. After the Georgia Power Company purchased it in 1982, the edifice gained a new lease on life. Turned into local offices for the firm's use, for two decades it fulfilled a worthy purpose. When TEA (Transportation Equity Act) funding of $1 million was awarded to the City of Macon in 2002, the jurisdiction bought the ex–Terminal Station from Georgia Power and renovated it. It has since supplied the community with a multimodal transportation center and added retail and office space.

SAVANNAH

Savannah, the largest port in Georgia — definitely a key to its earlier success as a rail town — currently may possess more depots than any other city in the Peach State. No fewer than four stations are there, although only one continues meeting its original purpose. The others are testament to the efforts of preservationists who have been triumphant in retaining some of the vintage landmarks that led to Savannah's being a progressive commercial center.

The zenith of those choice properties unfortunately was the victim of demolition-minded developers in 1962. That year Union Station was obliterated so approach ramps at the end of Interstate 16 could be fed into downtown Savannah. The imposing terminal was designed by New South architect Frank Pierce Milburn (1868–1926). A half-million-dollar edifice completed in 1902, it initially served trains of the Plant System (folded into Atlantic Coast Line Railroad about then), Seaboard Air Line Railroad and Southern Railway. A year hence draftsman Milburn's drawings for Augusta's Union Station culminated in opening that city's equally superlative facility. It met a similar fate as

Looking east, ca. early 1950s, an aerial view of Central of Georgia's Savannah properties depicts the vastness and complexity of the carrier's holdings in its hometown. The rail yard dominates the center with the roundhouse to its right and freight terminal to its left. The headhouse, Union Station, faces West Broad Street (since renamed M. L. King Jr. Boulevard) at the far end of inner covered platforms (*courtesy Allen Tuten and Central of Georgia Railway Historical Society*).

the wrecking ball reduced it to rubble in 1972. Milburn's handiwork is scattered around Georgia, incidentally; his designs of several courthouse structures dot the state and several more nearby Southern states.

Savannah's Union Station added remarkably to the city's skyline at the extreme western end of downtown. It was an imposing edifice on West Broad Street, renamed M. L. King Jr. Boulevard in 1990. With dual Spanish Renaissance towers separated by five archway entrances, the bi-level facility was — according to a modern Web site — "the center of life" for the city's Negroes. "All that changed, however, when the building was bulldozed to make way for the tail end of an Interstate."

There were plenty of earlier, and later, train stations in Savannah, however.

Although the Central of Georgia Railroad (CofG), organized in Savannah in 1833, and always headquartered there, maintained a small waiting station in its early years (possibly little more than a sheltered platform then), its usefulness had played out by mid-century. At that juncture an inclusive complex embracing passenger and freight traffic and shops for fabricating and repairing engines and rolling stock was called for by the line's superintendent, William M. Wadley. The resulting dual-story brick CofG depot that is still standing at 303 M. L. King Jr. Boulevard (formerly West Broad Street, at Liberty Street), slightly north of the later occupied Union Station site, was a masterpiece. It had truly become "the most complete and elegant railroad station in the country," according to the *New York Railroad Advocate*.

Begun in 1860, though incomplete until 1876, thanks to the War Between the States and financial reverses, the CofG station was designed by a German engineer in the company's employ, Augustus Schwaab. He later became one of the city's most versatile builders. The rectangular headhouse is marked by nine ceiling-to-floor arches on both levels across the front (16 are windows, two are entrances). A quartet of matched arching windows appears at the sides. A gable roof covers the brick building.

At the rear stands an example of old times (almost) forgotten. Trainsheds are not often seen today even when the main building has been preserved, but this one is still there. In keeping with the front end, its massive canopy displays at least

With a working turntable in place, the roundhouse of Central of Georgia's Savannah operations houses vintage locomotives and rolling stock. Some pull demonstration consists ferrying visitors on brief jaunts from the Savannah Roundhouse Museum alongside a once-prospering CofG yard. Self-guided tours propel visitors through adjacent shops that had bustled with activity for many decades (*courtesy Allen Tuten and Central of Georgia Railway Historical Society*).

two dozen arched entrances along each side extending far back from the headhouse. In its extended life, celebrating its sesquicentennial in 2010 since construction began, Union Station now hosts the Savannah History Museum and Visitors Center.

The depot and offices of the Savannah & Atlanta Railway remain intact on Stiles Avenue where the street dead-ends into Louisville Road. A sheltered drive-through extends in front of the square bi-level building. Brick towers flank the façade at opposite ends and similar thinner towers also appear at the front canopy's four corners. The facility serves a private business today although *S & A RY* is still prominently embedded in its stone signage along the roof line. Built in 1916 for Midland Railway, the station was acquired by S&A in 1924, shortly after Midland entered receivership.

The single-story Savannah & Tybee (S&T) depot represents a line that was ultimately absorbed into Central of Georgia after S&T was abandoned in 1933. The little station with dual windows on the front separated by a single door was erected at 130 Randolph Street where it crosses East President Street. That's at the edge of Savannah's downtown National Historic Landmark District, about four blocks below Front River. In 1988, the facility was transported a couple of miles east to the community of Thunderbolt on the route to Tybee Island. There it was pressed into service as a ticket office and gift shop for the historic Old Fort Jackson tourist attraction at 1 Fort Jackson Road. Nevertheless, on a sign above its door *Tybee Depot* is still identified as what it used to be.

Before Savannah's consummate Union Station was flattened in 1962, Atlantic Coast Line and Seaboard Air Line railroads—longtime occupants of that terminal and needing a place for their trains to call—jointly erected a new depot west of Savannah. Lying along the eastern side of the north-south mainline, a platform between tracks is reached by a pedestrian tunnel below the rails. The single-story facility is an outgrowth of a pact signed by the railroads, Georgia Ports Authority and the City of Savannah. "The agreement provides for all tenant roads and/or successor carriers [to] use of the facility in exchange for agreeing to the move" from Union Station, where the I-16 ramps were constructed, notes a modern Web site. Situated at what is now 2611 Seaboard Coastline Drive, the station was the local stopping place for trains of Seaboard Coast Line Railroad when the rival carriers merged operations in 1967.

Subsequently, on May 1, 1971, Amtrak began running SCL's passenger service. Today its runs through Savannah's Amtrak Station include four daily trains in each direction: *Auto Train*, which doesn't pause there on its route between Sanford, Florida, and Lorton, Virginia; *Palmetto*, between Savannah and New York; *Silver Meteor*, between New York and Miami on a route via Fayetteville, North Carolina, and Charleston, South Carolina; and *Silver Star*, also between New York and Miami, with intermediate stops at Raleigh, North Carolina; Columbia, South Carolina; and Tampa, Florida. In fiscal year 2008, Savannah ticket sales contributed $4.6 million to Amtrak's coffers while local ridership increased to 54,168 boardings and deboardings, 148 daily, up 11.5 percent over the year before.

Kentucky

BOWLING GREEN

The Louisville & Nashville Railroad pushed its way south from Louisville into Bowling Green by summer's end in 1859. While a waiting area for travelers was provided—in that pioneering epoch it may have been little more than a humble shelter or platform—it didn't last long. Shortly after the War Between the States began in 1861, the Confederates cited Bowling Green as the capital of their movement in the Bluegrass State. Steadily retreating in the wake of advancing federal forces sweeping down from Louisville, Rebel troops "destroyed bridges, trestles and track with reckless abandon and before leaving Bowling Green almost completely destroyed the railroad's facilities," a Civil War historian wrote. "Depots and other structures elsewhere had not escaped their blighting attention and damage to the railroad, either intentional, or otherwise, was enormous." It was a pattern to be repeated many times during that long conflict.

Even at that, however, by the spring of 1862, trains were once again running between the road's namesake cities, hinting that at least a makeshift station at Bowling Green was operating. While it may have been only an interim fixture, there was a depot at this strategic south central Kentucky city, likely of wood construction, for decades. It persisted until L&N significantly upgraded its Bowling Green facility in 1925 (although some sources allege 1923 is the more likely date).

At that juncture the intermediate city on L&N's mainline was gifted with a striking Classic Revival bi-level brick edifice. Featuring deep gateway arches and matching arched windows that reached past a front courtyard plaza, the exterior was constructed of limestone which had been mined locally. (The Bowling Green area mined huge deposits of the mineral.) The terminal's interior is expensively decorated with hand-laid hexagonal tile flooring selected from imported oak. Local chroniclers tout the art-deco edifice at 401 Kentucky Street where it intersects East 4th Avenue as "the last passenger depot [to be built] along the Louisville & Nashville line."

The *Floridian* led by SDP40F 640 and a second SDP40F pauses at the Bowling Green, Kentucky, station on its way south on September 25, 1976. This train will continue running three more years; when it ceases, no longer will there be regular passenger service on historic L&N tracks that have transported riders for 120 years (*courtesy Jay T. Thomson*).

One that missed the bulldozer is the ex–L&N station at Bowling Green, Kentucky, now a Historic Railpark run by volunteers. Beyond several pieces of rolling stock on tracks behind the mid–1920s edifice, exhibit halls on two floors, a theater screening train films, and a rail memorabilia shop keep visitors busy. Special events (speakers, socials, excursions) are calendared and the attraction produces a newsletter. A well-maintained facility, it seems like "only yesterday," through the image was captured May 4, 2009 (*courtesy Clyde Woodruff*).

Added to the National Register of Historic Places in 1979, it was restored after the trains stopped coming. Today it houses a dual-story Historic Rail-park Train Museum that has become one of the area's most acclaimed tourist attractions. The museum commemorates the history of the railroad and the lives of those who operated it. Visitors witness one of the district's largest model rail displays and several pieces of rolling stock, among them a 1911 L&N presidential office car, 1921 L&N railroad post office car, 1953 EBA diesel locomotive, 1949 Pullman Standard dining car, 1953 luxury Pullman sleeper car, and a Chessie Class caboose. Vintage railroad films are screened in a small theater while interactive historical and cultural exhibits related to passenger service are staged. Much of the tour is self-guided. All of it is a permanent memorial to an era when travel by train was at the forefront of Americans' aptitude for flaunting their mobility.

LEXINGTON

As early at 1851, the first of a series of precursors of the Louisville & Nashville Railroad (L&N) laid rails to the central Kentucky hamlet of Lexington. Three decades passed before the then-sprawling L&N, expanding an insatiable appetite for more trackage throughout the upper- and mid–South, gained the Louisville, Cincinnati & Lexington Railroad (1881). Not until then were permanent waiting stations to be increasingly evident in Lexington. After Kentucky Central Railroad (KC) formed in 1875, an outgrowth of multiple forerunners, too, it built a pioneer depot on [West] Short Street near [West] Main Street and Lexington Cemetery. A possibly makeshift operation served only until Chesapeake & Ohio (C&O) Railway erected a stable, elaborate full-service facility where Water Street joins [South] Limestone Street, the latter crossed by Vine Street. C&O arrived in town in 1880, after buying Elizabethtown, Lexington & Big Sandy Railroad. Kentucky Central soon joined C&O in occupying the new station on Limestone, perhaps hinting the earlier KC structure might have been makeshift.

A few years earlier (1877), Cincinnati Southern Railway—completing trackage through Lexington that linked Cincinnati, Ohio, with Somerset, Kentucky—opened a depot on South Broadway near its intersect with Angliana Avenue. In 1886, a fifth carrier came to town but Kentucky Union Railroad may never have transported travelers. Its purpose was hauling the wealth of mineral deposits and timber in the Bluegrass State's mountainous southeastern quadrant. After its reorganization as Lexington & Eastern Railroad (1894), the line was absorbed by L&N, which did provide passenger service to the hilly region.

The major roads of the early 20th century serving Lexington—namely C&O, L&N, and Southern—joined in a magnificent Union Station built downtown to process the city's rail riders through halcyon days. The bi-level edifice with a mammoth tri-story arched glass window above its main doors exhibited a cool classical portico that added dramatically to this distinctive work of art. Yet by the mid 1950s, most passenger service in Fayette County had halted. When the trains stopped departing, Union Station was abandoned then, finally, torn down. In the intervening decades all of the depots in town, in fact, also have been reduced to rubble with the notable exception of one.

At the time Union Station was about to be phased out in the early 1960s, C&O—still committed to its prestigious *George Washington* streamliner running through Lexington to Louisville from its dual eastern termini at Newport News/Norfolk, Virginia, and Washington, D.C.—constructed a new depot on its east Lexington property. Located on Delaware Street at Netherland Yard, the former yard and its facilities today are owned by a private brick-making firm. A C&O water tower still marks the location, nonetheless. C&O persisted in running its passenger trains until Amtrak assumed that duty on May 1, 1971.

LOUISVILLE

There were a handful of train depots in Louisville although Union Station has invariably tended to overshadow all the others. And, in the modern age, while trains no longer call at its platforms, the durable facility has managed to elude the bulldozer that blithely exterminated so many of its contemporaries in other environs. In spite of Union Station's dominance, which will be recounted momentarily, to ignore other Louisville stations would be to dismiss an important part of the city's illustrious railway heritage.

To begin with there were interurban stations serving the nearby regional towns like Lloydsboro (Pewee) Valley in Oldham County east of Louisville. The route to Pewee Valley via St. Matthews, Lyndon and Anchorage had its origin at 3rd and Liberty streets and its terminus in LaGrange, 25 miles away. When Illinois Central Railroad (IC) arrived in town in the late 19th century, it put up a temporary station on 4th Street. In 1884, 7th Street Union Depot was constructed on the west side of 7th at Main Street only a few hundred yards from the Ohio River. It served multiple lines, yet lost out to a tornado in 1890.

IC acquired the ruins and replaced the building in 1891 with a brick Richardsonian Romanesque architectural style terminal. From that time forward the facility was interchangeably known as both 7th Street Depot and Central Station, the latter terminology applied by its new owners. The most pronounced element of that tri-level edifice was a striking five- or six-story square tower at its southeast corner. The tower and the depot itself displayed tall narrow windows at every level. The tower was removed, incidentally, along with the depot's top floor, in the early 1940s, supposedly as an economy measure.

Passenger consists of the Baltimore & Ohio and Chesapeake & Ohio railroads also called at Central Station alongside Illinois Central trains. At its pinnacle the depot processed 36 passenger trains every day. Having been built after a tornado struck its predecessor, Central Station wasn't done with disaster quite yet. In 1908, much of it was leveled by fire, although it was reopened the following year. In the great flood of 1937, many of the tracks were underwater for a long siege while water reached the depot's second story.

In 1954, IC terminated its enduring Louisville–Paducah traffic, B&O pulled out next, and in 1963, C&O — Central Station's remaining tenant — shifted its trains to Union Station. Central's doors were shuttered forever. Before the wrecking ball arrived in the early 1970s, Actor's Theater staged dramatic and comedic productions there. As is the case in city after city, nevertheless, Central's property was ultimately cleared for construction of an in-terstate highway (64). As the trains had done, although worse, the expressway separated the city from its scenic riverfront. Not until the 21st century was the public well served by a mammoth Riverfront Park on a vast green apron between the road and river.

There was also a precursor to the impressive Union Station in Kentucky's largest municipality. Under one roof that earliest depot mingled freight and passenger operations of Louisville & Nashville Railroad (L&N), the chief long-distance transporter there. Occupying the southwest corner of 9th Street and [West] Broadway, that structure was erected in 1857-1858.

The archetypical depot was the design of an L&N employee, German-bred Albert Fink. Hired as a construction engineer, Fink's stock inflated rapidly as his employer elevated him to chief engineer (architecture, not trains), then as general superintendent and finally vice president. The draftsman earned accolades for skill in designing the first local rail bridge over the Ohio River, a model for which he was handsomely rewarded, having patented and then sold his blueprint to other railroads. He also drafted plans for Louisville's courthouse plus private homes, businesses and area landmarks.

In the early L&N years, much of the rail firm's

The crew of a southbound L&N E-unit 553, the *South Wind,* pauses at Louisville's Union Station in 1967. This passenger train initiated at Chicago will divide at Jacksonville into three continuing sections — to Miami, Tampa/Sarasota and St. Petersburg (*photograph by Charles B. Castner, Jr., courtesy Chuck Blardone*).

headquarters operations were handled at Fink's 9th & Broadway depot. As L&N outgrew that space those offices were scattered to a handful of buildings around town. Eventually (1877) they were collected again in a single spot at 2nd and [West] Main streets. In 1902, excavation began at the site of the original L&N station for an 11-story L&N office tower. It was readied by January 1907, a half-century after Fink's original depot premiered on the same spot. A matching annex, added in 1930, allowed L&N to maintain its base of operations there for the rest of its existence (1988) under its widely-recognized appellation. (The lighted letters remain on the exterior today.)

In the meantime the line relocated its passenger terminal one block west of the now almost hallowed 1857 site. The new depot debuted on September 7, 1891. Covering 40 acres of prime property at 10th and Broadway along downtown's western edge, at the time the edifice was billed as "the largest railroad station in the Southern United States." Construction on this grand new Union Station destined to serve multiple carriers began in 1880. Yet it took a decade to complete, a result of rapidly escalating expenses.

At a cost of $310,656 ($6.85 million in 2008 figures) the Richardsonian Romanesque structure exhibited Bowling Green, Kentucky, limestone for its exterior with limestone trim from Bedford, Indiana. A slate casing over an iron-and-wood roof topped the tri-level facility. In his design architect F. W. Mowbray incorporated a clock tower, three

smaller towers, turrets, immense façade and barreled vaulting. A large clerestoried trainshed covered a half-dozen platform tracks behind the station. Umbrella shelters were later added to tracks along the shed's west side.

Inside the imposing edifice a spacious atrium, dining room and ladies' "retiring rooms" awaited first-floor patrons. There was also a barber shop, newsstand, lunchroom and separate lounge on that main level. A wrought iron balcony overlooked the atrium with rose windows on either side that initially provided a profusion of soft lighting. That wasn't to last, however. A fire on July 17, 1905, almost 14 years into the station's occupancy, resulted in elimination of the rose windows. They were replaced by an 84-paneled stained glass skylight in a barrel-vaulting tower. The use of stained glass was prodigious, in fact, turning up not only in the head house but also in the trainshed. Ceramic-tiled floors were offset by walls fashioned of Georgian marble, and splendid southern oak and pine accented the great hall's extravagantly dazzling interior.

At its peak in the 1920s, Louisville's Union Station processed 58 consist arrivals and departures daily representing a quartet of carriers: L&N; Louisville, Henderson & St. Louis; Monon; and Pennsylvania. In time all but the latter were folded into the L&N aggregate. By mid 1963, these would be joined by Chesapeake & Ohio Railway when it vacated the smaller then-empty Central Station.

For decades, a modern Web site exclaims, the

Out of gray bleakness in at least two ways, Amtrak's *Floridian* rolls along on L&N tracks past the tiny community of Kenlite, Kentucky, on October 1, 1979. But for a court order this would be the passenger train's final run, a tradition dating to 1940 when antecedent *South Wind* launched this trek between Florida and Chicago via Louisville. The *Wind* shifted to *Floridian* six months after Amtrak acquired the legend in 1971. A judge ruled in favor of discontinuation effective October 9, 1979; the full route hasn't been provided regular passenger service in excess of three decades (***photograph by R. Lyle Key, Jr., courtesy Chuck Blardone***).

Louisville L&N–owned depot yielded the "first place of celebration" for the euphoric adherents of the annual Kentucky Derby. No less than a score of special trains traversed the rails to the River City from far-away places for the festivities. Pullman cars supplied the overnight accommodations for those travelers. And while the practice was nearly extinguished in the 1960s, there are still a few organized "special cars" that continue to haul party-goers to Louisville for the annual spring rite.

From May 1, 1971, to October 30, 1976, Amtrak's trains regularly stopped at Louisville's Union Station. The last of them, the *Floridian*, ran between Chicago and Florida points. It joined the *Auto Train* (Louisville–Sanford, Florida) operations at a small station south of the city on National Turnpike beginning in 1976. That lasted until October 8, 1979, when Amtrak dropped the all-passenger consist altogether.

From December 4, 2001, through July 4, 2003, a track on the west side of Union Station's parking lot was the southern terminus of Amtrak's daily *Kentucky Cardinal* from Chicago. (Since December 17, 1999, it had terminated across the river at Jeffersonville, Indiana.) Today Amtrak Thruway Motorcoach service runs between Chicago and Louisville every day, arriving and departing at the city's Greyhound Station at 720 West Muhammad Ali Boulevard, a few blocks from Union Station.

L&N eventually sold Union Station to the Louisville bus service Transit Authority of River City (TARC). Following a 1979 $2 million refurbishing, in April 1980, Union Station made the transition from a depot to TARC's administrative offices. After nearly 14 decades of service in Louisville, the conspicuous structure at 10th and Broad continues to meet some transportation necessities of its local community, albeit in ways no one could have dreamed at its debut in the 19th century.

OWENSBORO

When the Owensboro & Russellville Railroad fell into bankruptcy nine years after it inaugurated service in Owensboro in 1867, its assets were acquired by successor Owensboro & Nashville Railroad. Three years hence, in 1879, the Louisville & Nashville Railroad (L&N) bought the latter, giving the L&N a route to the western Kentucky burg on the south banks of the Ohio River. By then another carrier had established there — Louisville, Henderson & St. Louis Railroad (LH&StL). That line grew out of a reorganized Louisville, St. Louis & Texas Railroad in 1896. The LH&StL, too, was absorbed into the mounting L&N system in the early 1900s, although still operated under its own nomenclature for a time.

In 1905, the LH&StL's Owensboro depot was razed and replaced with an attractive Victorian limestone and slate Union Station at 1039 Frederica Street. Designed by draftsmen Henry F. Hawes and John B. Hutchings, the spacious bi-level facility was built by Walter Brashear Construction Company. It sported a Gothic façade with wooden barge boarding and brackets at its gabled entryway. On the first floor the passenger waiting room anchored the structure's western edge while the opposite end was occupied by freight traffic. Although the building accommodated a trio of railroads, including the Illinois Central, L&N and LH&StL, almost from its start it was clearly identified as "the L&N depot." On the building's second floor L&N maintained its administrative functions and support operations for the local district.

During the heyday of passenger rail in the 1920s, some 18 trains called at Owensboro Union Station every day. L&N won an appeal to cease passenger operations there in 1958, claiming annual losses of $130,000 after its travel business dropped sharply.

In the intervening years Union Station has been the home of a variety of commercial establishments and non-profit agencies, while also sitting idle during lengthy lapses between tenants. After periods as a discothèque followed by a pizza parlor in the 1970s, the building was abandoned for a while. It was subsequently refurbished not once but twice in the 1980s (1982, 1988). On the latter occasion a dual-story atrium and office on its eastern end were added to the edifice. Recent lessees have simultaneously included an adult day care center, architectural design firm, investment group and a preschool.

Louisiana

BATON ROUGE

The railways serving Baton Rouge, as elsewhere, underwent numerous alterations in appellations as time elapsed. The city's initial foray into rail traffic occurred in 1883, when the New Orleans & Mississippi Valley Railroad extended tracks west to Baton Rouge. Within a year that line's nomenclature was altered to Louisville, New Orleans & Texas Railway. By 1892, the company was absorbed into the expanding Illinois Central Railroad (IC) as that carrier increased its southerly direction and influence. In the meantime, in 1882, Yazoo & Mississippi Valley Railroad (Y&MV) had been formed to create a route extending west from Jackson, Mississippi. While Y&MV would also be folded into the IC ultimately, and aligned with it during most of its years of operation, unlike some others it was treated differently by IC. Y&MV was permitted to maintain its identity and distinctive "separateness," in fact, until 1946.

Fire insurance maps from early in the 20th century indicate that no fewer than three railway stations were erected in Baton Rouge within the railroad reservation on the levee at the foot of North Boulevard. The building in existence today is the second to be placed on the same site as a predecessor. In 1925, Yazoo & Mississippi Valley Railroad completed the current brick-and-stone Classic Revival passenger terminal in the Pelican State capital. It served travelers continuously to 1971, when Amtrak assumed that business and dropped existing routes through Baton Rouge. Grazing the banks of the Mississippi River, the double-decked edifice fronted by 10 imposing white columns at the center of its long, slender, rectangular design, the structure offered scenic vistas of riverboat traffic from its platforms. The facility was added to the National Register of Historic Places in 1994.

Even in the post-train epoch the structure continues to make a weighty impact, not only on its community but also on the state and region surrounding it. Purchased by the City of Baton Rouge, the old terminal at 100 South River Road was transformed into the Louisiana Art & Science Museum offering "educational entertainment for visitors of all ages." Fine art galleries, children's interactive art and science galleries, and a dome-topped planetarium were added to the depot's southern end; a store proffering train-related merchandise, lecture halls and classrooms have been included to achieve the museum's mission. The station's current use is a strong tie to its past while some of concepts inside project the future.

More recently, in early 2009, the Louisiana Department of Transportation announced plans to request federal funding to restore passenger rail service between Baton Rouge and New Orleans. It's one of scores of similar proposals throughout the country and its resolution will take time. Although an Amtrak Thruway bus (departing from an unattended, unsheltered curbside in Baton Rouge at 1253 Florida Street) makes the two-hour trip daily each way between Baton Rouge and New Orleans, there is no rail tie. Baton Rouge is the capital of one of five Southern states for which Amtrak rail service remains elusive.

HAMMOND

The local chamber of commerce proffers a fairly persuasive argument that — had there been no railroads — there would have been no Hammond. It started after a native Swede, entrepreneur Peter Hammond, moved to the area in 1830. He determined to fabricate goods from the resin of pine trees and ship them to the port at New Orleans.

Modern publicists establish: "Railroad is the reason behind the city's success, and in 1854, the New Orleans, Jackson and Great Northern Railroad pumped people and money into this small, pioneer town. A flag station just a block away from the current train depot was called 'Hammond's Crossing' and brought handfuls of new people to town. Peter Hammond was so convinced that the railroad would bring people to the city that he signed a contract with the rail company that forced the trains to stop every time they passed through Hammond." When some local residents at the turn of the century began growing strawberries, a growth explosion erupted, the little burg becoming a center for cultivating, processing and shipping seasonal fruit: "Boxcar loads of strawberries became a staple of the area and as trains left the city headed north, the money flowed south."

Today this thriving municipality on the northern rim of Lake Pontchartrain, some 30 miles east of the state capital at Baton Rouge and 55 miles northwest of New Orleans, boards and deboards more Louisiana Amtrak travelers than anyplace but New Orleans. In fiscal year 2008, the *City of New Orleans*, running daily between Chicago and its namesake conurbation, picked up or let off 14,695 riders in Hammond, a 3.5 percent rise in a year, an average of 40 patrons daily.

The *City of New Orleans* stops at a 1912 brick masonry single-level depot on NW Railroad Avenue. Erected by the Illinois Central Railroad which ran that train before Amtrak's arrival in 1971, the facility's principal tenant is now the City of Hammond where municipal offices are housed. Four blocks south, meanwhile, a restaurant occupies a wood-fabricated IC freight station built in 1927. In Hammond, it seems, they know how to put more to good use than mere berries.

NEW ORLEANS

Unremittingly a railway destination, New Orleans witnessed its first tracks only two years after the *Best Friend of Charleston* initiated steam-powered rail travel in America. That year (1832) the Pontchartrain Railroad began schlepping riders between the Mississippi River and Lake Pontchartrain. With that humble start the rails proliferated in and around New Orleans over the next century.

During the heyday of railway travel, five passenger stations and nine rail carriers concurrently served New Orleans. In a very real sense they all competed for that commerce. At the same time they collectively wreaked havoc at legions of grade crossings as they proffered trains throughout the Crescent City on copious tracks running hither and yon in a seemingly ungainly schematic. For decades this was a festering problem in 20th century New Orleans and growing worse with the passage of time. There were so many switch tracks there by the 1920s, for example, that it took a 254-page book to enumerate them all!

The city preferred a reduction in the number of terminal facilities: its best case scenario was "no more than one." The carriers were defiant for a while, however, remarkably resilient in favor of the status quo. Eventually there were to be no fewer than at least two surprises arising out of the prolonged discussions involving the rail barons and city leaders. First, while the railroads held their ground for years, their opposition eventually waned to the point they were persuaded that the city was actually "on to something" (surprise #1). Second, the attitudinal meltdown didn't occur until after initial cracks in the industry's armor were clearly visible — unmistakably hinting that the popularity of rail travel was about to be displaced by highways and airways (surprise #2). Only after city fathers came up with a plan they couldn't refuse — was it an ultimatum? — did the rail magnates acquiesce, signing on for "joint custody" at one edifice. But let's explore some background data that led to that point.

Among those five depots was the grand old Terminal Station which was sometimes locally identified as the Southern Railway terminal. And while Southern always dominated there, during some of the facility's life trains of two more railroads — Gulf, Mobile & Ohio and New Orleans & Northeastern — called there. Erected in 1908, this arresting edifice at 1125 Canal Street stood where that dramatic thoroughfare intersects with legendary Basin Street of jazz music fame. Renowned Chicago architect Daniel Hudson Burnham (1846–1912), who drew plans for Washington, D.C.'s Union Station (opened in 1907) and many of the towers that dot the skyline of the Windy City now, crafted drawings for Terminal Station in New Orleans. An elongated yet constricted facility, it was emblematic of the "shotgun house" architectural style that prevailed within the surrounding area's residential construction during that epoch. The bi-level building's elegant lines and curved archways were pleasing to the eye probably about as much as they were inviting to patrons and passersby.

One of the nine passenger carriers serving the Crescent City during these halcyon days of rail travel, on the other hand, felt it unwise to place all of its apples in a single basket. Missouri Pacific Railroad (MoPac) was purportedly the first line west of the Mississippi River, having started in that direction from St. Louis in 1851, finally reaching Kansas City 14 years hence. MoPac was convinced it could do a better job of helping its New Orleans customers by spreading its operations to a couple of depots. After buying Gulf Coast Lines in 1924, it received and dispatched Houston trains at Union Station on Howard Avenue. Three companies — MoPac, Illinois Central and Texas & New Orleans — sent their passengers to Union Station.

Designed by Louis Henry Sullivan (1856–1924), the "father of modernism" and mentor to superior architect Frank Lloyd Wright, New Orleans' Union Station, completed in 1892, was commemorated by one source as "a gracious slice of this Southern city." While its design was shamelessly Moderne, pitching clean lines and supplying a vivid, spacious, even soaring lobby, the new structure's facade invariably prompted illusions of a Beaux Arts colonnade. It witnessed tens of thousands of departures and arrivals over a span extending beyond six decades.

At the same time MoPac's consists coming from and leaving for northwesterly termini like St. Louis and Kansas City called at another New Orleans facility. They used the Beaux Arts depot between Melpomene and Thalia streets on Annunciation Street. MoPac shared that station with Texas & Pacific Railroad. A contemporary estimate lauded the depot as "the most impressive of all New Orleans passenger stations."

Kansas City Southern (KCS) and its ancillary Louisiana & Arkansas Railway (L&A) soon fused their passenger operations at 705 South Rampart Street where Rampart crosses Girod Street a few blocks south of the French Quarter. (The terminal was erected in 1923. L&A wasn't chartered until 1928, and absorbed into the KCS system in 1939.) Known forevermore as the Rampart Street Station, the facility's sobriquet also identified with the potent jazz presence of the Crescent City. More importantly perhaps, for the first time KCS had a direct route from its landlocked home base in Kansas City to New Orleans; and equally to the port city's strategic waterways linked to international freight and passenger carriers.

While some of those trains entered Rampart Street Station's stub-end tracks by pulling forward, unloading and then backing out for cleaning and servicing at nearby Jefferson Davis Yard, some more performed in the opposite fashion. The latter consists entered a wye at suburban Shrewsbury and backed into the terminal. They were subsequently transferred to Davis for overhauling and then backed into the station a second time for loading for departure to points north. When — in the 1950s — Rampart Street Station was abandoned by KCS, the facility was redeployed as a community fire station for the city.

The last of those New Orleans passenger carriers during the heyday of rail travel, and one of the mainstays evidenced by its early arrival in the Crescent City, was Louisville & Nashville Railroad (L&N). Unlike all the others L&N demonstrated its independence by maintaining a depot never shared with any other carrier. Occupied in 1902, it was at the foot of wide Canal Street, undoubtedly the city's most important northwest-southeast boulevard. The site was adjacent to the French Quarter, close by the banks of the winding Mississippi River with its tactically placed docks for ready freight transfer. A source branded the L&N depot "the most picturesque of New Orleans' old stations." New Orleans was the southern end of the company's mainline; in the opposite direction its "steamliners" and eventually streamliners headed for Mobile, Montgomery, Birmingham, Nashville, Louisville and Cincinnati. At those junctions connecting trains ferried riders to Atlanta, Washington, Chicago, St. Louis, Detroit and myriad supplementary destinations.

More specifics have been released about the L&N station in New Orleans than any of the others working in tandem at the time. A single-story brick edifice, it contained a 45 by 30 foot waiting room for white travelers, a 20 by 15 foot café within the waiting room, a 35 by 25 foot waiting room for black patrons, a 30 by 25 foot ladies' restroom and two smaller restrooms, a 60 by 30 foot baggage room, a 165 by 12 foot concourse extending along the building's north (track) side, and a 550-foot-long steel-roofed trainshed with sides open covering the station's trio of tracks. Two of those tracks were reserved for passenger consists while the remaining one was earmarked for baggage and express trade. It was almost always in use.

An eyewitness, in 1927, describes some of the congestion found at the L&N facility: "It is necessary to perform the seemingly impossible feat of getting out and in 22 trains daily on two tracks, one of which must be kept clear for freight and switching movements. To add to this difficulty, Iberville Street, which runs through the trainshed, must be kept open, and the available length for standing cars is only about sufficient to take seven or eight coaches. The operation is that of a through station, the trains being made up and received in the coach yard near Julia Street. The station is located between its own tracks and those of the Southern Pacific and the river, and is practically inaccessible at times. Taxis line up in the driveway along the south side of the station and to some extent in Canal Street where they obstruct traffic to the train tracks and wharf sheds."

After decades of this multiple facilities mishmash, Crescent City leaders negotiated a deal with the passenger carriers to stop the madness of calling at so many scattered depots. Instead they would thereafter converge all of their operations at a single facility. On October 22, 1947, New Orleans and the railroads signed a pact to construct a new passenger terminal next door to Union Station (a facility still serving the Illinois Central, Missouri Pacific, and Texas & New Orleans lines at that moment). The participating roads agreed to pay terminal construction and maintenance costs while the city was to own the property on which it sat and then to own the building upon completion. Allegorically and admittedly embellishing a tad, if the final out of a baseball game was just recorded, the scoreboard might read: New Orleans, 2; Railroads, 0.

Two years before its opening, an incomplete Louisiana Superdome bears witness to a pair of Amtrak E-units and IC E9A 4038 on rails beside it in September 1973. Amtrak E8A 203 once served B&O while Amtrak E10A 436, previously IC 2021, is an E10 rebuilt by Paducah from IC E8 4029 (*courtesy Jay T. Thomson*).

Or were the rail tycoons possibly more perceptive than they let on? Was this a plan to save them money? At the dawn of the twilight of America's dependency on rail travel, New Orleans Union Passenger Terminal (NOUPT) was to be erected at 1001 Loyola Avenue. Although it took six and a half years to build it (and why so long?), the deal was done. New Orleans Union Passenger Terminal officially welcomed the first trains to its stub-end tracks in April 1954, as the fortunes of that mode of travel were undeniably on the way out. NOUPT was the last great depot to rise in a major American metropolis, replacing multiple downtown terminals with one during the last hurrah of people-moving in the railroads' Gilded Age. One advantage in building it was the elimination of 80 level crossings where tracks previously intersected local streets.

After Amtrak began operating the nation's passenger trains on May 1, 1971, comparatively speaking, New Orleans fared especially well. Amtrak persisted in providing daily service between the Crescent City and Chicago and tri-weekly runs to Los Angeles. By 1993, the latter route was extended east to Miami, curtailed later at Orlando. That part of the route was discontinued after Hurricane Katrina struck the Gulf coast in 2005, although there is potentially serious current conversation about restoring it. Meanwhile, Southern Railway elected to continue operating its own trains after Amtrak began, doing so for nearly eight years. Southern terminated the southbound train four days weekly in Atlanta, continuing it to New Orleans the other three days. When Amtrak took over running Southern's *Crescent* in early 1979, the service was extended every day from New Orleans to New York.

NOUPT is now an intermodal facility serving intercity bus lines, the local transit carrier, taxis, shuttles, etc., in addition to trains. In Amtrak's fiscal year 2008, a total of 154,532 patrons boarded or deboarded one of its three long-distance runs (*City of New Orleans*, *Crescent*, *Sunset Limited*) at New Orleans, an average of 423 travelers per day. This netted a ridership increase of 22.6 percent over the previous year.

SHREVEPORT

Throughout much of its history Shreveport, in upper northwestern Louisiana near the Pelican State's borders with Texas and Arkansas, was a hotbed of railroad activity. While transportation firms emanating from it could only be measured as minor players among America's leading railway carriers, a couple of early Shreveport lines had substantial impact on the movement of freight and people back in the day. Their routes were strategically placed. One is still regularly applied now in transporting goods between Dallas and New Orleans.

Those humble beginnings were vested in German-born entrepreneur William Edenborn's Louisiana Railroad & Navigation Company (LR&N) and timber merchant William Buchanan's Louisiana & Arkansas Railroad (L&A). Edenborn's LR&N ran its first train in excess of 300 miles over tracks connecting Shreveport with New Orleans which his company laid. En route he sidestepped a costly Mississippi River bridge by traversing the water with an eight-mile ferry line hauling travelers on a tributary to the other side. Buchanan's L&A, on the other hand, laid tracks from Shreveport to the banks of the same river at Natchez, Mississippi. In the mid 1920s, this pair of regional pioneer capitalists died within three years of each other, leaving their respective enterprises to others.

A syndicate stepped in and bought both men's lines in 1928. Discarding the LR&N nomenclature, it ran the combined duo under the L&A banner. While still only a regional player, the Shreveport-based railway system soon extended its routes from Hope, Arkansas, to Alexandria, Louisiana; and from Minden, Louisiana, to Shreveport. It further operated a Lone Star State ancillary, the Louisiana, Arkansas & Texas Railway, which merged into the L&A on July 1, 1939. That year L&A itself was acquired by the much larger Kansas City Southern Railway (KCS). While L&A continued to operate as a separate line, it was folded into the KCS conglomeration and its name removed July 1, 1992, with its Shreveport operations substantially reduced.

Shreveport was perpetually recognized as a crossroads for railroads with lines running from the north to the Gulf coast and those with lines stretching east and west. Surprisingly for a city its size, in the 20th century Shreveport simultaneously claimed a quartet of rail depots instead of only one as might be anticipated at other locales with commensurate population. The owners included the Illinois Central Railroad; Kansas City Southern Railroad; St. Louis–Southwestern Railroad (Cotton Belt Line), with a structure erected in 1910; and Texas & Pacific Railroad, whose station opened in 1942.

Of the four, Kansas City Southern's downtown Union Station became a landmark. It impacted the city with a distinctive tall "watchman's tower," a symbol of Shreveport's long association with the rails. The oldest of Shreveport's passenger facilities, Union Station (sometimes labeled Union Depot) was erected in 1897 by the Kansas City, Shreveport & Gulf Terminal Company. It achieved its zenith in service during the postwar years of the 1920s. Typically 35 passenger trains called at Shreveport's most arresting railway center every day.

When Kansas City Southern began using those facilities on July 24, 1909, Shreveport was designated as a "Meal Station Stop" in KCS timetables. That notation persisted for nearly two decades, until 1928, when the carrier added diners to its passenger-coach consists. On November 2, 1969, the KCS *Southern Belle*—the only passenger train still passing through Shreveport at the end of the era—made its final trek north from New Orleans to Kansas City. It had been running since 1940.

The following day, November 3, Union Station shut its doors forever. On November 5, a blaze that commenced in the basement of the structure quickly engulfed the terminal in flames, literally burning it to the ground, leaving only rubble in its path. All that may be evidenced of that once proud transportation sanctuary today—beyond the memories of those it served—is a concrete footprint: stairs leading to the mount, ornamental tan-and-brown tiles at the front portal, green-and-white tiles on the restroom floors, and little more, according to an eyewitness.

As of 2009, a couple of former railway stations in Shreveport were still standing, although one was—according to a preservation Web site—on an "Endangered" list and subject to the impending possibility of a date with a wrecking ball. That is the vacant stone block Texas & Pacific depot on Common Street erected in 1942. The other, Central Station, erected in 1910, is a brick structure used during its lifetime by both Louisiana & Arkansas and St. Louis–Southwestern railroads. In the 1960s, east-west superhighway Interstate 20 was added alongside Central Station. The building, meanwhile, is currently occupied by commercial ventures, its security apparently not in imminent danger.

Mississippi

GULFPORT

When it hit the Gulf Coast in late August 2005, the destructive Hurricane Katrina altered everything in the way of train travel along heretofore scenic vistas embracing a pristine coastline from the Florida panhandle to the Crescent City. Amtrak, which had dispatched its tri-weekly *Sunset Limited* from Florida to California for a dozen years, terminated it eastbound at New Orleans. For a long while the tracks linking municipalities like Gulfport, Biloxi, Mobile and Pensacola were compromised. Even after they returned to freight service, Amtrak—for reasons not completely clear—didn't restore the train's run east of New Orleans. Legislators have since gotten into the debate over the issue. In early 2010, the matter was still unresolved, though cities like those mentioned plus Pascagoula, Tallahassee, Lake City and several more are hopeful of a positive outcome.

At Gulfport the *Sunset Limited* called at a passenger station built by the Louisville & Nashville Railroad (L&N). The structure, completed in 1907, is at 1419 27th Avenue where it intersects with 16th Street (formerly Railroad Street). At one time the Gulf & Ship Island Railroad also sent its trains to this facility. The site isn't quite four blocks north of Beach Boulevard, Gulfport's principal east-west thoroughfare (U.S. 90) that hugs the shoreline, so its tracks are well within reach of flooding and devastation from tempests in teapots.

The station remains extant and an update suggests it's unoccupied. The Gulfport Centennial Museum—depicting the history of the area for 100 years—which had been housed there also, closed when Katrina struck and (Web sites suggest) never reopened. The depot suffered extensive damage in that watery, windy melee. A report in the November 2009 issue of *Trains* magazine indicates Gulfport's depot is one of 13 along the eastern *Sunset Limited* route not yet ready to return to serviceable operation. The single-story brick structure is owned by CSX Transportation of which L&N was an ancestor.

At the depot's northwest corner there is a diamond crossing where CSX freights run east and west (Mobile–New Orleans and beyond) and Kansas City Southern freights run north and south (Hattiesburg–Gulfport wharf). The station's platform extends from the northwest corner along the CSX line and wraps around the building to the south along the KCS line. A reporter speculates on the facility: "Over the years the station has suffered a number of modifications, rendering it almost unrecognizable, one might imagine, from the original design."

HATTIESBURG

A captain in the Confederate Army, William Harris Hardy (1837–1917)—a native Alabamian who turned some discerning visions into realities in Mississippi—picked the site, laid the plans and named the city of Hattiesburg for his second wife, Hattie Lott. He was also the father of two more towns in the Magnolia State, Gulfport and Laurel. Hattiesburg's earliest recognition grew from a gargantuan long leaf pine virgin forest surrounding it. That lumber and its byproducts attracted residents who converted it into perpetual multimillion-dollar harvests.

The entrepreneurial-minded Hardy, in the meantime—an educator-turned-lawyer—married three times and fathered 12 offspring (his first two wives died at young ages of natural causes). He established a law practice and, with the passing of time, successively moved it to more prominent locales. In 1868, at Paulding, Mississippi, he became convinced the region must have a rail line that connected Meridian with New Orleans, a distance of slightly more than 200 miles. Over the next couple of years he advanced plans for a New Orleans & Northeastern Railroad. Relocating to Meridian in 1972, Hardy began to solicit financial aid for the venture just as a devastating panic in 1873 reversed the nation's economy, placing Hardy's intents on hold. For seven years he was unable to proceed.

When the crisis abated in 1880, he not only renewed his fundraising efforts but rode the distance from New Orleans to Meridian on horseback to settle the projected railway's route. He literally created Hattiesburg on that journey, ultimately establishing a small depot there. By 1887, Hardy was president of Gulf & Ship Island Railroad. He moved into public service in 1895, being elected to the state senate. A decade hence he was a circuit court judge, retiring from the post at 72 in 1909, and finishing his career as a Gulfport attorney.

Back in Hattiesburg, its first train came through in October 1883, and the town was incorporated five months later. Hardy's frame depot adequately served the community for a while. It was probably the center of activity, as the railroad was the town's reason for existence. That depot preceded the facility that still serves Hattiesburg today. Constructed by Southern Railway in 1910, the 14,000-square-foot bi-level Italian Renaissance station at 308 Newman Street is one of the striking landmarks in Hattiesburg. That's particularly so since a makeover earlier this century turned it into a majestic shrine celebrating past glories. Bathed in soft lighting at night, the station's facade is a vision of grandeur, a sterling testimony to local denizens' appreciation of their historic roots.

The 1910 structure was noted for its "interminable" 924-foot canopy-covered platform. When the roof finally fell into disrepair, it was downsized to the zone immediately fronting the building. Years ago the terminal's red tile roof was replaced by shingles. In the most recent makeover the original cover was replicated by installing flat red clay tiles. Dormers were reinstalled, skylights restored, and damaged rafters either repaired or replaced. A 4,000-square-foot Great Room (the depot's generous waiting hall) was renovated and restored to its previous ambience. Arched portals and windows in the Great Room, flanked by a tall exterior clock tower, make a hospitable impression on visitors and passengers.

In 1998, the City of Hattiesburg began talks with the depot's owner, Norfolk Southern Railroad, heir to Southern Railway, for the purchase of the site. Four years afterward the deed to the property was transferred. On April 21, 2007, an appropriate city-wide celebration followed completion of the total refurbishing of the edifice. Now on the National Register of Historic Places, the Hattiesburg depot was converted to an intermodal facility — the apex

of the local transit system and a taxi hub in addition to serving Amtrak. A total of 9,920 Hattiesburg patrons rode the *Crescent* in fiscal year 2008, 27 riders per day, a 9.7 percent increase in one year. The train runs daily in each direction between New Orleans and New York City.

Few, if any, railroad terminals elsewhere may be cited as the birthplace of a genre of popular music. Some local residents make that assumption about their depot nevertheless, believing rock 'n' roll was created there. In 1936, the station was the recording venue of a trio of rising blues artists, siblings Blind Roosevelt Graves and Uaroy Graves and pianist Cooney Vaughn. Their performances exhibited "fully formed rock & roll guitar riffs and a stomping rock & roll beat," *The Rolling Stone Illustrated History of Rock and Roll* insisted. The threesome, appearing as the Mississippi Jook Band, allegedly taped a couple of numbers at the Hattiesburg depot, *Barbecue Bust* and *Dangerous Women*. Tradition has it that this pair of records may have been the pioneering tunes of a musical form that was to sweep the nation in less than two decades.

Is there a railway terminal anywhere with a claim to fame equal to that?

JACKSON

The capital of Mississippi easily surpasses the nine other Amtrak stops in the Magnolia State in number of riders boarding and deboarding trains every day. With an aggregate 40,245 at Jackson stepping on or off the company's *City of New Orleans* (Chicago–New Orleans) in Amtrak's fiscal year 2008, there's no contest for first place. Greenwood, second, saw 14,085 riders come and go from the same train that year. Jackson witnessed a daily average of 110 patrons, an increase of 12.5 percent in one year among its *City* riders. While the late country singer Tammy Wynette warbled "Jackson ain't a very big town," in Amtrak ridership, size is enough to outclass anything else in the state.

The *City of New Orleans* stops twice daily, once in each direction, at Jackson's historic downtown Union Station at 300 West Capitol Street. (At the depot on one side of the train travelers are offered a fabulous view of the state capitol a few blocks east at the summit of a hill.) Built in 1927 by the Illinois Central Railroad (IC) and restored to its former grandeur between 2002 and 2004, Union Station is an intermodal facility today. In addition to Amtrak's *City*, it's home to a fleet of taxicabs plus Greyhound intercity buses and the principal hub of all Jatran buses, the local transit company.

The facility is composed of a connected series of basic structures. Its centerpiece is a bi-level brick-and-stone Georgian Revival headhouse extending beneath the elevated tracks. A single-story brick-and-stone shed runs alongside the tracks, providing roofing for about two-thirds of the station. In the makeover a few years ago exterior and interior masonry was scrubbed and refurbished, wooden windows restored, tile roof replaced, and interior systems upgraded, while cargo space was renovated.

Union Station is situated only a short distance west of another Jackson depot at 618 East Pearl Street also completed in 1927. It served routes of the Mobile & Ohio and New Orleans & Great Northern railroads, a couple of IC competitors. Today that extant facility is owned by the State of Mississippi and state offices occupy the brick structure.

MERIDIAN

Meridian, in central Mississippi and only a few miles from the Alabama border, is yet another Magnolia State town rich in rail history. A local account, published in 1907, terms the municipality "a child of the railroad." After John T. Ball, an enterprising Kemper County merchant-turned-realtor, purchased 80 acres of former Choctaw Indian land around 1853, new settlers were attracted.

Ball erected a depot on the existing Mobile & Ohio Railroad (M&O), formed in 1848, and called

Once the Magnolia State's largest city, Meridian — with a proud railway heritage — has lost population and Amtrak riders in modern times. A portion of the city's 1906 depot remains where Amtrak's *Crescent* calls twice daily and an occasional excursion train arrives. In October 1972, Southern 4501 led such a visit. This one carried area railfans into western Alabama for a brief outing, the principal thrill being to ride a steam-powered consist (*courtesy Clyde Woodruff*).

the stop *Sowashee* due to its proximity to Sowashee Creek. When the sobriquet *Meridian* was subsequently presented to Ball with the majority of denizens in favor, he liked it better, too. Soon Southern Railway of Mississippi (SRM) intersected M&O there. SRM president William Crosby Smedes prevailed on M&O officials to alter the nomenclature in their timetables to *Meridian*. On February 10, 1860, the town was incorporated under that name.

Four years hence, during the War Between the States' significant Battle of Meridian, General William Tecumseh Sherman — on a rampage through the South to render as much material damage as possible to break the Confederacy — led 20,000 Union troops to Meridian. The railroads were destroyed and much of the town was burned to the ground. "Meridian, with its depots, storehouses, arsenal, hospitals, offices, hotels, and cantonments no longer exists," Sherman assessed. His pronouncement and destruction to the contrary, within 26 working days the tracks were repaired and the trains were running.

Following resurgence in the postwar epoch, Meridian grew substantially, becoming a manufacturing center and the state's largest city from 1890 to 1930. After a brief economic slowdown following the Great Depression, the nation entered the Second World War and the railroads gained renewed momentum. That didn't persist forever; when they declined in the 1950s, locals sought employment elsewhere, and Meridian's population fell into a tailspin.

Some of the area's railroad impact may be gathered from the biographical account of William Harris Hardy reported in the article on Hattiesburg. At one time a quintet of passenger carriers brought their trains to Meridian: Alabama & Vicksburg, Alabama Great Southern, Mobile & Ohio, New Orleans & Northeastern, and Southern. All but Alabama Great Southern participated in Union Station, a 1905 one-story stucco-and-brick edifice partially remaining today at 1901 Front Street. A report states that 44 trains arrived or departed there daily during the halcyon days of passenger travel by rail.

A refurbished Mission Revival style depot and Railway Express Agency was completed in August 1906 at a cost of $250,000. While the original facility boasted a central tower demolished in the late 1940s, there was still more demolition in 1966, when all but the station's eastern wing was removed. Now on the National Register of Historic Places, the "revised" structure was formally dedicated by the city, its present owner, on December 11, 1997. As the Multi-Modal Transportation Center (MMTC), it occupies four city blocks on six acres donated by Alabama Great Southern Railroad. A railroad museum, provision for future rolling stock, a new terminal addition attached to the surviving portion of the 1905 depot, a farmers' market, landscaped park and space for festivals and citywide events sits on that land today.

The terminal itself has been expanded to encompass not only Amtrak's New York to New Orleans *Crescent* every day, but also Greyhound and Trailways buses, Meridian Transit System buses, and a fleet of local taxi providers. In fiscal year 2008, Amtrak saw 10,747 riders enter or leave the *Crescent* at Meridian, an average of 29 per day, and a loss of 6.3 percent over the previous year. As almost every Southern municipality experienced an increase in ridership in 2008, some doing so expansively, a potential explanation for the loss at Meridian is that its population remains in decline.

North Carolina

ASHEVILLE

Asheville's initial foray into railway depots came about October 3, 1880, when the owner of Western

North Carolina Railroad established a facility in the hamlet of Best, named after him. Until then getting to Best was inconvenient at best. Travelers coming from the flatlands of North Carolina's central Piedmont and eastern shore rode Best's trains to Old Fort, the terminus of the rail line at that time, some 30 miles east of Asheville. Between 1869 and 1880, the tourists stumbled along rocky roadbeds in stagecoaches for the final portion from Old Fort to Best.

Best's premiering depot was used by visitors and residents until wealthy Northeastern capitalist George W. Vanderbilt bought the town as the site for his Biltmore Estate mansion (America's largest house) and accompanying village in 1895. The small, undistinguished depot at Best was replaced with one designed by architect Richard Morris Hunt. Set on a brick foundation, it's a symmetrical, single-story structure with half-timbered pebbledash walls. Brick, stucco and wood were used in its construction. Its exterior is distinguished by a central porte cochere, low-hipped roof, wide overhanging eaves and heavy chambered brackets. Still in use to 2009, the depot along with other buildings crafted by Hunt in Biltmore Village is in striking contrast with his colossal design of the Biltmore Estate itself.

Built in 1896, Biltmore Village depot at 1 Biltmore Plaza is at 30 Brook Street on Asheville's suburban south side. Southern Railway trains called there in addition to stopping at the road's principal edifice in town. The Biltmore facility exhibits an interior that is typical of small railway stations of its epoch. Double waiting rooms—a large one for Caucasians on the right, a smaller one for Negroes on the left—were divided by a center ticket office and vestibule. Unquestionably the community's focal point, the depot was the key

The first station of much import that Southern Railway trains leaving Asheville heading east would encounter was in the rural mountain town of Black Mountain, 16 miles away. Captured April 15, 2005, Black Mountain's restored vintage depot parallels NS tracks now and looks much as it did a half-century or more in the past (*courtesy Michael B. Robbins*).

What better time to see the steam from a steam engine than at night? Here N&W Class J 611 prepares to depart Greensboro, North Carolina, for another fan trip. This one takes riders up the Blue Ridge Mountains into Asheville, a once-prominent crossroad for Southern Railway. There the *Asheville Special* to New York originated and terminated while the *Carolina Special* from Cincinnati (with legs from Chicago, Cleveland, Detroit and St. Louis) divided again: part of it continued to Goldsboro, in eastern North Carolina, and the rest persisted to Charleston, South Carolina (*courtesy Jay Miller*).

structure in Biltmore Village and is listed in the National Register of Historic Places. After the trains stopped running the station was molded into a restaurant and lounge.

The main station in town, meanwhile, anchored Asheville's Depot Street. It was razed after the final run of Southern Railway's *Carolina Special* to and from Greensboro, North Carolina, on December 5, 1968. At that time Southern's *Asheville Special* shifted to and from a Salisbury, North Carolina, terminus. At its westernmost destination it called at the Biltmore depot thereafter, relabeled "Asheville." The *Asheville Special* persisted as a tri-weekly run instead of daily as before to August 1975, after which passenger service to Asheville was discontinued altogether.

Tracks leading to the Asheville station paralleled the French Broad River, running several hundred feet east of it, 2.1 miles north of the Biltmore depot. They proceeded north from the station to destinations in far western North Carolina and Tennessee. The large two-story Asheville complex in the city proper exhibited a railroad yard to its west that included a roundhouse and repair shops. But in reality the terminal was about four stories tall at its center above the spacious waiting room. An ornate

rooftop and chimneys at each of its four corners created an imposing landmark on the local skyline. And if it looked familiar to anybody studying Southern depots, it should have: its designer was the tireless architect of the New South, Frank Pierce Milburn (1868–1926), whose depots dotted landscapes in many a Dixie conurbation (Augusta, Charlotte, Durham, Knoxville, Salisbury, Savannah, Winston-Salem, et al.).

In its heyday trains came and went from Asheville in four directions: west to Murphy, North Carolina; east to Greensboro or Salisbury, often connecting with Southern mainline consists at those cities; north to Knoxville and Cincinnati; and south to Spartanburg, Columbia and Charleston, South Carolina. When the final train rolled through, for the mountain people who had depended on that form of transportation for 95 years (1880–1975), it was the end of an era.

CHARLOTTE

After a half-century a quintet of functioning passenger rail stations in Mecklenburg County was reduced to one. Its successor has been in the planning stages since the 1990s, and could become reality within a few years. In the heyday of travel by train, following consolidations of previous carriers, a quartet of lines accessed the Carolinas' Queen City. Presented in the order in which those depots were built, they included the Seaboard Air Line Railroad (SAL), Southern Railway (SOU), Piedmont & Northern Railroad (P&N), a locally-based carrier with two passenger facilities in metropolitan Charlotte, and the original Norfolk Southern Railway (NS). As is often the case one terminal rose above the others in location, prestige, patronage, trains dispatched, and trade-marking the city's skyline. That one was blindsidedly obliterated when preservationists couldn't muster the forces to stop it and no organization stepped forward to buy it.

While the first tracks believed to reach Charlotte date to October 1852 — when the Charlotte & South Carolina completed a route from the Queen City via Columbia to the port at Charleston — another half-dozen years elapsed before anything approaching a real depot existed. That initial structure, a narrow, bi-level affair with a tin roof, was built by the Wilmington, Charlotte & Rutherfordton Railroad. It was the eastern terminus of a 31-mile line from the Queen City to the hamlet of Lincolnton, North Carolina, opened in April 1861. The station was set on the site that later would be occupied by the SAL terminal at 1000 North Tryon Street, 10 blocks above the city center. Tryon is one of dual thoroughfares (the other, Trade Street) whose long-recognized uptown intersect (known as "The Square" by locals) was commonly celebrated in the 20th century as "the Crossroads of the Carolinas" (Charlotte's city center is 10 miles north of South Carolina). Southern Railway subsequently established its station on Trade Street, the other half of that distinguished "crossroads."

The line to Rutherfordton wasn't completed until after the Carolina Central Railroad Company acquired the right of way on May 17, 1873. The Rutherfordton extension opened December 15, 1874. For the first time a coastal route from Wilmington through Charlotte continued to the foothills of the Blue Ridge Mountains 80 miles west of town. The Carolina Central dissolved into a mix of railways August 1, 1893, which together formed Seaboard Air Line. At that juncture, major additions to the Charlotte terminal were made including a ticket office and divided waiting rooms.

By mid century, after SAL passenger service was reduced to just one train daily, the railway extension to Rutherfordton was abandoned (December 1950). SAL replaced it with buses of the Queen City Trailways Coach Company, which honored SAL tickets. Daily passenger rail service persisted from Charlotte to Wilmington, linking with SAL mainline connections at Monroe and Hamlet. The last train rolled from Charlotte on November 3, 1958.

Charles Christian Hook (1870–1938), a native West Virginian of German parentage, arrived in the Queen City in 1890 to teach mechanical drawing at a local school. Hook is considered Charlotte's first architect of note. After designing homes in the newly-opened Dilworth section south of uptown, a few mansions (including White Oaks, home of James B. Duke, industrialist and transportation mogul), plus several landmarks like the original city hall and the clubhouse of the Charlotte Woman's Club, Hook quit his teaching job and opened an architectural practice. Railroad stations may have been his forte; in volume, they contributed heavily to his portfolio. The one he crafted for the SAL at Charlotte was among his earliest pursuits.

Hook's engagement resulted after the small tin-roofed terminal built in 1858 burned to the ground on February 11, 1895. SAL had only taken possession of the depot about 18 months earlier after a previous owner folded into SAL. Following the fire, for an interim period passenger sheds were enclosed as a makeshift waiting room and ticket office. On July 28, *The Charlotte Observer* announced the city's presumptive "leading architect" had been tapped to draw plans for a permanent replacement commensurate with SAL's increasing prominence as a key player in transportation in the South. Hook's drawings embraced a Classical Revival style of architecture which, when finished, were branded by one University of North Carolina history prof "relatively plain and austere." Depot construction by local contractor W. C. Williams began that December and a completed two-story 120 by 40 foot brick edifice with brown stone trim opened June 16, 1896, only 16 months after fire leveled the original.

Facing north, the outside walls followed an irregular pattern. Rectangular interruptions projected from both the center and southeast sides while a turreted polygonal bay, a classic Victorian feature, was pronounced on the northeast edge. A wide brim extended around the building except over the southeast façade. The southwest porch exhibited a centrally located porte cochere. A ticket office separated two waiting rooms on the SAL terminal's main floor, one 29 by 27 feet nearest Tryon Street for Caucasians, the other 27 × 16 feet beyond it for Colored patrons. Both rooms had their own toilet facilities. A baggage room, 27 by 12 feet, was adjacent to the Colored waiting room. A wooden staircase in the center rose to the second level, used by SAL for an engineers' dormitory and an office, 28 by 15 feet each; conductors' and train master's rooms, 15 by 12 feet each; telegraph room, 15 by 13 feet; and convenience areas.

Two decades later Seaboard gave a green light to a significant upgrading and refurbishing of the Charlotte terminal. Drafted by architects at the line's Norfolk, Virginia, headquarters, the makeover was awarded to A. M. Walkup Company of Richmond, Virginia. The improvement phase began August 7, 1916, and ended January 31, 1917. Single-story additions to the bi-level depot were made at northwest and southeast corners. Three bays were added on the north side and two square transom windows on the south. A chimney at one end of the original structure was incorporated within the interior. Steps outside the southernmost add-on led to a cellar. The façade was covered by brick veneer and there was a red tile floor throughout. A striking feature was the continuous umbrella shed that ran trackside 300 feet supported by 15 cast iron columns. During the renovation the baggage room was relocated.

After the final SAL train left the station in 1958, the structure became a yard office for the carrier, eventually serving Seaboard Coast Line Railroad when SAL and Atlantic Coast Line Railroad merged in 1967. A year earlier the Charlotte facility was altered yet again to meet needs of a functioning yard office. The main floor was partitioned, a wall removed upstairs to create a large room, and extensive electrical work brought it up to current code.

In its afterlife it appeared the Seaboard station was on the designated hit list after succeeding owner CSX Transportation abandoned it in 1987. In an arrangement spearheaded by the Charlotte-Mecklenburg Historic Landmarks Commission, on December 16, 1988, CSX donated the station and leased the property to the agency for $100 annually. The commission bought the land from CSX on December 31, 1990, and emergency roof repairs were made in hopes a buyer could be found to preserve it. A portion of the old Colored waiting room ceiling was destroyed in an electrical fire the following month (January 1991) but firefighters saved the rest of the building. On December 22, 1993, a coalition of uptown churches purchased the depot, expecting to spend a half-million dollars converting it to a daytime shelter and counseling center for the area's homeless. In 1996, a local railfan-historian wrote: "Now Charlotte can be assured that one of its few remaining railroad landmarks will be preserved for future generations."

Not so fast: A modern Web site indicates the aforementioned Urban Ministry Center departed the deteriorating ex–Seaboard terminal in 2006, relocating its homeless shelter in a nearby building at 945 North College Street. What became of the station? Viewed from the edge of the property in October 2009, it is dilapidated, falling down, overgrown foliage surrounds it, and it appears totally abandoned. If it isn't a prime candidate for removal it's probably because no one has expressed interest in the trackside property in a while. Its days could be numbered.

All of which segues naturally into Charlotte's second enduring railroad terminal, the most esteemed of the lot. It's the one that *was* demolished when a diversity of factors coalesced, eliminating it nearly two decades before its long-time landlord, Southern Railway, stopped running passenger trains. Prominent Dixie depot architect Frank Pierce Milburn (1868–1926), who subsequently drew sketches for terminals at Augusta and Savannah, Georgia, Knoxville, Tennessee, and other municipalities, plus scads of Southern county courthouses, was hired about 1901 to draft plans for a magnificent Charlotte station for Southern Railway. His work for an elegant, yet fancifully flamboyant and ornate Spanish Mission/Mediterranean edifice became a hallmark of Milburn's talent, frequently applied in the facilities he cultivated in later years.

Born at Bowling Green, Kentucky, Milburn opened an architectural practice at 17 in Louisville (1884–1889). He subsequently moved it to Kenova, West Virginia (1890–1895), and set up shop in Charlotte thereafter. He was well acquainted with the Queen City when tapped to design the inspired Southern Railway terminal. Milburn left Charlotte a few years after its completion, landing in Washington, D.C., about 1905. But he had already been employed three years earlier by Southern Railway as its chief architect, the same year (1902) his Charlotte temple of trains opened for traffic. Over a 57-year lifetime Milburn designed at least 250 salient public buildings including depots, courthouses, academic structures, and many more, plus scads of residences. Some of the 19 railway stations he drafted beyond Charlotte's included one in Asheville, Augusta, Durham, Knoxville, Salisbury, Savannah, and Winston-Salem. He died at Asheville. A biographer assessed: "Among architects working in the [Southeastern] region, the geographic scope and volume of his work were unprecedented."

Situated at 511 West Trade Street, the Charlotte station's main portal faced northeast. A large square tower at that entrance rose to heights of at least five stories. Several exits faced northwest, leading to a shed running alongside multiple tracks outside the rectangular bi-level edifice. SOU occupied a rather large tract of land in uptown Charlotte. It was bounded by South Graham Street on its back (southeast) side. The passenger station was enclosed by West Fourth Street on its southwest side but the railroad yard paralleling the tracks to the northwest extended south of Fourth Street several blocks. Grade crossings were a big concern for Charlotte drivers then, especially at major arteries like Trade where trains were constantly rolling. Some of this was eliminated when the block with the tracks crossing Trade — and the approaching roadway to it — was lowered, allowing a viaduct over Trade Street.

This didn't adequately satisfy the city fathers,

however. Southern Railway abandoned its station of grandeur in 1961, in favor of a cheaper-to-operate plain vanilla facility on the outskirts of town. The new one displayed almost no exterior semblance of railroading save a bank of taxis waiting out front as train time approached and for the tracks and shed behind the building. Once Southern was gone from its legendary uptown address, the city wasted no time: within months it removed from its midst one of Charlotte's most exalted architectural treasures. Today Greyhound buses pull onto the asphalt where Frank Milburn's spectacular beauty stood.

It's an area of uptown now surrounded by bars, bistros, vagrants, and — on Carolinas Panthers football game days — the neighborhood witnesses tens of thousands of patrons on foot hurriedly swarming through. Scores of vendors set up makeshift stands and hawk football regalia while the smell of brats, barbecue and beer punctuates the air at sidewalk and parking-lot grills, beckoning those on their way to or from the nearby coliseum. Few contemplate that on this site streamlined coach-and-sleeper consists with attractive-sounding sobriquets like *Peach Queen, Crescent, Southerner, Augusta Special, Piedmont Limited* and *Washington-Atlanta-New Orleans Express* ferried Charlotteans every day to faraway places with strange-sounding names. It's a faraway epoch this generation never knew.

Meanwhile the adjacent Piedmont & Northern Railroad was unique in every imaginable way. It was formed after William States Lee, vice president of Southern Power and Utilities Company, proposed it to the company's president, James B. Duke, in 1909. Lee envisioned "an electrically powered interurban railway system linking the major cities of the Piedmont Carolinas." Maybe rationalizing that harnessing and providing electrical power was the business they were already in and this would be a natural extension of it, Duke endorsed Lee's idea. (Parenthetically, Southern Power and Utilities already had the power monopoly in Charlotte, owning Charlotte Electric Railway also. In time the parent firm morphed into Duke Power Company, named after you-know-who, running not only the city's electric power supply but a gargantuan fleet of transit buses. Since then the firm has expanded into Duke Energy, a global player in a multifaceted industry.)

In 1910, subsidiary Piedmont Traction Company (PTC) was organized as a street railway, operating in and around Gastonia, North Carolina, about 25 miles west of Charlotte. A second ancillary, Greenville, Spartanburg & Anderson Railway Company (GS&A), was created in South Carolina as a street railway to run between those fixed termini. The pair of lines then united in a syndicate with PTC

acquiring the Charlotte street railway while GS&A bought the Belton to Anderson route. The 89-mile mainline in South Carolina ran between Spartanburg and Greenwood with a 31-mile spur connecting Anderson. Both companies built new lines and secured trackage rights over the lines of sundry street railways. The network was completed in April 1914, the divisional pair at last uniting on paper as Piedmont & Northern Railway.

The P&N's long-range plan had always been to connect its two sectors at Gastonia and Spartanburg. Further, it intended to continue northward from Charlotte to Winston-Salem and eventually to Washington, D.C., and southward to Atlanta. It never happened, however; in the 1930s, Southern Railway convinced the Interstate Commerce Commission it was a bad idea. (Southern Railway staffers took a jaundiced view of its competition, commonly referring to P&N as "that damned trolley line.") While P&N was heavily involved in transporting people, its freight tonnage was far weightier. Routinely it moved large quantities of coal and coke, cotton and cotton waste, paper and paper products, merchandise, building material, fertilizer and fertilizer products, grain and grain products, oil and gasoline, and textiles along its routes. Passenger service from Charlotte to Mount Holly, North Carolina, a distance of 11 miles — the first segment completed — was inaugurated April 3, 1912.

And do you recall the name Charles Christian Hook? Not only did he design the Hermitage Road manor that James B. Duke called home as well as the SAL station, Hook got the nod to prepare architectural drawings for *all* the P&N depots! The line's northern section terminated in the downtown block of Charlotte that is bounded between Mint and Graham streets and Third and Fourth streets. That's caty-cornered to the venerated terminal used by Southern Railway across Graham Street. P&N's freight depot operated in a second adjacent block bounded by Mint, Graham, Second and Third streets. A modern Web site suggests the Charlotte Knights AAA baseball team, which has been playing its home games in South Carolina since 1990, plans "to build a new ballpark on the two block site to open for the 2009 or 2010 season." But an agreement reached by the ball club with York County, South Carolina, in October 2009, indicates local baseball won't be played in North Carolina before 2014 at the earliest.

The P&N passenger station was also razed after its trains stopped running between Charlotte and Gastonia in 1951. Yet as all P&N depots had identifiable traits, it's a fair assumption that another extant Mecklenburg County P&N facility offers a pretty good indication of what riders downtown experienced. In use today as a commercial enterprise, this one is in the Paw Creek community on Old Mount Holly Road about seven miles northwest of the end of the line. On the timetables it was designated *Thrift* for an unincorporated community near it.

Hook's 1911 design combines simple forms with careful detailing to give the Thrift station functionalism and dignity. It's a long narrow building parallel to the tracks with a large freight room at one end and a small passenger waiting area at the opposite end. The stationmaster's office separates them, its brick bay window jutting out to offer unobstructed viewing up and down the tracks. Hook topped this customary form with a red Spanish tile roof. Wide eaves are carried on heavy wooden paired brackets, a motif adapted from the Spanish Colonial style popular then. Three cross-gabled attic vents are perched on the roof's ridgeline.

An eyewitness allowed: "The brick walls are almost devoid of decoration as are the tall double-hung windows with their simple concrete sills and lintels. Instead of applied ornament, the architect used the materials themselves to give visual interest to the structure. The main body of the walls is of yellow brick laid in an unusual running bond, the joints of one course not centered under the middle of the bricks above. Below the window sills, the brick changes to red and the walls thicken to give the building an added feeling of solidarity. These red bricks are rounded at the openings and the corners of the building to provide further interest. Another indication of Hook's thoughtful detailing is a cast concrete bench built into the east end of the station along Old Mount Holly Road, designed for passengers meeting trains when the waiting room was closed or crowded."

Hook used the design motifs and materials in the Thrift station in all his P&N buildings, including the large freight station that survived to 1980 in downtown Charlotte. The only variation in his design was size of structure, determined by the importance of a stop. All had a base of red brick with yellow brick walls topped by red tile roofs. The smaller depots, like the one at Thrift, combined freight and passenger operations under a single roof. "The architect used carefully functional forms for the structures, but gave them a quiet elegance through attention to detail," a historian observed.

P&N's initial interurban passenger service out of Charlotte included eight trains each way daily. Gradually the number was reduced to three round trips per day. Tickets were sold on "The Square" at Blake's Drug Store (later Liggett's Rexall Drugs) or the Mint Street depot for 20 cents one way. The line prospered because the company interchanged freight cars with steam railroads, industrial investors in the company shipped on the P&N whenever possible and Duke's development efforts marketed the company well. When the electric locomotives competing against steam engines were replaced by diesel power in the early 1950s, some of the electrics were shipped to South America while others were scrapped. On July 1, 1969, P&N's operations merged into the Seaboard Coast Line Railroad, ending business as "The Great Electric System of the South" precisely six decades after being conceived.

Norfolk Southern Railroad's (Railway, from 1942) presence in the Queen City occurred after that company purchased the Raleigh, Charlotte & Southern Railroad. (This NS company should not be confused with the Class 1 freight carrier of the same name established by the merger of the Norfolk & Western and Southern Railway systems in 1982.) The predecessor RC&S may never have gotten much of a foothold in Charlotte; apparently within months of its charter it was sold to NS. Since the first NS passenger train departed Charlotte on December 1, 1913, from outside the offices of *The Charlotte Observer*, it appears likely no station had yet been erected. Around that time the carrier selected a site at 6th and A streets, between North College and North Brevard streets, for a freight depot.

NS held off building a passenger depot as the four railroads in town—SAL, SOU, P&N, NS— negotiated a union station to serve them all. When that broke down NS determined to add a passenger waiting room to its freight facility and—with further modifications—created a joint freight-passenger terminal. The uptown rectangular structure extended more than four-fifths of the block between 6th and 7th streets. Four stub-end tracks from the north paralleled the depot's east side, abruptly ending at 6th Street. Although NS passenger service was suspended on January 31, 1948, the station continued handling NS freight until the carrier was folded into Southern Railway on January 1, 1974.

The "new" Southern Railway depot at 1914 North Tryon Street, meanwhile—a few blocks north of the SAL terminal—was opened in 1961. Southern sent its passenger traffic through it until 1979, when the company abandoned that business, relinquishing the throttle of its last train (*Crescent*) to Amtrak. The latter took over most of the nation's passenger service in 1971. Today Amtrak continues to run the daily *Crescent* between New Orleans and New York through Charlotte along with two more trains in conjunction with the North Carolina Department of Transportation: the *Carolinian* sprints from Charlotte to New York every day while the *Piedmont* travels from Charlotte to Raleigh. In fiscal year 2008, Amtrak's Charlotte patronage was 135,435, a rise of 23.7 percent in a year, and typically 371 travelers per day. In the Tar Heel State, Charlotte's ridership on Amtrak is second to

Raleigh, which also loads and receives passengers on yet another noteworthy train, the daily Florida–New York *Silver Star*.

Railfans in Charlotte await the next phase of travel by train for the area. A projected "Gateway Station" will return service uptown near the football stadium three blocks from the city center at a site bounded by West Trade, West Fourth, Graham Street and Norfolk Southern Railroad. If this sounds familiar, it should: Southern Railway's splendid unparalleled sanctuary occupied the site from 1902 to 1962; Greyhound buses stop there now. The intermodal facility on the drawing board embraces intercity rail as well as local, regional and intercity buses, rental cars, bicycles and pedestrians. Beyond providing better access to the region's commercial, entertainment and cultural venues, the edifice will connect with a county greenway system and a trio of parks. Assuming plans proceed on schedule, the state Department of Transportation anticipates that the facility will handle a half-million rail passengers annually by 2015.

FAYETTEVILLE

Unlike many other Dixie burgs of similar size, Fayetteville — situated in the coastal plain of eastern North Carolina — appears by some contemporary accounts to have been virtually uninvolved with railroading for a very long while. Particularly is this true as the economic dynamics are recounted that appreciably impacted the area's history. Some truncated chronologies of the city, in fact, ignore rail shipping and travel by train altogether. Named in 1783 for Frenchman Marquis de Lafayette, an American Revolutionary War hero who supported the colonies, Fayetteville prospered as an inland port. Sitting at the headwaters of the navigable Cape Fear River, which drains into the Atlantic Ocean 100 miles to the southeast, the city had a natural means of getting its goods to market and for accessing raw materials and commodities elsewhere. Unlike many of its sister cities without a watery advantage, Fayetteville didn't have to wait for the trains to come to ship its products.

After several unsuccessful attempts to add railroads to Fayetteville's landscape, connecting there with barges to the sea, the city's first durable line opened in 1861. Western Railroad of North Carolina laid tracks from the coal mines at Egypt, seven miles beyond Sanford, to Fayetteville, an aggregate of 43 miles. There "black gold" was transferred to barges for the continuation of its trip to world buyers. That strategic line was soon pressed into service by the Confederacy during the War Between the States. During his visit in April 1865, General William Tecumseh Sherman and 60,000 Union troops dismantled much of the route while inflicting severe material damage on Fayetteville.

Several other rail carriers appeared in the territory in the final decades of the 19th century: Fayetteville & Florence, Cape Fear & Yadkin Valley, Atlantic Coast Line, Red Spring & Northern, and a few more. Most combined, were abandoned or were absorbed into other lines. Aside from these, the original Norfolk Southern Railway was the only other line of enduring vintage at Fayetteville.

Atlantic Coast Line Railroad (ACL), the eventual predominant carrier there, didn't arrive in town until 1892. It constructed a trio of terminal facilities in succession, all on the same site. The address is 472 Hay Street on the city's most important downtown thoroughfare where Hay intersects with Hillsborough Street. Though the city wouldn't become a prime stop on ACL's mainline until the turn of the 20th century as the company laid tracks between Richmond, Virginia, 216 miles to the north, and Charleston, South Carolina, 178 miles to the south, Fayetteville lay directly in its path.

Today with 52,227 riders (143 daily) traversing that route in 2008, thanks to Amtrak's daily *Palmetto* (Savannah–New York) and *Silver Meteor* (Miami–New York) trains — showing an increase in Fayetteville patronage of 11.1 percent over the previous year — the city is now ranked fourth among Amtrak's 16 scheduled Tar Heel station stops. In fact, it's in a dead heat for third, only a handful behind sister city Rocky Mount, which shuffles not just two but four Amtrak trains every day. They include the *Palmetto* and *Silver Meteor* plus the *Carolinian* (Charlotte–New York) and *Silver Star* (Miami–Tampa–New York).

Local records are vague about when the first Fayetteville ACL depot was replaced by a second. The original was likely little more than a tar-paper shack made of wood and never designed for permanency or even large crowds. What we are sure of is that in 1911, the carrier erected its final facility on that commanding corner. Today, a century after its construction, the third building continues to welcome passenger trains.

Observed from either end of its longest expanse, the structure's exterior projects a four-sided roofline that typically resembles thousands of American barns. The interior of the brick Colonial Dutch Revival structure includes ticket windows, a passenger waiting room, baggage handling, restrooms, convenience areas, and a popular national chain's sandwich shop. For some years the building has been listed on the National Register of Historic Places. The station was restored to its earlier stateliness in 2005-2006, at the same time it was converted into handicapped-accessible. Platforms behind the depot alongside the tracks are narrowly covered by a continuous shed.

GREENSBORO

From 1899 to 1927, passenger trains of Southern Railway, Greensboro's dominant carrier, called at a two-story downtown depot at 460 South Elm Street. Architecturally, the long, narrow, flat-roofed L-shaped brick building left much to be desired. Although it may have been serviceable and in character with structures of its day, a rounded tower protruding at one corner of its otherwise straight lines was its sole distinguishing exterior attribute. Set next to a single door entryway at one end of its longest side, even that feature seemed out of place, as if added to break up a monotonous carton-looking façade. The platform and tracks ran along the structure's longest side. In its heyday in the 1920s, 42 passenger trains visited this station every day. A larger terminal was clearly needed.

Southern Railway's next Greensboro address was the spectacularly airy, high-ceilinged palace of grandeur at 300 East Washington Street facing Church Street. Designed by the architectural firm of Fellheimer and Wagner, veterans of New York City's Grand Central Terminal, its Beaux Arts classical style was warm and inviting, beckoning travelers for more than a half-century. Opened April 20, 1927, it contained 56,000-square-feet of space and cost $1 million to construct. The building's exterior is comprised of red brick and pale stone and an entryway surrounded by six Ionic columns topped by a balustrade. The portal's arched vestibule leads to a two-story grand hall and concourse which was then the station's Caucasian waiting room furnished with traditional railroad benches. Windows on the upper level, visible from the main floor, were rounded. A lighted map of the Southern Railway route system drew particular interest. On the building's west side another entrance led to the Colored waiting room.

The main floor included a handful of vendors: in addition to a dining room, there was a newsstand, drug store, shoeshine stand, barber shop, and Travelers Aid office. Southern Railway offices, baggage handling and Rural Electrification Administration (REA) facilities occupied the upper level. Passengers went to three platforms to board their trains by way of an underground tunnel. The terminal persisted until time ran out as Southern Railway pulled the plug on its last passenger train (1979). The carrier turned that portion of its business over to Amtrak, a firm that had assumed the service for most other U.S. freight rail lines in 1971.

Doors to the hall of grandeur in Greensboro were shuttered as Amtrak took the throttle of the surviving train operating through the city—the daily *Crescent* between New Orleans and New York. The grand edifice in Greensboro was replaced by a dinky cheap-to-maintain single-story facility on Oakland Avenue. The brick building's uninviting,

We can't see the physical structure—we can visualize its majesty—of the terminal Southern Railway opened in 1927 at Greensboro, North Carolina, shortly before this image that affirms its pace. Greensboro hosted 42 passenger trains daily in the 1920s. That grand, long overdue edifice was a beacon to passengers until Amtrak entered the picture in 1971. Shuttered but spared the wrecking ball, it was updated and reopened in 2005, now an intermodal center to meet the travel needs of new generations (*courtesy North Carolina State Archives*).

boxy exterior, distinguished by squared windows and a single portal under a small canopy, proffered a close resemblance to a Wendy's restaurant. Yet it was typical of scores of downsized Amtrak facilities currently in use.

In the meantime, for a quarter-century, the magnificence of the East Washington edifice was being lost. As that structure languished, the pages of the calendar turned into days, weeks, months, years and decades. Still no one came to rescue it. While idling all that time, by some measure it nevertheless avoided any unruly mob chanting "let's dismantle it now and take questions later." That mindset terrorized preservationists across the nation as dozens of unused train terminals that no longer added appreciably to local tax coffers met dire fates. Before it was too late in Greensboro, however, somebody advanced a better idea. Perceptive city fathers acted on a notion of easing several community concerns by combining multiple transportation forms at this unfulfilled facility. Following a $31.2 million makeover, the hall of splendor rose once again to its past glory.

The Greensboro Department of Transportation bills the newly-designated J. Douglas Galyon Depot at 300 East Washington Street "the state's largest historic station." Having gone intermodal on October 21, 2005, the edifice supports a variety of transportation means in the modern age. Not only does Amtrak run three trains every day, it's now home to intercity buses of Carolina Trailways, Greyhound and Piedmont Authority for Regional Transportation; local buses of Greensboro Transit Authority; and fleets of taxicabs, shuttles and rental vehicles. Four tracks and two platforms are accessed by way of a sub-track tunnel. A shed covers a portion of each platform and distinctive platform street-lighting is provided every few feet.

In addition to the *Crescent* calling at Galyon Depot daily, there's the *Carolinian* from Charlotte to New York and the *Piedmont* from Charlotte to Raleigh. The latter pair is sponsored by the state Department of Transportation in conjunction with Amtrak. In 2008, Greensboro's contribution to Amtrak's bottom line included 89,675 passengers, typically 245 daily, an increase of 22.9 percent in one year.

RALEIGH

Although at a passing glance it's difficult to distinguish the thriving transportation hub it once was, Raleigh's oldest extant railway depot, built in 1890, remains productive in a contemporary age. While no longer a stop for passenger trains — indeed, the tracks behind it were removed decades ago — that colossal two-story structure survives, converted into space for private commercial exploits. Historic Union Station at the intersection

of Dawson and West Martin streets, following its metamorphosis, overlooks a city park and flanks Central Fire Station at one side. Yet this depot proudly served travelers for decades that arrived and departed on the tracks of a quartet of carriers: Norfolk Southern, Raleigh & Gaston, Seaboard Air Line, and Southern.

An altered roof line, removal of a tall clock-tower at the right front corner, and multiple additions to the rear significantly distorted the exterior from its appearance back in the day. The interior of the old edifice was subdivided for business use. Yet when photographs taken in 2007 are compared with some from 1910, the differences in features aren't nearly that variable.

In the early 1890s, Seaboard inaugurated service at another Wake County facility. The Neuse Depot, a small wood frame structure set in a rural community named for the nearby Neuse River, is home to a private business today. At 9300 Durant Road, it's situated behind a North Carolina Communications agency in Raleigh proper, the city having grown to envelope Neuse.

After trains quit stopping there the station was transported from its original site on the south side of Durant Road to the north side. Now it rests about 600 feet west of the tracks and 500 feet east of another Raleigh fire station. Durant Nature Park, including hiking trails and provisions for recreation, is nearby. In addition to a new roof, stairs were added to Neuse Depot and the attic floored to provide more storage. A sliding freight door is still operable and its rollers are working smoothly after more than a century of use.

Perhaps Raleigh's most imposing railway edifice was built in the 1920s by Southern Railway during the heyday of travel by train. This inspired, rectangular, white-columned station at 320 West Cabarrus Street features a single story-plus-attic arrangement. Its pure white façade is in sharp contrast to the red-brick terminals that are typical in this area. A little east and across the tracks behind the structure lies the old Southern freight station, an area currently focused as a commercial plaza.

This Cabarrus station serves not only freight carrier Norfolk Southern Railroad, successor to Southern, but — since October 1986 — Amtrak, with a pair of through trains calling and another originating there every day. The *Carolinian* runs between Charlotte and New York while the *Silver Star* travels between Florida points on both coasts and New York. The *Piedmont*, meanwhile, runs back and forth between Raleigh and Charlotte. This usage currently places Raleigh at the head of the line in Amtrak's Tar Heel patronage: in fiscal year 2008, 141,291 riders boarded or detrained at Raleigh, about 387 per day and an increase of 18.7 percent in one year.

Seaboard's most prominent Raleigh outlet opened in 1942, at 707 Semart Drive. It's a strikingly contemporary single story-plus-attic facility proffering dual double-door white-columned entrances and framed by two fireplaces and chimneys. This station was eventually the calling place for Amtrak trains between May 1971 and October 1986. Yet it's possibly the adaptive reuse of this building that is most impressive — perhaps even more than its days of serving dozens of passenger trains schlepping affluent travelers to and from their Northeastern domiciles and the playgrounds of the rich and famous in the Sunshine State's tropical paradise.

The Shops at Seaboard Station spawned by the depot and encompassing a three-block commercial zone around it proffers 113,700 square feet of retail emporiums and restaurants today, largely occupying 1940s warehouses. It includes a full service grocery, wine store, soft goods sellers, hardware, art gallery, and upscale gym. Playing an integral role in the redevelopment of Raleigh's downtown, Seaboard Station is currently the capital city's only downtown shopping center. Well advertised community events are scheduled on the property throughout the year. A 112-unit residential rental section may be added to its north side. A landmark in the community, the enterprise is readily identified by the nomenclature "Seaboard Station." That's a pretty good track record for an out-of-business depot.

South Carolina

CHARLESTON

It began with *The Best Friend of Charleston* in 1830, the very first passenger train in America with front-end power supplied by a steam locomotive. "Tall oaks from little acorns grow" wrote David Everett in 1797, and from this acorn sprang a proliferating forest of soaring timber. While the resulting Charleston & Hamburg Railroad's 136-mile route from the Atlantic Ocean to the interior of the Palmetto State was impressive—celebrated at completion as the longest continuous trackage in the world under single management—those humble beginnings were but a foretaste of what was to come.

A byproduct, and an important one, in all of this was that owner South Carolina Canal and Rail Road Company (SCC&RR) proffered the development of an early railroad terminal facility. This eventually led from a primitive style which may have been little more than a marked spot at first to the modern temples of trains which exist in diminishing numbers today. Charleston's William Aiken home (founder of the SCC&RR) and allied railroad structures within a distinct historic district are considered "nationally significant" in the history and development of the railroad industry in the U.S., so claims the state's Department of Archives and History. The company with which they are linked was the first not only to apply steam but to operate an American-made locomotive and to haul U.S. mail. If for no other reasons than these, Charleston made its mark as a fundamental railroad town.

The principal carriers serving Charleston in the heyday of passenger rail traffic were Atlantic Coast Line (ACL), Seaboard Air Line (SAL) and Southern (SOU) systems. Charleston & Hamburg Railroad, by the way, was an ancestor of SOU. For a while this trio occupied Union Station built by ACL and SOU on the northwest corner of Columbus and East Bay streets. The stub-end facility facing Columbus with a shed covering the tracks opened in November 1907.

SAL trains didn't arrive there until the company's East Carolina mainline was completed into Charleston about 1915. Even then SAL wasn't an eternal tenant of Union Station. In 1934, its passenger operations transferred to the newly opened Grove Street Station. Over the years Seaboard gradually reduced its Charleston traffic, terminating service between there and Savannah in 1952, a route on which it competed with tapering results against ACL. In 1956, SAL withdrew its Charleston connection with its own mainline at Hamlet, North Carolina. Its last daily people-mover, the *Boll Weevil,* was habitually powered by doodlebugs. With that move SAL's passenger operations at the coastal city were brought to an end, at least until 1967: that year it returned to Charleston after SAL and ACL merged their operations, forming the Seaboard Coast Line Railroad. Prior to that SAL's prime route between Florida and the Northeast always turned due north out of Savannah as opposed to northeast toward Charleston, the route favored by ACL. SAL's mainline included Fairfax, Denmark, Columbia, Camden and Cheraw on its trek across South Carolina before hitting the key SAL junction at Hamlet.

Union Station burned on January 10, 1947. Whether that prompted or solidified moves by both ACL and SOU is left to conjecture. In 1948, both carriers found new Charleston addresses. ACL took up residence at North Boulevard Station while SOU moved to Line Street Station, all three major carriers then operating in an equal number of localities and relatively independently of one another. In 1967, Southern dismantled its Charleston passenger service altogether when it reduced the *Carolina Special* between Cincinnati and Charleston — the latter city's only SOU passenger consist still running — to a terminus at Columbia, South Carolina.

ACL, meanwhile, had already moved once again,

this time departing the corporate limits of Charleston when — in 1956 — its newly constructed station at 4565 Gaynor Avenue in North Charleston was ready for occupancy. Even now successor Amtrak continues to call there with the two passenger trains it sends down that route every day, including the *Palmetto* (Savannah–New York) and *Silver Meteor* (Miami–New York). In fiscal year 2008, North Charleston (listed as Charleston in Amtrak timetables) contributed to that firm's livelihood by boarding or deboarding 69,942 passengers, far and away Amtrak's most productive depot in South Carolina. That's an average of 191 riders per day and a rise of 4.9 percent over a year earlier.

COLUMBIA

Sitting in the middle of the state, Columbia was at the apex of major passenger routes back in the day. Like the spokes of a wheel, they ran north to Charlotte, northwest to Spartanburg, southwest to Augusta, south to Savannah, southeast to Charleston, and northeast to Raleigh. Today two of those lines continue to connect the capital city with much of the eastern seaboard as Amtrak's *Silver Star* rolls along between Miami and Tampa to Savannah, Columbia, Raleigh, and ultimately to New York. In the company's fiscal-year results in 2008, some 38,578 riders got on or off the train at Columbia, about 106 daily, and a boost of 11.4 percent in a year. The steel-constructed Amtrak station about three miles southeast of downtown is near the University of South Carolina at 850 Pulaski Street. The *Silver Star* began calling there upon the depot's completion in 1991.

Seaboard Air Line Railroad (SAL) erected a terminal in Columbia on Gervais Street near its intersection with Lincoln Street in 1902. It became the Seaboard Coast Line Railroad station in 1967, after SAL and Atlantic Coast Line Railroad joined forces. That depot is the oldest passenger rail facility still in existence in the city and served Amtrak for two decades after that provider assumed the service in May 1971. In the early 1990s, the tracks along Lincoln Street and a railroad trestle were removed by the city. Since 1991, when Amtrak relocated on Pulaski Street, the aging Gervais facility has been renovated and adapted for contemporary commercial use. Today it is the home of one of Columbia's leading restaurants with a specialized menu focused upon South Carolina Low Country delicacies. The old trainshed extending from the single-story depot along one side of Lincoln Street remains, convenient to patrons' vehicles and a welcome cover from car to restaurant during inclement weather.

In many communities where there are (or have been) multiple passenger rail terminals, one often may be viewed as the area's most prestigious. It rises above others in stature, in number of trains

and travelers served, and in recognition by locals and visitors as the facility placing an enduring brand on railroading there. In Columbia's case that undoubtedly would have been Union Station. Erected in 1904 by Atlantic Coast Line Railroad and Southern Railway in tandem, the mammoth brick tri-level edifice at 401 Main Street has been, in recent years, converted to one of Columbia's most popular restaurants and taverns. Even with the transformation it is still readily identifiable by those who recall the glory days when ACL trains between Augusta and Florence called there and Southern's consists crisscrossed the city on their way to and from Charlotte, Augusta and Savannah; and Greenville, Spartanburg and Charleston.

FLORENCE

The importance of Florence to the Atlantic Coast Line Railroad (ACL) during the golden age of rail travel cannot be overstated. The city situated in the farm belt of eastern South Carolina was as equally valuable to ACL as was Hamlet, North Carolina — 48 miles to the north — to rival carrier Seaboard Air Line Railroad (SAL). Both were not mere stopping places in the middle of mainline routes between Florida and New York termini; they furnished essential junctions for exchanging passengers, schlepping them in easterly and westerly directions there.

More importantly, the local economies were stimulated by gargantuan railroad shops at both cities where mechanical repairs were performed by large labor forces of skilled craftsmen. ACL maintained a sizeable freight yard at Florence and the city was also a crew-change point in the system. Thus, despite its relatively diminutive size, Florence loomed large in consequence among ACL–oriented municipalities. Those operations were nevertheless significantly downgraded after ACL and SAL combined their facilities into the Seaboard Coast Line Railroad in 1967. At that time many of the functions that had kept Florence on the railroad map were diminished or transferred to Hamlet even though the company retained a reduced presence at Florence.

Like so many sister cities, Florence owes its formation to the railroads. There was a trio of regional lines that met there in the early days: Wilmington & Manchester, North Eastern, and Cheraw & Darlington. The community even took its sobriquet from that industry. In honor of his daughter Florence Harlee, Wilmington & Manchester president William Wallace Harlee picked her given name to paint on the sign on the small depot he built there in 1853. With the completion of that structure, the town had its official start.

Florence's railways were busy during the War Between the States. Troops, artillery and supplies routinely passed through on their way to Richmond, Charleston and Savannah. Wounded Confederate troops were moved by rail to Florence's Wayside Hospital while detained Union troops were transported to town to be garrisoned in the Florence Stockade. Although the conflict exacted a heavy toll on trains, depots and tracks, all three Florence rail lines were running again shortly after the war's end in 1865. Local historians credit increasing railroad growth for doubling the city's middle-class inhabitants in the 1870s.

By taking over the assets of many small usually short-line companies, Atlantic Coast Line Railroad put together a principal route through Florence. Since assuming most of the nation's passenger service in May 1971, Amtrak has depended heavily on the ex–ACL/SCL North-South mainline. Currently it sends two trains daily through Florence, the *Palmetto* (Savannah–New York) and *Silver Meteor* (Miami–New York). Both stop at Amtrak's contemporary depot at 805 East Day Street, a structure gaining high marks from modern railfans. A Web site dedicated to the hobby insists: "The Amtrak station is nice — really nice. It's clean, modern, functional, and a credit to Florence and Amtrak. If only more Amtrak stations were so nice." No, "let's don't go there" from that source!

In fiscal year 2008, Florence generated 47,163 passengers (129 per day) for Amtrak's consists. That's a 5.2 percent upsurge in one year. Amtrak's total patronage at Florence is good enough to make it the firm's second busiest stop in the Palmetto State, well behind Charleston and well ahead of Columbia (in third place). Florence's numbers are categorically improved by its proximity to the coastal resort of Myrtle Beach. As the nearest station to that playground of sand, surf and sun — 58 miles east of Florence — the city benefits from beach-bound rail traffic, particularly during the warmer months.

GREENVILLE

In the foothills of the Blue Ridge Mountains, Greenville is situated in a region labeled by South Carolinians as "the upstate." After receiving a charter in 1845, construction began on the first trackage to transcend the upstate, the Greenville & Columbia Railroad. Its route persisted 111 miles to the southeast, down the western banks of the Saluda River to the piedmont center of the Palmetto State. Completed in 1853, the line was a principal feeder from the mountainous territories to the capital during the War Between the States. When corrupt politicians subsequently defrauded the railroad of $400,000, it failed.

Reorganized in the 1870s, it was renamed the Columbia & Greenville Railroad. By 1890, its route was divided into the Columbia, Newberry & Lau-

rens Railroad (CN&L) and the Charleston & Western Carolina Railroad (C&WC). The pair interconnected at Laurens with one of several C&WC branches leading to Greenville. After the turn of the century the Atlantic Coast Line Railroad gained control of both lines, using them to haul freight while hauling passengers between Columbia and Laurens. ACL maintained freight facilities in Greenville, a key spot in transporting goods to and from the foothills.

Another line with an influential presence in Greenville was the electrified Piedmont & Northern Railway (P&N) operating in South Carolina between Greenwood and Spartanburg via Greenville. (In 1911, track construction began at Greenwood. Three years later it reached Spartanburg.) For years all that remained of P&N's passenger station at the corner of South Academy and West Washington streets in Greenville was the carrier's insignia with three lightning bolts. That was integrated into the brick wall in front of P&N owner Duke Power Company (now Duke Energy at 400 North Academy Street).

P&N shop buildings, once part of River Junction Yard, were preserved just behind the Norfolk Southern yard. Today they are owned by a firm fabricating and refurbishing diesel locomotives for assorted railroads. The P&N station at Academy and Washington, razed long ago, was designed by architect Charles Christian Hook, who drafted plans for all P&N facilities. With many similarities shared by the remainder of the chain, the Greenville depot proffered a red Spanish tile roof, cross-gabled attic vents, yellow brick exterior with decoration almost nil, and yet with obvious attention to detail giving it a graceful presence. Much more on this company and its terminals is included in the entry on Charlotte, North Carolina, P&N's headquarters city.

The dominant rail carrier in Greenville during the Gilded Age was always Southern Railway. Its striking single-story brick temple to trains on West Washington Street near the junction of Willard Street was demolished decades ago. Although not an especially large facility, with a high tower rising several stories above its center portal, this turn of the century station was an impressive landmark on Greenville's early skyline. Eventually it was replaced by a much more contemporary structure that Amtrak operates today adjacent to the Norfolk Southern freight depot.

This passenger station, at 1120 West Washington Street, hosts Amtrak's New Orleans–New York *Crescent* twice nightly (actually, in the wee hours of the morning southbound). In 2008, the *Crescent* generated a ridership of 16,897 at Greenville (46 per night — and think what that might be if it arrived in the sunshine!). It was a gain for Greenville nevertheless, its patronage improving by 44.4 percent in a single year, one of the most substantial increases in the South that year.

Tennessee

CHATTANOOGA

During the first decade of the 20th century, when New York draftsman Donald Barber was picked in a competitive field to design a depot for Chattanooga, he submitted some original drawings that were several years old. After the city's Terminal Station opened on December 1, 1909, it looked very much like Barber's concept during the time (1900) he was enrolled at Paris' l'Ecole des Beaux-Arts.

Fronting 1400 Market Street downtown between Hotel and Elyria streets, the compressed station initially received trains from a dozen stub-end platform tracks. There were also a couple of other tracks— one reserved for express traffic, the other earmarked for private car treatment. The depot's baggage, mail and express commerce was accommodated in a three-sided annex set behind the south end of the head house. On past that facility an eight-track 65-car coach yard connected to the station throat by a wye also was linked to Southern Railway's mainline.

The airy open space of the waiting room in the head house was its most striking feature. Under an ornate 85-foot ceiling was an area 82 by 62 feet. Once riders passed the ticket windows, restaurant, café, smoking room, newsstand, shoeshine stand and restrooms they encountered a colossal 60 by 300 foot concourse that gave access to 700-foot umbrella-shed platforms alongside the tracks.

When Southern's *Royal Palm* left Terminal Station on August 11, 1970, it was—for Chattanooga— the end of an era. After that the facility closed its doors to passenger trains but not to patrons, especially those with an affinity for the railroads. Three years hence the structure was remodeled, refurbished and reopened as a Hilton Hotel property. In addition to sleeping rooms created inside the head house, a novel addition was added outside on the few surviving platform tracks. There a handful of parked railroad cars were reconfigured into deluxe suites, a couple of compartments in each car. A portion of the enormous waiting room inside the head house, meanwhile, was converted into an elegantly spacious dining room, a lounge, lobby, and meeting facilities. It was all branded as the "Chattanooga Choo Choo and Hilton Inn."

In 1989, with a $4 million refurbishing following, the hotel became a Holiday Inn property — and still is in 2010. It's one of a growing number of such ornate edifices to have missed the wrecking ball and be transformed into overnight accommodations. Here it would seem the essential functions of a trio of the four most important cars to many rail passengers (coach, diner, sleeper, tavern-observation) are once more in use in the same "consist."

KNOXVILLE

Although there was interest in Knoxville as early as 1836 in developing a rail line to connect the city with others, more than a decade-and-a-half elapsed before those pushing for it were finally rewarded. In 1852, the East Tennessee & Virginia Railroad received a charter to link Knoxville with Bristol, a burg straddling the Tennessee-Virginia border. Two years hence a detached East Tennessee & Georgia Railroad, inaugurated in 1837 as the Hiwassee line at Athens, Tennessee, brought its tracks to Knoxville. Multiple references to a local depot exist while at least one other succeeded it before the turn of the century. Those two early rail companies combined operations in 1869, being renamed the East Tennessee, Virginia & Georgia Railway. That route was a primary forerunner of Southern Railway that absorbed it in 1887.

The history is preliminary to the evolving rail story in this bastion of railway transportation, although Knoxville wasn't then and can't be considered now a metropolis of mammoth proportions. While significantly larger than any of its neighbors in northeastern Tennessee, the fact the conurbation of Knoxville — during the heyday of passenger rail traffic —could command separate facilities for the dual leading lines serving it begs the inevitable question "why?" That's left to others for answering, yet lingers as unsettling with no further elucidation. In addition to Southern Railway, Knoxville's other major carrier was the Louisville & Nashville Railroad (L&N).

The Southern terminal, erected in 1903, was sit-

In 2007, an identifying L&N logotype still hung from the exterior of the extant L&N depot in Knoxville. The 1905 structure was designed by Richard Montfort, who drew plans for a handful of L&N city terminals (*courtesy Michael Wall*).

uated at 306 West Depot Avenue. It covered extensive territory, by one account "roughly bounded" by Depot Avenue, North and South Central Avenue, Sullivan Street, Vine Avenue and North and South Gay Street. It was designed by draftsman Frank P. Milburn, whose handiwork sprouted about the same time in terminals at Augusta and Savannah, Georgia, at Charlotte, North Carolina, and several other Southern cities. The architectural style of the Knoxville facility is positioned as Classical Revival Italianate. Stone, brick, stucco, asphalt, metal and terra cotta were used in its construction. The waiting room and ticket windows occupied the second floor of the bi-level edifice while dining, baggage and mail rooms were below. Corbel-stepped gables were landmark features of the Southern terminal whose waiting rooms and restaurant proffered arched windows and coffered ceilings. Structural concerns resulted in removing an identifying clock tower in 1945.

Situated within Knoxville's Jackson Avenue Historic District, the station was later added to the National Register of Historic Places. It continued to host passenger trains for 67 years, the last one pulling out in 1970. The building lay dormant for many years thereafter. Following a renovation in 1989, it was converted into commercial office space.

Within two years following the opening of the Southern Railway facility, Southern's major competitor in the region, L&N, opened a new station in 1905 at 700 Western Avenue NW at its intersection with Henley Street. The site was to be at the north end of the 1982 World's Fair and that event triggered a sprucing up of the facility. The vacant station housed restaurants during the fair and in modern times has continued to prosper as a café and offices. Hence, both L&N and Southern stations in Knoxville have survived the demolition derby affecting depots in other towns thus far.

Richard Montfort, chief design engineer for L&N Railroad, crafted the original plans for the Vernacular Victorian Renaissance style L&N structure. It was built of stone, brick, ceramic tile and iron. Like its neighboring terminal a few blocks east, the L&N depot has also found its way onto the National Register of Historic Places.

MEMPHIS

Like some of its sizable sister metropolises in the South, during the halcyon days of passenger rail travel, Memphis was known for double depots which competed not only for traffic but also local prestige. In most of that epoch Central and Union stations hosted diverse railway carriers and were clearly identified with the companies they serviced. As Union opened its doors a couple of years before Central and handled trains of more lines, it is introduced first.

Union Station Company was chartered on September 25, 1909, for the purpose of building and operating the enterprise. At its outset five foremost passenger rail carriers entered into a joint pact that would ultimately bring their trains to the platforms at the future Union Station: Louisville & Nashville (L&N), Missouri Pacific (MoPac), Nashville, Chattanooga & St. Louis (NC&StL), St. Louis–Southwestern (SSW), and Southern (SOU).

The triple-level Beaux Arts edifice that was born of their collective efforts debuted on April 1, 1912, and could accurately boast of being the largest stone structure in town. It was situated in south Memphis on Calhoun Street between Second Street and Rayburn Boulevard (now Third Street). Two years afterward and two blocks west of Union Station, another major line, Illinois Central Railroad (IC), erected its own monument to the primary people-hauling mode. Grand Central Station — its moniker reduced in 1944 to Central Station — served a company that believed its largely north-south route and related operational interests were underrepresented in the planning for Union Station.

With a stub-end design, Union Station trains performed a "reverse movement" in accessing the terminal's platforms. Arriving trains reaching the end of their runs in Memphis pulled forward into the station to discharge their passengers and express packages. After unloading, they backed out. Meanwhile, trains passing through Memphis stopped on east-west tracks south of the station and then backed in. There were added tracks for servicing and storing passenger cars. Locomotive cleaning and overhauling were conducted onsite by way of a turntable and roundhouse.

In postwar America railway passenger traffic fell rapidly into a spiraling decline when upgraded roads, automobiles and airplanes came on strong. As a result in Memphis there was talk of consolidating passenger traffic at a single facility rather than attempting to maintain twin terminals. The various parties could never reach harmony on the matter, however, and as expenses mounted so did frustration within the industry. That didn't stymie alterations nevertheless. In October 1952, SSW brought its years of transporting travelers to and from Memphis to an end. In 1957, NC&StL — jointly operated by L&N since the previous century — became totally absorbed into that system. Those changes reduced the number of Union Station tenants from five to three. The number was condensed again after MoPac pulled out in 1964. That year it transferred its final passenger consist still running to Memphis from Union Station to an ex-freight facility down the street at 43 West Calhoun dubbed Iron Mountain Station.

Now with only L&N and SOU still operating and being responsible for maintenance at Union

Station, the overhead had simply become more than the pair of formidable players was willing to bankroll. L&N signed on as a new tenant at Central Station while SOU moved its operations to the antediluvian Memphis and Charleston freight facility on Lauderdale Street. By April 1, 1964, precisely 52 years after Union Station —filled with great promise — premiered, the facility shut its doors as a passenger rail terminal. Yet that wasn't quite the end of it. In an ensuing prolonged court battle, the city successfully argued against the railroads, claiming Union Station was abandoned without approval of the Tennessee Public Service Commission. As a result L&N and SOU reopened a small portion of the terminal on December 1, 1966. Even before that, nevertheless, on August 26, 1965, MoPac already severed its passenger ties with Memphis. By discontinuing its remaining solo train between the city and Little Rock, MoPac freed itself of binding by the court order to reopen Union Station.

Negligible passenger traffic to and from Memphis persisted for both L&N and SOU. The expense of reopening Union Station took a heavy toll on both carriers, then attempting to save a drowning ship in the form of decreasing numbers of travelers every year. Their answer was to pull the plug on Memphis trains altogether so they could be relieved of financing costly ventures like Union Station. On March 30, 1968, the edifice closed once again, and that time forever. The property was sold to the U.S. Postal Service for a new main post office in Memphis. By February 1969, the historic station that previously served millions who boarded trains of five major carriers was obliterated. A windowless postal center enclosed by barbed wire fencing occupies that land today with little visible reference to what once stood there.

Calhoun Street Station, an early Illinois Central Railroad depot, occupied the site that would eventually serve a small handful of railroads at Central Station. The new terminal was the result of an unresolved clash between IC and the carriers whose trains called at Union Station. Construction of the facility at 545 South Main at its intersection with East Calhoun Street began in September 1912 (Main and East G.E. Patterson Avenue now). Union Station had been open about five months then. Central Station debuted on October 4, 1914. At its peak it saw more than 50 passenger consists passing along its five stub-end and five through tracks daily. Across its long history Central Station, owned by IC, would also be home to passenger trains of the Chicago, Rock Island & Pacific (Rock Island), L&N, St. Louis-San Francisco (Frisco), and Yazoo & Mississippi Valley railroads, the latter eventually acquired by IC. (From April 1, 1964, to November 30, 1966, in the period Union Station was closed, Central hosted the L&N.)

But the diminishing fortunes of the railroads witnessed at Union Station eventually encompassed Central Station's owner and landlord — IC — too. Rock Island passenger service to Memphis ceased in November 1967; Frisco discontinued its service in December 1967. Once again only IC occupied the previously bustling Central Station. It was just too much. By 1970, with businesses in the South Main neighborhood closing and Union Station already being demolished, the handwriting on the wall wasn't hard to distinguish. It might take a miracle to prevent the same thing from happening again.

As Amtrak took over the throttle of Central Station's passenger train legacy, large sections of the facility were shuttered. IC offices upstairs were transferred. Soon Central earned the reputation as "one of the worst stations on the Amtrak system." Until 1982, when the South Main Historic District was established to focus on preserving the area, Central Station languished in dire uncertainty. After Memphis Area Transit Authority took an interest in it, however, spearheading restoration of the station to its original splendor, its future seemed assured. It now facilitates travelers as an intermodal transportation hub, serving not only Amtrak's *City of New Orleans* from Chicago to New Orleans daily but also Memphis Riverfront and Main Street trolley cars. In fiscal year 2008, Amtrak boarded or deboarded 54,879 patrons at Memphis, an average of 150 riders per day, and an increase of 8.8 percent over the previous year.

Adding to the structure's "next life," some other updates have been instituted. Since 2006, from mid–April through October, a Saturday Farmers Market has been conducted below the station's pavilion on South Front Street at G.E. Patterson Avenue. Part of Central Station was converted into a reception and banquet hall. Yet the most prolific alterations may have occurred on the structure's multiple-story upper floors: they were redesigned and transformed into moderately priced contemporary living space for apartment dwellers. Calling them "an address of distinction," a recent promotion for those quarters touts: "Our enormous one and two bedroom apartments and lofts range from 679 to 1536 square feet! All have high quality finishes and fixtures. With 8 foot windows and high ceilings, you'll enjoy expansive views of downtown Memphis and the Mississippi River from Central Station. Our luxurious community amenities include a rooftop deck, fitness center, controlled entry, on-site laundry, elevators and garage parking is available. You'll love our historic charm from being located in the former Amtrak Station. Central Station is just minutes south of downtown Memphis. Enjoy a nice walk down Main St. or ride the Main St. trolley to restaurants, shops, art galleries, the ball park, Mudd Island, Cook Convention Center and Beale Street." A legacy of luxury from the past, perhaps. Who could want more?

NASHVILLE

Although Nashville was home to a handful of scattered railway depots in the 19th century, when the ponderous Union Station opened its doors at 1001 Broadway on September 3, 1900, that edifice clearly marked the city as a maturing transportation hub. (A few historians believe the opening was delayed to October 9 but a preponderance of recorders appears to favor September 3.) Some of Union Station's operations literally rose from ground level beneath the downtown streets in what is still commonly branded as the "railroad gulch" separating the commercial structures above it at street level. The tracks passed under the viaducts of Church, Broadway and Demonbreun streets to reach the terminal.

A massive continuous clerestoried trainshed — 200 by 78 feet and capable of covering 10 trains simultaneously — was hemmed in by the Demon-

breun Street viaduct a block south of the station. Otherwise that protective top might have been extended further. Incidentally at its inception that roof was cited as the largest unsupported span in America. If you ever saw it (now gone), you could be rather easily persuaded. Meanwhile, the station's baggage, mail and express business was processed just across a covered breezeway behind the head house on its eastern perimeter. This was particularly convenient to passengers arriving or departing at the side portico, a semicircular affair on the building's east edge directly off 10th Avenue. The Nashville terminal encountered further good fortune when the main branch of U.S. Post Office ultimately relocated directly across 10th Avenue from the station. It proved to be a mutually rewarding convenience, saving vast amounts of time in merely transporting mail and express back and forth across the street as opposed to carrying it perhaps across town.

In a distinctively striking traffic flow not employed many places, boarding passengers waited in the breezeway at street level before a bank of esca-

A October 28, 1947, aerial scan of downtown Nashville shows the central business district with the dome-topped state capitol at its upper center. Left of center a trio of thoroughfares —(from top) Church, Broadway, and Demonbreun streets — bridge what is commonly referred to as "the railroad gulch." The dark-roofed trainshed backs up to Demonbreun; hard by its north side is Union Station on Broadway where L&N, NC&StL and Amtrak trains called (1900–1979). Flanked to the right by the U.S. Post Office, in the modern era the refurbished terminal thrives as a prominent chain hotel (*courtesy Tennessee State Library and Archives*).

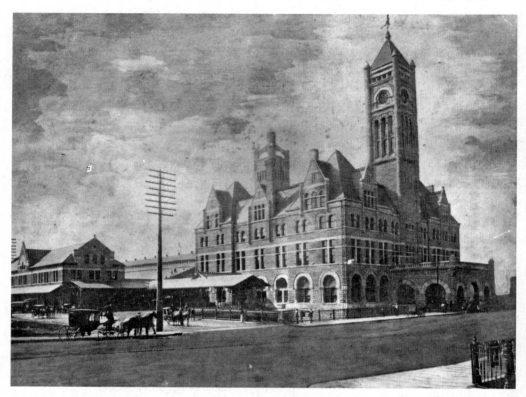

A picture postcard of Nashville's Union Station, ca. 1900, the year it opened, shows horse-drawn buggies on city streets, a basic mode of local transit then. Richard Montfort's Romanesque Revival terminal is one of arresting grandeur. The baggage, mail and express structure (left) and imposing headhouse foster an architectural magnificence not evident much earlier in Nashville, strikingly resembling an L&N facility erected a few years before in Louisville, also designed by Montfort. Trains, unseen here, came and went beneath the city streets on rails paralleling a massive shed, a small portion of its clerestoried roof poking directly from behind the headhouse (*courtesy Tennessee State Library and Archives*).

lators whisked them down to the tracks where their trains hissed while patiently waiting. Detraining passengers rode up those escalators first, however. Once the last rider arrived at the top, the escalators were stopped and their direction reversed. A bell sounded and patrons waiting upstairs were allowed to ride down and board. There was a cache of escalators running in tandem to keep the flow of pedestrian traffic moving. One escalator was reserved to run in the opposite direction of the bulk of traffic to ferry train personnel, vendors, visitors and the like, as well as straggling passengers that were late getting off an arriving train. The handicapped, baggage, mail and express traveled between floors by elevators, of course.

Union Station, which saw its final conveyance depart in 1979 (Amtrak's *Floridian*), pooled the passenger trains of the Louisville & Nashville Railroad (L&N) and Nashville, Chattanooga & St. Louis

Railway (NC&StL) under a single roof. The NC&StL, with its headquarters building sitting caty-cornered to the depot at 10th and Broad, was still operating under its own moniker at the station's debut. It had been controlled by L&N for years, nevertheless, and was to be fully integrated into the L&N system in 1957.

Meanwhile, the ornate Romanesque Revival station was a wonder to behold. It was drafted by Richard Montfort, L&N chief design engineer, who also drew plans for the Knoxville terminal a little later (it opened in 1905). The Nashville head house was 150 by 150 feet of magnificent grandeur rising 219 feet to the summit of its tallest rusticated stone tower. Multiple lofty towers and turrets were "a testament to U.S. ingenuity and energy," allowed one source. Two marble fireplaces—one at each end of the 125 by 67 foot waiting room—created an ambience that meshed well with an open area finished in Tennessee marble and oak. Like that of its earlier analogous L&N Union Station in Louisville, a stained-glass skylight graced the Nashville structure. Wall murals portrayed the Volunteer State's assets while sundry bas-relief forms added to its artistic and esthetic virtues. Bowling Green, Kentucky, limestone supplied the building's gray façade.

Nashville was a major junction point for passenger trains headed north, south, east and west. Out of Union Station rolled steam locomotives and eventually streamlined diesels pulling consists of coaches, sleepers and dining cars bound for Louisville, Cincinnati, Chicago and other points above the city; to Birmingham, Montgomery, Mobile, Pensacola and New Orleans below it; to Chattanooga, Knoxville, Atlanta, and all Florida destinations to its east; and to Memphis, Evansville, and St. Louis to its west.

One of the terminal's claims to fame was its complex passenger switching operation near or after midnight every night in postwar America, extending into the 1950s. It was a meticulous exchange for which timing was absolutely critical to make it work. Nor was it frequently repeated elsewhere. The *Georgian* heading south from Chicago and St. Louis to Chattanooga and Atlanta seamlessly shifted some of its Pullman cars bearing sleeping travelers onto the southbound *Humming Bird* consist heading south from Cincinnati and Louisville to Birmingham and New Orleans. At a different hour the reverse took place as northbound sleeping passengers from New Orleans were moved from the *Humming Bird* to the *Georgian* bound for St. Louis or Chicago. At the same time some of those northbound *Georgian* travelers from Atlanta and Chattanooga were connected to the Louisville- and Cincinnati-bound *Humming Bird*. It was an ingenious and absorbing accomplishment and the switching usually occurred 730 times a year, twice nightly—once in each direction.

For years after the trains stopped arriving at Union Station in Nashville, that once proud edifice lapsed into disrepair. Fortunately, there was never enough consideration given to razing it to see it done. Finally, in 1986, a multimillion-dollar conversion and refurbishing resulted in the prime piece of real estate—virtually left to thousands of birds and their droppings on sidewalks, terminal and passersby—being transformed into Union Station Hotel. For a while it was a Hilton property but in recent years the Wyndham chain has managed it.

Much of the structure's traditional atmosphere remains right down to the vintage arrivals and departures board, a backdrop to the hotel's front desk. Some of the guest rooms open three stories above the waiting room onto the original balconies overlooking it. In that great hall waiters serve diners seated at splendid white-clothed tables. It's a step back in time. And with train themes everywhere it is evocative of the heartbeat of a metropolitan transportation center through whose portals tens of thousands poured annually on their way to or from somewhere else.

Virginia

ALEXANDRIA

The Union Station still serving Alexandria, eight miles south of Washington's own Union Station, may be considered an anomaly among Dixie depots. There are at least two good reasons why: not only does it boast a protracted yet continuous lifespan that extends beyond a century, an element not all that common among depots still exclusively fulfilling their original intent, it has also undergone repeated refurbishing exploits, each time with caretakers—despite overseeing copious changes—making rigorous attempts to sustain a distinctive décor that retains and enhances the facility's earliest expression.

More than a half-century before it was built, Alexandria invested in five key railroad endeavors to link with other trading centers so it could contend with mounting commercial rivalry by an aggressive Baltimore. That city was quickly gaining status as a regional industrial trade center. Alexandria's city fathers hoped to cut into the market, attracting a huge piece of the action. Their ploys not only rewarded them well, they set in motion some unforeseen annoyances that were to haunt future generations of Alexandrians.

By the time gas-powered buggies surfaced on local streets, a calamitous hodgepodge of tracks, yards, depots and assorted rail facilities fostered by steam-driven, smoke-belching locomotives choked much of Alexandria and the surrounding environment. It soon presented grade-crossing nightmares, as motorists faced extended waits where tracks intersected with the town's thoroughfares. A big step in solving some of the region's headaches took shape when—in 1901—a half-dozen prominent rail carriers with interests in the area formed the Richmond-Washington Company. Together they sorted out extenuating circumstances to better manage their collective good fortune.

These operators included Atlantic Coast Line; Baltimore & Ohio; Chesapeake & Ohio; Pennsylvania; Richmond, Fredericksburg & Potomac; Seaboard Air Line; and Washington Southern systems. Not only did they consolidate freight traffic in a single district—Potomac Yard, north of the city, opened August 1, 1906—and coordinate train movements between Richmond and Washington through greater attention to scheduling detail, double-track some main lines and abandon others, but on September 15, 1905, all passenger consists passing through Alexandria were dispatched to a single terminal. It replaced as many as five more that existed concurrently. (Among the early depots were the 1854 "car shed" of Alexandria & Washington Railroad in a block bounded by Saint Asaph, Pitt, Queen and Princess streets; A&W and the newly formed Alexandria & Fredericksburg Railway, as of 1872, jointly called at passenger and freight stations in a block bounded by Henry, Cameron, Fayette and Queen streets; and about three blocks south, trains of Virginia Midland Railway anchored at a passenger facility at the southwest corner of Duke and Henry streets.)

Union Station is located at 110 Callahan Drive just below King Street in the city's Old Town district. It originally hosted three of the six long-distance carriers that strongly influenced the railroading milieu in the region: ACL, RF&P, and SOU. Today the edifice serves Amtrak intercity and Virginia Railway Express commuter rail lines. And now as an intermodal facility, its reach has broadened to be a true regional transportation hub encompassing the Washington Metro, Alexandria DASH and Metrobus lines in addition to those rail carriers.

As of early 2010, for its part Amtrak's trains call at Alexandria 12 times every day; three more trains stop there five days a week; one stops three days a week; two visit on Saturday and Sunday; one calls Friday while another on Sunday. They include the *Cardinal* (Chicago–New York), *Carolinian* (Charlotte–New York), *Crescent* (New Orleans–New York), *Northeast Regional* (Lynchburg, Newport News or Richmond originations to Washington, New York or Boston termini), *Palmetto* (Savannah–New York), *Silver Meteor* (Miami–New York), and *Silver Star* (Miami–Tampa–New York). For all of these the numbers can, of course, be doubled, as they are reported in only one direction. Alexandria's Union Station is a busy place! Amtrak's fiscal year 2008 patronage of 120,153 (329 daily) at Alexandria topped 2007's total by 22.9 percent, a healthy ascent.

As for the depot, it's a single-level brick edifice styled in Federal Revival architecture. That's an early 29th century mix of Neoclassical details borrowed from structures popular following the American Revolution, making it especially suitable around Alexandria. In addition to its waiting rooms, ticket windows and other conveniences, there was a baggage-handling building separated by a 20-foot open passageway. The two were connected on the depot's eastern edge adjacent to the tracks by a 370-foot-long shed-roofed portico. Together they cost $62,020.55 to erect in 1903–1905. A freight station next door, demolished in the early 1980s so a Metro station could be built, cost $25,086.11 to construct.

The name of the chief architect is lost to history but is believed to have been an in-house staff member employed by one of the underwriting rail lines. The structure's most inspiring features include highly detailed semicircular and elliptical brick arches with winged granite keystones and imposts around doors and windows. Four main porticos have double doors flanked by windows with overhead elliptical, spider-web fanlights. At the terminal's north side a pedestrian tunnel beneath the tracks ties the east and west sides of the passenger platform together. In 1943, a Railway Express Agency building was added south of the baggage facility and torn down in 1982.

Earlier, in 1929, Union Station's interior was altered substantially. The ticket office was enlarged with a square bay window for ease in viewing approaching trains. Angled ticket windows protruded into the lobby. Restroom facilities were moved and enlarged. The renovation was meticulously conducted with masonry and millwork matching construction of the initial project. There have been continuing upgrades of electrical, heating and air conditioning systems, restrooms have been enlarged again and other accommodations improved.

In conjunction with the restoration conducted in 1982, a portico on Union Station's western edge was reconstructed with the same form, location and Tuscan-style wood columns as originally exhibited but with glue-laminated beams and a stainless steel roof. This replaced the 4 by 10 yellow pine joists and tin roof that was there at its start. The porticos on the western and northern sides and on the eastern platform were removed during the same project, although not replaced. A slate roof and copper ridge flashing were superseded by black composition shingles. The north and west portico's concrete floor and wrought iron railing were supplanted. Neo-colonial light fixtures appeared where Victorian cast iron pole lights had been since 1905.

During a 1995-1996 refurbishing of Union Station's exterior and interior, the 20-foot passageway between the lobby and ex-baggage facility (by then a storage room) was enclosed with glass. Passenger, ticket and restroom areas were updated while mechanical, electrical and plumbing systems were modernized or replaced. Architectural elements were refurbished to their original appearance. Future improvements are on the drawing board to keep Union Station in touch with the present while attempting to retain its resolute ties to the past.

NEWPORT NEWS

On October 19, 1881, the first passenger train from the Lower Virginia Peninsula schlepped travelers from Lee Hall Depot to the Cornwallis Surrender Centennial Celebration. They proceeded between Newport News and Yorktown over a temporary track that had been laid by the Chesapeake & Ohio Railroad (C&O). The carrier had only recently erected Lee Hall Depot at the corner of Elmhurst Street and Warwick Road (now Boulevard) in Lee Hall Village, a district of Newport News. (The terminal was named after Lee Hall Mansion. Built in 1859, it was the manor of a prestigious local planter, Richard Decatur Lee.) At its inception Lee Hall Depot was the eastern terminus of an extensive east-west C&O route that connected Warwick Courthouse with Williamsburg and Yorktown. One recent assessment suggested the terminal habitually met the needs of Yorktown, Lee Hall and lower James City County denizens. It was "the social and economic focal point of the village of Lee Hall that grew around the station."

At one time the county was home to five railway stations: Lee Hall, Morrison, Newport News, Oriana, and Oyster Point. Today the only one left is Lee Hall. It furnishes a historical tie to early advances that transitioned into the modern city of Newport News. It has also been a pervasive part of the developing story of transportation in the area, too.

With the passing of time numerous additions were made to Lee Hall Depot that significantly altered its appearance. Although it premiered in 1881 as a one-story building, a dozen years later a bi-level section was created. Then came a new waiting room in 1918, followed by a storage shed in 1943, now no longer there. Passenger service ended in the late 1970s. In 1993, CSX Transportation, successor to C&O and other lines, determined that the depot's close proximity to the tracks made it unsafe. CSX announced it would give the structure to the city if it was moved away from the tracks.

Friends of Lee Hall Depot Foundation, a private group organized in 2000, accepted the challenge of shifting and restoring the station in tandem with the city. In a decade the preservationists raised about $1.5 million of an estimated $2.3 million required to push the depot 165 feet back from the tracks, to stabilize it and refurbish it to its previous quality. Following extensive planning, the move and stabilization was completed in the summer of 2009, and fundraising continues for its rehabilitation. When fully restored, Lee Hall will provide a light rail transit stop, special exhibitions, meeting space and a gift shop. It's now administered and maintained by the Division of Museums & Historic Services of Newport News.

In the meantime a functioning Amtrak station at 9304 Warwick Boulevard hosts two *Northeast Regional* trains daily plus one operating Monday–Friday, one running weekends only, and one traveling southbound on Friday and northbound on Sunday. Those trains sprint between Newport News and Washington, New York and Boston. In fiscal year 2008, Amtrak boarded or deboarded 117,114 patrons at Newport News, about 321 riders per day, and a 21.7 percent increase in one year. A published local newspaper account in 2008 outlined a future Amtrak facility in downtown Newport News. It would be built to alleviate burgeoning conditions inside the Warwick station and on its parking lot, the report said, although nothing further has been released as of this writing. Newport News is the closest Amtrak station to Chesapeake, Hampton, Norfolk, Portsmouth, Suffolk, Virginia Beach and several more Tidewater municipalities, thereby drawing heavily from the greater metropolitan community. Limited Amtrak Thruway Motorcoach service links Norfolk and Virginia Beach to the Newport News station.

RICHMOND

A quartet of enduring railway stations serving Virginia's capital, a couple of them spawning spectacularly signature images on the city's skyline while two continue their original functions today, offer illustrious links to the area's role as a railroad Mecca. Although the Seaboard Air Line Railroad's headquarters were ensconced in Richmond, a handful of long-distance roads maintained powerful divisions there, too.

A pair of carriers serving the city — Richmond & Petersburg (a precursor of Atlantic Coast Line) and Richmond, Fredericksburg & Potomac — combined their ventures in a depot opened in 1887. It replaced a seven-year-old RF&P facility at Pine and Broad streets that was already considered obsolete for current needs. The city fathers prompted the rail duo to obliterate their downtown tracks and stations in the interest of diminishing hazards and congestion (which presumably included stagecoaches, buckboards, and people on horseback and foot!). The joint terminal affirmed better connections between the lines. Obstruction continued unabated, however, particularly around the turn of the 20th century with the arrival of the automobile.

In 1913, the dual roads decided to scrap their 1887 structure and project yet another new, palatial terminal northwest of the city's center. It was to occupy ex-fairgrounds property bought by the RF&P in 1904, since then home of the Hermitage Country Club also fostered by the railroad. The RF&P developed it to encourage the uppercrust to ride excursion trains to the city's western edge where the club was situated. The site had earlier witnessed Civil War military encampments and a ballpark where a few early professional baseball teams played.

Some pointed acrimonious debate ensued between the dual roads and local civic leaders, the latter faction protesting vigorously the establishment of a "second" new station. An imposing facility had opened in 1901 southeast of the city's center (to be visited presently) hosting trains of the Chesapeake & Ohio (C&O) and Seaboard Air Line (SAL) systems. The C&O consolidated the ex–Richmond & Allegheny and Virginia Central railroads which had previously operated separate depots. Some city fathers believed a single operation where all the lines could call was better for the municipality and travelers alike. But the RF&P and Atlantic Coast Line (having succeeded R&P) would have none of it and went ahead with plans for a separate facility. In time Norfolk & Western Railway joined the band of feisty mavericks, securing a spot within the confines of the city's newest terminal.

The resulting structure went by several designations across its durable history. Initially known as the *Hermitage Station*, an outgrowth of the property where it was built, for years it was interchangeably labeled *Union Station*. But because of its prominent location on the corner of Davis and West Broad streets, the latter a widely recognized thoroughfare, it was soon dubbed *Broad Street Station* by locals. The nomenclature stuck and today it's still commonly branded by that term even though train service ended there several decades ago.

New York architect John Russell Pope (1874–1937), a devout Classicist — who designed the District of Columbia's Jefferson Memorial, National Archives, and National Gallery of Arts— gained the nod for drafting the bi-level Union Station. Combining multiple architectural styles, his work reflects the Beaux Arts trend so prevalent in the opening decades of the 20th century. Hallmarks of Pope's Neoclassical Revival masterpiece were a central copper dome-covered rotunda, Doric portico and colonnade of Indiana limestone.

A lapse of nearly four years occurred before work began on Broad Street Station on January 6, 1917. The intervention of the First World War, heavily diminishing an inventory of available skilled craftsmen, plus material cost overruns, delayed the opening to January 6, 1919, exactly two years after construction began. The capital outlay approached $3 million (after inflation, $42.5 million in 2008).

Union Station's track layout was unique with a non-conventional approach to the station. Rather than being on the artery for ACL and RF&P through trains, a loop at the end of a pithy branch off the mainline circled the edifice. The branch joined the main by wye tracks so consists heading north or south entered the loop and station headed southeast, no matter from which direction they

A southbound Amtrak train with numerous cars calls at the suburban Richmond passenger station in July 1976. Opened the year before, the platform can accept lengthy passenger trains. The motive power is furnished by dual EMD SDP40Fs, each delivering 3,000 hp. Both are equipped with generators that supply steam for conventional lightweight passenger cars. Numerous freight and passenger trains navigate 113-mile RF&P dual bridge-line trackage daily from Richmond to Washington, D.C. (*courtesy Michael B. Robbins*).

came. Departing trains completed the residue of the brief trip through the loop to revisit the mainline and turn north or south. A historian branded the configuration "ingenious." Innovative locomotive-servicing operations staged at an end of the terminal were considered a plus, a concept of civil engineer Harold Frazier.

During the Second World War Broad Street realized its greatest potential, processing nearly 60 trains daily and, in 1943, it saw some 10 million patrons come and go in a single year. After the last train left on November 15, 1975, Broad Street Station miraculously escaped a planned date with the wrecking ball. The Commonwealth of Virginia bought it in 1976, intending to raze it and build a satellite state office complex on the site. But after a nascent Science Museum of Virginia was allowed to temporarily occupy a portion of it in 1976, things changed. Revised thinking led to the governor dedicating the facility as the permanent home of that temporary tenant on the 58th anniversary of Broad Street Station's opening, January 6, 1977. Pope's splendid hall of grandeur now survives as an interactive educational exhibition embracing a planetarium, Imax theater and other compelling treasures. Traces of the depot's rail legacy are still in evidence today, nevertheless, including a trio of platform tracks reinstalled for rail equipment. A model railroad club also utilizes the structure for its gatherings.

The other major depot in Richmond—Main Street Station—was completed in 1901 by Chesapeake & Ohio Railway and Seaboard Air Line Railroad, opening that year on November 27. It's located at 1500 East Main Street and the intersection of 16th Street, three blocks south of Broad. The Philadelphia architectural firm of Wilson, Harris and Richards designed it. A French Renaissance paradigm, Main Street's large gathering hall is framed by tiled walls and a high ceiling buttressed by 22-foot columns, some damaged in a 1983 fire, although restored since. Candlestick light fixtures bearing C&O and SAL logos in the halcyon days are still present. The concourse proceeds to a waiting room and train platform where original bench seating is replicated and currently used.

The clock on the concourse once operated at Broad Street Station. Standing 110 feet above the city, Main Street's four-faced clock tower is observed by travelers passing by on nearby Interstate 95. A 400-foot metal trainshed behind the head house as well as the station itself went on the U.S. National Register of Historic Places in 1970. The terminal is in close proximity to 18th Street, where the planet's only tri-level railroad tracks prevail.

In 1958, Seaboard transferred its passenger rail operations from Main Street to Broad Street, leaving behind C&O as Main's chief caretaker. C&O already maintained some administrative offices on the upper levels at Main Street. At Broad Street, SAL joined ACL to become dominant tenants and its only carriers when the pair pooled resources to form Seaboard Coast Line Railroad in 1967.

Both Broad and Main structures witnessed their final passenger train departures in 1975. Unlike Broad Street however—where "The End" meant exactly that—some 28 years hence Amtrak resurrected passenger service at Main Street. In the interim, there was a 28-year gap to be accounted for, however. A developer bought the station in 1983, expecting to transform it into a mall. That was delayed by a fire that year which destroyed the roof. Main Street was the victim of more than one unfortunate incident. Hurricane Agnes caused the James River to overflow its banks and flood the terminal in 1972, leaving a high watermark identifiable today. Devastating fires erupted in both 1976 and 1983. Despite that it has survived and is deemed structurally sound.

After restoration the impending mall seemed doomed: it opened and closed in 1985. Five years afterward the Virginia Department of Health moved into offices at Main Street Station. Finally, the City of Richmond purchased the property from the Commonwealth of Virginia to revive it as a commuter rail station. After a $51.6 million renovation by the city and state, Main Street was again opened to rail traffic on December 20, 2003.

Planners eventually expect to see Amtrak trains to and from the South again stopping at Main Street (including the *Carolinian, Palmetto, Silver Meteor, Silver Star*, and any additions that may increase that cluster). It's also anticipated by some sources that the station may become the northern terminus of a projected Southeast High Speed Rail Corridor which would greatly enhance its visibility and value. It could be an intermodal complex, too, providing a central transfer point for Richmond's transit bus service. In 2006, meanwhile, the three upper floors were refurbished to allow for a second tenant, a Richmond-based advertising firm.

In 1975, Amtrak shifted the passenger business that had been calling at Broad Street Station since 1901 to a new location. The company erected a suburban station about five miles northwest of downtown at 7519 Staples Mill Road. With few distinguishing features, certainly not rivaling the architectural gems elsewhere in the city, it provides a commodious waiting room "with lots of uncomfortable seats" according to a modern blog, plus the usual basic services. Through this gateway passes a throng of passenger consists, most daily: *Auto Train* (nonstop Lorton, Virginia–Sanford, Florida), *Carolinian* (New York–Charlotte), *Northeast Regional* (Boston-Richmond or Newport News, or Richmond–Newport News—an aggregate of 10 to 14 trains daily), *Palmetto* (New York–Savannah), *Silver Meteor* (New York–Miami), *Silver Star* (New York–Tampa–Miami).

Only some of the *Northeast Regional* consists call at both Main Street and Staples Mill stations while all others are limited to Staples Mill. The latter led Virginia boardings and deboardings in Amtrak's fiscal year 2008 with 275,479 riders, an increase of 17.4 percent over 2007. Main Street added another 19,390 travelers in 2008, up 51.8 percent over a year earlier, one of the best percentage increases in the nationwide system.

Beyond all of this there is yet another major passenger carrier in Dixie whose presence in Richmond — while minimal when compared to other lines — prevailed throughout rail travel's heyday. Southern Railway maintained its own facilities independent of the competition. In that epoch it ran two daily consists between Richmond and Danville, Virginia. They connected at Danville with mainline Southern trains bound for and from Greensboro, Charlotte, Atlanta, Birmingham or Montgomery, and New Orleans. The company opened a waiting room on Richmond's Mill Street near the end of the 19th century. It was soon outmoded, however. Southern revealed it would combine passenger and freight operations, then at separate sites, at a single facility to be built in South Richmond at 102 Hull Street. Following that announcement in June 1914, passenger trains arrived in the interim at Main Street Station. That lasted only briefly for the timetables show — after the Mill Street Station disappeared from listings — Hull Street Station was Southern's local destination. The single-story rectangular brick structure alongside the tracks, though simple in design, was functional and practical for its dual purposes.

Today Hull Street Station is a key provision of Old Dominion Railway Museum. It has become a project of the local chapter of the National Railway Historical Society, whose area members are dedicated to the preservation of railroadiana in the middle of the Old Dominion State. Operating out of an adjacent RF&P express car, the group closed Hull Street Station to visitors for renovation in September 2009. When finished in 2010, their efforts were expected to produce displays of artifacts and documents pertaining to a wide range of railroading interests in central Virginia.

ROANOKE

A city known for its railroad history where first or secondary mainlines of a handful of leading carriers crossed and where one (Norfolk & Western) based its gargantuan headquarters, Roanoke's fortunes as an industry player petered out as people-hauling services evaporated. Passenger trains haven't rolled through Roanoke, in the Blue Ridge and Allegheny mountains, on any consistent basis in more than three decades (1979). Despite that circumstance the freight-line successor of two railways gracing the city then — Norfolk Southern Corporation with Norfolk & Western (N&W) and Southern (SOU) as ancestors, both Roanoke mainstays — still maintains a large presence in the city. The N&W shops were known far and wide for fabricating powerful steam locomotives during the Gilded Age prior to the arrival of diesels.

Thanks to southwest Virginia's pervasive Pocahontas bituminous coal that fueled half the world's navies, N&W was an enormously prosperous operation back in the day. Tonnage by the zillions of "black gold" was lifted from the earth and transported by rail to waiting steamships at Tidewater coastal ports. N&W's piers at Lambert Point, Virginian Railway's Sewells Point wharf and docks of the Chesapeake & Ohio Railway at Newport News — all three situated in Hampton Roads — collectively became the planet's utmost coal-shipping zone.

SOU ran a crucial southwestly route that branched off its mainline between New York and New Orleans at Lynchburg, Virginia. There travelers heading west were routed onto it, encountering Roanoke, Bristol, and Knoxville before reaching a major Southern junction point at Chattanooga. There riders might proceed west to Huntsville, Decatur and Sheffield-Tuscumbia before encountering Memphis. Or they might travel south from Chattanooga to Atlanta, Birmingham, Meridian and New Orleans.

At the same time mainlines of both the Norfolk-based Virginian and Roanoke-based N&W ran from the Old Dominion State's coastal region to the depths of West Virginia coal-mining country. Both carriers paralleled one another much of the way and while each offered passenger service via Roanoke, the Virginian's was a mere token to that of almost any other carrier. Virginian erected a passenger station at Williamson Road Southeast and South Jefferson Street in downtown Roanoke in 1909. With its blond brick facade, red tile roof and terrazzo floors, it was then one of the city's most distinctive buildings and doubtlessly was the most lavish depot in Virginian's system.

N&W leased Virginian in 1926. After Virginian discontinued passenger service altogether on January 29, 1956, it was ultimately folded into chief rival N&W's more extensive organization in 1959. By combining routes with those of other carriers, N&W was able to offer patrons through travel between Norfolk and Roanoke to termini at Buffalo, Chicago, Cincinnati, Columbus (Ohio), Kansas City and St. Louis.

For more than four decades after the Virginian's Roanoke depot was shuttered, a private commercial venture—a feed-and-seed merchant—occupied the premises. But after the edifice went up in flames on January 29, 2001, exactly 42 years after the last passenger consist left the station, the enterprise was out of business there. The structure subsequently languished, lapsing into deterioration.

As a consequence the National Railway Historical Society, in tandem with the Roanoke Valley Preservation Foundation, staved off a visit by the bulldozer, which might have been anticipated and even deemed inevitable. (Norfolk Southern gave the property and structure to the NRHS in 2003.) With a goal of raising $2.4 million, the dual groups spearheading a drive to save the depot intend to stabilize, repair, replace and refurbish the facility. Once that's done they expect to create a lasting tribute to Virginian Railway by exhibiting and storing archived materials. To pay the bills, once they arrive at that point they hope to engage a permanent tenant capable of meeting the ongoing financial obligations. No completion date is projected but the vision is gaining local momentum.

West Virginia

CHARLESTON

Charleston's Chesapeake & Ohio Railroad (C&O) depot shows how a community can turn an otherwise partially useless property from its past into something of value today. In a historic station fronting the Kanawha River just across that body of water separating the terminal from downtown Charleston, a farmer's market shares the space with Amtrak.

The carrier dispatches a single passenger train, the *Cardinal*, on its scenic sojourn across the Mountain State every Sunday, Wednesday and Friday in each direction. The consist, with endpoints in Chicago and New York City, generated 9,178 local Amtrak patrons during the company's fiscal year 2008, or about 25 per day. While those figures represent some of the lowest in Dixie for a city of Charleston's considerable influence—and particularly so among Southern state capitals—nevertheless, the numbers register a 6.6 percent uptick in ridership over a year earlier.

The striking two-story station, meanwhile, proffers expansive views of the river at an upper-level restaurant. Large picture windows overlook the water in a contemporary edifice. The facility is easily accessed from downtown by vehicle or on foot. A pedestrian walkway bridge adjacent to the depot connects the city with the other side of the river. As the first permanent viaduct across the Kanawha in 1891, the overpass was replaced in 1936 with today's South Side Bridge. The South Side was originally designed as a two-lane toll-way with a

fee assessed for crossing it (a toll office remains at the south end).

In the meantime a previous C&O depot in Charleston, built early in the 20th century and situated within a couple of blocks of the present Amtrak facility, hasn't gone to waste. Some enterprising Charlestonians put the imposing structure at 350 MacCorkle Avenue, Southeast, to excellent use in 1979, after Amtrak moved out. Retaining some of its historic charms and with fabulous waterside views, the old station proffers an upscale fine dining restaurant featuring continental cuisine. While food is pricey, reviews are positive and reservations are suggested, hinting of its attainment.

HINTON

When the Chesapeake & Ohio Railway (C&O) built its rail line across southeastern West Virginia in the early 1870s, Hinton was founded as a salient route stopover. At a spot where the water encounters the mountains, in 1872, Hinton was established at the confluence the Greenbrier and New rivers and chartered eight years later. Summers County attorney John (Jack) Hinton owned the property where it was formed and the resulting town was given his name. There the C&O's steam locomotives were serviced or swapped for fresh ones on their trek across the Mountain State journeying west and over the neighboring Old Dominion State of Virginia traveling east.

Shortly after the turn of the 20th century, Hinton proudly boasted almost 6,000 denizens. Commensurate with its habitation there was a well-appointed hospital, trio of thriving banks, superior hotel, foundry and machine shop, a couple of grain mills, multiple wholesale enterprises and retailers, competing news journals, and mammoth C&O repair shops staffed by hundreds of skilled craftsmen and laborers. A half-century hence much of the bustling activity that was the underpinning of life in Hinton dried up and moved on followed by many of the locals as population significantly declined. Much of the blame was placed on the railroad, which shifted from steam to diesel power. That required fewer workers and engine crews to maintain and operate trains from the Hinton terminal. Local streets once congested were no longer busy. As the nation's demand for coal diminished—the "black gold" that had put West Virginia on the country's economic map—so did Hinton's influence as a key staging area for putting together coal trains. By the mid 1980s engaged Hinton yards that had bustled with hundreds of railroad cars were virtually empty.

Today Hinton's streets, much quieter than a century ago, are flanked by "architectural gems" of the past. Community leaders and the National Park Service, since 1987, have labored in concert to revitalize the town as a living museum. Domiciles and public and private enterprises have been renovated while the Hinton Railroad Museum was created. One of the extant treasures targeted for refurbishing and preservation is the C&O passenger station, a lengthy, rectangular affair alongside the tracks in the heart of the city. While a mostly bi-level structure, at its center the brick depot exhibits a third story complete with chimney rising above its central portico.

Amtrak's stop in Hinton at 100 Second Avenue at its intersect with Maple Avenue is on the banks overlooking the broad New River. The company threads its Chicago–New York *Cardinal* consist through the city on Sundays, Wednesdays and Fridays in each direction. Although the numbers aren't hefty, the aggregate local Amtrak patronage of 10,162 in 2008, about 28 per day, placed Hinton second on West Virginia's ridership roster that year. That's a 16.7 percent gain over the previous year.

HUNTINGTON

Collis P. Hunington, one of the rail barons of America at the turn of the 20th century, not only had a major hand in developing some of the nation's prime trackage but was determined (or brazen?) enough to name one of the evolving burgs after himself. Huntington, the city, founded in 1870 and incorporated a year later, became the western terminus of the Chesapeake & Ohio Railway (C&O). It occupied property west of the mouth of the Guyandotte River at the Ohio River.

Created as a railroad town when the C&O stretched from the Ohio to Richmond, Virginia, the West Virginia town named after the rail magnate still houses voluminous railroad shops. (The first train to Huntington arrived from Richmond on January 29, 1873.) That line, of course, later expanded much farther — west to Cincinnati and Chicago and east to Newport News, the latter complete with newly constructed coal piers. And now with the Collis P. Huntington Railroad Historical Society active in the area, the founding father's impact likely won't soon be forgotten.

That organization took an active part recently in renovating C&O's early 20th century Mid-Georgian Palladin style passenger depot and administrative office complex at 935 7th Avenue. The facility is presently owned by CSX Transportation, which concurred with refurbishing the imposing tri-level brick structure. Arched windows along its exterior at street level and six three-story columns supporting a central portico cover make an impressive frontispiece for the wide, narrow rectangular edifice. In the enhancement of interior facilities, an adaptive use program was created to modify the space, furnishing convenient, modern and appropriately decorated rooms that kept with the original architecture. An accessible elevator to meet Americans with Disabilities Act requirements was added during the updating.

A superior location in the downtown commercial zone gave the Baltimore & Ohio Railroad (B&O) some distinct advantages when it erected its original passenger station in Huntington in 1887. The fact B&O was the nation's oldest continuous passenger line still operating under its initial nomenclature, then dating more than a half-century, added to its prestige even in a town already committed to rival carrier C&O. B&O set up shop in the 1100 block of 2nd Avenue between 11th Street and what is now Veterans Memorial Boulevard (formerly 1st Avenue) just across the river from Ohio. There it prospered for many years.

Upon the B&O terminal's debut a horse cart shuffled patrons between it and the C&O depot. When, in the 1930s, the Greyhound bus station in Huntington burned, a pioneering concept of putting train and bus patrons side-by-side in the same facility was implemented. For several years it worked well for B&O and Greyhound operations. Think of it as an early start on intermodal transportation hubs sprouting everywhere now. After the last train left the Huntington station B&O closed its doors and locked them tight. The aging edifice hasn't been razed but neither has it been pressed into other use. Languishing on the banks of the river now, it's always potentially a step away from the proverbial wrecking ball.

Amtrak, in the meantime, took over the three-day-a-week *Cardinal* passenger consist formerly run by C&O in May 1971. The train stops Sundays, Wednesdays, and Fridays in Huntington. Amtrak's contemporary facility at 1050 8th Avenue where it meets with 10th Street is across the tracks from the refurbished C&O depot. The Amtrak station is set back from the river a few blocks and also isn't far from the unoccupied B&O depot. It's a very small, almost square and nearly windowless single-story modern brick structure. The roofline extends over a concrete walkway that surrounds the building. A total of 12,610 riders boarded or deboarded the *Cardinal* at Huntington in fiscal year 2008, almost 35 daily, an increase of 13.8 percent over a year earlier. Despite the low patronage Huntington easily tops the other nine stops this train makes across the Mountain State.

F: Dixie Rail Chronology

1830 The Commonwealth of Virginia charters the Petersburg Railroad Company, the oldest ancestor of the future Atlantic Coast Line Railroad.

On Christmas day, the first completely American-built steam engine going into scheduled passenger service, the *Best Friend of Charleston*, hauls its first travelers along six completed miles of the Charleston & Hamburg Railway at Charleston, South Carolina. Fabricated at New York's West Point Foundry, it performs well for several months after starting regular service January 15, 1831. That is, until the boiler explodes by the actions of a reckless fireman, terminating its—and his—careers concurrently. (Actually, what is left of the engine is salvaged, reconfigured, and returned to work in a short while as the *Phoenix*.)

1831 The *South Carolina* becomes the first eight-wheeled engine, another successor to the *Best Friend of Charleston*.

Native Southerner Andrew Jackson is the nation's first chief executive to advocate the potential of railroads. In an address to Congress on December 6 he signifies "those most isolated by the obstacles of nature" in "the extreme parts of our country" will be included by rails' proliferation. Two years hence, he's the first sitting president to ride a train.

1832 The Portsmouth & Roanoke Railroad is certified, the earliest in a strain of antecedents that—a few decades from now—will coalesce to form the Seaboard Air Line Railroad. The initial 79-mile segment links a Virginia Tidewater settlement at Portsmouth with the hamlet of Weldon in neighboring northeastern North Carolina. The P&R originates with horses pulling wooden coaches along a crude track on a shaky roadbed that of necessity will be rebuilt in a couple of decades.

1833 When the full 136-mile Charleston & Hamburg line is completed in October it is the longest continuous rail right-of-way on the planet.

On December 20, the Central Rail Road and Canal Company is organized at Savannah to compete with South Carolina's Charleston & Hamburg Railroad to move natural resources, raw materials and finished goods from the interior to a coastal port. It will be renamed the Central of Georgia Railway in 1895, popularly known in the Peach State as "the Central." In spite of a modest start the line will grow to afford dependable transportation for travelers between Atlanta and Savannah and between Columbus and Atlanta.

1834 *Native*, the first steam locomotive to be constructed in the South from the ground up, is placed into service on the Charleston & Hamburg line.

1839 Five Southeastern states rank third through seventh in miles of railway tracks laid by now, right behind Pennsylvania and New York. In order: Virginia, Alabama, North Carolina, Tennessee, and Louisiana.

1848 Some enterprising visionaries at Mobile embark on laying a north-south rail line to connect their burg with Ohio River traffic at Cairo, Illinois. That undertaking, the Mobile & Ohio Railroad, won't reach the river for 26 years (1874). In the next century, nevertheless, M&O will donate incredibly to the backbone of an indispensable regional carrier: Gulf, Mobile & Ohio Railroad.

1850 On March 5, the Commonwealth of Kentucky issues a charter to a Louisville deputation hoping "to build a line of railroad between Louisville and the Tennessee state line in the direction of Nashville." Sanctioned by the Tennessee General Assembly on December 4, 1851, their venture nets the Louisville & Nashville Railroad. Construction is delayed; tracks are open 42 miles south of Louisville by mid 1958, when momentum picks up. The first train rolls into Nashville, 187 miles below Louisville, October 27, 1859. The L&N mainline will extend from Cincinnati to New Orleans; secondary mains will link Atlanta to both Cincinnati and St. Louis. Foremost branches will run to Lexington, Memphis, Pensacola and other municipalities.

1862 Southern-born President Abraham Lincoln signs the Pacific Railway Act that finally geographically unifies the nation when a transcontinental rail system is opened in 1869.

1869 Covington & Ohio and Virginia Central railroads combine their operations into the Chesapeake & Ohio Railway with headquarters at Norfolk. The passenger service, while modest, will eventually see consists running between Newport News and Chicago, and calling en route at Norfolk, Richmond, Charleston, Cincinnati, Indianapolis and other upper South and Midwest conurbations, with more trains to Louisville, Cleveland, and Washington, D.C.

1870 Under the nomenclature Atlantic, Mississippi & Ohio Railroad, a coalition of three lines unifies 400 miles of track between Norfolk and Bristol, Virginia. By May 1881, the outfit is named Norfolk & Western Railway and based at Big Lick, soon to be christened Roanoke, for most of its life. Only a tiny portion of its revenues will be earned transporting people. N&W will become widely recognized as a coal-hauler, largely gathered from West Virginia mines.

1871   The nomenclature *Atlantic Coast Line* is initially applied when Baltimore capitalist William T. Walters and cohorts buy a few shortline railways to connect Richmond, Virginia, with Wilmington, North Carolina. In evolving terminology, their venture is branded *Atlantic Coast Line of Railroads*, then *Atlantic Coast Line System*, and eventually *Atlantic Coast Line Company*. By 1900, their endeavor will be repositioned as a homogeneous outfit with a moniker that will be known for two-thirds of a century as *Atlantic Coast Line Railroad*.

1874   The Illinois Central gains access to the port city of New Orleans by acquiring dual Dixie lines for which it holds bonds. After some evolving name changes it shakes out as Chicago, St. Louis & New Orleans Railroad, a wholly owned IC auxiliary. A 550-mile segment built on a 5-foot gauge between Cairo, Illinois, and New Orleans will be converted July 29, 1881 to standard gauge (4 feet 8.5 inches) in one incredible day!

1876   Extending from multiple precursors dating to 1849, the St. Louis–San Francisco Railway emerges under that handle September 7. Operating out of St. Louis, it's commonly referenced by "Frisco" and its tracks not only traverse Missouri but dip into the Deep South's Arkansas, Alabama, Tennessee, Mississippi and Louisiana. San Francisco will turn out to be a pipe dream, at least without connections; the mainline won't make it west of Ellsworth, Kansas.

1880   To curtail the bidding by Nashville, Chattanooga & St. Louis Railway for inflated trackage in Illinois, Indiana and Kentucky, rival Louisville & Nashville Railroad buys the bulk of NC&StL's stock. Not only is a threat squashed, it boosts L&N's route system by 1,000 miles and workforce by 4,000. L&N is at once the South's third largest rail line and the 16th in size in the U.S. Outwardly NC&StL continues to run independently from its Nashville base, retaining its separate identity until it is folded into L&N in 1957.

1884   Industrial financier Henry Morrison Flagler realizes that if affluent Northerners are to be lured to the luxurious hotels he is building along Florida's Atlantic seaside, they must have a compelling means of getting there. Dipping once more into an endless personal fortune, Flagler commits to creating the Florida East Coast Railway. He will turn a piece of desolate geography into a perennial tourist and residential draw, one that continues proliferating.

1893   On August 1, five roads with routes between Portsmouth, Virginia, and Atlanta unite forces under the Seaboard Air-Line System umbrella. By dates of premier they are Seaboard & Roanoke (1832), Raleigh & Gaston (1835), Carolina Central (1857), Raleigh & Augusta Air-Line (1871), and Georgia, Carolina & Northern (1888). This coalition sets traffic policy without legal backing. Seaboard's deputation also controls a fleet of steamers in Baltimore–Norfolk–Old Point Comfort–Portsmouth channels. By owning shares in another steamship firm, Seaboard System gains access to the New York City port, too.

1894   International financier J. Pierpont Morgan and some allies gain control of the Richmond & Danville Railroad and reorganize it as *Southern Railway Company*. Around the turn of the century, it will be rechristened *Southern Railway System*. What began in 1847 as a 140-mile local line will expand into 8,883 route miles in due course.

1900   On April 21, the Atlantic Coast Line Railroad is launched in six Southeastern states: Alabama, Florida, Georgia, North Carolina, South Carolina, and Virginia. Until 1960, its nerve center occupies multiple adjacent structures in downtown Wilmington, North Carolina, after which its base will shift to Jacksonville, Florida. While ACL is one of Dixie's prime freight carriers, the company becomes a formidable rival in the competitive market of schlepping Northeastern denizens between their homes and Florida each winter.

On April 30, at Vaughn, Mississippi, a man who is to become a legend in the annals of railroad lore, John Luther "Casey" Jones, loses his life at the throttle of a southbound mail as it strikes a parked freight that hasn't cleared the IC mainline. Jones gains immortality after coworker Wallace Saunders pens a ballad crediting the heroism of the brave engineer. Mississippi will honor his memory at the crash site in 1953, and name a nearby state park for him in 1980.

On July 1, Seaboard Air Line Railway is officially in business with mainline tracks extending 850 miles between Richmond and Tampa. A distinguishing advantage it touts to shippers and travelers is that its route is 79 miles shorter than rival Atlantic Coast Line's between those two key endpoints.

1901   An "equal share" pact controlling traffic over the "Richmond-Washington Line" (Richmond, Fredericksburg & Potomac and Washington Southern) is signed by six roads effective July 1. Together they own the New Jersey–based Richmond-Washington Company overseeing operations and maintenance. The fraternity encompasses Atlantic Coast Line, Baltimore & Ohio, Chesapeake & Ohio, Pennsylvania, Seaboard Air Line, and Southern.

1902   Atlantic Coast Line Railroad gains appreciably in a deal between it and Southern Railway. ACL acquires control of the Louisville & Nashville Railroad and its auxiliary Nashville, Chattanooga & St. Louis Railway; plus half-interest in the Georgia Railroad (the rest held by L&N); and half the Monon Route between Chicago and Louisville (the rest held by SOU). All these lines will operate as independent carriers for decades, retaining their own sobriquets.

ACL completes its core route map by absorbing the Plant System, its seminal acquisition. The consortium of railways gathered by Henry Bradley Plant of Tampa adds 2,200 miles to ACL's pool encompassing the gateway cities of Albany, Jacksonville, Montgomery, Orlando, St. Petersburg, Savannah, Tampa, and Waycross. It also opens ACL routes to Atlanta and Birmingham. The purchase of this crown jewel lets patrons stay on one train from New York or Chicago to either Florida coast, creating a passenger business climate that ACL will never exceed.

1903   Although few recall his name, the September 27 death of Joseph A. Broady in a fiery mishap on Southern Railway near Danville, Virginia, places that episode second among notorious fatal crashes in the annals of Dixie railroading. It occurs when the southbound *Fast Mail* takes a trestle at accelerated speed and leaps from the tracks, falling into a creek below. Engineer Broady and 12 others die. Tunesmiths immortalize him and the more infamous Casey Jones in ballads about their disasters. In 1900, Jones lost his life at Vaughn, Mississippi, after his Illinois Central southbound mail struck a parked freight. Both engineers were running late and attempted to make up time deficiencies.

1907   Assets of the Central of Georgia Railway pass into the hands of Illinois Central Railroad, which will manage them for 35 years, to 1942.

1908   Seaboard Air Line is driven into bankruptcy in a competitive milieu in which it tries to gain a niche in passenger, freight, mail and express arenas against two wealthier rivals: to the east, Atlantic Coast Line; to the west, Southern. Though SAL survives and prospers, it will meet bankruptcy again.

1912   The "Route to the Sea," rail magnate Henry M. Flagler's Overseas Railroad between Miami and Key West, and an extension of his Florida East Coast Railway from Jacksonville open to raucous fanfare when the first train arrives in Key West bearing its owner on January 22.

1925   On January 21, Seaboard Air Line Railroad opens a 204-mile extension from its mainline between Jacksonville and Tampa at Coleman, Florida, to reach West Palm Beach, 204 miles south. Until now SAL hasn't had a direct link of its own with rapidly expanding southeast Florida. This exploit has profound implications: still greater effects result after the area's other carrier — Florida East Coast Railway — is shut down by strikers in 1963. Thenceforth the SAL tracks see the trains of not just one but two passenger haulers, SAL and ACL.

The Carolina, Clinchfield & Ohio Railroad (known hereafter as the Clinchfield) — a strategic bridge route between other lines at both Elkhorn, Kentucky, and Spartanburg, South Carolina — is jointly leased by Atlantic Coast Line and Louisville & Nashville railroads. While Clinchfield's prime commerce is hauling coal between Appalachia and coastal links, until 1954, it will also persist in schlepping travelers through the mountains.

1928   The Perry Cutoff, opened by the Atlantic Coast Line Railroad, trims many miles off some routes between the Midwest and Florida's west coast. From Thomasville, Georgia, Perry Cutoff trains travel east of Tallahassee to Dunnellon, Florida, before accessing Tampa. At Tampa they may persevere to south Florida resorts (Everglades, Fort Myers, Naples, Punta Gorda, St. Petersburg, and Sarasota). The Perry Cutoff eliminates costly, congested, time-consuming Jacksonville jaunts only to double back across the peninsula to the Gulf.

1930   After the bottom drops out of the national economy 14 months before, Seaboard Air Line Railroad enters bankruptcy a second time in December.

1932   Central of Georgia Railway enters a 16-year receivership.

1934   Seaboard Air Line becomes the first carrier in Dixie to supply its passenger equipment with air conditioning, instigating it with a trio of premier trains between Florida and the Northeast. Key rivals will have little choice about adding this feature.

1935   On July 29, the *Rebel*, two passenger trainsets launched by the Gulf, Mobile & Northern Railroad (a predecessor of the Gulf, Mobile & Ohio), debuts as the first streamlined consist in Dixie. The pair travels daily in opposite directions between Jackson, Tennessee, and New Orleans, setting a high watermark for similar introductions by Southern competitors that still won't happen for another four years.

When a devastating hurricane strikes the Florida Keys on September 2, the Overseas Railroad is washed out to sea. The end to Henry Flagler's dream is a nightmare as the epoch of that fateful line swiftly erodes. From now on southbound FEC passenger trains will again terminate at Miami.

1939   Seaboard is the first line in the Atlantic

coastal states— and second in the South — to in-augurate streamliner service. On February 2, to rave reviews, the *Silver Meteor* lightweight coach consist makes a maiden voyage between New York and Miami, increasing the urgency for the leading carriers to follow suit.

ACL introduces a stunning livery, one of its most distinctive eye-catching features for nearly two decades. Plum-tinted locomotives with yellow stripes and aluminum-gray bands supply head-end power for stainless steel cars adorned with matching royal purple letterboards and aluminum-gray lettering. The costumed bodies stand in a sea of conventional hues exhibited by almost every other line.

1940   Amalgamation of the Gulf, Mobile & Northern and Mobile & Ohio railroads nets a crucial regional carrier, Gulf, Mobile & Ohio Railroad, later linking the Gulf with St. Louis while accessing Kansas City and Chicago. Calling at many places that would be circumvented otherwise, the Jackson, Tennessee–based GM&O is an alternate to behemoths Illinois Central and Louisville & Nashville, both far more powerful north-south route neighbors.

Unable to withstand the pressure of multiple lines ahead of it, plus enduring tumultuous howls from Atlantans for action, Southern Railway — with a dominant presence in Atlanta — reveals its buy of five diesel locomotives and 44 lightweight cars to equip dual streamlined trains. *The Southerner*, between New Orleans and Washington, and *The Tennessean*, between Memphis–Nashville and Washington, will provide seamless extensions at D.C. to New York City.

1944   Atlantic Coast Line Railroad fruitlessly tries to acquire the Florida East Coast Railway now in receivership. ACL is solely reliant on FEC to transport its passengers between Jacksonville and Miami, having no tracks as rival Seaboard Air Line Railroad does between those cities.

1948   Central of Georgia Railway exits receivership after 16 years.

1949   The first rail carrier in the U.S. to totally dieselize its entire fleet of locomotives is in the South and isn't one of the region's three or four largest movers: Gulf, Mobile & Ohio.

1956   The assets of Central of Georgia Railway pass into the hands of St. Louis–San Francisco Railway. The Interstate Commerce Commission

Separated from the ocean by trees at left at Edgewater in Volusia County, Florida, south of New Smyrna Beach, northbound 88 *Florida Special* led by FEC E7s 1008 and 1011 rolls along to Jacksonville in mid afternoon on February 21, 1951. Despite ACL's attempts to buy it, FEC remains out of the clutches of its peer, still supplying ACL's meal ticket to Miami (**photograph by Robert Malinoski, courtesy Richard C. Beall**).

SW9 227 switches passenger cars out in 1958, crossing N.E. 29th Street running through FEC's Buena Vista Yard at Miami. The wooden structure at left is the yard office, while the water tower in the distance stands immediately south of the line's Gold Coast roundhouse and turntable (*photograph by Fred Carnes, courtesy Richard C. Beall*).

takes a dim view of the purchase, however, believing it stymies competition in the region, and orders its divestiture in 1961.

1957 By August 30, Nashville, Chattanooga & St. Louis Railway, an ancillary of Louisville & Nashville Railroad since 1880, is fully integrated into L&N. Proffering an illustrious history, NC&StL dates from 1845, when it began as Nashville & Chattanooga Railway. It extends to Atlanta, Memphis, Paducah and Hickman, Kentucky, but never to St. Louis except over L&N routes.

1958 Enduring archrivals ACL and SAL put aside their sticking points to launch an intensive self-examination designed to settle whether a fusion of their systems might appreciably respond to the eroding business climate both face. It's prompted by a growing reliance upon highways and airways, including passenger transport and trucking shipments. The inquiry will take nine years to complete, after which the pair will blend their operations.

Starting this year Gulf, Mobile & Ohio, with its roots and most of its tracks deep in Dixie, will no longer run any passenger trains south of St. Louis. The last of its consists, *Gulf Coast Rebel*, is purged to Mobile and Montgomery.

1959 Norfolk & Western adds substantially to its substance by finally acquiring a longtime thorn in its side, the smaller but hardy Virginian Railway. The latter coal-hauler's 600-mile route between Deepwater, West Virginia, and Newport News, Virginia, encounters fewer grades, superior roadbed, smoother turns and nets faster delivery than opponents. For decades it has been coveted by N&W and Chesapeake & Ohio and likely others after the same commodity.

1960 Norfolk & Western Railway is the last major U.S. rail carrier to switch from steam to diesel-electric motive power. There's a chief reason for its delay: in its shops at Roanoke, N&W fabricated, repaired, rebuilt, and refurbished steam engines used by N&W and other lines. N&W is celebrated throughout the industry for its excellence with steam. After steam passes, those shops continue building and repairing other rolling stock, with Norfolk Southern as a beneficiary.

1963 Eleven non-operating unions strike the Florida East Coast Railway on January 23, resulting in an abrupt and total work stoppage. Partner ACL can no longer get its passengers between Miami and Jacksonville after relying on FEC for 67 years. ACL quickly hammers out another deal with archrival SAL to access its tracks at Auburndale, where their lines cross, and run on SAL rails 220 miles to Miami. The deal lasts until Amtrak takes over in 1971.

Central of Georgia, getting out from under the thumb of the St. Louis–San Francisco Railway in 1961, is approved by the Interstate Commerce Commission for takeover by Southern Railway effective June 17. Precautions to protect CofG employees, it turns out, aren't worth the paper on which they are written. A tyrannical Southern president summarily discharges 1,500 CofG workers "without prior notice, without implementing agreements, and without attempting to merge seniority rosters." Central's board chairman is sacked, too.

1967 ACL and SAL merge their operations into a newly formed Seaboard Coast Line Railroad on July 1, based in ACL's home (as of 1960) of Jacksonville.

1969 Louisville & Nashville Railroad makes one of its last two major acquisitions, the easternmost route of the Chicago & Eastern Illinois Railroad. The 287-mile segment gives L&N direct access to Chicago from Evansville. Until now traffic from the central South, Gulf Coast and Southeast has depended on other carriers for connections with the crucial Windy City gateway.

1970   Congress passes the Rail Passenger Service Act creating Amtrak, a quasi-government corporation that will assume running the nation's passenger trains. Southern Railway and a few smaller carriers will opt out of the system and continue running their own trains.

1971   The Class 1 freight carriers terminate their passenger services on April 30; on May 1, Amtrak takes over with severely reduced service. Hundreds of communities in the South are left without passenger trains while six or more consists on a handful of primary routes are reduced to one or two trains daily. It's a vastly different environment for travel by rail, one most inhabitants have never experienced in their lifetimes.

In its last ambitious acquisition, on August 1, Louisville & Nashville Railroad buys the 541-mile Monon Railroad, gaining a second direct route into Chicago while obtaining access to Indianapolis and a few more Indiana burgs.

In November, Seaboard Coast Line Industries, Inc., increases its holdings in L&N from 33 to 98 percent.

On December 6, Auto-Train Corporation appears. This privately owned firm begins transporting passengers and their cars between Lorton, Virginia, and Sanford, Florida. It will add a route between Louisville, Kentucky, and Sanford in 1974, but it won't ever be as successful as the original, and will be abandoned in 1977. Eventually Amtrak will assume this business and turn it into one of its most lucrative ventures, still operating daily.

1972   The Chesapeake & Ohio, Baltimore & Ohio, Western Maryland and a few lesser roads combine operations to form Chessie System, Inc., a holding company for the merged lines. Its headquarters is Cleveland, Ohio. In eight years this amalgamation will join Seaboard to create CSX.

On August 10, longtime rivals Gulf, Mobile & Ohio and Illinois Central merge into a single 9,600-mile unit initially recognized as Illinois Central Gulf Railroad. Many of their tracks serve the same locales and some are therefore sold, traded or abandoned. The "Gulf" reference in

the nomenclature remains to February 29, 1988, yet the more powerful IC dictates many decisions. The independency lasts to February 11, 1998, when a stronger Canadian National Railway buys all of IC. That carrier allows the name to continue to 2001 when it is shifted to CN identifying marks.

1979   On January 31, Southern Railway sends its final *Crescent* on the mainline between New Orleans and the Northeast. After today the throttle will be in Amtrak's hands, a transfer SOU resisted in 1971. This takes SOU out of passenger travel forever, the last Class 1 line in the South to persist at it this late.

The *Floridian*, Amtrak's sole consist on the most direct route from Chicago to Florida (over L&N tracks to Indianapolis, Louisville, Nashville, Birmingham, and Montgomery, and ACL to Jacksonville) is withdrawn October 9. Louisville, Nashville and Montgomery are left without passenger service.

1980   CSX Corporation is formed November 1. It includes combined operations of the Seaboard and Chessie systems, the latter a holding company that embraces a handful of lines like Chesapeake & Ohio, Baltimore & Ohio, Western Maryland, and some minor roads. CSX is one of the nation's most powerful Class 1 amalgamations running in the eastern third of the country and dominant in the Southeast. Its Jacksonville base is a durable railroad hub.

Burlington Northern Railroad acquires the St. Louis–San Francisco Railway (Frisco) on November 21. In 1995, BN will join the Santa Fe Railroad to create BNSF, one of the nation's major Class 1 freight haulers.

1982   To have a chance of competing successfully against the powerful CSX Corporation in the eastern third of the nation, Southern and Norfolk & Western railways merge operations into a single entity, Norfolk Southern Corporation, with headquarters in Norfolk.

2009   The future of rail travel in America gains a more solid footing as a new U.S. president pledges his efforts to equip the country with the foundations for a high speed rail system starting regionally. If this proceeds as announced the South could fare very well.

G: *Powerful Railway Personalities*

Presented here are brief biographies of individuals who influenced the early railroads of the South, and whose influence is still evident today. In several cases their influence extended north of the Mason-Dixon Line. Those leaders put their personal stamps on railroading in places where magnolias and dogwoods are uncommon and orange groves and pecan trees don't grow. Whether they are recognized inside or outside the South, the impressions they made on their industry helped maintain and guide it through both perilous and profitable times.

BROSNAN, DENNIS WILLIAM (BILL). b. April 14, 1903, Albany, Georgia. d. June 14, 1985, Asheville, North Carolina. A polarizing figure, Brosnan was unpopular as president of Southern Railway (1962–1967) and at last was forced out. Joining SOU at Macon as a track laborer (1926), he moved up to general manager (1947), VP-operations (1952), and executive VP before gaining the top office. He initiated efficiencies and reforms that became commonplace elsewhere in the trade while sharply cutting costs, personnel and services. Honored by peers in the industry, Brosnan wasn't esteemed at home. His staff distrusted him, viewing him as an autocratic tyrant. In acquiring Central of Georgia Railroad (1963), he fired 1,500 workers without prior notice, without implementing agreements and without merging seniority rosters. Sensing the approaching end of passenger trains, Brosnan was jubilant. He focused squarely on freight as the key to profitability, directing marketing toward shippers. Board chairman from 1967 to 1976, Brosnan remained a director to 1983.

CLAYTOR, WILLIAM GRAHAM, JR. b. March 14, 1912, Roanoke, Virginia. d. May 14, 1994, Bradenton, Florida. Recruited to Southern Railway as VP (1963), Claytor had been an attorney with a Washington, D.C., firm 25 years. He acceded to SOU's top job in 1967, and his tenure was widely acclaimed. He repaired human relations at a time *Dun's Review* labeled Southern "one of America's best managed enterprises." Claytor refused Amtrak's bid for SOU's last passenger services in 1971, figuring it would "go to hell, very fast." Chairman in 1976, he "retired" in 1977. Serving the nation under President Jimmy Carter, Claytor was secretary of the Navy (1977–1979), acting secretary of transportation (1979), and deputy secretary of defense (1979–1981). When Amtrak beckoned, surprisingly he answered! He presided (1982–1993) over an agency he had strongly criticized, and reduced federal subsidies 40 percent while securing Amtrak's future on solid turf.

DAVIS, CHAMPION McDOWELL. b. July 1, 1879, Hickory, North Carolina. d. January 28, 1975, Wilmington, North Carolina. Davis was a lifelong bachelor who worked on the railroad 64 years (1893–1957). He rose from a telegraph messenger with Wilmington & Weldon Railroad through the ranks of Atlantic Coast Line Railroad to vice president and ultimately president (1942–1957).

Some think the ACL directors' high esteem for Champ Davis influenced their choice in naming the *East Coast Champion* and *West Coast Champion* when ACL added streamliners to the fleet in 1939.

FINK, ALBERT. b. October 27, 1827, Lauterbach, Germany. d. April 3, 1897, Ossining, New York. A mechanical engineer-turned-administrator starting in 1850, Fink began as a bridge-design draftsman at the Baltimore & Ohio. Creating a patented trestle known as the Fink Truss, he earned status and wealth. In 1857, he joined L&N and moved up, eventually claiming a vice presidency. His ability at the drawing board served him well, yet Fink's vision and managerial skills rose to the forefront. He was a strong negotiator and judiciously steered the L&N ship in turbulent economic crises. He fostered plans doubling the mainline, extending it 300 miles from Nashville south to Montgomery. "Retiring" at 47, Fink wasn't idle long; he became first commissioner of two agencies— Southern Railway and Steamship Association (1875–1877) and Trunk Line Association (1877–1889). He directed hundreds of minions as a rail rate-setter at the latter. *The New York Times* observed: "No single man ever wielded so potent an influence directly upon the railway traffic of this country as did Albert Fink." He was an L&N director late in life.

FLAGLER, HENRY MORRISON. b. January 2, 1830, Hopewell, New York. d. May 20, 1913, Palm Beach, Florida. Flagler was a grain merchant who met John D. Rockefeller in 1863, forming a tie leading to an oil refining partnership which made both stunningly prosperous. Standard Oil, begun in 1870, was within two years at the forefront of all similar activity in America. Flagler's Florida sojourns from 1878 led him to cultivate a tourism industry. With endless capital he put gargantuan sums into building palatial resorts for affluent frozen Yankees seeking to escape winter's blast. To get them there he bought short rail lines south of Jacksonville and added new tracks along the ocean's fringe, increasing permanent as well as temporary populations. In 1896, his tracks arrived at what was to be Miami, where he literally built a town. Flagler increased his holdings by investing in steamship lines and real estate ventures. His crowning achievement was a 156-mile extension of his Florida East Coast Railway from Miami to Key West. The last 128 miles over water (constructed 1905–1912) were washed away by a 1935 hurricane.

HARRIMAN, EDWARD HENRY. b. February 25, 1848, Hempstead, New York. d. September 9, 1909, Orange County, New York. A stockbroker before entering railroading, Harriman honed managerial skills at Illinois Central. Then he launched a syndicate to obtain a bankrupt Union Pacific (1898)

Henry M. Flagler died 45 years before this 1958 photograph, thus he never encountered diesels like E6 1005 and E7 1013 powering FEC 38, the *East Coast Express*. But the entrepreneur was proud of what he amassed nevertheless. Northbound 38 is departing Miami for Jacksonville. The low pointed station roofline rises above the train's furthermost cars; the tall edifice to the side of it is the Dade County Court House (*photograph by Fred Carnes, courtesy Richard C. Beall*).

and turn it into a profitable venture. Subsequently he took control of Southern Pacific and many smaller lines including Central of Georgia (1907). After helping launch the railway holding corporation Northern Securities Company (NSC) in 1901, Harriman suffered a "blighted public image" from wide-reaching financial reverses on Wall Street tied to his involvement in NSC. He was president of Southern Pacific (1901) and Union Pacific (1903) at the same time. A shrewd businessman, Harriman's influence over SP, UP & IC allowed him to perpetuate similar organizational structures and philosophies for that trio. Standardization and uniformity resulted in broad purchasing and maintenance economies of scale saving millions of dollars.

HUNTINGTON, COLLIS POTTER. b. April 16, 1821, Harwinton, Connecticut. d. August 13, 1900, Raquette Lake, New York. A successful mercantilist in New York and later in California, Huntington joined a cadre of capitalists surveying the Sierra Nevada Mountains to create a transcontinental railroad. They plotted a California system of nearly 9,000 miles next before opening a rail line from Portland, Oregon, to New Orleans. They formed Southern Pacific Company with rails linking San Francisco and Los Angeles and extending to New Orleans. The rail magnate participated heavily in founding and becoming first president of Chesapeake & Ohio (1869) by rescuing predecessor Vir-

ginia Central in the post–Civil War era, leading to a second transcontinental line. Huntington did what no other man in America had done, said a source: Connecting westward through West Virginia, Kentucky, Tennessee and Mississippi, "he was able to ride his own private car over his own tracks from the gateway of the Old Dominion on the Atlantic to the Golden Gate on the Pacific coast." Beyond rail construction, Huntington (his name is borne by a rail-induced West Virginia city) was invested in Pacific Mail Steamship Company with extensive water routes, and founded Newport News, Virginia, where 4,000 workers fabricated battleships.

KENDALL, WILLIAM H. b. March 24, 1910, Somerville, Massachusetts. d. March 31, 1989, Jacksonville, Florida. A veteran of four railroads (Ann Arbor, Pennsylvania, ACL, Clinchfield) before arriving at L&N in 1954, within three years he was vice president; in two more, president. In the early 1970s, Kendall oversaw the transition to Seaboard Coast Line Industries, Inc. He relinquished the L&N presidency in 1972 to spend three years before retiring as vice chairman of the holding company.

MORGAN, JOHN PIERPONT. b. April 17, 1837, Hartford, Connecticut. d. March 31, 1913, Rome, Italy. Born with the proverbial silver spoon in his mouth, Morgan learned banking from his dad before launching a financial empire of his own (1871).

Revered as J. P. Morgan & Company now, his worldwide venture is one of the most powerful in its trade. For years he dominated railroads, consolidating lines in the East including Southern Railway, which he and others organized July 1, 1894, from some Dixie forebears. The feds heavily scrutinized Morgan for creating controlling monopolies which prevented others from competing fairly against his businesses. In 1901, he formed U.S. Steel Corporation, also topping that manufacturing sector worldwide.

OSBORN, PRIME F., III. b. 1915, Greensboro, Alabama. d. January 4, 1986, Jacksonville, Florida. Osborn, staff attorney for Gulf, Mobile & Ohio Railroad starting in the mid 1940s, joined L&N in 1951 as general solicitor, becoming vice president-general counsel at ACL in 1957. An architect of the merger netting Seaboard Coast Line in 1967, he became Seaboard Industries president two years later. Osborn returned to L&N as president (1972–1980) and was chairman of the newly-formed CSX Corporation two years until his 1982 retirement.

PLANT, HENRY BRADLEY. b. October 27, 1819, Branford, Connecticut. d. June 23, 1899, New York, New York. Leaving the Northeast in 1854 to manage an express business at Augusta, Georgia, an entrepreneurial Plant was to preside over an aggregate of Southern railroads, steamship lines, hotels, express, real estate, and auxiliary interests. He dredged the port of Tampa in 1885, and amassed more than 2,200 miles of railroad right-of-way from Tampa to Charleston, South Carolina, to Montgomery. His steamship lines, connected with Plant System rails at Tampa, linked to Mobile, Key West and Havana. From Winter Park to Fort Myers his Florida resorts were prime winter retreats for shivering, affluent Yankees. After Plant's death his railways opened a route for Atlantic Coast Line to extend its Richmond to Charleston mainline all the way to Tampa.

POWELL, LEGH RICHMOND, JR. b. March 10, 1884, Portsmouth, Virginia. d. October 14, 1969, Norfolk, Virginia. An auditor for Seaboard Air Line at 18, Powell gave his life to the company. Moving steadily up, at 34 he was vice president and controller, and at 43, president (1927–1952). Leasing tracks to link SAL through the Florida panhandle to Montgomery, he opened a new gateway. In 1930, Powell was a receiver for the railroad. With upgrades in passenger equipment and attention to creature comforts, he attracted loyal clientele while focusing on stabilizing the line's financial health. In the postwar years SAL finally realized the intents of John Williams and Davies Warfield as Powell thrust it into "one of the premier railroads" of the Southeast.

RICE, WILLIAM THOMAS. b. June 13, 1912, Hague, Virginia. d. March 5, 2006, Richmond, Virginia. Hired at 22 by Pennsylvania Railroad, Rice rose to track supervisor there before taking the presidency of Richmond, Fredericksburg & Potomac on January 1, 1955. Moving to ACL on August 1, 1957, he presided over a firm in transition. Rice led the 1960 ACL headquarters shift from Wilmington to Jacksonville and conducted merger talks with archrival SAL to sustain profitability by pooling resources. That resulted in Seaboard Coast Line Railroad's formation July 1, 1967. Rice became SCL president and chairman of ancillary L&N, adding SCL chairman and CEO titles later. Retiring in 1977, he returned to foster a 1980 Chessie and Seaboard systems merger that created CSX Corporation.

ROBINSON, JOHN MONCURE. b. October 22, 1835, Philadelphia, Pennsylvania. d. February 14, 1893, Baltimore, Maryland. A colonel in the Confederacy, following the war Robinson joined the Seaboard & Roanoke Railroad as superintendent. In quick succession he acquired the top jobs of a multiplicity of railroads and steamship carriers. He ultimately presided over a handful of roads that coalesced operations in the months after his death to form Seaboard Air-Line System on August 1, 1893. Robinson was a catalyst in establishing partnerships for the common benefit and a visionary whose reach exceeded his grasp. Given more time he would very likely have been Seaboard's first chief executive.

SMITH, JOHN W. b. July 20, 1900, Baltimore, Maryland. d. May 1972, Richmond, Virginia. Starting in Seaboard Air Line corporate engineering in 1925, Smith oversaw construction of the rail extension from West Palm Beach to Homestead, Florida, through Miami (1926). Rising through the ranks, he took tasks that led to administrative VP in 1951 and the top job a year hence. His presidency was marked by upgrading equipment and facilities. Smith is best recalled, however, for bringing on the merger with SAL's longstanding competitor, ACL. Discussions began in 1957 that led to its implementation in 1967. At that juncture Smith became successor Seaboard Coast Line's chairman and served to retirement in 1970.

SMITH, MILTON HANNIBAL. b. September 12, 1836, Green County, New York. d. February 22, 1921, Louisville, Kentucky. With a tenure of more than three decades as L&N president (1884–1886, 1891–1921), Smith was the carrier's most influential. Entering railroading as a telegrapher, he joined L&N as a freight agent (1866). His service was interrupted by a brief period with the B&O and Pennsylvania roads before returning to L&N to move up the corporate ladder. In his presidential years Smith "shaped the L&N from a small regional carrier into one of America's major railroad systems." He oversaw significant expansion of the

L&N Pacific 295 on May 16, 1941, is one of the originators of both *South Wind* and *Dixie Flagler* passenger trains. The venerated passenger consists ran alternate days and on separate routes between Florida points and Chicago. In the era prior to E-units that became commonplace in supplying motive power for such trains, locomotives like this one were key members of L&N's stable, worthy of its "The Old Reliable" slogan (*photograph by E.G. Baker, courtesy Chuck Blardone*).

company's routing, nearly doubling it. Smith presided in L&N's final golden age of home rule as ACL acquired the company but let it run independently under its own management and name; it was a transitory period for which Smith was well equipped.

SPENCER, SAMUEL. b. March 2, 1847, Columbus, Georgia. d. November 29, 1906, Lawyers, Virginia. First president of Southern Railway (1894–1906), Spencer was a Confederate soldier prior to surveying for the Savannah & Memphis in sequences that took him to several roads. Appointed manager at two lines—Virginia Midland (1877), Long Island (1878)—he made upwardly mobile steps at B&O leading to its presidency (1887). That ended when directors believed he was a pawn for financier J. P. Morgan's banking interests (1889). Morgan hired him, made him a partner (1890), letting Spencer actively share in organizing Southern Railway, launched July 1, 1894. For decades Spencer Shops repaired the carrier's rolling stock and locomotives at Spencer, North Carolina, a town named for him.

TIGRETT, ISAAC (IKE) BURTON. b. September 15, 1879, Friendship, Tennessee. d. May 2, 1954, Northwood, Tennessee. A banker-turned-rail baron, Tigrett eased into the latter as a sideline, becoming treasurer and chief fundraiser for an unremarkable shortline in west Tennessee. By 1911, he was elevated to president of that line and learned many lessons to be applied throughout his future. Eight years later he moved to the top job at a larger Gulf, Mobile & Northern which segued into Gulf, Mobile & Ohio. In 1940, he bought Mobile & Ohio. With access to Birmingham, East St. Louis (Illinois),

Jackson (Mississippi *and* Tennessee), Mobile, Montgomery, and New Orleans, he was poised to haul people and freight between the mid and upper South and Gulf Coast. His empire would eventually be extended to embrace Chicago, Kansas City, and St. Louis. A perceptive railman, Tigrett introduced streamliners to Dixie in 1935, only a year after their premier elsewhere, getting a four-year start on competition in the South. He hired young women to work on the new trains, the nation's original train hostesses. In 1949, Tigrett's GM&O became the first totally dieselized road in Dixie as the last of its steam power was retired.

WALTERS, HENRY ("HARRY"). b. September 26, 1848, Baltimore, Maryland. d. November 30, 1931, New York, New York. The son of a transportation industrialist, Harry Walters built on his dad's groundwork. He finished the dream of rail passage from the East to Florida, establishing ACL on April 21, 1900, and acquiring the Plant System in 1902. Walters' friendship with rail tycoon J. P. Morgan allowed ACL to gain control of L&N and its ancillary NC&StL (1902). ACL also took a half-interest in the Georgia Railroad and Chicago, Indianapolis & Louisville (Monon Route). Its position as a carrier from Northeast and Midwest to Dixie's lower depths was secure yielding a competitive edge in some markets.

WALTERS, WILLIAM THOMPSON. b. May 23, 1819, Liverpool, Pennsylvania. d. November 22, 1894, Baltimore, Maryland. A wealthy Baltimore mercantilist, banker and capitalist, he invested heavily in railroads of the South, tying many short lines together. At his death an account claimed he "was prominent in every great Southern company organized for transportation of freight and travel." The senior Walters laid groundwork for the ACL, a vision his son, Henry, saw completed.

WARFIELD, SOLOMON DAVIES. b. September 4, 1859, Baltimore, Maryland. d. October 24, 1927, Baltimore, Maryland. Receiver of the Seaboard Air Line Railroad in 1908-1909, the prosperous financier played a large role in shaping the company's destiny. Elected chairman of its board in 1912, he occupied the presidential suite (1918– 1927), the years in which aggressive expansion shaped SAL's permanent physical assets. Most of this was focused on Florida, where Warfield created a cross-state line extending from Coleman to West Palm Beach while he developed new territory on the west coast at St. Petersburg, Fort Myers and Naples. Earlier Baltimore's U.S. postmaster, Warfield presided over banks and Baltimore Steam Packet Company while holding numerous directorships. He exhibited a lifelong love for the South through philanthropy for the arts and environmental issues there and considered himself a Southerner.

WILLIAMS, JOHN SKELTON. b. July 6, 1865, Powhatan County, Virginia. d. November 4, 1926, Richmond, Virginia. Building on the work of predecessors, Williams was in the right place at the right time to organize Seaboard Air Line Railroad. The banker-turned-capitalist and some cohorts bought the Savannah, Americus & Montgomery Railroad (1895), then negotiated a lease linking Alabama's capital with the sea under Georgia & Alabama taxonomy. Shrewdly making subsequent deals, Williams put together a coalition of strategically placed roads to form SAL on April 10, 1900. At 34, he presided over a 850-mile mainline from Richmond to Tampa. In 1904, he borrowed to finance an extension from Atlanta to Birmingham, mistakenly turning to an enemy for help. His fortunes with SAL soon turned 180 degrees and he was out. Williams' contributions weren't over, however: he served President Woodrow Wilson as a financial officer (1913–1921). Late in life he was president of a Richmond bank and, weeks before his death, was elected chairman of a newly-reorganized Georgia-Florida Railroad.

H: Dixie Lines

The following provides an overview of railroads that figured in the development of transportation in the South during the 19th, 20th, and 21st centuries. It is not exhaustive.

Aberdeen & Asheboro — *See Raleigh, Charlotte & Southern.*

Aberdeen & Rockfish — A family-run line since 1892, A&R still operates. It moved the owners' timber and turpentine goods to market then and hauls mostly agricultural products in the modern age. A&R's 47-mile route ties Aberdeen to Fayetteville in eastern North Carolina, linked with key north-south routes of CSX Transportation (ex–SAL at Aberdeen; ex–ACL at Fayetteville) and NS at both. In the halcyon days of rail travel, A&R ran a single round-trip passenger consist Monday through Saturday.

Air-Line Railroad Company of South Carolina — Formed by Palmetto State lawmakers (1856), ALRCSC eventually came under control of a powerful Richmond & Danville along with neighboring Georgia Air-Line Railroad Company. Evidence that either laid track is missing. R&D consolidated the pair (1870), naming the combo Atlanta & Richmond Air-Line. R&D wanted tracks between Charlotte and Atlanta but couldn't build them under its own appellation. A&RAL laid rail by fall 1873. Emerging from foreclosure afterward, the route was renamed Atlanta & Charlotte Air-Line (1877). Southern Railway absorbed R&D and its ancillaries (1894).

Alabama & Gulf Coast — Dating only to 1997, A&GC maintains 425 track miles from a Pensacola, Florida, yard and base at Monroeville, Alabama. Yet it claims a heritage reaching the Civil War epoch. Over those rails people and products moved via a series of lines. The earliest was Pensacola & Mobile (1870), which opened a route from a tie with Florida & Alabama at Cantonment, Florida, to mill and logging facilities five miles west at Muscogee, Florida. Pensacola & Perdido arrived next (1874) to run five miles from yards and ports at Pensacola to Millview on the Perdido River. Passenger service was provided that early with a single P&P coach. The line joined with Pensacola, Alabama & Tennessee (later named Gulf Port Terminal Railway) to add tracks from Millview to Muscogee. More lines figured into Alabama & Gulf Coast's ancestry: Gulf, Florida & Alabama; Muscle Shoals, Birmingham & Pensacola; St. Louis–San Francisco (which ran daily passenger trains in the halcyon days); Burlington Northern; and Burlington Northern Santa Fe. A&GC gained trackage rights over Norfolk Southern from Kimbrough, Alabama, to Mobile, and over BNSF between Columbus and Amory, Mississippi.

Alabama & Vicksburg—A&V's roots date to 1831, when precursor Clinton & Vicksburg was formed to build a 30-mile route tying Vicksburg to Clinton, Mississippi. Construction began and the line changed owners in the same year (1833). Resolve remained to retire dreadfully slow oxen pulling carts to the Vicksburg wharf with 3,000 pounds of cotton, movement cited by one source as so slow "motion was scarcely perceptible." The road was mainly built by slave labor and it, too, was slow. Rail was added to Jackson (1848). C&V's name changed to Vicksburg & Jackson (1850). With moves encompassing multiple small carriers, an unbroken 152-mile route with sidings opened June 3, 1861, to cross the state from Vicksburg to Meridian. Built as narrow gauge, in 16 hours the full route was changed to standard on October 22, 1885. Beginning in 1889, taxonomy of V&M altered to Alabama & Vicksburg. Managed by Illinois Central from that year, A&V was absorbed into IC June 2, 1926. Advocates believed A&V would play a role in the nation's first transcontinental railway. The Civil War intervened; by the time it ended work was underway on a northerly course.

Alabama Great Southern—Succeeded Alabama & Chattanooga (1877), having completed 230 miles of a 293-mile route from Chattanooga to Meridian via Birmingham, some of it in northwest Georgia and most crisscrossing Alabama northeast to southwest. It was one of five carriers late in the 19th century participating in a pivotal Queen and Crescent Route between Cincinnati and New Orleans. For five years starting in 1890, AGS was jointly owned by East Tennessee, Virginia & Georgia and Richmond & Danville; from 1895, Southern Railway, the previous owners' successor, controlled AGS. Since 1982, it has been a property of Norfolk Southern.

Alabama Midland—Because his Savannah, Florida & Western ended abruptly at Bainbridge, Georgia, rich rail baron Henry B. Plant sought a means of extending the route farther west. He found it in Alabama Midland and invested heavily, providing new rails between Bainbridge and the Alabama capital at Montgomery. Shortly after the new route opened in 1890, Plant purchased it and added it to his extensive Plant System portfolio.

Albany & Northern—With origins in Albany, Florida & Northern in 1889, a 35-mile route linking southwestern Georgia townships Cordele and Albany, AF&N was leased to Savannah, Americus & Montgomery (1892). After foreclosure and sale of SA&M (1895), AF&N was reorganized as Albany & Northern. New owners (1910) altered taxonomy to Georgia, Southwestern & Gulf, intending to run passenger and freight trains from Cordele to the Gulf of Mexico. They never got beyond those 35 miles. GS&G entered receivership (1932), was dis-

solved (1942), and operated as A&N again. Southern Railway bought it (1966) and abandoned it (1977).

Albany & Salem—1847 forerunner of renamed Louisville, New Albany & Chicago (1859), which became Chicago, Indianapolis & Louisville (1897), renamed Monon (1956). Bought by L&N just as its passenger service ended (1971), still opening another freight gateway to Chicago for L&N.

Albany, Florida & Northern—*See Albany & Northern.*

Albemarle & Pantego—Formed 1887, A&P ran a 30-mile route connecting Belhaven with Mackey's Ferry, North Carolina, plus a 12-mile stem. It was folded into the original Norfolk Southern on June 1, 1891.

Alton—A Northern-based carrier until merging into Gulf, Mobile & Ohio on May 31, 1947. With roots in multiple precursors traced to Alton & Sangamon (1847), Alton was owned by Baltimore & Ohio (1931–1942). Its impact stemmed from linking Chicago, St. Louis and Kansas City. That was a draw to GM&O with a main from Illinois to the Gulf; it helped create more traffic between the Windy and Crescent cities. Alton ran George Pullman's first sleepers and diners from Chicago to East St. Louis (1859). GM&O was the final carrier to offer sleepers on that route, through 1969.

Alton & Sangamon—*See Alton.*

Americus, Preston & Lumpkin—Chartered (1884), a regional carrier based in Americus, Georgia; reached Lumpkin (1886), extended from Louvale to Abbeville (1887). Name altered to Savannah, Americus & Montgomery (1888) as tiny southeast Georgia village of Lyons linked 263 miles to Montgomery. Steamboats at Abbeville took traffic down Ocmulgee and Altamaha rivers to Brunswick and Savannah ports. John Skelton Williams and cohorts bought SA&M and extended track from Lyons to Savannah, giving uninterrupted Savannah–Montgomery rail route as Georgia & Alabama. Williams soon became president of a newly organized SAL (1900).

Amtrak, a.k.a. National Railroad Passenger Corporation—A federally subsidized and supervised for-profit company that assumed operation of the nation's passenger rail service on May 1, 1971. It was created after Congress approved allowing the existing railroads to abandon that traffic and to focus on more profitable freight shipping.

Anniston & Atlantic—*See Eastern Alabama.*

Appomattox—Nine-mile City Point Railroad in central Virginia, formed 1836, is the original rail of Norfolk & Western. Reorganized in 1847 as Appomattox Railroad, then sold to Southside Railroad (1854). Station at Appomattox was site of final Civil War battle (1865). Southside and two more lines blended as Atlantic, Mississippi & Ohio (1870), renamed Norfolk & Western (1881).

Arkansas & Ozarks — *See Eureka Springs.*

Arkansas, Louisiana & Mississippi — Begun 1906 to link Monroe, Louisiana, and Pine Bluff, Arkansas. Pine Bluff was never accessed; the line ended at Hamburg and Crossett (1908). Entering receivership (1913), reorganized (1914), it leased Arkansas, Louisiana & Gulf and Ashley, Drew & Northern. Many transactions followed including property abandonments. Recent owner Georgia-Pacific reorganized again, adopting AL&M as the name (1991).

Ashburn, Sylvester & Camilla — After Hawkinsville & Florida Southern entered receivership in 1922, the Ashburn–Camilla route of H&FS ancillary Gulf Line Railway was bought by a private investor. Ashburn, Sylvester & Camilla was its new name as a subsidiary of Georgia Northern Railway. Southern Railway acquired AS&C (1966) and merged it into Georgia Northern (1972). In the 1980s, much of the original route was abandoned.

Asheville & Craggy Mountain — Organized 1890, A&CM initially was a steam-powered single-car open-coach trolley from Asheville, North Carolina, to Golf Course. Electrified (1900) when a 1.5-mile extension to Locust Gap was added (1902), the little conveyance returned to steam power. A&CM also owned Asheville Southern, a route totally within Buncombe County connecting with Southern Railway that persisted principally through the French Broad River valley. SOU purchased A&CM and its subsidiary (1906), later absorbing

it (1926). It's unclear when A&CM quit running, although there is evidence that may not have been until in the 1940s.

Asheville & Eastern Tennessee — When A&ET purchased Weaverville Electric Railway & Power Company (1909), it gained not only a local utility but an electrified interurban rail line running since 1901. It linked western North Carolina towns Grace and Weaverville with downtown Asheville's Pack Square. At its zenith it made more than 10 round trips daily. A serious accident finally pushed it into receivership (1922). In 1925, new owner Asheville Electric Company (another utility) renamed it Carolina Power & Light Company (a curious moniker for a rail line). The operation chugged along the mountains to 1934, when it finally reached the end of the line.

Asheville & Spartanburg — Forerunner Spartanburg & Asheville (chartered 1873) commenced building a rail route in 1876 from Spartanburg, South Carolina, to the North Carolina state line "in the direction of Asheville." Encountering financial trouble early, S&A entered receivership after just 26 miles were finished. Reorganized as A&S (1891), construction toward Asheville faced daunting obstacles. A lack of capital prevented A&S from circumventing Saluda Mountain, a steep 4.7 percent grade. So the work proceeded slowly. Twenty-nine men died on Saluda during construction. The first train to the summit arrived July 4, 1878. Thirteen months hence the road accessed

The ex–Southern Railway passenger station in Biltmore Village at Asheville, North Carolina, is captured on May 26, 2007. It's next to Southern's Saluda line south to Spartanburg, Columbia and Charleston, South Carolina, on which a portion of the *Carolina Special* ran. Those tracks were closed just beyond Hendersonville, North Carolina, a few years ago. The Biltmore station, dubbed "The Depot" in the modern era, was a trendy restaurant and lounge which ceased in 2009, leaving the future uncertain (*courtesy Michael B. Robbins*).

Hendersonville, North Carolina. It reached Best (now Biltmore, an Asheville suburb) in 1886. Tracks laid at 5-foot gauge were standardized in the late 1880s. Richmond & Danville began operating S&A/ A&S (1881). When that carrier helped form Southern Railway (1894), A&S was folded into SOU. The route became vital to SOU not only for transporting freight but delivering passenger consists between cities like Cincinnati, Louisville and St. Louis to the northwest and Charleston, Greensboro and Jacksonville to the south and east.

Atlanta & Birmingham Air Line—Seaboard Air Line renamed a new holding, East & West Railroad (linking Cartersville, Georgia and Pell City, Alabama) as A&BAL in 1903. Forty-three miles of new rail was laid from northwest Atlanta's Howells community to E&W's tracks at Rockmart, Georgia. At the other end new rail was laid from Coal City, Alabama (now Wattsville), to Birmingham. It created an unbroken SAL route between Atlanta and Birmingham (1904) with Seaboard absorbing A&BAL (1909).

Atlanta & Charlotte Air-Line—Reorganization of Atlanta & Richmond Air-Line (1877) resulted in the new taxonomy A&CAL. A&RAL built a route between Atlanta and Charlotte accessing Suwanee, Buford, Gainesville, Lula, and Toccoa, Georgia; Westminister, Seneca, Easley, Saluda, Greenville, Greer, Spartanburg, and Gaffney, South Carolina; and Kings Mountain, Gastonia, and Lowell, North Carolina. Fostered by Richmond & Danville, a precursor of Southern Railway (1894), the route became a major segment of Southern's main. Travelers were carried over it maybe on a dozen passenger consists daily in opening decades of the 20th century.

Atlanta & Richmond Air-Line—Formed 1870 in North Carolina and owned by Richmond & Danville, A&RAL was a consolidation of Air-Line Railroad Company of South Carolina and Georgia Air-Line Railroad Company. R&D constructed a route from Charlotte to Atlanta (completed 1873). R&D's charter prevented it from doing that under its own nomenclature. Entering receivership a year later, A&RAL was sold under foreclosure (1876) and reorganized as Atlanta & Charlotte Air-Line Railway (1877).

Atlanta & St. Andrews Bay—Founded by an individual in 1905, completed in 1908, A&SAB's 82-mile route tied Panama City, Florida, with Dothan, Alabama (a far cry from Atlanta). Trackage rights over CofG let trains reach Atlanta, nonetheless, in a roundabout way: from Dothan to Albany, Macon, and the Peach State capital. Beyond CofG, two more interconnections with Class 1 carriers (ACL, L&N) occurred. While hauling freight (wood and wood products mostly) was its chief motivation, A&SAB transported passengers, too (1908–1957).

By 1947, all its power was converted from steam to diesel. Granted Class 1 status, it was the nation's first Class 1 railway to be 100 percent dieselized. After its founder died, A&SAB was owned by some big names—Coca-Cola, United Fruit, International Paper. When a new owner took over in 1994 it was renamed Bay Line. It merged with A&G Railroad (1996), allowing Bay Line access to Abbeville-Grimes tracks. Bay Line's route now is from Panama City to Abbeville, Alabama, with trackage rights on CSX from Dothan to Grimes, Alabama.

Atlanta & West Point—Began in 1847 as Atlanta & LaGrange with a terminus at East Point, a few miles below Atlanta. Extended 80 miles to access hamlet of West Point, Georgia, in 1854; name altered to A&WP three years hence. Georgia Railroad financed construction and controlled it; that passed to CofG, L&N, and ACL. In joint ownership with Western Railway of Alabama, pair was dubbed "West Point Route." The dual lines were vital to Southern Railway's 1200-mile course from Mobile to Washington, D.C.

Atlanta, Birmingham & Atlantic, a.k.a. Atlanta, Birmingham & Coast—Formed to buy Atlanta & Birmingham (1905) chartered as Waycross Air Line (1887), AB&A was a 641-mile route from Waycross in southeast Georgia to Atlanta and Birmingham. After foreclosure (1922), ACL bought it (1926) and altered its appellation to AB&C. The line gave ACL prime connections for Florida traffic from the Midwest.

Atlanta, Birmingham & Coast—*See Atlanta, Birmingham & Atlantic.*

Atlantic & East Carolina—*See Atlantic & North Carolina.*

Atlantic & Gulf—Chartered 1856, A&G's route took it from Screven to Thomasville in south Georgia by 1860. It and Savannah, Albany & Gulf merged during the war. A&G and Pensacola & Georgia fused to add a stem from Lawton (now Dupont), Georgia, to Live Oak, Florida, in that same era. Interrupted earlier, A&G was extended to Bainbridge, Georgia (1867). Rail tycoon Henry B. Plant bought the line at a foreclosure sale (1879) and renamed it Savannah, Florida & Western. It had a 237-mile main from Bainbridge to Savannah with stems placing its total mileage above 350.

Atlantic & North Carolina—Chartered in 1854 with two-thirds of its capital from the state, A&NC's debut saw trains running between Goldsboro and Charlotte (1856). Ninety-six more miles opened from Goldsboro to Beaufort Harbor via New Bern (1858). Efforts to join A&NC with North Carolina Railroad began in 1866 but it took 123 years to consummate the deal (1989). North Carolina leased the road to Southern Railway for 99 years (1896). A&NC's operating company was renamed Atlantic & East Carolina (1939), bought by

Southern Railway and given subsidiary status (1957). The line merged into NC to open an unbroken pathway from Morehead City to Charlotte (1989).

Atlantic Coast Line—The name can be traced to 1871, when William T. Walters and some cohorts purchased some smaller lines connecting Richmond, Virginia, to the port city of Wilmington, North Carolina. It was called Atlantic Coast Line of Railroads, Atlantic Coast Line System, Atlantic Coast Line Company, and in 1900, Atlantic Coast Line Railroad. Following a plethora of mergers and acquisitions, ACL was to eventually operate in Virginia, North and South Carolina, Georgia, Florida and Alabama, the feather in its cap being service to the vacation state of Florida. This was one of two highly successful rail endeavors in the South (the other being rival Seaboard Air Line) at a time when most rail lines would have preferred to move only freight. Favorable routes, attention to maintenance and passenger service, efficient double tracking, creative marketing and modern equipment and facilities were factors in its favor. It merged with competitor SAL in 1967 to form Seaboard Coast Line Railroad, which was absorbed by the CSX Corporation in 1980. *See Chapter 3.*

Atlantic, Gulf & West India Transit—A striking new moniker given Florida Railroad (1872), more commonly dubbed Transit Road. It was sold under foreclosure (1881), re-emerging as Florida Transit Railroad. Earlier, Transit Road revived a venture predating the War Between the States, adding a branch from Waldo south to Tampa Bay and Charlotte Harbor. Before the war 45 miles of right-of-way was bought and graded between Waldo and Ocala. Transit Road organized Peninsular Railroad (1876) to complete the mission. In 1879, Peninsular opened the route from Waldo to Ocala with a two-mile stem to Silver Springs, a major tourist attraction in the century ahead. Transit Road leased the operation to Peninsular to 1883 when Peninsular joined with it to form Florida Transit & Peninsular.

Atlantic, Mississippi & Ohio—Formed in 1870 after a trio of Virginia carriers—Norfolk & Petersburg, Southside, Virginia & Tennessee—pooled resources to gain a line from Norfolk to Bristol, Virginia–Tennessee, expecting to go farther. AM&O entered receivership in a nationwide panic (1873). Pennsylvania Railroad gained control at a foreclosure sale (1881), the year it was renamed Norfolk & Western Railroad. After another foreclosure, it was renamed N&W Railway (1896).

Atlantic, Valdosta & Western—Chartered 1897, AV&W constructed a route between Jacksonville and Valdosta via Fargo, Georgia, touted as the "Jacksonville Short Line." Georgia, Southern & Florida bought AV&W (1902); it's now part of Norfolk Southern.

Augusta & Savannah—Preceded by Augusta & Waynesboro (opened 1854), it was relabeled A&S on February 16, 1856, linking Augusta to Millen, Georgia. Leased by Central Railroad and Banking Company (1862) and Central of Georgia (1895), A&S was bought by CofG and absorbed in 1948.

Augusta & Waynesboro—53-mile route from Millen, Georgia, to Augusta opened in 1854, chartered in 1838. Renamed Augusta & Savannah (1856), six years hence it was leased to Central Railroad and Banking Company and—in 1895—to Central of Georgia. CofG bought and absorbed A&S in 1948.

Auto-Train—AT Corporation ferried passengers and their vehicles between Lorton, Virginia, and Sanford, Florida (1971–1981). The advantages of the concept survived that unlucky operator who departed after failing dismally. Amtrak resumed the promising service on its own, however (1983). The segment, running daily, has proven to be one of its most profitable ventures and plays to a near capacity crowd much of the time.

Baltimore & Ohio—One of the most powerful Eastern carriers whose quest to link its namesake city with lucrative Ohio River traffic originated with horse-drawn passenger carts (1830). B&O built a mainline through West Virginia and a stem to Louisville before reaching a western terminus at St. Louis (1893). Its control shifted to Chesapeake & Ohio (1963), launching the Chessie System so-named in 1972, merging at last into CSX (1980). *See Appendix B.*

Barnesville & Thomaston—In some sources, the Georgia names 16 miles apart are reversed; the line was chartered in 1839 and opened 17 years later. Reorganized as Upson County Railroad (1860) and destroyed in the Civil War, it was rebuilt by 1870. Central of Georgia bought it in 1891.

Barren County—*See Glasgow.*

Bay Line—*See Atlanta & St. Andrews Bay.*

Birmingham & Northwestern—An early 1900s 48-mile shortline struggling to be viable, it ran across west Tennessee from Dyersburg to Jackson. Banker Ike Tigrett got his start in a new career as B&N treasurer and fund-raiser and accepted the line's presidency (1911). Soon he was a director of a more promising Gulf, Mobile & Northern, elected its president in 1919. Tigrett's career as a rail tycoon was set with B&N having pointed the way.

Birmingham Southern—In 1878, tracks were laid from Birmingham to where Pratt City, Alabama, is today. In 1887, they extended to Ensley, carrying coal from Pratt Fields to blast furnaces at Ensley and Birmingham. L&N and Southern bought BS (1899), selling it to Tennessee Coal, Iron & Railroad Company (1906). After U.S. Steel bought the plants and mines served by BS, it acquired BS. BS was sold to transportation holding outfit Transtar (1988). Mobile & Ohio, a precursor of Gulf, Mobile & Ohio, negotiated for a connection from Montgomery to Birmingham with BS (1899). L&N and Southern, controlling BS stock, voided that. Having awakened a sleeping giant, however, SOU took control of M&O (1901).

Blue Ridge—Chartered 1852, it's a railroad with a grand design that wasn't realized. Proposed in 1936 by John C. Calhoun, who envisioned a rail line descending across the lower Appalachians to Charleston, South Carolina, BR was to connect Knoxville, Tennessee, with existing tracks to the coast at Anderson, South Carolina. But the 34 miles of rails laid between Anderson and Walhalla in 1859, plus a 10-mile extension from Anderson to Belton, was all. Southern Railway acquired it in 1894, reorganized it in 1901, and ran several passenger trains daily between Walhalla and Belton.

Blue Ridge—Reaching Clifton Forge, BR was leased to Virginia Central that year (1857) with four tunnels bored through the Blue Ridge Mountains. Among the world's longest, one was 4,263 feet between Mechum's River and Waynesboro (1858). It cost nearly a half-billion in today's dollars yet opened the Shenandoah Valley and west with an easy route for western Virginia militiamen to reach Richmond if summoned in the Civil War.

Bonhomie & Hattiesburg Southern—See *New Orleans, Mobile & Chicago*.

Bonlee & Western—An example of a community-oriented shortline, family-run B&W included a single coach pulled by steam engine that ran 11 miles between Chatham County, North Carolina's small hamlets of Bonlee and Bennett in the state's central Piedmont district. While most of its income was produced by hauling timber to a Southern Railway connection at its namesake town, B&W provided passenger service for area residents from its inception in late 1910 to 1927. The line was abandoned in 1932.

Boston & Albany—See *Georgia Northern*.

Brinson—See *Savannah & Northwestern*.

Brunswick & Albany—Taking over a defunct Brunswick & Florida (1869), B&A replaced tracks confiscated by the Confederacy in 1863. Within a few months it was running trains again between Brunswick and Tebeauville (now Waycross), Georgia. Trains didn't reach Albany until late 1871. An earlier route to Glenmore was dumped. When bonds were invalidated by the state's General Assembly, B&A fell into receivership (1872). Sold the next year, it was reorganized again later as Brunswick & Western (1882).

Brunswick & Florida—Chartered 1835, B&F expected to open south Georgia and north Florida trade to the Brunswick, Georgia, port. In two dozen years B&F laid only 60 rail miles from Brunswick to Glenmore (Ware County). A branch to Albany

ran but a few miles to Waresboro when the Civil War halted it. The Confederacy seized B&F in 1863, taking up its tracks to satisfy martial needs elsewhere. In 1869, $6 million in state-backed bonds helped a private investor who reorganized B&F as Brunswick & Albany.

Brunswick & Western—In 1882, B&W—tying Albany and Brunswick, Georgia, over a 171-mile route—was preceded by Brunswick & Florida (1835) and Brunswick & Albany (1869). Bought by Plant System's Savannah, Florida & Western (1884), B&W was absorbed into that line (1901). An extensive Plant System was acquired the following year by Atlantic Coast Line.

Buena Vista & Ellaville—A line with persistent nomenclature and location problems, it was chartered as Buena Vista (1880) before BV&E five years later. Oglethorpe, Georgia, was the intended eastern terminus; that was altered to Andersonville, then Americus. Controlled by Central of Georgia, BV&E mingled with a handful of CofG roads, blended in CofG's Savannah & Western (1888). A 30-mile stretch from Americus to Buena Vista opened (1889) as a 35-mile tie to Columbus was built.

Cairo & Fulton—See *Little Rock & Fort Smith*.

Canadian National—Illinois Central Corporation today is part of CN Railway Company. IC is the only major American rail carrier to operate under its own moniker nearly 15 decades (1851–2001) with only fundamental alterations. For a short while from 1972 it used the handle Illinois Central Gulf Railroad after IC and Gulf, Mobile & Ohio merged.

Cape Fear & Northern—Chartered 1892, constructed from Durham to Dunn, North Carolina, 1898–1903, renamed 1906. See *Durham & Southern*.

Cape Fear & Yadkin Valley—Chartered in 1879 when Western Railroad of North Carolina and Mt. Airy & Ore Knob merged. In 1881, CF&YV purchased Fayetteville & Florence. Reorganized 1883, it entered a pact with South Carolina Pacific to interconnect at the state line—SCP was to run north from Bennettsville, South Carolina to the border. Construction south from Fayetteville reached the state line in October 1884 and Bennettsville in December. CF&YV added extensions to Greensboro (1884), Mt. Airy (1887), and Wilmington (1890). It fell into receivership (1894). For three decades an imbroglio languished until the state Supreme Court rendered a verdict (1924). CF&YV passed into and out of many owners' hands meanwhile, some multiple times. Southern Railway finally gained the northern segment; the southern went to Atlantic Coast Line. In 1894, ACL took over CF&YV and dispensed with some redundant routes. Still more miles were trimmed as Seaboard

Air Line and ACL merged to establish Seaboard Coast Line (1967), part of a future CSX Transportation (1980).

Carolina & Northwestern — Completed in 1884 by Chester & Lenoir, a 22-mile narrow gauge line (standardized 1902) connecting Lenoir and Hickory, North Carolina. C&N was absorbed into Southern Railway later. Owning C&N when it purchased an original Norfolk Southern Railway (with tracks from Charlotte to Norfolk) in 1974, SOU dubbed both auxiliaries NS. But as the owner merged with Norfolk & Western (1982), its subsidiary was relabeled C&N to free Norfolk Southern, chosen for the combined carriers. After Rail Link didn't renew a four-year lease in 1994, NS sold C&N to Caldwell County, which leased the shortline to Caldwell County Railroad.

Carolina, Atlantic & Western — 1914 heir to Georgetown & Western and North & South Carolina railways, CA&W operated only months until SAL absorbed it (1915). It gave SAL a second main from Hamlet, North Carolina, to Savannah, Georgia. The 263-mile route dubbed "East Carolina Line" accessed Dillon, Poston, Andrews, Charleston, and Wiggins. SAL gained sizeable operating savings through tonnage increases with a three-tenths percent grade from Charleston to Savannah. Fewer freight tons took the route by Columbia. "East Carolina Line" was left almost totally for cargo like perishables from Florida needing high-speed transit.

Carolina Central — CC grew from forerunner Wilmington, Charlotte, and Rutherfordton (1857). WC&R finally linked Rutherfordton in the foothills with the Piedmont's Charlotte and coastal Wilmington, 267 miles distant. Reorganized as CC in 1873, rails tied Wilmington and Charlotte only. Controlled by Seaboard & Roanoke by 1883, CC accessed Rutherfordton in 1887. By 1893, it operated as Seaboard Air Line Railway and folded into SAL's 1900 startup. The route offered a secondary main that saw daily passenger traffic between Charlotte and the coast into the late 1950s, and ferried Atlanta SAL consists along its tracks between Hamlet and Monroe.

Carolina, Clinchfield & Ohio — Principally a coal-hauler, CC&O also carried passengers on its 1909 route from Spartanburg, South Carolina, to Elkhorn, Kentucky (terminus reached 1915) via Marion, North Carolina; Erwin, Tennessee; and Dante, Virginia. Leased by Atlantic Coast Line and Louisville & Nashville (1925), Clinchfield (new name) finally proceeded under "Family Lines," Seaboard System and CSX flags.

Central Mississippi — Trackage rights over CM allowed Illinois Central to access Jackson, Tennessee, in the early 1870s. Within a few years CM helped form IC wholly owned ancillary Chicago,

St. Louis & New Orleans as IC improved access to those points.

Central of Georgia — This railway was shorter than some of its surrounding contemporaries, but was celebrated for two famed consists and for providing a vital link through the Peach State. The Central Rail Road and Canal Company was chartered in late 1833 by businessmen in the port city of Savannah, Georgia, who perceived a threat to commerce from a new rail connection between Charleston, South Carolina, a port city 100 miles to their north, to the interior of Georgia. Construction was launched in 1835; by 1843 it had reached the periphery of populous Macon. In 1851 a bridge over the Ocmulgee River extended it into Macon proper, where it tied into the Macon & Western railroad to form a link between the coast and Atlanta (then Marthasville) and form Central's main line. A connection to Augusta & Waynesville provided access to Augusta. A string of acquisitions, name changes, mergers and financial woes ensued. In 1888 the Richmond Terminal Company gained control of Central; in time RTC would become part of Southern Railway. In its heyday, the Central boasted two showpiece passenger consists named for famed race horses: the *Nancy Hanks* (daily between Savannah and Atlanta) and the *Man O' War* (daily between Columbus and Atlanta). *See Chapter 4.*

Charleston & Hamburg — Completed October 1833, it linked raw materials, fresh produce and finished goods from the interior arriving at Hamburg on the Savannah River with the port at Charleston 136 miles east. C&H is best recalled for running the first passenger-hauling steam locomotive in America (1830) and providing the first such scheduled train service.

Charleston & Savannah — Chartered 1854, C&S laid 120 miles of track to tie two key Southeast antebellum ports. Sections were savagely attacked in General William T. Sherman's campaign in 1865 as the War Between the States drew to a close. The full line didn't reopen until repairs were done (1870). Entering bankruptcy (1873), C&S was sold to rail tycoon Henry B. Plant (1880), added to a growing inventory of Plant System roads. Plant holdings were bought by Atlantic Coast Line (1902); when Seaboard Coast Line appeared (1967), the route went there and later to CSX (1980). In the heyday a 20-mile portion from Hardeeville to Savannah allowed Southern Railway to link its Columbia–Hardeeville route.

Charleston & Western Carolina — Organized 1896, it extended northwesterly from Port Royal, South Carolina, to Augusta, Georgia, into South Carolina again to Anderson and Spartanburg. Roots included Port Royal & Augusta (1878) and Port Royal & Western Carolina (1886), both with predecessors. Atlantic Coast Line Railroad of South

Carolina gained control in 1897, with successor ACL taking over early in the 20th century. C&WC didn't merge into the parent until 1959.

Charleston, Sumter & Northern— A route claimed by Atlantic Coast Line (1900), CS&N had been absorbed by Wilmington & Weldon (1895).

Charlotte & South Carolina —Organized 1851 as a narrow-gauge line, C&SC was upgraded to standard (1869). That year it merged with Columbia & Augusta to form Charlotte, Columbia & Augusta, a 191-mile route between endpoints. C&SC was consolidated by Richmond & Danville (1886) and into R&D's successor, Southern Railway (1894). Rails from the Carolinas to Georgia were an integral part of SOU passenger traffic. Its most durable train in the heyday was *Augusta Special*, daily between Washington, Charlotte, Columbia and Augusta and connecting service north to New York and Boston. Norfolk Southern has controlled those rails since 1982.

Charlotte, Columbia & Augusta —*See Charlotte & South Carolina.*

Chatham —*See Raleigh & Augusta Air-Line.*

Chattanooga, Rome & Columbus— Launched as Rome & Carrollton (1881), never laying track under that sobriquet, a renamed CR&C (1887) initially built a 20-mile narrow gauge road from Rome to Cedartown, Georgia. It was replaced by standard width and a 140-mile route opened in 1888 tying Chattanooga and Carrollton. Owners intended to persist 90 miles south to Columbus but a Central of Georgia auxiliary, Savannah & Western, bought it first (1891). CofG and S&W went into foreclosure soon after; when they emerged in 1894, federal judges returned CR&C to previous owners. Facing more financial hurdles, CR&C was sold again (1897) and renamed Chattanooga, Rome & Southern. CR&S was bought by CofG May 16, 1901.

Chattanooga, Rome & Southern—*See Chattanooga, Rome & Columbus.*

Cheraw & Darlington—Chartered in 1849, opened 1853, awarded rights of Northwestern Railroad by South Carolina legislature (1863). C&D was part of an 1898 amalgamation that folded into Atlantic Coast Line (1900).

Chesapeake & Ohio Railway— Largely a bituminous coal hauler, the C&O nonetheless made its mark as a long distance people mover with a modern fleet and emphasis on creature comforts. It connected major Eastern and Midwestern cities with a mainline from the Atlantic seaboard to the Ohio River and numerous branches. It changed hands frequently over its lifetime and was for a time part of the Chessie System with its trademark kitten logo, and eventually provided the "C" in the modern day CSX Corporation. One of its precursors, the Blue Ridge Railroad, famously conquered the first barrier of mountains to the west with a quartet of tunnels. Another precursor, Virginia Central, was an important transportation link to the Confederacy in the Civil War, and as such was damaged severely by the Union. After the war new life was infused by New York capitalist Collis P. Huntington, under whose watch the Chesapeake & Ohio Railroad grew. After the Panic of 1872 it went into receivership (1875) and came out as the Chesapeake & Ohio Railway (1878). Later owners included magnates J.P. Morgan, William K. Vanderbilt and siblings O.P. and M.J. Van Sweringen. *See Chapter 5.*

Chesapeake, Ohio & Southwestern —Built between 1854 and 1892 with a mainline between Louisville and Memphis, CO&S was acquired by rail magnate Collis P. Huntington. He sought a Memphis tie with a carrier to haul traffic to New Orleans to meet Southern Pacific and persist to the

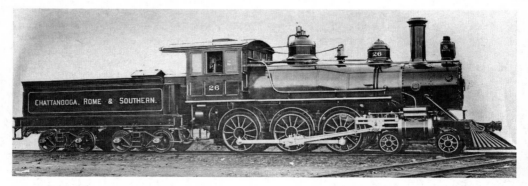

A 1898 Baldwin-built 4-6-0 steam locomotive 26 and its tender furnish motive power for Chattanooga, Rome & Southern, 1897 successor to Chattanooga, Rome & Columbus with ancestry to 1881. Independency was fleeting for the fledgling carrier; in a quadrennial CR&S folded into a better positioned CofG (1901). The engine was sold to CofG subsidiary Wrightsville & Tennille in 1917, its ultimate disposition unknown (**courtesy Allen Tuten** and **Central of Georgia Railway Historical Society**).

West Coast. An aggressive Illinois Central outfoxed Huntington, however, buying multiple mid South routes and, by 1893, CO&S.

Chicago & Alton—Formed 1862, growing out of a string of predecessors, it chartered the Alton & St. Louis in 1864, extending rails to East St. Louis, Illinois. All of it merged into Gulf, Mobile & Ohio (1947). *See Alton.*

Chicago & Eastern Illinois—A Midwest carrier with a route between St. Louis and Chicago, it was formed as a trio of lines merged (1877). Acquired by Frisco (1902), it was run in the ground and into bankruptcy (1913). Pulling out (1920s), C&EI returned to receivership (1933–1940). After long prosperity, MoPac gained control (1967) and L&N—which relied on trackage rights to and from Chicago—bought a route from Evansville, Indiana, to Woodland Junction, Illinois. It gave L&N a gateway to the Windy City. C&EI vanished in 1976 when it merged into MoPac. Its tracks are now controlled by MoPac successor Union Pacific and L&N successor CSX.

Chicago & Mississippi—An antecedent of the Alton, C&M was a name change for the Alton & Sangamon in the early 1850s. In a continuing progression of new taxonomy, its moniker shifted to St. Louis, Alton & Chicago about 1855, and Chicago & Alton about 1862. *See Alton.*

Chicago, Indianapolis & Louisville—From 1897 to 1956, known as Monon thereafter, it ran almost totally in Indiana. It was renamed Monon because its four key routes met at Monon, Indiana (to the municipalities named plus Michigan City, Indiana). Its final passenger train ran September 30, 1967. In 1971, it merged into L&N, giving that carrier another direct route to the Windy City. Today much of its right-of-way is operated by CSX. Genealogy began with New Albany & Salem (1847), renamed Louisville, New Albany & Chicago (1859), combined with Chicago & Indianapolis Air Line Railway (1881), and reorganized as CI&L (1897).

Chicago, Rock Island & Pacific—*See Rock Island.*

Chicago, St. Louis & New Orleans—In 1874, Illinois Central reorganized a couple of shortlines into New Orleans, St. Louis & Chicago. In 1877, NOSL&C was broken into a trio of roads: New Orleans; Jackson & Northern; Central Mississippi. They were eventually consolidated as Chicago, St. Louis & New Orleans, a wholly owned subsidiary of IC. Like many Southern tracks of that vintage the route from Cairo, Illinois, to New Orleans was built on a 5-foot gauge. On July 29, 1881, the 550-mile line was converted to a standard 4-foot, 8.5-inch gauge in one day.

Choctaw, Oklahoma & Gulf—In 1894, CO&G took over the assets of Choctaw Coal and Railway Company and launched a large scale expansion.

Based in Oklahoma, it made multiple advancements there before reaching out to add Memphis & Little Rock (chartered 1853) to its portfolio (1898). Choctaw completed the 151-mile M&LR route that included a bridge over the Arkansas River at Little Rock. It then extended its Oklahoma lines to connect at Little Rock. CO&G was bought by Rock Island on April 1, 1904.

Cincinnati, New Orleans & Texas Pacific—CNO&TP is a route from Cincinnati to Chattanooga that now forms a portion of Norfolk Southern. Tracks access Lexington, Danville and Somerset, Kentucky, and Oakdale, Tennessee. In its heyday as a passenger route CNO&TP witnessed several SOU consists moving daily on its tracks between Cincy and destinations like Atlanta, Jacksonville, Memphis, and New Orleans. The line is owned by the City of Cincinnati and leased to CNO&TP under a pact ending 2026, the only long-distance carrier of a U.S. municipality. Fearing losing Ohio River shipping in a downturn, the city built it in 1869. CNO&TP is now a wholly owned subsidiary of NS. In excess of 50 freights ply the route daily.

City Point—Chartered 1836, it created a nine-mile rail link from City Point (renamed Hopewell) to Petersburg in central Virginia—the original N&W trackage. City Point was sold to the City of Petersburg in 1847 and renamed Appomattox Railroad.

Clinchfield—*See Carolina, Clinchfield & Ohio, also Appendix B.*

Clinton & Vicksburg—*See Alabama & Vicksburg.*

Columbia & Augusta—*See Charlotte & South Carolina.*

Columbia & Greenville—*See Greenville & Columbia.*

Columbia, Newberry & Laurens—*See Greenville & Columbia.*

Columbus & Atlanta Air Line—A line organized in 1870 and overtaken by Central of Georgia by that decade's end.

Columbus & Rome—Initially operating as North & South Railroad (1871), C&R reached 23 miles to Hamilton, Georgia by 1875, a year after entering receivership. It got to Greenville by 1888, 50 miles from Columbus, when it was folded into Central of Georgia's Savannah & Western line.

Columbus & Western—Begun to tie Columbus, Georgia, and Birmingham, Alabama (1880). C&W initially obtained Savannah & Memphis, a 66-mile route from Opelika to Goodwater, Alabama, then bought a 55-mile branch of Western Railroad of Alabama from Columbus to Opelika (1882). C&W built an extension from Goodwater to Birmingham (1888) and merged into the Savannah & Western, a Central of Georgia auxiliary, that year.

Covington & Lexington—*See Kentucky Central.*

Covington & Ohio—Part of a planned rail link in the 1850s between eastern Virginia and the Ohio River, C&O was never formally incorporated. Instead it formed part of Chesapeake & Ohio (1868), opened to traffic in 1873. In the early 21st century, it supplies some of a CSX path from West Virginia bituminous coal mines to Newport News coal piers.

CSX Transportation—Class 1 freight carrier operating primarily in the eastern U.S., formed 1980, when Chessie and Seaboard systems merged.

Dublin & Southwestern—Chartered in 1904, it intended to build south from Dublin, Georgia, to Eastman (completed 1905) and Abbeville (uncompleted). Bought by Wrightsville & Tennille (1907), D&S was operated separately as a branch off W&T's mainline from Tennille to Hawkinsville via Dublin. Original D&S tracks were abandoned (1941).

Dublin & Wrightsville—*See Wrightsville & Tennille.*

Durham & Charlotte—*See Raleigh, Charlotte & Southern.*

Durham & South Carolina—Organized in 1905 to replace Mount Hope Valley (organized August 1904), never starting construction. D&SC built from a point on Durham & Southern almost 28 miles to Bonsal, North Carolina, finished June 1906. Another 10 miles was added from Bonsal to Duncan (1913). From the tie with Durham & Southern, D&SC ran to a small depot a quarter-mile east of Durham's Union Station via rails of D&S and Seaboard Air Line. Original Norfolk Southern leased D&SC route (1920). Five years later NS laid tracks into Durham, contending with N&W for American Tobacco Company traffic. In 1957, NS bought D&SC.

Durham & Southern—Preceded by Cape Fear & Northern chartered in 1892 with construction from 1898 to 1903, the road's moniker was altered to D&S (1906). Running southeast from Durham, North Carolina, it persisted through Apex, Fuquay-Varina, Angier, and Coats to a terminus at Dunn, northeast of Fayetteville. A stem to Erwin left the mainline below Coats. Angier and Coats sprang up because D&S was there. The line operated to late 1981 when Seaboard Coast Line, heir to Atlantic Coast Line and Seaboard Air Line, acquired it. D&S shifted to CSX Transportation which absorbed SCL. In late 1987, CSX sold the rails to Aberdeen & Rockfish which chartered Dunn-Erwin, later merged into A&R (1990). Abandoned in 2000, D-E was transformed into a 5.3-mile rail trail. Mainly a freight-hauler, D&S and precursor CF&N ran passenger trains. They were reduced to mixed trains about 1943; human transport ended in 1950.

East Alabama—*See East Alabama & Cincinnati.*

East Alabama & Cincinnati—Chartered 1868, EA&C planned a 37-mile route between Opelika and Roanoke, Alabama, but finished just 20 miles from Opelika to Buffalo before foreclosure (1880). Renamed East Alabama, it opened to Roanoke (1887). Central of Georgia bought EA (1888), folded it into Savannah & Western, and it was reacquired by CofG (1895).

East & West—Chartered 1882, E&W began building a 64-mile winding narrow gauge line from Esom Hill in western Georgia to Broken Arrow in eastern Alabama. E&W bought a 46-mile route from Esom Hill to Cartersville, Cherokee Railroad, in 1886. Intents to extend to Gainesville on the east end, connecting with Atlanta & Charlotte Air-Line Railway there, and connecting Birmingham on the west were never completed. Bankruptcy intervened (1888). In 1902, Seaboard Air Line bought E&W, dispatching it to ancillary Atlanta & Birmingham Air-Line. After a re-build by SAL, E&W tracks were a major factor in helping SAL access Birmingham.

Eastern Alabama—EA connects Talladega and Sylacauga, Alabama. An earlier separate line linking Wellington and Anniston, Alabama was abandoned (1992). Constructed as narrow-gauge shortline Anniston & Atlantic (1883), its control passed to L&N (1889) via its Alabama Mineral Railroad. L&N folded into Seaboard System (1982) and CSX Transportation (1986). Since then the road was acquired by Eastern Alabama Railway (1990), an ancillary of Kyle Railways, and then by recent owner RailAmerica.

East Florida—*See Savannah, Florida & Western.*

East Tennessee & Georgia—*See East Tennessee, Virginia & Georgia.*

East Tennessee & Virginia—*See East Tennessee, Virginia & Georgia.*

East Tennessee, Virginia & Georgia—Amalgamation of East Tennessee & Virginia (Knoxville to Bristol, Tennessee–Virginia) with East Tennessee & Georgia (Knoxville to Dalton, Georgia) in 1869 netted a new company and name, ETV&G. In 1881, the carrier made two strategic purchases that incredibly expanded its routes. It bought Macon & Brunswick, a 174-mile road connecting those namesake cities, and the Dalton–Selma, Alabama, road Georgia Southern (ex–Selma, Rome & Dalton). With lines widely separated, ETV&G constructed a 158-mile Atlanta Division from Rome to Macon via Atlanta (1882). Ultimately ETV&G reached west to Memphis, south to Meridian, east to Brunswick and north to Bristol, all routes converging between Cleveland, Tennessee, and Rome, Georgia. Sold under foreclosure (1886), the line re-emerged as property of Richmond Terminal Company (1887–1892), closely identified with Richmond & Danville. In this period Rome & Decatur joined ETV&G (1890). ETV&G and R&D were keys to forming Southern Railway (1894). *See Western North Carolina.*

Eatonton & Machen —*See Middle Georgia & Atlantic.*

Eatonton Branch— 22-mile connection finished in 1853 between Georgia hamlets Eatonton and Milledgeville. EB and Milledgeville & Gordon ferried traffic to Gordon, Georgia, where Central of Georgia persisted to the state capital. EB and M&G combined in 1855, leased to CofG. The lease was acquired by Middle Georgia & Atlantic (1893), opening a 64-mile route tying Milledgeville to Covington. MG&A was overtaken by CofG (1897) with the Eatonton–Milledgeville segment operated by Norfolk Southern today.

Elizabeth City & Norfolk —Earliest ancestor of original Norfolk Southern, chartered 1870, opened 1881 running from Berkeley, Virginia, to Elizabeth City and Edenton, North Carolina. Renamed Norfolk Southern in 1883. *See Norfolk Southern.*

Elizabethtown, Lexington & Big Sandy —Chartered 1869, it succeeded Lexington & Big Sandy Railroad. Big Sandy River was referenced in its name along with two Bluegrass cities. From its inception the West Virginia to central Kentucky line was leased and operated by Chesapeake & Ohio, which bought it in 1892. Most passenger service ended in the 1960s and the route was abandoned in the 1980s.

Empire & Dublin —Chartered 1888, before entering receivership two years hence, E&D opened a line between Dublin and Hawkinsville via Empire in south Georgia. It completed surveying for an extension from Hawkinsville to Grovania. Reorganized as Oconee & Western (1892), the company sold its Dublin–Hawkinsville segment to Wrightsville & Tennille (1896).

Eureka Springs —Launched 1882 between Eureka Springs, Arkansas, and Seligman, Missouri. In 1899, its name was changed to St. Louis & North Arkansas; in 1906, to Missouri & North Arkansas; in 1935, to Missouri & Arkansas; in 1949, to Arkansas & Ozarks, ending in 1961 with tracks removed in 1964. At its peak the route extended 369 miles between Helena, Arkansas, and Joplin, Missouri. The carrier was replaced by Eureka Springs & North Arkansas in 1981, a steam excursion daytripper with a 1912-1913 depot and a 1881–1883 roadbed on a 2.1-mile route.

Eureka Springs & North Arkansas —*See Eureka Springs.*

Evansville, Owensboro & Nashville —*See Owensboro & Nashville.*

Fayetteville & Florence— Line tying named termini, chartered 1862, persisted to 1873 under F&F taxonomy; ancestor on mainline of Atlantic Coast Line (1900). Florence was major ACL repair, maintenance, crew change point.

Florida—Construction began in 1855 at Fernandina on the upper Atlantic Coast to cross the state southwest to the Gulf of Mexico and end untimely voyages around keys between the oceans. A 156-mile route to Cedar Key on the Gulf opened March 1, 1861, in time to see War Between the States action with plenty of destruction. Rebuilding began after the war. The road's name was altered to Atlantic, Gulf & West India Transit Company (1872).

Florida & Alabama —*See Alabama & Gulf Coast.*

Florida, Atlantic & Gulf Central —Initiated 1851, FA&CG construction began 1857 heading west from Jacksonville. Completed in 1860, the road reached Alligator Town (now Lake City) 60 miles from Jacksonville. There it was to meet with Pensacola & Georgia then under construction heading east from Tallahassee. By fall 1861, the route was open from Tallahassee to Jacksonville in time to serve the Confederacy during most of the War Between the States. Damaged heavily in the conflict, FA&GC was sold to private investors (1868) and reorganized as Florida Central.

Florida Central —In 1868, Florida Atlantic & Gulf Central was reorganized as FC. It was closely tied to Jacksonville, Pensacola & Mobile, which owned tracks west of Lake City and temporarily leased FC (1870-1871). Finances plagued those carriers and both went into receivership. Sold at auction on January 6, 1882, to a private investor, FC was consolidated with JP&M to form Florida Central & Western.

Florida Central & Peninsular —A 940-mile route acquired in February 1899 by organizers and owners of Seaboard Air Line (established July 1, 1900). Growing from multiple ancestors, FC&P operated in Florida, Georgia and South Carolina. Its earliest forebear, Tallahassee Railroad, dated to 1834. FC&P developed in 1889 when Florida Railway & Navigation Company (derived from consolidations in 1884) was renamed. FC&P equipped SAL with links between Columbia, South Carolina, and Jacksonville through Savannah; between Waldo, Florida, and Tampa; and more. Once a connection was made between Hamlet, North Carolina, and Columbia, SAL was to have continuous trackage from Richmond to Tampa. Buying FC&P was indeed consequential.

Florida Central & Western —Formed by joining dual lines sold at foreclosure, Florida Central and Jacksonville, Pensacola & Mobile (1882), FC&W ran a 209-mile main between River Junction (now Chattahoochee) west of Tallahassee and Jacksonville with stems to Monticello and St. Marks. Two years hence FC&W consolidated with Florida Transit & Peninsular to form Florida Railway & Navigation Company. The lines intersected at Baldwin.

Florida Coast & Gulf —*See Jacksonville, St. Augustine & Halifax River.*

Florida East Coast—This Sunshine State railroad's most famous component was a 128-mile line that extended from the end of the peninsula over the ocean to Key West. With only sparse earth rising above the sea to support tracks, the line took from 1905 to 1912 to build. It lasted until an unnamed hurricane brought destruction 23 years later. The FEC was the creation of Standard Oil magnate Henry M. Flagler, who saw possibilities for new resorts in the Sunshine State after visiting St. Augustine with his second wife in 1883. He knew transportation would be a key to getting building materials and people to his destinations. In 1895 he opened the St. Augustine & Halifax Railway, the original underpinning of the new Florida East Coast Railway. In 1888 the line opened the lower half of Florida to rail traffic. In 1894 it reached Palm Beach; afterward Flagler accepted the invitation from the residents of Fort Dallas to extend his tracks another 60 miles. With his infusion of infrastructure, the little burg grew and became known as Miami. By 1905 Flagler had visions of going even farther: a line extending 28 more miles to the end of the peninsula and 128 miles over deep sea to the island of Key West. Flagler envisioned a deep sea port close to the new Panama Canal and a link to resorts in Havana, Cuba. The port wasn't to be, but Flagler wasn't deterred. The rails were completed in January 1912. The line operated until a hurricane packing winds over 200 miles an hour surged over the keys and the Overseas Railway on September 2, 1935. By then Flagler was deceased. The road bed and remaining bridges later provided the impetus and route for U.S. 1 between Miami and Key West. *See Chapter 6.*

Florida Railway & Navigation—The Sunshine State's first large rail system encompassing over 500 miles of track was founded by an 1884 fusion of a trio of lines: Florida Central & Western, Florida Transit & Peninsular, and Fernandina & Jacksonville. Partially completed Leesburg & Indian River running 11 miles from Wildwood to Leesburg was absorbed. The union boasted three narrow-gauge lines altered to standard on June 1, 1886: Fernandina to Cedar Key ("The Gulf Coast Route"), Waldo to Panasoffkee, Leesburg, and Silver Springs ("The Golden Fruit Route"), and Jacksonville to River Junction ("The Tallahassee Route"). The firm ran a steamboat from Fernandina to Savannah. In receivership 1886–1889, FR&N extended its Leesburg stem 10 miles to Tavares (1885) and Peninsular's route below Panasoffkee 53 miles to Plant City (1887). Other auxiliaries were added. On July 12, 1888, the properties were sold to a new party, reorganized as Florida Central & Peninsular after taking over the operations in 1889.

Florida Transit—*See Atlantic, Gulf & West India Transit.*

Florida Transit & Peninsular—Formed in 1883 by an amalgamation of three roads: Florida Transit, Peninsular and Tropical Florida. The combined lines operated 258 miles of track linking Fernandina–Jacksonville–Gainesville–Cedar Key with Panasoffkee. FT&P was folded into Florida Railway and Navigation Company with other lines the following year.

Florida West Shore—Running to or near the Gulf in central and south Florida, FWS was pivotal to SAL in the 20th century in cargo and human traffic. Shortly before its selection as SAL's route to counties below Tampa Bay in 1903, FWS became alluring by expanding from Manatee River to Sarasota, Fruitville and Bradenton. It served well, giving access to an unexploited area where fruits and vegetables grew profusely. SAL shipped them to distant points. After FWS folded into SAL in 1909, tracks were extended farther south to Venice and north to Inverness and Hernando, the latter burgs well above Tampa. The southern route impacted tourism at the resort town of Venice, a major destination for several passenger trains.

Frankfort & Lexington—Precursor of Louisville, Cincinnati & Lexington. *See Louisville, Cincinnati & Lexington.*

Georgia—With a mainline from Augusta to Atlanta, Georgia Railroad traversed 525 miles with daily except Sunday passenger service. Investors led by James Camak launched the line in 1833 in Athens, Georgia. It became Georgia Railroad & Banking Company in 1836; headquarters moved to Augusta in 1840, when the line came under new owners. By 1847 steam had replaced livestock as a means of locomotion. It eventually extended the breadth of the Peach State to Selma, Alabama. Its various incarnations eventually ended up as part of CSX Transportation formed in 1986. *See Appendix B.*

Georgia Air-Line—Chartered in 1856. Capitalists behind GAL purposed to create a route northeast from Atlanta to the upper reaches of neighboring South Carolina. Their desire was to make the Peach State capital a prime stop on any potential Washington–New Orleans route. Although it happened, it was no thanks to them. In many years they never laid any track. A like imbroglio played out next door. Air-Line Railroad Company of South Carolina (formed 1856) planned to lay rail along the same route. But they did nothing. Both lines were bought by a powerful Richmond & Danville. R&D combined the duo (1870), naming it Atlanta & Richmond Air-Line. R&D wanted tracks from Charlotte to Atlanta but couldn't build them under its sobriquet due to a charter stipulation. A&RAL opened the rails in fall 1873. Emerging from foreclosure later, the route was renamed Atlanta & Charlotte Air-Line (1877). Finally, Southern

Railway, out of which R&D was partially created, absorbed the auxiliary line (1894).

Georgia & Alabama—It was a 263-mile line linking the hamlet of Lyons in southeast Georgia with Montgomery. Its history under other monikers is colorful. Originating as Americus, Preston & Lumpkin (1884), it added tracks to Louvale (1887), Abbeville (1887) and steamboat connections from Abbeville to waterways at Brunswick and Savannah (1889). Its appellation was altered to Savannah, Americus & Montgomery, and in 1895, to Georgia & Alabama. With pressure from John S. Williams (who organized SAL in 1900) in 1896, CofG reluctantly allowed him to send G&A trains 17 miles from Lyons to Savannah, providing a surface rail route between Montgomery and the coast. G&A was purchased by SAL in 1902.

Georgia & Florida—Established by capitalists led by John Skelton Williams after his ouster as SAL president, G&F (which locals branded "Gone & Forgotten" and a historian dubbed "a hard luck road") operated 1906–1971. Serving Georgia wiregrass sawmill towns like Sparks, Valdosta, Douglass, Hazlehurst, Swainsboro and Vidalia, G&F connected Greenwood, South Carolina with Madison, Florida, through Augusta, its only decent-sized municipality. Joining smaller roads into a shortline, G&F intended to transport locally grown tobacco, watermelons, onions and more crops to Northern markets. With undercapitalization, aging rolling stock and bankruptcies more than three decades, it seldom met expectations. For years it proffered passenger service which was eventually dropped. In 1963, Southern Railway—having outbid ACL for it—bought G&F and turned it into a wholly-owned subsidiary. The G&F name faded in 1971 after Southern dispatched it to another auxiliary, Central of Georgia.

Georgia, Ashburn, Sylvester & Camilla—Organized in 1922, GAS&C bought a route between Camilla and Ashburn, Georgia, as part of a larger Georgia Northern system. The previous owner was Gulf Line, a subsidiary of Hawkinsville & Florida Southern. GAS&C came under Southern Railway control in 1966, which consolidated it in Georgia Northern.

Georgia, Carolina & Northern—Organized in 1888 (some sources say 1886), before running its first train GC&N was leased for life by dual lines in 1889: Seaboard & Roanoke and Raleigh & Gaston. GC&N became SAL's Atlanta Division (1901) when it merged into SAL, the 268-mile route from Monroe, North Carolina, to Atlanta having opened in 1892. CG&N terminated at a tie with Georgia Railroad at Inman Park on Atlanta's east side (1892). To outmaneuver an embargo preventing it from entering Atlanta from the east, GC&N built a Seaboard Air Line Belt Railroad, an eight-mile line meeting GC&N near Emory University at Belt Junction. Trains ran west to link with Nashville, Chattanooga & St. Louis tracks at Howells on Atlanta's northwest side. Despite the ban, GC&N—with NC&StL trackage rights—sent its trains to downtown Atlanta anyway.

Georgia, Florida & Alabama—Chartered in 1895 as Georgia Pine Railway, it acquired the GF&A handle in 1901. The 180-mile route ran from Richland, Georgia, to Carrabelle, Florida. In 1928, SAL controlled GF&A, opening a way through the Florida panhandle for its trains to reach Montgomery. The line was leased in 1930. Commonly dubbed "The Sumatra Leaf Route," it was so branded for a strain of tobacco grown in that territory.

Georgia Northern—Southwest Georgia's Boston & Albany, chartered 1891, failed, its assets then bought by a family. Renamed Georgia Northern, it accessed Albany in 1905. Through the 1930s its owners bought more regional lines. GN was sold to Southern Railway (1966) which merged it into other lines (1972) but retained Georgia Northern taxonomy for all.

Georgia Pacific—Chartered 1881, GP absorbed dual lines, Georgia Western and Georgia Pacific Railroad Company of Alabama. Jointly controlled by Southern Railway precursors Richmond & Danville and Richmond & West Point Terminal, GP was acquired by Southern in 1894. With its full route open (1889), it linked Atlanta to Greenville, Mississippi via Birmingham.

Georgia Pine—Chartered 1895 with shops in Bainbridge, it built 29 miles to Damascus by 1898, with another 10 miles to Arlington by 1900. The taxonomy was altered the next year. *See Georgia, Florida & Alabama.*

Georgia Railroad & Banking Company—Formed in Athens (1833), power shifted to Augusta (1840). Augusta–Atlanta main reached Montgomery after Georgia gained control of Atlanta & West Point and Western Railway of Alabama. Autonomy ended (1881), Georgia's ownership passing among Central of Georgia, Louisville & Nashville, and Atlantic Coast Line. Its separate identity was kept through the Seaboard Coast Line era to 1972; it was a unit of "Family Lines System" before its absorption into CSX (1982).

Georgia Southern—*See East Tennessee, Virginia & Georgia.*

Georgia, Southern & Florida—Chartered 1885, its mission was to construct a 285-mile rail line tying Macon, Georgia with Palatka, Florida. Opened south to Valdosta, Georgia, in February 1889, its full route was finished 13 months later. It entered receivership in 1881 and was reorganized (1895), by then controlled by Southern Railway. Labeled "Suwanee River Route" because it crossed the Suwanee at White Springs, Florida, GS&F bought Atlantic, Valdosta & Western between Valdosta and Jacksonville. It also owned two more roads: Macon & Birmingham, Hawkinsville & Florida Southern. The route now ends at Lake City, Florida, not Palatka, owned by Norfolk Southern, which designates AV&W tracks as the area's main route.

Girard—Chartered in 1845, Girard may not have been running until 1868, some records say. It connected Girard, Alabama, with Columbus, Georgia, and then extended to Alabama cities Troy (1870) and Andalusia (1899). Before its 1886 leasing to Central Rail Road and Banking Company, Girard was renamed Mobile & Girard. Central of Georgia bought M&G in 1895.

Glasgow—Organized 1856 as Barren County Railroad Company, Glasgow linked with L&N then under construction. Acquired by a trio of Glasgow, Kentucky citizens, it was renamed Glasgow Railroad Company (1868). "Railroad" was changed to "Railway" when they sold it to new investors (1899). Glasgow's surviving rolling stock is passenger car 109, one of few extant in Jim Crow configuration. Now on a siding near the Glasgow end, this car was in a mixed consist daily or twice daily between the town and L&N connection (formerly Glasgow Junction, now Park City). The old car is decaying rapidly. The freight-only line serves local factories today. Owned by a Glasgow clan, it runs under long-term lease by CSX, successor to L&N. Glasgow has no locomotives or rolling stock of its own in service.

Greenville & Columbia—Chartered 1845, G&C built the first rails to transcend South Carolina's upstate. Running southeast from Greenville 111 miles by the western banks of the Saluda River, it arrived at Columbia in the central Piedmont. Completed 1853, its tracks were a conduit linking mountains and capital during the War Between the States. But in the postwar era G&C failed after corrupt politicos defrauded it of $400,000. Reorganized (1870s), it was renamed Columbia & Greenville with its route divided into Columbia, Newberry & Laurens and Charleston & Western Carolina (1890). The duo met at Laurens, where a C&WC branch persisted to Greenville. Early in the 20th century Atlantic Coast Line gained control of both roads for freight and to ferry travelers from Columbia to Laurens.

Greenville, Spartanburg & Anderson—Formed 1910, GS&A constructed an interurban (electric-powered) passenger line between its South Carolina namesakes. Its main was extended from Greenville to Greenwood (1912). The whole route was eventually consolidated in Piedmont & Northern, another interurban operator based in Charlotte, North Carolina (1914). P&N was ultimately folded

into Seaboard Coast Line (1969); a series of mergers ensued sending the route to CSX (1980). In 2006, CSX spun off the Pelzer–Belton portion to another owner which renamed it Greenville & Western. A 13-mile G&W route persists today linking Belton and Pelzer.

Gulf & Chicago—*See Ripley.*

Gulf & Ship Island—Absorbed into Illinois Central (1945), the G&SI 160-mile main extends from Gulfport at the waterfront to Jackson, the state capital. Chartered 1882, from Gulfport it took 15 years to make Hattiesburg (70 miles) but just three more years to access Jackson (90 miles farther).

Gulf, Florida & Alabama—*See Alabama & Gulf Coast.*

Gulf Line—Established by Southern Railway in 1907 to fold multiple south Georgia shortlines into a minor system. Hawkinsville & Florida Southern (Hawkinsville–Worth) was leased; Flint River & Gulf (Sylvester–Ashburn) purchased; Georgia Southern & Florida, a SOU property, gave trackage rights to both at Worth and Ashburn connecting points. GL extended its route from Sylvester to Camilla with new rail (1908). H&FS, still under SOU control, bought and absorbed GL (1913). Entering into receivership (1922), H&FS's Camilla–Ashburn segment was sold to upstart Georgia, Ashburn, Sylvester & Camilla and the remainder of its routes abandoned.

Gulf, Mobile & Northern—One of two key roads that combined to form Gulf, Mobile & Ohio (the other, Mobile & Ohio) September 13, 1940. GM&N contributed a main artery linking Mobile, Alabama, to Jackson, Tennessee. A stem ran west from that route to Jackson, Mississippi, where it turned south, persisting to New Orleans. That gave GM&N port ties at Mobile and New Orleans. GM&N dates to 1917 when bankrupt New Orleans, Mobile & Chicago connecting Mobile with Middleton, Tennessee, was reorganized. By the mid 1930s, GM&N ran a streamliner, the *Rebel*, between Jackson and Mobile with a section also bound for New Orleans. Not only was it the first true streamliner below the Mason-Dixon Line, it was also purportedly the country's first train with hostesses aboard.

Gulf, Mobile & Ohio—Not one of the major players the Southern passenger train realm, GM&O nonetheless ran people moving consists for 18 years in Dixie. The line and its predecessors were innovators, though, and GM&O was a solid passenger and freight transporter in the mid 20th century. GM&O was launched in 1938 to accommodate the merger of Gulf, Mobile & Northern and the Mobile & Ohio Railroad, which it completed in 1940. Alton was a major acquisition in 1947. At its peak the line owned 258 engines and

2,734 miles of track, headquartered at Jackson, Tennessee. It was merged with Illinois Central Railroad in 1972 to form Illinois Central Gulf Railroad, which later dispersed redundant trackage to other companies and, as Illinois Central, was purchased by the Canadian National Railway in the late 1990s. *See Chapter 7.*

Gulf Port Terminal — *See Alabama & Gulf Coast.*

Hawkinsville & Florida Southern — Chartered 1889, in a dozen years H&FS constructed a 43-mile route linking middle Georgia's Hawkinsville and Worth. At Worth a Georgia Southern & Florida tie ferried trains to and from the Sunshine State. GS&F's main from Macon to Valdosta, Georgia, had split branches beyond to Jacksonville and Palatka, Florida. H&FS built a 15-mile stem from Davisville (now defunct) to Fitzgerald, Georgia. Leased to Gulf Line Railway (1907), the lines joined (1909) but retained their own monikers. GL was absorbed by H&FS (1913), its main routed from Ashburn to Camilla, Georgia. In the 20th century's early decades two daily passenger trains plied tracks between Hawkinsville and Camilla. After entering receivership (1922), H&FS didn't recover. Its Hawkinsville branch and original Hawkinsville–Worth main were abandoned; a new Georgia, Ashburn, Sylvester & Camilla bought the Ashburn–Camilla route.

Illinois Central — In 1850, IC became the first line in America to be supported by a large (2.6 million-acre) federal land grant; such grants helped railroads create the first transcontinental system by 1869. When its mainline within Illinois was completed in 1856, the 705-mile road was the longest on the planet. Its "Chicago Branch" from Centralia (named after the carrier) to Lake Michigan, opened in 1855, was the nucleus of its activity. It was a vital transportation link during the American Civil War (1861–1864) carrying Federal troops and supplies down the Mississippi River as far as the Gulf of Mexico. It hauled people and products between the South and Chicago; was a route north for the "Great Migration" of about 1916 to 1930; and was a major commuter system for Chicago. In 1998 IC and its 2,600 miles of track became a subsidiary of Illinois Central Corporation, a branch of Canadian National Railway Company. Until 2001 it conducted business under its own moniker. One of IC's engineers, John Luther "Casey" Jones, was immortalized in a ballad written after the train wreck that killed him in 1900. *See Chapter 8.*

Jackson & Eaton — A 15-mile route between Mississippi's state capital and the community of Eaton acquired in 1925 by Gulf, Mobile & Northern (an ancestor of Gulf, Mobile & Ohio). This gave GM&N access not only to Jackson but a connection with New Orleans & Great Northern and ongoing access to the Crescent City, of great subsequent value to GM&O.

Jacksonville & Southwestern — Dating to 1890s, J&S was bought by ACL in 1904 to open traffic to Newberry, Florida. ACL added three short lines to gain direct access to St. Petersburg as the route bypassed Tampa.

Jacksonville, Pensacola & Mobile — Formed in 1869 by joining Pensacola & Georgia and Tallahassee roads, JP&M leased Florida Central (1870-1871), gaining an unbroken 189-mile route from Jacksonville to Quincy with stems to Monticello and St. Marks. P&G tracks were sold (1870). A 20-mile addition west of Quincy to River Junction (now Chattahoochee) was completed in 1872. JP&M and FC spent most of 1870s in receivership; a private investor consolidated the pair as Florida Central & Western (1882).

Jacksonville, St. Augustine & Halifax River — Seeing no quality means of overland transport beyond Jacksonville, diminishing the ability to attract affluent cold-weather Yankees to the magnificent resorts he was building beside Florida's sunny shores, Henry Flagler bought the narrow gauge rail line opened in 1884 from Jacksonville to St. Augustine. It had begun as JSA&HR, was subsequently renamed Jacksonville, St. Augustine & Indian River, and briefly Florida Coast & Gulf when Flagler acquired it in 1885. After its conversion to standard measure, the route became the first rails of Florida East Coast Railway, ultimately ferrying travelers to Key West.

Jacksonville, St. Augustine & Indian River — *See Jacksonville, St. Augustine & Halifax River.*

Jacksonville, Tampa & Key West — Initially Tampa, Peace Creek & St. Johns River (1879), the moniker altered to JT&KW (1881). That year Palatka & Indian River was chartered to run from Palatka to the St. Johns River port at Sanford. JT&KW bought it (1887). JT&KW's main linked Jacksonville to Sanford, where a separate South Florida persisted to Tampa. On February 20, 1886, the full line opened from Jacksonville to Tampa. After JT&KW entered bankruptcy (1893), it reorganized as Jacksonville & St. Johns River and was sold to Savannah, Florida & Western, a member of the Plant System. Plant joined Atlantic Coast Line (1902), merging into Seaboard Coast Line (1967) and later CSX Transportation (1980).

Kansas City Southern — Formed in 1897 in Kansas City, Missouri, when entrepreneur Arthur E. Stilwell envisioned extending his local trackage to the Gulf of Mexico. His Kansas City, Pittsburg & Gulf Railroad reached Port Arthur, Texas, by 1897 and became Kansas City Southern Railway. It later added links to New Orleans and Dallas, among others. As part of its passenger traffic it ran a luxury consist between Kansas City and New Orleans from 1940 to 1969. After passenger business faded, it extended freight routes by acquiring several other in-

This 1974 view is from a highway bridge crossing an old SAL and ACL diamond located directly below a bridge at Auburndale, Florida. At the time the tracks were owned by successor SCL. The mainline shown is SAL's route north with an unseen ACL crossing east-west. In this period Amtrak used both mainlines but it doesn't utilize the SAL route any longer (*courtesy Michael B. Robbins*).

terests. An ancillary, Kansas City Southern de Mexico, was formed in 2005. *See Appendix B.*

Kentucky Central—KC originated as Covington & Lexington (1849), operating until Kentucky Central Railroad Association acquired it (1861). Kentucky Central Railroad was its next owner (1875). After a year in receivership, the line emerged as KC Railway (1887), bought by L&N (1891), giving L&N access to southeast Kentucky's rich coal fields. Until it had a direct route to Cincinnati, Chesapeake & Ohio accessed it by traveling in east Kentucky over Elizabethtown, Lexington & Big Sandy and connecting at Lexington on Kentucky Central tracks leading to Cincinnati (1881–1888).

Lake Monroe & Orlando—Organized with a charter to build from St. Johns River port at Sanford south to Orlando (1875), LM&O was in danger of losing its land grants when South Florida (organized 1878) stepped up in late 1879 and offered to build the road LM&O never did. Taking over LM&O's charter, SF ran its first trains on a completed Sanford–Orlando route in late 1880. Its intents were more extensive, however, with plans to reach the Gulf. *See South Florida.*

Lexington & Big Sandy—Chartered 1852 and opened to traffic 1857, it was folded into Elizabethtown, Lexington & Big Sandy (1869), absorbed into Chesapeake & Ohio later. *See Elizabethtown, Lexington & Big Sandy.*

Little Rock & Fort Smith—Charter of ex–Cairo & Fulton's Fort Smith branch was renewed April 12, 1869, as Little Rock & Fort Smith. Its route completed in 1874, LR&FS was acquired by Missouri Pacific in 1882.

Live Oak & Rowlands Bluff—Chartered 1881, a Plant System member, LO&RB built a line from Live Oak to Brandford, Florida (now Branford). It connected at Brandford with Live Oak, Tampa & Charlotte Harbor.

Live Oak, Tampa & Charlotte Harbor—To extend below Live Oak, Florida, about 25 miles from the Georgia border, financier Henry B. Plant launched Live Oak & Rowlands Bluff to open a route to Brandford (now Branford). Live Oak, Tampa & Charlotte Harbor, chartered 1881, advanced the cause below Brandford, extending trackage to Fort White, High Springs and, in 1883, to Newnansville (near present Alachua). Making a pact with Florida Southern, Plant continued the line to Gainesville, where LOT&CH ended.

Louisa—Organized by Louisa County, Virginia, farmers in 1836, Louisa was a means to get crops to market. Tying into Richmond, Fredericksburg & Potomac, owners built their own route to the capital at Richmond (1837) and added a leg to Charlottesville. Louisa was renamed Virginia Central.

Louisiana & Arkansas—Incorporated 1897, a 300-mile mainline between L&A's base in Shreveport and New Orleans didn't open until 1907. It was extended west through Texas with the purchase of a line from a bankrupt Katy system. Kansas City Southern bought L&A in 1939, gaining links with New Orleans and Dallas, plus from Shreveport to Minden, Louisiana, plus Hope, Arkansas. From 1940 to 1969, it ran a daily luxury consist between Kansas City and New Orleans via Shreveport as a key slice of its passenger traffic.

Louisville & Frankfort—*See Louisville, Cincinnati & Lexington.*

Louisville & Indiana—L&I is a 106-mile freight line running due north from Louisville to Indianapolis. Purchased from Conrail (1994), it was owned by Penn Central earlier and still earlier by Pennsylvania. At Louisville it interchanges with CSX, Indiana, and Paducah & Louisville. L&I ferried Amtrak's *Kentucky Cardinal* (1999–2003), a failed attempt to capture express business from Louisville's UPS hub while transporting passengers to and from Chicago. Inconvenient departure and arrival times and a prevailing 30 mile-an-hour limit on the L&I route led to its demise.

Louisville & Nashville—The L&N was born of a need for better travel between Louisville, Kentucky, to the center of Tennessee. Trade mostly traversed on water and was subject to its eccentricities, while passengers paid for slow and expensive stagecoaches. In 1850 and 1851 the two state governments authorized a line between the two namesake cities. The line's construction crept south from Louisville and reached Elizabethtown, 42 miles south, in five years. Railbuilding picked up steam past the tunnel through Muldraugh's Hill and reached Nashville in 1859, adding through passenger service to Memphis in 1861. After the Civil War ended in 1865, L&N jumped on the expansion bandwagon and reached to many other Southern and Midwestern cities, including Cincinnati, Mobile, New Orleans, Pensacola and St. Louis. One of its last major acquisitions was the Nashville, Chattanooga & St. Louis Railway in 1957. It eventually spread 6,574 miles of rail over 13 states as it standardized tracks, modernized equipment and introduced Centralized Traffic Control (CTC). Its luxury passenger consists during the heyday of rail travel included the *Humming Bird* and *Pan-American*. L&N finally lost its

own identity in 1980 with the creation of the CSX Corporation. *See Chapter 9.*

Louisville & Wadley—Organized 1872 and in operation 1879, a 10-mile route in south Georgia sold to Central of Georgia (1898). CofG sold it to Louisville & Wadley Railway (previously Railroad) in 1961 which—a decade later—abandoned all but two miles between Wadley and Gibson Junction.

Louisville, Cincinnati & Lexington—In 1869, two Kentucky shortlines, Louisville & Frankfort and Frankfort & Lexington, consolidated operations to form a 175-mile Louisville, Cincinnati & Lexington. From Frankfort it accessed Covington on the south bank of the Ohio River opposite Cincy. A rail bridge to downtown Cincy opened in 1872. LC&L was bought by L&N in 1881. LC&L became part of Seaboard System (1982) and CSX (1986).

Louisville, Henderson & St. Louis—Louisville, St. Louis & Texas reorganized as LH&SL (1893). Reorganized again (1896), LH&SL was acquired by L&N early in the 20th century, though allowed to operate under its own moniker. Commonly dubbed "The Henderson Route," it ran an extensive passenger service, part of L&N's main linking Cincinnati with St. Louis.

Louisville, New Albany & Chicago—Launched as New Albany & Salem (1847), a carrier operated mostly in Indiana with expanded horizons as LNA&C (1859). It joined the lineage of Chicago, Indianapolis & Louisville (1897) with altered name of Monon (1956). It was bought by L&N as its passenger service ended (1971). *See Chicago, Indianapolis & Louisville.*

Louisville, New Orleans & Mississippi Valley—*See Louisville, New Orleans & Texas.*

Louisville, New Orleans & Texas—Launched as New Orleans & Mississippi Valley (1883), the route completed from Memphis to New Orleans via Vicksburg and Baton Rouge (1884) was backed by rail baron Collis P. Huntington. He intended to link his Chesapeake, Ohio & Southwestern with Southern Pacific at New Orleans, opening a second transcontinental. In its early stages NO&MV was renamed LNO&T. Huntington's empire soon ran into foul territory nevertheless and Illinois Central stepped in, bought LNO&T and his Mississippi & Tennessee (Grenada, Mississippi, to Memphis) and joined the pair with Yazoo & Mississippi Valley. IC also took the Louisville to Memphis sector of Huntington's CO&S route (1893).

Lynchburg & Tennessee—An early predecessor in 1848 of Virginia & Tennessee, L&T was an ancestor of Atlantic, Mississippi & Ohio (1870) and Norfolk & Western (1881). Its 204-mile route (opened 1856) linked Lynchburg with Bristol and eventually was a vital trackage route for SOU.

Macon & Birmingham—Owned by Georgia

Southern & Florida, chartered in 1888, completed in 1891, M&B was nicknamed "The LaGrange Route" and "The Pine Mountain Route." Never profitable, M&B tied central Georgia's Macon with LaGrange at the state's western border. Entering receivership (1891) and reorganized (1895), the route was finally abandoned (1922).

Macon & Brunswick — *See East Tennessee, Virginia & Georgia.*

Macon & Western — Opened in 1846, M&W's route between Macon and Atlanta supplied a way for Central of Georgia to move its trains from Savannah to the state capital. That occurred after a trestle over the Ocmulgee River at Macon was in place (1851). M&W's roots were in Monroe Railroad tying Macon to Forsyth (built 1834–1838). Bankruptcy intervened with the line reorganized as M&W (1845), and funneled into CofG in 1871-1872.

Manchester & Augusta — Precursor of Atlantic Coast Line (1900), absorbed by Atlantic Coast Line Railroad Company of South Carolina two years before.

Mandeville & Sulphur Springs — *See New Orleans & Northeastern.*

Memphis & Charleston — Incorporated in 1846, M&C was the final link in a chain of early railways tying the Atlantic with the Mississippi River. Its route from Memphis to Chattanooga through Tennessee, Mississippi, and Alabama still plays a vital role in commerce. It became part of Southern Railway (1894) and remained until Norfolk Southern was created (1982).

Memphis & Little Rock — Chartered in 1853, by 1858, the first rail line in Arkansas was laid from Hopefield (now West Memphis) to Madison on the St. Francis River, M&LR's initial segment. On August 21, 1871, the 133-mile narrow-gauge route opened between Memphis and Argenta (now North Little Rock). Seventeen miles between Brinkley and DeValls Bluff weren't in use until a bridge opened over the White River late that decade. Until then connections were made by steamboat or stagecoach from Clarendon to DeValls Bluff. Sold four times at foreclosure between 1873 and 1898, M&LR was later bought by Choctaw, Oklahoma & Gulf. The Choctaw Route became property of Chicago, Rock Island & Pacific (1904).

Memphis & Ohio — Chartered 1852, completed 1861, M&O played a significant part during the Civil War. Its main ran northeast from Memphis to Paris, Tennessee, connecting with Memphis, Clarksville & Louisville. After both lines were disrupted by ravaged track during the conflagration ending in 1865, Louisville & Nashville came to the rescue. It helped both carriers regain their business and then absorbed them into L&N inventory.

Memphis, Clarksville & Louisville — Chartered 1852, completed 1859, its 82-mile route ran between Guthrie, Kentucky, and Paris, Tennessee. At Guthrie, it met Louisville & Nashville for a run northeast to Louisville. At Paris, it linked with Memphis & Ohio, heading southwest to Memphis. While the Louisville–Memphis course didn't open to 1861, it was disrupted by the Civil War, which demolished tracks of MC&L and M&O lines. Louisville & Nashville helped them after the war and took control of both carriers.

Meridian & Memphis — Another case of a misnomer title. Incorporated in 1911, M&M purposed to haul lumber of eastern Mississippi to more profitable markets. Yet it never went beyond Union, 32 miles past its start at Meridian, opening late 1913. In 1919, Gulf, Mobile & Northern — one of dual ancestors of Gulf, Mobile & Ohio — began buying M&M shares. It took total control in time, though the ICC didn't OK its acquisition until 1929.

Middle Georgia & Atlantic — Successor to a trackless Eatonton & Machen, a 64-mile MG&A route from Milledgeville to Covington, Georgia, was built in 1890–1894. A line from Eatonton to Machen (finished 1891) was followed with addition from Machen to Covington (1893). MG&A leased a 22-mile route from Milledgeville to Eatonton — Eatonton Branch Railroad (1893). Central of Georgia bought MG&A at foreclosure in late 1896, operating it as a stem from Milledgeville to Covington. In 1959, the Eatonton–Machen route was abandoned. Norfolk Southern maintains Milledgeville-Eaton and Great Walton runs Machen–Covington.

Milledgeville & Gordon — Chartered in 1837 but not open for 15 years, M&G ferried traffic 17 miles between its namesakes, linked with Central of Georgia at Gordon for continuation to and from Atlanta. Paired with Eatonton Branch at Milledgeville, the two combined in 1855, leased to CofG.

Mississippi & Tennessee — Route linking Memphis with Grenada, Mississippi, bought by rail tycoon Collis P. Huntington (1884). When Huntington got into trouble, IC bought the line along with other Huntington properties.

Mississippi Central — Under construction from 1853 to 1860, MC linked Canton, Mississippi, with Jackson, Tennessee. With connections at both ends, for the first time traffic flowed between the Great Lakes and Gulf. Illinois Central gained MC trackage rights in the 1970s to access Jackson.

Missouri & Arkansas — *See Eureka Springs.*

Missouri & North Arkansas — *See Eureka Springs.*

Missouri Pacific — From its beginnings in 1849, the Pacific Railroad extended from St. Louis to a dozen states. After financial difficulties in 1872 it became Missouri Pacific (MoPac), eventually extending its routes from Chicago to the Southwestern United States. Its passenger consists included the *Houstonian, Southern Scenic* and *Texas Eagle.* Passenger service ended in 1971 with the creation of Amtrak. The Missouri Pacific Railroad folded into Union Pacific Railroad in 1997. *See Appendix B.*

Mobile & Girard—*See Girard.*

Mobile & Montgomery—Chartered 1874, M&M was created to tote cotton and other crops from Alabama's interior to the port at Mobile. Trackage rights were granted to Louisville & Nashville in 1880. By gaining rights on New Orleans & Mobile, too, L&N expanded its mainline to the Crescent City from Cincinnati. L&N absorbed M&M into its system in 1900.

Monon—*See Chicago, Indianapolis & Louisville.*

Monroe—Chartered in December 1833, its intent was to tie Macon, Georgia, with the Monroe County burg of Forsyth. In December 1838, the first trains ran over the line. The Monroe was extended to Griffin south of Atlanta in 1842, after which the money ran out. Sold in 1845, it re-emerged as the Macon & Western, supplying a link to Atlanta the following year.

Montgomery—*See Western Railway of Alabama.*

Montgomery & Eufaula—Central of Georgia entered Montgomery after buying M&E, chartered January 13, 1860. Delayed by the Civil War, it didn't reach Eufaula until October 1, 1871. It entered receivership (1873), was sold (1879), and emerged under CofG (1895). Controlled by Illinois Central (1909), it again entered receivership (1932). M&E was acquired by Southern Railway in 1963 and merged into Norfolk Southern in 1982. Passenger service was brisk ferrying trains between Louisville, Kentucky, and Florida, ending May 31, 1952.

Montgomery & West Point—*See Western Railway of Alabama.*

Mount Airy & Ore Knob—*See Cape Fear & Yadkin Valley.*

Mount Hope Valley—*See Durham & South Carolina.*

Muscle Shoals, Birmingham & Pensacola—*See Alabama & Gulf Coast.*

Muscogee—50-mile route linking Georgia cities Columbus and Butler chartered in 1845, expected to reach Central of Georgia's main at Macon. When it fell short Southwestern Railroad added a stem connecting Muscogee with Fort Valley to create a continuous line between Columbus and Macon (1853). Southwestern absorbed Muscogee in 1856 and CofG in 1868.

Nashville & Chattanooga—This 151-mile road linked namesake cities. Chartered in 1845, it was the first flourishing railway in Tennessee at completion (1854) with stems to varied Tennessee and Alabama towns. Mainline dipped into northern Alabama before resurfacing at Chattanooga. There it

connected with Western & Atlantic to Atlanta and a link to Savannah's port. In Nashville, N&C met Louisville & Nashville (1859), forwarding travelers and goods to Louisville. With expansion to Memphis and more west Tennessee and Kentucky points, N&C altered its sobriquet to Nashville, Chattanooga & St. Louis (1873). L&N bought it (1880) and allowed it to remain under its own brand until NC&StL was folded into L&N (1957).

Nashville & Decatur—N&D emerged from consolidation of Tennessee & Alabama and Central Southern railroads. In 1872, L&N leased Nashville & Decatur (Alabama) and South & North Alabama to open a continuous route south of Nashville through Birmingham that led to Alabama's state capital at Montgomery. L&N completed unfinished tracks on S&NA tying Decatur to Montgomery. Birmingham, according to a historian, "came into being, largely as a result of the above acquisitions."

Nashville & Knoxville—*See Tennessee Central.*

Nashville & Northwestern—Chartered in 1852; it took 16 years to construct a 168-mile route between Nashville and Hickman, Kentucky, on the Mississippi River, severely hampered by Civil War destruction. The carrier was ultimately absorbed into Nashville, Chattanooga & St. Louis.

Nashville, Chattanooga & St. Louis Railway—Although NC&StL began as a separate and older entity, it merged in the mid 20th century with the Louisville & Nashville, to eventually become the second most extensive system in the South. NC&StL was a bridge carrier that joined lines in Midwestern cities like Chicago and St. Louis to destinations beyond the end of its route, including Florida. Western & Atlantic Railway, organized in 1936 by the government of Georgia, was its earliest predecessor. The 151-mile Nashville & Chattanooga Railway became one of its most important precursors, ultimately to be the NC&StL's most traveled route, including passenger service. By 1854, N&C offered passenger service to Atlantic coast cities of Savannah, Georgia, and Charleston, South Carolina. Another precursor was the Nashville & Northwestern Railway ultimately connecting Nashville with the Mississippi River 168 miles to the west. NC&StL became part of the L&N system in 1957. *See Chapter 10.*

New Albany & Salem—*See Louisville, New Albany & Chicago.*

New Orleans & Mississippi Valley—*See Louisville, New Orleans & Texas.*

New Orleans & Mobile—In the years after the Civil War, Louisiana and New Orleans prompted new rail expansion by offering land grants to emerging ventures. Wharf-side parcels were assigned to New Orleans, Mobile, and Chattanooga (1869). A route opened in 1870 along the Gulf. It may have been reduced to a more realistic New Orleans & Mobile over time (sources aren't clear on origination). Buying NO&M in 1940 allowed Gulf, Mobile & Northern — a forerunner of Gulf, Mobile & Ohio— to take trains to East St. Louis, Illinois. That was a key link in the route system of a coming GM&O.

New Orleans & Northeastern — Incorporated by the Louisiana legislature in 1868 under the sobriquet Mandeville & Sulphur Springs, it was altered to NO&N (1870). NO&N was a standard-gauge, single-track, 196-mile route between New Orleans and Meridian, encountering Slidell, Louisiana, and Picayune, Poplarville, Hattiesburg, and Laurel, Mississippi, en route. It was controlled by Southern Railway from 1916, adding it to the lower end of a main beginning nearly a thousand miles distant at Washington, D.C. The route sees heavy freight traffic and — in its heyday — many SOU passenger consists daily to and from the Crescent City. Norfolk Southern absorbed the rails in 1982. Amtrak has schlepped travelers along them since 1979.

New Orleans Great Northern — Chartered in 1905, NOGN was leased by Gulf, Mobile & Northern in 1933 to gain a route into the Crescent City. GM&N was one of two key antecedents of Gulf, Mobile & Ohio formed in 1940.

New Orleans, Jackson & Great Northern — Organized in 1851, it survived to 1874, merging with Mississippi Central to form New Orleans, St. Louis & Chicago. NOJ&GN linked the Crescent City with the rest of the nation prior to Civil War, reaching 206 miles north from New Orleans to Canton, Mississippi, meeting with MC, which ran to Jackson, Tennessee.

New Orleans, Mobile & Chattanooga — Built under an act of the Alabama legislature (1866), NOM&C was sold and reorganized as New Orleans, Mobile & Texas (1880), its 140-mile route running between namesake Gulf cities. Acquired by L&N in 1881, NOM&C formed the southern terminus of a L&N mainline beginning in Cincinnati.

New Orleans, Mobile & Chicago — Mobile, Jackson & Kansas City, chartered in 1890, opened 50 miles between Merrill, Mississippi, and Mobile in 1898. Tracks extended to Beaumont (1902) with a link to Hattiesburg over Bonhomie & Hattiesburg Southern. New owners bought MJ&KC and a 62-mile narrow gauge Gulf & Chicago tying Middleton, Tennessee, with Pontotoc, Mississippi, then filled in 240 miles to connect the pair. MJ&KC was bankrupt when construction ended in 1906. Out of receivership, it appeared as New Orleans, Mobile & Chicago (1909). L&N and Frisco assumed NOM&C control in 1911 but the road collapsed again in 1913. It emerged from receivership as Gulf, Mobile & Northern (1917), a vital antecedent of Gulf, Mobile & Ohio (1940). *See Gulf, Mobile & Northern.*

New Orleans, Mobile & Texas — *See New Orleans, Mobile & Chattanooga.*

New Orleans, St. Louis & Chicago — Organized 1874, it is easily confused with Chicago, St. Louis & New Orleans, which came later. Formed by merging New Orleans, Jackson & Great Northern, and Mississippi Central, NOSL&C connected Jackson, Tennessee, with New Orleans. It was divided into three roads in 1877: New Orleans; Jackson & Northern; and Central Mississippi. In 1882, they were consolidated as Chicago, St. Louis & New Orleans, a wholly owned ancillary of Illinois Central.

New River — Chartered 1872, NR planned to run rails into the heart of Virginia coal fields. When N&W bought the unfinished line it altered the projected course by buying property around Pocahontas, Virginia. On May 2, 1883, a new route from New River, Virginia, to Bluefield, West Virginia, opened to traffic. It bore Pocahontas coal bound for the port at Norfolk. Overnight coal became N&W's chief product that led to vast profitability.

Norfolk, Albemarle & Southern — *See Norfolk, Virginia Beach & Southern.*

Norfolk & Petersburg — Completed in 1858, it tied Virginia's Tidewater with its central section. After N&P's president, William Mahone, concurrently gained the top job at Southside Railroad, he urged merger with Virginia & Tennessee to form a route from Bristol to Norfolk. He accomplished it in 1870 as the three carriers formed the Atlantic, Mississippi & Ohio based in Lynchburg. In 1881, AM&O reorganized as Norfolk & Western.

Norfolk & Virginia Beach — *See Norfolk, Virginia Beach & Southern.*

Norfolk & Western Railway — N&W was primarily a coal hauler, but ran a handful of passenger trains from its base in the Appalachian Mountains. It didn't have a populated region from which to draw traveling customers, but did serve as a link for people traveling long distances. Its hallmark was carrying enormous amounts of coal to various points, all the while operating in fine financial health with an excellent fleet with steadfastly devoted employees. It achieved no fewer than 200 mergers in 150 years. Norfolk and Western Railroad was created in 1881 when new owners netted the Atlantic, Mississippi and Ohio Railroad and changed its name. Fifteen years later, after a foreclosure sale, it was renamed Norfolk and Western Railway, which stuck throughout its years as an independent carrier. Roanoke, Virginia, was the base of its operations for most of its existence; the enormous Roanoke Shops became legendary for manufacturing steam locomotives and other rolling stock. Its flagship passenger consists *Powhatan Arrow* and *Pocahontas* offered luxury travel, which continued until the formation of Amtrak in 1971. N&W was merged into Norfolk Southern Corporation in 1998, after earlier becoming a subsidiary. *See Chapter 11.*

Norfolk Southern—Its oldest appellation, Elizabeth City & Norfolk, dated to 1871; original Norfolk Southern received its durable name (NS) in 1883. Ultimately it ferried people and products over a 622-mile main from Norfolk to Charlotte. Meandering through Carolina countryside, branches broke off the route to Virginia Beach, Fayetteville, New Bern and others. NS was one of Southern Railway's final acquisitions (1974). When SOU merged with Norfolk & Western (1982), NS was designated Carolina & Northwestern, freeing "NS" for a new SOU–N&W combo. *See Appendix B.*

Norfolk Southern—Class 1 freight carrier operating primarily in eastern U.S., formed 1982, when Norfolk & Western and Southern systems merged. *See Appendix B.*

Norfolk, Virginia Beach & Atlantic—*See Norfolk, Virginia Beach & Southern.*

Norfolk, Virginia Beach & Southern—Name changes of the initially narrow-gauge line are legion. Built to connect namesake cities as Norfolk, Virginia Beach Railroad and Improvement Company (1883), it was reorganized as Norfolk & Virginia Beach (1887), again as Norfolk, Albemarle & Southern (1891), sold to re-emerge as Norfolk, Virginia Beach & Atlantic (1896), with stem added from Virginia Beach to Munden Point from which

steamers plied Currituck Sound (1898), and finally renamed NVB&S as the original Norfolk Southern bought it (1900). NS passenger traffic was vulnerable to highways within a quarter-century, prompting it to launch Norfolk Southern Bus Corporation (1926) with routes largely paralleling rails.

North and South Railroad of Georgia—Organized at Columbus on August 11, 1871, with a planned narrow gauge route to Hamilton, LaGrange, Franklin, Carrollton, Cedartown and Rome. Beset by financial difficulties, it was sold to an individual in 1878 and reorganized as Columbus & Rome (1879). Merged with Savannah & Western (1882) and shifted in foreclosure to Central of Georgia (1895). A decade later CofG standardized its track and extended it to Raymond, Georgia, tying into CofG's Griffin–Chattanooga line.

North Carolina Railroad—Chartered 1856, the inaugural 223-mile state-owned NC was leased to Richmond & Danville (1871), a forerunner of Southern Railway, to which NC was leased at SOU's inception (1894), then to heir Norfolk Southern (1982). NC had absorbed Atlantic & North Carolina in 1989, essentially gaining its present route. Now its 317-mile line runs from the central Piedmont's Charlotte to Morehead City at the coast.

Northeastern—Chartered 1851 and opened 1856, Northeastern persisted from Charleston north

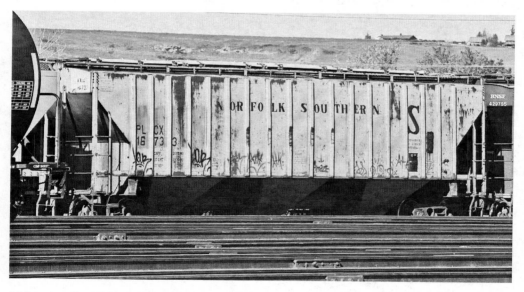

A historic relic, PLCX (General Electric Rail Services) covered hopper 16733 is a lingering piece of rolling freight stock of an unmistakably Norfolk Southern Railway—the original one launched in 1883, not 1982, after the Norfolk & Western and Southern roads amalgamated. On June 21, 2008, this hopper was far from its eastern seaboard roots at the Burlington Northern Santa Fe yards in Great Falls, Montana. While it has surely seen better days, it nevertheless remains a symbol of long ago glory in Dixie (***courtesy Robert W. Thomson***).

to Florence, South Carolina, linking with Wilmington & Manchester. It joined Wilmington, Columbia & Augusta (W&M renamed) and a few more carriers to form Atlantic Coast Line Railroad Company of South Carolina (1898), a fundamental part of Atlantic Coast Line (1900).

Oconee & Western — Organized 1892, O&W took over a failed Empire & Dublin. E&D built a 39-mile road between Dublin and Hawkinsville in the south Georgia counties of Laurens and Pulaski (1889-1890). It expected to extend its route another 30 miles from Hawkinsville to Grovania but it's unclear if that occurred. In 1896, Wrightsville & Tennille bought the Dublin–Hawkinsville route, extending W&T's mainline from Tennille.

Overseas Railroad — Colloquial term still in widespread use referring to the ambitious overwater extension of the Florida East Coast. It ran between Miami and Key West from 1912 until an unnamed hurricane washed some of its tracks to sea in 1935, sealing its end as a viable transport carrier.

Owensboro & Nashville — O&N was built under a charter granted Owensboro & Russellville (1867), subsequently altered to Evansville, Owensboro & Nashville. Only 36 miles of track was laid in western Kentucky when it went into receivership. In 1879, Nashville, Chattanooga & St. Louis made overtures for O&N. This and other NC&StL buys in the region set off alarm bells in the Louisville headquarters of L&N, which intended to control the area. In 1880, L&N outmaneuvered NC&StL, making a secret deal to buy its threatening competition and gain control of the market.

Paducah and Louisville — Purchased from Illinois Central Gulf (1986), P&L is a 223-mile freight carrier linking namesake Kentucky cities, and 47 branch line miles. In much earlier days these tracks saw passenger consists daily trekking between the state's largest city and westernmost large town.

Paducah, Tennessee & Alabama — PT&A reached Paducah from Hazel, Kentucky, near the Tennessee border (1890). Acquired by L&N (1895) PT&A was leased to L&N's NC&StL subsidiary (1896). Combined with Tennessee Midland — also leased to NC&StL by L&N — the pair formed a 230-mile route linking Paducah and Memphis, those lines meeting at Lexington, Tennessee. The course saw people and products hauled between Ohio and Mississippi rivers. At Memphis they transferred to other rail lines or seagoing vessels and were forwarded to more interior destinations or port cities (Mobile, New Orleans, Beaumont, Galveston).

Palatka & Indian River — *See Jacksonville, Tampa & Key West.*

Peninsular — *See Atlantic, Gulf & West India Transit.*

Pennsylvania — Organized in 1846, it was one of two most powerful lines in the East, linking New York with its Philadelphia headquarters, Chicago and St. Louis. Its main crossed West Virginia at Wheeling while branches brushed Dixie at Norfolk (via steamer), minor Virginia termini, and Louisville with a north-south route to Chicago. PRR ferried trains of four Dixie carriers (Atlantic Coast Line, Chesapeake & Ohio, Seaboard Air Line, Southern) on its busy Washington, D.C., to New York line. With rival New York Central, PRR formed Penn Central (1968); Conrail emerged from that (1975), with the spoils divided by CSX and Norfolk Southern (1999). *See Appendix B.*

Pensacola, Alabama & Tennessee — *See Alabama & Gulf Coast.*

Pensacola & Atlantic — *See Savannah, Florida & Western.*

Pensacola & Georgia — Chartered 1853, intending to build east from Pensacola, Florida. Plans changed and construction started east from Tallahassee (1856) to meet Florida, Atlantic & Gulf Central, then built west from Jacksonville. P&G took control of Tallahassee Railroad in 1856. P&G's terminus at Lake City (formerly Alligator Town), where it met FA&G in 1860, was 106 miles from Tallahassee. From 1861 to 1863, P&G built a 24-mile extension west from Tallahassee to Quincy. Never a financial success, P&G was in "a wretched condition" at war's end. P&G and Tallahassee were sold at foreclosure to form Jacksonville, Pensacola & Mobile (1869).

Pensacola & Mobile — *See Alabama & Gulf Coast.*

Pensacola & Perdido — *See Alabama & Gulf Coast.*

Petersburg — Chartered in 1830; visionaries saw benefits of trading with North Carolinians who were doing brisk commerce with Virginia's Tidewater area. Petersburg gained substantially when Richmond & Petersburg was organized, adding a link to the state capital (1838). Petersburg's chief distinction is as the oldest component of Atlantic Coast Line (1900).

Piedmont & Northern — P&N ran passenger trains over 150 miles of track between Charlotte and Gastonia, North Carolina, and Greenwood and Spartanburg, South Carolina, along with freight hauling operations. It was created in 1909 when power company VP William Lee States proposed an electrically powered railway linking major cities of the two states. Another segment to Atlanta and Washington, D.C., never materialized. Passenger service ended in 1951, and the rest of the operations merged with Seaboard Coast Line Railroad in 1969. *See Appendix B.*

Plant System — An amalgamation of railroads and steamboats in Alabama, Florida, Georgia and South Carolina in the latter decades of the 19th cen-

In 1977, a short Amtrak *Floridian* with seven heritage cars is led from Tampa Union Station to Chicago by EMD SDP40F 612. Behind the head-end power a dormitory-baggage car is followed by a dome coach and five more passenger cars. A SCL Budd boat-tail diesel locomotive observation car converted for instruction is between the *Floridian* and headhouse. Many platform tracks and canopies that used to be in the foreground have been removed. Today the site is improved, Union Station was refurbished and the Tampa skyline is dotted with modern skyscrapers, a more impressive vista (*courtesy Michael B. Robbins*).

tury. Spawned by Connecticut Yankee self-made millionaire Henry B. Plant, a rail tycoon and luxury resort hotel owner; Plant's first railway was Savannah, Florida & Western, chartered 1847, connecting Savannah and Albany, Georgia. The Plant venture was sold to Atlantic Coast Line in 1902.

Pontchartrain—Built in 1830-1831, Pontchartrain was the first line west of the Alleghenies and thereby first to provide New Orleaneans with a taste of rail travel, spawning complex future lines. Affectionately dubbed "Old Smoky Mary" after a popular 1920s streetcar ("Smoky Mary") that ran from the French Quarter to the lakefront at Milneburg, by 1831 the railway hauled riders five miles from the Mississippi River to Lake Pontchartrain at Milneburg. It was the second U.S. steam-powered passenger-carrying railway, the first also launched in Dixie at Charleston, South Carolina (1930). A seawall added at Milneburg in 1930 displaced some attractions, sealing the area's fate as a trendy tourist destination for the middle class.

Port Royal & Augusta—Chartered in 1878, this was a precursor of Charleston & Western Carolina (1890). *See Charleston & Western Carolina* and *Greenville & Columbia.*

Port Royal & Western Carolina—Chartered in 1886; an ancestor of Charleston & Western Carolina (1890). *See Charleston & Western Carolina* and *Greenville & Columbia.*

Portsmouth & Roanoke—Chartered 1832, P&R was the founding father of the future Seaboard Air Line. Construction from Portsmouth, Virginia, to Weldon, North Carolina, 79 miles distant, began in 1833. The following year horse-drawn wooden coaches ferried travelers twice daily from Portsmouth to Suffolk, Virginia. It was little more

than a stagecoach run over a defined route with a better roadbed. By September 1834, a four-wheel five-ton steam engine (*John Barnett*) ran the tracks at 15 miles an hour, vastly improving the 75-minute trip. In 1836, *Barnett* went all the way to Weldon. It was sold to new owners in 1843 who renamed P&R Seaboard & Roanoke; rails were replaced—61 miles from Portsmouth to the state line by S&R and 18 miles to Weldon by Roanoke Railroad. Roanoke was absorbed by S&R in 1849. Purchases, construction and interline connections increased the route system in future decades. On August 1, 1893, S&R was the oldest of five carriers to form SAL.

Prescott & Northwestern—Chartered in 1890 to construct a rail line north-northwest from Prescott, Arkansas, to timberlands of a private lumber mill. Track added later ran to Arcadia, Blevins, McCaskill, Belton, Tokio, and Highland. While forest products dominated freight, for years Elberta peaches grown at Highland made the journey during harvests. At Prescott, refrigerator cars carried them to northern markets via Missouri Pacific. By the 1950s, lumber and cement—the latter from a Highland plant—comprised most of P&N's cargo. Passenger service was offered during the road's heyday although it was discontinued in November 1945. When the cement plant shuttered (1980), P&N's reach was numbered. Unused tracks north of Prescott were retained for potential use after second growth timber was harvested. Abandonment and dismantling occurred with ownership strategy changes (1994). P&N now maintains five miles of Prescott switching track mostly between a sawmill and MoPac (now Union Pacific).

Raleigh & Augusta Air-Line—Debuting as

Chatham Railroad 1871, R&AAL —from its start a subsidiary of Raleigh & Gaston —built a 98-mile route from Raleigh to Hamlet, North Carolina (completed 1877). It joined east-west carrier Carolina Central there.

Raleigh & Gaston —Chartered 1835, begun 1836, completed 1840, an 86-mile R&G connected North Carolina's state capital with Roanoke River hamlet of Gaston. R&G created a way (using three railroads) to travel unimpeded from Raleigh to Richmond. At a foreclosure sale in 1845, the State of North Carolina became its owner. R&G was reorganized (1851-1852) with the state remaining majority owner. R&G merged with Seaboard Air Line (1900) and eventually became part of CSX Transportation (1980).

Raleigh & Southport —*See Raleigh, Charlotte & Southern.*

Raleigh, Charlotte & Southern —Acting independently in less than two years under its moniker (1912-1913), RC&S still got a lot done. It absorbed Aberdeen & Asheboro, Raleigh & Southport, Durham & Charlotte, and Sanford & Troy. On January 1, 1914, RC&S was folded into the original Norfolk Southern, then running its mainline from Norfolk to Charlotte.

Red Springs & Northern —An old route of Cape Fear & Yadkin Valley created in 1884 from Parkton to Red Springs, North Carolina; changed hands after 1967. Renamed RS&N, it has since interchanged with CSX at Parkton.

Richmond & Allegheny —In 1880, Kanawha Canal was deeded to R&A and laying track on a water-level route began from Virginia's capital to the Appalachians. R&A built from Richmond beside the James River and Kanawha Canal to near Buchanan, Virginia (west of Lynchburg), where it met Buchanan & Clifton Forge to access Clifton Forge. Chesapeake & Ohio leased (1888) and later bought R&A. Today the route is a part of CSX.

Richmond & Danville —A 140-mile line linking dual Virginia towns, chartered in 1847 and opened in 1856. Financier J.P. Morgan and others took control of R&D and reorganized it as Southern Railway on July 1, 1894. SOU became one of Dixie's dominant transporters, encompassing 13 states and 8,883 route miles. For several decades in the late 19th century, meanwhile, R&D was a potent manager of rail lines throughout the Southeast, buying numerous carriers and otherwise significantly influencing ownership.

Richmond & Petersburg —Strategic route chartered 1830; opened two years hence to link Virginia's capital to Petersburg Railroad with connections to North Carolina trade. In the Civil War, R&P was a vital channel in hauling men and material from the Wilmington, North Carolina, port. It played a part in forming the Atlantic Coast Line (1900).

Richmond, Fredericksburg & Potomac —Critical bridge route that linked Richmond, Virginia, and the nation's capital (1842). RF&P served trains of a half-dozen carriers forming the Richmond-Washington Company (1901) to oversee its operations: Atlantic Coast Line, Baltimore & Ohio, Chesapeake & Ohio, Pennsylvania, Seaboard Air Line, and Southern. After multiple fusions, RF&P was acquired by CSX in 1991. *See Appendix B.*

Richmond, Petersburg & Carolina —The 1892 heir to Virginia & Carolina (established 1882), in 1897, Virginia-based RP&C was taken over by John Skelton Williams and others putting together Seaboard Air Line (1900).

Richmond Terminal —A holding company that at its peak (1890) controlled all or portions of nearly 9,000 miles of Dixie rails. In 1893, financier and rail magnate J.P. Morgan turned the Terminal from a holding company into one operating Southern Railway System.

Ripley —Chartered 1872; soon renamed Ripley, Ship Island & Kentucky and later Gulf & Chicago. Owner ran a line from his Ripley, Mississippi, plantation connecting with Memphis & Charleston at Middleton, Tennessee. RSI&K gained its third moniker when the route was extended through New Albany, Mississippi, to Pontotoc. Ultimately G&C was absorbed into Gulf, Mobile & Northern, an antecedent of Gulf, Mobile & Ohio (1940).

Ripley, Ship Island & Kentucky —*See Ripley.*

Roanoke —*See Portsmouth & Roanoke.*

Rock Island —This line began operating in 1852 as Chicago & Rock Island Railroad, in time reaching Dallas, Denver, El Paso, Houston, Minneapolis and St. Louis. It ran its *Choctaw Rocket* passenger consist from Memphis to Amarillo, downgrading it in 1952 and again in 1964, but RI was one of few rail lines that continued passenger service beyond the creation of Amtrak in 1971. With additional routes came an addition to its name, which is now Chicago, Rock Island & Pacific Railroad. *See Appendix B.*

Rome & Carrollton —Never laying any tracks, R&C was chartered in 1881 to connect its dual north Georgia namesakes. In 1887, it was renamed Chattanooga, Rome & Columbus with control passed to Central of Georgia.

Rome & Decatur —*See East Tennessee, Virginia & Georgia.*

St. Louis, Alton & Chicago —One of several handles applied starting with Alton & Sangamon (1847). The carrier evolved into Chicago & Mississippi, SA&C about 1955, Chicago & Alton about 1862, and merged into Gulf, Mobile & Ohio on May 31, 1947, under Alton nomenclature. *See Alton.*

St. Louis & Cairo —In 1886, Mobile & Ohio purchased the narrow gauge SL&C connecting East St. Louis with Cairo, Illinois, on the Ohio River banks.

Once widened to standard gauge, M&O celebrated a 650-mile system tying Mobile with St. Louis. M&O was to segue into Gulf, Mobile & Ohio (1940).

St. Louis & North Arkansas—*See Eureka Springs.*

St. Louis & Southeastern—NC&StL took an interest in Illinois and Indiana sectors of St. Louis & Southeastern Railway in 1879. That line joined East St. Louis, Illinois, on the Mississippi River's east bank, with Evansville. That same year L&N bought a line from Evansville to Nashville. St. Louis & Southeastern Railway completed those tracks a short time before. Then threatened by a number of purchases by the smaller NC&StL, L&N reacted by becoming the majority stockholder of its rival. The new route was to be beneficial to L&N in ferrying traffic between Nashville and St. Louis.

St. Louis–San Francisco—Five of the nine states where the "Frisco" operated were in Dixie and the rest were in the South Central and Midwest, though it never reached San Francisco at all. It was incorporated in St. Louis, Missouri, in 1876 from some established lines. During its heyday it had two main routes, one between St. Louis and Oklahoma City and another from Kansas City to Birmingham. The routes crossed at Springfield, Missouri, where the company's shops were located. The *Texas Special* was jointly the passenger flagship of this rail and the Missouri-Kansas-Texas Railroad. It upgraded from steam to diesel in 1947. The *Sunnyland* traversed tracks in the South, as did the *Kansas City–Florida Special.* Amtrak took over the passenger business in 1971. The company was acquired in 1980 by the Burlington Northern Railroad. *See Chapter 12.*

Sanford & Troy—*See Raleigh, Charlotte & Southern.*

Savannah, Albany & Gulf—Chartered as Savannah & Albany (1847), it was to link Savannah and Albany, Georgia; renamed SA&G (1853). Completed in 1858, it ran from Savannah to Screven. SA&G merged with Atlantic & Gulf (1863) to provide an uninterrupted line from Savannah to Thomasville.

Savannah, Americus & Montgomery—As Americus, Preston & Lumpkin, it laid narrow gauge tracks from its Americus base to Richland, Lumpkin, Louvale and Abbeville, Georgia (1884–1887). Reorganization as SA&M in December 1888 produced an extension to Lyons to connect with Central of Georgia auxiliary Savannah & Western (1890). Shortly thereafter an expansion from Louvale carried SA&M to the Chattahoochee River. At Abbeville it linked with its own fleet of watercraft plying the Ocmulgee and Altamaha rivers to Darien, Brunswick and Savannah. SA&M leased Albany & Northern tying Albany and Cordele

(1892). Sold at foreclosure (1895), SA&M emerged as Georgia & Alabama with A&N spun off.

Savannah & Atlanta—Chartered in 1915, completed in 1916, the 142-mile route from Savannah terminated between Warrenton and Camak, Georgia, at S&A Junction on Georgia Railroad's mainline (Atlanta to Augusta). S&A's import is manifold: Georgia relied on it to access Savannah; S&A absorbed Savannah & Northwestern (1917), an outfit operating it in its first year; and the S&A line was 28 miles shorter between its namesake cities than Central of Georgia. S&A entered receivership (1921), was bought by an individual (1929), bought by CofG (1951), folded into Southern Railway (1971), and absorbed by Norfolk Southern (1982).

Savannah & Atlantic—*See Savannah & Tybee.*

Savannah & Columbus—In two months since its charter was issued in May 1888, S&C didn't start on its mission to construct a line between Georgia villages Eden and Americus. It was grouped instead with a handful of carriers by owner Central Railroad and Banking Company of Georgia, fused into Savannah & Western in July 1888, a Central of Georgia unit.

Savannah & Memphis—With roots in Opelika & Talladega (1854) renamed Opelika & Tuscumbia (1861), neither of which laid any track, a reorganized Savannah & Memphis (1866) took a stab where others failed. It took S&M eight years to lay 55 miles of rail from Opelika to Goodwater, Alabama. S&M was sold at foreclosure to Columbus & Western (1880) before C&W was folded into Central of Georgia ancillary Savannah & Western (1888).

Savannah & Northwestern—Launched as Brinson Railway (1910), S&N acquired its name in 1914 after its founder departed. By adding existing tracks to some new construction, Brinson opened a route from Savannah to St. Claire, Georgia, connecting at the latter with Georgia & Florida. In 1916, Savannah & Atlanta linked with S&N at St. Claire. It ran to Georgia Railroad's main near Camak and then over it to Atlanta. For a year S&N operated S&A; in 1917, S&A absorbed S&N.

Savannah & Tybee—An 18-mile route tying Savannah, Georgia, with the coast; in quick succession S&T was chartered (1886), completed (1887), entered receivership (1888), sold (1889), dubbed Savannah, Tybee & Atlantic (1890), and dubbed Savannah & Atlantic (1890). Its stock was acquired by Central of Georgia (1890), which operated it until abandonment (1932).

Savannah & Western—Central of Georgia created a key subsidiary in S&W (1888). Seven CofG–held roads were folded into it and 57 miles of new track built between Georgia hamlets Meldrim and Lyons (1890). That created a line linking Americus, Georgia, and Birmingham via Columbus. S&W acquired Savannah, Griffin, and North Alabama

Central of Georgia may have been dominant regional carrier in the Peach State. Yet when the route of Savannah & Atlanta running northwest from Savannah to Georgia Railroad's main (Augusta-Atlanta). at Camak, Georgia, was combined with it, it provided the shortest — dare we say fastest?— tracks to the state capital. After S&A was bought by CofG in 1951, its rolling stock like this GP-35 locomotive went with it. In 2004, 2715 was part of the heritage of a noble rival exhibited at CofG's Savannah Roundhouse Museum (*courtesy Clyde Woodruff*).

(1890) tying Griffin to Carrollton, Georgia, and bought Chattanooga, Rome & Columbus (1891), a Carrollton to Chattanooga route. S&W and CofG emerged (1894) from subsequent receivership; courts returned CR&C to former owners and CofG gained it in 1901. S&W was sold and assigned to CofG (1895). The Meldrim and Lyons stretch was leased to Georgia & Alabama (1896).

Savannah, Florida & Western — At a 1879 fore-closure sale, rail and hotel magnate Henry B. Plant bought assets of a defunct Atlantic & Gulf and re-organized it as SF&W. It built 71 miles of track for ancillaries Waycross & Florida and East Florida in southeast Georgia and northeast Florida (1881). It created a 32-mile route between Climax, Georgia, and Chattahoochee, Florida, connecting with L&N ancillary Pensacola & Atlantic. Several Florida roads plus W&F were consolidated into SF&W (1884). Brunswick & Western (bought 1884) was added to SF&W's portfolio (1901). A stem from Thomasville, Georgia, to Monticello, Florida, was constructed in 1888. As part of a larger Plant System, SF&W was folded into Atlantic Coast Line when Plant's roads were acquired in 1902.

Savannah, Griffin & North Alabama — Sixteen years after chartering in 1854, SG&NA ran trains between Georgia burgs Griffin and Newnan, reaching Carrollton in two more years (1872). There is evidence this road operated under Central of Georgia auspices then; proof exists SG&NA in foreclosure was sold to Savannah & Western, a CofG ancillary, in 1890.

Savannah, Tybee & Atlantic — *See Savannah & Tybee.*

Seaboard Air Line — In existence well before air travel was a reality, this company's "air line" name implied that travel was in a straight line, as the crow flies perhaps, to reach its destinations quickly. SAL's earliest antecedent was the Portsmouth & Roanoke Railroad, chartered in 1832 to link Portsmouth, Virginia, with Weldon, North Carolina, in its earliest days plying wooden coaches pulled by literal horse power. After further transitions and improvements, P&R reopened the route in 1851. The Seaboard Air-Line System came into being in 1893, combining five separate companies with tracks extending from Portsmouth through the Carolinas to Atlanta. Further expansion brought about the Seaboard Airline Railroad. Its crack passenger train, the *Orange Blossom Special* running from New York to Florida, was immortalized in a song written by Ervin T. Rouse in 1938. SAL launched streamlined equipment on its rails in 1939. After the mid-twentieth century brought widespread alternatives in transportation, SAL merged with rival Atlantic Coast Line in 1967 to form Seaboard Coast Line Railroad Company, which later folded into the CSX Corporation. *See Chapter 13.*

Seaboard Air Line Belt — When an embargo threatened competition by preventing trains of the Georgia, Carolina & Northern — a line from Monroe, North Carolina, to Atlanta completed in 1892 — from actually entering the Georgia capital, GC&N found a way around the injunction.

It built an eight-mile SAL Belt Railroad from Inman Park at Belt Junction near Emory University on Atlanta's east side across the city's northern side. GC&N trains went west to Howells, a community northwest of Atlanta, where they met up with Nashville, Chattanooga & St. Louis. Gaining trackage rights there, GC&N entered downtown Atlanta.

Seaboard & Roanoke — *See Portsmouth & Roanoke.*

Selma, Rome & Dalton — *See East Tennessee, Virginia & Georgia.*

Shenandoah Valley — Organized 1867, construction began in 1879 and ended in 1882, with tracks from Hagerstown, Maryland, to Roanoke, where it linked with Norfolk & Western. In receivership (1885) SV was sold to N&W (1890). N&W merged with Southern Railway to become Norfolk Southern in 1982.

Silver Springs, Ocala & Gulf — Assigned land grants on March 12, 1879, by Florida's legislature, the finish line had to be met by law to exercise those grants. Completion was extended twice, finally to September 1, 1897, 18 and a half years after proffer. On January 9, 1893, meanwhile, the Plant System bought SSO&G, adding it to a large inventory.

SSO&G's 43-mile mainline ran from Ocala to Inverness to join South Florida, another Plant property with a main between Sanford and Tampa and branches north and south. Thirty-two miles of SSO&G stems led to Homosassa and phosphate mines. The mines, previously dependent on a distant Fernandina wharf for exporting, reached Tampa's larger, deeper, closer port when SSO&G opened. Completing about 60 miles of new track from Dunnellon to High Springs, Plant controlled a continuous line from Tampa to Montgomery, reportedly the shortest route for western traffic to and from south Florida.

South & North Alabama — A route original owners didn't complete between Montgomery and Decatur starting at the southern end and accessing only Birmingham. At that juncture L&N leased S&NA (1872), and then finished track-laying north to Decatur. Tying in to Nashville & Decatur there, which it also leased, L&N created a continuous route extending its mainline south of Nashville to Montgomery. Eventually L&N ran trains still farther — to the Gulf ports of Mobile, New Orleans and Pensacola.

South Bound — Launched construction in 1888, completing a 135-mile course from Cayce Junction

One of numerous railroad diamonds near the historic passenger station at Plant City, Florida, east of Tampa, is shown on May 5, 2007. Here former ACL and SAL mains cross — both now CSX property. Their routes from Jacksonville to Tampa and more of the west coast ran in contrary courses. Each had a backstory. An important segment of SAL's is recounted in histories of the South Bound and Florida Central & Peninsular lines. Some of ACL's legacy, meanwhile, is invested in the precursor Plant System (*courtesy Michael B. Robbins*).

(near Columbia, South Carolina) and Savannah in 1891. In 1892, South Bound's tracks were leased to Florida Central & Peninsular for 99 years effective October 1, 1893. That was the time FC&P's new rails from Jacksonville were expected to reach Savannah, forming a continuous line from Columbia to Plant City, Florida. FC&P soon bought all South Bound stock. FC&P itself was bought by investors, creating a line of still more imposing proportions (1899) to run from Richmond, Virginia, to Tampa. To be labeled Seaboard Air Line, it opened August 1, 1900.

South Carolina Canal & Railroad Company—Exhibited the first U.S. steam-driven train with locomotive, *Best Friend of Charleston*, on the Charleston & Hamburg line in 1830, setting a new benchmark for motive power.

South Carolina Pacific—*See Cape Fear & Yadkin Valley.*

Southern—The SOU's beginnings date back to 1827, when the South Carolina Canal and Railroad Company was organized. On Christmas Day 1830 SCC&R debuted a steam engine, *Best Friend of Charleston*, which then supplied continuous trips over its six miles of tracks at 25 miles an hour, making it the first regularly scheduled engine-driven passenger service. With additional trackage, it was also the first to carry U.S. troops and mail. Over its life span Southern had 150 forebears. Southern Railway, established in 1894, resulted when the strapped Richmond & Danville Railroad blended with the East Tennessee, Virginia & Georgia Railroad. John Pierpont Morgan was prominent in its formation. It maintained first class passenger service through much of the 20th century (including the *Crescent* and *Southerner*) and had rails traversing 14 states in the South and adjacent areas. Southern's *Fast Mail* and engineer Joseph A. Broadey (Broady) were the subject of a famous ballad, "Wreck of the Old 97," written following a tragic accident near Danville, Virginia, in 1903. Southern was one of few systems continuing passenger service beyond the formation of Amtrak in 1971. It finally handed over that service in 1979; Amtrak continues to run a consist named *Crescent* between New York and New Orleans daily. As the sun began to set on the 20th century, Southern became a component of Norfolk Southern Corporation in 1982 and was renamed Norfolk Southern Railway in 1990. It remains a strong competitor to the behemoth CSX Corporation. *See Chapter 14.*

Southern Pacific—Launched in San Francisco, California, in 1865, this system expanded into the South. It extended to St. Louis, Dallas, Memphis and Shreveport, and was entrenched in the South with an enduring line to New Orleans. It plied freight routes to and from Gulf and Mississippi River ports and ran the *Sunset Limited* passenger consist between the bayous of Louisiana and the Pacific Coast. Its passenger service ended with the creation of Amtrak in 1971. The name was lost in further mergers in the 1980s and 1990s; the system became part of Union Pacific Railroad in 1996. *See Appendix B.*

South Florida—Incorporated 1878 by an Orange County, Florida, businessmen who intended to lay rail from Sanford to Charlotte Harbor on the Gulf of Mexico. Denied a charter, SF gained that of fading Lake Monroe & Orlando. After indecision over the route direction (1881), an extension from Orlando to Kissimmee was opened (1882). In May 1883, Connecticut Yankee Henry B. Plant, who was to line central and west Florida with a string of resort hotels and amass a fortune in Southeast railways, bought South Florida. "With Plant at their helm the South Florida changed from a kitten to a roaring lion," observed a historian. Plant made copious deals with competing lines to attain right-of-way to Tampa. Construction began from Tampa and Kissimmee in mid 1883. On January 20, 1884, five days before a charter was to expire, dual ends were connected. It was Tampa's first railroad and gained the best wharf by creating Port Tampa southwest of the city on Old Tampa Bay. The route was upgraded from narrow- to standard-gauge (1886). Stems were added to the mainline to Bartow and a point east of Brooksville. South Florida merged into the Plant System and was in an expansive purchase by Atlantic Coast Line (1902). Almost all of South Florida survives as CSX still relies on the Sanford–Tampa main.

South Georgia & Florida—Before running any trains, SG&F was absorbed by Atlantic & Gulf as its Albany, Georgia, branch. SG&F constructed a route from Thomasville to Pelham (1869), adding Camilla and Albany (1870).

Southside—Chartered 1846, Southside connected with Richmond & Danville at Burkesville (1852) and linked Virginia cities of Petersburg and Lynchburg (1854). It bought City Point Railroad in 1854 to gain navigable water traffic on the James River at City Point. Southside, with two more lines (Norfolk & Petersburg and Virginia & Tennessee), formed Atlantic, Mississippi & Ohio in 1870, reclassified as Norfolk & Western in 1881.

South Western—Central of Georgia was instrumental in chartering the line in December 1845 between Albany, Americus, Columbus, and Fort Gaines, Georgia. A common carrier in Dawson, Georgia, that emerged in 1989 as Georgia Southwestern currently operates in some of the same territory.

Spartanburg & Asheville—*See Asheville & Spartanburg.*

Tallahassee—Chartered in 1834, this was the earliest antecedent of 940-mile Florida Central & Peninsular acquired by John S. Williams and others forming what would become Seaboard Air Line (1900). FC&P supplied some valuable routes linking Columbia, South Carolina, with Jacksonville via Savannah; Waldo, Florida with Tampa; and multiple other key Sunshine State connections.

Tampa & Gulf Coast—Formed in 1909, T&GC followed a 15- or 20-mile course (sources disagree) from Lutz, on Tampa's northern edge, west to Tarpon Springs on the Gulf of Mexico. Reorganized in 1913, it was leased to Seaboard Air Line (1927).

Tampa & Thonotosassa—Thonotosassa is a hamlet in Hillsborough County, Florida, on a picturesque lake 15 miles northeast of Tampa, surrounded by citrus groves. Organized in 1893, T&T purposed to help local farmers transport their fruit to market. Urbanites, meanwhile, were drawn to the lake on weekends for picnics and boating excursions. The train had a negative effect upon the community, causing Thonotosassa to stagnate as people began relocating to Tampa, diminishing the number of residents. Very early T&T was folded into the burgeoning Plant System of railroads.

Tampa Northern—A 49-mile route extending due north from Tampa to Brooksville, Tampa Northern was bought by Seaboard Air Line (1912).

Tampa, Peace Creek & St. Johns River—*See Jacksonville, Tampa & Key West.*

Tennessee Central—Initiated in 1883 as Nashville & Knoxville and never completed under that name, N&K was soon renamed TC. Its eastern terminus was never Knoxville but Harriman, where it connected with a SOU route to Knoxville (1904). Attention meanwhile was focused northwest of Nashville as a 95-mile extension was completed to Hopkinsville, Kentucky, where TC connected with Illinois Central. IC bought that Hopkinsville-Nashville sector from a bankrupt TC in 1968. At the same time L&N stepped in to buy the Nashville-Crossville mainline while Southern picked up the rest, Crossville–Harriman. *See Appendix B.*

Tennessee Midland—Chartered in 1886, TM ran from Lexington, Tennessee, to Memphis. After L&N took control (1895), TM was joined with Paducah, Tennessee & Alabama (north from Lexington to Paducah) and leased by L&N to ancillary NC&StL (1896). The dual roads featured continuous track between Ohio and Mississippi rivers. At the latter, traffic flowed by rail or barge to inland sites and a choice of several port cities on the Gulf.

Transit Road—*See Atlantic, Gulf & West India Transit.*

Upson County—*See Barnesville & Thomaston.*

Vicksburg & Brunswick—In 1879, Central of Georgia gained control of a regional carrier between Vicksburg, Mississippi, and Brunswick, Georgia.

Vicksburg & Jackson—*See Alabama & Vicksburg.*

Virginian—This line, based in the port city of Norfolk, Virginia, was the eventual product of an industrialist-philanthropist's efforts to haul coal from West Virginia to the neighboring state's coast for shipping around the world. Formed in 1907, by the 1930s, the Virginian offered the shortest and easiest route to the Atlantic. Its operations included a modest passenger service on the mainline and key stems. Passenger operations faded with the transportation boom of the 20th century and was out of business altogether by the late 1940s. Realizing that railways now needed to compete with other forms of transportation rather than each other, the Interstate Commerce Commission allowed it to merge with Norfolk & Western in 1959. *See Appendix B.*

Virginia & Carolina—Chartered in 1882, renamed Richmond, Petersburg & Carolina in 1892, and acquired by investors in 1897 who included it in forming Seaboard Air Line (1900).

Virginia & Tennessee—Chartered as Lynchburg & Tennessee Railroad (1848), its horizons soon expanded and name with it. In 1870, it was one of three (Norfolk & Petersburg, Southside also) to form Atlantic, Mississippi & Ohio headquartered at Lynchburg. It opened a continuous route from Bristol to Norfolk. Reorganized in 1881, AM&O became Norfolk & Western.

Virginia Central—Growing out of Louisa Railroad, VC continued its route farther west from Charlottesville. By 1856, it arrived at the present Clifton Forge. The line was a key benefit to the Confederacy in the Civil War as men and material moved along its rails. In 1869, Covington & Ohio and Virginia Central joined to form Chesapeake & Ohio. *See Louisa.*

Washington & Plymouth—Connecting namesake North Carolina hamlets on Pamlico and Albemarle sounds respectively, the 33-mile narrow-gauge line was bought by original Norfolk Southern (1904). W&P was built in 1888-1889 to serve commercial lumbering interests of a private owner. Reorganized as a common carrier (1902), W&P offered passenger service for the first time. NS replaced the tracks with heavier standard-gauge rail and incorporated it in a planned mainline between Norfolk and Raleigh.

Waycross & Florida—*See Savannah, Florida & Western.*

Western & Atlantic—Organized in 1836 by the State of Georgia, W&A is the earliest forebear of NC&StL. Tracks connected a future Atlanta with Chattanooga (1850) and were a critical link not only to NC&StL but to its future owner, L&N (1880). Trains went not merely to Atlanta but beyond—the port at Savannah, many Florida points, and still other places. W&A was leased to a group of private investors in 1870 and to NC&StL in 1890. Still owned by the state, it is currently under a long-term lease to L&N successor CSX Transportation.

Old Fort, North Carolina, was a strategic spot on the Western North Carolina map at the foot of a treacherous summit. Rails accessed Old Fort in 1873, seven years before reaching Asheville. In the interim travelers were shuttled to the state's far western tourist and commercial Mecca by stagecoach, a jarring ride leaving much to be desired. The ex–SOU station at Old Fort is in pristine condition, now a museum, seen June 17, 2007. NS tracks show a long double-ended bypass siding fabricated of welded rail. The grade crossing accesses U.S. 70 immediately to the right and I-40 about a mile to the left (*courtesy Michael B. Robbins*).

Western North Carolina — Created by North Carolina lawmakers in 1855, WNC opened with a 84-mile route from the Piedmont district's Salisbury west, nearly to Morganton (1858). The first train arrived in Marion in 1870 and Old Fort in 1873. For a while the state operated WNC (1875–1880). A group bought it and resold it to a powerful Richmond & Danville. Until 1880, when it reached Asheville, stagecoaches met trains at Old Fort—30 miles east—for the arduous trek up steep inclines on jarring, often muddy terrain to the future Ridgecrest, as they ferried travelers to western North Carolina's largest city. The road gradually extended west from Asheville in expectation of reaching Ducktown, Tennessee. It never made it. After nine years accessing Murphy in the state's far corner (1891), WNC owners decided enough had been invested: linking with Marietta & North Georgia at Murphy was sufficient. The extended route was acquired by R&D (1886) and WNC and part of R&D banded under East Tennessee, Virginia & Georgia taxonomy. Entering bankruptcy (1892), ETV&G and the rest of R&D coalesced to form Southern Railway (1894). WNC ran passenger trains the full extent of its route for years but SOU is best recalled from that era for consists like *Asheville Special* (New York–Washington–Asheville) and *Carolina Special* (Chicago–Cincinnati–Golds-

boro), making the eastern line memorable. SOU ran its last passenger train on the route in 1975, four years after Amtrak took over most similar services.

Western Railroad of North Carolina — *See Cape Fear & Yadkin Valley.*

Western Railway of Alabama — Begun as Montgomery Railroad on January 20, 1832, financing kept WRofA from reaching an ultimate terminus of West Point, Georgia, for 19 years. Reorganized as Montgomery & West Point (1842), it was relabeled Western Rail Road Company of Alabama (1854). Refined further, WRofA was bought by Central of Georgia and Georgia (1875); Georgia's interest transferred to Louisville & Nashville in 1881 with control moving to Atlantic Coast Line later. Then jointly operated with the Atlanta & West Point and commonly called "West Point Route," the lines met there while ferrying prestigious passenger trains for ACL and SOU.

"West Point Route" — *See Atlanta & West Point and Western Railway of Alabama.*

Wilmington & Manchester — Chartered 1846, opened 1853, W&M's route ran from Wilmington, North Carolina, to Camden Crossing, South Carolina, on a Camden branch of South Carolina Railroad. W&M was reorganized as Wilmington, Columbia & Augusta (1870). That sent it farther southwest, to Columbia (1873), although it never accessed Augusta, Georgia. Leasing Wilmington & Weldon (1872), WC&A offered an unimpeded path through Wilmington from Columbia to Weldon, North Carolina, and marketed as Atlantic Coast Line. Bankruptcy in 1878 forced the lease's termination; the carrier was sold in 1879 and reorganized in 1880. On July 18, 1898, WC&A, Northeastern, and a few more lines blended to form Atlantic Coast Line Railroad of South Carolina, a key part of ACL (1900). Its destiny was set.

Wilmington & Raleigh — Opened in 1840, W&R tied the port city with Weldon, North Carolina, linking to the Petersburg and Richmond & Petersburg roads to finish a route to Virginia's capital. Renamed Wilmington & Weldon (1855), it was an antecedent of Atlantic Coast Line (1900).

Wilmington & Weldon — *See Wilmington & Raleigh.*

Wilmington, Charlotte & Rutherfordton — Chartered in 1857, it ran 267 miles from the sea at Wilmington through North Carolina's southern Piedmont, accessing Charlotte and the Appalachian foothills at Rutherfordton, though it didn't reach the latter till 1887. When WC&R was reorganized as Carolina Central (1873) it was open from Wilmington to Charlotte. Seaboard & Roanoke took control of CC in the early 1880s and CC provided

a powerful east-west route to the future Seaboard Air Line (1900) at its intersect with SAL's north-south mainline at Hamlet. Traffic flowing west over original WC&R rail might persist to Charlotte, the state's largest city, or turn southwest at Monroe to proceed to Atlanta and Birmingham.

Wilmington, Columbia & Augusta — This was a portion of Atlantic Coast Line Railroad Company of South Carolina organized July 18, 1898, a forerunner of ACL. *See Wilmington & Manchester.*

Wrightsville & Tennille — Chartered in 1883, W&T (dubbed "Wiggle and Twist" by locals for a curvaceous route) launched a 17-mile line linking rural south Georgia hamlets Tennille (Washington County) and Wrightsville (Johnson County). The shortline took advantage of its opportunities. A just-completed 19-mile Dublin & Wrightsville folded into W&T (1886) to give access to Laurens County's largest city. W&T bought the Dublin–Hawkinsville segment of Oconee & Western (1896) to add 39 miles through Dodge and Pulaski counties to Hawkinsville, 75 miles from Tennille. Daily passenger trains made a Tennille–Hawkinsville trek in about three hours. Central of Georgia bought W&T (1899), letting it run independently. When W&T purchased Dublin & Southwestern (1907), a 28-mile branch was added from Dublin to Eastman (Dodge County). W&T abandoned stems west of

In this 2004 shot, an unrestored Central of Georgia 1223 Consolidation 2-8-0 constructed in Baldwin's shops occupies a stall at the Central of Georgia Roundhouse Museum at Savannah (*courtesy Clyde Woodruff*).

After volunteers give painstaking hours to refurbishing **Central of Georgia 1223, the job is at last done. It's been converted to Wrightsville & Tennille 223 and is still exhibited at the Savannah facility** (*courtesy Jay Miller*).

Dublin (1941). CofG — bought by SOU (1963) — absorbed W&T (1971). W&T is now a branch of Norfolk Southern (1982).

Yadkin — Chartered in 1871 though not operational until 1891 (the first spade of dirt was turned in 1874), Yadkin planned a route from Salisbury to Albemarle, Norwood and Wadesboro, North Carolina. An influential Richmond & Danville soon gained control and financed construction to Norwood; Yadkin never went any farther and historians can't tell why. It was a lousy investment nonetheless; Southern Railway (successor to R&D, 1894) lost money on Yadkin almost every year. In 1916, SOU dumped it. Operating on its own, Yadkin deleted the Albemarle–Norwood bit in 1938. Reorganizing,

it rejoined SOU via a Carolina & Northwestern subsidiary in 1951. Beyond its bread-and-butter freight business (mostly stone, ore, aluminum, timber, cotton, and peaches), Yadkin offered passenger service from the start in 1891. That persisted to December 2, 1928. When 30 miles of concrete highway linking Salisbury to Albemarle opened in 1927, a death blow to revenues generated from travelers was dealt.

Yazoo & Mississippi Valley — Launched in 1882; built west from Jackson to Yazoo City. Illinois Central later united it with Mississippi & Tennessee and Louisville, New Orleans & Texas. IC absorbed Y&MV in 1946.

I: Streetcars, Commuter Lines and Monorails (by State)

Here is a log of municipal mass rail transportation systems that can be substantiated in the South at the time this material is prepared (first quarter 2010). It is a follow-up to Chapter 20 and is presented here as supplementary to that material.

Arkansas

FORT SMITH
    System: Fort Smith Trolley

Operator: Fort Smith Streetcar Restoration Association, Inc.
Type: Traditional (Modern) Streetcar
Debut: December 25, 1990
Miles: 1.5
Power: Electrification supplied by overhead wire
Inventory: 1 car
Abstract: Discounting stagecoaches, Fort Smith's earliest public transportation appeared in the form of a trio of mule-drawn cars in 1883. Within a decade they were supplanted by electrically-pow-

ered trolleys. By the 1920s, the trolley cars were upgraded, enclosed and heated as they moved over a 30-mile track in and near the state's second largest city. Yet in 1933, the trolley was discontinued, the victim of a pervasive bus line as well as automobiles and fallout from the Great Depression. As tracks and rolling stock vanished, one of the cars, #224, ca. 1926, was shipped to Ashdown, Arkansas, and stationed as a commercial bistro, Streetcar Café. When a faction of Fort Smith citizens learned "their car" was for sale in the 1980s, they swung into action: launching fund-raisers to acquire and restore it, their mission was triumphant after #224 was returned to service in 1990. Today, in addition to the Fort Smith Trolley Museum at 100 South 4th Street, #224 stops at the city's convention center, a history museum and a national historic landmark as it winds its way through the older sector of downtown. A planned extension, if it happens, will ferry riders from hotels and a convention complex to east end museums and restaurants. The Fort Smith Light & Traction trolley runs daily from May through October and on weekends in other months.

LITTLE ROCK/NORTH LITTLE ROCK

System: River Rail Streetcar
Operator: Central Arkansas Transit Authority
Type: Heritage Trolley
Debut: November 1, 2004
Miles: 3.4
Stations: 14
Power: Electrification supplied by overhead catenary
Gauge: 4 feet 8.5 inches (standard)
Inventory: 5 cars
Abstract: River Rail Streetcar (RRS) is a 21st century variation of a longstanding tradition of mass transport organisms in Little Rock present in each of the two previous centuries. The city's first horse tramway operated from 1876 to 1895. Concurrently for a year, 1888 to 1889, a steam tramway functioned. Also overlapping the horse-drawn conveyance, on December 13, 1891, electric traction was introduced. For more than a half-century electrically-powered streetcars plied the thoroughfares of Arkansas' capital and were discontinued September 1, 1947. By then they had been extended west from the Arkansas River to the Hillcrest and Stifft's Station neighborhoods. The city's fourth entry in the arena, RRS, premiered with 2.5 completed track miles in 2004, linking Little Rock with its opposite number across the river, North Little Rock. A second phase, a 0.9-mile extension to the William J. Clinton Presidential Center, opened in 2006. In addition to the Clinton Library, RRS calls at Little Rock's downtown convention center and historic River Market district. In North Little Rock it accesses a new downtown sports arena. More ex-

tensions are planned, among them a 2.5-mile route to Little Rock National Airport. "If the expansion is completed," a historian allowed, "the status of the line could take a role in some form of light rail line, instead of its current role as a heritage trolley." With similar systems operating in Savannah and Tampa, RRS is classified as a hybrid transportation mode branded *rapid streetcar*. If it grows into a more effective rapid transit network, it could be an early (if not inaugural) model of that layout in the U.S. In third quarter 2009, RRS transported 340 riders daily.

Florida

JACKSONVILLE

System: Skyway
Operator: Jacksonville Transportation Authority
Type: Automated Guideway Transit (Elevated Peoplemover/Monorail)
Debut: 1989
Miles: 2.5
Stations: 8
Power: Electrification supplied by third rail
Abstract: The peoplemover was inserted in a sweeping mobility scheme in Jacksonville in 1971. After a feasibility study, the U.S. Urban Mass Transit Administration chose it as a peoplemover project that would receive federal assistance. (Others: Detroit; Irving, Texas; Miami; and Morgantown, West Virginia.) Construction of an initial phase, launched in 1987, netted three stations and two vehicles in 1989. When the supplier and city couldn't agree on an extension in the 1990s, the technology was revamped to a monorail layout (matching one at Tampa International Airport) and additions made. Cars with Automatic Train Control (no operator) run on a beam resting on a guideway. A high parapet wall on each side reduces noise, aids drainage, and protects workers. The Skyway bridges both sides of the St. Johns River dividing Jacksonville's core. There are eight stations handling trains with two to six cars each. Three stations are intermodal, giving riders ready access to city buses. The system is handicapped in not reaching local sports venues. Proposals to extend east and south have met with reluctance. "It doesn't go anyplace," allowed an ABC-TV report. Skyway reaches Northbank and Southbank riverwalks, a few upscale hotels and restaurants, a couple of museums, a performing arts center, and a community college. Lack of ridership is a thorn in Jacksonville's side. An initial projection of 56,000 riders daily, one source insisted, was outrageous; latest figures indicate less than 2,000 daily, and frustrating to proud Jacksonvillians and taxpayers.

MIAMI

System: Metrorail

Operator: Miami-Dade Transit

Type: Elevated Heavy Rail Rapid Transit

Debut: May 20, 1984

Miles: 22.4 miles

Stations: 22.6

Power: Electrification supplied by third rail

Gauge: 4 feet 8.5 inches (standard)

Inventory: 136 cars typically seating 164 per car

Abstract: Running at a top speed of 58 miles an hour and averaging 31, Miami's Metrorail is Florida's only metro system and one of but two heavy rail rapid transit networks in the Southeast (the other in Atlanta). Following a population boom, a 1971 study called for rapid transit. Within a year Dade County voters ok'd a bond issue and the state granted more. Feds picked up 80 percent of the initial phase and earth was turned in 1980. More than 125,000 rode a portion of Metrorail's first trips gratis on opening day in 1984. In third quarter 2009, 62,100 boarded daily. As rails were extended incrementally to 2003, more stations opened. Construction of a 23rd stop at the airport's new Miami Intermodal Center is expected to be ready in early 2012, maybe sooner. An addition expected in 2020 will access the airport, stadium and a university. Long range plans call for extensions to Coral Gables and west Kendall southwest of downtown and Aventura between Miami and Fort Lauderdale. Stations can receive trains of at least six car lengths, although some trains run with as few as two cars. In 42 minutes Metrorail races from the Palmetto Expressway at its north end to Dadeland South, a Kendall, Florida, shopping mall.

MIAMI

System: Metromover

Operator: Miami-Dade Transit

Type: Automated Guideway Transit (Elevated Peoplemover)

Debut: April 17, 1986

Miles: 4.4

Stations: 22

Power: Electrification supplied by third rail

Inventory: 29 cars

Abstract: Starting as a downtown circulator in 1986, Miami's peoplemover train system was extended to Brickell's financial district in 1994. Metromover connects major office structures, residential facilities, hotels and retail centers in Miami and Brickell. A government complex, arena, performing arts center, cultural plaza and college are among its stops. Metromover is one of a small handful of peoplemover projects fostered by the U.S. Urban Mass Transit Administration (including Jacksonville's, which hasn't gained Miami's out-

pouring of acceptance). Ridership has typically exceeded 30,000 daily, attesting to the fact it's not only free but Metromover goes where people want to go safely, efficiently, and quickly, and is available every 90 to 180 seconds.

MIAMI/FORT LAUDERDALE/WEST PALM BEACH

System: Tri-Rail

Operator: South Florida Regional Transportation Authority

Type: Regional Commuter Rail

Debut: 1987

Miles: 70.9

Stations: 18

Power: Diesels running on biodiesel fuel (since 2008)

Gauge: 4 feet 8.5 inches (standard)

Inventory: 18 locomotives, 32 cab cars, coaches and diesel multiple units (some bi-level cars seat up to 188 each)

Abstract: Under auspices of the state DOT, Tri-Rail was to briefly supply commuter rail while paralleling I-95 and Florida's Turnpike were widened. Adding stations and trains in the interim, it became such a necessity to riders it was retained after construction ended. In 1989, the DOT bought the track from CSX (shared with Amtrak's Silver Meteor and Silver Star and CSX's Miami subdivision). Tri-Rail's owner is to take on dispatching and upkeep from CSX when pending upgrades are finished. Initially running 67 miles between West Palm Beach and Hialeah Market in 1998, the line was opened north to Mangonia Park and south to a new Miami Airport station. Its full length was double-tracked in 2007. In addition to numerous small cities on the southeast coast, Tri-Rail accesses three major airports (Miami, Fort Lauderdale, West Palm Beach). When a new Miami Central Station opens in 2012, its airport stop will shift there with ties to Miami Metrorail, Amtrak, Metrobus, MIA Mover, and Miami Intermodal Center. Long range plans call for Tri-Rail to occupy the Florida East Coast rail corridor. In replacing the present route, reliance on shuttle buses will shrink as riders hop off within walking distance of many destinations. Ridership in third quarter 2009 was 11,600, qualifying it as the nation's 12th busiest commuter rail system. In December 2009, Florida lawmakers included expanded Tri-Rail funding in a financial and administrative accord that permits a long-planned SunRail network in central Florida to proceed, linking the pair of systems under state oversight in the future.

ORLANDO

System: SunRail

Operator: Central Florida Commuter Rail Commission

Type: Regional Commuter Rail
Debut: Not Yet Available — Under Construction
Miles: 61
Stations: 18
Power: Diesels
Gauge: 4 feet 8.5 inches (standard)
Inventory: Unknown
Abstract: In December 2009, with a federal deadline for action looming, Florida lawmakers approved financial arrangements permitting regional commuter rail project SunRail—until then in limbo—to proceed. In the future it will be overseen by the state with Tri-Rail in southeastern Florida. SunRail's initial phase is expected to be operational in 2012, with the entire system functioning in 2014. Its route follows the CSX "A" Line (ex–Atlantic Coast Line Railroad mainline) from DeLand south through downtown Orlando to a point below Kissimmee at Poinciana, Florida. Its tracks are now occupied by Amtrak's *Silver Meteor* and *Silver Star* and CSX cargo traffic. The state agreed to buy the route from CSX which—with the exception of a few night trains—will reroute most of the freight to other rails. Leaving DeLand, SunRail trains will call at Sanford, Lake Mary, Longwood, Altamonte Springs, Maitland, Winter Park, Orlando, Kissimmee and a few more.

TAMPA
System: TECO Line Streetcar System
Operator: Hillsborough Area Regional Transit Authority
Type: Heritage Light Rail Trolley
Debut: October 19, 2002
Miles: 2.4
Stations: 12
Power: Electrification supplied by overhead catenary
Gauge: 4 feet 8.5 inches (standard)
Inventory: 11 cars
Abstract: Tampa was initially introduced to electric streetcars in 1892. For more than a half-century, locals relied on them for transit until the cars were pulled from the streets on August 4, 1946. Another half-century elapsed until they returned. Today TECO Line (so named after branding rights were sold to Tampa Electric Company) services a route from downtown's Transportation Plaza to Tampa's famed historic Latin cultural zone, Ybor City, to the east. A one-third mile extension in 2010 accesses a Fort Brooke parking garage, TECO's largest station, capable of processing three cars at once as four wait on side rails. The line accesses varied tourist attractions like the convention center, Ice Palace, Garrison Seaport, Florida Aquarium, and Ybor City. TECO uses single track and largely segregated rights-of-way along city streets and multiple passing sidings. Nine replica double-truck cars proffer welded steel bodies with cosmetic rivets to make them appear older. They are wheelchair-accessible, air-conditioned, with automated stop announcements and on-board ticket dispensers. Reversible wooden seats allow adaptations when a car's direction changes. An original Birney Safety Car in TECO Line's inventory was discovered as a residence in Tampa's suburban Sulphur Springs. Refurbishing it returned it to past glory days; it was added to the fleet along with a replica open-bench "Breezer" car. Some 700 patrons daily boarded TECO vintage streetcars in third quarter 2009.

Georgia

ATLANTA
System: MARTA Rail System
Operator: Metropolitan Atlanta Rapid Transit Authority
Type: Elevated/Surface/Subway Heavy Rail High Speed Transit
Debut: June 30, 1979
Miles: 47.6
Stations: 38
Power: Electrification supplied by third rail
Gauge: 4 feet 8.5 inches (standard)
Inventory: 338 cars
Abstract: The original building blocks for MARTA date at least to 1965, when the Georgia legislature created it to supply rapid transit to metropolitan Atlanta's key contiguous counties. Not all wanted to play, however, yet voters in Fulton and DeKalb counties passed a one percent sales tax to fund it in 1971. MARTA purchased Atlanta Transit Company (buses) the following year to gain control of all local public transit. Construction of its extensive rail system began in 1975, with initial service commencing four years hence. While most of its intended lines were built plus stations at Sandy Springs and North Springs not in the original mix, numerous extensions have been proposed. Traveling at speeds up to 70 miles an hour, two- to eight-car trains hauled 259,900 riders daily in third quarter 2009. MARTA is the nation's seventh busiest rapid transit system (topped by New York, Washington, Chicago, Boston, San Francisco, and Philadelphia). Over four main routes (east, west, north, south—converging at downtown's Five Points core), trains intercept MARTA bus lines at numerous stations with commodious, well-lit parking lots. The one percent sales tax and passenger revenues cover all operational costs, making MARTA the largest U.S. transit agency that doesn't tap state funding to run it.

SAVANNAH
  System: River Street Streetcar
  Operator: City of Savannah
  Type: Heritage Streetcar
  Debut: February 11, 2009
  Miles: 1
  Stations: 7
  Power: Biodiesel-fueled generator and batteries
  Gauge: 4 feet 8.5 inches (standard)
  Inventory: 1 car
  Abstract: Savannah's foray into mass transit began in 1869 when horse-drawn cars arrived. Electric streetcars replaced them in 1890 and persisted to August 26, 1946. In the years afterward Norfolk Southern Railway—which owned the River Street branch line—ran a local freight train there, *River Street Rambler*. Savannah purchased that right-of-way in 2004. That's where the River Street Streetcar runs today fronting the Savannah River along abandoned tracks, some set within cobblestones. Plying the middle of its namesake thoroughfare, the River Street Streetcar encounters a thriving entertainment district as it passes east and west of City Hall. The urban circulator is as much a tourist draw as a solution for locals to access points near its route without needing a vehicle on crowded streets with little parking room. The city bought a 1920s W5 class streetcar from Melbourne, Australia, and converted it to a hybrid drive. Nicknamed "Dottie," it was dubbed for the Department of Transportation, instrumental in its acquisition. Although only one mile is in service, the city owns 4.3 track miles, hinting that the route could be extended if the demonstrator shows promise. Possibilities include adding a second car to create a dual-car bidirectional train. Local railfans hope the line will reach Savannah's Roundhouse Railroad Museum and Visitor Center (requiring new rail to do so). The present operation is fueled by an internal combustion engine but future lines might be powered by overhead wires.

In 1831, they contemplated the city's second railway, New Orleans & Carrollton, launched in 1833, following the Pontchartrain's inception (1831). Initially pulled on streets without a dedicated right-of-way by a steam locomotive, NO&C later met burgeoning urbanization. As soot and noise were intolerable to residents, the cars were powered next by horses and mules. To increase speed, propulsion by overhead cables in the 1870s netted many drawbacks; electric streetcars, in 1884, weren't perfected to be viable. After a few more years, they improved and the line was electrified February 1, 1893. The St. Charles Avenue route, from 1923, is the world's oldest surviving street railway. Its 7-mile line almost from the Mississippi River encounters Audubon Park, Tulane and Loyola universities, then traverses the Garden District to the central business core at the edge of the French Quarter. The line and two more were out of sync after Hurricane Katrina devastated New Orleans in August 2005. They returned to service incrementally. The Canal Street route, with horse-drawn streetcars traceable to 1861, plies the city's most prominent thoroughfare. Electrification in 1892 was replaced by buses in 1964 and rail returned in 2004. That year Canal proffered dual destinations: one from the river to the cemeteries to the north; the other an extension to City Park, an art museum and in walking distance of the fairgrounds. The Riverfront streetcar is a 2-mile trip by a tourist trade area paralleling the waterfront. Opened August 14, 1988, it was the Crescent City's first new line in 62 years. In third quarter 2009, the trio of New Orleans routes ferried 10,700 riders collectively to their destinations each day. The future of these revered historic conveyances—many dating to the 1920s—are assured. Parenthetically, Tennessee Williams' play *A Streetcar Named Desire* was titled after a New Orleans trolley running to Desire Street (1920–1948), earning it credence as the most famous streetcar of all time.

Louisiana

NEW ORLEANS
  System: New Orleans Streetcars
  Operator: New Orleans Regional Transit Authority
  Type: Traditional (Modern) Light Rail Streetcar
  Debut: September 26, 1835
  Miles: 21.5 (3 routes)
  Stations: Stops on request
  Power: Electrification supplied by overhead catenary
  Gauge: 5 feet 2.5 inches (broad)
  Inventory: 58 cars
  Abstract: New Orleans transit planners were at work in 1830, the year railroads began in America.

North Carolina

CHARLOTTE
  System: Charlotte Trolley
  Operator: Charlotte Area Transit System
  Type: Heritage Trolley
  Debut: 1996
  Miles: 2.1
  Stations: 11
  Power: Electrification by overhead wire
  Gauge: 4 feet 8.5 inches (standard)
  Inventory: 3 cars
  Abstract: While Charlotte Trolley is functional in hauling riders to businesses up and down its slightly curving route south of Uptown to the Atherton Mill area, the attraction's unabashed ap-

peal is to good-time excursions. Beyond the transit operator's extensive bus system and newly added light rail, it's the arm pitched to nostalgia, not commuter passage. Linked to its Charlotte Trolley Powerhouse Museum, the project — a weekend daytime operation — is about fun, letting riders experience "what used to be." The museum recovers Charlotte's past through exhibitions of the Gilded Age of local transportation, a celebrated history. Charlotte Street Railway Company, formed in 1883, laid track along Tryon and West Trade streets. Cars were pulled by two mules, upgraded to horses within a year. When Charlotte Consolidated Construction Company acquired four lines and electrified them May 18, 1891, six cars, 20 horses and 40 harness sets swelled the city's transit portfolio. Ownership passed to Charlotte Electric Railway, Light & Power Company in 1896, which grew the stockpile to 30 cars and 21 miles of track. It sold the operation to Southern Public Utilities Company, soon renamed Duke Power Company, in 1910. Duke launched Piedmont & Northern Railway as a side venture while controlling the Charlotte transit enterprise to 1951. Adding buses to city streets in 1935, it discontinued trolleys entirely on March 14, 1938, replacing them with buses. Today Charlotte Trolley, instituted in 1996, travels down the middle of the street on tracks laid in 1852 by Charlotte & South Carolina Railroad. C&SC, Charlotte's first rail line, ferried trains to and from Columbia, the Palmetto State capital. Laying those tracks was dubbed "the single most important event in Charlotte's economic history," a local source maintained. Who says a little nostalgia can't be a good thing?

CHARLOTTE

System: LYNX Rapid Transit Services
Operator: Charlotte Area Transit System
Type: Light Rail (contrary to its name, it isn't rapid transit)
Debut: November 24, 2007
Miles: 9.6
Stations: 15
Power: Electrification supplied by overhead catenary
Gauge: 4 feet 8.5 inches (standard)
Inventory: 20 cars
Abstract: Streetcars left Charlotte's streets in 1938 but their pragmatic service wasn't forgotten. When a Charlotte-Mecklenburg Planning Commission evaluated the area's mushrooming growth in 1984, light rail reappeared on the horizon. Prolonged acquisition of rights-of-way and spiraling costs delayed action almost 15 years. In 1998, Mecklenburg County voters ok'd a half-cent sales tax to launch a light rail network. When a referendum surfaced in 2007, the tax's repeal was rejected 7–3 by voters. More studies, surveying, and escalating

land and construction costs for an initial route delayed its finish to 2008. The Blue Line runs south from Uptown almost to Pineville on the South Carolina border. LYNX was adopted as its moniker based on a big cat theme in pro sports sobriquets (Carolina Panthers, Charlotte Bobcats) and a homophonous tie to "links" that portends bonding. With free rides on opening day, 60,000 jumped on board. Daily ridership in third quarter 2009 was 20,000, qualifying it as the 20th busiest light rail system in the U.S., leading Dixie. The South Corridor Blue Line will have many peers if modern planners prevail. A mixture of Light Rail, Commuter Rail, Rapid Transit and Streetcar services may be added between 2015 and 2034. Expansion calls for an 11-mile Northeast Corridor Blue Line extension to UNC–Charlotte; a 30-mile Red Line north from Uptown's planned Gateway Station (an intermodal facility) to Huntersville, Cornelius and Davidson; a 13.5-mile Silver Line from Gateway Station east to Matthews; a 9.9-mile Center City Corridor linking structures east and west of Uptown by streetcar; and a 6.4-mile West Corridor streetcar accessing the airport. If money can be found and the voters of Charlotte maintain their resolve, it could happen as planned.

Tennessee

MEMPHIS

System: MATA Trolley
Operator: Memphis Area Transit Authority
Type: Heritage Light Rail Trolley
Debut: April 29, 1993
Miles: 7 (3 routes)
Stations: 24
Power: Electrification by overhead catenary
Gauge: 4 feet 8.5 inches (standard)
Inventory: 18 cars
Abstract: Memphis' original streetcar network was dismantled in the 1940s. A return to it was driven by a need to resuscitate a failing pedestrian mall in a fading downtown. A projected 4.9-mile line by the Mississippi River was reduced by the City Council in January 1990 to a 2.5-mile route on Main Street. Construction took almost two years; with car restoration and tests, service commenced on a 12-stop course in 1993. The route from Butler to Overton avenues encounters famed Beale Street, Civic Center Plaza and the convention center. A second 2-mile Riverfront line with six stops came next, opening in 1997. Endpoints are the Pyramid at Auction Avenue and Central Station, linking ends of the Main Street line over a right-of-way shared with Amtrak. A third line with six stops, extending 2.5 miles on Madison Street from Fourth to Cleveland streets, opened March 15,

2004. It connects downtown to the Medical Center complex tying the two largest employment centers via rail. These combined routes transported 4,100 riders daily in third quarter 2009. The Memphis trolley fleet of vintage cars—or made to appear so—is cosmopolitan. They descended from Portuguese, Australian, Brazilian and American builders and users.

NASHVILLE

System: Music City Star

Operator: Tennessee Department of Transportation

Type: Regional Commuter Rail

Debut: September 18, 2006

Miles: 32

Stations: 6

Power: Rebuilt EMD F40PH diesel locomotives (3)

Gauge: 4 feet 8.5 inches (standard)

Inventory: 7 bi-level gallery cars

Abstract: With six more routes to satellite cities in a circle around Nashville planned, Music City Star's inaugural line to Lebanon, Tennessee, is a "starter" project. It exhibits the viability of a commuter rail service by reclaiming existing tracks; the initial route follows ex–Nashville & Eastern, later Tennessee Central. The concept lets MCS "build" lines at far less than buying land and laying rails. Operators claim it's "the most cost efficient commuter rail start-up in the nation." Nashville's Riverfront Station sits by the Cumberland River at the foot of Broadway. It's within walking distance of arenas, stadium, legendary Ryman Auditorium and more entertainment, educational, historical and tourism venues. As trains arrive buses extend commuters' trips without charge, carrying them to the university district west of town or on a loop through downtown. Leaving Riverfront Station, the East Corridor encounters Donelson, Hermitage, Mount Juliet, and Martha before arriving Lebanon. Trains include double coaches with controlling cab cars in push-pull configuration. Seats are reversible and may be rearranged for groups. MCS hasn't yet reached its potential, hauling 800 riders daily in third quarter 2009. Backers are nevertheless optimistic its trains will one day radiate from Riverfront to Ashland City, Columbia, Dickson, Franklin, Gallatin, and Murfreesboro.

Virginia

NORFOLK

System: The Tide

Operator: Hampton Roads Transit

Type: Light Rail

Debut: 2011 projected

Miles: 7.4 projected

Stations: 11 projected

Power: Electrification by overhead catenary

Gauge: 4 feet 8.5 inches (standard)

Inventory: 9 cars projected

Abstract: When Virginia Beach voters refused to join neighboring Norfolk in a light rail line to the sea in 1999, Norfolkians plowed ahead to build one in its city limits. The projected route, expected to open in 2011, parallels I-264 from Eastern Virginia Medical School to Newtown Road. Accessing downtown Norfolk on its way, it encounters city hall, a park and two colleges. The Tide is the first major light rail service in Hampton Roads, embracing multiple cities in Virginia's coastal Tidewater. Projections forecast 7,100 to 11,400 riders daily at the line's start. Now Virginia Beach officials appear ready to play. There are signs an extension from The Tide's eastern end through Virginia Beach to the Oceanfront Convention Center might be added. A station at Virginia Beach's Town Center would tie the beach to Norfolk's downtown, something Norfolkians were angling for in the 1990s. Tide owners are hopeful more extensions of their starter line will reach the Naval Station, Portsmouth and Chesapeake. If the original route flourishes, who's to say it won't happen?

NORTHERN VIRGINIA COUNTIES

System: Virginia Railway Express

Operator: Transportation Partnership of the Potomac and Rappahannock Transportation Commission and Northern Virginia Transportation Commission

Type: Regional Commuter Rail

Debut: June 22, 1992

Miles: 90

Stations: 18

Power: Diesel Locomotives (3)

Gauge: 4 feet 8.5 inches (standard)

Inventory: 83 cars

Abstract: Following a 1984 feasibility study and discussions dating to 1964, northern Virginians and District of Columbia planners were psyched. Working together they launched a regional rail transit system to largely haul commuters to and from Washington's Union Station. Virginia Railway Express serves Prince William and Stafford counties and the cities of Alexandria, Fredericksburg, Manassas, Manassas Park and a handful more. In 1988, a two percent motor fuels tax was instituted to support it and an operating board named. The first of dual lines—between Bristow, Virginia and Union Station with Manassas, Manassas Park and Alexandria among eight stops en route—commenced June 22, 1992. The second—from Fredericksburg starting July 20, 1992—stopped at Quantico, Lorton and Alexandria and seven more times. VRE operates Monday through Friday and is reduced or suspended some holidays. The network ferried 11,600 travelers on weekdays in third quarter 2009. VRE runs on tracks owned by CSX (ex–Richmond, Fredericksburg & Potomac) and Norfolk Southern (ex–Southern). Several Amtrak trains ply the former route; the *Cardinal* (thrice weekly) and *Crescent* (daily) run the latter. A French outfit, Keolis, was to begin running VRE trains in mid 2010, handled previously by Amtrak.

NORTHERN VIRGINIA COUNTIES
System: Metrorail
Operator: Washington Metropolitan Area Transit Authority
Type: Rapid Transit Commuter Rail
Debut: March 27, 1976
Miles: 106.3
Stations: 86
Power: Electrification by third rail
Gauge: 4 feet 8.5 inches (standard)
Inventory: 1,126 cars
Abstract: With 998,000 daily riders in third quarter 2009, the Washington Metro (also known as Metrorail)—second busiest rapid transit system in the nation—exceeds anything else dipping into Dixie. (The inauguration of President Barack Obama in 2009 set a peak of 1,120,000 passengers in a single day.) Established by Congress in 1968, construction commenced the next year with the first 4.6 miles open in 1976. By July 1, 1976, Arlington County, Virginia, was added with 11 stations. Not till December 17, 1983, was Fairfax County, Virginia (with 3 stations), and the city of Alexandria (with 3) brought "on line." The route now being built will add eight more stations in Fairfax County and three in Loudoun County, Virginia. Departing Metro Center in Washington, the Blue Line extends to Franconia–Springfield, Virginia. The Orange Line proceeds to Virginia's Vienna/Fairfax–GMU station. The Silver Line underway will access Dulles International Airport on its course to Virginia Route 772 and a 2015 finish.

West Virginia

MORGANTOWN
System: Morgantown Personal Rapid Transit
Operator: West Virginia University
Type: Automated Guideway Transit (Customized Peoplemover)
Debut: 1975
Miles: 8.2
Stations: 5
Power: 3-phase 575-volt A.C. altered to drive 70 hp DC motor
Inventory: 73 mini buses (each seats 8 with standing room for 12)

Abstract: When dire circumstances, creative ingenuity, and political clout converge, almost anything is possible, West Virginia University learned. At Morgantown (1970s pop. 20,000), hard by the Pennsylvania line 57 miles south of Pittsburgh, WVU faced a crisis of epic proportions. Geographically constrained by mountainous terrain in a valley beside the Monongahela River, its growth (20,000 students) forced it to create dual sites two miles apart separated by the city. Free busing wasn't adequate; with all roads passing through the town's center, traffic gridlock resulted like a megacity. A Personal Rapid Transit (PRT) craze in the late 1960s coupled with federal funds for testing and promising outcome prevailed on powerful U.S. Senator Robert Byrd to push it for WVU. Construction didn't begin to 1974 but the first phase opened a year later and was ready totally in 1979. It's the only commercial model of this rapid transit genre. The PRT hauls 16,000 riders daily through Morgantown to town and three campuses. Unlike wholly elevated peoplemover systems, it reaches highs and lows: 65 percent is on elevated bridges and viaducts while 35 percent is at or below ground level. Running at 30 miles an hour, the Morgantown PRT is a practical solution for an academic community confronting reality. Other places may not have seen an explosion of PRTs for two reasons: an absence of (a) federal funding and (b) an influential politician.

Monorails

OPERATING
Jacksonville, Florida: Connects both sides of the St. Johns River in downtown Jacksonville.
Memphis, Tennessee: Connects Mud Island in the Mississippi River with downtown Memphis.
Miami, Florida: Connects major exhibitions at Metrozoo.
Orlando, Florida: Connects Disney hotels and attractions at Walt Disney World.
Orlando, Florida: Connects main terminal with gate areas at Orlando International Airport.
Tampa, Florida: Connects main terminal with gate areas at Tampa International Airport.

DISCONTINUED
Charlotte, North Carolina: Carowinds theme park (1973–1994).
Miami, Florida: Miami Seaquarium (1963–1991).
Richmond, Virginia: Kings Dominion theme park (removed 1993).
Tampa, Florida: Busch Gardens theme park (removed 1999).

J: Advertising and Passenger Information

On the following pages you will find reproductions of magazine and newspaper advertising, posters, handbills, timetables, brochures and company literature that marketed trips to the South by passenger trains. Except where noted, the material was supplied by Chuck Blardone and the author acknowledges those contributions with gratitude.

The **Southland**

THE SCENIC ROUTE
to Florida

Daily train through the Picturesque Cumberland and Blue Ridge Mountains by Daylight.

Through sleepers Chicago to Tampa, serving Sanford, Winter Park, Orlando and Lakeland.

Observation-Club Car, sleeping cars, dining car and coaches.

Lv. Chicago 9:15 p. m. daily

Passengers for St. Petersburg may transfer en-route into St. Petersburg sleepers on same train. Excellent service to Jacksonville and all Central Lake Region and West Coast Resorts.

Via Cincinnati and the L. & N. R. R.

For Tickets Apply to Local Agents, or Address A. E. Hoadley, Dis. Passenger Rep. 813 Metropolitan Life Bldg., Minneapolis

Pennsylvania Railroad

November 6, 1925

the *Dixie Flagler*

...takes you straight through to *Florida fun!* Your trip on the Dixie Flagler is a vacation in itself...a luxury trip highlighted by superb accommodations that invite relaxation...by excellent food that is a compliment to your good taste...by attentive service that says "we're glad to have you aboard!"

Once Every Three Days During the Winter Season

CHICAGO-MIAMI THROUGH SERVICE

On Board the Flagler You Enjoy

The Accommodation of Your Choice ...Pullman sleepers with berths, compartments or rooms...or, if you prefer...Streamlined Coaches with really comfortable reclining seats.

Excellent Food...Attentive Service ...Two dining cars...Lounge-Tavern ...Club Lounge.

And you go the best route...the scenic, historic route that adds to the pleasure of your trip.

NASHVILLE-MIAMI SLEEPER
(schedule)

Lv. Nashville	6:00 PM CT	Lv. Miami	11:45 AM ET
Lv. Chattanooga	10:15 PM ET	Lv. Jacksonville	7:10 PM ET
Ar. Atlanta	1:20 AM ET	Lv. Atlanta	3:15 AM ET
Ar. Jacksonville	9:25 AM ET	Ar. Chattanooga	6:20 AM ET
Ar. Miami	4:45 PM ET	Ar. Nashville	8:35 AM CT

LEAVE NASHVILLE

Dec. 14, 17, 20, 23, 26, 29
Jan. 1, 4, 7, 10, 13, 16, 19, 22, 25, 28, 31
Feb. 3, 6, 9, 12, 15, 18, 21, 24, 27
Mar. 2, 5, 8, 11, 14, 17, 20, 23, 26, 29
Apr. 1, 4, 7, 10, 13, 16, 19, 22, 25, 28
and every third day thereafter

LEAVE MIAMI

Dec. 15, 18, 21, 24, 27, 30
Jan. 2, 5, 8, 11, 14, 17, 20, 23, 26, 29
Feb. 1, 4, 7, 10, 13, 16, 19, 22, 25, 28
Mar. 3, 6, 9, 12, 15, 18, 21, 24, 27, 30
Apr. 2, 5, 8, 11, 14, 17, 20, 23, 26, 29
and every third day thereafter

THE NASHVILLE, CHATTANOOGA & ST. LOUIS RY.

N.C.&St.L.

Winter Season 1952-1953

ALL-EXPENSE TOURS

Ask your travel agent or ticket agent about low-cost all-expense tours from Chicago to Florida; write for descriptive folder to Mr. R. C. Caldwell, Div. Pass. Agt., Pennsylvania Railroad, 33 N. La Salle St., Chicago, Ill.

Go Now . . . Pay Later

The Travel Credit Plan makes it possible for you to enjoy a Winter Holiday NOW without paying one cent down. You can finance any trip costing $50.00 or more and pay in small monthly installments. And that includes Pullman or coach fares . . . meals . . . even hotels. Ask your ticket or travel agent about this amazing plan.

Take Your Car . . . By Train

Here's your chance to enjoy the comfort, speed, and safety of rail travel on your trip South and yet have your automobile when you get there. Ask your ticket agent about shipping your car by train; you can do it for only 4 cents a mile, plus two rail fares good in Pullmans or three in coaches, and the fares can be used for your own transportation. (Minimum charge $54)

FAST THROUGH TRAIN SERVICE DAILY TO FLORIDA AND THE SOUTH

PENNSYLVANIA RAILROAD
WABASH RAILWAY
LOUISVILLE & NASHVILLE R. R.

ca. 1950

December 16, 1962 (*courtesy Michael Wall*).

Florida Sunbeam

Air-Conditioned Train Direct To and From Both Coasts of Florida

Effective from Chicago and Detroit, Thursday, December 12; from Toledo, Cleveland and Cincinnati, Friday, December 13; from Columbus, Saturday, December 14; and from Miami and St. Petersburg, Saturday, December 14.

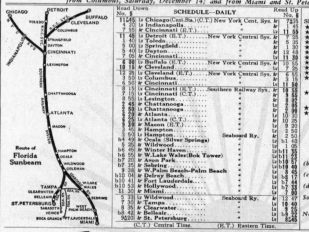

SOUTHERN RAILWAY SYSTEM

FASTER AND BETTER THAN EVER

CRESCENT LIMITED

ALL PULLMAN EQUIPMENT
NEW YORK---NEW ORLEANS

ONE HOUR and
TEN MINUTES quicker to
Atlanta and New Orleans

ONE HOUR QUICKER
to Washington and
New York.

DOUBLE-BED ROOM
CRESCENT LIMITED

DOUBLE-BED ROOM
and
PRIVATE SECTION CARS,
AN ADDED CONVENIENCE

Club and Observation Cars . . . Maid and Valet Service

Shower Baths for Men and for Women

Women's Lounging Room

Serving Gulf of Mexico-Mississippi Resorts of Pascagoula

Ocean Springs . . . Biloxi . . . Edgewater Park

Gulfport . . . Pass Christian . . . and Bay St. Louis; also
New Orleans, La.

EXCELLENT DINING CAR SERVICE

"There Is No Finer Train Than This"

OTHER SPLENDID TRAINS
Between NEW YORK and NEW ORLEANS

PIEDMONT LIMITED

NEW YORK--WASHINGTON--ATLANTA
and NEW ORLEANS EXPRESS

WASHINGTON---CHATTANOOGA
and NEW ORLEANS EXPRESS

PRIVATE SECTION
CRESCENT LIMITED

July 31, 1932

Plan Your Vacation
to the
Virginia Seashore

Make your plans NOW for a vacation at wonderful
Virginia Beach. Take the family or get up your own "Beach Party"
— enjoy the blue Atlantic . . . miles of golden seashore . . . swimming,
fishing, boating, golfing, tennis. You'll enjoy every minute of
your trip to the Beach and back, too, if you go by N. & W. . . . in
luxurious, air-conditioned coaches with adjustable,
deep-cushioned seats at wide Vista-Vue windows.
Go by N. & W.
— Every Mile's A Memory!

On Line Excursion Rates

Rate includes round-trip
transportation from Norfolk to
Virginia Beach.* Leave any
Friday or Saturday from June
10 to September 10 inclusive
—return any time within 12
days from date of departure.

avoid heavy highway traffic —

Go N&W

*Round-trip fares to Norfolk
only, are slightly less.

July 21, 1955

Seaboard STILL LEADS THE WAY!

. . . with the only complete diesel-electric powered all-Pullman, and streamlined, stainless-steel coach service between New York, Washington, central and both coasts of Florida.

SPEED . . . and plenty of it behind giant diesel-electric locomotives. 40,000 horsepower in the Seaboard fleet! Remarkable "on-time" performance record.

COMFORT unsurpassed. Modern air-conditioned equipment. Tight-lock couplers, rubber draft gear, in addition to smooth-running diesel-electric locomotives produce a velvet-smooth ride.

TRAVEL NOW! PAY LATER! Ask any Seaboard representative about this new, convenient, credit plan. No money down.

December 13, 1940

September 27, 1936

THE Powhatan Arrow

Trains 25 and 26

RESERVED SEAT, STREAMLINED COACH TRAIN

NORFOLK - CINCINNATI

THE MIDWEST AND WEST

Train 25 Daily		TABLE No. 1			Train 26 Daily
AM					**PM**
7 15	Lv.	Norfolk (Terminal Station) (E. T.) .... N. & W.	Ar.		11 25
7 38	"	Suffolk .... "	Lv.		10 57
8 35	Ar.	Petersburg .... N. & W.	Lv.		10 00
9 35	Ar.	Richmond .... A. C. L.	Lv.		9 00
7 35	Lv.	Richmond .... A. C. L.	Ar.		10 35
8 35	Lv.	Petersburg .... N. & W.	Ar.		10 00
B9 16	"	Blackstone .... "			**B9 17**
9 35	"	Crewe .... "			9 05
10 01	"	Farmville .... "			8 34
11 03	Ar.	Lynchburg .... N. & W.			7 38
See Note ^	Ar.	Durham .... N. & W.	Lv.		**See Note ^**
11 03	Lv.	Lynchburg .... N. & W.	Lv.		7 38
12 10	Ar.	Roanoke .... "	Lv.		6 35
4 25	Ar.	Winston-Salem			2 00
12 20	Lv.	Roanoke .... "	Ar.		6 25
1 04	"	Christiansburg .... "			5 39
A1 52	"	Pearisburg .... "			**A4 48**
2 50	"	Bluefield .... "			4 00
3 48	"	Welch .... "			2 53
5 35	"	Williamson .... "			1 15
7 14	"	Kenova .... "			11 25
7 28	"	Ironton .... "			11 10
8 05	"	Portsmouth .... "			10 40
10 45	Ar.	**Cincinnati** .... N. & W.	Lv.		8 10
C11 50	Lv.	Cincinnati (E. T.) .... P. R. R.	Ar.		7 20
7 00	Ar.	Chicago (C. T.) .... P. R. R.	Lv.		**D10 50**
N11 15	Lv.	Cincinnati (E. T.) .... N. Y. C.	Ar.		7 15
5 40	Ar.	Chicago (C. T.) .... N. Y. C.	Lv.		**D10 45**
E11 15	Lv.	Cincinnati (E. T.) .... N. Y. C.	Ar.		7 15
7 15	Ar.	St. Louis (C. T.) .... N. Y. C.	Lv.		**F10 40**
J11 30	Lv.	Cincinnati (E. T.) .... N. Y. C.	Ar.		6 45
7 00	Ar.	Detroit (E. T.) .... N. Y. C.	Lv.		**K11 35**
L10 45	Lv.	Cincinnati (E. T.) .... N. Y. C.	Ar.		7 00
5 27	Ar.	Cleveland (E. T.) .... N. Y. C.	Lv.		**M11 59**
E11 59	Lv.	Cincinnati (E. T.) .... B. & O.	Ar.		7 50
7 40	Ar.	St. Louis (C. T.) .... B. & O.	Lv.		**F11 30**
G11 45	Lv.	Cincinnati (E. T.) .... B. & O.	Ar.		6 55
7 20	Ar.	Detroit (E. T.) .... B. & O.	Lv.		**H11 40**
10 50	Lv.	Cincinnati (E. T.) .... L. & N.	Ar.		7 45
1 20	Ar.	Louisville (C. T.) .... L. & N.	Lv.		3 45
AM					**AM**

REFERENCE MARKS FOR TABLE No. 1

Note ^—Mixed train, daily except Sunday, leaves Lynchburg 8:25 A. M., arriving Durham 4:02 P. M.; leaves Durham 6:33 A. M., arriving Lynchburg 2:45 P. M. N. & W. tickets between Lynchburg, Va., and Durham, N. C., will also be honored by Virginia Trailways Buses. Consult Ticket Agent.

A—Stop to discharge or receive revenue passengers from or to Roanoke and beyond, or to receive or discharge revenue passengers for or from Williamson and beyond.

B—Stop to discharge or receive revenue passengers.

C—Sleeper Cincinnati to Chicago, open for occupancy 9:30 P. M.

D—Sleeper Chicago to Cincinnati, open for occupancy 9:30 P. M.

E—Sleeper Cincinnati to St. Louis, open for occupancy 9:30 P. M.

F—Sleeper St. Louis to Cincinnati, open for occupancy 9:00 P. M.

G—Sleeper Cincinnati to Detroit (except Saturdays), open for occupancy 9:30 P. M.

H—Sleeper Detroit to Cincinnati (except Saturdays), open Detroit 10:00 P. M., may be occupied Cincinnati until 7:30 A. M.

J—Sleeper Cincinnati to Detroit, open for occupancy 9:30 P. M., may be occupied at Detroit until 7:30 A. M.

K—Sleeper Detroit to Cincinnati, open Detroit 10:00 P. M., may be occupied Cincinnati until 7:30 A. M.

L—Sleeper Cincinnati to Cleveland, open for occupancy 9:30 P. M., may be occupied at Cleveland until 7:30 A. M.

M—Sleeper Cleveland to Cincinnati open Cleveland 9:30 P. M., may be occupied Cincinnati until 7:30 A. M.

N—Sleeper Cincinnati to Chicago open for occupancy 9:30 P. M., and may be occupied at Chicago until 7:00 A. M.

SEATS RESERVED WITHOUT ADDITIONAL CHARGE. NO CHECKED BAGGAGE HANDLED.
For explanation of Reference Marks, see side of this Table.

Tavern-Lounge-Observation Car -- Luxury Coaches -- De Luxe Diners

PAGE **6**

July 21, 1955

(Courtesy Allen Tuten and Central of Georgia Railway Historical Society)

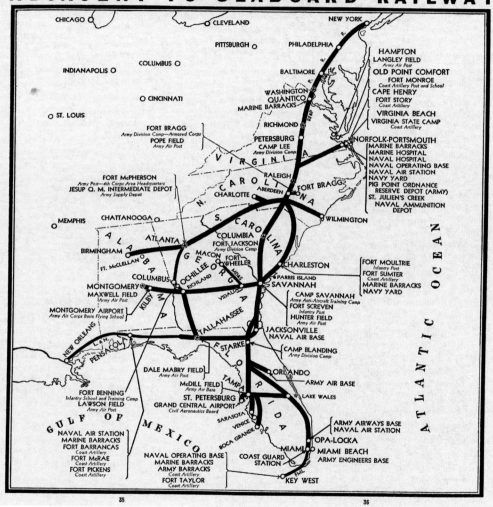

December 13, 1940

NEW! Improved
ORANGE BLOSSOM SPECIAL
AND
SILVER METEOR SERVICE

The Only Streamlined, Stainless-Steel Coach Service and Only Diesel-Electric Pullman Service between Eastern Cities and Both Coasts of Florida.

West Coast ORANGE BLOSSOM SPECIAL All-Pullman for First Time

BOTH EAST AND WEST COAST "BLOSSOMS" MAKE FIRST TRIPS FROM NEW YORK DEC. 13
DECEMBER 15 FROM FLORIDA

...GO MODERN GO SEABOARD!

Florida's west coast resorts will be served by all-Pullman ORANGE BLOSSOM SPECIAL service with equipment matching the magnificence and luxury of the famous East Coast ORANGE BLOSSOM SPECIAL. Both "Blossoms" will contain lounge and club feature cars, latest type section-compartment-drawing room-bedroom sleeping cars. All air-conditioned, of course, and equipped with anti-noise devices to add to the pleasantness of your journey.

December 13, 1940

FASTEST SCHEDULES
Ever Operated between Eastern Cities and Florida
25 Hours New York - Miami
23 Hours FIFTY MINUTES New York - St. Petersburg

December 15, 1939

It's **FLORIDA** for Sun, Fun and Rest

Go on the
Streamlined, Winter-Season

NEW ROYAL PALM

THERE'S NO FINER TRAIN TO FLORIDA

The NEW ROYAL PALM offers luxurious, daily through service between the Great Lakes Region and the East Coast of sunny Florida.

Save WITH
ROUND-TRIP TICKETS

SOUTHERN RAILWAY SYSTEM

No. 5 Southbound Read Down			DAILY SCHEDULE		No. 6 Northbound Read Up
10:45 PM	Lv.	Chicago (C.T.)	N. Y. C. Sys.	Ar.	5:40 AM
3:47 AM	Lv.	Indianapolis (C.T.)	"	Ar.	12:35 AM
7:15 AM	Ar.	Cincinnati (E.T.)	"	Lv.	11:15 PM
11:30 PM	Lv.	Detroit (E.T.)	N. Y. C. Sys.	Ar.	7:10 AM
1:15 AM	Lv.	Toledo	"	Ar.	5:15 AM
4:35 AM	Lv.	Springfield	"	Ar.	1:20 AM
5:22 AM	Lv.	Dayton	"	Ar.	12:45 AM
6:50 AM	Ar.	Cincinnati	"	Lv.	11:30 PM
7:10 PM	Lv.	Buffalo (E.T.)	N. Y. C. Sys.	Ar.	9:45 AM
8:55 PM	Lv.	Erie	"	Ar.	8:02 AM
11:15 PM	Ar.	Cleveland	"	Ar.	6:10 AM
11:59 PM	Lv.	Cleveland	"	Ar.	5:50 AM
3:35 AM	Lv.	Columbus	"	Ar.	2:05 AM
7:10 AM	Ar.	Cincinnati	"	Lv.	11:00 PM
8:30 AM	Lv.	Cincinnati (E.T.)	Sou. Ry. Sys.	Ar.	10:15 PM
7:30 AM	Lv.	Cincinnati (C.T.)	"	Ar.	9:15 PM
9:10 AM	Lv.	Lexington (C.T.)	"	Ar.	7:30 PM
4:00 PM	Lv.	Chattanooga (E.T.)	"	Ar.	2:15 PM
4:10 PM	Lv.	Chattanooga	"	Ar.	2:05 PM
7:40 PM	Ar.	Atlanta	"	Ar.	10:30 AM
7:50 PM	Lv.	Atlanta	"	Ar.	10:10 AM
9:50 PM	Lv.	Macon	"	Ar.	8:10 AM
10:00 PM	Lv.	Macon	"	Ar.	8:00 AM
4:05 AM	Ar.	Jacksonville	"	Lv.	1:50 AM
4:25 AM	Lv.	Jacksonville	F. E. C. Ry.	Ar.	1:30 AM
5:01 AM	Ar.	St. Augustine	"	Lv.	12:46 AM
b5:43 AM	Ar.	Ormond Beach	"	Lv.	b12:03 AM
5:55 AM	Ar.	Daytona Beach	"	Lv.	11:55 PM
6:15 AM	Ar.	New Smyrna Beach	"	Lv.	11:35 PM
f7:03 AM	Ar.	Titusville	"	Lv.	b10:46 PM
7:19 AM	Ar.	Cocoa-Rockledge	"	Lv.	10:28 PM
7:37 AM	Ar.	Melbourne	"	Lv.	10:07 PM
8:13 AM	Ar.	Vero Beach	"	Lv.	9:33 PM
8:32 AM	Ar.	Fort Pierce	"	Lv.	9:18 PM
b9:02 AM	Ar.	Stuart	"	Lv.	8:45 PM
b9:16 AM	Ar.	Hobe Sound	"	Lv.	b8:28 PM
9:44 AM	Ar.	West Palm Beach	"	Lv.	8:03 PM
b9:57 AM	Ar.	Lake Worth	"	Lv.	7:48 PM
b10:11 AM	Ar.	Delray Beach	"	Lv.	7:37 PM
b10:22 AM	Ar.	Boca Raton	"	Lv.	c7:26 PM
b10:31 AM	Ar.	Pompano Beach	"	Lv.	b7:18 PM
10:44 AM	Ar.	Fort Lauderdale	"	Lv.	7:08 PM
10:57 AM	Ar.	Hollywood	"	Lv.	6:56 PM
11:25 AM	Ar.	Miami	"	Lv.	6:30 PM

b—Stops to let off or receive passengers from or for Jacksonville and beyond.   c—Stops to let off passengers from Miami and receive for Fort Pierce and points north.   f—Flag stop.

EQUIPMENT

SLEEPERS—   Diesel Power Cincinnati-Miami

South	North	Between	Type
700	F-700	Detroit-Miami	5-Double Bedroom, Lounge-Observation
701	F-701	Detroit-Miami	4-Compt., 4-Dble. Bedroom, 2-Drawingroom
702	F-702	Detroit-Miami	10-Roomette, 6-Double Bedroom
703	F-703	Detroit-Miami	13-Double Bedroom
704	F-704	Cincinnati-Miami	10-Roomette, 6-Double Bedroom
705	F-705	Cleveland-Miami	4-Compt., 4-Dble. Bedrm., 2-Drawingroom
*706	F-706	Cleveland-Miami	10-Roomette, 6-Double Bedroom
707	F-707	Buffalo-Miami	14-Roomette, 4-Double Bedroom
708	F-708	Chicago-Miami	10-Roomette, 6-Double Bedroom

*—Operates from Buffalo, Tuesday, Thursday and Saturday, from Cleveland balance of week; operates from Miami to Buffalo, Sunday, Tuesday and Thursday, from Miami to Cleveland balance of week.

RECLINING-SEAT COACHES—Detroit-Miami, Cincinnati-Miami. (Coach seats reserved at slight extra cost.)
LOUNGE-COACH—Cincinnati-Miami.
DINER—Cincinnati-Miami.
TRAIN PASSENGER REPRESENTATIVE-HOSTESS.

Southbound—Sleeping cars open for occupancy 9:30 PM at Chicago and Cleveland, 10:00 PM at Detroit.   Northbound—Sleeping cars may be occupied until 7:15 AM at Chicago, 7:30 AM at Detroit, 8:00 AM at Cleveland.

March 7, 1954

March 25, 1956

5

KANSAS CITY FLORIDA *Special*

Reaches MIAMI at Midday

Schedule Effective December 12 southbound; December 15 northbound

Lv Kansas City	(Frisco Lines)	7:00 PM
Lv Memphis	"	7:20 AM
Lv Birmingham	(Sou. Ry. Sys.)	1:40 PM
Lv Atlanta (C. T.)	"	a6:55 PM
Ar Jacksonville (E. T.)	"	a4:35 AM
Ar West Palm Beach	(F. E. C. Ry.)	a10:45 AM
Ar Miami		a12:40 PM
Lv Miami	(F. E. C. Ry.)	b12:55 PM
Lv West Palm Beach	"	b2:30 PM
Lv Jacksonville (E. T.)	(Sou. Ry. Sys.)	9:30 PM
Ar Atlanta (C. T.)	"	6:20 AM
Ar Birmingham	"	11:35 AM
Ar Memphis	(Frisco Lines)	6:50 PM
Ar Kansas City	"	7:45 AM

a-Effective first trip from Atlanta Dec. 13; prior to that date Lv Atlanta 8:10PM, Ar Jacksonville 6:05AM, connecting with F.E.C. Ry. "Vacationer," coach train No. 79, Ar West Palm Beach 12:01PM, Miami 1:30PM. b-Effective Dec. 15; prior to that date connects with F.E.C. Ry. "Vacationer," coach train No. 70, Lv Miami 11:55AM, West Palm Beach 1:23PM.

NOTE—Effective first trip from Atlanta Dec. 13, the Kansas City-Florida Special will operate southbound via Valdosta and northbound via Jesup.

Through Sleeping Cars between Kansas City and Miami, Kansas City, Birmingham, Atlanta and Jacksonville • Lounge Car Service available between Kansas City and Miami • Dining Cars Serving All Meals • Chair Cars or Coaches • All Cars Air-Conditioned

LEAVE WINTER BEHIND . . .
Greet summer at its best

The SUNNYLAND

Through Air-Conditioned Sleeping Car Between Memphis and Atlanta

Lv St. Louis	(Frisco Lines)	8:55 AM
Lv Memphis	(Frisco Lines)	11:00 PM
Ar Atlanta	(So. Ry. Sys.)	a12:05 PM
•		
Lv Atlanta	(So. Ry. Sys.)	3:40 PM
Ar Memphis	(Frisco Lines)	6:50 PM
Ar St. Louis	(Frisco Lines)	3:45 PM

a—Effective Dec. 15; prior to that date Ar Atlanta 11:50 AM

Air-Conditioned Dining Car and Coaches

SOUTHERN RAILWAY SYSTEM

FRISCO LINES
ST. LOUIS-SAN FRANCISCO RY.

December 1940

LUNCHEON

THE CRESCENT

LUNCHEON SELECT

Price opposite entree includes complete meal. Please write each item on check.

Chilled Grapefruit Juice
    Chicken Broth, Rice

Chilled Tomato Juice
Jellied or Hot Consomme, Clear

°FRIED FISH, TARTAR SAUCE 2.75
°GRILLED HAMBURGER STEAK, MUSHROOM SAUCE 2.75
°HAM OR CHEESE OMELET 2.40

Choice of Two

Mashed Potatoes   Navy Beans   Turnip Greens   Green Peas, Butter

Head Lettuce—French Dressing

Deep Dish Berry Pie   Ice Cream   Chilled Melon

Coffee   Tea   Milk

*Above items prepared to order.

LUNCHEON A LA CARTE

Sliced Tomatoes .50   Chilled Grapefruit Juice .40   Chilled Tomato Juice .40
Chicken Broth, Rice, Cup .35; Tureen .60   Jellied or Hot Consomme, Clear (cup) .35

ENTREES

°BROILED OR FRIED FISH, TARTAR SAUCE 2.00
°GRILLED HAMBURGER STEAK, MUSHROOM SAUCE 2.00
VEGETABLE PLATE, POACHED EGG 1.50
°HAM OR CHEESE OMELET 1.50

(The above entrees include Bread and Butter, Coffee, Tea or Milk)

SANDWICHES	VEGETABLES	SALADS
American Cheese .80	Mashed Potatoes .35	(Served with French Dressing or Mayonnaise)
Baked Ham .80	Navy Beans .35	
Comb. Ham and Cheese .80	Green Peas, Butter .35	Lettuce and Tomato .90
Lettuce and Tomato .80	Turnip Greens .35	Head Lettuce .80
Chicken Salad on Toasted Bread 1.35		Chicken Salad—Crackers 1.60
Ham and Egg 1.35		
Bacon, Lettuce and Tomato .90		

Hot Corn Bread .25   Dry or Buttered Toast .25   Flake Crackers or Ry-Krisp .20

Chilled Melon .40
Vanilla Ice Cream .40

Deep Dish Berry Pie .45; A la Mode .60
Bleu Cheese, Crackers .45

Coffee, Pot .35   Hot Tea, Pot .35   Iced Tea, Pot .35   Cocoa, Pot .35   Instant Postum, Pot .35
Instant Sanka Coffee, Pot .35   Grade "A" Pasteurized Milk .20

*Above items prepared to order

● Place settings gladly furnished without extra charge to parents who desire to share their portions with children, or half-portions will be served at half-price to children under ten years of age.

● The States of Alabama, Florida, Georgia, Louisiana, Mississippi, North Carolina, South Carolina, and Tennessee assess a sales tax on the value of meals served, which must be collected from the buyer.

● Meals served in Pullman Space, 50c extra per person; available when waiter can be spared from Dining Car.

R&C 67859

SOUTHERN RAILWAY SYSTEM ● ATLANTA & WEST POINT RAILROAD
WESTERN RAILWAY OF ALABAMA ● LOUISVILLE & NASHVILLE RAILROAD
F. C. THOMAS, MANAGER DINING CARS ● SOUTHERN RAILWAY SYSTEM ● ATLANTA 31, GA.

1959

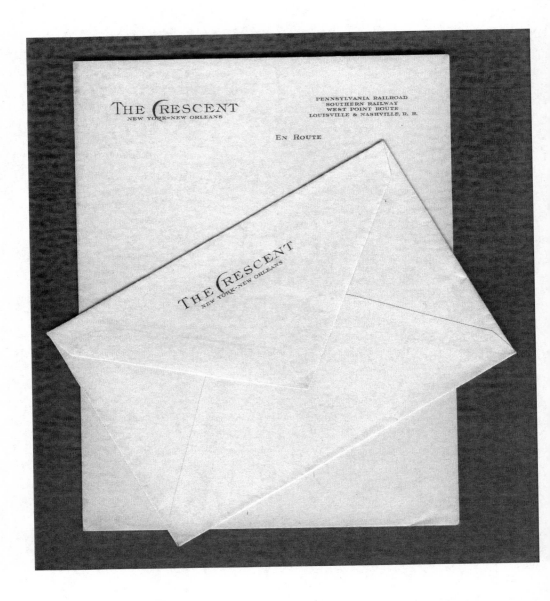

CHAPTER NOTES

Introduction

1. Richard E. Prince, *Atlantic Coast Line Railroad: Steam Locomotives, Ships, and History*. Bloomington: Indiana University Press, 2000, p. 22.
2. Ibid.

Chapter 1

1. Lucius Beebe and Charles Clegg, *The Age of Steam: A Classic Album of American Railroading*. New York: Promontory Press, 1994, p. 77; Louis Warburton, *Railroads: Bridging the Continents*. San Diego: Lucent Books, 1991, pp. 8, 11; John P. Hankey, "Fact or Fiction? Standard Gauge Originated with a Roman Chariot." *Trains*, July 2009, p. 25.
2. Warburton, pp. 8, 11.
3. http://www.knowledgerush.com/kr/encyclopedia/Timeline_of_railway_history/.
4. http://www.knowledgerush.com/kr/encyclopedia/Timeline_of_railway_history/.
5. Warburton, p. 11.
6. Hankey, p. 25.
7. Ibid.
8. Warburton, p. 5.
9. Jim Cox, *Sold on Radio: Advertisers in the Golden Age of Broadcasting*. Jefferson, N.C.: McFarland, 2008, p. 9.
10. Anthony J. Bianculli, *Trains and Technology: The American Railroad in the Nineteenth Century*. Vol. 1. Newark: University of Delaware Press, 2001, p. 33.
11. Arthur M. Wellington, *The Economic Theory of the Location of Railways*. New York: John Wiley and Sons, 1887, p. 48.
12. http://www.vahistorical.org/onthisday/3198.htm.
13. Wellington, p. 48.
14. http://www.sdrm.org/history/timeline/; http://www.irs.gov/businesses/article/o,,id=175287,00.html; http://www.knowledgerush.com/kr/encyclopedia/Timeline_of_railway_history/; http://www.aar.org/AboutAAR/AAR%20History.aspx; http://www.narprail.org/cms/index.php/resources/more/railroad_history/; Bianculli, p. 34; Warburton, pp. 8–9, 64.
15. Bianculli, p. 21.
16. Warburton, p. 64.
17. Bianculli, p. 21.
18. Stewart H. Holbrook, *The Story of American Railroads*. New York: Crown, 1947, p. 3.
19. Sources of track measurements: Bianculli, pp. 18–20; Warburton, p. 65.
20. Warburton, p. 32.

Chapter 2

1. Jim Loomis, *All Aboard: The Complete North American Train Travel Guide*. 2nd ed. Rocklin, Calif.: Prima, 1998, pp. 18–19.
2. http://www.american-rails.com/golden-age-of-railroading.html.
3. George W. Hilton, *Amtrak: The National Railroad Passenger Corporation*. Washington, D.C.: American Enterprise Institute for Public Policy Research, 1980.
4. Donald M. Itzkoff, *Off the Track: The Decline of the Intercity Passenger Train in the United States*. Westport, Conn.: Greenwood, 1985.
5. Louis Warburton, *Railroads: Bridging the Continents*. San Diego: Lucent Books, 1991, pp. 9, 65.
6. http://www.american-rails.com/golden-age-of-railroading.html.
7. Loomis, p. 21.
8. http://www.narprail.org/cms/index.php/resources/more/railroad_history/.
9. Stephen B. Goddard, *Getting There: The Epic Struggle Between Road and Rail in the American Century*. New York: HarperCollins, 1994.
10. There is a misnomer in the reference cited. William Peters Hepburn (1833–1916) was never a senator, as allowed. An Iowa Republican, Hepburn was in the U.S. House of Representatives on two occasions, 1881–1887 and 1893–1909, losing his seat to other contenders twice. See http://en.wikipedia.org/wiki/William_P._Hepburn.
11. The fare increased from 3 cents to 3.6 cents per passenger mile in August 1920, according to the National Association of Railroad Passengers.
12. Restrictions on commercial aviation and automobile travel at a time of high war-related demand for intercity transportation brought the number of passengers back to the level of the early 1920s and actually caused passenger miles to reach double the 1920 level, Amtrak reported. In 1944, the railroads carried 916 million travelers an aggregate 95.7 billion passenger miles.
13. http://www.narprail.org/cms/index.php/resources/more/railroad_history/; http://en.wikipedia.org/wiki/William_Gibbs_McAdoo; Gregory Lee Thompson, *The Passenger Train in the Motor Age: California's Rail and Bus Industries, 1910–1941*. Columbus: Ohio State University Press, 1993.
14. A sleeper surcharge of a half-cent per passenger mile was reinstituted by the railroads in August 1920, the National Association of Railroad Passengers reports.
15. Lucius Beebe and Charles Clegg, *The Age of Steam: A Classic Album of American Railroading*. New York: Promontory, 1994, p. 77.
16. http://library.duke.edu/digitalcollections/adaccess/rails-history.html.

17. Anthony J. Bianculli, *Trains and Technology: The American Railroad in the Nineteenth Century*. Vol. 1. Newark: University of Delaware Press, 2001, pp. 39–40, 44.

18. Applying the Gross Domestic Product deflator using the value of consumer bundle, $4,000 in 1830 is estimated to have been $92,968.71 in 2007, the most recent year's data available as this is written. See http://www.measuringworth.com/calculators/uscompare/result.php.

19. Bianculli, pp. 44–45.

20. Stewart H. Holbrook, *The Story of American Railroads*. New York: Crown, 1947, p. 6.

21. Warburton, pp. 31–32.

22. Ibid., p. 32.

23. Beebe and Clegg, p. 77.

24. http://www.american-rails.com/passenger-railroading.html.

25. Bianculli, pp. 39–40.

26. Ibid.; http://www.sdrm.org/history/timeline/.

27. Ibid., p. 45.

28. Warburton, p. 32.

29. Stewart H. Holbrook, *The Story of American Railroads*. New York: Crown, 1947, p. 23.

30. Fourteen U.S. presidents serving in the 73-year span from 1872–1945 principally relied upon the railroads of America for their domestic travel while in office, finding it safe and fast. They included, in order: Ulysses S. Grant, Rutherford B. Hayes, James A. Garfield, Chester A. Arthur, Grover Cleveland, Benjamin Harrison, Grover Cleveland (second term), William McKinley, Theodore Roosevelt, William H. Taft, Woodrow Wilson, Warren Harding, Calvin Coolidge, Herbert Hoover, Franklin D. Roosevelt. Sources: http://www.irs.gov/businesses/article/0,,id=175287,00.html; http://www.whitehouse.gov/history/presidents/chronological.html.

31. Warburton, p. 32.

32. Holbrook, p. 24. Figures adapted from H.S. Turner's *A Description of Canals and Rail Roads in the United States*, research completed and published in 1840.

33. Bianculli, p. 35.

34. Sources: http://www.sdrm.org/history/timeline/; http://www.irs.gov/businesses/article/0,,id=175287,00.html; Warburton, pp. 8–9, 11; Mirco De Cet and Alan Kent. *The Complete Encyclopedia of Locomotives*. Lisse, The Netherlands: Rebo International, 2006, p. 46; Loomis, p. 13.

35. http://www.american-rails.com/streamliners.html.

36. http://www.american-rails.com/streamliners.html.

Chapter 3

1. http://www.american-rails.com/the-champion.html.

2. Ibid.

3. While the "Overseas Railroad" will be mentioned again later in this chapter, there is a great deal more to this portion of the fascinating Florida East Coast tale to be revealed in Chapter 6.

4. The "purple stage" alludes to the ACL's distinguished mid 20th century livery dominated by purple hues as well as carriages (stages) that were pervasive in an earlier railroad epoch. It's a throwback to Zane Grey's esteemed frontier novel based on incidents in 1871 and published in 1912, *Riders of the Purple Sage*, a moniker subsequently adopted by no fewer than a trio of cowboy singing troupes.

5. While Amtrak took over the passenger service in 1971, the Seaboard Coast Line Railroad persisted as a freight carrier until the SCL was absorbed into the newly formed CSX Corporation in 1980.

6. Excludes a handful of pithy routes of a few hours' duration where multiple daily trains persist without requiring overnight travel.

7. See Chapter 2.

8. http://www.csa-railroads.com/Wilmington%20&%20Weldon.htm.

9. http://en.wikipedia.org/wiki/Atlantic_Coast_Line_Railroad.

10. Richard E. Prince, *Atlantic Coast Line Railroad: Steam Locomotives, Ships and History*. Bloomington: Indiana University Press, 2000, p. 105.

11. Some sources claim Walters was born in 1920. On a ship's manifest in early May 1848, he gives his age as 28; he didn't turn 29 until two weeks later, adding credibility to 1919 as his birth year.

12. *The New York Times*, November 23, 1894.

13. Tom Murray, *Southern Railway*. St. Paul, Minn.: MBI Publishing, 2007, pp. 15, 34–35, 38.

14. Prince, p. 106.

15. Ibid.

16. By 1925, the ACL's mainline from Richmond to Jacksonville was comprised of either double track or two parallel single-tracked routes equipped with automatic block signals. Later, 60 miles of the west coast route were double-tracked from Dunnellon to Vitis, Florida. Four brief stretches between Jacksonville and Tampa via Orlando also received a second track.

17. For additional comments on the Plant System, see the Introduction to this volume.

18. See Chapter 6 on the Florida East Coast Railway.

19. Larry Goolsby, *Atlantic Coast Line Passenger Service: The Postwar Years*. Lynchburg, Va.: TLC, 1999, p. 11.

20. Ibid., p. 23.

21. Ibid., p. 31.

22. Ibid., pp. 31–32.

23. Ibid., p. 39.

24. On June 29, 1956, President Dwight D. Eisenhower, without ceremony or fanfare, lying in a hospital bed at Walter Reed Army Medical Center recovering from an attack of ileitis, signed into law the Federal-Aid Highway Act of 1956. It was a landmark bill for which he had long lobbied that authorized the nation's interstate highway system.

25. Goolsby, p. 46.

26. Goolsby, p. 8.

27. http://www.american-rails.com/atlantic-coast-line.html.

28. Hays T. Watkins, Jr., was born at Louisville, Ky., on January 26, 1926. He joined the Chesapeake & Ohio Railway as a staff analyst in 1949, becoming treasurer in 1961. An affiliation of the C&O and Baltimore & Ohio Railroad in 1964 advanced him to vice president for finance for both firms. He was elected president and CEO of those companies in 1971, adding chairman of the board to his status two years later. In 1975, Watkins became chairman, president and CEO of Chessie System, Inc.; in 1980, president and co–CEO of CSX Corp.; in 1982, chairman and CEO of CSX; and 1989, chairman of CSX board of directors. He retired in 1991, in Richmond, Va.

29. http://en.wikipedia.org/wiki/Atlantic_Coast_Line_Railroad.

30. Goolsby, p. 71.
31. Ibid., p. 75.

Chapter 4

1. http://www.georgiaencyclopedia.org/nge/Article.jsp?id=h-1282.
2. Ibid.
3. The 600 horsepower SW1 was manufactured at McCook, Illinois, by General Motors' Electromotive Corporation shortly before GM merged EMC with Winton Engine to create Electro-Motive Division (EMD), a better remembered locomotive maker. SW1 was sold to Atlanta, Stone Mountain and Lithonia Railroad in 1957, which sold it to Greenville Northern Railroad early in the 1990s. The line altered its name to Carolina Piedmont Railroad a few years hence before returning the CofG's premier diesel to the Savannah roundhouse. At least nine CofG diesels were still intact—some still working, some in museums—in 2009. Sources: http://cofg.org/index.php?option=com_content&task=view&id=279Itemid-1; http://cofg.org/index.php?option=com_content&task=view&id=280Itemid-1.
4. This account is presented in some detail in Chapter 2.
5. http://railga.com/cofg.html.
6. http://www.georgiaencyclopedia.org/nge/Article.jsp?id=h-1282.
7. http://www.georgiaencyclopedia.org/nge/Article.jsp?id=h-1282; http://www.georgiahistory.com/containers/154.
8. http://cofg.org/index.php?option=com_content&task=view&id=66&Itemid=1.
9. http://en.wikipedia.org/wiki/Central_of_Georgia_Railway.
10. http://railga.com/cofg.html.
11. http://cofg.org/index.php?option=com_content&task=view&id=66&Itemid=1.
12. Ibid.
13. Murray, Tom. *Southern Railway*. St. Paul, Minn.: Voyageur Press, 2007, p. 25.
14. http://railga.com/cofg.html.
15. Ibid.
16. That same summer the parent owner, Richmond Terminal Company, suffered a similar setback. It entered receivership along with auxiliary carriers Richmond & Danville Railroad and the East Tennessee, Virginia and Georgia Railway.
17. If the name Harriman is memorable, it probably should be. W. Averell Harriman (1891–1986), son of Edward H. Harriman, followed in his father's footsteps in 1915, serving as chairman of the board of directors of both the Illinois Central and Union Pacific railroads from 1932 to 1946. Active in Democratic politics, the younger Harriman was U.S. secretary of commerce from 1946 to 1948, governor of New York from 1954 to 1958, and a U.S. diplomat to Europe, the Far East and the Soviet Union. In 1956, he made an unsuccessful bid for his party's nomination for president.
18. Most details of Edward Harriman's life supplied by http://answers.com/topic/e-h-harriman.
19. http://eh.net/bookreviews/library/0287.
20. Ibid.
21. According to one reporter, at the time of Harriman's death he controlled the Central of Georgia, Illinois Central, Saint Joseph and Grand Island, Southern Pacific and Union Pacific railroads; Pacific Mail Steamship Company; and Wells Fargo Express Company. His estate, left completely to his wife, was estimated at between $200 million and $600 million.
22. http://railga.com/cofg.html.
23. Ibid.
24. The Southern Railway annual report for 1967 indicates that Southern owned 99 percent of the CofG's stock at that point.
25. Murray, p. 109.
26. Ibid., p. 87.
27. Murray, p. 130.
28. Ibid., pp. 130–131.
29. http:/en.wikipedia.org/wiki/Central_of_Georgia_Railway.
30. Adapted from http://cofg.org/index.php?option=com_content&task=view&id=66&Itemid=1.
31. Details of this racehorse supplied by http://www.spiletta.com/UTHOF/manowar.html.
32. http://horseracing.about.com/od/famoushorses/a/aa05304a.htm.
33. From an old ballad, author unknown, appearing in *The Macon Telegraph* on May 1, 1971.
34. "Nancy Hanks was named in honor of the mother of the greatest of Kentucky's sons, Abraham Lincoln," pontificated one wag, "and you might say Nancy Hanks was going to be one of the greatest daughters of Kentucky." Source: http://www.mm-online.se/standardbred/Standardbred/Stories/nancy_hanks.htm.
35. Ibid.
36. http://www.queenandcrescent.org/coach_660.html.
37. Ibid.
38. Excerpts from a story about the Nancy's last ride by city editor Archie McKay of *The Macon Telegraph*, appearing in that paper's May 1, 1971, edition.
39. http://www.queenandcrescent.org/coach_660.html.
40. The Old Gray Mare gained fame in the 1840s as a top Standardbred competitor. The Old Gray Mare was Lady Suffolk (1833–1855), dubbed "Queen of the Turf." She was forever remembered in the folk song "The Old Gray Mare."

Chapter 5

1. While there was more than three, only a triumvirate gained consistent widespread marketing exposure in the company's promotional campaigns.
2. http://www.american-rails.com/george-washington.html.
3. Some of this history is adapted from these websites: http://www.american-rails.com/george-washington.html, http://www.pmhistsoc.org/, http://www.pmhistsoc.org/timeline.shtml, http://en.wikipedia.org/wiki/Chesapeake_and_Ohio_Railway, http://csx.history.railfan.net/history/histco.html, http://www.pmhistsoc.org/maxpmmap.shtml.
4. Scott Reynolds Nelson, *Steel Drivin' Man: John Henry, the Untold Story of an American Legend*. New York: Oxford University Press, 2006, p. 7.
5. Ibid., p. 11.
6. By proclamation of U.S. President Abraham Lincoln, West Virginia became a state on June 20, 1863, an area separated from Virginia. It was "the only state born out of the armed conflict of the Civil War," said one source. Three primary reasons formed the basis for residents' preference for separation from Virginia: inequal-

ity in taxation, unequal representation in the legislature and unequal distribution of funds for public works in which the eastern part of the state was favored.

7. http://csx.history.railfan.net/history/histco.html.

8. Nelson, p. 5.

9. C&O "Railroad" was changed to "Railway" in 1878.

10. http://csx.history.railfan.net/history/histco.html.

11. Eugene L. Huddleston, *Appalachian Conquest: C&O, N&W, Virginian and Clinchfield Cross the Mountains.* Lynchburg, Va.: TLC, 2002, p. 1.

12. http://en.wikipedia.org/wiki/Chesapeake_and_Ohio_Railway.

13. The Pere Marquette Historical Society, Inc., formed in 1995, claims the original road operated trackage from Buffalo, New York, to Chicago, and Bay View, Michigan, to Toledo, Ohio. PM also maintained railway car ferries on the Detroit and St. Clair rivers plus a fleet of car ferries from Ludington across Lake Michigan to Milwaukee, Kewaunee and Manitowoc, Wisconsin. Almost all CSX tracks across Michigan currently in use emanated from the PM system.

14. http://www.american-rails.com/george-washington.html.

15. "CSX Eyes Selling Greenbrier Resort," *Trains,* April 2009, p. 10.

16. http://en.wikipedia.org/wiki/Chesapeake_and_Ohio_Railway.

17. Actually, there were some pretty impressive exceptions to the sweeping assumption that other mergers weren't going nearly as well. In 1957, for instance, having waited 77 years after buying it, the Louisville & Nashville Railroad appeared well prepared to swallow the Nashville, Chattanooga & St. Louis Railway. After pausing a full decade before implementing another well-reasoned business plan, the Atlantic Coast Line and the Seaboard Air Line systems merged in 1967. Both examples occurred before the union of the C&O and B&O; was the latter fusion simply following a model already in play?

18. Material from Huddleston, pp. 50, 52, 55, with direct quotes from researcher Jessie J. Smith.

19. Huddleston, p. 56.

20. http://appalachianhistory.blogspot.com/1008/dining-in-style-in-ffv.html.

21. Ibid.

22. A request to the C&O Historical Society did not produce an answer.

23. It depends on whom is asked, although a contemporary American Rails website designates it in that fashion.

24. George Washington was actually born on February 11, 1731, of the Julian calendar in use before England's calendar reformation in September 1752. His birthday is equivalent to February 22, 1732, in the Gregorian calendar used since 1752. Later in life, Washington considered the 22d to be his birthday.

25. http://www.american-rails.com/george-washington.html.

26. Adapted from Louis Decimus Rubin, Jr., *A Memory of Trains: The Boll Weevil and Others.* Columbia: University of South Carolina Press, 2000.

Chapter 6

1. Seth H. Bramson, *Speedway to Sunshine: The Story of the Florida East Coast Railway.* Erin, Ontario: Boston Mills, 2003, p. 47.

2. Ibid., p. 52.

3. At one point Flagler claimed a personal vendetta was instigated against him by President Theodore Roosevelt, whom he earlier supported for the New York governorship. Elected to the post, Roosevelt rapidly passed bills taxing corporate franchises, acts Flagler viewed as betrayal. In succeeding years Flagler's contempt for Roosevelt grew epically. "I have no command of the English language that enables me to express my feelings regarding Mr. Roosevelt," he said in a letter found by biographer David Leon Chandler.

4. Bramson, pp. 52–53.

5. Les Standiford, *Last Train to Paradise: Henry Flagler and the Spectacular Rise and Fall of the Railroad That Crossed an Ocean.* New York: Crown, 2002, p. 77.

6. Ibid.

7. Ibid., p. 72.

8. Pat Parks, *The Railroad That Died at Sea: The Florida East Coast's Key West Extension.* Key West, Fla.: Langley Press, 1968, p. 4.

9. The U.S. Congress had made provision for the Overseas Highway in 1928. Already bankrupt and in the hands of a receiver, the FEC was in no position to rebuild anything. Desperate for cash, the FEC sold the right-of-way to the state for $640,000, a lousy return on a project costing $30 million over seven years of labor and the lives of some of the project's 40,000-member workforce.

10. Standiford, p. 32.

11. Ibid., p. 257.

12. Parks, p. 7.

13. Bramson, p. 49.

14. For about three years Mary Lily Flagler divided her time between Whitehall in Palm Beach and a home the couple maintained in New York state. In that period she encountered an old friend, an intrepid, stressed Louisville lawyer, Robert Worth Bingham, whose ambitions exceeded his grasp. From 1933 to 1937, he was appointed by Franklin D. Roosevelt as U.S. ambassador to Great Britain. Bingham and Mary Lily Flagler married in 1916. She altered her will to earmark $5 million for him although a secret codicil supposedly specified he was to receive nothing. (See http://www.findagrave.com/cgi-bin/fg.cgi?page=gr&GRid=10351761.) Eight months after their nuptials and quite mysteriously, Mary, then 50, was dead, reportedly of acute alcohol and opium abuse. Despite the confusion over the will, Bingham nevertheless received $5 million, purchased his city's two daily newspapers, *The Courier-Journal* and *The Louisville Times,* and paid off some indebtedness. His transactions "fueled rumors that if Bingham hadn't actually been involved in Mary Lily's death, he did little to prevent it." (Standiford, p. 219.) Other revelations surfaced: an incomplete autopsy speculated that traces of arsenic were found in her system. In *The Binghams of Louisville,* the authors argue that Bingham had clearly aided and abetted Mary Lily's death. There have been other theories advanced in subsequent works, some of which are startling and do not involve Robert Bingham. *The Patriarch: The Rise and Fall of the Bingham Dynasty,* for one, purports that cardiovascular syphilis may have been her cause of death, indicating that Henry Flagler could have been its source.

15. The FEC had contracts with other carriers, too. It ferried passengers arriving in Jacksonville on Southern Railway between Jacksonville and Miami as well as those whose trips began or ended with a diverse lot of Midwest and upper South carriers.

16. Obstructions included a stubborn Interstate Commerce Commission, state claimants alarmed by potential loss of jobs and rivalry, and fierce resistance by both SAL and SOU systems (Southern competed as far south as Palatka and sent some of its through customers beyond via interline connections at Palatka and Jacksonville). There was also a new ACL president in the late 1950s pushing merger with SAL which might (and did) render exchanges with FEC virtually worthless.

17. The *Florida Special* was also streamlined throughout, effective December 15, 1949. It had been plying the New York–Florida route since 1887, readily surpassing the longevity records of most other trains.

18. High's two campaigns for the governorship, in 1964 and 1966, ended in defeat. He was considered a progressive liberal. His greatest legacy may have been diluting racial barriers.

Chapter 7

1. To clarify, note that the rail lines that predominate in this chapter using Ohio in their monikers refer to the Ohio River as their destination and not the state of Ohio. Those tracks didn't run anywhere near the Buckeye State, which was never an intended part of their companies' routes.

2. http://www.gmohs.org/SecondaryPages/A%20ondensed%20History%20of%20the%20G....

3. Falkner, a colonel in the Confederate Army, was to have at least limited impact as a journalist, author and writer. Of his efforts, *The White Rose of Memphis* (1881) received the most acclaim, an entertaining work of post–Reconstruction fiction and landmark in literary history of the Falkner family and Mississippi. The importance of his life and work on his great-grandson, William Falkner, named for him, was considered large.

4. *The New York Times*, December 26, 1937, p. I29.

5. *Time*, May 7, 1945.

6. By one count he combined parts of about 50 railroads. One of them was his former line, the Birmingham & Northwestern, folded into the GM&N in 1927. In 1925, he acquired the Meridian and Memphis, then the 15-mile Jackson & Eaton, gaining entry to Jackson, Mississippi, and a direct connection with the New Orleans & Great Northern. That didn't satisfy him, however; Tigrett subsequently leased the latter line, assuring permanent access to the Crescent City.

7. Adapted from *Time*, May 7, 1945.

8. *The New York Times*, December 30, 1938, p. 37.

9. Ibid., October 14, 1938, p. 35.

10. *The New York Times*, July 7, 1938, p. 27.

11. Ibid., October 14, 1938, p. 35.

12. Ibid., August 6, 1947, p. 33.

13. Streamliners appeared originally in the U.S. in February 1934, when the Union Pacific Railroad put one into service. Obviously impressed and convinced this would have great bearing on the future of train travel, Tigrett introduced streamliners in the South in 1935. He was four years ahead of the second southern system (Seaboard Air Line) to adopt this eye-popping flash.

14. *Time*, June 24, 1940.

15. http://www.stocklobster.com/gumoohraco.html.

16. *The New York Times*, May 3, 1954, p. 25.

17. Godfrey lived a colorful life. As a young man he served with a gunboat flotilla in the War of 1812, then made and lost fortunes as a sea captain plying West Indies trade and as a merchant businessman in Mexico.

He made a third fortune in New Orleans in Mississippi River shipping and commerce and in 1832, moved his family to Alton. With a partner he co-founded Godfrey, Gilman & Company. In 1834, the Godfreys settled north of Alton in present day Godfrey, a town later named for him. He gave liberally to churches and underwrote a women's seminary. The father of eight daughters, he championed education for females. He was fond of saying: "If you educate a man, you educate an individual; educate a woman and you educate a whole family."

18. At least one source claims the C&M was reorganized in 1857, becoming the Chicago, Alton & St. Louis that year, and that it wasn't renamed Chicago & Alton until 1862.

19. http://en.wikipedia.org/wiki/Timothy_Blackstone.

20. Harriman already controlled the Illinois Central and Union Pacific lines and by 1901, controlled the Southern Pacific in a seemingly relentless quest to dominate the industry. Numerous other lesser lines found their way into his portfolio. One of his objectives was a second transcontinental route, a mission fulfilled by putting multiple lines together.

21. Mike Schafer and Joe Welsh, *Streamliners: History of a Railroad Icon*. St. Paul, Minn.: MBI, 2002, p. 21.

22. Stewart H. Holbrook, *The Story of American Railroads*. New York: Crown, 1947, p. 143.

23. http://www.american-rails.com/the-rebel.html.

24. Schafer and Welsh, p. 21.

25. *The New York Times*, May 30, 1937, p. 31.

26. Ibid., June 17, 1935, p. 29.

27. Schafer and Welsh, p. 21.

28. *The New York Times*, June 22, 1938, p. 40.

29. One source intimates that the third trainset may have been implemented as early as 1937.

30. http://www.gmohs.org/SecondaryPages/A%20Condensed%20History%of%20the%20G....

31. *The New York Times*, March 14, 1950, p. 37.

32. http://www.stocklobster.com/gumoohraco.html.

33. Holbrook, p. 321.

34. Schafer and Welsh, p. 123.

Chapter 8

1. The Illinois Central Railroad wasn't merely an Illinois-based line; in its formative years it was focused almost wholly on its home state. Its early investors-directors left their mark in diversified fields, some far beyond Illinois, including David A. Neal, president, Eastern Railroad (Massachusetts); John F. A. Sanford, fur trader and Indian agent; Morris Ketchum, pioneer locomotive manufacturer; and Robert Rantoul, Massachusetts senator.

2. Illinois had, in the 1830s, launched a concerted program of internal improvements, attempting to open its prairie areas to settlement and agricultural development. The endeavor was largely a failure. But the rise of railroading offered prospects for finally accomplishing its aims. The Illinois General Assembly made unsuccessful attempts to link the northern and southern portions of the state with rail lines prior to the assistance generated by the federal land grant legislation.

3. Stewart H. Holbrook, *The Story of American Railroads*. New York: Crown, 1947, p. 99.

4. Ibid., p. 110.

5. http://icrrhistorical.org/icrr.history.html.

6. The fascinating account of New York City rail

baron Collis P. Huntington's involvement with U.S. rail-roads, and especially those in the South, is recalled in greater detail in this text's Chapter 5 on the Chesapeake & Ohio Railway. Not only was he heavily invested in the Central Pacific Railway in the era when it linked with the Union Pacific to form a transcontinental route in 1869, Huntington combined the Virginia Central and Covington & Ohio railroads to form the Chesapeake & Ohio, becoming its president. This dreamer envisioned another lower transcontinental route linking the Atlantic and Pacific coasts. By tying the Southern Pacific between Los Angeles and New Orleans to the C&O via a connection from Louisville to New Orleans, his feat could be accomplished. Yet it would take a successor, E.H. Harriman, who gained control of the Southern Pacific and Central Pacific lines while also dominating the Illinois Central and Union Pacific, to make it happen.

7. http://icrrhistorical.org/icrr.history.html.

8. A fascinating account of these nocturnal transitions in Nashville is reported in some detail in Chapter 9.

9. In 1969, the L&N bought the eastern route of the Chicago & Eastern Illinois Railroad. In 1971, it acquired the Monon Railroad in Indiana.

10. http://eh.net/bookreviews/library/0287.

11. http://en.wikipedia.org/wiki/E._H._Harriman.

12. http://www.answers.com/topic/e-h-harriman.

13. Composite details adapted from Lucius Beebe and Charles Clegg, *The Age of Steam: A Classic Album of American Railroading*. New York: Promontory, 1994, p. 87; Mirco De Cet and Alan Kent, *The Complete Encyclopedia of Locomotives*. Lisse, The Netherlands: Rebo International, 2006, p. 44; Warburton, Lois Warburton, *Railroads: Bridging the Continents*. San Diego: Lucent, 1991, p. 63; http://www.metrolyrics.com/casey-jones-lyrics-johnny-cash.html; http://en.wikipedia.org/wiki/Vaughn,_Mississippi.

14. Holbrook, p. 429.

15. Jones' infamous rise to stardom rivaled that of a lesser known Southern Railway engineer, Joseph A. "Steve" Broadey (or Broady), at the helm of the *Fast Mail* on September 27, 1903. At high speed it jumped the tracks and plunged Broadey and eight co-workers aboard to their deaths from a trestle near Danville, Virginia. They were immortalized in "The Wreck of the Old '97," a tune attributed to various authors.

16. A museum honoring Jones at the state park named for him closed its doors in 2004, perhaps hinting that some of the aura surrounding the legend had been tarnished with the passing of more than a century.

17. In the modern age Casey Jones Village has become a highly commercialized operation, a destination for railroad memorabilia buffs, touted as "The Best Whistlestop between Memphis and Nashville." See http://www.caseyjones.com.

18. Warburton, p. 63.

19. Beebe and Clegg, p. 87.

20. Figures adapted from http://www.encyclopedia.chicagohistory.org/pages/2716.html.

21. *A Tale of Two Cities*, Book 1, Chapter 1.

22. *Trains*, February 2009, p. 41.

23. http://www.encyclopedia.chicagohistory.org/pages/627.html.

24. http://www.american-rails.com/panama-limited.html and http://www.american-rails.com/city-of-new-orleans.html.

25. Operational integration began July 1, 1999.

26. *Trains*, February 2009, p. 41.

27. http://en.wikipedia.org/wiki/Illinois_Central_Railroad.

28. http://www.american-rails.com/panama-limited.html.

29. When country singer Willie Nelson recorded it in 1984, the lyrical tune topped the charts.

30. Mike Schafer and Joe Welsh, *Classic American Streamliners*. Osceola, Wis.: Motorbooks International, 1997, pp. 22–23.

31. Mike Schafer, *Streamliner Memories*. Osceola, Wis.: MBI, 1999, pp. 20–31.

Chapter 9

1. Maury Klein, *History of the Louisville & Nashville Railroad*. Lexington, Ky.: University Press of Kentucky, 2003, pp. 2–3, 4, 5.

2. Ibid., p. xiv.

3. Kincaid A. Herr, *The Louisville & Nashville Railroad, 1850–1963*. Lexington: University Press of Kentucky, 2000, p. 3.

4. Charles B. Castner, Ronald Flanary, and Patrick Dorin. *Louisville & Nashville Railroad: The Old Reliable*. Lynchburg, Va.: TLC, 1996, p. 1.

5. Klein, p. 10.

6. Despite the fact Muldraugh's Hill tunnel was one of the prized antebellum achievements of the L&N, it was abandoned in 1926 when a 4,600-foot cut in the mountain replaced it. The cut was 70 feet at its deepest, 40 feet wide at the bottom, 75 feet wide at the top and cost about $450,000 (Herr, p. 238).

7. Castner, Flanary, and Dorin, p. 1.

8. The date is uncertain. About half of the sources on the L&N that have surfaced in the 1990s and since give the date shown while the other half offer November 1, 1859, as the first regular run.

9. Ibid., p. 66.

10. Klein, p. xiv.

11. Castner, Flanary, and Dorin, p. 3.

12. Ibid., p. 5; Herr, p. 79: While the change to five feet, nine inches became "standard" on many roads in the South, the L&N converting to it on May 30, 1886, a decade later those same roads revised the "standard" slightly — to four feet, eight and one-half inches. Conversions were costly including added man hours, parts, tools and significant rolling stock.

13. Beginning in 1980, as many L&N and Seaboard Coast Line departments merged in Jacksonville, Florida, L&N leased some floors of its headquarters to the Commonwealth of Kentucky's Department of Human Resources. In 1984, the state purchased the structure and permitted the railroad to lease some space. Final CSX departments transferred to other Louisville locations in 1988. A large illuminated "L&N" sign added in 1959 to the facility's east side remains. Because of the edifice's prominence in the community, it is still locally identified as "the L&N building."

14. Klein, p. 13.

15. http://www.answers.com/topic/albert-fink.

16. "In the early days of the war, L&N President James Guthrie spoke out in defense of the South, and the L&N shipped vital supplies for the Confederate army. But, after the ban on trade with the Confederacy, the company reduced its southern shipments and shifted support to the Union. The L&N's assistance to the Union turned out to be profitable as the company emerged

from the war in comparatively stable physical and economic condition." http://tennesseeencyclopedia.net/imagegallery.php?EntryID=R004.

17. Stewart H. Holbrook, *The Story of American Railroads*. New York: Crown, 1947, pp. 128, 124.
18. http://www.answers.com/topic/albert-fink.
19. Ibid.
20. *Railway Gazette*, May 30, 1874.
21. http://www.answers.com/topic/albert-fink.
22. Klein, p. 350.
23. *The New York Times*, April 4, 1897.
24. Smith left L&N in a huff when President E.D. Standiford reversed his decision in an incident during a yellow fever epidemic in 1878. Montgomery, Alabama, citizens threatened Smith with firearms as he arrived to protest local action barring trains from stopping there for fear of contagion. Smith responded by halting southbound cargo destined for Montgomery. An angry city council intervened with Standiford prompting Smith's resignation.
25. Smith's presidency was interrupted during a particularly harrowing financial episode in which Dutch interests among the stockholders prevailed on L&N directors to install vice president Eckstein Norton as president. Norton, a native of Russellville, Kentucky, was in cotton exchange commerce in New York City, and had the ear of those Dutch interests. Smith was appointed vice president in charge of the railroad's operations and his work was deemed of equal importance. Norton's and Smith's salaries were the same.
26. Castner, Flanary, and Dorin, p. 8.
27. Klein, p. 235.
28. Ibid., p. 223.
29. Ibid., p. 235.
30. Ibid.
31. *The New York Times*, April 2, 1959, pp. 43, 45.
32. Charles B. Castner, Robert E. Chapman, and Patrick C. Dorin, *Louisville & Nashville Passenger Trains: The Pan-American Era, 1921–1971*. Lynchburg, Va.: TLC, 1999, p. 17.
33. In April 1933, for instance, the *Pan-American* lost its Pullman-only status and some of the services that set it apart from other trains. Remodeled coaches with one-two seating were added and a three-compartment, single drawing room solarium lounge car replaced the observation lounge car. However, other advancements occurred as time passed. All *Pan-American* cars were air conditioned between 1934 and 1936. In 1938, new double-bedroom/drawing room sleepers and mid-train lounge cars were added to its consists.
34. Castner, Flanary, and Dorin, p. 65.
35. Ibid., p. 66.
36. According to Castner, Chapman, and Dorin (p. 111): "Meat for the 'Country Ham' breakfast was sliced from sugar-cured, hickory-smoked hams specially prepared for the L&N by the Old Hickory Farm near Peewee Valley, Ky. Mr. and Mrs. Ellis Henry, owners of the farm, were among the top producers of Kentucky hams and long supplied quality hams to the railroad and its dining cars."
37. Castner, Flanary, and Dorin, p. 14.
38. To be candid, organized in 1836, the Western & Atlantic Railway was actually the oldest precursor of the NC&StL. Source: Charles B. Castner, Jr., *Nashville, Chattanooga & St. Louis Railway: The Dixie Line*. Newton, N.J.: Carstens, 1995, p. 4.
39. Castner, Flanary, and Dorin, pp. 17, 18.
40. Herr, p. 298.

41. Castner, Chapman, and Dorin, p. 78.
42. From the 1920s onward the C&EI was a major player in providing the L&N, NC&StL and other southeastern roads with sizeable through passenger service between Chicago and Atlanta plus Chicago and Florida. By 1940, some of those trains were streamlined and were running faster.
43. The origin of "Monon" is in doubt. One source claims it is a Potawatomi Indian word meaning "to carry." Another dubs it "swiftly moving." The Monon evolved from the New Albany & Salem Railroad organized in 1847, which became the Louisville, New Albany & Chicago (1859), and by 1897, Chicago, Indianapolis & Louisville, the official title it retained at the middle of the 20th century, although popularly referred to then as the Monon Route. For more detail see Appendix H.
44. Castner, Flanary, and Dorin, p. 41.
45. Klein, p. xvi.
46. Ibid.
47. Herr, p. 337.
48. Castner, Chapman, and Dorin, p. 111.
49. Herr, p. 340.
50. Ibid., p. 348.
51. Ibid.
52. Ibid., pp. 253–254.
53. Herr, p. 273.
54. Charles B. Castner, Ronald Flanary, and Lee Gordon, *Louisville & Nashville Diesel Locomotives*. Lynchburg, Va.: TLC, 1998, p. 6.
55. Castner, Chapman, and Dorin, pp. 139–140.
56. American Car & Foundry, headquartered in St. Charles, Missouri.
57. Herr, p. 275; Klein, p. 534.
58. Herr, pp. 283, 294.
59. *The New York Times*, April 2, 1959, p. 43.
60. Ibid., p. 45.
61. *The New York Times*, January 6, 1986, p. B7.
62. Castner, Flanary, and Dorin, pp. 109–110.
63. Castner, Flanary, and Dorin, p. vii.
64. Klein, p. xviii.
65. Plans are on the drawing board to connect Louisville to Chicago with high speed rail at a future undetermined date. As this is written there are no known plans to include Nashville with any proposed links.

Chapter 10

1. Charles B. Castner, Ronald Flanary, and Patrick Dorin, *Louisville & Nashville Railroad: The Old Reliable*. Lynchburg, Va.: TLC, 1996, p. 1.
2. Kincaid A. Herr, *The Louisville & Nashville Railroad, 1850–1963*. Lexington: University Press of Kentucky, 2000, p. 3.
3. *The New York Times*, April 2, 1959, p. 43.
4. An allegation that "none of the company's tracks ever actually entered St. Louis, Missouri" (http://en.wikipedia.org/wiki/Nashville,_Chattanooga_and_St._Louis_Railway) could be debated. Between 1879 and 1881, the Louisville & Nashville Railroad, majority stockholder of the NC&StL from 1880, bought short lines in Illinois, Indiana and Kentucky, gaining trackage to St. Louis. L&N timetables of the 1950s and 1960s show trip starts and termini at St. Louis' Union Station and don't suggest L&N (which had fully merged with NC&StL in that era) relied on any carrier's tracks other than its own to and from the city. The quote may be a matter of se-

mantics; while NC&StL initially stopped at East St. Louis, its parent eventually operated into and out of downtown St. Louis. Food for thought: At what point were the NC&StL tracks owned by L&N?

5. Charles B. Castner, Jr., *Nashville, Chattanooga & St. Louis Railway: The Dixie Line.* Newton, N.J.: Carstens, 1995, p. 4.

6. When interstate highway planners came along more than a century after the ride of John Edgar Thompson, they too found their most direct route blocked by the mountains. Instead of constructing their super road alongside the railway tracks, however, they also dipped into another state. They found a preferred route through northwest Georgia. As a result today I-24 vehicles between Nashville and Chattanooga spend most of their trip in Tennessee before turning south a few miles into Georgia, curving back into Tennessee to encounter a "Welcome to Tennessee" border station. That facility most likely beckons travelers from Alabama, who have by then joined the flow into Chattanooga via I-59.

7. Charles B. Castner, Robert E. Chapman and Patrick C. Dorin, *Louisville & Nashville Passenger Trains: The Pan-American Era, 1921–1971.* Lynchburg, Va.: TLC, 1999, pp. 78–79.

8. Castner, p. 9.

9. Atlanta, originally a Cherokee and Creek Native American village known as "Standing Peachtree," was sold to white men in 1822. The city developed as a terminus to the state-owned Western & Atlantic Railway, built by the Georgia Assembly, which — in 1837 — dubbed the southern end of the line "Terminus." That persisted to 1843, when the city was briefly renamed "Marthasville." That moniker didn't please everybody, however. In 1845, when the chief engineer of the Georgia Railroad suggested "Atlantica-Pacifica" for their fair burg, townspeople rallied, shortened it to "Atlanta," and embraced the latest appellation.

10. Castner, p. 10.

11. Through sleeping car service between St. Louis and Nashville was originated by L&N in 1886.

12. Castner, p. 13.

13. http://en.wikipedia.org/wiki/Nashville,_Chattanooga_and_St._Louis_Railway.

14. http://www.american-rails.com/Nashville-chattanooga-and-saint-louis-preservation-society....

15. While the *Georgian* debuted as a St. Louis–Atlanta run, when it didn't draw sufficient response to meet marketing forecasts, its route was altered in June 1948. Split sections to and from Evansville originated and terminated in St. Louis and Chicago, turning it into a viable business venture.

16. Castner, Chapman, and Dorin, p. 85.

Chapter 11

1. http://www.nwhs.org/about_nw.html.

2. Ibid., adaptation.

3. http://www.american-rails.com/norfolk-and-western.html.

4. http://en.wikipedia.org/wiki/City_Point_Railroad; http://en.wikipedia.org/wiki/South_Side_Railroad_(Virginia).

5. http://en.wikipedia.org/wiki/South_Side_Railroad_(Virginia).

6. O. Winston Link and Tim Hensley, *Steam Steel & Stars: America's Last Steam Railroad.* New York: Harry N. Abrams, 1987, p. 27.

7. Although it was Mahone's swan song with the railroad, it wasn't the last Virginians heard of him. Active in politics, he channeled some proceeds from sale of AM&O to a forerunner of Virginia State University as well as to the beginnings of Central State Hospital, both near his home at Petersburg. He also influenced the election of William E. Cameron of Petersburg as governor and was elected to a U.S. Senate seat, dying of a stroke in Washington, D.C., in 1895. While Mahone lost control of the railroad in 1881, he owned vast tracts of land in the coal regions and was in that epoch "one of the wealthiest men in Virginia," according to a biographer.

8. http://www.wvrailroads.net/index.php/Norfolk_&_Western_Railway.

9. http://en.wikipedia.org/wiki/Norfolk_and_Western_Railway.

10. Eugene L. Huddleston, *Appalachian Conquest: C&O, N&W, Virginian and Clinchfield Cross the Mountains.* Lynchburg, Va.: TLC, 2002, p. 1.

11. http://www.wvrailroads.net/index.php/Norfolk_&_Western_Railway.

12. N&W tracks were extended to coal piers at Lamberts Point in Norfolk County on the Elizabeth River in 1886. One of the world's busiest coal export facilities was erected to access Hampton Roads shipping. By 1900, Norfolk was the East Coast's leading coal exporting port.

13. As availability and infamy of high quality Pocahontas bituminous coal amplified, economic forces intruded. Coal operators and employees settled scores of southern West Virginia villages and as demand for coal increased some citizens became extravagantly prosperous. These hamlets flourished for four decades before the stock market crash of 1929. Bramwell, West Virginia, was one: it laid claim to more millionaires per capita then than anyplace else in the U.S.

14. http://en.wikipedia.org/wiki/Norfolk_and_Western_Railway.

15. http://www.american-rails.com/norfolk-and-western.html.

16. http://en.wikipedia.org/wiki/Norfolk_and_Western_Railway.

17. http://www.american-rails.com/norfolk-and-western.html; Link and Hensley, p. 34.

18. http://www.american-rails.com/powhatan-arrow.html.

19. O. Winston Link and Thomas H. Garver, *The Last Steam Railroad in America.* New York: Harry M. Abrams, 1995, pp. 8–9.

20. Ibid., p. 9.

21. http://en.wikipedia.org/wiki/Norfolk_and_Western_Railway.

22. Huddleston, p. 55.

23. http://www.american-rails.com/powhatan-arrow.html.

24. Mike Schafer and Joe Welsh, *Streamliners: History of a Railroad Icon.* St. Paul, Minn.: MBI, 2002, p. 47.

25. Link and Hensley, p. 31.

26. Ibid.

27. http://en.wikipedia.org/wiki/Pocahontas_(passenger_train).

28. Link and Hensley, p. 30.

Chapter 12

1. Some informants state the road wasn't opened to Rolla until 1861.

2. Included among those lines were the Arkansas

Valley & Western; Atchison, Topeka & Santa Fe; Burlington Northern Santa Fe; San Francisco & San Joaquin Valley; and Santa Fe Pacific.

3. Lovers of railroad history who investigate the successive adventures of the previously footnoted railroads likely will not be disappointed. The fact that the San Francisco Bay area was accessed at last under other sobriquets in January 1899, nearly a quarter-century after that enduring quest began, speaks of American determination and rugged ingenuity in making good on a pledge in spite of great odds. Those roads pieced together links forming another transcontinental route.

4. While not yet fully integrated, those roads were cooperating with each other as early as 1978.

5. http://www.american-rails.com/the-frisco.html.

6. http://thelibrary.springfield.missouri.org/loc hist/frisco/about.cfm.

7. A caveat is in order: Katy removed the diesel engine every day at Waco, where it was serviced before its next trip northbound. A Pacific class 4-6-2 steam locomotive usually replaced the diesel for the final 207-mile leg to San Antonio.

8. http://en.wikipedia.org/wiki/Texas_Special.

9. This branch of the *Meteor* originally ran between Monett, Missouri, and Paris, Texas, but was eventually truncated to terminate at Fort Smith, Arkansas.

10. Originally, in the steam engine era, the *Meteor*'s locomotives bore a zephyr blue, white and gray scheme with the train's sobriquet appearing in bold red lettering across the tender.

11. Other key Frisco passenger consists included the *Black Gold*, running from Tulsa to Fort Worth; *Bluebonnet*, from St. Louis to San Antonio; *Firefly*, from Tulsa to Oklahoma City; *Oklahoman*, originally from Kansas City to Tulsa but later from St. Louis to Oklahoma City; and *Will Rogers*, from St. Louis to a pair of terminating cities, Oklahoma City and Wichita.

12. http://www.cbu.edu/~mcondren/MRP/Mem phisCentralStation/Frisco_Operations.htm.

13. Late in the *Sunnyland*'s existence a continuing coach between St. Louis and Atlanta was provided, blunting some of the manipulations, although there was a multiple-hour layover at Memphis that was never satisfactorily addressed.

14. Ibid.

15. *The Memphis Press-Scimitar*, December 9, 1967.

16. In November 2007 this author was aboard Amtrak's *City of New Orleans*, which traveled through Memphis where this account was reported. Contrasting the recollections of Charles Ross with that experience, on our train two employees were assigned to the dining car: a cook and a steward-waitress-cashier, the latter serving patrons at all tables for the full length of the trip (New Orleans to Chicago). It was virtually impossible to perform either's duties in timely fashion and get it all right, although they gave it their very best. Getting an order taken, and delivered, took forever. Gone were the silver and the "silverplate stuff" Ross remembered. In their place were plastic throw-away bowls and plates. Times had definitely changed; they had done so long before this trip.

Chapter 13

1. Robert Wayne Johnson, *Through the Heart of the South: The Seaboard Air Line Railroad Story*. Erin, Ontario: Boston Mills, 1995, p. 7.

2. The Gulf, Mobile & Northern, a precursor of the Gulf, Mobile & Ohio Railroad (1940–1972), both headquartered at Jackson, Tennessee, began running the *Rebel* streamliners between Jackson and New Orleans on July 29, 1935. The *Rebel* name proliferated when a series of streamliners appeared under the GM&O flag. For more details see chapter 7 in this text.

3. Johnson, p. 7. The "two stronger rivals" referred to were the paralleling Atlantic Coast Line on the east and the Southern Railway on the west.

4. Ibid.

5. Portsmouth, boasting miles of waterfront terrain, is situated on the western banks of the Elizabeth River opposite Norfolk in the natural harbor of Hampton Roads. The harbor is connected by Chesapeake Bay with the Atlantic Ocean, all of it making the area a major shipping port. Weldon is a tiny burg south of the Virginia state line in the upper coastal plains of northeast North Carolina. The impetus in selecting Weldon and, indeed, creating the line itself lay in completion of the Petersburg Railroad in 1833. That route, unaffiliated with the SAR, ran between Petersburg in central Virginia and Blakely, North Carolina, lying on the north banks of the Roanoke River opposite Weldon. That was to become the oldest predecessor of the Atlantic Coast Line Railroad, the Seaboard's eventual chief rival. By building a route to the sea, however, the P&R (antecedent of the Seaboard) was to have quick access for delivering goods from the interior hinterlands to distant markets over water route options.

6. William E. Griffin, Jr., *Seaboard Air Line Railway: The Route of Courteous Service*. Lynchburg, Va.: TLC, 1999, p. 5.

7. John Barnett was signified as first Caucasian to scale the Roanoke River above its grand falls.

8. Griffin, p. 5.

9. Weldon, which may have appeared to have had little to offer as a railway terminus, effectively became an important crossing in train traffic. The Wilmington & Raleigh Railroad, opened in 1840, tied the port of Wilmington, North Carolina, to Weldon, where a connection with the Petersburg Railroad moved traffic along to Petersburg, Virginia, where it was met by the Richmond & Petersburg Railroad. All of this became part of the Atlantic Coast Line Railroad, the Seaboard's principal competitor, at the turn of the century. But its historical importance was secured much earlier in the Civil War: "This was one of the most important roads in the South, being the main line for carrying supplies from the Deep South to Richmond and the main route for sending blockade runner supplies from Wilmington to Richmond," said a source. The completion and connection of these three lines was absolutely indispensable to the Confederacy. Along the interline road, soldiers, equipment and provisions arriving by freighter in the port of Wilmington were transported by rail to the Southern cause's headquarters at Richmond.

10. Griffin, p. 5.

11. Shallow water, sand bars and perilous capes on the North Carolina coast led local freight-handlers to secure a route to Norfolk in preference to Tar Heel ports.

12. Griffin, p. 7.

13. Alan Coleman, *Images of Rail: Railroads of North Carolina*. Charleston, S.C.: Arcadia, 2008, pp. 126, 127; http://www.carolana.com/NC/Transportation/rail roads/nc_rrs_carolina_central.html; http://www.car olana.com/NC/Transportation/railroads/nc_rrs_car olina_central_railway.html.

14. Details from *The New York Times*, February 15, 1893.

15. Coleman, p. 51.

16. Griffin disagrees with this date. He states the SAR and RAG railroads jointly took control of the GC&N effective July 1, 1889 (p. 7).

17. Griffin, pp. 7–10.

18. Johnson, p. 20.

19. It had originated as the Americus, Preston & Lumpkin Railroad Company in 1884, before picking up "steam"—first by adding track to Louvale, Georgia (1887), track to Abbeville, on the Ocmulgee River (1887), and adding steamboat service on the Ocmulgee and Altamaha rivers from Abbeville to the coastal ports of Brunswick and Savannah (1889) under the revised nomenclature of Savannah, Americus & Montgomery Railway Company (1888).

20. Johnson, p. 37.

21. Griffin, p. 10.

22. Johnson, p. 39.

23. Ibid.

24. John L. Williams & Sons, John Skelton Williams' dad's bank, helped finance the Confederate operation during the Civil War. Both remained true throughout their lives.

25. To reach Birmingham, SAL bought and rebuilt East & West Railroad between Cartersville, Georgia, and Pell City, Alabama. SAL organized Atlanta & Birmingham Air Line Railway to add trackage from Birmingham to Coal City, Alabama, where it joined the existing East & West. A 43-mile extension at Rockmart, Georgia, carried traffic to and from Atlanta's northwest side.

26. Seaboard's route between New York and Memphis could by no means be considered the shortest. Comparing a trio of streamlined carriers in the early 1950s, SAL's *Cotton Blossom* made the 998-mile southbound trek via Richmond, Atlanta and Birmingham in 36 hours. Southern's *Tennessean* made the same jaunt via Roanoke, Knoxville and Chattanooga — a 927-mile route — in 33 hours 10 minutes. In the same era the Pennsylvania and L&N combined to offer the *Pan-American* over a 1,249-mile Pittsburgh, Cincinnati and Louisville course in 28 hours, 20 minutes! In this instance, at least, there may have been bragging rights for everybody *except* SAL.

27. Griffin, p. 12.

28. Born in poverty at Lovington, Virginia, on October 17, 1851, and orphaned at an early age, T.F. Ryan — by the time of his death in New York City on November 23, 1928 — was "one of the world's richest men," having amassed a cache estimated at between $100 million and $500 million. Retiring from active business two decades prior to his death, Ryan was a commanding but seldom encountered presence on Wall Street, overseeing $1.5 billion in public utilities investments. "Rarely in the foreground but always potently in the background, he exerted great power upon the men and the events of the Street," affirmed an appraisal in *The New York Times* at his death. Entering the New York brokerage business in his early twenties, he focused on lighting and transit systems in numerous cities before adding banking interests to that. Ryan assisted in forming the American Tobacco Company, which reportedly controlled 80 percent of the U.S. tobacco market. He was a faithful supporter of Democratic office-seekers as well as Catholic charities. Often controversial, he exhibited genius for organization and blending divergent points of view.

29. *The New York Times*, October 26, 1927, p. 2.

30. *The New York Times*, December 4, 1927, p. 21.

31. Interestingly, a maximum three-tenths percent grade distinguished the "East Carolina Line" between Charleston and Savannah. This permitted the SAL to realize substantial savings in operating costs by allowing tonnage increases per train on the route as opposed to fewer tons for trains traveling the Hamlet-Columbia-Savannah line. The "East Carolina Line" was reserved almost altogether for freight over which perishables from Florida and other high-speed, high-tonnage cargo journeyed. The shorter route via Columbia carried most of SAL's passenger fleet.

32. Griffin, p. 13.

33. Figures adapted from Griffin, pp. 100–101.

34. Mike Schafer and Joe Welsh, *Streamliners: History of a Railroad Icon*. St. Paul, Minn.: MBI, 2002, p. 101.

35. Griffin, p. 20.

36. Johnson, p. 67.

37. Ibid., p. 70.

38. Ibid., p. 76.

39. That changed in January 1963, when FEC went on strike and ACL's trains joined the SAL line half-way down the peninsula, proceeding to Miami. But in the early years of merger deliberations that was not the case.

40. Johnson, p. 69.

41. The naming of the "new" line would be no different than what was coming in a brief spell, however: think CSX (Chesapeake & Ohio-Seaboard Coast Line) Transportation, Norfolk Southern (Norfolk & Western, Southern), BNSF (Burlington Northern–Santa Fe).

42. Johnson, p. 70.

43. The Baltimore & Ohio was not fully in the camp until 1987, being absorbed by the Chesapeake & Ohio on April 30 of that year. On August 31, C&O completed the merger with CSX.

44. Griffin, p. 24.

45. Excluded were a few passenger, freight and mail trains moving over a separate line between Jacksonville and St. Petersburg via Gainesville, Williston, Dunnellon, Brooksville, and Clearwater.

46. The *Carolina-Florida Special* was the last SAL passenger train over the Florida East Coast tracks. It departed Miami northbound on December 31, 1925; afterward all SAL people-movers traversed SAL trackage within Florida as some trains had been doing since November 1925.

47. Effective with the opening of a new west coast line on January 9, 1927, the *Seaboard Florida Limited* offered service to Fort Myers and Naples in addition to its usual handful of Gulf side cities and resorts.

48. Johnson, p. 133.

49. Schafer and Welsh, p. 102.

50. Its moniker was submitted by 30 winners in a "name the train" competition in 1939, drawing more than 76,000 entries. When the lucky champs split the advertised $500 prize, to their dismay each received $16.67 before taxes!

51. Johnson, p. 135.

52. Ibid., p. 136.

Chapter 14

1. Some would argue that "The Standard Railroad of the South" (ACL), "The Dixie Line" (NC&StL) or "Through the Heart of the South" (SAL) could be substituted. A couple of short lines might also qualify: "Thru the Heart of Dixie" (Columbus and Greenville

Railway) and "Best Little Railroad in Dixie" (Eastern Alabama Railway).

2. Southern didn't own any rails in the District of Columbia but accessed the capital from Alexandria, Virginia, by way of the Richmond, Fredericksburg & Potomac Railroad and the Long Bridge over the Potomac River. The latter was successively owned by the Pennsylvania, Penn Central, Conrail and CSX railroads.

3. You may have already read about these epic, precedent-setting transactions in the emerging development of U.S. transportation revealed in Chapters 1 and 2.

4. http://www.srha.net/public/History/history.htm.

5. Ibid.

6. For the reader desiring a brief overview, go to: http://www.modelrailways.info/southern-railway-system-history.html.

7. *The New York Times*, August 2, 1894.

8. Morgan's close ties with Henry Walters, another Dixie rail tycoon who wielded a big stick in the developing Atlantic Coast Line Railroad during the same epoch, is recounted in Chapter 3. Their dynasties warded off competing lines (SAL in particular) while they turned money into greater advantage through steamship line purchases. Morgan "gave" Walters several plums, none more beneficial than control of the L&N and its NC&StL subsidiary, plus interests in both the Georgia and Monon roads.

9. http://www.answers.com/topic/samuel-spencer.

10. http://members.tripod.com/generaljimlivil/theerielackawannalimited/id29.html.

11. http://en.wikipedia.org/wiki/Norfolk_Southern_Railway.

12. http://www.american-rails.com/southern-railway.html.

13. http://www.american-rails.com/crescent.html.

14. Lucius Beebe and Charles Clegg, *The Age of Steam: A Classic Album of American Railroading*. New York: Promontory, 1994, p. 84.

15. Aside from the folklore of such traditions, the personal experiences of some of Southern's workforce — some personal, some eyewitness, some hearsay — are recounted in the unpolished style of James Leslie Helper's illustrated *The Southern Railway Remembered* (TLC, 2001). SOU hired Helper as a fireman in 1943, at Alexandria, Virginia. By the time he gained retirement in 1970, he had engineered manifold steam and diesel freights and even a few passenger trains on the mainline south of Washington and its stems. Autobiographical, for railfans it's a treasure trove of men interacting with machines in the period Helper was there.

16. Mike Schafer and Joe Welsh, *Streamliners: History of a Railroad Icon*. St. Paul, Minn.: MBI, 2002, p. 105.

17. http://www.american-rails.com/crescent.html.

18. In 2010, sightseer lounge cars appear on the *Empire Builder* (Chicago–Seattle/Portland), *California Zephyr* (Chicago–Emeryville, California), *Southwest Chief* (Chicago–Los Angeles), *Texas Eagle* (Chicago–San Antonio–Los Angeles), *Sunset Limited* (New Orleans–Los Angeles) and *Coast Starlight* (Seattle–Los Angeles).

19. There was a connecting train to the *Southerner* from Boston, although for some of its life it arrived at New York's Grand Central Terminal. Continuing patrons had to make the transition to Pennsylvania Station where the *Southerner* (and other SOU trains) arrived and departed.

20. http://www.american-rails.com/southerner.html.

21. In actual practice service was trimmed to tri-weekly between Birmingham and New Orleans at the end of 1970. It was diminished to tri-weekly from Atlanta to New Orleans later as daily service was maintained to New York (to Washington on Southern's route).

22. Tom Murray, *Southern Railway*. St. Paul, Minn.: Voyageur, 2007, p. 115.

23. Ralph Ward, *Southern Railway Varnish, 1964–1979*. Asheboro, N.C.: R. Ward, 1985.

24. Brosnan, historians attest, was not universally appreciated, particularly by some members of Southern's board of directors and staff. He was "one of the most polarizing figures in U.S. railroad history," allowed one reporter — ruthless in cutting expenses and employees while instituting efficiencies that became commonplace in the trade. Brosnan terminated company officers impulsively and was a bitter enemy of labor unions. Before his election as president some directors had serious doubts. Ultimately he was forced out, though he stayed on the board to 1983.

25. These facts on Brosnan's career are from obituaries appearing in *The Atlanta Journal-Constitution* on June 17, 1985, and *The Washington Post* on June 19, 1985.

26. Murray, p. 130.

27. Ibid., p. 111.

28. Bob Claytor is recalled by N&W railfans for his efforts in reactivating its steam program which rebuilt steam locomotives J-611 and A-1218 at the line's Roanoke Shops. He also promoted excursion trips. On rare occasions Graham Claytor occupied the engineer's cab on those steam jaunts.

29. http://enc.slider.com/Enc/W._Graham_Claytor,_Jr.

30. That was interrupted by some years of service in the U.S. Navy during the Second World War. In August 1945, Claytor's rapid response led to the rescue of nearly 100 men who had been aboard a sunken U.S. cruiser in the Pacific, then in life jackets floating in shark-infested waters for many hours. His bravery was deemed heroic with the potential for discovery by lurking Japanese submarines nearby. He returned to his Washington law digs following the war.

31. Murray, pp. 130–131.

32. Schafer and Welsh, p. 107.

33. Adapted from *Railway Age*, June 1994, by Luther S. Miller, in which Miller quotes from Frank N. Wilner's *The Amtrak Story* published by Simmons-Boardman (New York, 1994).

34. *The New York Times*, May 15, 1994.

35. http://www.american-rails.com/class-i-railroads.html.

Chapter 15

1. Jim Crow was a system of laws and customs that enforced racial segregation and discrimination throughout the United States, evident in the South from the late 19th century through the 1960s. The laws didn't mention race but spelled out and supported practices victimizing Negroes.

2. Peter Lauranzano, "Resistance to the Segregation of Public Transportation in the Early 1840s." http://www.primaryresearch.org/bh/research/lauranzano/index.php.

3. Ibid.

4. "Treatment of Colored Passengers." *The Liberator*, November 15, 1844.

5. Harvey Fireside, *Separate and Unequal: Homer Plessy and the Supreme Court Decision That Legalized Racism*. New York: Carroll and Graf, 2004, p. 154.

6. Ibid.

7. A sterling example may be viewed today in the separate entrances for whites and blacks at Macon, Georgia's Terminal Station opened in 1916. The striking grandeur of the magnificent Beaux Arts edifice, preserved for other uses in the present, is offset by a separate yet irrefutably disproportionate entryway to a colored waiting room at the far left of its long rectangular façade. While it is constructed in the same style and material as the rest of the building, it exists as a reminder of a time very different in American life and particularly in the South.

8. "The Train Down South: A Trip to Segregation." National Public Radio, *Morning Edition*, June 15, 2007.

9. Raymond Arsenault, *Freedom Riders: 1961 and the Struggle for Racial Justice*. New York: Oxford University Press, 2006, p. 14.

10. http://www.encyclopediaofalabama.org/face/Article.jsp?id=h-1248.

11. *The Railroad Gazette*, 1901, now exhibited at the Spencer railway museum.

12. http://www.kawvalley.k12.ks.us/brown_v_board/segregation.htm.

13. In 1914, Louisiana forbade the races from using the same entrance to public places. A year later, Oklahoma required separate telephone booths. By 1920, Mississippi declared it a crime to encourage "social equalities" or anything promoting interaction "between whites and Negro's [*sic*]." Arkansas segregated racetracks; Texas segregated boxing matches; Kentucky segregated schools, with a stipulation no textbook issued to a Negro could be reissued to a white; Georgia prohibited Negro ministers from officiating at marriages of white couples; and New Orleans specified different districts for white and Negro prostitutes.

14. On that occasion National Association for the Advancement of Colored People lawyer Thurgood Marshall had pressed 14th Amendment arguments to the U.S. Supreme Court, asking for separate but equal to be struck down in the *Brown v. Board of Education* case. He got his wish.

15. Keith Weldon Medley, *We as Freemen: Plessy v. Ferguson*. Gretna, La.: Pelican, 2003, pp. 135, 137.

16. *The New Orleans Daily Picayune*, June 9, 1892.

17. Wayne Anderson, *Supreme Court Cases Through Primary Sources: Plessy v. Ferguson — Legalizing Segregation*. New York: Rosen, 2004, p. 18.

18. *The New Orleans Times-Democrat*, October 19, 1892.

19. http://www.bgsu.edu/departments/acs/1890s/plessy/plessy.html.

20. Anderson, p. 43.

21. Ibid., p. 50.

22. New Albany, Indiana, situated on the northern embankment of the Ohio River opposite Louisville, Kentucky, on the southern bank, was Indiana's largest metropolis with 8,181 inhabitants when the New Albany & Salem was incorporated in 1847.

23. Stewart H. Holbrook, *The Story of American Railroads*. New York: Crown, 1947, p. 115.

24. In 1902, the Mobile, Alabama, town council issued an edict requiring "separation of the races" on city streetcars. It mandated that Negroes sit in the back. Hundreds of other communities throughout the South enacted similar legislation affecting their public transit systems.

25. Samuel Augustus Jennings, "Reflections in Black and White." *Passenger Train Journal*, March 1988.

26. http://en.wikipedia.org/wiki/Champion_(passenger_train).

27. Fireside, p. 191.

28. Ibid., pp. 230, 268.

Chapter 16

1. The SCC&R line eventually ran from the Atlantic port city of Charleston to the interior hamlet of Hamburg, South Carolina, some 136 miles distant. When completed in 1833, it was the longest continuous railroad right-of-way in the world.

2. Thomas Curtis Clarke, et al., *The American Railway: Its Construction, Development, Management, and Appliances*. New York: Benjamin Blom, 1972, p. 246.

3. Ibid.

4. Pullman's sold-out maiden voyage of a rudimentary sleeping car left Bloomington for Chicago the night of September 1, 1858. The Chicago & Alton Railroad had given him a sixth of its rolling stock — two day coaches — to convert to sleepers at his expense. Demand soon warranted converting a third. For the next quadrennial, however, Pullman panned for gold and operated a mercantile store in Colorado during a mining surge, reconfiguring details of an improved sleeping car as a sideline.

5. The concept of the vestibuled train was first demonstrated in June 1886 by the Pennsylvania Railroad, even before a patent was granted.

6. Clarke, pp. 246, 249.

7. In 1893, the *Vestibule* was marketed as "A magnificent train of Pullman Vestibuled Palaces, consisting of Drawing-room, Dining, Sleeping and Library cars of the latest and most magnificent and luxurious designs, built expressly for this service, and run daily."

8. Clarke, p. 245.

9. This followed a trend begun in the early decades of U.S. rail travel as maids and secretaries appeared on a few luxury limited trains traversing a tiny handful of routes principally between Midwest and Northeast points.

10. August Mencken, *The Railroad Passenger Car: An Illustrated History of the First Hundred Years with Accounts by Contemporary Passengers*. Baltimore: Johns Hopkins University Press, 2000 (originally released 1957), pp. 13–15.

11. Henry Deedes, *Sketches of the South and West, or Ten Months' Residence in the United States*. Edinburgh: William Blackwood and Sons, 1869, p. 80.

12. Walter Thornbury, *Criss-Cross Journeys*. London: Hurst and Blackett, 1873, pp. 25–26.

13. Holbrook, p. 12.

14. Ibid.

15. Ibid., p. 326.

16. Jim Loomis, *All Aboard! The Complete North American Train Travel Guide*. 2nd ed. Rocklin, Calif.: Prima, 1998, p. 14; Mike Schafer and Joe Welsh, *Classic American Streamliners*. Osceola, Wis.: Motorbooks International, 1997, p. 34; Mike Schafer, with Joe Welsh and Kevin Holland, *The American Passenger Train*. St. Paul, Minn.: MBI, 2001, p. 45.

17. Since the age of heavyweights, sleepers received number designations like 12–1 and 10–6. The figures are confusing and have different meanings for heavyweight and streamlined cars. They refer to space in heavyweight

cars as this: a 12–1 sleeper had 12 open sections (berths) and a lone bedroom. Figures for streamlined sleepers noted the number of private rooms. A 4-4-2 sleeper had four compartments, four double bedrooms and two drawing rooms. Private rooms were preferential to open sections after streamlining arrived. Roomettes were direct replacements for sections, offering a fold-down bed, folding toilet and clothes locker. Compartments held a private sitting room by day and two beds by night. Adjacent double bedrooms could be joined in a single large room with four beds. Drawing rooms had more space and doubled as conference rooms.

18. Harry Bruinius, "Pullman Porters Tell Tales of a Train Ride Through History." *The Christian Science Monitor*, February 29, 2008.

19. Numerous historians of these incidents report that Pullman paid black hires only a fraction of the compensation he meted out to white staffers. Blacks working for him were normally kept in subservient roles to whites, answering to whites who were in positions of superiority.

20. Bruinius.

21. Holbrook, pp. 325–326. Pullman also operated a large plant at Worcester, Massachusetts.

22. There are published accounts intimating that while Pullman was alive his company never paid his black help at all, to wit: "For roughly the first thirty-five years, Pullman paid no salary to these workers, who were glad for the opportunity to travel the country extensively and work for tips. They worked for tips only until around the turn of the century." Mauris L. Emeka, *Amtraking: A Guide to Enjoyable Train Travel.* Port Orchard, Wash.: Apollo, 1994, p. 8.

23. Loomis, p. 15.

24. http://www25.uua.org/uuhs/duub/articles/georgemortimerpullman.html.

25. http://www.u-s-history.com/pages/h3065.html.

26. Lois Warburton, *Railroads: Bridging the Continents.* San Diego: Lucent Books, 1991, p. 59.

27. Karl Zimmerman, *All Aboard! Passenger Trains Around the World.* Honesdale, Pa.: Boyds Mills, 2004, p. 15.

28. Loomis, p. 18.

29. Ibid., p. 140.

30. Schafer and Welsh, 1997, p. 34.

31. Jill Jonnes, *Conquering Gotham: A Gilded Age Epic — The Construction of Penn Station and Its Tunnels.* New York: Viking Penguin, 2007, p. 6.

Chapter 17

1. Hans Halberstadt and April Halberstadt, *The American Train Depot & Roundhouse.* Osceola, Wis.: Motorbooks International, 1995, p. 9.

2. Jeffrey Richards and John M. MacKenzie, *The Railway Station: A Social History.* Oxford, England: Oxford University Press, 1986, p. 385.

3. Halberstadt and Halberstadt, pp. 30–31.

4. Richards and MacKenzie, pp. 385–386.

5. Ibid., p. 3.

6. Halberstadt and Halberstadt, p. 9.

7. James Scott, *Railway Romance and Other Essays.* London: Hodder and Stoughton, 1913, p. 71.

8. Kevin J. Holland, *Classic American Railroad Terminals.* Osceola, Wis.: MBI, 2001, p. 9.

Chapter 18

1. http://www.ehow.com/facts_5135596_history-rail-travel.html.

2. http://library.duke.edu/digitalcollections/adaccess/rails-history.html.

3. Lois Warburton, *Railroads: Bridging the Continents.* San Diego: Lucent Books, 1991, p. 65; 2005 estimates by U.S. Bureau of Transportation Statistics.

4. National Railroad Passenger Corporation figures.

5. Second World War figures from U.S. Congressional Budget Office; 2005 estimates by U.S. Bureau of Transportation Statistics.

6. http://www.american-rails.com/decline-of-passenger-railroading.html.

7. Interstate Commerce Commission: *Transport Statistics in the United States*; Stanley Berge, *Railroad Passenger Service Trends 1950–1960.* Evanston, Ill.: Chandler's, 1961.

8. http://www.american-rails.com/decline-of-passenger-railroading.html.

9. National Railroad Passenger Corporation figure.

10. http://history.howstuffworks.com/american-history/decline-of-railroads.htm/printable.

11. Editors of Publications International in "Modern Decline of Railroads." http://history.howstuffworks.com/american-history/decline-of-railroads.htm/printable.

12. Ibid.

13. http://www.experiencefestival.com/a/Amtrak_-_History/id/4790630.

14. *Trains*, March 2009, p. 28.

15. Ibid., p. 30.

16. Ibid., p. 28.

17. Anthony Perl, *New Departures: Rethinking Rail Passenger Policy in the Twenty-first Century.* Lexington: University Press of Kentucky, 2002, pp. 95–96.

18. George W. Hilton, *Amtrak: The National Railroad Passenger Corporation.* Washington, D.C.: American Enterprise Institute for Public Policy Research, 1980, p. 16.

19. National Railroad Passenger Corporation figures.

20. http://history.howstuffworks.com/american-history/decline-of-railroads.htm/printable.

21. *Amtrak Source Book.*

22. http://www.experiencefestival.com/a/Amtrak_-_History/id/4790630.

23. J. Bruce Richardson, president of the United Rail Passenger Alliance, in an address to the Florida Coalition of Rail Passengers at Jacksonville on November 7, 2009.

24. Rush Loving, Jr., "Trains' Formula for Fixing Amtrak." *Trains*, March 2009, p. 31.

25. Joseph Vranich, *Supertrains: Solutions to America's Transportation Gridlock.* New York: St. Martin's Press, 1991, p. 241.

26. "This Week at Amtrak." Vol. 6, No. 31, August 24, 2009, twa@unitedrail.org.

27. "This Week at Amtrak." Vol. 6, No. 48, December 7, 2009, twa@unitedrail.org.

28. Ben Jervey, "Train in Vain." GOOD.IS/Magazine, June 5, 2008. http://www.good.is/post/train-in-vain/

29. Loving, pp. 28–29.

30. Vranich, p. 243.

Chapter 19

1. Jim Cox, *Sold on Radio: Advertisers in the Golden Age of Broadcasting.* Jefferson, N.C.: McFarland, 2008, pp. 129–130.

2. Anthony Perl, *New Departures: Rethinking Rail Passenger Policy in the Twenty-first Century*. Lexington: University Press of Kentucky, 2002, p. 16.

3. Joseph Vranich, *Supertrains: Solutions to America's Transportation Gridlock*. New York: St. Martin's Press, 1991, p. 372.

4. http://en.wikipedia.org/wiki/High-speed_rail.

5. Ibid.

6. Amtrak owns 363 miles of the 456-mile "Northeast Corridor" between Boston and Washington. Controlling much of the route allows Amtrak to dedicate that part to passenger traffic exclusively, speeding its trains without interference from host railroads running freight traffic on the same line.

7. High Speed Rail USA depicts itself as "a grassroots movement of concerned citizens who promote the development of a national high speed rail system at 220 mph on separate dedicated tracks."

8. According to *Trains* News Wire of November 18, 2009, Tim Schweikert, president of General Electric Transportation in China, said: "China currently is a leader in high speed rail technology for speeds of 220 miles per hour." He advocated a deal inked by GE and China's Ministry of Railways that will bring both parties together to "develop the best solutions faster to serve America's high speed rail needs for many years."

9. http://en.wikipedia.org/wiki/High-speed_rail.

10. Maglev technology was successfully tested in 2002 at Shanghai, China, using a German-made train. In December 2003, commercial traffic began using it along a 19-mile route connecting the city center with the airport. Maglev covers the distance in less than 10 minutes at an average speed of 267 miles per hour and it replaced an hour-long trip by taxi. A 99-mile extension to the route connecting Hangzhou to Shanghai — the first maglev line between two cities — was expected to be open by a 2010 Shanghai Expo.

11. Vranich, p. 375.

12. http://trains4america.wordpress.com/2008/06/21/obama-speaks-up-again-on-high-speed-rail/.

13. http://green.autoblog.com/2009/04/16/obama-outlines-high-speed-rail-plan-for-u-s/.

14. Esther 4:14.

15. http://www.cnn.com/2009/POLITICS/04/16/obama.rail/index.html.

16. http://www.highspeedrailusa.com/blog/whatishighspeedrail.html.

17. http://www.highspeedrailusa.com/blog/resources/faq.html.

18. David Grossman, "The Case for High Speed Rail in America." *USA Today*, August 22, 2008.

Chapter 20

1. George W. Hilton and John F. Due, *The Electric Interurban Railways in America*. Stanford, Calif.: Stanford University Press, 2000 (re-release of a 1960 edition).

2. http://xroads.virginia.edu/~Hyper/INCORP/interurbanrail/index.html.

3. http://en.wikipedia.org/wiki/Interurban.

4. http://xroads.virginia.edu/~Hyper/INCORP/interurbanrail/index.html.

5. A little comparison in the dialectical differences between the Brits and Americans may help the inquisitive reader sort some of this out. The application of a generic *light rail* shuns some serious incompatibilities in British and American English. *Tram* would be understood in the United Kingdom and ex–Brit colonies as a synonym for *streetcar* while it could refer to an *aerial tramway* in North America. The British identification for that is *cable car*; in the U.S. that often designates a ground-level car pulled by subterranean cables. In America *trolley* may substitute for *streetcar*. In the U.K. and elsewhere, that's usually taken to mean a cart and in particular a shopping cart. North American transportation officials usually reserve *streetcar* for traditional vehicles that exclusively run in mixed traffic on city streets. At the same time they apply light rail to more modern vehicles principally in exclusive rights-of-way, as they may operate parallel and be pitched to varied passenger groups. A difference in the two countries' English surfaced late in the 19th century as Americans, perhaps influenced by a large segment of German immigrants then residing in the Northeast, adopted "street railway" instead of "tramway" with vehicles being "streetcars" as opposed to "trams." While the Brits discarded all their *trams* except at Blackpool following the Second World War, seven North American cities persisted, maintaining large *streetcar* operations in Boston, Newark, New Orleans, Philadelphia, Pittsburgh, San Francisco, and Toronto. When these were upgraded to new technology, it was branded *light rail* to distinguish it from existing *streetcars* that continued to run both old and new systems.

6. H.D. Quinby, "Major Urban Corridor Facilities: A New Concept." *Traffic Quarterly*, Vol. 16, No. 2, April 1962, pp. 242–259.

7. Gregory L. Thompson, "Defining an Alternative Future: Birth of the Light Rail Movement in North America." 9th National Light Rail Transit Conference: *Experience, Economics & Evolution — From Starter Lines to Growing Systems*. Portland, Oregon, November 16–18, 2003.

BIBLIOGRAPHY

Anderson, Wayne. *Supreme Court Cases Through Primary Sources: Plessy v. Ferguson — Legalizing Segregation.* New York: Rosen Publishing, 2004.

Arsenault, Raymond. *Freedom Riders: 1961 and the Struggle for Racial Justice.* New York: Oxford University Press, 2006.

Beebe, Lucius, and Charles Clegg. *The Age of Steam: A Classic Album of American Railroading.* New York: Promontory Press, 1994.

Berge, Stanley. *Railroad Passenger Service Trends 1950–1960.* Evanston, Ill.: Chandler's, 1961.

Bianculli, Anthony J. *Trains and Technology: The American Railroad in the Nineteenth Century.* Vol.1. Newark: University of Delaware Press, 2001.

Bramson, Seth H. *Speedway to Sunshine: The Story of the Florida East Coast Railway.* Erin, Ontario: Boston Mills, 2003.

Brennner, Marie. *House of Dreams: The Bingham Family of Louisville.* New York: Random House, 1988.

Castner, Charles B., and Thomas E. Bailey. *The Dixie Line: Nashville, Chattanooga & St. Louis Railway.* Newton, N. J.: Carstens, 1995.

Castner, Charles B., Robert E. Chapman, and Patrick C. Dorin. *Louisville & Nashville Passenger Trains: The Pan-American Era, 1921–1971.* Lynchburg, Va.: TLC, 1999.

Castner, Charles B., Ronald Flanary, and Patrick C. Dorin. *Louisville & Nashville Railroad: The Old Reliable.* Lynchburg, Va.: TLC, 1996.

Castner, Charles B., Ronald Flanary, and Lee Gordon. *Louisville & Nashville Diesel Locomotives.* Lynchburg, Va.: TLC, 1998.

Chandler, David Leon, with Mary Voelz Chandler. *The Binghams of Louisville: The Dark History Behind One of America's Great Fortunes.* New York: Crown, 1987.

Clarke, Thomas Curtis, et al. *The American Railway: Its Construction, Development, Management, and Appliances.* New York: Benjamin Blom, 1972.

Coleman, Alan. *Images of Rail — Railroads of North Carolina.* Charleston, S.C.: Arcadia, 2008.

Cox, Jim. *Sold on Radio: Advertisers in the Golden Age of Broadcasting.* Jefferson, N.C.: McFarland, 2008.

De Cet, Mirco, and Alan Kent. *The Complete Encyclopedia of Locomotives.* Lisse, The Netherlands: Rebo International, 2006.

Deedes, Henry. *Sketches of the South and West, or Ten Months' Residence in the United States.* Edinburgh: William Blackwood and Sons, 1869.

Emeka, Mauris L. *Amtraking: A Guide to Enjoyable Train Travel.* Port Orchard, Wash.: Apollo Publishing, 1994.

Fireside, Harvey. *Separate and Unequal: Homer Plessy and the Supreme Court Decision That Legalized Racism.* New York: Carroll & Graf, 2004.

Fistell, Ira. *America by Train: How to Tour America by Train.* New York: Burt Franklin, 1983.

Goddard, Stephen B. *Getting There: The Epic Struggle Between Road and Rail in the American Century.* New York: HarperCollins, 1994.

Goolsby, Larry. *Atlantic Coast Line Passenger Service: The Postwar Years.* Lynchburg, Va.: TLC, 1999.

Griffin, William E., Jr, *Seaboard Air Line Railway: The Route of Courteous Service.* Lynchburg, Va.: TLC, 1999.

Halberstadt, Hans, and April Halberstadt. *The American Train Depot and Roundhouse.* Osceola, Wis.: Motorbooks, 1995.

Hankey, John P. "Fact or Fiction? Standard Gauge Originated with a Roman Chariot." *Trains,* July 2009.

Helper, James Leslie. *The Southern Railway Remembered.* Lynchburg, Va.: TLC, 2001.

Herr, Kincaid A. *The Louisville & Nashville Railroad, 1850–1963.* Lexington: University Press of Kentucky, 2000.

Hilton, George W. *Amtrak: The National Railroad Passenger Corporation.* Washington, D.C.: American Enterprise Institute for Public Policy Research, 1980.

_____, and John F. Due. *The Electric Interurban Railways in America.* Stanford, Calif.: Stanford University Press, 2000.

Holbrook, Stewart H. *The Story of American Railroads.* New York: Crown, 1947.

Holland, Kevin J. *Classic American Railroad Terminals.* Osceola, Wis.: MBI, 2001.

Huddleston, Eugene L. *Appalachian Conquest: C&O, N&W, Virginian and Clinchfield Cross the Mountains.* Lynchburg, Va.: TLC, 2002.

Itzkoff, Donald M. *Off the Track: The Decline of the Intercity Passenger Train in the United States.* Westport, Conn.: Greenwood, 1985.

Johnson, Robert Wayne. *Through the Heart of the South: The Seaboard Air Line Railroad Story.* Erin, Ontario: Boston Mills, 1995.

Jonnes, Jill. *Conquering Gotham: A Gilded Age Epic — The Construction of Penn Station and Its Tunnels.* New York: Viking Penguin, 2007.

Klein, Maury. *History of the Louisville & Nashville Railroad.* Lexington.: University Press of Kentucky, 2003.

Lemly, James H. *The Gulf, Mobile and Ohio: A Railroad That Had to Expand or Expire — A Dynamic History of the Tigrett Road.* Homewood, Ill.: Richard D. Irwin, 1953.

Link, O. Winston, and Thomas H. Garver. *The Last Steam Railroad in America.* New York: Harry M. Abrams, 1995.

Link, O. Winston, and Tim Hensley. *Steam, Steel and Stars: America's Last Steam Railroad.* New York: Harry N. Abrams, 1987.

Loomis, Jim. *All Aboard: The Complete North American Train Travel Guide.* 2nd ed. Rocklin, Calif.: Prima, 1998.

Medley, Keith Weldon. *We as Freemen: Plessy v. Ferguson.* Gretna, La.: Pelican, 2003.

Mencken, August. *The Railroad Passenger Car: An Illustrated History of the First Hundred Years with Accounts by Contemporary Passengers.* Baltimore: Johns Hopkins University Press, 2000.

Murray, Tom. *Southern Railway.* St. Paul, Minn.: MBI /Voyageur, 2007.

Nelson, Scott Reynolds. *Steel Drivin' Man: John Henry, the Untold Story of an American Legend.* New York: Oxford University Press, 2006.

Norris, John R., and Joann Norris. *The Historic Railroad: A Guide to Museums, Depots and Excursions in the United States.* Jefferson, N.C.: McFarland, 1996.

Parks, Pat. *The Railroad That Died at Sea: The Florida East Coast's Key West Extension.* Key West, Fla.: Langley, 1968.

Perl, Anthony. *New Departures: Rethinking Rail Passenger Policy in the Twenty-first Century.* Lexington: University Press of Kentucky, 2002.

Prince, Richard E. *Atlantic Coast Line Railroad: Steam Locomotives, Ships and History.* Bloomington: Indiana University Press, 2000.

Richards, Jeffrey, and John M. MacKenzie. *The Railway Station: A Social History.* Oxford, England: Oxford University Press, 1986.

Rubin, Louis Decimus, Jr. *A Memory of Trains: The Boll Wevil and Others.* Columbia: University of South Carolina Press, 2000.

Schafer, Mike. *Streamliner Memories.* Osceola, Wis.: MBI, 1999.

_____. *Vintage Diesel Locomotives.* Osceola, Wis.: MBI, 1998.

_____, and Joe Welsh. *Classic American Streamliners.* Osceola, Wis.: Motorbooks, 1997.

_____. *Streamliners: History of a Railroad Icon.* St. Paul, Minn.: MBI, 2002.

Scott, James. *Railway Romance and Other Essays.* London: Hodder and Stoughton, 1913.

Smyth, George Hutchinson, and George Sherwood Dickerman. *The Life of Henry Bradley Plant.* New York: Putnam's, 1898.

Standiford, Les. *Last Train to Paradise: Henry Flagler and the Spectacular Rise and Fall of the Railroad That Crossed an Ocean.* New York: Crown, 2002.

Thompson, Gregory Lee. *The Passenger Train in the Motor Age: California's Rail and Bus Industries, 1910–1941.* Columbus: Ohio State University Press, 1993.

Thornbury, Walter. *Criss-Cross Journeys.* London: Hurst and Blackett, 1873.

Tifft, Susan E., and Alex S. Jones. *The Patriarch: The Rise and Fall of the Bingham Dynasty.* New York: Summit Books, 1991.

Vranich, Joseph. *Supertrains: Solutions to America's Transportation Gridlock.* New York: St. Martin's Press, 1991.

Warburton, Louis. *Railroads: Bridging the Continents.* San Diego: Lucent, 1991.

Ward, Ralph. *Southern Railway Varnish, 1964–1979.* Asheboro, N.C.: R. Ward, 1985.

Wellington, Arthur M. *The Economic Theory of the Location of Railways.* New York: John Wiley and Sons, 1887.

Wilner, Frank N. *The Amtrak Story.* New York: Simmons-Boardman, 1994.

Wojtas, Edward J. *Travel by Train.* New York: Rand McNally, 1974.

Zimmerman, Karl. *All Aboard! Passenger Trains Around the World.* Honesdale, Pa.: Boyds Mills, 2004.

In addition to these published works several thousand Web sites supplied supplementary facts for this reference.

INDEX